THE LANGUAGE

AND

ITS USAGE

Prentice-Hall
Series in Automatic Computation

AHO, ed., *Currents in the Theory of Computing*

AHO AND ULLMAN, *The Theory of Parsing, Translation, and Compiling,*
  Volume I: *Parsing*; Volume II: *Compiling*

ANDREE, *Computer Programming: Techniques, Analysis, and Mathematics*

ANSELONE, *Collectively Compact Operator Approximation Theory and Applications to Integral Equations*

BATES AND DOUGLAS, *Programming Language/One,* 2nd ed.

BLUMENTHAL, *Management Information Systems*

BRENT, *Algorithms for Minimization without Derivatives*

BRINCH HANSEN, *Operating System Principles*

COFFMAN AND DENNING, *Operating Systems Theory*

CRESS, et al., *FORTRAN IV with WATFOR and WATFIV*

DAHLQUIST, BJÖRCK, AND ANDERSON, *Numerical Methods*

DANIEL, *The Approximate Minimization of Functionals*

DEO, *Graph Theory with Applications to Engineering and Computer Science*

DESMONDE, *Computers and Their Uses,* 2nd ed.

DRUMMOND, *Evaluation and Measurement Techniques for Digital Computer Systems*

ECKHOUSE, *Minicomputer Systems: Organization and Programming (PDP-11)*

FIKE, *Computer Evaluation of Mathematical Functions*

FIKE, *PL/1 for Scientific Programmers*

FORSYTHE AND MOLER, *Computer Solution of Linear Algebraic Systems*

GEAR, *Numerical Initial Value Problems in Ordinary Differential Equations*

GORDON, *System Simulation*

GRISWOLD, *String and List Processing in SNOBOL4: Techniques and Applications*

HANSEN, *A Table of Series and Products*

HARTMANIS AND STEARNS, *Algebraic Structure Theory of Sequential Machines*

JACOBY, et al., *Iterative Methods for Nonlinear Optimization Problems*

JOHNSON, *System Structure in Data, Programs, and Computers*

KIVIAT, et al., *The SIMSCRIPT II Programming Language*

LAWSON AND HANSON, *Solving Least Squares Problems*

LORIN, *Parallelism in Hardware and Software: Real and Apparent Concurrency*

LOUDEN AND LEDIN, *Programming the IBM 1130,* 2nd ed.

MARTIN, *Computer Data-Base Organization*

MARTIN, *Design of Man-Computer Dialogues*

MARTIN, *Design of Real-Time Computer Systems*

MARTIN, *Future Developments in Telecommunications*

MARTIN, *Programming Real-Time Computing Systems*

MARTIN, *Security, Accuracy, and Privacy in Computer Systems*

MARTIN, *Systems Analysis for Data Transmission*

MARTIN, *Telecommunications and the Computer*

MARTIN, *Teleprocessing Network Organization*
MARTIN AND NORMAN, *The Computerized Society*
MCKEEMAN, et al., *A Compiler Generator*
MEYERS, *Time-Sharing Computation in the Social Sciences*
MINSKY, *Computation: Finite and Infinite Machines*
NIEVERGELT, et al., *Computer Approaches to Mathematical Problems*
PLANE AND MCMILLAN, *Discrete Optimization: Integer Programming and Network Analysis for Management Decisions*
POLIVKA AND PAKIN, *APL: The Language and Its Usage*
PRITSKER AND KIVIAT, *Simulation with GASP II: A FORTRAN-based Simulation Language*
PYLYSHYN, ed., *Perspectives on the Computer Revolution*
RICH, *Internal Sorting Methods Illustrated with PL/1 Programs*
SACKMAN AND CITRENBAUM, eds., *On-Line Planning: Towards Creative Problem-Solving*
SALTON, ed., *The SMART Retrieval System: Experiments in Automatic Document Processing*
SAMMET, *Programming Languages: History and Fundamentals*
SCHAEFER, *A Mathematical Theory of Global Program Optimization*
SCHULTZ, *Spline Analysis*
SCHWARZ, et al., *Numerical Analysis of Symmetric Matrices*
SHAH, *Engineering Simulation Using Small Scientific Computers*
SHAW, *The Logical Design of Operating Systems*
SHERMAN, *Techniques in Computer Programming*
SIMON AND SIKLOSSY, eds., *Representation and Meaning: Experiments with Information Processing Systems*
STERBENZ, *Floating-Point Computation*
STOUTEMYER, *PL/1 Programming for Engineering and Science*
STRANG AND FIX, *An Analysis of the Finite Element Method*
STROUD, *Approximate Calculation of Multiple Integrals*
TANENBAUM, *Structured Computer Organization*
TAVISS, ed., *The Computer Impact*
UHR, *Pattern Recognition, Learning, and Thought: Computer-Programmed Models of Higher Mental Processes*
VAN TASSEL, *Computer Security Management*
VARGA, *Matrix Iterative Analysis*
WAITE, *Implementing Software for Non-Numeric Application*
WILKINSON, *Rounding Errors in Algebraic Processes*
WIRTH, *Systematic Programming: An Introduction*
YEH, ed., *Applied Computation Theory: Analysis, Design, Modeling*

RAYMOND P. POLIVKA

IBM Corporation

SANDRA PAKIN

Consultant

THE LANGUAGE

AND

ITS USAGE

Prentice-Hall, Inc., Englewood Cliffs, New Jersey

Library of Congress Cataloging in Publication Data

POLIVKA, RAYMOND P.
    APL: the language and its usage.

    (Prentice-Hall series in automatic computation)
    Bibliography: p.
    Includes index.
    1. APL (Computer program language) I. Pakin, Sandra,
joint author. II. Title.
QA76.73.A27P64   001.6′424   75-4943
ISBN 0-13-038885-8

APL: The Language and Its Usage
Polivka   /   Pakin

© 1975 by Prentice-Hall, Inc.
Englewood Cliffs, N. J.

Printed in the United States of America

10   9   8

PRENTICE-HALL INTERNATIONAL, INC., *London*
PRENTICE-HALL OF AUSTRALIA, PTY. LTD., *Sydney*
PRENTICE-HALL OF CANADA, LTD., *Toronto*
PRENTICE-HALL OF INDIA PRIVATE LIMITED, *New Delhi*
PRENTICE-HALL OF JAPAN, INC., *Tokyo*

To Our Families

CONTENTS

LIST OF ILLUSTRATIONS

PREFACE

APL is a versatile programming language providing a direct means for problem-solving by students, engineers, scientists, educators, and businessmen. It is used interactively on typewriter or cathode ray tube (CRT) terminals.

APL has many primitive functions, each invoked by a symbol in the APL symbol set. With these supplied functions, the APL user can evaluate an expression for immediate results, such as one for finding the solution to a set of simultaneous linear equations. And he can define functions of his own, such as those for maintaining inventory control on a set of warehouse items or for presenting computer-assisted instructional material. By defining functions, the user tailors the language to meet his needs, expressed in ways best suited for him. The user can also interface with other processors for maintaining files and for input and output of data. Simple keyboard entries are provided for managing system resources and otherwise communicating with the APL system's environment.

APL: *The Language and Its Usage* is a complete and comprehensive presentation of APL. It is intended for the problem-solver. The text has grown out of several years of teaching APL. Its organization is such that the reader will be able to solve real and significant problems as he is introduced to APL functions and concepts. New functions and concepts are grouped so that problems requiring similar operations can be solved most satisfactorily. That is:

Chapter 1: *Basic APL*

Presents a working set of APL functions and operations

Chapter 2: *Function Definition*

Presents the principal conventions and mechanics of defining functions

Chapter 3: *The Shape of Data*

Discusses data and its shape and the interrelationship between data and the APL functions that manipulate it

Chapter 4: *Elementary Functions*

Presents APL functions for solving most problems whose solution is gained by the evaluation of formulas

Chapter 5: *Extensions of the Scalar Dyadic Functions to Arrays and other Array Handling Capabilities*

Presents additional functions for operations on the elements of an array

Chapter 6: *Additional Techniques and Capabilities of Defining Functions*

Presents branching, interacting defined functions, format control, debugging tools, and recursive functions

Chapter 7: *Data Selection and Rearrangement*

Presents further functions for data manipulation on arrays

Chapter 8: *Communications with the APL Supporting System*

Discusses system commands and system variables and functions

Chapter 9: *Data Communication—The Shared Variable Facility*

Discusses the shared variable communication facility and the TSIO processor of APL.SV

When access to an APL system is available, the reader should supplement his reading with terminal sessions as often as possible. He should develop an experimental, try-and-see attitude.

APL: The Language and Its Usage contains 181 illustrative solved problems. These illustrations show sample applications or useful programming techniques. Each APL function is illustrated in at least one way to demonstrate its usage.

APL: The Language and Its Usage contains more than 400 problems. These follow each section of each chapter and are keyed to the text presentation. Sample data is provided with most problems and the result anticipated from this data is given. By solving these problems, the user gains familiarity with a functions's responses to various arguments, practices applying the function in a problem situation, and develops techniques in the preparation of data. There is a sufficient range of problems in terms of applications and difficulty so that all readers should find problems to satisfy, teach, and challenge them.

The bibliography provides extensive material. For instance, the section on applications lists books and articles discussing APL applications in education, business, engineering and science, computers and computing, and mathematics and statistics.

The first four appendices provide a reference section, describing APL functions and operations and error reports. The last two appendices describe alternative approaches to data communication.

While some of the text, particularly the early chapters, can be used successfully by readers at the high school level, later chapters and some illustrations and problems expect more background—academically or professionally—than that normally possessed by a high school student. College and professional readers should find *APL: The Language and Its Usage* replete with detail on APL.

IBM's APL/360 program product (5734-XM6) has over the years formed the essential core of APL. In 1973 IBM introduced APL.SV (5799-AJF) extending APL/360 to include both a generalized communications facility through the use of shared variables and some additional primitive functions. *APL: The Language and Its Usage* is based on APL.SV. Differences between APL/360 and APL.SV are noted. Other companies such as Burroughs, Computer Innovations, Scientific Time Sharing, and Xerox Data Systems have added their own enhancements to APL/360, especially in the areas of function and line editing, formatted output, and file input/output. The Burroughs APL/700 file system and the Scientific Time Sharing APL*Plus file subsystem are summarized in appendices as examples of file systems that differ from that of APL.SV. Users of all APL systems should find that *APL: The Language and Its Usage* provides them the foundation for successful work in APL.

ACKNOWLEDGMENTS

We are indebted to our colleagues and friends who painstakingly read the manuscript of *APL: The Language and Its Usage* and made suggestions for improvements and who willingly contributed illustration and problem ideas. In particular we would like to thank W. Asprey, P. Berry, P. Calingaert, D. Martin, D. Polivka, L. Solheim, and S. Van Shaik for their critical reading of the manuscript; K. Haralson for reading and teaching from the manuscript; L. Breed for his reading of Appendix E and J. Ryan for his reading of Appendix F; and P. Benkard, P. Berry, T. Borden, P. Calingaert, P. Carrol, L. Coleman, R. Doyle, K. Haralson, P. Nicholson, S. E. Pakin, B. Randolph, J. Sowa, and L. Woodrum for contributing illustrations and problem ideas. Nevertheless, any errors or omissions in the text are our responsibility and not those of the people listed here.

We are also indebted to Science Research Associates for use of exercise material in problem sections, and to IBM for their support and cooperation.

Special thanks are owed to the many students who used various drafts of the text and problems, to J. Marsden, D. Walsh, and L. Williams of IBM for their help and support, and to J. Polivka, D. Polivka, A. Polivka, and A. Preis for their help in proofreading the text.

To our families—Joanne, David, and Anne Polivka and Sherwin, Scott, and Stacy Pakin—we owe our gratitude for their understanding, patience, and encouragement. And finally, we are indebted to K. Iverson and A. Falkoff, without whom this fine and exciting tool would never have been.

THE LANGUAGE

AND

ITS USAGE

CHAPTER

1

BASIC APL: A WORKING SET
OF APL FUNCTIONS

Data items in APL can be numeric or character. They can be structured in arrays such as a vector and can be operated on by any of the APL primitive functions. Data can be represented by variables and can be stored and later retrieved for further use.

Section 1.1 FOUR FAMILIAR FUNCTIONS

The APL keyboard is shown below:

Appendix A names and describes each of the keyboard symbols.

Adding, subtracting, multiplying, and dividing are as easy to do on an APL terminal as on the simplest desk calculator. After signing on,* one simply types the appropriate digits and the symbol for the arithmetic function desired: + for addition, − for subtraction, × for multiplication, and ÷ for division; and then strikes the RETURN key to signal that the expression typed in should be evaluated. For example,

```
      95 + 117      ← you type (followed by RETURN)
212                  ← computer responds

      338 - 182     ← you type (followed by RETURN)
156                  ← computer responds

      3965 × 217
860405

      36937 ÷ 479
77.113
```

Examples in the text, such as these, are shown as they would appear in APL.SV. This means that, in general, what you type is automatically indented six spaces from the left margin and that the computer response starts at the left margin. Results in the examples are shown carried to five decimal places.†

Of course, one does not ordinarily sit down with paper and pencil, slide rule, adding machine, desk calculator, or computer merely to add, subtract, multiply, or divide numbers at random. Typically, the numbers have some purpose: They are related to a problem to be solved. For example,

What is the per share cost if I purchase 16 shares of ITBO Products at a net cost of $2191.74?

Suppose that the air fare for a wife traveling with her husband is three-fourths of his fare. How much will it cost for both tickets if the husband's fare is $197?

What is the maximum tax I will have to pay on a long-term capital gain of $1937.62 if the tax rate is 25 percent.

Evaluating simple arithmetic expressions gives the answers to these problems:

```
      2191.74 ÷ 16
136.98375
```

---

*Instructions for signing on an IBM 2741 communications terminal with a Data-Phone acoustic coupler are given in Appendix *D*.

†In IBM S/360 (370) the calculations are carried to 16 significant digits. However, the actual number of digits printed is controlled by the user through a system command or system variable (digit display is discussed in Chapter 8).

```
      1.75 × 197
344.75
      .25 × 1937.62
484.41
```

Typing each of these lines at an APL terminal produces the results shown. Notice that while we might expect an answer in dollars and cents, the results are not automatically rounded to hundredths. A method for rounding is shown in Illustration 4.11.

Here are two problems requiring a different kind of solution:

How many seconds are there in a year if a year has 365 days?

What is the cost, including a 5% sales tax, of purchasing four shirts at $9.95 a shirt?

The solution for each of these problems is a sequence of products. In the first, the solution is the product of the seconds per minute (60), minutes per hour (60), hours per day (24), and days per year (365). In the second, the solution is the product of the tax converted to a decimal and added to 1 (1.05), the number of shirts (4), and the price per shirt (9.95). The APL solutions are

```
      60 × 60 × 24 × 365
31536000
      1.05 × 4 × 9.95
41.79
```

Still other problems may require the use of two or more functions for their solutions. For example,

What is the income tax due on a taxable income of $576,890 if the tax is $55,490 plus 70% of the excess over $100,000?

This problem can be solved by subtracting first to find the excess, then multiplying the remainder by the percentage to find the additional tax, and finally adding that amount to the base tax to find the total tax. The order in which the functions are applied—the order of execution—is first subtraction, second multiplication, and last addition. The APL solution that describes this procedure is

```
      55490+.7×576890-100000
389313
```

The expression is read from left to right. It says to 55490 add the result of taking seven-tenths of the result of subtracting 100000 from 576890. Stated in general terms, the APL rule of evaluation is that every function operates on the value to its immediate left and the value of the entire expression to its right.

The order of execution of the functions to obtain the result to the income tax problem stated above is subtraction, multiplication, and addition. And in the solution expression subtraction is the rightmost function, multiplication is the next rightmost, and addition is the leftmost function. From this it can be seen that the evaluation is performed from right to left, with the rightmost function applied first, then the next rightmost, and so forth. The arrangement of functions in an APL expression—called the *syntax of the expression*—is dictated by the way the expression is evaluated. That evaluation is from right to left. In fact, the evaluation rule is often called the *right-to-left* rule.

The diagram below shows how the tax expression is evaluated following the right-to-left rule. The parenthesized numbers indicate the order in which the intermediate results are calculated.

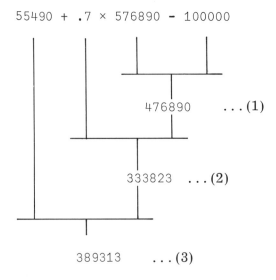

```
55490 + .7 × 576890 - 100000
```

476890   ...(1)

333823   ...(2)

389313   ...(3)

The right-to-left rule of evaluation is the only rule of evaluation in APL. A corollary to it concerns parentheses. Parentheses, properly paired (a left parenthesis for every right parenthesis and vice versa), are always permitted. The expression in parentheses is evaluated first. In the event that there are nested parentheses, the innermost expression is evaluated first.

Sometimes parentheses are necessary to alter the order of execution of an expression so that it can produce the desired result. For example,

What is the average cost of three yachts whose costs were $12,750, $23,896, and $18,975?

One way to solve this problem satisfactorily is to add first and then divide by 3. Parentheses are needed to indicate that the addition should occur before the division:

(12750 + 23896 + 18975)÷ 3

The evaluation is shown in the following diagram:

(12750 + 23896 + 18975) ÷ 3

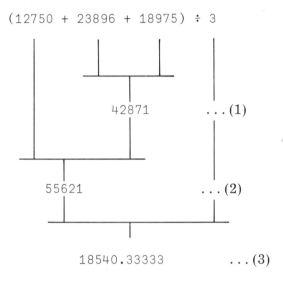

Note that within parentheses the evaluation follows the right-to-left rule. Had parentheses not been used in the solution, the expression `12750+23896+18975 ÷ 3` would have been evaluated by dividing `18975` by `3`, then adding `23896` to the quotient, and finally adding `12750` to the intermediate sum. This results in the value `42971`, much more than the value of any one yacht. The evaluation of the expression without parentheses is shown in the following diagram:

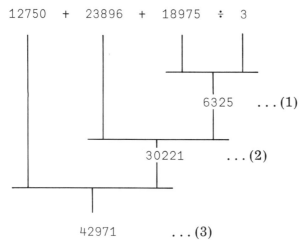

```
12750  +  23896  +  18975  ÷  3
```

                              6325   ...(1)

                    30221   ...(2)

        42971   ...(3)

Extra or unnecessary parentheses in an expression properly placed do not harm the evaluation of that expression. The tax expression could have been written

    (55490+.7×(576890-100000))

and the result still would have been `389313`. The parentheses here do not alter the order of execution and so do not alter the result.

Illustration 1.1   Cigarette Smoking and Life Expectancy

According to Linus Pauling an individual aged 50 who smoked a pack of cigarettes or more daily since the age of 21 has shortened his life expectancy by 8.5 years. On the basis of a pack of 20 cigarettes a day, the number of minutes each cigarette smoked shortened his life can be calculated as follows:

    8.5×365×24×60÷20×365×50-21
21.103

PROBLEMS

1. Evaluate expressions (a)-(n):
   (a) 2+6×7
   (b) 2×6+7
   (c) (2×6)+7
   (d) 2+3+4+5
   (e) 2×3×4×5
   (f) 2÷3÷4÷5
   (g) ((2×3)+4)+5
   (h) ((2×3)×4)×5
   (i) ((2÷3)÷4)÷5
   (j) (330÷15)×42-37
   (k) 3×4+2
   (l) 0÷0
   (m) 2÷0
   (n) 1+1÷1+1÷1+1÷1

2. Use the general expressions shown below:

   5 α 6 ω 2

   6 α 5 ω 2

   2 α 5 ω 6

   For α and ω in the above expressions, substitute the following functions and evaluate the resulting expressions:

	α	ω
(a)	+	×
(b)	×	+
(c)	+	÷
(d)	÷	+

3. In the sets of expressions (a)-(e) which expressions are equivalent?
   (a) (1) $A \times B + C$
       (2) $(A \times B) + C$
       (3) $A \times (B + C)$

   (b) (1) $(A+B)-C+D$
       (2) $A+B-C+D$
       (3) $A+(B-C)+D$
       (4) $A+B-(C+D)$
       (5) $(A+B)-(C-D)$
       (6) $(A+B+C)+D$

   (c) (1) $A-B \times C+D$
       (2) $(A-B) \times C-D$
       (3) $A-B \times (C+D)$
       (4) $A+B \times (C+D)$
       (5) $(A-B \times C)+D$
       (6) $(A-B) \times (C-D)$

   (d) (1) $B \times B - 4 \times A \times C$
       (2) $(B \times B) - 4 \times (A \times C)$
       (3) $(B \times B) - 4 \times A \times C$
       (4) $(B \times B - (4 \times (A \times C)))$
       (5) $B \times B - (4 \times A) \times C$

   (e) (1) $A \div B \div C \div D$
       (2) $A \div (B \div C) \div D$
       (3) $A \div B \div (C \div D)$
       (4) $(A \times C) \div B \times D$
       (5) $A \times B \div C \times D$
       (6) $(A \times B) \div (C \times D)$

4. Construct expressions for each of the following:
   (a) The sum of 5 and 11.

   (b) The difference between 19.23 and 3.57.

   (c) 8.6 more than 0.451.

5. (a) The formula for determining the number of calories needed by an infant between 6 months and 1 year old is calories = pounds × 45.5. Write an expression to determine how many calories an 8-month-old, 19-pound infant needs.

   (b) The formula for determining the number of grams of protein for an infant between 6 months and 1 year old is grams of protein = pounds × .8. Write an expression to determine how many grams of protein an 8-month-old, 19-pound infant needs.

   (*Source: Nutritive Values of Foods*, Home and Garden Bulletin No. 72, U. S. Department of Agriculture, Washington, D. C., 1971.)

6. A file contains a coded date format which is computed by multiplying the last two digits of the year by the number of intervals per year (months, weeks, quarters, etc.) and adding the current interval to the result. For example, the code for May 1970 on a monthly basis is 5 + 12 × 70.
   (a) Write an expression to determine the code for the twenty-third week, 1968 on a weekly basis.

   (b) Write an expression to determine the code for the third quarter, 1984 on a quarterly basis.

Section 1.2   DATA REPRESENTATION

The four arithmetic functions operate on numbers to produce numbers. These numbers may be integral or rational (fractions) and may have positive or negative values. Numbers may be represented in *standard notation* as a string of digits such as 12 or 456 or in *exponential notation*.

Exponential notation consists of the product of

1. A rational number and

2. Ten raised to an appropriate integral power

Thus, 1492 in exponential notation is 1.492×10^3. Within APL (and most computing languages) an E is used to represent the ×10 (times 10 to the) in exponential notation. Hence 1.492×10^3 using an E would be $1.492E3$. Also, $2.345E6$ is 2345000, that is, 2.345 *times 10 to the* sixth power. Exponential notation is useful for expressing very large or very small numbers. For example, a light year, expressed in exponential notation, is $5.88E12$ (5,880,000,000,000) miles.

Numbers can always be entered in either standard notation or exponential notation at the preference of the user. However, for very small numbers, APL.SV automatically displays numbers less than 0.00001 in exponential notation. For very large numbers, the shift to exponential notation depends on the digits display. If the number of significant digits displayed is five, as it is in the examples in the text, APL.SV automatically displays numbers greater than $1E5$ in exponential notation.

In general, decimal numbers are displayed in exponential notation if their value is greater than 10 raised to the digits display setting.

Nonintegral rational numbers (or fractions) are represented with the decimal point, such as 3.45 or .5. Positive numbers and zero are represented without a sign. Negative numbers are represented with the negative sign ‾, such as ‾45 or ‾7.8. The negative sign symbol is raised to distinguish it from the minus symbol -. Not only is there a visual distinction between the negative symbol and the minus symbol, but there is a distinction in their meanings. The negative sign is a part of the number; it indicates something about the number, specifically that it is less than zero. The minus symbol is a function symbol; it specifies a function to be performed on a number or set of numbers. Nonintegral rational numbers between ‾1 and 0 and between 0 and 1 can be represented in exponential notation by indicating a negative number following the E, such as 2.345E‾4 (.0002345). An angstrom, for instance, expressed in exponential notation is 1.0E‾7 (.0000001) millimeters.

Commas must not be used in the representation of a single number. The number three-thousand five-hundred seventy-four should be written 3574 *not* 3,574. Neither can spaces be used in the representation of a single number. For example, a light year cannot be represented 5.88 E 12.

Some functions that will be discussed can operate on character data as well as numeric data. A *character* data item is represented by enclosing the character in quotes, such as 'H' or '$*$'. Any character on the APL keyboard, the return, and the defined composite characters formed by typing one symbol over another are valid character data.

Numbers and/or characters are called *arguments* when they are data associated with a function. For example, in the expression 9×8, the numbers 9 and 8 are arguments of multiplication. 9 is the *left argument* because it appears to the left of the function symbol, and 8 is the *right argument* because it appears to the right of the function symbol. An expression might also be an argument of a function. For example,

```
      (95+86+21)×2÷3
134.67
```

The left argument of multiplication is the parenthesized expression (95+86+21), and the right argument of multiplication is the expression 2÷3. In the expression

```
      95+86+21×2÷3
195
```

the left argument of multiplication is 21, and the right argument is 2÷3.

Illustration 1.2   How Much Is a Billion Dollars?

On January 6, 1972 someone wrote to Ann Landers saying he had read that if a person had a billion dollars and he went into business the year Christ was born and he lost $1000 every day, he would still be in business and could stay in business for another 765 years before the billion dollars ran out. He wanted to know whether this was true or false. Ann's answer was "I am also rotten in arithmetic, but I asked a professor at MIT and he said, 'Yes, it's true'."

The following expression which computes the difference between a billion dollars and such a rate of spending verifies the reply:

```
    1E9-(765+1972)×1000×365.25
3.1075E5
```

With $310,750 remaining, the person could continue in business for almost another year.

Illustration 1.3   The Optimum Lecture

John Von Neumann is said to have defined the optimum length of a lecture as one micro-century. The number of minutes in a micro-century can be determined by the expression

```
    1E⁻6×100×365×24×60
52.56
```

PROBLEMS

1. Evaluate expressions (a)–(t):

   (a) 10-13
   (b) ⁻10+13
   (c) 5-3-6
   (d) 5+⁻3-6
   (e) (5-3)-6
   (f) 5-(3-6)
   (g) 2-3-4-5
   (h) ((2-3)+4)-5
   (i) 2+3-4+5
   (j) (2+3)-4+5
   (k) 2+(3-4+5)
   (l) 2+(3-4)+5
   (m) (16-11)+⁻3×4
   (n) (16-11)-3×4
   (o) 3×4+⁻2
   (p) 3×⁻4+2
   (q) ⁻6×⁻4+2
   (r) ⁻2×⁻6.34E4
   (s) 5×⁻1.6÷⁻.2
   (t) ⁻5×⁻1.6÷⁻.2

2. Use the general expressions shown below:

   5 α 6 ω 2
   6 α 5 ω 2
   2 α 5 ω 6

   For α and ω, substitute the following functions and evaluate the resulting expressions:

	α	ω
(a)	-	×
(b)	×	-
(c)	-	÷
(d)	÷	-

3. Write the numbers (a)–(j) in exponential notation:

   (a) 4.32   (b) 132   (c) 76135.1
   (d) ‾734.63   (e) ‾2678   (f) 0.00357
   (g) 0.0132   (h) ‾0.07346   (i) ‾0.132
   (j) ‾0.00389

4. Write the numbers (a)–(d) in standard notation:

   (a) 8.367E5
   (b) ‾2.141E3
   (c) 1.46215E‾4
   (d) ‾7.86214E‾6

5. Construct expressions for each of the following:
   (a) 3.725 times negative 9.5.
   (b) Negative 8.6 more than .451.
   (c) 3.75 times a value which is ‾9.1 more than .451.
   (d) Three and two-fifths of 34.5.
   (e) The sum of the two products 3 times 4.5 and one-half of negative 6.
   (f) The product of the two sums 3 plus 4.5 and one-half plus negative 6.

6. (a) Light travels at approximately 186,000 miles per second. Express this value in exponential form.
   (b) A light year is the distance light travels in a year, approximately 5.88E12 miles. Express this in standard notation.
   (c) The miles in a light year given in part (b) was based on 186,272 miles per second. Write an expression to determine the number of miles that light travels in 1 year if light travels at 186,000 miles per second.
   (d) Write an expression to compute the difference in miles in a light year if 186,000 miles per second is used instead of 186,272 miles per second.

7. Some quasars (quasi-stellar objects) are as remote as 10 billion light years away.
   (a) Write this distance in exponential form.
   (b) How many miles, expressed in exponential form, would this be?

8. One centimeter is equivalent to 100,000,000 angstrom units.
   (a) Express in exponential form the number of angstrom units in a centimeter.
   (b) Express in exponential form the number of centimeters in an angstrom unit.

Section 1.3 VECTORS

Section 1.3.1　Vectors Introduced

Consider the following problem in which the same process must be applied again and again to similar data:

A discount music store sells its records at 70% of the retail price. The records retail for $5.95, $4.95, $3.95, and $1.95. What does the music store sell its records for?

One way of getting the answer is to enter four expressions, each a record retail price, times the net percentage expressed as a decimal:

```
      .7×5.95
4.165
      .7×4.95
3.465
      .7×3.95
2.765
      .7×1.95
1.365
```

While this method produces the answers, a far simpler way is to use the concept of a *vector*. A vector is an ordered set or list of data. The retail prices can be made into a vector simply by listing the data in a line with each data element separated from the others by a space, like this: 5.95 4.95 3.95 1.95. Then the vector can be multiplied by .7, like this:

```
      .7×5.95 4.95  3.95  1.95
4.165 3.465 2.765 1.365
```

The result is a four-component vector; each component of the result is the result of multiplying .7 by the corresponding component of the data vector. Both arguments of a function might be vectors. For example, suppose that another record store has a varying discount depending on the list price of the record—perhaps 55%, 60%, 70%, and 75% for the $1.95, $3.95, $4.95, and $5.95 records, respectively. The selling prices of the records can be found by using a vector of percents as decimals and a vector of costs.

```
       Percents as Decimals          Retail Prices
      ⎧⎯⎯⎯⎯⎯⌃⎯⎯⎯⎯⎯⎫     ⎧⎯⎯⎯⎯⎯⌃⎯⎯⎯⎯⎯⎫
        .55  .6  .7  .75  ×   1.95  3.95  4.95  5.95
1.0725 2.37 3.465 4.4625
```

Again the result is a four-component vector. This time it is the result of multiplying corresponding components of the vectors. As you can see, using vectors is a means of consolidating data. What might appear to be several problems is not only more easily identifiable as a single problem but can be treated as a single problem.

A *numeric vector* is a vector of numbers, each separated by at least one space from those adjacent to it. Each number in the list is a *component* or *element* in

the vector. The *length* of a vector is its number of components. For example, the
vector 56   8.9   ⁻4   23   0   is a five-component vector; its length is five. Each
component in a numeric vector can be represented in any of the ways available to
represent numbers (see Sec. 1.2), for example,

```
    6   8   9   3   6   7

    6.8   9   4   ⁻6.7

    78   5.6E13   5.9E⁻10

    897   6.78   ⁻45   6.7E10   5.4   8.8E⁻15   ⁻3.47
```

A *character vector* is represented as a list of characters enclosed in quotes. For
example, 'HELLO' is a five-component character vector. Within quotes, the space is
considered a character, so the vector 'HI THERE' , for example, has eight components, not seven. If one of the characters in a character vector is a quote, it must be
entered as a double quote, for example, 'DON''T ASK' must be entered to produce
DON'T ASK. If a return is entered as part of a character vector, the closing quote is
automatically printed on the next line. Thus the return is the last character of the
character string. If the return is part of the character vector, the printed quote can
be erased by the sequence backspace-attention and the character string continued.*
    A character vector made up of digits such as '123' does not represent a num-
ber. '123' is a character vector made up of three components. Also it is not possible
to have both numeric data and character data in the same vector.
    Evaluating expressions with vectors proceeds component by component. The
result is a vector with a component corresponding to each component in the vector
argument(s). For example,

```
    5 + 7  9  3  8
12 14  8 13
```

That is, the components of the result are (5+7),(5+9),(5+3), and (5+8).
    If both the arguments are vectors, they must have the same number of compo-
nents. The first component of the result is the result of having operated on the
first component of each vector; the second component of the result is the result of
having operated on the second component of each vector, and so forth. For example,

```
    6 8 9 3 + 9 7 2 1
15 15 11  4
```

That is, the components of the result are (6+9),(8+7),(9+2), and (3+1).
    Evaluating expressions containing vectors follows the right-to-left rule. Each
vector is a single argument. If you have trouble seeing the vector, you might enclose

---

*APL.SV only. In APL/360 a carrier return does not automatically provide a closing quote.

it in parentheses; for example, (6 8 9 3)+(9 7 2 1). This does not affect the evaluation of the expression. If a vector is to the immediate left of a function, the entire vector, *not* the last component of the vector, is the left argument of the function. For example,

```
      6.95 10.95 14.5 × 1774 ÷ 9
1369.9 2158.4 2858.1
```

The result is a three-component vector obtained by first dividing 1774 by 9 and then multiplying each of the components of the vector 6.95 10.95 14.5 by that quotient.

Illustration 1.4   Total Cost of Items in a Purchase

A company places an order for three items as follows:

Item	Number of Units	Cost Per Unit
A	24	2.61
B	18	3.02
C	15	1.93

A 5% sales tax is added. The total cost of each item can be determined by the expression

```
      1.05×24 18 15×2.61 3.02 1.93
65.772 57.078 30.398
```

Section 1.3.2   A Vector of Consecutive Integers—Index Generator

A vector of consecutive integers such as 1 2 3 4 5 can be generated by the *index generator* function. The general form of this function is

$$\iota B$$

ι is the function symbol and is called *iota*. The argument B must be a nonnegative integer; that is, it can be any positive integer or zero. The argument must be a single number. The result of ιB is the vector of integers from 1 through the value of the argument. For example,

```
      ι5
1 2 3 4 5

      ι10
1 2 3 4 5 6 7 8 9 10
```

The expression $\iota 0$ is a special case and is known as the *empty vector*. The empty vector is a vector of no components and is discussed in Chapter 3. A blank line is printed in response to $\iota 0$: The computer line-feeds and indents for the next input.

Warning: There is a great temptation for a user who has just learned about index generator to try an expression like ⍳1000 on the terminal to see what happens. The typing speed of a terminal is approximately 15 characters per second. After watching the first 100 numbers or so type out, the user usually deplores his action and wants a way to stop the seemingly endless display. Pressing the attention key (ATTN) on the terminal halts the execution and display of any expression.

Illustration 1.5 Arithmetic Progressions

The index generator is useful for creating *arithmetic progressions*, for example, a progression of even numbers or a progression of odd numbers:

```
     2×⍳5
2 4 6 8 10

     ⁻1+2×⍳5
1 3 5 7 9
```

A general formula for creating an arithmetic progression using ⍳ is

$$S+D\times\iota N$$

where N is the number of terms in the progression, D is the difference between adjacent terms, and S is the amount added to get the first term. For example, the expression for the progression 4 7 10 13 16 19 22 is 1+3×⍳7 ($S=1$, $D=3$, $N=7$).

Other progressions and the expressions that create them are shown below:

Progression	Expression
2 7 12 17 22 27 32 37	⁻3+5×⍳8'
.1 .2 .3 .4 .5 .6 .7 .8 .9 1	.1×⍳10 (0+.1×⍳10)
5 8 11 14 17 20	2+3×⍳6
⁻1 ⁻3 ⁻5 ⁻7 ⁻9	1+⁻2×⍳5

PROBLEMS

1. Evaluate expressions (a)–(r):

(a) 2+3 5 ⁻5 6.1 7

(b) 2−3 5 ⁻6 6.1 7

(c) 2 ⁻3 6 − 4 7 2

(d) 3 2×6 ⁻9

(e) 6÷2 3

(f) 2+3 ⁻4+5

(g) 2+3−4 5

(h) 2 3−4+5

(i) 2 ⁻3−4+5

(j) 2×3 4 5

(k) 2 3 4×5

(l) 2 3×4 5

(m) .5 1 1.5 + 150.5 ⁻3.15E⁻2 ⁻204

(n) (.5×1 2 3)+150.5 ⁻3.15E⁻2 ⁻204

(o) .5×1 2 3+150.5 ⁻3.15E⁻2 ⁻204

(p) 2 3+1.23E2 2.012E⁻2

(q) 3 ⁻5.5E2+3.5E⁻2 6.098

(r) ⁻3 17 + 75 ⁻33

2. Construct an expression for each of the following:

    (a) One-third of the numbers negative 1.739, negative 1.5, and 2.49E3.

    (b) The component-by-component difference between the set of numbers 15.25, 75.34, and negative 100 and the set of numbers 4.2, negative 3.12, and negative 57.5.

3. A speedometer reads 3% too high. Write an expression to determine what the real speed is when the speedometer reads 30, 40, 50, and 60 miles per hour.

4. A company purchases the following:

    24 units of product A for $2.41 per unit

    15 units of product B for $1.47 per unit

    28 units of product C for $3.58 per unit

    (a) Write an expression to determine the total cost for each product.

    (b) Write an expression to determine the total cost for each product including a 5% sales tax.

    (c) Write an expression to determine the total cost for each product if handling charges are added to the cost including sales tax as follows:

    A: $\frac{1}{2}$ cent per unit

    B: $\frac{3}{5}$ cent per unit

    C: $\frac{3}{8}$ cent per unit

5. One hundred-fifteen people responded to the five questions on a survey questionnaire. The results were as follows:

	#1	#2	#3	#4	#5
Yes Responses	108	111	103	109	108

    Write an expression to determine what percentage of the respondents answered yes to each question.

6. A music store has its records classified into four categories A, B, C, and D with the corresponding list prices $5.95, $4.95, $3.95, and $1.95. Write an expression to determine the cost for a record in each of the categories if the records in categories A and B are discounted 40%; category C, 30%; and category D, 15%.

7. The daily protein need for an adult male is 65 grams. Write an expression to determine the percentage of the daily requirement the following foods fulfill:

Peanut butter	4 grams
Bacon	5 grams
Milk	9 grams
Wholewheat bread	3 grams

8. Business X wishes to purchase 1475 units of item A, which has a list price of $5.80 per unit. Distributor A allows a 5% discount and has a shipping charge of $35. Distributor B allows a

4% discount and has a shipping charge of $28. In both cases a 3% sales tax is present on the purchase price excluding shipping. Write an expression to determine the cost of business X of ordering from each distributor.

9. The directions for reconstituting dehydrated potatoes to make 12 servings specifies $4\frac{1}{2}$ cups of water, 6 tablespoons of butter, $\frac{1}{2}$ teaspoon of salt, and $1\frac{1}{4}$ cups of potato flakes. Write an expression to determine the amount of each ingredient to make 4 servings.

10. Write an expression to generate each of the following arithmetic progressions:

(a) 3   7   11   15   19   23
(b) ¯10   ¯7   ¯4   ¯1   2
(c) ¯2.25   ¯1.5   ¯0.75   0   0.75   1.5

11. Refer to problem 6 of Sec. 1.1. What are the codes for each month of 1976?

Section 1.4 VARIABLES AND SYSTEM COMMANDS

Consider this problem:

Last year's earnings per share of a stock portfolio of six common stocks were $2.80, $1.50, $1.35, $2.08, $8.21, and $1.18, respectively. At the end of each week prepare a list of current price-earnings ratios.

The price-earnings ratio can be found by dividing the week's prices by the earnings. During the year the earnings values are the same each week; however, the prices will vary. To avoid the repetitive typing of earnings and likely copying errors, it is far better to store earnings. This can be done by using *variables* and *workspace saving*.

Section 1.4.1 Variables

A *variable* is a name which represents a value. The word *variable* comes from "vary" and indicates that the value represented by the variable may be changed. For instance, the variable Y may have the value 10 or the value 6.7, depending on what value the specifier of Y wants it to have. A *constant*, on the other hand, always has the same unalterable value, for example, 3 is 3. A *specification* or *assignment statement* is the expression that gives a value to a name. The value may be a single number (also called a *scalar*) or a vector (or other array)*; it may be numeric or character. For instance, the specification statement below names the earnings for the example above *EARN*:

EARN←2.8 1.5 1.35 2.08 8.21 1.18

---

*A vector is one form of *array*. Arrays of all forms, such as the matrix or table, are discussed in Chapter 3. Most of what applies to vectors applies similarly to all arrays. In the remaining sections of this chapter, the phrase "vectors (or other arrays)" is used to indicate this, even though arrays are not defined and discussed until Chapter 3.

This expression establishes *EARN* as the name of a six-component vector made up of the numbers 2.8, 1.5, 1.35, 2.08, 8.21, and 1.18. Once a variable has been assigned a value, it can be used in any expression. The expression

```
    45 89 123 56 324 213 ÷ EARN
16.071 59.333 91.111 26.923 39.464 180.51
```

gives the price-earnings ratio if the week's prices for the stocks were $45, $89, $123, $56, $324, and $213.

The parts of a specification statement are

Name of Variable	Symbol	Expression
EARN	←	2.8 1.5 1.35 2.08 8.21 1.18

Names of variables can be made up of letters and numbers. Some examples are

```
   I    BEST    MNTR    SYS3    Z2B2
```

All names in APL follow the same naming rules. These rules are stated formally in the summary to this chapter.

The symbol ← is called the *specification arrow.* It is a left-pointing arrow and can be read "is specified by." The expression to the right of the arrow may be any valid APL expression, such as

```
3987

3 9 8 7

9 ¯7 16 6

9×8÷75

'HELLO'

45  89  123  56  324  213÷EARN

PRICE÷EARN

PRICE1-PRICE
```

In the fifth example, the expression is a character vector. In the last three examples, where variables are used, a value must have been assigned to the variable before it is used; otherwise a *VALUE ERROR* report is given.

The value of a variable can be seen by simply typing in the name of the variable. For example, the variable *EARN* was previously specified. If *EARN* is typed, the computer responds with the value of *EARN*:

```
   EARN
2.8 1.5 1.35 2.08 8.21 1.18
```

Since a specification statement is itself an expression, it may appear to the right of the arrow, such as

    A←B←3

    A←1+B←3

In the first example, both A and B are given the value 3. In the second example, B is given the value of 3 and A is given the value of 4, one more than B, because of the rule of evaluation. When more than one specification arrow appears in a line, as above, it is called *multiple specification*.

   The specification arrow behaves like a function, so the value assigned to A in an expression like A←1+B←3 is everything to the right of the leftmost arrow. Another ramification of this is that the same variable can appear on both sides of the arrow. For example,

    A←4

    A←A+1

The first expression assigns the value 4 to A. The second statement reassigned to A the value of 5, one more than the old value of A. A variable can be respecified as above where the new value is somehow dependent on the old value of the variable, or it can be respecified with an entirely new value. For example,

    A←98 75

respecifies A to be the vector 98 75. Whatever its former value was is lost. Only when the name appears to the left of the arrow does its value change. For example, examine the sequence below:

        ART←9 8 7
        ART×4
    36 32 28
        ART
    9 8 7
        ART+ART
    18 16 14
        ART←75
        ART
    75
        ART+ART
    150
        SALT←2+ART

```
        ART
75
        SALT
77
```

The value of the variable *ART* changes only once even though it was used in eight expressions following its original specification.

The rule of evaluation can now be stated more completely to include variables:

> Every dyadic function takes as its left argument a constant or a variable or a parenthesized expression to its immediate left. Every function takes as its right argument the entire expression to its right or up to the right parenthesis of the pair that encloses it.

Parentheses can be used to change the order of execution. In general, parentheses alter the execution of a function when they make the left argument an expression other than the constant or variable to the immediate left of the function symbol.

Illustration 1.6 Multiple Specification

A set of variables can be set to the same value or to related values by multiple specification.

```
        A←B←C←D←1
```

The values of *A*, *B*, *C*, and *D* are each 1.

```
        A←1+B←1+C←1+D←0
```

The value of *A* is 3; of *B*, 2; of *C*, 1; and of *D*, 0.

Illustration 1.7 Percentage Yield of a Two-Step Process

The percentage yields for three products from step 1 of a process are 95%, 96%, and 90% and from step 2, 95%, 94%, and 91%. Assuming that the number of starts for the three products is 2000, 3000, and 4000, a *single* expression can be used to assign the value of the yield at the end of each step to a variable.

```
        STEP2←.95 .94 .91×STEP1←.95 .96 .90×2000 3000 4000
        STEP1
1900 2880 3600

        STEP2
1805 2707.2 3276
```

Section 1.4.2   System Commands

System commands provide the means for storing, retrieving, transferring, and erasing work; for transmitting messages; and for making inquiries about the contents of the active workspace.* The *active workspace* is the work area in which the user's APL work takes place. The four most basic system commands are discussed in this section. The details of complete workspace control are discussed in Chapter 8.

A system command is identified by an initial right parenthesis) . This right parenthesis is followed by a mnemonic group of letters; for instance, the commands discussed in this section are)*VARS*,)*ERASE*,)*SAVE*, and)*LOAD*.

The command)*VARS* lists alphabetically all the variable names in current use in the workspace. For example,

```
      )VARS
A ART EARN SALT
```

The command)*ERASE* followed by a list of names erases all those names and the associated data from the workspace. For example,

```
      )ERASE EARN A
```

eliminates the variables *EARN* and *A*.

```
      )VARS
ART SALT
```

As long as the terminal is signed on, all variables remain in the workspace and retain their values unless they are erased or are respecified to have new values or if a new workspace is activated. Once the terminal is signed off, however, all the work disappears unless it is saved. The easiest way to do this is with a simple)*SAVE* command. Each saved workspace has a reference name, for example, *ASSETS*. When first establishing a workspace, the)*SAVE* is followed by a name, for example,

```
      )SAVE ASSETS
```

Once this is entered, a confirmation message stating the time on a 24-hour clock and the date is printed:

```
10.21.04 03/23/76
```

If anything is wrong with the save command, an error report pinpointing the error

---

*System commands may vary on different systems. These described here are accurate for APL.SV.

is printed. (Error reports that might occur with system commands are listed in Appendix C along with their causes.)

If a confirmation message is printed after a save command, two things have happened. First, a storage area named *ASSETS* has been entered in a library identified by the terminal's sign-on number and a duplicate of all the work in the active workspace has been placed in the storage area. Second, the active workspace has been given the name *ASSETS*. As long as the storage area and the active workspace have the same name, the storage area can be updated with either *)SAVE* or *)SAVE ASSETS*. Either command replaces the entire storage area *ASSETS* with a duplicate of the current active workspace. If the active workspace does not have the same name as the storage workspace being named in the commands, an error report is given:

```
NOT SAVED THIS WS IS .......
```

The workspace called *CLEAR WS* which is sometimes named in this error report indicates that the active workspace is associated with no name, such as when the terminal is first signed on.

Once a stored workspace has been established, it can be retrieved and brought into the active workspace at any time with a *)LOAD* command. For example,

```
      )LOAD ASSETS
10.21.04 03/23/76
```

After the command is entered, a confirmation message stating the last time and date the workspace was saved or an error report pinpointing the difficulty is printed. If there is confirmation, what will have happened is that a duplicate of the entire work space named *ASSETS* is brought into the active workspace, completely obliterating anything that had been there. (Another command, the *)COPY* command, can be used to bring in selected material without destroying what is in the active workspace. See Sec. 8.1.1.) The saved version of the workspace *ASSETS* is still in the storage library.

PROBLEMS

1. Use the following variables to evaluate expressions (a)–(f):

```
A←2 4 6
B←5 ¯3 9
C←5 1 ¯.5
```

(a) $A+10$	(b) $2 \times A + B$
(c) $C+(A-B) \div 2$	(d) $C+1\ 2\ 3$
(e) $C+A \div 2$	(f) $B-C-A$

2. For the following sequence of statements, the questions apply at the point in the sequence where they appear. (Assume a clear workspace.)

```
A←2
2×A
```

(a) What value is displayed?
(b) What is the value of A?

```
B←2
2×B
B←17 2.5
```

(c) What is the value of B?

```
C←2.75
D←'HOW ARE YOU?'
)SAVE WS1
C←3.5×2
```

(d) What is the value of C?

```
D←B-C
```

(e) What are the values of A, B, C, and D?

```
)VARS
```

(f) What is displayed?

```
)ERASE B
)VARS
```

(g) What is displayed?

```
)LOAD WS1
)VARS
```

(h) What is displayed?
(i) What are the values of each of the variables?

```
A←A×10
```

(j) What is the value of A?

```
B←4×A←A-30
```

(k) What are the values of A and B?

```
)LOAD WS1
```

(l) What are the values of A, B, C, and D?

3. Write an expression to assign to the name *INTEREST* the interest paid on the sum of money *AMT* at the rates of 4%, 5%, $5\frac{1}{2}$%, and 6%.

4. To find the equivalent Fahrenheit temperature for a Celsius (centigrade) reading, one adds 32

to nine-fifths of the Celsius reading. Write the expressions to convert

(a) Celsius C to Fahrenheit.

(b) Fahrenheit F to Celsius.

5. A 1971 Volvo advertisement gave the following statistics: In New York 73,000 cars were abandoned last year. In Chicago cars are abandoned at the rate of one per 7 minutes. In Los Angeles there are 1400 abandoned cars per month. In Detroit 20,000 cars are abandoned per year.

(a) Write an expression to determine how many cars are abandoned per year in Chicago and Los Angeles (365 days per year).

(b) Write an expression to compare the abandonment rates in New York, Los Angeles, and Chicago to that of Detroit.

(c) Write an expression to determine the total car abandonment in the average month in each of the four cities.

6. It has been recommended that the foods we eat should have a minimum of 2 grams of protein for every 100 calories. Here are the grams of protein and calories for normal servings of selected foods:

Food	Grams of Protein	Calories
Buttermilk	9	90
Yogurt	8	125
Hot dog	7	170
Asparagus	3	30
Corn	3	70
Cantaloupe	1	60
White bread	2	70
Apple pie	3	350
Spaghetti	5	155
Sherbet	2	260

(a) Write an expression to determine the calorie-protein ratios for each.

(b) Write an expression to determine what percentage of the adult male daily requirements of protein (65 grams) each food fulfills.

(c) Write an expression to determine what percentage of the adult male daily calorie needs (2800) each food fulfills.

Section 1.5 ERRORS

An error in an expression when you are working on paper is detected by you (or by some person checking your work) or not at all. However, if an erroneous expression is entered at the terminal, the computer may not accept it. If it does not, an error report is printed. For example,

```
      (9+6÷.3
SYNTAX ERROR
      (9+6÷0.3
         ∧
```

Another type of error called a *CHARACTER ERROR* can occur if a character not recognized by the system is typed. This happens most often if an illegal composite character is typed. When a character error occurs, the line is printed out up to the first character error and the keyboard is released to allow you to finish the line.* For example,

    'STOP! YOU MUST NOT HOP ON POP!'   (' overstrike : was typed
                                                instead of ' overstrike .)

CHARACTER ERROR
   'STOP
     ↑ carrier waits here for further entry

The report *RESEND* is given when there is a faulty transmission of data. This usually indicates a hardware failure rather than a user-produced error, although it can occur if the user hits two keys simultaneously.

With the material presented in Chapter 1 thus far, a number of errors in expressions that the computer detects and signals can occur. These are

SYNTAX ERROR: The expression is not properly constructed—a typical result if parentheses are not properly paired.

DOMAIN ERROR: The function is not defined for the given arguments—a typical result if a nonzero number is divided by zero.

LENGTH ERROR: The vector arguments do not have the same number of components. This might occur if a minus sign is used instead of a negative sign in representing a negative number.

VALUE ERROR: No value is associated with the name. This report might be given if an *L* were used instead of a 1 or an *X* instead of an × in an expression.

RANK ERROR: The argument(s) used are not permitted with this function—a typical result if a vector argument is used with index generator.

Appendix B has a complete list of error reports and a description of their causes.

Another kind of error exists—one that is not detectable by the computer. This occurs when the result is not what you anticipated because of misuse of the symbols of APL. This can occur if a comma is used in the representation of a single number or if a minus sign is used instead of a negative sign or if the syntax of the expression causes it to be evaluated one way when you intended it to be evaluated in another way.

Whether an error report or an unanticipated result is printed, the correction procedure (for all errors but the character error) once the expression has been entered is the same: Reenter the entire expression with the correction. Note that only one error

---

*APL.SV only. In APL/360 an illegal overstruck character produces the error report *CHARACTER ERROR*. The entire expression has to be reentered.

is signaled in any error report so that on reentering the expression another error might be detected. For example,

```
      ι6X.3
SYNTAX ERROR
      ι6   X   .3
               ∧

      ι6×.3
DOMAIN ERROR
      ι6×.3
      ∧
```

Sometimes you recognize the error as soon as the computer starts printing the error report. The printing of the error report can be stopped by striking the ATTN key.

     If an error is spotted before the expression containing it is entered, it can be corrected by first backspacing to the error and then hitting the ATTN key to "erase" that character and everything to its right. The expression is then retyped correctly from that point right. For example,

678.L9÷2.3	Typed an L for a 1
∨	Inverted caret—the result of attention after backspacing
19÷2.3	Retyped correction and everything to the right
294.87	Value of the expression 678.19÷2.3

     Backspacing without using the attention key does not erase and does not harm the expression. The general rule is "What you see the system sees." This is called *visual fidelity*. For example, suppose that you are finding the perimeter of a 4 by 3 rectangle. You type 4+3 and realize that you forgot to multiply by 2. To do this without erasing you need to insert parentheses or to precede that expression with 2× to avoid parentheses. In either case, you need to backspace. After typing 4+3 you can backspace five times and then type 2×. What you see is 2×4+3, and that is what is evaluated. Or, after you have typed 4+3, you can backspace four times, type a left parenthesis, space three times, and then type)×2. What you see is (4+3)×2 , and this is what is evaluated.

PROBLEMS

1. Each of the expressions (a)–(h) contains an error. Identify it.

     (a) (9+(8×6)×4   (b) (¯6×2+)1.4−6   (c) 221÷(1.5X6)−3×3

     (d) 8 6 2+2 1×7   (e) L32 ÷ 14   (f) ι2.6

     (g) ι3 5 7   (h) 14ι

Section 1.6   CATENATION

The vector *EARN* discussed in Sec. 1.4 is a list of the last year's earnings for a portfolio of six stocks. Suppose that the portfolio is increased by three stocks whose earnings last year were \$1.51, \$1.18, and \$2.09. How can the earnings vector be updated to reflect the addition in the portfolio? Dismissing retyping the vector again as inefficient and error-prone, there is a function to do this. It is called *catenation*. The function *catenation* is represented by the comma:

       A,B

"To catenate" means "to string together", and this is what the function catenation does. It strings the right argument to the left, forming a single vector with as many components as there are components in both arguments.

Using catenation, *EARN* can be respecified to be the old *EARN* catenated with the new stocks' earnings like this:

```
EARN←EARN,1.15 1.18 2.09

EARN
2.8 1.5 1.35 2.08 8.21 1.18 1.15 1.18 2.09
```

Here are some other examples of catenation:

```
        A←5
        B←7
        C←9 7 6
        D←2 1 ¯3 8

        A,B
5 7

        A,C
5 9 7 6

        C,A
9 7 6 5

        A,B,C
5 7 9 7 6

        A,C,B
5 9 7 6 7

        C,D
9 7 6 2 1 ¯3 8

        C,C
9 7 6 9 7 6
```

Catenation is the only way of including a variable in a vector. For example, the expression 9 8 7 *W* results in a *SYNTAX ERROR* even though *W* may have been assigned a value and is a scalar or a vector, but the expression

    9 8 7, *W*

gives a result, as will the expressions

    9 8, *W*, **7**

    W,9 8 7

Similarly, if the value of a parenthesized expression is to be a component of a vector, catenation is required. For example,

    (3×8÷.67),8 9

Because the comma represents a function, it cannot be used in the representation of a single number, as you saw if you accidentally used one. For example, the result of the expression 5,689 is the two-component vector 5 689. Generally catenation is not used when all the components are numeric, although it could be. Typing 9 8 7 5 or 9,8 7 5 or 9, 8, 7, 5 or 9 8 7,5 all result in 9 8 7 5 being printed. The difference between the first expression and the others is that the first uses no function to produce the result (it is a constant), whereas the others do.

Both arguments of catenation must be numeric or both must be character. It is not possible to catenate a numeric argument and a character argument. An attempt to do so results in a *DOMAIN ERROR* report.

The right-to-left rule of evaluation prevails with catenation (as indeed it does with all functions) as the following four diagrams (a)–(d) demonstrate:

(a)

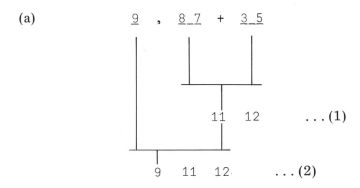

...(1)

...(2)

(b)

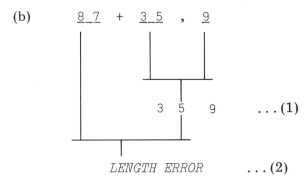

...(1)

...(2)

(c)

$$\underline{2} \times \underline{7} , \underline{3} , \underline{9} \div \underline{5}$$

```
                    1.8              ...(1)

                3 1.8                ...(2)

            7 3 1.8              ...(3)

        14 6 3.6             ...(4)
```

(d)

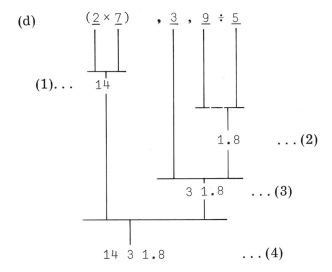

Catenation is the first function that we have discussed that can have character arguments. For example,

```
    'HI' ,' THERE'
HI THERE
```

Note that if the space had not been included as a character, that is, within quotes (here preceding *T*), no space would have been included in the result:

```
    'HI' ,'THERE'
HITHERE
    'HI' , ' THERE'
HI THERE
```

Illustration 1.8   Forming Words

Variables containing parts of words can be catenated in different ways to form new words. For example,

```
    A←'OUT'
    B←'IN'
    C←'DOWN'
    D←'PUT'
```

```
      A,D
OUTPUT

      B,D
INPUT

      D,C
PUTDOWN

      B,D,'/',A,D
INPUT/OUTPUT
```

Illustration 1.9   Creating a Vector with Data
                    Longer than the Typing Line

Catenation is useful for creating a vector which has more components than can be typed on one line. For example,

```
      VEC←234 567 34 5 67 89 234 678 98 7 6 555 4 5 7 89 12 34 566
      VEC←VEC,5 8 9 65 23 56 7 8 9 0 9 123 5 8 3 2 1 678 4 5 656
```

PROBLEMS

1. Evaluate expressions (a)–(m):

   (a) `2,3+4 5`   (b) `2 3+4,5`   (c) `¯2,3+4,5`
   (d) `2,3-4 5`   (e) `2, (3+4),5`   (f) `(2 3+4),5`
   (g) `2 3 4+5 6`   (h) `2,3 4+5 6`   (i) `(2 3 4+5),6`
   (j) `(2 3 4+5) 6`   (k) `'X','Y'`   (l) `'X''Y'`
   (m) `'X' 'Y'`

2. Use the following variables to evaluate expressions (a)–(p):

   ```
   A←14 ¯35            B←¯3 10            C←'QUITE'
   D←'RIGHT'
   ```

   (a) `A,B`   (b) `B,A`   (c) `A B`
   (d) `2,A`   (e) `2 A`   (f) `2,2×B`
   (g) `2×B,A`   (h) `(2×B),A`   (i) `(2×B) A`
   (j) `A, 7, B`   (k) `A, ¯5 7, B`   (l) `C,D`
   (m) `C,' ',D`   (n) `C,B`   (o) `C,' CORRECT'`
   (p) `'NOT ',D`

3. Write an expression to append the test scores 85 and 78 to the vector *TESTSCORES*, a vector of test scores.

4. Use the following variables:

   ```
   A←'THE'
   B←'EARNINGS'
   ```

C←*'P/E RATIO'*
D←*'QUARTER'*

(a) Write an expression to produce the statement *THE P/E RATIO*.

(b) Write an expression to produce the statement *THE 2ND QUARTER EARNINGS*.

Section 1.7   TYPES OF FUNCTIONS
AND CONFORMABILITY RULES

APL functions may have one argument like index generator or they may have two arguments like addition and catenation. Functions of one argument are called *monadic* functions; functions of two arguments are called *dyadic* functions. Monadic and dyadic functions can be further grouped depending on the types of arguments they permit.

The four arithmetic functions that we presented in Sec. 1.1—addition, subtraction, multiplication, and division—are *scalar functions*. Scalar functions are defined first on single-number (called *scalar*) arguments and extend to vectors *component by component*. The following rules guide the operation of all the scalar functions on their arguments:

1. If the arguments are scalar, the result is scalar.

   Example: 7+6 is 13.

2. If both arguments are vectors (or other arrays), they must have the same size and shape.

   Example: 5 6 8 + 1 2 7 is 6 8 15.

3. If one argument is a scalar and one is a vector, the result is a vector of the same size and shape as the vector argument.

   Example: 7 + 5 8 9 is 12   15   16.
              9 2 5 + 9 is 18   11   14.

Rules such as these that state the conditions under which arguments can be combined are known as *conformability rules*.

A function is called *mixed* when a vector appears in its primary definition either as an argument or as the result, and the result may or may not be the same length and shape as the argument(s). Index generator, for example, is a mixed function. Its argument must be scalar, but its result is a vector. Catenation is another mixed function. Its arguments may be scalars or vectors or scalar and vector. Also the lengths of the vector arguments do not have to be the same for catenation as they do for the scalar functions.

Besides APL primitive functions, there are APL primitive *operators*. These operators can be thought of as special extensions to arrays of the scalar dyadic functions. They are characterized as having functions as their argument(s).

Finally, as part of the APL.SV system there are also a number of *system functions* which dynamically describe or affect the environment of the system.*

In addition to the conformability rules associated with a function, a function may have *restrictions* associated with it, limiting in some way the type of arguments permitted. One restriction on division is that a *divisor* must be nonzero if the dividend is nonzero. Note that this restriction is slightly different from the restriction imposed on division in arithmetic. Namely, the expression $0 \div 0$ is permitted in APL and has the value of 1.† A restriction on the arguments of addition, subtraction, multiplication, division, and index generator is that the arguments must be numeric; character arguments are not permitted with these functions. ($2 + 2 = 4$, but what is the sum of the letters *a* and *p*? They cannot be added.) Character arguments are permitted with catenation, however.

The arguments of the scalar functions can be single numbers, vectors, or other arrays (discussed in Chapter 3). This is not so with the mixed functions. Some mixed functions, like index generator, must have a scalar argument; others must have a vector argument; some must have a numeric left argument but may have a character right argument; and so forth. When the definition of a function is given in the text, the conformability rules and restrictions associated with it are also given, except that the conformability rules for all scalar functions are the same as stated above and so are not repeated each time.

Section 1.8 SUMMARY

Functions are either *monadic*, taking one argument, or *dyadic*, taking two arguments. Whether arguments combine is called *conformability*. Functions are grouped for convenience by the conformability requirements on their arguments. For example, all scalar functions operate on a component-by-component basis when combining the arguments.

---

*APL.SV only. In APL/360 there exists a lesser set of *system-dependent* functions.

†It was decided that this result might be useful. Justification for it comes from the fact that the limit of X÷X as X approaches zero is 1.

Functions Introduced in Chapter 1

Name	Function Symbol	Syntax	Definition	Type/ Conformability
Addition	+	$L+R$	Arithmetic sum	Scalar
Subtraction	−	$L-R$	Arithmetic difference	Scalar
Multiplication	×	$L×R$	Arithmetic product	Scalar
Division	÷	$L÷R$	Arithmetic quotient, except $0÷0=1$	Scalar
Catenation	,	L,R	The vector of the components of R appended to the components of L	Mixed; L and R can be scalar or vector; character arguments permitted
Index generator	ι	$ιR$	The vector of integers 1 through R	Mixed; R must be a nonnegative integer

Syntax and Evaluation of Expressions

All but one (index generator) of the APL functions introduced in Chapter 1 are dyadic functions. Dyadic functions have two arguments.

The syntax of an expression with a dyadic function is

$$L \qquad FN \qquad R$$

left   function   right
argument   symbol   argument

The syntax of an expression with a monadic function is

$$FN \qquad R$$

function   right
symbol   argument

An argument is a scalar or a vector or other array, either numeric or character, a variable, or an expression. Every function takes as its right argument the entire expression to its right or up to the right parenthesis of the pair of parentheses that encloses it, and as its left argument, if it has one, the constant, variable, or parenthesized expression to its immediate left. The effect of this rule is that the rightmost expression is evaluated first, then the next rightmost, and so forth. The rule of evaluation is known as the right-to-left rule. Parentheses can be used to change the order of execution.

Naming Rules

The following rules define the naming conventions of APL. These rules hold whether the name applies to a variable, a defined function, or a workspace:

1. A name must begin with a letter, an underscored letter, the symbol Δ, or the symbol $\underline{\Delta}$.

2. After the first character, a name may consist of any combination of letters, underscored letters, digits, Δ, and $\underline{\Delta}$ except for combinations beginning with *S*Δ or *T*Δ

3. A name must not contain any embedded spaces.

4. A name may be of any length. Only the first 77 characters are significant for variables and functions, and only the first 11 characters are significant for workspaces. Characters in a name in excess of 77 (or 11) are ignored.

FUNCTION DEFINITION

AND FUNCTION EDITING

APL has two basic kinds of functions—primitive and defined. Primitive functions like the functions discussed in Chapter 1 are indigenous to APL; they are functions that are part of the language. Defined functions are named collections of expressions formulated by the user and can be thought of as user extensions to the language. They may or may not be used in the same manner as the primitive functions. It is through defining functions that the versatility and power of APL is realized.

Section 2.1 FUNCTION DEFINITION

A defined function is a named collection of expressions that performs a set of calculations. The expressions are executed when the function name and its arguments, if any, are typed. For example, given the height H in inches and the weight W of an overweight woman of average frame as arguments of the defined function $REDUCE$, typing $H\ REDUCE\ W$ causes a four-component vector to be printed: The first component is an average ideal weight for that height; the second, the approximate number of calories necessary to maintain that weight; the third, the approximate number of calories needed daily to reduce 2 pounds a week; and the fourth, the approximate number of weeks it should take to reduce with the reduced calorie input. To find the diet information for a woman who is 5 feet, 6 inches tall and weighs 145 pounds, the parameter information (the values of H and W) and the name of the function ($REDUCE$) are entered:

```
    66 REDUCE 145
130 2200 1200 7.5
```

The results are printed without any expressions for the calculations being typed. (The function definition for $REDUCE$ is shown in Sec. 2.4.)

As an example of function definition, let us define a function to perform the following calculations for a portfolio of common stocks:

Increase/decrease in price over last period

Yield

Price-earnings ratio

The following variables, selected arbitrarily, are used

EARN : Last year's earnings

CMV :   Current market value

OMV :   Old market value

DIV: Annual dividend paid

The expressions for the three calculations are

$CMV-OMV$:   Increase/decrease over last period

$100 \times DIV \div CMV$:   Yield

$CMV \div EARN$:   Price-earnings ratio

These three expressions make up the body of the function. The *body* of a defined function is the collection of expressions that define the function, that is, the way the function behaves. In addition to a body, a defined function has a *header* which defines the syntax of the defined function. A header always contains a name for the function. It may also indicate that the function has arguments such as those of *REDUCE*. The name of a function follows the same naming conventions as those for the naming of a variable (detailed in the summary of Chapter 1); that is, it is an alphameric name.

Function definition is entered and ended by means of the special symbol ∇ —called *del*. The del on the header line indicates a request for *function definition mode*. (The work in Chapter 1 was done in *calculation* mode.) Suppose that we call the stock computation function *STOCK*. To start function definition, we type

    ∇*STOCK*

The del must be the first character. It says "Enter function definition for the function whose name follows." The header ∇*STOCK* indicates that there are no arguments to be entered at the time of the function call. The computer response to the header is

[1]

The bracketed number is the number of the statement to be entered. (On a first definition, the number in brackets is always 1. For additions or other editing to the function this number may not be 1.) The bracketed number indicates definition mode. This means that an expression entered following the brackets is part of the definition. Expressions entered in definition mode are not evaluated at definition time, and, consequently, errors in them are not detected until the function is called. Now the first statement can be typed:

[1]   *CMV-OMV*

Once the expression is entered, a new statement number in consecutive integer sequence is given:

[2]

We continue the definition:

[2] $100 \times DIV \div CMV$
[3] $CMV \div EARN$
[4]

The next statement number given is [4], but there is no fourth expression to enter. When function definition is completed, another ∇ ends function definition and returns the computer to calculation mode.

[4]   ∇

Alternatively, the del could have been placed at the end of the expression of statement \ 3, like this:

[3] $CMV \div EARN∇$

This is the more common method of ending definition mode. Either way, typing the second del puts you back into calculation mode. All expressions entered after the second of a pair of dels are executed immediately and, as usual, are not numbered. The function *STOCK* as it has been defined is

      ∇ *STOCK*
[1]   *CMV-OMV*
[2] $100 \times DIV \div CMV$
[3] $CMV \div EARN$
      ∇

It has been entered but it has not been called or executed. To avoid value errors, the variables used in the function definition must be assigned values before the function is executed. For example,

```
OMV←71   97.5 22.5   29.125
CMV←69.75   96 25   32.5
EARN←2.45   4.58 1.10   1.30
DIV←.49   1.3   .6   .66
```

EARN and *DIV* are constants that do not change each time; they have to be typed once only and saved. After the first week's run of the program, the expression *OMV←CMV* gives the old market value without retyping. *CMV* is the only variable that has to be retyped each week. An analysis of the variables such as this helps determine whether the function should have arguments.

To execute the function, its name is entered:

```
    STOCK
¯1.25 ¯1.5 2.5 3.375
0.68817 1.3542 2.4 2.0308
24.474 26.816 22.727 25
```

The three vectors following the function call are the results of executing each of the expressions in the defined function in order. The function can be executed as often as needed. Each time *STOCK* is executed, the same results print unless the values for *OMV*, *CMV*, *EARN*, or *DIV* are changed.

PROBLEMS

1. Define a function named *STOCKDESCRIBE* which describes the function *STOCK* defined in Sec. 2.1. It should tell what the variables mean and how to specify them.

2. Define a function named *AC* to determine the following information about air conditioners given the Btu's (British thermal units) delivered per hour (*BTU*), the dimensions of the units in cubic inches (*DIM*), and their prices (*PR*).

   (a) How many Btus are delivered per cubic inch for each air conditioner?

   (b) The cost per Btu for each conditioner.

   (c) The cost per cubic inch for each conditioner.

   (d) The ratio of Btu per cubic inch to the cost per cubic inch for each conditioner.

   Test:

   ```
   BTU←24000 29000 36000 48000
   DIM←23 23 23 30.5 × 34.25 38.25 38.25
   42 × 32.25 39.875 39.875 50
   PR←449 559 649 789
   .......*
   0.9447 0.82668 1.0262 0.74941
   0.01871 0.01928 0.01803 0.01644
   0.1767 0.01593 0.0185 0.01232
   53.452 51.878 55.47 60.836
   ```

---

[*]In the test for each problem . . . . . indicates the solution expression or function. The values following . . . . . are the anticipated result.

Section 2.2 FUNCTION EDITING

Section 2.1 presented the essential elements of function definition—entering and ending definition mode, the function header, and the numbered statements of the function body. Functions often require some alterations or deletions to the definition. Accomplishing this is done by means of *function editing.*

The first form of function editing you are likely to perform is a *display* of the function definition. This is done by means of the statement

$$\nabla STOCK[\square]\nabla$$

The quad $\square$ within brackets means that the entire function is to be displayed. The computer responds with

```
    ∇  STOCK
[1]    CMV-OMV
[2]    100×DIV÷CMV
[3]    CMV÷EARN
    ∇
```

Let us examine the meaning of all the symbols on the line

$$\nabla STOCK[\square]\nabla$$

The first del of this statement reestablishes function definition mode; the name identifies the function; the information within brackets indicates what should be done. The closing del indicates a return to calculation mode after the editing is performed. (If the closing del is omitted, the computer remains in definition mode and function editing can continue.) This is a basic format for function editing. What you put between the brackets establishes what you want done. For example, the quad $\square$ within brackets is a display symbol.

The quad is used for three different editing displays. The first, $\nabla NAME[\square]\nabla$, displays the entire function; the second, $\nabla NAME[N\square]\nabla$, displays line N of the function; and the third, $\nabla NAME[\square N]\nabla$, displays the function from line N to the end of the function. Striking the ATTN key at any time during a display stops the display.

Let us continue editing the function. Suppose that we want to identify each of the results printed in the function $STOCK$. Then three statements will have to be inserted in the function definition, each one a character vector display. To make an insertion, a fractional number locating the place of the insertion is indicated between brackets. For example,

$$\nabla STOCK[.1]$$

indicates an insertion before statement 1. Any fractional number from .0001 to .9999 can be used. Either the insertion can be added after the closing bracket on the line or RETURN can be entered. (If the latter, the computer responds with [.1] as the next numbered statement. Then the insertion can be made.) Ordinarily the insertion is done at once as shown below:

$\nabla STOCK[.1]$'*INCREASE OVER LAST PERIOD*'

The computer responds with [.2] as the next statement number.

Since another insertion is not needed here, but rather between statements 1 and 2, the statement number displayed by the computer is *overridden* with another bracketed number followed by the insertion statement:

[.2]   [1.5]   '*YIELD*'

The response is [1.6], which can again be overridden:

[1.6]   [2.7] '*PRICE/EARNINGS RATIO*'

The response is [2.8]. There is no more editing to do, and so function definition can be closed with a second del:

[2.8] ∇

After the closing del, the statements are renumbered by the APL system to consecutive integers, as you can see by a subsequent display of the function:

$\nabla STOCK[\square]\nabla$

```
     ∇ STOCK
[1]    'INCREASE OVER LAST PERIOD'
[2]    CMV-OMV
[3]    'YIELD'
[4]    100×DIV÷CMV
[5]    'PRICE/EARNINGS RATIO'
[6]    CMV÷EARN
     ∇
```

Overriding a statement number can also be used to *replace* an existing statement. For example, suppose that we wanted to reword the first statement. We could enter function definition mode and do this:

$\nabla STOCK[1]$'*CHANGE OVER LAST PERIOD*'∇

The last statement entered for a statement number overrides previous statement.

Before definition mode is closed, fractional statement numbers remain in effect. This means that a display of the function will include the fractional numbers (although these are changed to integers after the close of definition mode) and editing may be to a statement with a fractional number. For example, after the insertion of the commentary to the *STOCK* function, the statement number [2.8] appears. If, instead of closing definition, [$\square$] is entered, the function is displayed with fractional line numbers:

```
[2.8]    [☐]
    ∇   STOCK
[0.1]   'INCREASE OVER LAST PERIOD'
[1]     CMV-OMV
[1.5]   'YIELD'
[2]     100×DIV÷CMV
[2.7]   'PRICE/EARNINGS RATIO'
[3]     CMV÷EARN
    ∇
[2.8]
```

Statement .1 can be edited and then the definition can be closed:

```
[2.8]    [.1]'CHANGE OVER LAST PERIOD'∇
```

Once definition is closed all statements are renumbered by the APL system to consecutive integers.

Suppose now that we want to add cost and price information to the function. To *add* statements to the end of a function, simply enter definition mode:

```
    ∇STOCK
```

The computer responds with the next available statement number, and we continue entering statements:

```
[7]     'NET INCREASE'
[8]     CMV-COST
[9]     'INVESTMENT IN EACH STOCK'
[10]    CMV×NSH
[11]    ∇
```

The function is now lengthened. If it is executed, this happens:

```
    STOCK
CHANGE OVER LAST PERIOD
¯1.25 ¯1.5 2.5 3.375
YIELD
0.68817 1.3542 2.4 2.0308
PRICE/EARNINGS RATIO
24.474 26.816 22.727 25
NET INCREASE
VALUE ERROR
STOCK[8] CMV-COST
         ∧
```

We added several lines to the function but neglected to specify values for the variable *COST*. Function execution has halted, but it has not terminated; it is in a suspended state. To terminate the function, enter the symbol $\rightarrow$. A value can be assigned to *COST* and to *NSH* and the function reexecuted:

```
        →
        COST← 68 100 20.25 30
        NSH← 7 5 20 31
        STOCK
CHANGE OVER LAST PERIOD
¯1.25 ¯1.5 2.5 3.375
YIELD
0.68817 1.3542 2.4 2.0308
PRICE/EARNINGS RATIO
24.474 26.816 22.727 25
NET INCREASE
1.75 ¯4 4.75 2.5
INVESTMENT IN EACH STOCK
488.25 480 500 1007.5
```

A statement can also be *deleted*. This is done by striking the ATTN key after the statement number. When lines have been deleted, the statements are renumbered by the APL system to consecutive integers after function definition is ended.

Overrides and deletions are irrevocable actions. Once a statement has been replaced or deleted, the former statement is gone and cannot be retrieved. A means of overcoming this is to save the workspace before editing is done. If the editing is not right, the previously saved workspace can be loaded and editing started again. If the editing is all right, the workspace with the edited version can be saved. Before deleting a line or overriding it, it is advisable to look at that line to be sure it is the one that you want to change. This is done using the line number and the display quad within brackets. For example, to see line 7 of *STOCK* we type

```
    ∇STOCK[7□]
[7]     'NET INCREASE'
[7]
```

The line gets displayed and then [7] appears on the next line so that a change can be made if desired. If you enter ∇*STOCK*[7□]∇, that is, showing a closing del, the line is displayed and the computer returns to calculation mode.

A function can be erased from a workspace by using the)*ERASE* command in the same way as with variables. For example,

```
    )ERASE STOCK
```

eliminates the name and definition of *STOCK*.

PROBLEMS

1. Suppose that your active workspace contains a function *FCN*1 which contains 16 lines.

Indicate the sequence of events at the terminal which would allow you to perform the following activities:

(a) Display the entire function.

(b) Display the twelfth line of the function.

(c) Display the eleventh line if you are already in definition mode of $FCN1$.

(d) Display from line 10 to the end of the function.

(e) Display lines 10 through 13.

(f) Delete line 8 if it is $I \leftarrow I+1$; otherwise leave it unchanged (do without displaying the whole function).

(g) Replace line 5 by the expression $I \leftarrow 0$.

(h) Replace line 5 by the expression $I \leftarrow 0$ only if it was $I \leftarrow 1$; otherwise leave it unchanged (do without displaying the entire function).

(i) Insert after line 7 the expression $A \leftarrow B \div C$.

(j) Insert before line 13 the two expressions

    $D \leftarrow B \times J$
    $L \leftarrow J \times 2$

2. What is a convenient way of determing how many statements the function $LONGFCN$ has?

3. Edit function AC of problem 2 in Sec. 2.1 to include appropriate commentary.

Section 2.3 ARGUMENTS OF A DEFINED FUNCTION

$STOCK$ was a defined function of no arguments and no single result. Other functions that might be defined, however, do have arguments and a single result. For example, a function named $TEMP$ for converting Fahrenheit temperatures to Celsius (centigrade) temperatures is a function of the Fahrenheit temperature, which is its argument, and yields as a single result, the Celsius temperature. The header for this temperature conversion function is

    $\nabla C \leftarrow TEMP \ F$

The header of the function $TEMP$ indicates that the argument will be called F in the body of the function and that the result will be called C. C will be replaced by the last value assigned to it in the function body. Here is the definition of $TEMP$:

```
   ∇ C←TEMP F
[1]   C←(F-32)×5÷9
   ∇
```

During the execution of $TEMP$ the variable F is replaced by the value indicated as the argument of $TEMP$ at the time of function call. The expression of line 1 is evaluated and the result is output automatically. The argument of the function is part of the function call. It may be a constant, an expression, or a variable that has been previously assigned a value. It must be separated from the function name by a space. For example,

```
    TEMP 68
20
```

```
    MANY←32  50  75  90
    TEMP MANY
0 10 28.889  32.222
```

The result name and specification arrow in the header indicate that the defined function has an explicit result. This result name should appear in the body of the defined function to the left of a specification arrow. In executing *TEMP* the syntax established by the header must be used. Compare

```
    TEMP 68
20
```

```
F←68
TEMP
SYNTAX ERROR
TEMP
∧
```

TEMP is a function of one argument. Its function call must include the argument.

A function *SPEED* to determine the miles per hour that a car is moving given the diameter of the wheel in inches and the number of revolutions per minute that the wheel is traveling is a function of two arguments with a single result. Here is the definition of *SPEED*:

```
    ∇ MPH←RPM SPEED D
[1]    MPH←RPM×D×3.14159×60÷5280×12
    ∇
```

Again the arguments are part of the function call in the same order as established in the header. For example,

```
    500 SPEED 25
37.187
    500 1000 1500 SPEED 25
37.187 74.375 111.56
    500 SPEED 45 60
66.937 89.25
```

It is the explicit result indicated in the header that makes the defined function usable in the same ways that a primitive function is used; that is,

1. The result may be displayed automatically.
2. The function may be used within a longer expression.
3. The result may be assigned a name.

The similarities between a defined function with an explicit result and a primitive function can be seen by comparing the function *TEMP*, a monadic defined function, to the function index generator, a monadic primitive function:

	Defined Function	Primitive Function
Syntax	$\nabla C \leftarrow TEMP\ F$	ιN
Execution	*TEMP* 68	$\iota 6$
Result	20	1 2 3 4 5 6
In an expression	273+*TEMP* 68	$2 \times \iota 6$
Result	293	2 4 6 8 10 12
In a specification statement	*CEL*←*TEMP* 68	$ODD \leftarrow {}^-1+2 \times \iota 6$

The explicit result indication is independent of the number of arguments associated with the defined function, and so it is also possible to define monadic or dyadic functions with no explicit results. A defined function without an explicit result cannot be used *within* an expression; that is, a defined function with no explicit result must be the leftmost function in an expression. Thus had the Fahrenheit to Celsius conversion function been defined as

```
      ∇ TEMP F
[1]      Z←(F-32)×5÷9
[2]      Z
      ∇
```

then

```
      TEMP 50×2
37.778
```

but

```
      25+TEMP 50×2
37.778
VALUE ERROR
      25+TEMP 50×2
           ∧
```

As we saw with the function *STOCK*, a defined function may have no arguments. A function of no arguments is called a *niladic defined function*. If a function does have arguments, the kind of argument(s) it can have—whether scalar or vector, positive, negative, integers, characters, and so forth—depends on the definition of the function. For example, both *TEMP* and *SPEED* can have vector arguments; *TEMP* may have a negative argument but *SPEED* should not; neither accepts character arguments.

There are six possible headers for defined functions. These are summarized in the following table:

Number of Arguments	Name	Without Explicit Result	With Explicit Result
0	Niladic	∇*FN*	∇*Z←FN*
1	Monadic	∇*FN X*	∇*Z←FN X*
2	Dyadic	∇*A FN B*	∇*Z←A FN B*

Which of the six headers you should use depends on the intended purpose of the function. For example, Illustration 2.2 shows a function that might be defined as either a monadic or dyadic function. The illustrations that follow show functions with different headers.

Illustration 2.1 Functions with No Explicit Results

A defined function with no arguments and no explicit result is very commonly used to provide some verbal description of the workspace or function contents. For example, by a convention established in the early days of APL, the defined function *DESCRIBE* in a workspace gives a prose description of the material in the workspace.

Within workspace *NEWS* in library 1 which is distributed with APL.SV there is a monadic function without an explicit result whose header is

∇*APLNOW D*

The argument *D* is a three-component vector made up of the month, day, and year. This function provides the most recent APL news items entered into this workspace on or after the given date. No explicit result is needed and none appears in the header.

Within library 1 in workspace *PLOTFORMAT* there is a dyadic function without an explicit result for plotting whose header is

∇*A PLOT B*

where *A* provides scaling information and *B* provides the data to be plotted.

Illustration 2.2 Computing Surtax

Suppose that a surtax of 2.5% were placed on all tax payments *T*. The following monadic function with an explicit result *SURTAX* computes the surtax and adds it to the previously computed tax *T*:

```
     ∇ TAX←SURTAX T
[1]    TAX←T+.025×T
     ∇
```

For example,

```
     SURTAX 1500
1537.5
```

If the surtax rate might vary, a dyadic function can be defined where one argument is the rate and the other the computed tax:

```
     ∇ TAX←R SURTAX2 T
[1]    TAX←T+T×.01×R
     ∇
```

For example,

```
     3 SURTAX2 2200
2266
```

Illustration 2.3　Effective Rate of a Loan

A discounted loan is a loan in which the amount of interest charged is deducted in advance of the loan. So, for example, if a loan is made for $100 for 1 year at 8% per year, the borrower receives $92 and pays back $100 at the end of the year. The *effective* rate of such a loan is not 8%, the *nominal* or quoted rate, but 8.7%. The relationship between R, the effective rate of interest, and the nominal rate of interest D is

$$R = \frac{.01 \times D}{1 - T \times .01 \times D}$$

where T is the time in units which correspond to the time period of the interest rate. For example, if the interest rate is per year, T represents the number of years in which the loan is to be repaid. The dyadic function with an explicit result *RATES* determines the effective rate of interest given a nominal rate *NOM* and a time period *YRS*:

```
     ∇ EFF←YRS RATES NOM
[1]    EFF←100×(.01×NOM)÷1-YRS×.01×NOM
     ∇
```

For example,

```
     1 RATES 5
5.26
```

Illustration 2.4   The Value of π

The function *PI* has no arguments but has an explicit result. It supplies the value of π as a constant.

```
    ∇ Z←PI
[1]    Z←3.141592654
    ∇
```

Using a function with no arguments but with an explicit result is a common way of representing constants that will be used often. The advantage of using a function instead of a variable is that the function's value cannot be respecified inadvertently. For example, compare the results of respecifying the function *PI* and of respecifying the variable *PI*:

PI as a Function	*PI* as a Variable
Definition shown in Illustration 2.4	`PI←3.141592654`
`    PI` `3.141592654`	`    PI` `3.141592654`

`    PI←'A PIECE OF PIE'`
`SYNTAX ERROR`
`    PI←'A PIECE OF PIE'`
`    ∧`
	`    PI←'A PIECE OF PIE'`
	`    PI`
	`A PIECE OF PIE`

When a defined function is used within the defining body of another defined function, we say that the functions are *nested*. For example, suppose that we have the function *ATR*, which converts angles in degrees to their equivalent radian units:

```
    ∇ Z←ATR ANGLE
[1]    Z←PI×ANGLE÷180
    ∇
```

PI, as defined in Illustration 2.4, is a function with no arguments and an explicit result:

```
    ATR 30
0.5236
```

It is common to nest a function that does calculations within a function that explains the arguments, calculations, or result. For example, the function *RATES* from Illustration 2.3 could be embedded as follows:

```
    ∇ T INT D
[1]   'INTEREST RATES'
[2]   'QUOTED - EFFECTIVE'
[3]   D, T RATES D
    ∇

    1 INT 5
INTEREST RATES
QUOTED - EFFECTIVE
5   5.26
```

The advantage of this approach is that the function that does the calculations is thus available to be used in other functions or expressions where the commentary would be inappropriate.

PROBLEMS

1. For the functions *SWAP1* and *SWAP2* shown here,

```
    ∇ SWAP1
[1]   C←A
[2]   A←B
[3]   B←C
    ∇

    ∇ A SWAP2 B
[1]   C←A
[2]   A←B
[3]   B←C
    ∇
```

fill in the blanks:

```
                                              A←1
                                              B←2
A←1                                           C←3
B←2                        SWAP1              A SWAP2 B
C←3                        A,B,C              A,B,C
A,B,C

   (a)_____           (b) _____          (c) _____
```

2. Each of the following three defined functions computes the area of a triangle given its base B and height H:

```
     ∇ AR1
[1]    Z←B×H×.5
     ∇
```

```
     ∇ Z←AR2 B
[1]    Z←B×H×.5
     ∇
```

```
     ∇ Z←B AR3 H
[1]    Z←B×H×.5
     ∇
```

Let

```
A←2
B←3
C←8
H←5
Z←13
```

State the values associated with each of the five variables A, B, C, H, Z, after the execution of

   (a) *AR1*   (b) *AR2 C*   (c) *H←AR2 C*   (d) *Z←B AR3 H*

3. Define a function *FUELCOST* to find the actual per unit cost of heat output for gas, oil, and electric heating units. Let E be the percent efficiency of a home heating unit (electricity is considered 100%; 60-80% for gas and oil are considered good). Let C be the cost in cents of the fuel in whatever the common units are. The formulas for converting cost into costs per unit of heat output are

                natural gas = cost per 100 cubic feet × 10

                oil = cost per gallon × 7.15

                electricity = cost per kilowatt × 293

   Test:

```
E←70 70 100
C←9.4  19.61  1.55
• • • • •
1.34  2  4.54
```

4. (a) Define a set of functions such that a person may enter an addition question at the terminal such as

     WHAT IS 21 PLUS 5

   and receive the correct answer. The set of functions should be written so that any numbers can be used in place of 21 and 5.

 (b) Modify the set of functions such that the answer to the inquiry is

     THE ANSWER IS
     26

5. The formula

$$H. P. = \frac{TV}{550}$$

gives the horsepower exerted by the propeller of an airplane, where T is the thrust in pounds and V is the velocity in miles per hour. Define a function HP to determine the horsepower exerted by the propeller of a plane.

> *Test:*
>
> $T \leftarrow 1214$
> $V \leftarrow 180$
>
> • • ○ • •
> 397.31

6. The evaluation of a polynomial function of the form

$$C_0 x^n + C_1 x^{n-1} + \cdots + C_{n-1} x + C_n$$

can be done using addition and multiplication by rewriting the function as

$$C_n + X \times C_{n-1} + \cdots + X \times C_1 + X \times C_0$$

For example, the polynomial

$$6x^3 + 5x^2 + 4x + 3$$

can be evaluated by the expression

$$3 + x \times 4 + x \times 5 + x \times 6$$

Define a function POL to evaluate the polynomial

$$3x^4 + 9x^3 - 2x^2 + 5x - 12$$

for various values of x.

> *Test:*
>
> $X \leftarrow 2$
>
> • ○ • • •
> 110

Section 2.4 LOCAL AND GLOBAL VARIABLES

The function $REDUCE$ was described in Sec. 2.1 but not shown. Here is its definition:

```
     ∇ DIET←H REDUCE W;IW;DMC
[1]    IW←100+5×H-60
[2]    DMC←1750+10×W-100
[3]    DIET←IW,DMC,(DMC-1000),.5×W-IW
     ∇
```

where IW is the ideal weight and DMC is the number of calories needed to maintain that weight.

The header of *REDUCE* indicates that it is a dyadic function with an explicit result and local variables *IW* and *DMC*. *Local variables* are variables that exist and have meaning only within the defined function. Local variables are used like scratch paper in hand calculations. They hold intermediate results while arriving at an answer but are not needed once the final result is gained. The variables *IW* and *DMC* specified in lines 1 and 2 of *REDUCE* are used to represent intermediate results that are not needed once the function is completed. *IW* and *DMC* will have no values once the execution of *REDUCE* is completed. For example,

```
      54 REDUCE 148
70 2230  1230    39
      IW
VALUE ERROR
      IW
      ∧

      DMC
VALUE ERROR
      DMC
      ∧
```

A variable name is called a *local variable* because it exists and has meaning only during the execution of the defined function. This is in contrast to a *global variable*, which is a variable name that has value before, during, and after the execution of a function. A global variable, once specified, exists in the workspace until it is erased. If the header does not explicitly declare that a name is local, it is global.

A function has its local variables declared in the function header by separating the local variable names from the function syntax and from each other by semicolons. Thus the header that indicates that the monadic function *FNC* has three local variables—*I*, *J*, and *K*—is

$$\nabla Z \leftarrow FNC\ X;I;J;K$$

During the execution of *FNC*, the local variables *I*, *J*, and *K* take precedence over any global variables of the same name. Any global variables or defined functions with the same names are *not* accessible. In this sense, all the names in the header except the function name are local names. The argument and result names, too, take precedence over any global ones of the same name. Functions *FN1*, *FN2*, *FN3* and *FN4* shown below use variables *I*, *J*, and/or *K*, either as local or global names:

```
     ∇ FN1;I;J  |      ∇ FN2;I   |      ∇ FN3;I;J  |      ∇ FN4;I;J
[1]     I←20    | [1]     I←20   | [1]     I←10    | [1]     I←20
[2]     J←30    | [2]     J←30   | [2]     J←30    | [2]     I,J
[3]     I,J     | [3]     I,J    | [3]     I,J,K   |         ∇
     ∇          |      ∇         |      ∇          |
```

The following sequences of events using these functions illustrate some of the differences between local and global variables. First consider sequence *FN1*:

Step	Sequence *FN*1
1	$I \leftarrow 'TEST'$
2	$J \leftarrow 'CASE'$
3	I,J
	TESTCASE
4	*FN*1
	20 30
5	I,J
	TESTCASE

During the execution of *FN*1 any reference to I or J as in line 3 of the function *FN*1 results in the values associated with the local names I and J. However, after the execution of *FN*1 any reference to I or J results in the values associated with the global names I and J. Now consider sequence *FN*2:

Step	Sequence *FN*2
1	$I \leftarrow {}^-100$
2	$J \leftarrow {}^-200$
3	I,J
	${}^-100 \ {}^-200$
4	*FN*2
	20 30
5	I,J
	${}^-100 \ 30$

In this second sequence the final value of J (step 5) differs from the final value of J (step 5) of the previous sequence. Since J was not declared local to *FN*2, the specification of J as 30 in *FN*2 was to the global variable J. Similarly, function *FN*3 does not have a local variable K, and so the value of the global variable K is used, as in sequence *FN*3.

Sequence *FN*3

```
    I←⁻100
    J←⁻200
    K←⁻300
    I,J,K
⁻100  ⁻200 ⁻300
    FN3
10 30 ⁻300
    I,J,K
⁻100  ⁻200  ⁻300
```

Finally, consider sequence *FN*4:

Sequence *FN*4
_____

$$I \leftarrow {}^{-}100$$
$$J \leftarrow {}^{-}200$$
$$FN4$$
VALUE ERROR
*FN*4[2] *I*,*J*
      ∧

The variable name *J* is declared local in *FN*4. Any reference to *J* during the
execution of the function, then, is to the local value of *J*. Local variables, if used
within a function, must be specified within the function. Note, however, that it is
possible to declare variable names local in the function header that do not appear at
all in the function body:

```
        ∇ FN7;K
[1]       I←20
[2]       J←30
[3]       I,J
        ∇

        FN7
  20 30
```

Section 2.5   NESTED FUNCTIONS AND LOCAL VARIABLES

When defined functions with and without local variables are nested, complications
may occur. Consider the following functions:

```
        ∇ FN5;J;K                            ∇ FN6;I;K
[1]       I←50                       [1]       I←20
[2]       J←60                       [2]       K←40
[3]       K←70                       [3]       I,J,K
[4]       I,J,K                      [4]       J←30
[5]       FN6                        [5]       I,J,K
[6]       I,J,K                              ∇
        ∇
```

When *FN*5 is executed, values for *I*, *J*, and *K* are displayed four times: twice
explicitly at lines 4 and 6 and twice implicitly through function *FN*6 at lines 3
and 5. Now examine the following sequence of events:

```
      I←100
      J←200
      K←300
      I,J,K
100 200 300

      FN5
50 60 70                    from FN5[4]
20 60 40                    from FN6[3] via FN5[5]
20 30 40                    from FN6[5] via FN5[5]
50 30 70                    from FN5[6]

      I,J,K
50 200 300
```

J and K were declared local variables in $FN5$. $FN5$ also called function $FN6$, which declared local variables I and K. Any specifications in $FN6$ to variable J are made to the local variable J which is in effect at the time $FN6$ is executed. This is the variable J which is local to function $FN5$. $FN6$ does not change the global variable J because the local variable J from $FN5$ is blocking or shadowing the global variable J. Since K was declared local to $FN6$, a second level of locality was created. Hence $FN6$ does not change either K, which is local to $FN5$, or the K, which is global. In general, the name to which the nested function refers is the name currently in effect.

Caution: If a function is suspended, because an error was encountered during its execution or for any other reason (see Sec. 6.5), the values displayed for requested names are those associated with the name currently in effect.

PROBLEMS

1. Consider the following set of defined functions:

```
      ∇ F1
[1]      I←1
[2]      J←2
[3]      K←3
[4]      I,J,K
      ∇

      ∇ F2 I
[1]      J←4
[2]      I,J,K
      ∇

      ∇ F3;J;K
[1]      I←5
[2]      J←6
[3]      K←7
[4]      I,J,K
      ∇
```

```
    ∇ F4 J;K
[1]    K←8
[2]    I,J,K
[3]    F2 9
[4]    I,J,K
[5]    F3
[6]    I,J,K
    ∇

    ∇ RESET
[1]    I←100
[2]    J←200
[3]    K←300
    ∇
```

Indicate the values at the various blanks in the following sequence:

(a) *RESET*
    I,J,K

————————

(b) *F1*   value of *I,J,K* from line 4 of *F1*

————————

(c) *I,J,K*

————————

(d) *RESET*
    F2 31

———————— value of *I,J,K* from line 2 of *F2*

(e) *I,J,K*

————————

(f) *RESET*
    F3

———————— value of *I,J,K* from line 4 of *F3*

(g) *I,J,K*

————————

(h) *RESET*
    F4 ⁻3

———————— value of *I,J,K* from line 2 of *F4*
———————— value of *I,J,K* from line 2 of *F2*
———————— value of *I,J,K* from line 4 of *F4*
———————— value of *I,J,K* from line 4 of *F3*
———————— value of *I,J,K* from line 6 of *F4*

(i) I,J,K

_____

2. Fill in the blanks:

```
    ∇ A SWAP3 B;C
[1]     C←A
[2]     A←B
[3]     B←C
[4]     A,B,C
    ∇
```

(a) $A←1$
             $B←2$
             $C←3$
             A,B,C

_____

(b) $A\ SWAP3\ B$

(c) A,B,C

_____

Section 2.6   LINE EDITING

In Sec. 2.2 we discussed many editing capabilities applicable to defined functions. Each of the editing procedures discussed concerned at least a whole line of the function; however, errors within a line of a function—perhaps in only one or two characters—often occur. None of the editing procedures discussed in Sec. 2.2 can be used for editing within a line. Editing within a line is called *line editing*.

In general, line editing is a three-step process. Each step is followed by a RETURN. First enter definition mode; then

1. Within brackets indicate line number, quad, and the approximate position of the carrier in spaces from left:

    [*line number* ☐ *spaces*]

    If the number of spaces indicated is zero, step 2 is skipped and the carrier in step 3 stops at the end of the line.*

2. Indicate changes by typing any of the following symbols placed below the appropriate characters:

_____

* APL.SV only. In APL/360, step 2 is not skipped. If spaces are indicated as zero, the carrier waits at the left margin.

Symbol	Purpose
A digit, 1 . . . 9	Insert that many spaces to the left of this character
An alphabetic character *A* . . . *Z*	Insert five times the position of the letter in the alphabet spaces to the left of this character; *A* is 5 spaces; *B* is 10 spaces, . . .; *F* is 30 spaces, and so forth
A slash, /	Delete this character

Spacing and backspacing to get to the appropriate character are permitted.

3. Type the new characters needed on the line, if any. If only deletions have been indicated, or if the number of spaces indicated in step 1 is zero, the carrier rests at the end of the line. At this point the line can be extended or modified by backspace-attention. If spaces have been indicated within the line, the carrier stops at the leftmost created space.

Suppose that when we were entering the body of the dyadic function *SPEED* in Sec. 2.3, we had typed

$$MPH \leftarrow RPM \times D \times 3.4159 \times 600 \div 5280 \div 12$$
$$\qquad\qquad\quad \uparrow \qquad\quad \uparrow \qquad\quad \uparrow$$
$$\qquad\qquad (1) \qquad (2) \qquad (3)$$

There are three errors in this line as indicated by the arrows and parenthesized numbers. Correcting the first, reading from the left, requires inserting a 1; correcting the second requires deleting an extra 0; and correcting the last requires changing the ÷ symbol to a × symbol. This line is corrected using line editing by typing

$\nabla SPEED[1\square13]$

This expression tells the system to enter function definition mode, to display line 1 of *SPEED*, to position the carrier 13 spaces from the left margin, and to release the keyboard. When the keyboard is released, changes are indicated by digits, letters, and/or slashes:

[1] $MPH \leftarrow RPM \times D \times 3.4159 \times 600 \div 5280 \div 12$
$\qquad\qquad\quad 1 \qquad\quad / \qquad\quad /1$

The leftmost 1 will create a space to the left of the 4 so that a 1 can be inserted; the slash under the 0 will delete the extra 0; and the /1 will delete the ÷ and create a space to the left of 1 so that × can be inserted. After the RETURN, the system displays the line following the instructions indicated:

[1] $MPH \leftarrow RPM \times D \times 3. \quad 4159 \times 60 \div 5280 \quad 12$
$\qquad\qquad\qquad \uparrow$
$\qquad\qquad\qquad$ carrier waits here

The carrier is automatically positioned at the leftmost created space or if no spaces were created at the end of the line. Getting to all other spaces requires manual spacing and backspacing. To make changes, type

1   ×

and RETURN. This concludes the line editing on this line. A display of the line shows that the editing did take place:

```
[2]     [1□]∇
[1]     MPH←RPM×D×3.14159×60÷5280×12
```

Line editing permits editing of any character on the line including the line number. For example,

```
        ∇FNC1[3□2]
[3]     I←I-1
  ↑
carrier
```

A copy of this line can be placed at some other line—line 14, for example:

```
[3]     I←I-1
 /2
```

This returns as

```
[ ]     I←I-1
  ↑
carrier
```

During the third step, the number 14 can be typed, and in so doing, a copy of line 3 will have been placed at line 14 of the function, destroying what had formerly been line 14. Line 3, as it was, still exists and must be deleted if it is not needed.

Just as the body of a function can be line-edited, so may the header of a function be line-edited. The header is assigned a line number of 0 for editing purposes only. For example, the following sequence changes the name of a function from *OLDNAME* to *NEWNAME*:

```
        ∇OLDNAME[0□6]
[0]     ∇OLDNAME
         ///3
[0]     ∇   NAME
          ↑
         carrier
```

At this point *NEW* can be typed, thereby changing the name of the function to *NEWNAME*. The name of the function can be changed completely, but it is not possible to edit away the entire name of the function. For example,

```
        ∇  FN
[1]     5
        ∇

        ∇FN[0□9]
[0]     FN
        //
[0]     ∇

        ∇FN[□]∇
      ∇FN
[1]     5
        ∇
```

A function can be removed only by erasing it explicitly. Also the name of a function cannot be changed to a name already in use in the workspace. For example,)*FNS* is the function name list. (See Sec. 8.1.3.)

```
        )FNS
FN1     FN2
        ∇FN1[□]∇
      ∇  FN1
[1]     'ONE'
        ∇

        ∇FN1[0□9]
[0]     FN1
        /
[0]     FN2
DEFN ERROR
[0]     FN2
        ∧
[0]     [0□9]
[0]     FN1
        /
[0]     FN3
[1]     ∇

        )FNS
FN2     FN3
```

Editing the function header is most often done to add or delete local variables. A function definition might be entered without naming any local variables; then before definition is closed [0□0] is entered, local variables are added, and the function is closed. For example,

```
        ∇  FCN
[1]     I←I+1
```

[2] $J \leftarrow J \times I$

.

.

.

[10] [0□0]
       ∇ *FCN*
              ↑   carrier waits here
              $;I;J$∇

If the attention key is used during the entry of characters in the third step of line editing, all the characters on the line to the right of where the carrier is when the attention key is struck are lost. For example, the response to the second step

[3] $A \leftarrow 2+A)\times B$

Should be

[3] $A \leftarrow\ 2+A)\times B$
          ↑
          carrier

But suppose that in our haste to insert the (symbol we forgot to upshift and typed a bracket instead:

[3] $A \leftarrow [2+A)\times B$
          ↑
          carrier

Having caught this error almost immediately, we would be tempted to use the backspace-attention correction sequence. If we did, the result would be an erasure of everything to the right of ←, leaving just part of the line:

[3] $A \leftarrow$

       Finally, line editing cannot be performed on a line which has more characters than fit on a single line or on a character vector which includes a carrier return as one of its characters.

PROBLEMS

1. If during the second step of character editing the line appeared as illustrated, how would the line be displayed at the beginning of the third step?

    (a) [4] $TAX \leftarrow T+0.025 \times T$
                //   /

    (b) [4] $TAX \leftarrow T+0.025 \times T$
                2   ///A

(c) [4] $TAX \leftarrow T + 0.025 \times T$

/3   3   /1

2. Consider the functions

```
   ∇ FNA;I
[1]   I←31
   ∇
```

```
   ∇ FNB
[1]   J←I+2
   ∇
```

Suppose that the value of I created in FNA were to be used in FNB. Then the header of FNA must be changed. Indicate the character editing procedure to be followed to change it.

3. Consider the function

```
   ∇ DF
[1]   A←3
[2]   B←4,C
[3]   C←5
   ∇
```

Assume that you are in execution mode. Write the sequence of steps using character editing to

(a) Insert the contents of line 2 as line 4.

(b) Interchange lines 2 and 3.

(c) Interchange lines 1 and 3.

(d) Change the name of the function to $AFCN$.

Section 2.7 SUMMARY

Function definition, header forms, the nature of global and local names, and function editing techniques have been presented in Chapter 2.

Function Definition

All defined functions contain two parts, the header and the body. A header must contain a del and the name of the defined function. The header allows a collection of APL statements to be grouped together with a name. The body contains the defining statements of the function and must conclude with a ∇.

Function Headers

The possible function headers are summarized in the following table:

	Without Explicit Result	With Explicit Result
Niladic	∇FN	$\nabla Z \leftarrow FN$
Monadic	$\nabla FN\ X$	$\nabla Z \leftarrow FN\ X$
Dyadic	$\nabla X\ FN\ Y$	$\nabla Z \leftarrow X\ FN\ Y$

Defining functions that have arguments permits the user to provide the data at the time of the function call. Defining functions that have an explicit result allows the defined functions to be used like a primitive function; that is, the defined function may be used in any expression or statement.

Local and Global Variables

Variable names that are created and have meaning throughout the workspace are called *global* variables. Variable names that are created and have meaning only during execution of a defined function are called *local* variables. All variable names are global unless they have been made local explicitly. A variable name is made local by placing it in the header of a defined function and separating it from the rest of the header by semicolons. Thus in the header

$$\nabla RES \leftarrow A\ FCN\ B;I;J;K$$

the names I, J, and K are all local variable names. The names RES, A, and B are the result and argument names used in the function and behave like local variable names. The only name which is not local in the header of a function is the name of the function itself. When a local variable is in effect, any identically named global variable is not accessible.

Function Editing

Function editing can be done either while in function definition mode or by entering definition mode. Editing procedures are shown in the illustrations while in function mode at statement 7 and by entering function definition mode in terms of the function FN. A closing del is shown in the function editing commands. The closing del indicates a return to calculation mode after the current editing. If the closing del is omitted, the computer remains in definition mode. In this section if a closing del is not shown, it is not possible to include it in the command.

1. *Displaying a function*:

    $\nabla FN[\Box]\nabla$

or

    [7]   [$\Box$]∇

Note: A display while in definition mode shows fractional numbers if they have been used.

 2. *Displaying a line, for example, line 3:*

∇*FN*[3☐]∇

or

[7]   [3☐]∇

Note: To stop the display, strike the ATTN key (see terminal instructions).

 3. *Adding statements by insertion:*

∇ *FN*[3.1] *expression* ∇

or

[7]   [3.1] *expression* ∇

Note: 3.1 inserts between 3 and 4. 3.11 inserts between 3.1 and 3.2. Any fractional part between .0001 and .9999 may be used for insertion.

 4. *Adding statements to the end of the function:*

∇*FN*

Note: The computer responds with the next available statement number.

 5. *Changing statements by deletion:*

∇*FN*[7]   ATTN followed by RETURN

 6. *Changing statements by complete replacement:*

∇*FN*[7]   *new expression* ∇

 7. *Erasing functions from a workspace:*

)*ERASE FN*

Line Editing

Individual characters within a given line of a defined function may be edited. Once function definition mode has been established, the line-editing process requires three steps:

1. Within brackets, indicate line number, quad, and approximate position of carrier in spaces from the left: [line number □ spaces].

2. Indicate spaces to insert to the left by digits or letters and deletion of characters by slashes.

3. Type the new characters needed on the line, if any.

All characters on a line may be line-edited, including the line number. Use of the attention key during the third step causes a loss of all the characters to the right of the carrier. Only lines that do not exceed the line width setting of the workspace and do not include a carrier return as a character may be line-edited.

THE SHAPE OF DATA

Data is usually organized in some fashion. For instance, we speak of the *set* of even numbers meaning 2, 4, 6, 8, . . . or of a postage rate *table* where the rows are weights and the columns mailing zones. The organizing form for data in APL is the *array*. The term *array* is a generic term that applies to an orderly grouping or arrangement of numbers or characters. In this chapter we shall explore the concepts of order and arrangement as they relate to specific forms of arrays and discuss some of the APL functions on arrays that facilitate data handling.

Section 3.1 ARRAYS

One form of array, which we have already used, is the *vector*. The elements of a vector are arranged *linearly* or in one dimension; that is, for a vector there is a first component, a second component, a third component, and so forth to a last component. We made use of this orderly grouping of the components of a vector when we discussed how a vector is formed by listing its components or by catenation and how these elements combine component by component when operated on by scalar functions.

Another form of array is the *matrix*, a two-dimensional array whose components are arranged by rows and by columns. Interest tables and trigonometric tables are examples of data arranged as matrices. How matrices are formed is discussed in later sections of this chapter. Once formed, however, the elements combine component by component when operated upon by scalar functions like addition, subtraction, multiplication, and division. For example, A is a two-row by three-column (2 by 3) matrix of odd numbers and B is a 2 by 3 matrix of even numbers. A and B can be added:

```
        A
  1   3   5
  7   9  11

        B
  2   4   6
  8  10  12

        A+B
  3   7  11
 15  19  23
```

The result of adding two matrices conformable for addition, that is, matrices which have the same number of rows and columns, is a matrix: The component in the first row, first column of the result is the sum of the component in the first row, first column of *A* and the component in the first row, first column of *B*; the component in the first row, second column of the result is the sum of the component in the first row, second column of *A* and the component in the first row, second column of *B*; and so forth, component by component. Addition is not defined for matrices that are not conformable for addition.

Three-dimensional arrays and higher-dimensional arrays have no special names. Their components are arranged in an orderly fashion by row, column, plane, hyperplane and so forth.* Like the vector and matrix, these higher-dimensional arrays combine component by component when operated upon by scalar functions.

The importance of the orderly grouping of data is apparent when you consider how often component by component operations on data are performed. For example, percentages might be applied over a set of numbers, or ratios between sets of numbers might be found. The requirement for an orderly arrangement of data occurs, even more often, when only selected data is needed for an array. In the use of a compound interest table, for instance, you select the data only for the rate of interest which is of concern to you.

The orderly grouping of the elements in an array makes it possible to identify or select any element unambiguously in an array by referring to its position. The positional reference of an element in an array is known as the *index* of that element. (In mathematics the positional reference of an element is known as the *subscript*. The terms *subscript* and *index* are synonymous.) Thus, when we speak of the fourth element of a vector, we are speaking of that element in the vector whose index (or subscript) is 4.

The *index* identifies an element of an array. The function of *indexing*, which is discussed in detail in Sec. 3.5, selects specific components from an array. Indexing is denoted by the index values in square brackets following the array. For example, in the vector

$$V \leftarrow {}^{-}2 \quad {}^{-}4 \quad {}^{-}6 \quad {}^{-}8 \quad {}^{-}10 \quad {}^{-}12$$

---

*For arrays of rank higher than 2 the labels attached to the various dimensions vary. One may speak of hyper-hyperplanes, hyperplane, planes, and so forth. Another set of terminology comes from using a book analogy—columns, rows, pages, chapters, books, and so forth.

the fourth component is selected by

$$V[4]$$
‾8

the sixth component is selected by

$$V[6]$$
‾12

and the first, third, and fifth components are selected by

$$V[1\ 3\ 5]$$
‾2 ‾6 ‾10

   Each dimension of an array has a range of possible index values associated with it. The range of values that any index may take on in an array is *independent* of the index values taken on by the other indices. As an example of the independence of indices in an array, compare the two sets of asterisks below:

```
            ****              ******
            ****              ***
            ****              ****

            (A)               (B)
```

In set (A) the range of possible values for the column index for each row is the same. And therefore the row index and column index are independent. This is not so in set (B). Here the range of possible values of the column index depends on the selected value for the row index. The index values for columns range between 1 and 6 for the first row, but between 1 and 3 for the second row, and between 1 and 4 for the third row. The indices of an array are always independent.   Set (A), then, is an array; set (B) is not.

   An index value is needed for each dimension of an array in order to select an element. In indexing, these values are separated by semicolons. For example, recall the matrix A:

```
      A
  1   3   5
  7   9  11
```

The component in the first row, third column is selected by

$$A[1;3]$$
5

The first index value in an index to a matrix always refers to the row index, and the second index value always refers to the column index:

    A[2;2]
9

    A[2;1 3]
7 11

One form of array is distinguished from another by the number of independent indices necessary to refer unambiguously to a single element of the array. An element can be selected from a vector by a single index, referring to its position from the left. For example, in the stock earnings vector *EARN* of Chapter 1, the third element can be identified unambiguously:

    EARN
2.8 1.5 1.35 2.08 8.21 1.18
           ↑
         third
         component

    EARN[3]
1.35

An element of a matrix, however, needs two indices to refer to its position unambiguously: one placing it in a row, and the other placing it in a column. For example, finding the compound interest on $1 for 4 years at 3% in an interest-principal table means that we have to look in the 4-year row and the 3% column for the amount:

Years	2%	3%	4%
1	1.020	1.030	1.040
2	1.040	1.061	1.082
3	1.061	1.093	1.145
4	1.082	1.126	1.170
5	1.104	1.159	1.217

If the body of the table of values is called *INT*, the accumulated value at 3% for 4 years can be selected with the expression

    INT[4;2]
1.126

Likewise it takes three independent index values to select a single element from a three-dimensional array—plane, row, column—and four independent index values to select a single component from a four-dimensional array—hyperplane, plane, row, and column.

The term *rank* is used in APL to identify one form of array from another. The rank of an array indicates the number of independent indices which are necessary to get to a single data item in the array; that number corresponds to the number of dimensions of the array. A vector is an array of rank 1. It requires only one index value to "reach" or specify the position of a single element. The data in a vector are one-dimensional (linearly ordered). A matrix is an array of rank 2; it requires two independent indices to reach a single element. The data in a matrix are two-dimensional (doubly ordered). A three-dimensional array is an array of rank 3; it requires three independent indices to reach a single element. The data in a three-dimensional array are triply ordered. This pattern extends similarly to arrays of higher rank.

Based on the above discussion, we can now give a more precise definition of an array: *A rank-r array is an ordered collection of data structured to have r dimensions; hence to select a single element from it requires r indices whose ranges are independent.*

PROBLEMS

1. Use the following variables to evaluate expressions (a)–(e):

    U

    ```
     0   1   2  ¯2
     4   8  12  ¯6
    10  20  30   4
    ```

    P

    ```
    1 2
    3 4
    5 6
    7 8
    ```

    L

    ```
    5 7 1 2
    6 3 2 5
    2 1 6 7
    ```

    (a) $U+L$ (b) $P\times.5$ (c) $5\times U-L$
    (d) $P\div L$ (e) $U\div L$

2. Using the variables from problem 1, write expressions for the following:
    (a) Add the matrix U to the matrix L.
    (b) Halve each component of P.
    (c) Multiply the matrix L by the matrix U component by component.
    (d) Take one-tenth of the result of multiplying component by component the matrix L by the matrix U.

Section 3.2 SHAPE AND RANK

In APL a variable name may represent a single item or an array, and so given a name like MPH or $ST1$ or $ALPHA$ it is not possible to know what structure the name represents. Any of these names might be a scalar, a vector, or a matrix. The function *shape* reports the shape of the data associated with a name. The general form of shape is

   ρA

where the argument A may be a scalar or any array. The result of ρA is *always* a vector whose components represent the number of elements in each dimension of the array A, and thus the degree of freedom one has in choosing an index in the corresponding dimension of A. For example,

   PRICE←257 48.675   10.5   72.25

   $\rho PRICE$
4

The number of components in the first (and only) dimension of *PRICE* is 4. The indices of *PRICE*, then, are 1 through 4. *PRICE* is linear since there is only one component in $\rho PRICE$.

Suppose that *INT* is the interest table shown in Sec. 3.1; then

```
     INT
1.02      1.03      1.04
1.04      1.061     1.082
1.061     1.093     1.145
1.082     1.126     1.17
1.104     1.159     1.217
```

and

   ρINT
5 3

The number of components in the first dimension (row dimension) of *INT* is 5 (there are five rows) and the number of components in the second dimension (column dimension) of *INT* is 3 (there are three columns). The index values of the row dimension are 1 through 5, and the index values of the column dimension are 1 through 3. *INT* is doubly ordered since there are two components in ρINT.

Similarly, if ρB contains three components, the array B is three-dimensional and is triply ordered. There is a connection, as you might have observed, between the number of components in the vector ρB and the rank of B. In fact, the number of components in ρB is the rank of B. An expression for the rank of B, then, is $\rho\rho B$:

   $\rho\rho PRICE$
1

```
      ρρINT
2

      ρρB
3
```

Note that regardless of the shape of the array, the rightmost component of the vector returned, in response to applying the shape function, indicates the number of columns in the array. The next rightmost component (the second from the right) indicates the number of rows. If the named array has more than two dimensions, the components indicating the degrees of freedom in the additional dimensions are appended to the left. For example, if *ARRAY* is a rank-3 array of two planes, three rows, and four columns,

```
      ρARRAY
2 3 4
```

Rows and columns are always the rightmost components of the result of shape.

Section 3.3 BUILDING ARRAYS

As you know, a vector can be created by listing its components or by catenation. Neither of these methods is sufficient for creating other arrays. In this section we shall discuss a common way of creating arrays.

Two things are necessary for creating an array:

1. The data which will be the components of the array

2. An indication of the desired shape of the data.

This information is provided as the right and left arguments, respectively, of the array-building function *reshape*. The general form of reshape is

```
      VρA
```

where *V*, the left argument, is a scalar or a vector specifying the shape of the result, and *A*, the right argument, is the data that makes up the components of the result. The right argument may be a scalar or any array. For example, a character matrix *MONTHS* can be created in which each row contains a three-character abbreviation of the name of a month. This matrix, then, has 12 rows and 3 columns. To create *MONTHS* we write

```
      MONTHS←12  3 ρ 'JANFEBMARAPRMAYJUNJULAUGSEPOCTNOVDEC'
```
shape   data

The left argument of reshape is 12 3, while the right argument is the character string of month abbreviations. A display of *MONTHS* produces

        MONTHS

JAN
FEB
MAR
APR
MAY
JUN
JUL
AUG
SEP
OCT
NOV
DEC

There is a   relationship between the functions represented by monadic and dyadic ρ, namely

       If: $R \leftarrow V\rho A$
       Then: $(\rho R) = V$

In words this means that the shape (ρR) of the result of reshape $(V\rho A)$ is the left argument (V). $\rho MONTHS$, for example, is 12 3.

     The number of components in the left argument of reshape defines the rank of the resulting array. The value of each component defines the degree of freedom available in indexing the corresponding dimension. If the left argument is a scalar or one-component vector, the result is a vector, and the value of the left argument defines the number of components in the result. If the left argument is a two-component vector, the left component defines the number of rows, and the right component defines the number of columns in the reshaped data. In general, the left argument A, B, C, D of the reshape function can be interpreted as follows:

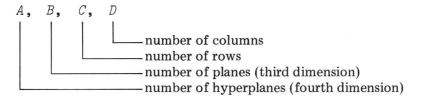

For example, if $R \leftarrow 2\ 3\ 4\rho A$, the resulting array R has two planes, three rows, and four columns.

     The right argument of reshape contains the data. The array is shaped with this data row by row. Recall that the data in the right argument that were used to create the matrix *MONTHS* were a vector arranged so that when the array was shaped the abbreviation for each month occupied one row:

MONTHS←12 3ρ*'JANFEBMARAPRMAYJUNJULAUGSEPOCTNOVDEC'*

Suppose that we wish to group the abbreviations of the months by quarters. The matrix *MONTHS* can be reshaped into a 4 by 3 by 3 array with this expression:

```
    QUART←4 3 3ρMONTHS
    QUART
JAN
FEB
MAR

APR
MAY
JUN

JUL
AUG
SEP

OCT
NOV
DEC
```

The data are taken from the right argument row by row and reshaped into the new array row by row.

Filling an array row by row can be interpreted more formally in this way. For *R←VρA*, each data item from *A* is assigned a set of independent indices. The number of indices assigned to each data item is ρ*V*. In the creation of the *MONTHS* matrix each character of the character string is assigned two indices (since *V* has two components), and in the creation of the *QUARTS* array each character is assigned three indices (since *V* has three components). Each index value is initialized to 1. Then the rightmost index is varied most rapidly. For instance,

```
    J is assigned the indices 1 1
    A, the indices 1 2
    N, 1 3
    F, 2 1
    E, 2 2
    B, 2 3
    etc.
```

This is identical to the manner in which the odometer (mileage count) on a car operates and can be referred to informally as the *odometer principle*. If the right argument is an array, the elements of the array are selected by applying the odometer principle to its current set of indices. Essentially this means that the elements are chosen row by row. Each element as it is selected is assigned a new set of indices as defined by the left argument.

In the construction of the *MONTHS* matrix, there were exactly 36 data characters in the right argument, just enough to fill the array. This is not a necessary restriction on the data. The right argument may have more data than needed or less data than needed. The reshape function takes as much data as it needs to construct the specific array as specified by the left argument. If there are too much data, it takes only what it needs. If there are too little data, it uses the data present, repeatedly cycling through them as often as necessary. For example,

> *R2←3ρ'STYLE'*

Only the first three components are used; thus

> *R2*

STY

and:

> *ρR2*

3

And if:

> *R3←6ρ'HIHO'*

then:

> *R3*

HIHOHI

and

> *ρR3*

6

It often happens in creating large arrays that the data are too long to fit on a single typing line. One means of overcoming this is to specify a vector of the data first, using catenation to continue to add typing lines, as shown in Illustration 1.9, and then to restructure that vector into the desired array using the reshape function.

The rank of the arrays that might be created is restricted only by the limitation of the implementation on the host computer. However, the question of the representation of these higher-rank arrays on paper is always present. An array of rank 3 or greater in APL.SV prints as a sequence of matrices; for example, if *AR3* is a rank-3 array such that *ρAR3* is 3 2 4, *AR3* is printed as a sequence of three 2 by 4 matrices. The display of *AR3* would appear as follows:

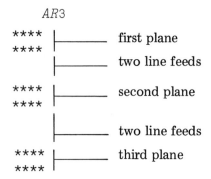

If *AR4* is a rank-4 array such that ρ*AR4* is 2   3   2   4 , the display of *AR4* is also printed as a sequence of matrices. There are two hyperplanes, each of which contains three planes and is separated from the other by three line feeds. The display of *AR4* would be as follows:

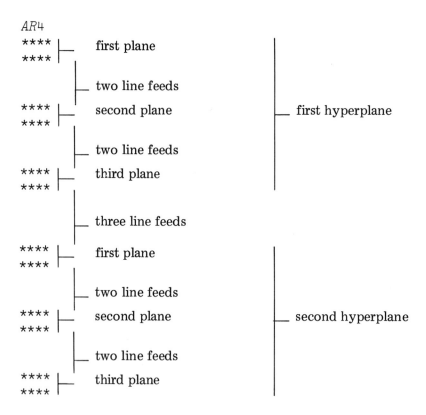

Each increase in dimension provides one more line feed to separate this higher dimension from the rest.

In addition to how the terminal system represents higher-rank arrays, there is a question of how the user might represent such higher-rank arrays on paper.

Typically he would follow the convention established for terminal printing, or he can use a graphic representation. The following is a graphic technique which is extendable to higher-rank arrays. *AR3* could be represented as

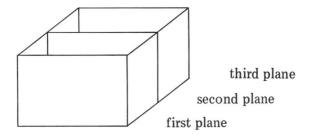

and *AR4* could be represented as

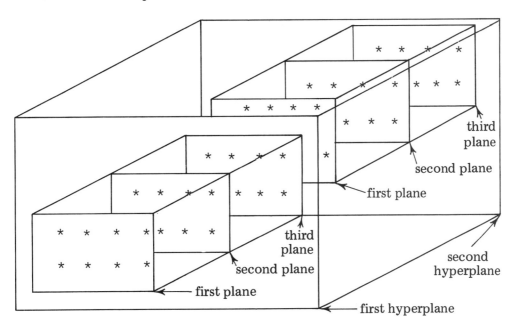

Note: The function symbols for the monadic function shape and the dyadic function reshape are the same:

SHAPE: ρA RESHAPE: $V\rho B$

However, there is never a problem in determining which function the symbol represents. The syntax of the expression indicates whether a function symbol represents a monadic or dyadic function. To see how this works, consider the following expressions:

(a) $5\rho2\ 3\ 4$ (b) $\rho2\ 3\ 4$ (c) $5\rho\rho2\ 3\ 4$

The first two expressions cause no problem. In the first, since the function symbol is between two arguments, it must be dyadic and hence represents reshape. In the second, there is only one argument, and so the function is monadic. It is shape. The rule of evaluation tells what functions the symbols represent in the third expression. The leftmost ρ has two arguments: Its left argument is 5 and its right argument is everything to its right or ρ2 3 4. It is reshape. There is no left argument to the second ρ and so it is monadic. It is shape. The results of the three expressions are

(a) 2 3 4 2 3   (b) 3   (c) 3 3 3 3 3

It is the syntax of the expression that determines without a doubt whether a symbol is being used in its monadic or dyadic sense.

Illustration 3.1 Duplicating Consecutive Components in a Vector

Entering a vector with duplicated consecutive components can be simplified by using reshape and catenation. For example, to create the vector

6 6 6 6 6 6 5 5 5 5 5 5 5 9 9 9 9 9

use the expression

(6ρ6),(7ρ5),5ρ9

Illustration 3.2 Creating an Identity Matrix

An identity matrix is a matrix that contains 1s on the main diagonal and 0s elsewhere. The expression 5 5ρ1 0 0 0 0 0 creates a 5 by 5 identity matrix:

```
1 0 0 0 0
0 1 0 0 0
0 0 1 0 0
0 0 0 1 0
0 0 0 0 1
```

Thus only six data elements are necessary to create this matrix with 25 components.

Section 3.4 THE SCALAR

In the preceding sections we discussed arrays and their shape. The shape of the data associated with a name can be determined via the monadic function ρ. The number of components in the result indicates the rank of the array, and the value of each of the components indicates the degree of freedom available in choosing indices in the corresponding dimension. For example, for the rank-4 array *AR*4,

```
      ρAR4
2  3  2  4
      ρρAR4
4
```

Consider now the vector OC:

```
      OC
⁻13
      ρOC
1
```

OC is a one-component vector, but its display is identical to that of the scalar S:

```
      S
⁻13
```

What is the difference between a one-component vector and a scalar? The most important difference is that a one-component vector, like all vectors, has shape but a scalar does not.

```
      OC←1ρ⁻13                       S←⁻13
      OC                             S
⁻13                         ⁻13
      ρOC                            ρS   (♭ is used in the text to
1                             ♭              indicate a blank return)
```

A scalar is shapeless data, and so an inquiry about its shape produces a null answer, indicated by the blank return. A name assigned to a scalar has only data associated with it. A name assigned to an array has both data and shape assigned to it.

To understand the distinction between a scalar and a one-component vector fully, it is necessary to consider the concept of the *null* or *empty* array. A null array is a data structure which has shape but no data associated with it.

The shape function (ρA) by definition always responds with a vector result, indicating the shape of the right argument. If we ask for the shape of a scalar, for example,

```
      ρ5
♭
```

we receive a reply which says "It has no shape." This reply is in the form of a null or empty vector. The terminal indicates this situation by printing a blank line.

How many components are there in the vector $\rho 5$; that is, what is the rank of a scalar?

```
      V←ρ5
      V
♭
```

```
        ρV
0
```

A scalar has no components in its shape vector. The rank of a scalar, then, is zero. Hence you have zero choices for index values for it, and so a scalar cannot be indexed.

Besides the null vector, there are null arrays which have no components in one or more dimensions. It is not possible to determine what the null array is from its display. A blank return is the response for all null arrays. The shape and rank of scalars and various arrays are illustrated in the following table:

For

```
        A←7

        B←2  4  6  8

        C←0ρ5

        D←2  3ρ6

        E←0  3ρ6

        F←2  0ρ6

        G←0  0ρ6

        H←2  3  4ρ1  2  3
```

X	ρX	ρρX
A	⌿	0
B	4	1
C	0	1
D	2 3	2
E	0 3	2
F	2 0	2
G	0 0	2
H	2 3 4	3

There are two forms of the null array, numeric and character. They are distinct and distinguishable, although in most cases they can be used interchangeably. (See also the discussion of the function expansion in Chapter 7.) The form of the null array is determined by the nature of the data supplied when the array was created. For example, the null vector can be represented by any of the following expressions:

$\rho 5$ the shape of a scalar number

$0\rho 5$ reshape 5 into an array with zero components

$\iota 0$ special case of ι (see Chapter 1)

$'\;'$ open and close quote

$\left. \begin{array}{l} \rho\,'A' \\ \\ \rho'\;' \end{array} \right\}$ the shape of a scalar character

The last three expressions are representations of a character null vector.

There are two very common applications for the null vector (array). First, it can be used to initialize a vector. For example, suppose that you wish to build a vector WT whose components represent the daily usage of a local library for the past week. The vector WT can be augmented each day as follows:

        $WT \leftarrow WT, DU$

where DU contains the daily usage data. But on the first day, this expression results in a value error because WT has not been previously specified:

VALUE ERROR
        $WT \leftarrow WT, DU$
            $\wedge$

WT can be specified initially as the null vector; thus

        $WT \leftarrow \iota 0$

This does not affect the validity of the data in WT.

Initializing a variable to be the null vector is not the same as initializing it to be 0, as the following example demonstrates:

$WT \leftarrow \iota 0$	$WT \leftarrow 0$
$WT \leftarrow WT, 5$	$WT \leftarrow WT, 5$
$WT \leftarrow WT, 8$	$WT \leftarrow WT, 8$
$WT \leftarrow WT, 4$	$WT \leftarrow WT, 4$
WT	WT
5 8 4	0 5 8 4
ρWT	ρWT
3	4

A second commonly used application of the null vector is in conditional branching. This is discussed in Chapter 6.

If the null vector is one of the arguments of a scalar function, the result is the null vector. For example,

      $NV \leftarrow \iota 0$

      $NV \times 3$

♭

      $NV \div 0$

♭

PROBLEMS

1. Use the following variables:

      $A \leftarrow 0\ \ 0\ \ 1\ \ 1\ \ 0\ \ 0\ \ 1\ \ 1$

      $B \leftarrow 10\ \ \ 5\ \ \ 3\ \ \ 6\ \ \ 4$

      $C \leftarrow 'THE\ \ YEAR\ \ 1776'$

```
    U
 0   1   2  ¯2
 4   8  12  ¯6
10  20  30   4
    P
1 2
3 4
5 6
7 8
    L
5 7 1 2
6 3 2 5
2 1 6 7
    Q
GOOD
NITE

     AR
AB
CD
EF

GH
IJ
KL
```

For X in each of the expressions (a) and (b), substitute A, B, C, U, P, L, Q, and AR, and evaluate the resulting expressions.

(a) ρX

(b) $\rho\rho X$

2. Use the variables shown in problem 1, when needed, to evaluate expressions (a)–(z):

(a) 2 3ρι6   (b) 3 2ρ2×ι6   (c) 4ρι3

(d) 2 3 2ρι12   (e) ρ5 4   (f) ρρ5 4

(g) ρ54   (h) ρρ54   (i) ρι5

(j) 2×ι1   (k) 2×ι0   (l) 6+ι0

(m) ρι0   (n) ρ6+ι0   (o) 0 3ρ7

(p) 6+2 0ρ7   (q) ρ0 3ρ7   (r) ρ6+2 0ρ7

(s) ρ''   (t) 2 4ρAR   (u) ρ' '

(v) 3 2ρQ   (w) 3 4ρQ   (x) 2 4ρP

(y) 2 3 2ρL   (z) ρρ'H'

3. Use the variables shown in problem 1, when needed, to evaluate expressions (a)–(o):

(a) 1 8ρQ   (b) 9ρL   (c) ρ1 8ρQ

(d) 2 2 2ρA   (e) 8 1ρQ   (f) (8ρP)×A

(g) ρ8 1ρQ   (h) ρB,6ρU   (i) ρ2×ι1

(j) (8ρC),' 1976'   (k) ρ2×ι0   (l) 5×ρL

(m) (ρA),ρB   (n) 3 2ρB   (o) ρA,ρB

4. For the variable A defined as $A \leftarrow (\iota 0)\rho 5\ 6\ 7$, evaluate the following:

(a) A (b) ρA   (c) ρρA

5. For the variable B defined as $B \leftarrow 1\rho 5\ 6\ 7$, evaluate the following:

(a) B (b) ρB   (c) ρρB

6. Using the vector C defined as $C \leftarrow$ 'THE YEAR 1776', create the following:

(a) The vector *THE YEAR*.

(b) The vector *THE YEAR THE YEAR*.

(c) The matrix *THE YEAR*
                  THE YEAR.

7. Write an expression to create the matrix MT:

```
1 1 1 1 1 1 1 1
2 2 2 2 2 2 2 2
3 3 3 3 3 3 3 3
```

8. Write an expression to create the figure

```
+---+
|   |
+---+
```

9. Write an expression to produce 10 returns/line feeds.

10. Write an expression to create a matrix M entirely of the constant 5 with as many rows as there are components in vector A and as many columns as there are components in vector B.

Test:

    A←2 3 9 8

    B←1 7 3

    . . . .

    5 5 5
    5 5 5
    5 5 5
    5 5 5

11. (a) Write an expression to create a matrix M from data S with as many rows and columns as there are indicated in the two-component vector V.

Test:

    S←9 3 8 5 4 6 2 1

    V←2 4

    . . . .

    9 3 8 5
    4 6 2 1

(b) Create a matrix N from S with as many rows and columns as there are components in R.

Test:

    R←9 ⁻7 2 1

    . . . .

    9 3 8 5
    4 6 2 1
    9 3 8 5
    4 6 2 1

12. (a) Define a function called *PAGE* to print a heading and a page number right-justified on a page. Leave three spaces between the page number and title. Assume a page width of 55 characters per line. For example, the response to the function call might be

        APL: THE LANGUAGE AND ITS USAGE   12

(b) Modify the function to take a variable page width.

13. (a) Define a function $ADD1$ to add a vector V to each row of a matrix M. Assume that V is as long as M is wide.

Test:

M←3 4ρι12

V←4 1 3 8

• • • • • • •

5	3	6	12
9	7	10	16
13	11	14	20

(b) Define a function *ADD2* to add a vector *V* to each even row of *M*.

Test: Use *V* and *M* from part (a).

• • • • • • •

1	2	3	4
9	7	10	16
9	10	11	12

Section 3.5 INDEXING

In Sec. 3.1 an array was defined in terms of the number of independent indices needed to select a single component from it. The function *indexing* does the selecting. Specific components can be selected from a given array by specifying their indices enclosed between square brackets following the array or the array name. For the vector *A*, for example, the expression *A*[*I*] selects those components whose indices are *I*. The array being indexed may be either numeric or character; the index expression must be numeric.

Section 3.5.1 Indexing Vectors

As an illustration of indexing, consider the character vector *V*:

V←'*REASON*'

Various components of *V* can be selected depending on the index expression. For example,

Expression	Selects	Result
V[3]	The third element	*A*
V[2 5 6]	The second, fifth, and sixth elements	*EON*
V[5 6 2]	The fifth, sixth, and second elements	*ONE*
V[2 1 3 4 2 1]	The first and second elements twice	*ERASER*

In general, the order in which the elements are selected is the order in which the set of indices is stated. The same element may be selected more than once.

Suppose that $J\leftarrow4\ 2\ 3$. The expression $V[J]$ yields the characters *SEA*. Furthermore, the expression $V[J-1]$ yields the characters *ARE*. Thus not only may integers themselves be indices, but also names and expressions can be indices as long as their values are integral. Both the names and the expressions must produce a valid set of indices. In our example, neither $V[J+3]$ nor $V[J\div2]$ is possible. The seventh character of V cannot be selected if V contains only six characters. The expression $V[7]$, if ρV is 6, exceeds the degree of freedom possible. Had such a request been attempted at a terminal, it would have received an *INDEX ERROR* report. An *INDEX ERROR* means that an index value did not stay within the domain of definition. It can arise when the index value is an integer beyond the amount of freedom permitted in the selection of the index value or when the index has a negative value. A *DOMAIN ERROR* report is given if the index has a nonintegral value. Thus

$V[.5]$	$V[{}^-1]$	$V[J+3]$
DOMAIN ERROR	*INDEX ERROR*	*INDEX ERROR*
$V[0.5]$	$V[{}^-1]$	$V[J+3]$
$\wedge$	$\wedge$	$\wedge$

If $J\leftarrow6\ 2\ 3\ 1$ and $R\leftarrow V[J]$, R is the vector of characters *NEAR* and ρR is 4. If $K\leftarrow2\ 6\ 4\ 6\ 3\ 1\ 2$ and $R\leftarrow V[K]$, R is the vector of characters *ENSNARE* and ρR is 7. And if $KK\leftarrow2\ 3\rho\iota6$ and $R\leftarrow V[KK]$, R is the character matrix

REA
SON

and ρR is 2 3. In general, for $R\leftarrow A[B]$, the shape of R is the same as the shape of B, the index. That is,

$$(\rho R) = \rho B$$

And, as we have seen in the above examples, the shape and rank of the result need not be the same as the shape and rank of the array being indexed.

An index expression may itself contain an indexed expression. For example, with the V and KK defined above, the expression $V[(\rho KK)[2]]$ extracts from V the element which corresponds to the number of columns in KK or the letter A. Actually nested indexing is only one specific case of the general case: Any expression producing a valid set of indices is acceptable.

At this point, let us pause to reiterate a general property of APL: The arguments of a given function may be *any* expression which produces a valid argument for the particular function. Because the specification statement is a special type of expression, it may also be used. The following expression, for example, extracts the subscript components of V in reverse order:

$$V[1+(\rho V)-\iota\rho V]$$
NOSAER

And if the index expression were useful enough to name (perhaps because it will be used to index other vectors), it could be assigned a name within the index expression:

$$V[IV\leftarrow1+(\rho V)-\iota\rho V]$$
NOSAER

$$IV$$
6 5 4 3 2 1

Returning once more to the mainstream of our discussion of indexing, suppose that you wish to replace the character R in V by the character S. The expression $V[1]\leftarrow'S'$ accomplishes this. Thus indexing is also possible to the left of specification. And, in fact, indexing is the only function permitted on the left side of the specification arrow.

When an index expression appears on the right of the specification symbol, a selection is performed. However, when an index expression appears on the left of the specification symbol, a replacement is performed. Both may occur within the same statement. For example, the expression $V[1]\leftarrow V[4]$ replaces the character R in V with the character S:

$$V$$
SEASON

To replace items in an array by using indexing, the array has to have been previously defined; otherwise you get a *VALUE ERROR* report. An expression such as $V[2\ 4]\leftarrow'RPQ'$ produces a *LENGTH ERROR* report. This occurs because the statement attempts to insert three characters into two slots. They do not fit. For a replacement A to occur in W at positions I,

$$W[I]\leftarrow A$$

it is necessary that the shape of the index conform with the shape of the replacement data. These shapes conform if either

1. They match, that is, $(\rho I)=\rho A$, or

2. The replacement is a scalar quantity or a one-component array.

Thus for $W\leftarrow'WRENS'$ either $W[1\ 5]\leftarrow'AA'$ or $W[1\ 5]\leftarrow'A'$ replaces the first and fifth components of W with the character A, resulting in *ARENA*.

Illustration 3.3 "Drawing" a Letter

The following expression draws the letter L with the character □ on a 6 by 5 grid:

```
L←' □'[6 5ρ(25ρ2 1 1 1 1),5ρ2]
    L
```

□
□
□
□
□
□□□□□

The expression of Illustration 3.3 demonstrates that very compact statements can be written as single statements or "one liners." However, for clarity the user may not wish to do this, since quite often the statement of an algorithm[*] in a single line undermines the understanding of the algorithm. Whether you should program a one liner should depend on the clarity of the resulting expression.

Section 3.5.2   Indexing Arrays

We have seen how vectors are indexed. Let us now consider the details of indexing all arrays. Let

```
    M←3 5ρ'BLOODSWEATTEARS'
    M
BLOOD
SWEAT
TEARS
```

Since the rank of M, $\rho\rho M$, is 2, two independent indices are necessary to extract a single element of M. Also, since the shape of M, ρM, is 3 5, there are three choices possible for the first index and five choices for the second index. The independent indices are separated from each other in the index expression by using the semi-colon (;) as a *delimiter* or separator. The expression $M[3;4]$ selects the element of M which is in the third row and fourth column, that is, the character R. The expression $M[2;3\ 4\ 5]$ selects from M those elements which appear in the second row, third, fourth, and fifth columns, the vector EAT. And the expression $M[1\ 2;3\ 4]$ selects from M those elements which appear in the first and the second rows, third and fourth columns of the matrix M

```
OO
EA
```

---

[*]An algorithm can be defined as a sequential procedure consisting of a finite number of un-ambiguous instructions or actions working on some initial data or information and producing some final result. For an excellent and more detailed discussion of algorithms, see D. E. Knuth, *The Art of Computer Programming*, Vol. 1, Addison-Wesley, Reading, Mass., 1968, pp. 1-9.

Another way of interpreting the expression $M[1\ 2;3\ 4]$ is to say that it selects from M all those elements in the first row, third and fourth columns, and those elements in the second row, third and fourth columns. The row and column indices are *not* paired off. They cannot be since there is no restriction stating that the number of index values in each dimension must be the same. For instance, $M[1\ 3;1\ 3\ 5]$ results in the matrix

```
BOD
TAS
```

The expression $M[3\ 2]$ results in a *RANK ERROR* report. The error occurs because there is an ambiguity in the meaning of the expression. It could be interpreted as referring to the third and second rows of M or the third and second columns of M, or the third row and second column of M. To remove ambiguity, the semicolon delimiter must be used.

The expression $M[2;\iota5]$ selects all those components of M which lie in the second row and the first through fifth columns. For M this is simply the second row, *SWEAT*. The expression $M[\iota3;4]$ extracts the fourth column from M, *OAR*. When an entire row or column is to be extracted, the index expression can be simplified by eliminating the index values for the row or column but maintaining the semicolon. Therefore $M[2;]$ is the same as $M[2;\iota5]$, and $M[;4]$ is the same as $M[\iota3;4]$. The absence of any expression for an independent index means that the index varies over all possible values.

When we discussed indexing of vectors, we said that the shape of the result was the same as the shape of the index; that is, for $R\leftarrow V[I]$, $(\rho R) = \rho I$. This also applies to other arrays. Consider

```
R←M[1 2;3 4]
```

Here ρR is 2 2. Thus, the shape of the result is equal to the catenation of the shape of the row indices and the shape of the column indices. Formally, for

```
R←M[I;J]
```
$$(\rho R) = (\rho I),\rho J$$

if $R\leftarrow M[;2]$, ρR is 3, that is, $\rho R = (\rho\iota3),\rho2$, $\rho\iota3$ is 3, and $\rho2$ is the null vector.

Arrays with more components and a greater rank than the array being indexed can be built by selective indexing. For example, with

```
M←3 3ρ'ABCDEFGHI'
M
```
```
ABC
DEF
GHI
```

```
I←2 3
N←2 3ρ3 2 2 1 3 1
```

M can be indexed with the index list *I*;*N* as follows:

```
M[I;N]
```

This results in a 2 2 3 shaped array whose elements are

```
FEE
DFD

IHH
GIG
```

The components were selected by using the expression

```
2 2 3ρM[2 3;3 2 2 1 3 1]
```

The information within brackets can be considered a list, the index list. The elements of the list are separated by semicolons. The number of entries in such a list depends on the rank of the object being indexed, but the shapes of each item within the list are independent.

Illustration 3.4 Extracting Information from a Matrix

RESULTS is a data matrix of election results as indicated in the body of the table below:

		Precinct				
		1	2	3	4	5
	A	102	175	81	123	86
Party	B	93	120	88	127	163
	C	137	71	195	87	91

The expression *RESULTS*[2;] states the vote record of party B by precinct. The expression *RESULTS*[3;4] states how party C did in the fourth precinct. And the expression *RESULTS*[;1] states how the first precinct voted by party.

Illustration 3.5 Functions of More than Two Arguments

A defined function can have none, one, or two arguments indicated in its header. If the function requires more than two arguments—for example, a function to compute the volume of a rectangular solid whose arguments are length, width, and height—it can be defined by using the monadic or dyadic header and by requiring that one or both arguments be arrays. The function *YIELD* is a generalization of Illustration 1.7, "Percentage Yield of a Two-step Process." The percentage yields are collected in a two-row matrix *PY* and the number of starts are collected in a vector *STARTS*:

```
     ∇ STEPS←STARTS YIELD PY
[1]    STEPS←(ρPY)ρ0
[2]    STEPS[1;]←PY[1;]×STARTS
[3]    STEPS[2;]←PY[2;]×STEPS[1;]
     ∇
```

For example,

```
     2000 3000 4000 YIELD 2 3ρ.95 .96 .9 .95 .94 .91
 1900    2880      3600
 1805    2707.2    3276
```

The matrix has been used to illustrate the means of indexing arrays of rank greater than 1. The principles stated for matrices extend to higher-rank arrays. For instance, if *AR* is a rank-3 array such that ρ*AR* is 2 3 4 , the expression *AR*[2;1;4] selects the element in the second plane, first row, fourth column. In general, if *A;B;C* is the expression within the index brackets, it is interpreted as follows:

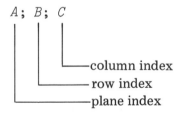

A; B; C

────column index
──── row index
──────plane index

Any higher-dimension indices are appended to the left, again delimited by semicolons. If *W* is a vector, no semicolons appear in the indexing. If *W* is a matrix, one semicolon appears. If *W* is a rank-3 array, two semicolons appear. In general, the number of semicolons is equal to ¯1+ρρ*W*. It is not necessary to separate the set of independent indices from each other by parentheses; the semicolon acts as a sufficient delimiter.

The shape of the result of indexing an array is the catenation of the shapes of each of the independent indices. For example, the shape of *A*[1 2;2 3ρι3;4] is 2 2 3.

If *AR*←2 3 4ρ3×ι24, the expression *AR*[1;2;3] produces the element from

AR that is in the first plane, second row, and third column, the element 21. Likewise, *AR*[2;;] produces the second plane:

```
39   42   45   48
51   54   57   60
63   66   69   72
```

AR[1;3;] produces the third row in the first plane:

```
27 30 33 36
```

And *AR*[;2;4] produces the elements which lie in the second row and fourth column in both planes:

```
24   60
```

The null array is also a permissible index for an array. Thus, if

$$R \leftarrow 'AB'[\iota 0]$$

then

```
        ρR
0
```

and

```
        R
ϸ
```

The result *R* is a null vector because

$$(\rho R) = \rho \iota 0$$

PROBLEMS

1. Use the following variables to evaluate expressions (a)–(z):

$$B \leftarrow 10 \quad 5 \quad 3 \quad 6 \quad 4$$

$$C \leftarrow 'THE \ YEAR \ 1776'$$

```
      U
   0  1  2  ‾2
   4  8 12  ‾6
  10 20 30   4

      P
  1 2
  3 4
  5 6
  7 8

      L
  5 7 1 2
  6 3 2 5
  2 1 6 7

      Q
 GOOD
 NITE

      AR
 AB
 CD
 EF

 GH
 IJ
 KL
```

(a) B[4]   (b) B[3 5 2]   (c) B[2 5 3]

(d) ρB[4]   (e) ρB[3 5 2]   (f) C[3 4ρι12]

(g) ρC[3 4ρι12]   (h) Q[1;4]   (i) ρQ[1;4]

(j) Q[1;2 4 4]   (k) ρQ[1;2 4 4]   (l) U[1;3]

(m) U[;1 3]   (n) U[;3]   (o) ρU[1;3]

(p) ρU[;3]   (q) L[1;]   (r) ρL[;1]

(s) U[1 3;2]   (t) ρU[1 3;2]   (u) U×L[3;2]

(v) U[2;],L[;1]   (w) U[1 3;2 1]   (x) ρU[1 3;2 1]

(y) U[1 2;3 2]×P[1 4;]   (z) U[;3 2]

2. Use the variables of problem 1 to evaluate expressions (a)–(x):

(a) (ρU)[2]   (b) ρU[2]   (c) U[1 3;1 2]

(d) U[3 1;1 2]   (e) U[3 1;2 1]   (f) AR[2;3;1]

(g) AR[;3;2]   (h) AR[1;2;2 1]   (i) AR[2;1 3;2]

(j) AR[1;3;]   (k) AR[2;;]   (l) AR[;2 3;1]

(m) ρAR[2;3;1]   (n) ρAR[2;1 3;1]   (o) ρAR[2;;]

(p) ρAR[;2 3;1]   (q) ρAR[;2 3ρ1 3 2;1]   (r) AR[;2 3ρ3 2;1]

(s) C[2 5ρ3+ι10]   (t) P←2 2 2ρP   (u) B[1+(ρB)−ιρB]
                                P[1;;]×P[2;;]

(v) 'ARET'[3 3ρ1 2 3 4]   (w) 'AMIABLE'[L]   (x) C[B]

3. Write an expression to select from a matrix M the element E whose row and column indices are indicated by the vector V.

    Test:

       $M\leftarrow2$ $4\rho9$ 6 2 4 1 3 7 8

       $V\leftarrow2$ 3

       • • • • •

      7

4. Write an expression for each of the following using the variables shown in problem 1:
   (a) The sum of the first and third components of B.
   (b) The extraction of the date 1776 from C.
   (c) The extraction of the date 1667 from C.
   (d) The character null vector.
   (e) The numeric null vector.
   (f) The extraction of the second row of Q.
   (g) The replacement of the last row of Q by *MORN*.
   (h) The extraction of the second plane from the array AR.
   (i) The replacement of the third row in the first plane of AR by the characters XY.
   (j) The replacement of the elements J and D in the array AR by the characters R and P respectively.

5. Write a concise one-statement specification of a matrix M where M has the following characteristics:

   (ρM) = 3 4
   $M[1\ 3;1\ 3]$ = 2 2ρ0 2 8 10
   $M[1\ 2;2\ 3]$ = 2 2ρ1 2 5 6
   $M[;4]$ = $^{-}1+4\times\iota3$
   $M[2;1]$ = 4
   $M[3;2]$ = 9

6. Write a concise one-statement specification of a matrix C where C has the following characteristics:

   (ρC) = 3 4
   $C[1\ 3;4]$ = '$D!$'
   $C[;2]$ = 'O'
   $C[2\ 3;1\ 3]$ = 2 2ρ'$FRYU$'
   $C[1;1]$ = 'G'
   $C[1;3]$ = $C[1;2]$
   $C[2;4]$ = ' '

7. Write an expression to convert the vector V, a vector whose components are a set of positive digits between 0 and 9, into the corresponding character digits CD.

> *Test:*
>
>   V←2 6 7 1
>   • • • • •
>   2671

8. Given a matrix M where $(\rho M) \geq 3\ 3$, write the statement to

   (a) Exchange the first and third rows.

   (b) Exchange the second and third columns.

   (c) Replace the second column by the first row, assuming that M is a square matrix.

9. Write an expression to replace a row whose index is X of an arbitrary matrix M with a given vector R. Assume that $(\rho R) = (\rho M)[2]$

> *Test:*
>
>   X←3
>   M←4 2ρι8
>   R←9   15
>   • • • • • • •
>   1 2
>   3 4
>   9 15
>   7 8

10. Write an expression to reverse the rows of a matrix M.

> *Test:*
>
>   M←3 4ρι12
>   • • • • •
>   9 10 11 12
>   5 6 7 8
>   1 2 3 4

11. The following table shows student enrollment and number of teachers in six Great Lakes states:

	Pupils		Classroom Teachers	
State	Elementary	Secondary	Elementary	Secondary
Illinois	1,688,269	656,247	60,847	41,186
Indiana	675,901	531,611	24,713	24,194
Michigan	120,003	922,836	47,284	40,203
Minnesota	498,182	401,424	21,609	23,691
Ohio	1,747,327	676,504	57,295	43,244
Wisconsin	672,643	307,421	29,106	15,703

Write an expression to do each of the following:

(a) Define a matrix ED to contain the figures in the table.

(b) Define a corresponding matrix $STATES$ to contain the names of the states.

(c) Rearrange ED so that columns 1 and 2 are the elementary pupils and teachers and columns 3 and 4 are the secondary pupils and teachers.

(d) Determine the ratio of pupils to teachers for elementary and for secondary schools. Determine the ratio for all schools.

(e) Determine how many more or fewer elementary pupils Illinois has than the other states.

(f) If the annual yearly expenditure per pupil is as follows,

State	Amount Per Pupil
Illinois	737.77
Indiana	819.33
Michigan	655.58
Minnesota	742.00
Ohio	701.81
Wisconsin	875.00

Determine the total expenditure each state makes.

12. The following table shows the mean annual income of elementary, high school, and college graduates:

Annual Mean Income

Year	Elementary	High School	College
1949	2829	3784	6179
1956	3631	5183	7877
1961	4206	5946	9817
1967	5189	7629	11924
1968	5467	8148	12938

Write an expression to do each of the following:

(a) Define matrix INC to contain the figures in the table.

(b) Determine the difference between elementary school and college graduate incomes.

(c) Determine the percentage increase of college over high school incomes for each year.

(d) Determine the figures for 1961.

(e) Determine the figures for college graduates.

(f) Determine the monthly mean income for each year for each type of graduate.

(g) Determine the weekly mean income for each year for each type of graduate.

(h) Determine the percentage increase for all mean incomes of 1967 over 1956.

(i) The consumer price index, 1957–1959 $= 100$, for all items was

1945	62.7
1954	93.6
1959	101.5
1968	121.2

Adjust the mean income figures in *INC* to reflect as closely as possible the purchasing power of that income. Since the price index years do not match the table years, use a straight-line interpolation. For example, assume that 1949 is the 1945 index plus four-ninths of the difference between the 1945 and 1954 indices.

13. Create the following figures:

(a)

(b)

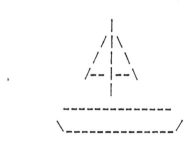

(c)

(d)

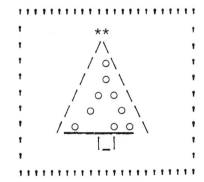

14. What are the values of expressions (a)–(k) with matrices A and B defined as

$A \leftarrow 3\ 3\rho 1$
$B \leftarrow 2 \times A$

(a) A (b) B (c) $A[\ ;1] \leftarrow \iota 3$
                                                      $A[\ ;\bar{1}]$

(d) $A[\ ;1] \leftarrow 5$ (e) $C \leftarrow A[\ ;1] \leftarrow 6$ (f) C
    $A[\ ;1]$ $A[\ ;1]$

(g) ρC (h) $A[\ ;1],A[\ ;1] \leftarrow 7$ (i) $B[2;\ ] \leftarrow A[\ ;1] \leftarrow 8$

(j) $A[\ ;1]$ (k) $B[2;\ ]$

15. V is a vector of items. Assume that items are appended to the right-hand end of V. Write an expression to select an item by

   (a) LIFO (last in, first out).

   (b) FIFO (first in, first out).

16. Suppose that the vector V is rearranged by indexing it with the vector of indices P, resulting in the vector W. Given P and W, define a function $ORIG$ to determine V.

   Test:

   $P \leftarrow 6\ 2\ 5\ 3\ 4\ 1$
   $W \leftarrow 1\ 2\ 3\ 6\ 8\ 9$
   $\cdots\cdots$
   $9\ 2\ 6\ 8\ 3\ 1$

17. Define a function $PROG1$ that generates an arithmetic progression given the following information vector V:

   $V[1]$ The number of terms

   $V[2]$ The first term

   $V[3]$ The difference between consecutive terms

   Test:

   $V \leftarrow 5\ 8\ 6$
   $\cdots\cdots$
   $8\quad 14\quad 20\quad 26\quad 32$

18. Define a function $PROG2$ that generates an arithmetic progression given the information vector F:

   $F[1]$ The number of terms

   $F[2]$ The last term

   $F[3]$ The difference between consecutive terms

19. Define a function DEL to delete the first or last column from a matrix Y, whichever is specified. Let 0 mean that the last column is deleted and 1 mean that the first column is deleted.

    Test:

    ```
        M←3 4ρι12
          0 DEL M
    1   2   3
    5   6   7
    9  10  11
          1 DEL M
    2   3   4
    6   7   8
   10  11  12
    ```

20. Define a function $CORRECT$ to replace a component in a matrix M, given the row and column index RC and the replacement value NEW.

    Test:

    ```
    M←2 3ρ9 3 6 5 8 2
    RC←2 3
    NEW←¯10

    . . . . . . . .
    9   3      6
    5   8   ¯10
    ```

Section 3.6 INDEX-OF

With indexing, information is accessed by providing an index or set of indices for selecting the desired data. Now consider the converse. Rather than supplying the index value and retrieving the data associated with it, the data might be available and the positions of some of its elements in the array needed. For example, this book, like many others, has an index. A particular data item in the index such as the sine function has associated with it a page number placing its occurrence in the text. This page number is the *index-of* that information in the text. The *index-of* function locates data items in a vector and returns the indices of those data items relative to the vector. The general form of index-of is

$$V \iota A$$

where A is a scalar or any array made up of the data to be located and V is the vector of data being scanned. V must be a vector.

The index-of function provides an index value for each of the elements of the right argument A. Each index value represents the first occurrence of each element of A relative to the vector left argument V. This left argument V must be a vector. For example,

        $U\leftarrow{}'ABCDE'$

        $U\iota{}'C'$
3

The result 3 indicates that the index of the character C with respect to the character vector $ABCDE$ is 3. Also,

        $U\iota{}'DAD'$
4   1   4

Index-of supplies the index of the first occurrence of each of the elements of the right argument.

    If the vector left argument contains duplicate elements, index-of returns the index of the *first* occurrence only. Thus

        $'ABAC'\iota{}'A'$
1

If the right argument contains an element or elements which do not appear in the vector left argument, the value given for each such element is one more than the shape of the left argument, that is, $1 + \rho U$. Thus

        $U\iota{}'F'$
6

        $U\iota{}'GADS'$
6 1 4 6

    The shape of the result of $V\iota A$ is identical to the shape of the right argument A. For example,

        $M \leftarrow 2\ 3\ \rho\ 'BEEBED'$

        $U\ \iota\ M$
    2 5 5
    2 5 4

    Index-of provides a set of index values relative to a given vector V. If these values are used as indices on the vector V, the result is the corresponding components. For example,

```
      ALPH←'ABCDEFGHIJKLMNOPQRSTUVWXYZ'
      I←ALPHι'CAT'
      I
3  1  20
```

If I is used as an index on $ALPH$, CAT comes back:

```
      ALPH[I]
CAT
```

Illustration 3.6   A Mapping Function

The book *System Structure in Data, Programs, and Computers* by L. R. Johnson, published by Prentice-Hall, Englewood Cliffs, N. J., 1970, p. 23, defines a mapping operation

$$M \int B$$

as producing a vector C with the property that

$$C_I = B_{M_I}$$

For example,

$$1 \quad 2 \quad 3 \quad 4 \quad \int \quad 17 \quad 12 \quad 6 \quad 9 \quad \text{yields} \quad 17 \quad 12 \quad 6 \quad 9$$

$$4 \quad 3 \quad 2 \quad 1 \quad \int \quad 17 \quad 12 \quad 6 \quad 9 \quad \text{yields} \quad 9 \quad 6 \quad 12 \quad 17$$

$$2 \quad 1 \quad 4 \quad 3 \quad 3 \quad \int \quad 17 \quad 12 \quad 6 \quad 9 \quad \text{yields} \quad 12 \quad 17 \quad 9 \quad 6 \quad 6$$

The expression $B[M]$ defines this mapping function.

But suppose that M_I is outside the indexing range of B. The function MAP defines a mapping function similar to the one above except that C_I is a zero whenever M_I is outside the indexing range of B:

```
      ∇ Z←M MAP B
[1]      Z←(B,0)[(ιρB)ιM]
      ∇
```

For example,

```
      2 1 6 2 4 MAP 17 12 6 9
12 17 0 12 9
```

PROBLEMS

1. Use the following variables to evaluate expressions (a)-(m):

$$B \leftarrow 10 \quad 5 \quad 3 \quad 6 \quad 4$$

$$C \leftarrow 'THE \ YEAR \ 1776'$$

$$U$$

$$\begin{array}{rrrr} 0 & 1 & 2 & ^-2 \\ 4 & 8 & 12 & ^-6 \\ 10 & 20 & 30 & 4 \end{array}$$

$$P$$

$$\begin{array}{rr} 1 & 2 \\ 3 & 4 \\ 5 & 6 \\ 7 & 8 \end{array}$$

$$Q$$

$$GOOD$$
$$NITE$$

(a) $B\iota 5$ (b) $B\iota 7$ (c) $B\iota 5 \ 6$ (d) $B\iota 5 \ 7$ (e) $5 \ 6\iota B$

(f) $6 \ 5\iota B$ (g) $B\iota U$ (h) $B\iota B$ (i) $C\iota '1776'$ (j) $C\iota '1677'$

(k) $C\iota '1 \ 7 \ 7 \ 6'$ (l) $C\iota Q$ (m) $R \leftarrow 2 \ 4\rho P$
$$R + C\iota Q$$

2. Write an expression to determine the index of the first occurrence of the character $'.'$ in a character string D.

Test:

$$D \leftarrow 'GOOD. \ THERE \ IS \ THE \ PERIOD.'$$
$$\cdot \ \cdot \ \cdot \ \cdot \ \cdot$$
$$5$$

3. Write an expression to convert a character string CS into a unique numeric vector. Assume that the conversion is to be based on the prescribed collating or ordering sequence SEQ.

Test:

$$SEQ \leftarrow 'ABCDEFGHIJKLMNOPQRSTUVWXYZ'$$
$$CS \leftarrow 'SCOTT'$$
$$\cdot \ \cdot \ \cdot \ \cdot \ \cdot \ \cdot$$
$$19 \quad 3 \quad 15 \quad 20 \quad 20$$

4. Write an expression to convert a character string CS which consists only of digits to a vector whose components correspond to the numeric characters in the character string.

Test:

$$CS \leftarrow '12345'$$
$$\cdot \ \cdot \ \cdot \ \cdot \ \cdot$$
$$1 \quad 2 \quad 3 \quad 4 \quad 5$$

5. Define a function *DFROMH* to convert a character string *CS* which represents a three-digit hexadecimal (base-16) number to its corresponding decimal value.

> *Test:*
>
> >   *CS*←'*A5F*'
> >   · · · · · · ·
> > 2655

6. Define a function *FROM* to remove the first occurrence of the component *R* from a vector *V*. Assume that *R* is a member of *V*.

> *Test:*
>
> >   *R*←4
> >   *V*←6 4 2 8 0 5 4
> > · · · · · · ·
> > . 6 2 8 0 5 4

7. Define a function *WHATIS* to translate a word string of uppercase APL symbols to its corresponding lowercase APL letters as found on the APL keyboard:

> *Test:*
>
> >   *APL*←'⌈∈α⌈∆○ρ∈'
> > · · · · · · ·
> > *SEASHORE*

Section 3.7 RAVEL

The shape of data or the interrelationship of data can be changed dynamically by the dyadic ρ function and by indexing. Frequently it is useful to consider data as a vector regardless of what their former shape was; for instance, to determine the indices of some data *A* with respect to other data *B* using the index-of function requires that *B* be a vector. The function which accomplishes this is the function *ravel*. The general form of ravel is

>   ,*A*

where the argument *A* can be a scalar or any array. The result of a ravel expression is always a vector.

The ravel of an array *A*, ,*A* , produces a row-by-row or *row-major* raveling of the array *A* . For example,

```
      M←2 6ρ'HIHO'
      M
HIHOHI
HOHIHO

      ,M
HIHOHIHOHIHO
```

In the formation of the components of the raveled vector, the odometer principle is applied to the set of associated indices. Each component is chosen by cycling through the rightmost index values first. When the rightmost index values have cycled through all their possible values, the next rightmost index value is stepped up by 1 and the rightmost index is cycled again. This continues until all the indices have been cycled through once. At this point, all the elements have been selected. Suppose that

$$AR \leftarrow 2\ 3\ 2\rho\ 'ABCDEFGHIJKL'$$

$$AR$$

```
AB
CD
EF

GH
IJ
KL
```

Listing the elements of AR and their corresponding indices following the odometer principle in the listing, we have

Indices	Elements
1 1 1	A
1 1 2	B
1 2 1	C
1 2 2	D
1 3 1	E
1 3 2	F
2 1 1	G
2 1 2	H
2 2 1	I
2 2 2	J
2 3 1	K
2 3 2	L

Then, $,AR$ is $ABCDEFGHIJKL$.

Illustration 3.7   Creating a One-Component Vector

The ravel function can be used to produce a one-component vector from a scalar. For example,

```
      S←5
      ρS
```
b
```
      T←,S
      ρT
```
1

A one-component vector is often needed because scalars cannot be indexed, whereas vectors, even one-component vectors, may be.

Illustration 3.8   Generalizing an Indexing Expression

In Sec. 3.5.2 an example of creating a larger array by indexing a matrix was shown. A general form for determining the result of $M[I,N]$ where I and N are any arrays is

$$((\rho I),\rho N)\rho M[,I;,N]$$

Raveling the index expression assures vector lists. For example, with

```
      M←3 3 ρ 'ABCDEFGHI'
      I←2 3
      N←2 3 ρ 3 2 2 1 3 1
```

the above expression would be

```
      2 2 3 ρ M[2 3;3 2 2 1 3 1]
FEE
DFD

IHH
GIG
```

PROBLEMS

1. Use the following variables to evaluate expressions (a)–(g):
```
        Q
GOOD
NITE
        C←'THE YEAR 1776'
```

AR

AB
CD
EF
GH
IJ
KL

(a) $,Q$ (b) $C,,Q$ (c) $\rho,5$

(d) $\rho5$ (e) $5[1]$ (f) $(,5)[1]$

(g) $3\ 5\rho(,AR)[3,R,6,R,2,R\leftarrow12\ 1\ 3\ 11]$

2. Write an expression to create the character vector $ABCDEFGHIJKL$ from AR as defined above in problem 1.

3. Write an expression to create by selective indexing on $,AR$ a matrix of at least three rows where each is a word formed by the letters of AR.

4. Ravel always makes an array into a vector. Write an expression for always making a scalar from a one-component array Z.

5. The left argument of index-of must be a vector. Suppose that index-of is used within a function where the left argument is supplied by the function user. How can you assure that a domain error will not occur on the left argument during execution of the function?

6. (a) Define a function $TO1$ to append a row R to a matrix M. For example, the response to the function call for appending the row $\iota3$ to $3\ 3\rho\iota9$ would be

```
1   2   3
4   5   6
7   8   9
1   2   3
```

(b) Define a function $TO2$ to append one row or several rows to a matrix. Assume that the appended rows can be in the form of a vector or in the form of a matrix. That is, the function $TO2$ should work equally well if the appending information is $4\ 7\ 8\ 2\ 4\ 6$ or $2\ 3\rho4\ 7\ 8\ 2\ 4\ 6$.

Section 3.8 GRADE UP, GRADE DOWN

Consider the following vector of numbers:

$GOLF\leftarrow82\quad 80\quad 75\quad 83\quad 77$

If you were asked where the smallest element was in $GOLF$, you would reply that it is the third from the left. Similarly, the largest element is the fourth. It is a small extension to state the position of not only the smallest but also the next larger and so forth until you reach the position of the largest component. If you write down the indices of these components as you select them, the list would be $3\ 5\ 2\ 1\ 4$. This is simply a rearrangement or *permutation* of the indices associated with the vector data.

The monadic function *grade up* produces such a permutation. Its general form is

$$\spadesuit V \quad (\spadesuit \text{ is formed by } \triangle \text{ overstrike } |)$$

where V is a numeric vector. The result of $\spadesuit V$ is the permutation on the indices of V which describes the arrangement of the elements of V in *ascending* order. Thus the first component of the result is the index of the smallest element in V, the Ith component of the result is the Ith smallest, and the last component of the result is the index of the largest element of V. If the result is used as the indices on V in the expression $V[\spadesuit V]$, the elements of V are rearranged into ascending order. For the vector *GOLF*,

```
    GOLF[⍋GOLF]
75  77  80  82  83
```

If *GOLF* is a vector of golfing scores, this creates a rearrangement of the scores with the best first and the poorest last.

An analogous function is the function *grade down*. Its general form is

$$\psi V . \quad (\psi \text{ is formed by } \triangledown \text{ overstrike } |)$$

where V must be a numeric vector. The result of ψV is the permutation which describes the arrangement of V in *descending* order. The first component of the result is the index of the largest element of V, the Ith component of the result is the Ith largest element of V, and, of course, the last component of the result is the index of the smallest element of V. If the result is used as indices on V in the expression $V[\psi V]$, the elements of V are rearranged into descending order. For example,

```
    BOWLSCORES←185 255 173 261 159
    BOWLSCORES[⍒BOWLSCORES]
261  255  185  173  159
```

If *BOWLSCORES* is a vector of bowling scores, this creates a rearrangement of the scores with the best first and the poorest last.

Illustration 3.9 Ordering Data

Suppose that the matrix *STOCKPRICE* has as its first row the current prices of a number of stocks and as its second row the corresponding earnings. (If the stock had a loss, the earnings component is negative.) Thus

```
    STOCKPRICE
250.62 74.5  11.5   49.125
 11     4.25  ¯1     6.31
```

The following expression arranges the stocks and their associated earnings in the *STOCKPRICE* matrix in ascending order by price to earnings:

 STOCKPRICE←STOCKPRICE[;⍋STOCKPRICE[1;]÷STOCKPRICE[2;]]

 STOCKPRICE

11.5	49.125	74.5	250.62
⁻1	6.31	4.25	11

Illustration 3.10   The Mesh of Two Vectors

   The *mesh* of the two vectors A and B consists of the merging of the components of these vectors into a single vector R. The order of the merge of the components of A and B is defined by a binary vector V whose shape is $(\rho A)+\rho B$. The components of A are chosen wherever the components of V are 0 and the components of B are chosen wherever the components of V are 1; that is, the Ith component of R is equal to the Ith component of A if the Ith component of V is 0; otherwise it is equal to the Ith component of B.
This mesh of A and B with respect to the binary vector V can be produced as follows:

 Z←A,B

 Z[⍋V]←,Z

For example,

 A←' LBS   OZS'

 B←'4312'

 V←1 1 0 0 0 0 0 1 1 0 0 0 0

 Z[⍋V]←,Z←A,B
 Z
43 *LBS* 12 *OZS*

   Alternatively, the sequence ⍋⍋ applied to the binary vector V will also produce the mesh of the two vectors A and B. For example, with the A, B, and V defined above,

 Z←(A,B)[⍋⍋V]

43 *LBS* 12 *OZS*

Indexing appears in its selective role using this technique, whereas it appears in its replacement role in the first procedure.

Illustration 3.11   Reversing the Integers from 1 through N

The integers ιN can be reversed with the expression $\Phi\iota N$. Combined with indexing, this constitutes a means of reversing a vector. For example,

   $V\leftarrow{}'STOP{}'$

   $V[\Phi\iota\rho V]$

POTS

*Illustration 3.12   Ordinality of a Vector Sorted by
               Ascending Order*

The elements of a vector of numbers V can be sorted into ascending order with the expression $V[\Delta V]$. Without sorting the elements, the ordinal numbers associated with the elements of V can be obtained by the expression

      $\Delta\Delta V$

That is, the expression $\Delta\Delta V$ gives the indices associated with the individual elements of V were they sorted. For example,

   $V\leftarrow7\ \ 5\ \ 9\ \ 7\ \ 6$

   $\Delta\Delta V$

3   1   5   4   2

Thus the first component of V, 7, would become the third of the sorted elements. The second, 5, would be the first; the third, 9, would become the fifth; and so forth:

   $V[\Delta V]$

5   6   7   7   9

PROBLEMS

1. Use the following variables to evaluate expressions (a)–(j):

   $B\leftarrow10\ \ 5\ \ 3\ \ 6\ \ 4$

   $A\leftarrow0\ \ 0\ \ 1\ \ 1\ \ 0\ \ 0\ \ 1\ \ 1$

   U

   0   1   2   ‾2
   4   8 12   ‾6
  10 20 30   4

```
      Q
GOOD
NITE
      L
 5 7 1 2
 6 3 2 5
 2 1 6 7
```

(a) $⍋B$ (b) $⍒B$ (c) $B[⍋B]$

(d) $B[⍒B]$ (e) $\text{'}ABCDE\text{'}[⍋B]$ (f) $A[⍋A]$

(g) $A[⍒A]$ (h) $\text{'}ABCDE\text{'}[⍋⍋B]$ (i) $U[;⍋4\rho B]$

(j) $Q[;⍒L[2;]]$

2. Write an expression to rearrange an alphabetic character string S so that all the As appear before all the Bs and so forth.

    Test:

$$S←\text{'}MISSISSIPPI\text{'}$$

        • • • • • • •

$$IIIIMPPSSSS$$

3. Let X be a vector whose components are arranged in ascending order. Define a function *MESH* to insert the components of a vector Y so that the resulting vector *NEW* is still in ascending order.

    Test:

```
      X←9   13   15   22
      Y←16   3   25
      • • • •
 3 9 13 15 16 22 25
```

4. The set of golf scores GS has associated with it a matrix *PLAYERS* of names, where each row of the matrix represents a name. The names in the matrix are in the same order as the golf scores. Write an expression to display the names so that the first name has the best score on down to the last name with the worst score.

    Test:

```
      PLAYERS←5 4ρ'TED NED JED ED  FRED'
      GS←89   77 93   101   85
      • • • •
NED
FRED
TED
JED
ED
```

5. M is the body of the three-column inventory table shown below:

Item Number	Units On Hand	Units Ordered
1763	125	18
9261	98	6
4012	25	3
6347	106	31
1462	133	15

   (a) Write an expression to rearrange the rows of M in ascending order based on the on-hand figures of each item number. The smallest on-hand item should comprise the first row.

   (b) Write an expression to rearrange the rows of M in descending order based on the on-order figures. Thus the item with the largest on-order figure should be the first row.

6. Refer to problem 11 of Sec. 3.5. Rearrange the matrices ED and $STATES$ so that

   (a) The matrices are arranged such that the state with the greatest pupil enrollment is first, and so forth.

   (b) The matrices are arranged so that the state with the fewest number of teachers is first.

Use the matrix as initially shown in the problem and not as altered during execution of the problem.

7. Define a function CNT to count the number of 1s in a vector V of 1s and 0s.

    Test:

```
        V←1 0 1 1 0 1 1 0 0 1
. . . . .
6
```

8. Define a function $ORDER$ to list all names in a character matrix M alphabetically. Assume that each row contains a name and that no two names begin with the same letter.

    Test:

```
        M←4 5ρ'SAM  TERRYFRED ELROY'

    ∘ ∘ • • •

ELROY
FRED
SAM
TERRY
```

Section 3.9   DEAL AND ROLL

Section 3.9.1 Definition

The functions grade up ⍋ and grade down ⍒ were introduced in the previous section from the point of view of producing two specific permutations of a set of indices. Another useful permutation of the indices is a random arrangement.

For example, consider a household in which five daily chores are to be performed, each by one of five different people. One method of dealing out the five chores among the five people is randomly, much like one might shuffle and deal a deck of cards.

This can be accomplished by establishing a random permutation among the first five integers which then can be used as indices to the identification of the involved persons. The generation of such a random permutation can be accomplished by using the function *deal*. The general form of deal is

```
A?B
```

where A is the shape of the result vector and ιB is the set of integers from which the random selection of A integers is made. For example,

```
    5?5
1 5 2 3 4
    3?5
1 2 4
```

The integers are selected *without replacement*. This means that once an integer is selected, it is not available for selection again; that is, 5?5 , for example, can *never* result in 1 3 1 3 5.

The assignment of tasks from the introductory example can be accomplished in this way, using deal and indexing:

```
NAMES←'ABCDE'

    NAMES[5?5]
CAEDB
```

The same expression executed again might produce

```
    NAMES[5?5]
 ACEBD
```

From the nature of its definition, deal has some inherent restrictions. Both arguments must be nonnegative integers—either scalars or one-component arrays. Any other shaped argument results in a *RANK ERROR*. Also, since deal produces random integers *without* replacement, A must always be less than or equal to B. An expression like 6?3 results in a *DOMAIN ERROR* since it is meaningless to ask for a set of six integers chosen at random from the integers $\iota 3$.

There are times, however, when it is desirable to select numbers at random *with replacement* so that the possibility of the same number occurring more than once exists, for example, when test data are being simulated. Random selection with replacement can be achieved from the scalar function *roll*. The general form of roll is

```
      ?A
```

where ιA is the set of integers from which a random number is selected.

Roll is a scalar function, unlike its dyadic counterpart deal, which is a mixed function, and so its argument may be a scalar or an array of any rank. Roll is applied to its argument component by component, and the shape of the result is the same as the shape of the argument. For example,

```
      ?5 4 8
3 2 7
```

Here three integers are chosen; the first from the set ι5 , the second from the set ι4 , and the third from the set ι8 . If all the components of the argument are the same, the component-by-component application of the function to its argument results in the generation of random numbers *with replacement*. For example,

```
      ?5 5 5 5 5
 5 3 2 5 4
      ?6 6
 4 3
```

The expression ?6 6 describes the roll of a pair of dice—hence the name *roll* for the function. Replication can be achieved using the reshape function, for example,

```
      ?5ρ5
2 1 2 3 4
```

Illustration 3.13   Generating Test Data

The random functions are quite useful in the generation of test data. Suppose that you wish to generate a random bowling score which could range between 90 and 300 to test your average-keeping and handicap function. The expression 89+?211 does this. And the expression 89+?10ρ211 generates 10 such scores.

Suppose that you wish to generate a matrix M with three rows and four columns containing random integers between ‾30 and 30. The expression M←‾31+?3 4ρ61 does this.

Illustration 3.14   Shuffling a List of Names

NAMES is a matrix of names, for example,

```
      NAMES
ADAMS
BROWN
JONES
SMITH
SMYTH
```

The expression *NAMES*[5?5;] arbitrarily rearranges the names in the matrix. Such a listing of names is useful for arranging names on a ballot or assigning chores.

Section 3.9.2 Nature of the Number Generation

The numbers generated by roll and deal have been referred to as *random numbers*. Actually they are not truly random numbers but merely pseudorandom. A random number is one which cannot be generated by a describable algorithm. Hence it is impossible to produce pure random numbers on a computer (a machine whose operations are based on algorithms); however, there are good techniques which produce close approximations to pure random numbers. These approximations, called *pseudorandom*, are what the computer can produce. Thus although we speak of random numbers, we should realize that they are only pseudorandom.

Let us consider the nature of the generation of such numbers. Initially when a workspace is cleared, the algorithm which generates the pseudorandom numbers begins at a standard starting value or *seed*. The seed that is used in APL.SV is 7^5 .*

After the generation of each pseudorandom number, a new seed is generated. Suppose that after generating a series of random numbers, for instance, ?100ρ100, you sign off without saving your workspace. When you return later, you load the workspace and again generate ?100ρ100. The pseudorandom numbers are the same as those you received the first time. The sequence of pseudorandom numbers is the same because the starting seed in each case is the same. This has the advantage of permitting the generation of the same sequence several times, which can be quite useful in debugging a function. If you wish to avoid this, however, the workspace should be saved before sign-off. The current seed is the one saved. Upon reloading the workspace this saved seed becomes the starting seed.

PROBLEMS

1. From each of the set (a)–(f) below, select an expression that will satisfy the given statement.

   (a) Select with replacement three random integers chosen from the set of integers between ⁻5 and 6, excluding both ⁻5 and 6 .

   (1) ⁻6+?3ρ10

   (2) ⁻6+3?10

   (3) ⁻6+3?11

   (4) ⁻6+?3ρ11

   (5) ⁻5+?3ρ10

   (6) ⁻5+?3ρ11

   (7) ⁻5+?10

---

*For a more detailed discussion of the generation of pseudorandom numbers and the merits of the seed 7^5, see B. A. W. Lewis, A. S. Goodwin, and J. M. Miller, "A Pseudo-random Number Generation for the System 360," *IBM Systems Journal*, 8, No. 2, 1969, 136–146.

(b) Select without replacement three random integers chosen from the set of integers ι10 .

   (1) ?3ρ11

   (2) ?3ρ10

   (3) 3?10

   (4) 3?11

(c) Select with replacement three random integers chosen from the set of integers ι10 .

   (1) ?3ρ11

   (2) ?3ρ10

   (3) 3?10

   (4) 3?11

(d) Select without replacement three random integers from the set 2 4 6 8 10 .

   (1) ?2×3ρ5

   (2) (2×ι5)[3?5]

   (3) (2×ι5)[?3ρ5]

   (4) 2×3?5

(e) Select with replacement three random integers chosen from the set of integers between ¯5 and 6 inclusive.

   (1) ¯6+?ι12

   (2) ¯5+?3ρ12

   (3) −5+?3ρ12

   (4) ¯5+3?12

   (5) −6+3?12

   (6) ¯6+3?12

   (7) ¯6+?3ρ12

   (8) −6+?3ρ12

(f) Select without replacement three random integers chosen from the set of integers between ¯5 and 6 inclusive.

   (1) ¯6+?12

   (2) ¯5+?3ρ12

   (3) −5+?3ρ12

   (4) ¯5+3?12

   (5) −6+3?12

   (6) ¯6+3?12

   (7) −6+?3ρ12

   (8) ¯6+?3ρ12

2. Write an expression to represent each of the following situations:

   (a) The roll of a single die.

   (b) The roll of six dice.

   (c) A vector of dimension 5 with each of its components a random positive integer less than 10.

(d) A vector such that (1) its dimension is random but no greater than 10 and (2) each component is a random positive integer less than or equal to 100.

(e) A matrix such that (1) its dimensions are random but always less than 11, and (2) each component is a random positive integer no greater than 500.

(f) The selection at random of an element from a matrix M.

(g) The generation of a 12-component vector V which will contain random integral temperatures between minus 40 and plus 120 degrees.

3. Consider *NAMES* to be the same NAME matrix as in Illustration 3.14. Write an expression to assign several tasks arbitrarily to the same name.

4. Write an expression to generate a random number between negative 1 and plus 1 (but excluding both end points). The random number should have three decimal places.

5. Define a function called *HI* that produces a message chosen at random from a given set when the function is called. For example, successive calls could produce

GOOD DAY
HI YOURSELF
HOWDY PARDNER
GO AWAY, I'M BUSY

6. Define a function *PROB* to print out N arithmetic problems for either $+$ $\times$ $-$ chosen at random with D digits per operand. For example, response to the function call might be

```
  456
 -183
 ----

  678
 ×319
 ----

  913
 -190
 ----

  612
 +319
 ----
```

Warning: The first digit of any line should not be zero.

Section 3.10 SUMMARY

The nature of arrays and scalars and their construction and manipulation have been covered in Chapter 3. Several related functions were introduced.

The Scalar and the Array

An array is a collection of data structured in an orderly fashion such that the indices necessary to select a single element from it are independent of each other.

The number of independent indices necessary to select a single element from an array is called the *rank* of the array. A scalar is shapeless data. A named scalar has only data associated with the name. A named array has both data and shape associated with it. A *null* or *empty* array is a data structure that has shape but no data associated with it.

Function	Syntax	General Description	Right Argument	Left Argument	Conformability	Shape and Rank of Result
Shape	ρA	Reports the shape of an array. The value of each component reports the degree of freedom available in the corresponding dimension. The rightmost component defines the number of columns, the next rightmost the rows, then planes, hyperplanes, etc.	Data array of any shape and rank—numeric or character	None		Shape: As many components as there are dimensions in the argument. Rank: Always a vector, 1.
Reshape	$V \rho A$	Restructures data A into the array form specified by shaping information V	Data array of any shape and rank—numeric or character. If too much data, as much as needed to create result is used. If not enough data, repeatedly cycles through provided data.	The shaping information. Must be scalar or vector numeric, nonnegative integers. Rightmost column defines number of columns, next rightmost, number of rows of result, then planes, hyperplanes, etc.		Shape: The same as V Rank: The number of components of V or if V is a nonzero scalar, 1 If V is 0, rank is 0.
Indexing	$A[B]$ $A[\,\bullet\bullet\bullet;\bullet\bullet\bullet\,]$	Selection (indexing to the right of specification): Selects those elements in the B positions of A. Replacement (indexing to the left of specification): Replaces those elements in the B positions of A	Index array of any shape and rank of valid index values—numeric	Data array of any shape and rank, not a scalar—numeric or character	The number of independent indices necessary in B is equal to $\rho \rho A$. The indices related to each dimension are separated by semicolons.	Shape: The catenation of the shape of each index dimension. Rank: The sum of the ranks of each index dimension.
Index-of	$V \iota A$	Determines the index of the *first* occurrence for each of the data items in A with respect to vector V. If a component of A does not appear in V, the index provided is $1 + \rho V$.	Data array of any shape and rank—numeric or character.	Must be a vector— numeric or character.		Shape: Same as A. Rank: Same as A.
Ravel	$,A$	Restructures the data into a vector.	Data array of any shape and rank—numeric or character.	None		Shape: The product of ρA, or if A is a scalar, 1. Rank: Always a vector.
Grade up	$\triangle V$	Gives indices for arranging the elements of V in ascending order.	Must be a numeric vector.	None		Shape: ρV. Rank: 1, always a vector
Grade down	$\triangledown V$	Gives indices for arranging the elements of V in descending order.	Must be a numeric vector.	None		Shape: ρV. Rank: 1, always a vector
Roll	$?A$	Generates a random number from the set ιA.	Data array of any shape and rank—numeric and nonnegative integers.	None	Scalar function	Shape: ρA. Rank: $\rho \rho A$.
Deal	$S ? T$	Generates S distinct random numbers from set ιT.	Nonnegative integer numeric scalar.	Nonnegative integer—numeric scalar— less than or equal to T.		Shape: S. Rank: 1, always a vector

CHAPTER

4

ELEMENTARY FUNCTIONS

Cognates abound between the functions of mathematics and APL. Besides the arithmetic functions introduced in Chapter 1, there are several others such as absolute value, exponentiation, logarithm, sine, cosine, and tangent. With these functions and some others that are unique to APL, it is possible to solve most problems whose solutions are gained by the evaluation of formulas.

Section 4.1 SCALAR MONADIC FUNCTIONS: ABSOLUTE VALUE, NEGATION, and RECIPROCAL

The function roll $?A$ introduced in Sec. 3.9 was the first scalar monadic function discussed. A scalar monadic function is applied to each element of its array argument component by component. For example, the expression

        ?5   10   15

is equivalent to

        (?5), (?10), ?15

The result is an array of the same shape and rank as the argument.

The functions of finding the absolute value of a number, of negating a number, and of taking the reciprocal of a number are three common scalar monadic functions. These functions are described in the following paragraphs.

The *absolute value* function $|$ is like the mathematical absolute value. Its general form is

        $|B$

where B is any array. Absolute value removes the sign of the argument, leaving only the magnitude. For example,

```
      | ¯23 23  4.6  ¯3.7
23 23   4.6  3.7
```

Illustration 4.1   Squaring a Number Without Changing its Sign

Multiplying a number by itself, or squaring it, always results in a positive number. For example,

```
      3×3
9
      ¯3×¯3
9
```

However, at times it is desirable that the result maintain the sign of the original number. This can be achieved by multiplying the number by its absolute value. For example,

```
      A←4  ¯4  6  ¯6
      A×|A
16  ¯16  36  ¯36
```

The *negation* function ¯ changes the sign of the argument. Its general form is

```
      -B
```

where B is any array. A positive argument becomes a negative result; a negative argument becomes a positive result. Zero is always unsigned. For example,

```
      -35  ¯35  6.7  ¯7.25  0
¯35  35  ¯6.7  7.25  0
```

Negation rather than a negative sign must be used with variables. Using a negative sign with a variable results in a *SYNTAX ERROR* report.

Illustration 4.2   Slope and x and y Intercepts of a Straight Line

The general equation of a straight line is

$$Ax + By + C = 0 \text{ (where A and B are not both 0)}$$

If $B \neq 0$, the slope is $-A/B$; if $A \neq 0$ the x intercept is $-C/A$; and if $B \neq 0$, the y intercept is $-C/B$. The function *INFO* results in a three-component vector containing the slope and the x and y intercepts of a straight line given A, B, C as a vector *LINE*:

```
      ∇ Z←INFO LINE
[1]     Z←-LINE[1 3 3]÷LINE[2 1 2]
      ∇
```

The result of the *reciprocal* function $\div$ is the value 1 divided by the argument B. Its general form is

$$\div B$$

where B is any array. No component of the array can be zero. For example,

```
      ÷5   .25   ¯2
0.2   4   ¯0.5
```

Illustration 4.3   Creating a Harmonic Progression

A harmonic progression is built from an arithmetic progression (see Illustration 1.5) by taking the reciprocal of each term of the arithmetic progression. For example,

```
      N←4

      ÷ιN
1   0.5   0.33333   0.25

      ÷¯1+2×ιN
1   0.33333   0.2   0.14285
```

PROBLEMS

1. Evaluate expressions (a)–(l)
   - (a) -1 2 4 8 (b) $\div$1 2 4 8 (c) $-\div$1 2 4 8 (d) $\div-1$ 2 4 8
   - (e) 23$-$14 (f) 23$-$¯14 (g) 23$--$14 (h) 12$-$24
   - (i) ¯12$-$24 (j) $-$12$-$24 (k) $\div$0 (l) 4$\div\div$2

2. A computer developed in the late 1940's could do 10,503 additions per second. Write an expression to determine how long it took to do a single addition.

3. Under optimal conditions the IBM 370/195 executes one instruction every machine cycle. The machine cycle is 54 nanoseconds (1 nanosecond $= 1.0E$¯9 seconds). Write an expression to determine how many instructions can be executed in 1 second at this rate of execution.

Section 4.2   FUNCTIONS WITH LIMITED RANGES

The *range* of a function is the set of all possible values of the result of the function. The range of reciprocal, for example, is all numbers but zero. The range of absolute value, on the other hand, is only positive numbers and zero. We say therefore that the range of absolute value is limited to the positive numbers and zero.

The *domain* of a function is the set of all possible values of the argument(s) of the function. The domain of negation, for example, is all numbers. The domain of roll, on the other hand, is only the positive integers.

Many APL functions have limited domains and/or ranges. Several of these are discussed in the following sections.

Section 4.2.1 Floor and Ceiling

When making rough approximations on the amount of money we owe, we are likely to truncate *down* to the nearest dollar, whereas we are likely to truncate *up* to the nearest dollar on amounts owed to us. Two useful scalar monadic functions—*floor* $\lfloor$ and *ceiling* $\lceil$—are used for truncation to integers. The general form of floor is

$$\lfloor B$$

where B is any array. The result of the function floor $\lfloor B$ is the largest *integer* algebraically less than or equal to B. For example,

```
     ⌊6.2  6.8  ¯6.2  6
 6   6  ¯7   6
```

The general form of ceiling is

$$\lceil B$$

where B is any array. The result of the function ceiling is the smallest integer algebraically greater than or equal to B. For example,

```
     ⌈6.2  6.8  ¯6.2  6
 7   7  ¯6   6
```

Notice that floor or ceiling applied to integers results in those integers. Notice also that the range of floor and ceiling is limited to integers. There is no domain restriction other than that the argument must be numeric.

Illustration 4.4 Determining Costs when Purchasing Unbreakable Lots

Many items are purchased in unbreakable lots, such as reams of paper (500 sheets), gallons of paint (covers 450 square feet), and rolls of wallpaper (covers 36 square feet). The function ceiling can be used to round up to the nearest unit. For example, the function $COSTS$ determines the various paper costs for a newsletter where K copies are needed each month and paper costs D per ream. The size of the newsletter varies from one through seven pages:

```
     ∇ Z←K COSTS D
[1]    CST←D×⌈(K×ι7)÷500
[2]    Z←2 7ρ(ι7),CST
     ∇

      1535 COSTS 2.32
  1      2      3      4      5      6      7
  9.28  16.24 · 23.2  30.16  37.12  44.08  51.04
```

Illustration 4.5 Median

The median, a statistical measure of central tendency, is found by first sorting the numbers involved from highest to lowest and then selecting the one in the middle. If there are an even number of components, the median is found by dividing the sum of the middle two numbers by 2. The function *MEDIAN* determines the median of a set of numbers. Note the use of floor and ceiling in line 3:

```
     ∇  Z←MEDIAN X;N
[1]     X←X[⍋X]
[2]     N←.5×1+ρX
[3]     Z←.5×X[⌊N]+X[⌈N]
     ∇
```

Section 4.2.2   Relational Functions

A set of dyadic functions whose results have even a more limited range than those of floor and ceiling are the six relational functions—<, ≤, =, ≥, >, and ≠— each of which returns a 1 if the relationship it represents holds true and a 0 if it does not.

The names of the symbols generally explain the relationship they represent and are shown below with an example:

Name	Function Symbol	Syntax	Examples
Less than	<	$A<B$	9 ‾8 3<11 ‾1 ‾5 1 1 0
Less than or equal	≤	$A\le B$	6 ‾3 4≤6 ‾2 ‾5 1 1 0
Equal	=	$A=B$	9 4 3=9 3 1 1 0 0 'FIX'='SIX' 0 1 1
Greater than	>	$A>B$	9 ‾8 8>12 ‾1 6 0 0 1
Greater than or equal	≥	$A\ge B$	4 6 2≥‾4 6 8 1 1 0
Not equal	≠	$A\ne B$	9 4 3≠9 3 1 0 1 1 'FIX'≠'SIX' 1 0 0

Only the functions equal and not equal may have character arguments as shown by the examples. The other relational functions cannot have character arguments. To ask if `'A'<'B'` is meaningless unless some ordering of character data is established. The order of character data can be established by creating a vector of the characters. For example, for an alphabetic order, a vector of the alphabet can be created.

ALPHA←'ABCDEFGHIJKLMNOPQRSTUVWXYZ'

The order between two characters relative to this vector can be determined using index-of:

$$(ALPHA\iota'A') < ALPHA\iota'B'$$

In APL no preestablished ordering or collating sequence for characters exists, but as shown above, any desired collating sequence can be created based on the arrangement of characters in a vector.

Illustration 4.6   Test Conditions

The relational functions are frequently used in conjunction with other primitive functions to make up test conditions. For example,

1. Either of the following expressions tests whether a number M is an integer:

    $M=\lfloor M$
    $M=\lceil M$

    A result of 1 means that M is an integer.

2. The following expressions provide test conditions to distinguish between various shapes of data:

    $1=\rho,Q$
    $1=\rho\rho Q$

    The first expression returns a 1 if Q is a scalar or one-component array; otherwise it returns a 0. The second expression returns a 1 if Q is a vector and a zero otherwise.

3. Suppose that $FLAG$ is to be set to 7 only if a condition C is equal to zero; otherwise $FLAG$ is defined as a null vector. This can be done with the expression

    $FLAG\leftarrow(,7)[\iota C=0]$

    The scalar 7 was raveled into a one-component vector so that it could be indexed. Thereafter if $C=0$, the variable $FLAG$ is set to 7. If $C\neq0$, the variable $FLAG$ becomes the null vector.

Illustration 4.7   Discounting a Purchase

A firm gives a 1% discount if the money due it is paid before the tenth of the month. A test condition is used in the function $DISC$ in determining the amount owed.

```
     ∇  Z←DAY DISC AMT
[1]     Z←AMT×.99+.01×DAY≥10
     ∇
```

Section 4.2.3 Membership

The relational functions can be used to determine which components of a vector meet certain requirements. Sometimes, however, it is necessary to determine only whether a given item is present in a set of data, for example, whether there is an 8 in the vector M. The dyadic mixed function *membership* ϵ can be used to determine whether there is an 8 in M. The general form of membership is

$$A \epsilon B$$

where A and B can be any arrays. There are no conformability requirements between the arguments. The result has the same shape as the left argument. The range of membership, like that of the relationals, is 0,1. A component of the result is 1 if the corresponding component of the left argument is present anywhere in the right argument. A component of the result is 0 if the corresponding component of the left argument is not present anywhere in the right argument. The arguments may be characters. Examples are shown below:

```
      8∈8
1
      9∈8 9 6
1
      9∈6 2 1
0
      8 9 6∈9
0 1 0
      9 7 4 2 ∈ 2 7 9 8 3 6 5
1 1 0 1
      'A'∈'BROAD'
1
      'CRAZY'∈'DAISY'
0  0  1  0  1
```

For   P←3 4ρ'ABCDEFGHIJKL'
         Q←2 3ρ'HOTDOG'
         Q∈P
```
  1  0  0
  1  0  1
```
         P∈Q
```
  0  0  0  1
  0  0  1  1
  0  0  0  0
```

Illustration 4.8 Determining Whether Two Arrays Are Identical

At times it is necessary to determine whether two arrays T and S of the same shape are identical. The expression $T=S$ produces an array of 1s and 0s. If $T=S$ contains a zero, the two arrays are not identical. The expression $0 \in T=S$ tells us whether there is a 0 in $T=S$. A result of 1 in the expression $0 \in T=S$ indicates that a zero is present; that is, the two arrays are not identical.

Section 4.2.4 Logic Functions

If we would prefer a result of 0 to indicate that the arrays of Illustration 4.8 are not identical (since 1 generally indicates true and 0 false), we could use the scalar monadic function *not* $\sim$ in the expression

$$\sim 0 \in T=S$$

The general form of *not* is

$$\sim B$$

where B is any array whose components are 1s and 0s. *Not* simply changes an argument of 0 to a 1 and an argument of 1 to a 0. For example,

        ~ 1
0

        ~ 0
1

Not is a function that has a limited range and a limited domain. Both the range and domain are 0,1. There are four scalar dyadic functions that have the same limited domain as not. These are *and* $\wedge$, *or* $\vee$, *nand* $\barwedge$, and *nor* $\veebar$. ($\barwedge$ is formed by $\wedge$ backspace $\sim$; $\veebar$ is formed by $\vee$ backspace $\sim$).

The result of $A \wedge B$ is 1 only if both A and B are 1. The result of $A \vee B$ is 1 if either A or B or both A and B are ones. The result of $A \barwedge B$ is 1 if A and B are not both 1. The result of $A \veebar B$ is 1 if both A and B are 0. These definitions are summarized by the table below, which shows the result for each combination of arguments:

A B	$A \wedge B$	$A \vee B$	$A \barwedge B$	$A \veebar B$
0 0	0	0	1	1
0 1	0	1	1	0
1 0	0	1	1	0
1 1	1	1	0	0

Each of the five functions—not, and, nand, nor, or—is often called a *logic* or *Boolean function*, that is, a function whose arguments and result are 0s or 1s—false or true. A vector made up of 0s and 1s is known as a *logic* (or *Boolean*) *vector*. The results of the functions $<, \leq, =, \geq, >, \neq, \lor, \land, \not\lor, \not\land, \sim, \epsilon$ are known as *logic arrays* (or scalars).

Illustration 4.9 Determining Whether a Number Meets Multiple Conditions

The logic functions are often used to determine whether a number meets multiple conditions. For example,

1. Is N a nonnegative integer?

   $(N=\lfloor N)\land N\geq 0$

2. Is N either less than 10 or greater than 25?

   $(N<10)\lor N>25$

3. Is N an integer between ¯100 and 100?

   $(N=\lfloor N)\land (N>\text{¯}100)\land N<100$

4. Is M a matrix whose components are integers?

   $(2=\rho\rho M)\land \sim 0\epsilon M=\lfloor M$

Section 4.2.5 Signum

Another function with a limited range is the scalar monadic function *signum* ×. It is used when the only information needed about a number is that it is positive, negative, or zero. The general form of signum is

   $\times B$

where B is any array. The results of $\times B$ are as follows:

Result	Meaning
1	Positive B
¯1	Negative B
0	Zero B

An example of signum is shown below:

```
     ×6 ¯9 0 2.1 ¯7.3
1 ¯1 0 1 ¯1
```

Illustration 4.10   Restoring a Sparse Matrix

A sparse matrix is a matrix containing many zeros. Suppose that the nonzero components are either 1 or ¯1. Instead of storing the sparse matrix G as a matrix, storage space can be conserved if the matrix is raveled into a vector SG, the zeros suppressed, and the 1s and ¯1s replaced with their index numbers. The index number contains a negative sign if a ¯1 occupies the index position. The last two components of SG contain the shape of G. For example, the vector SG

    1 ¯4 10 ¯11 14 16 21 ¯23 5 5

is stored instead of the matrix G:

    1 0   0 ¯1 0
    0 0   0   0 1
   ¯1 0   0   1 0
    1 0   0   0 0
    1 0 ¯1   0 0

The original matrix G can be restored from SG with the function *RESTORE*. Note the use of signum in line 4.

```
      ∇ G←RESTORE SG;S
[1]     S←SG[¯1 0+ρSG]
[2]     SG←SG[ι¯2+ρSG]
[3]     G←,Sρ0
[4]     G[|SG]←×SG
[5]     G←SρG
      ∇
```

PROBLEMS

1. Evaluate expressions (a)–(z):

   (a) ⌈2.5 3 ¯4.3 0

   (b) ⌊2.5 3 ¯4.3 0

   (c) 3=5 ¯3 3 2

   (d) 3≥5 ¯3 3 2

   (e) 3 ¯2 ¯1 4>2

   (f) 3 ¯2 8 =3 2 ¯8

   (g) 3 ¯2 8≠3 2 ¯8

   (h) 5 3 ='AZ'

   (i) 'B'≠'ABBA'

   (j) 'ACERY'='ECAPY'

   (k) 'AB'='BA'

   (l) 'AB'≤'DE'

   (m) 3 4='34'

   (n) 3<'A'

   (o) 2 4 6<3 4 7

   (p) 2 4,6<3 4 7

   (q) 2 4,(6<3),4 7

   (r) ~2 4 6<3 4 7

   (s) 2 4,~6<3 4 7

   (t) 2 4~6<3 4 7

   (u) 34=34

   (v) 3 4=3 4

   (w) 2,4=2 4

   (x) 2,(4=2),4

   (y) 2,4=2,4

   (z) 1=1≠1<1≤1≥1>1

2. Evaluate expression (a)–(i):

 (a) $\div\times4\quad {}^{-}4$

 (b) $\times\div4\quad {}^{-}4$

 (c) $\times8\quad 0\quad {}^{-}8$

 (d) $2\ 4\ 6\ 8\in1\ 2\ 3\ 4\ 5$

 (e) $'SMITH,J.E.'\in'E'$

 (f) $'A\ B'\in'B\ A'$

 (g) $1\ 2\ 3\ 4\ 5\in2\ 4\ 6\ 8$

 (h) $'A'\in'VOWEL'$

 (i) $'ACERY'\in'ACAPY'$

3. Assume the following:

 $Y\leftarrow10\quad 5\quad 3\quad 6\quad 4$

 $A\leftarrow1\ 1\ 1\ 1\ 0\ 0\ 0\ 0$

 $B\leftarrow0\ 0\ 1\ 1\ 0\ 0\ 1\ 1$

 $C\leftarrow0\ 1\ 0\ 1\ 0\ 1\ 0\ 1$

 Evaluate expressions (a)–(q):

 (a) $5<Y$ (b) $5\geq Y$ (c) $A\wedge B$

 (d) $A\neq B$ (e) $B\not= C$ (f) $A\vee B\wedge C$

 (g) $(\sim A\wedge B)\vee A\wedge B$ (h) $(\sim B)\vee C$ (i) $(\sim B)\vee\sim C$

 (j) $Y=Y$ (k) $\sim5\geq Y$ (l) $A\leq B$

 (m) $A\vee B$ (n) $A\wedge B\vee C$ (o) $(\sim A)\wedge B\wedge\sim C$

 (p) $\sim B\vee C$ (q) $\sim B\vee\sim C$

4. Write an expression to produce a binary vector B corresponding to a given vector V. B should have a 1 in each position where the corresponding component of V is described in (a)–(k) below. If you wish, use test data

 $V\leftarrow{}^{-}5\ 4\ 3\ 0\ {}^{-}2.1\ 3\ {}^{-}4.3\ 0\ {}^{-}.75\ 6\ {}^{-}.25\ 5.1\ 4\ {}^{-}3$

 (a) Not equal to 3.   (b) Not less than negative .75.

 (c) Less than 2.   (d) Positive (does not include zero).

 (e) Nonnegative (includes zero).   (f) Positive or less than negative .75.

 (g) Less than 3 and not less than negative .5.   (h) Positive and not equal to 4.

 (i) An integer   (j) A nonnegative integer.

 (k) Positive integers.

5. Produce a scalar S which has a result of

 (a) One if a vector V has no integer components.

 (b) One if no elements of a vector V are positive integers.

6. Write an expression to select a random time in hours, minutes, and seconds on a 24-hour clock. Midnight is 24:00:00. There is no 24:00:01, etc.

7. Assume that V is a vector with only integer components. Write an expression to produce a binary vector indicating where the one-digit integers are.

> *Test:*
>
> $V\leftarrow 9\ 15\ ^-3\ 12\ 134\ ^-45\ ^-6$
>
> • • • • • • •
>
> 1 0 1 0 0 0 1

8. Given two character strings A and B of equal length, write an expression to determine whether they are identical.

> *Test:*
>
> $A\leftarrow'BEAR'$
> $B\leftarrow A$
>
> • • • • • • •
>
> 1
>
> $B\leftarrow'BARE'$
>
> • • • • • • •
>
> 0

9. Let LO and HY be two values where LO is less than HY. Write an expression to

(a) Determine whether a scalar S lies within the range LO,HY inclusively (the expression should produce a 1 if S is in the range).

> *Test:*
>
> $LO\leftarrow 34$
> $HY\leftarrow 100$
> $S\leftarrow 78$
>
> • • • • • • •
>
> 1
>
> $S\leftarrow 15$
>
> • • • • • •
>
> 0

(b) Produce a binary vector B with 1s corresponding to the components of a vector V which lie within the range LO,HY inclusively.

> *Test:*
>
> $V\leftarrow 10\ 56\ 123\ 45\ 78$
>
> • • • • • • • •
>
> 0 1 0 1 1

(c) Produce a 1 if any of the components of the vector V lie within the range LO,HI inclusively.

> *Test:*
>
> • • • • • • •
>
> 1

(d) Produce a 1 if all the components of the vector V lie within the range LO,HY inclusively.

> *Test:*
>
> ```
> . . . . . . .
> 0
> ```

10. Given a numeric vector V, write an expression to make negative all the components of V which are less than a given quantity K.

> *Test:*
>
> ```
> V←10  56  123  45  78
> K←50
> . . . . . . .
> ¯10  56  123  ¯45  78
> ```

11. The exclusive-or logic function is defined by the following table:

A B	A exclusive-or B
0 0	0
0 1	1
1 0	1
1 1	0

What is the APL expression for exclusive-or?

12. Write an expression to find the index of the first nonblank character in the character vector C.

> *Test:*
>
> ```
> C←'  HI THERE'
> . . . . . . .
> 3
> ```

13. Write an expression to select all of the even-indexed components of the vector R.

> *Test:*
>
> ```
> R←2  6  8  9  1
> . . . . . . .
> 6  9
> ```

14. A guide number for a camera's electronic flash unit is used to determine the lens opening (f-stop) needed to take a picture of a subject at a particular distance. One way of determining the guide number is to select a film standard, say one with ASA 32 (film speed rating) and take a series of pictures of a subject 10 feet away from the light at varying f-stops. The guide number is the result of dividing the f-stop of the best exposed shot by 10. Thereafter, guide numbers for any film can be related to this standard by determining the times faster (new film ASA divided by standard film ASA) and multiplying by the appropriate factor. The factors are shown in the following table:

Times faster	2	2.5	3	4	5	6	8	10
Factor	1.4	1.6	1.7	2	2.2	2.4	2.8	3.2

The f-stop for a particular shot with direct flash exposure is determined by dividing the guide number by the footage. Assume that the factors available are only those stated in the table

(a) Define a function $GUIDE$ for giving the guide number of any film whose ASA is F, given the guide number GN and the ASA of the film standard S.

>   *Test:*
>
> $F \leftarrow 165$
> $GN \leftarrow 44$
> $S \leftarrow 25$
>   . . . .
>
> 105.6

(b) Define a function $EXPOSE$ which will, given the guide number GN, determine the f-stops to one decimal place for direct flash exposure from X to Y feet.

>   *Test:*
>
> $GN \leftarrow 96.8$
> $X \leftarrow 5$
> $Y \leftarrow 10$
>
>   . . . .
> 19.4 16.1 13.8 12.1 10.8 9.6

15. Modify Illustration 4.6, item 3, so that, with $FLAG$ a previously defined scalar, $FLAG$ is set to 7 if $C=0$, and otherwise $FLAG$ is left unchanged.

16. Write an expression to determine how many reams of paper it is necessary to purchase in order to print 1725 copies of a 29-page document. Assume that there are 500 sheets per ream and that the document is to be printed on both sides of a sheet.

17. Write an expression for determining

(a) Whether the character string CS contains a comma. If it does, the result is 1; if not, 0.

>   *Test:*
>
> $CS \leftarrow 'IF,THEN'$
>   . . . .
>   1

(b) Whether a character string C contains any of a set of special characters SC, returning 1 if any of the special characters is present and 0 otherwise.

>   *Test:*
>
> $SC \leftarrow '.?(;.'$
> $C \leftarrow 'NICE? NO!'$
>   . . . .
>   1

18. Assume that $(\rho M) = R,C$ and let $V\leftarrow,M$. Define a function IND that gives the corresponding row and column indices for any component I of $\iota\rho V$, that is, the vector of indices of V.

    Test:

    ```
    (ρM)=3 4
    I←7
    ```
    · · · · · · · ·
    ```
    2   3
    ```

19. Given an array A which is supposed to be binary, write an expression to determine whether there is a component other than 0 or 1 present. Let the expression return a value of 1 if there exists a nonbinary component.

    Test:

    ```
    A←2 2 2ρ1 0 1 1 0 ¯1 1 1
    ```
    · · · · · · ·
    ```
    1
    ```

20. Write an expression to set the Ith component of a vector V to the value R if C is equal to 1.

    Test:

    ```
    V←9 6 3 2 4
    I←2
    R←15
    C←1
    ```
    · · · · · · ·
    ```
    V
    9   15 3 2 4

    C←4
    V←9 6 3 2 4
    ```
    · · · · · · ·
    ```
    V
    9 6 3 2 4
    ```

Section 4.3 MORE COMMON FUNCTIONS

A number of APL functions parallel common arithmetic and algebraic operations. These are discussed in the following sections.

Section 4.3.1 Exponentiation

Consider this problem:

Two wealthy golfers play an 18-hole round of golf. They bet \$2 on the first hole, \$4 on the second, and \$8 on the third and continue to double the bet on each successive hole. How much money will the winner of the eighteenth hole receive?

Starting with 2 and doubling it each time suggests a pattern:

Hole(#):	1	2	3	4	5	· · ·	18
Bet ($):	2	4	8	16	32	· · ·	?

The amount is a power of 2. At the third hole the bet is 2^3, at the fourth hole 2^4, at the fifth hole 2^5, and at the eighteenth hole it must be 2^{18}. How much is 2^{18}? The scalar dyadic function *exponentiation* $\star$ computes this:

```
      2*18
262144
```

The general form of exponentiation is

```
      A*B
```

The left argument A is the *base*; the right argument B is the *exponent*. If the exponent B is a positive integer, the result is the product obtained by using A as a factor B times; that is,

```
      3*4 = 3×3×3×3 = 81
```

If the exponent B is a positive fraction $N \div D$, the result is the Dth root of A raised to the Nth power. Roots are often represented in mathematics by the special symbol $\sqrt[n]{}$. In APL a root is always represented as the base raised to a fractional power. For example,

```
      25*.5
5
      2*.5
1.4142
      64*÷3
4
      27*2÷3
9
```

If B is a fraction $N \div D$, A must be positive if D is even; otherwise the result is imaginary and in APL produces a *DOMAIN ERROR* report, for example,

```
      ¯25*.5     (.5=1÷2; D is 2 and even)
DOMAIN ERROR
      ¯25*0.5
         ∧
      ¯64*÷3
¯4
```

If the exponent B is negative, the result is equivalent to the reciprocal of A raised to a positive power, that is, $(\div A)*|B$:

```
      5*¯2
0.04
      16*¯.5
0.25
```

Illustration 4.11   Rounding a Number

The function *ROUND* rounds the number N at any position P to the left or right of the decimal point:

```
    ∇ R←P ROUND N
[1]   R←(10*-P)×⌊.5+N×10* P
    ∇
```

For example,

```
      2 ¯1   0  ROUND 126.346
126.35   130   126
```

Section 4.3.2   Logarithm

Returning once more to the golf-bet example of Sec. 4.3.1, on what hole will $8,192 be bet? That is, for what exponent N does $2*N$ equal 8192? The scalar dyadic *logarithmic* function ⊛ is used to find the exponent. The general form is

$A⊛B$ (⊛ is formed by ○ overstrike *)

A is the base. The result is the power that A must be raised to in order to produce B. Thus if

$R←A*B$

then

$B←A⊛R$

A and B must be greater than 0 and A cannot be 1 unless B is also 1. The evaluation of the expression $2⊛8192$ tells us that $8192 is bet on the thirteenth hole.

Illustration 4.12   Number of Decimal Places in an Integer

The function *PLACES* determine the number of decimal digits in an integer B:

```
     ∇ Z←PLACES B
[1]    Z←1+⌊10⊛|B+B=0
     ∇
```

For example,

```
     PLACES 362 ¯4567 0
3   4   1
```

The scalar monadic functions *exponential* *B and *natural logarithm* ⊛B are related to the dyadic exponentiation and logarithmic functions. For each the base is assumed to be the transcendental value *e* (approximately 2.718281828459045), and so *B is the same as *e*B and ⊛B is the same as *e*⊛B.

Illustration 4.13 Comparing Interest Rates

Principal X is invested in one account at $R\%$ and principal Y is invested in another account at $T\%$, where X is less than Y and R is greater than T. The function YEARS determines how many years it will take for the two accounts to contain the same amount of money and how much money there will be in each account. The argument A represents the vector X,R and the argument B represents the vector Y,T.

```
     ∇ Z←A YEARS B
[1]    N←(⊛A÷B)[1]÷⊛((1+0.01×B)÷1+0.01×A)[2]
[2]    Z←N,A[1]×(1+0.01+A[2])*N
     ∇

     1500 5.75 YEARS 2000 5.25
60.7008  44661.12
```

Note: Line 1 of YEARS is the solution after solving the equality $X(1 + R)^n = Y(1 + T)^n$ for n.

Section 4.3.3 Factorial, Combination, and Residue

Three more APL functions with counterparts in mathematics are factorial, combinations, and residue. These are explained by means of the following problems.

First, suppose that a sociology student has to conduct a survey in which five questions are asked. He does not want the order of the questions to bias the results, and so he decides to prepare his questionnaires so that no two have the questions arranged in the same order. How many unique questionnaires can he have?

The solution to this is the product of the ways each position on the page can be filled:

```
     5×4×3×2×1
```

This product is, as you may recognize, 5 factorial and is represented in APL by the scalar monadic function *generalized factorial* !.

The general form is

$!B$ ($!$ is formed by $'$ overstrike $.$)

If B is a positive integer, $!B$ produces the result of the product:

$1 \times 2 \times 3 \times \cdots \cdots \times B$

For example,

        $!4$
24

        $!2\ 5\ 4$
$2\quad 120\ 24$

If B is not an integer, the result is the value of the gamma function[*] evaluated at $B+1$. For example,

        $!.25$
0.9064

The argument of $!$ cannot be a negative integer. If B is 0, $!B$ is 1.

Warning: The symbol $!$ is formed by $'$ overstrike $..$ If you forget to backspace when creating this symbol, you will have typed $'.$ or $.'$, and the computer will be accepting everything that follows as character data until you strike RETURN.

Illustration 4.14 Permutations

Any arrangement of a set of n elements in a definite order is called a *permutation*. For example, *cba*, *acb*, and *bac* are permutations of the letters *a*, *b*, and *c*. The number of permutations that can be formed from N different elements when taken R at a time is

$(!N) \div !N-R$

For example, the number of permutations of 3 things taken from a set of 10 different items is

        $(!10) \div !10-3$
720

Note that the number of permutations of N items taken from a set of N different items is simply $!N$.

The number of permutations of N items taken from a set of N items in which

---

[*]The gamma function is used in advanced mathematics.

K elements are alike is

$$(!N)÷!K$$

For example,

```
    (!5)÷!ı5
120 60  20   5   1
```

Thus there are 120 permutations of 5 unlike items; 60 permutations of 5 items when 2 of the items are alike; 20 permutations when 3 are alike; 5 permutations when 4 are alike; and one permutation when all are alike.

Next suppose that a teacher gives a test composed of eight questions. Each student can answer any four he wishes. How many combinations of answers might the teacher get? The dyadic scalar function *generalized combination* ⋮ is used to solve this. The general form is

$$A!B$$

where A and B can be any arrays. The result is the number of combinations of B things taken A at a time. The expression `4!8` provides the solution for the above example. Here are some examples of combinations:

```
    4!8
70
    2!26 10
325    45
```

Illustration 4.15 Coefficients of a Binomial Expansion

The coefficients of the binomial expansion

$$(a + 1)^n \qquad \text{(where } n \text{ is a positive integer)}$$

can be determined by the expression

$$(0,ıN)!N$$

For example,

```
    (0,ı6)!6
1   6   15   20   15   6   1
```

Finally suppose that six people are playing fan-tan, a card game in which all the cards are distributed. How many people will get an extra card? The dyadic scalar function *residue* | can be used to solve this problem. Its general form is

$$A|B$$

where A and B can be any arrays.

In its most common use residue behaves like a remainder function; that is, if A and B are positive, the result is the remainder after dividing A into B. The expression

        6|52
    4

answers the above question. Four people get an extra card. The result of the residue function depends on the sign of the left argument. For $R \leftarrow A | B$, the result lies between A and zero.* It is equal to $B - Q \times A$ for some integer Q. Q can be determined by the expression

        $\lfloor B \div A + A = 0$

If A is 0, the result is B. For example,

        3|11   (11-3×3)
    2

        ⁻3|11   (11-⁻4×⁻3)
    ⁻1

        3|⁻11   (⁻11-⁻4×3)
    1

        ⁻3|⁻11   (⁻11-3×⁻3)
    ⁻2

Note: The residue function can be used to deal with numbers in a modulo fashion; that is, $A | B$ can be interpreted as B *modulo* A.

Illustration 4.16   The Fractional Part of a Number

The following expression yields the fractional part of decimal numbers N:

        1| |N

For example,

        M←12.34   0.56   ⁻3.89
        1| |M
        0.34   0.56   0.89

And the expression

        (×N)×1| |N

yields the signed fractional part of the decimal numbers N.

---

*APL.SV only. In APL/360, the result is the least nonnegative value R satisfying the equation $B = R + A \times Q$ for some integer Q. The result of $⁻3|11$ is 2 and of $⁻3|⁻11$ is 1.

For example,

```
    (×M)×1||M
0.34   0.56  ‾0.89
```

Illustration 4.17 24-Hour Clock Conversion

The left argument of the residue function may also be noninteger. For example, given the hour of the day based on a 24-hour clock, that is, from 1 to 24, the expression

```
    ⌈12.01|H
```

converts it to its 12-hour clock equivalent:

```
    ⌈12.01 |  5  12  17  21  24
5  12  5  9  12
```

Illustration 4.18 Even or Odd

The expression $2|N$ determines whether the integer N is even or odd. If the result is 0, N is even. If the result is 1, N is odd. For example,

```
    N←6 8 12 4 7 5 8
    2|N
0  0  0  0  1  1  0
```

This can become part of an index if the result of a problem depends on whether an argument is odd or even. For example, the function $FCN1$ subtracts 2 from its integer argument if it is odd and adds 3 to it if it is even:

```
    ∇ Z← FCN1 N
[1]   Z←N+‾2 3[1+2|N]
    ∇
```

Section 4.3.4 Minimum and Maximum

There are two related dyadic scalar functions which are quite useful. Consider this problem:

The standard deduction on the 1970 federal income tax is $1000 or 10% of income whichever is less. What is the standard deduction for an income I?

The dyadic scalar function *minimum* ⌊ selects the lesser of two arguments. Its general form is

```
    A⌊B
```

where A and B are any arrays. The result is A if $A \le B$ and B if $B \le A$. A function that solves the standard deduction problem is

```
    ∇ Z←DEDUC I
[1]    Z←1000⌊.1×I
    ∇
```

For example,

```
    DEDUC 9876.57
987.657

    DEDUC 12762.17
1000
```

The dyadic scalar function *maximum* ⌈ is analogous to minimum except that the *greater* of the two arguments is selected. Its general form is

$$A⌈B$$

where A and B are any arrays. The result is A if $A≥B$ and B if $B≥A$. For example,

```
    1  8 ¯4 6⌈2 6 ¯5 7
2 8 ¯4 7
```

Illustration 4.19 Mileage Reimbursement for Company Travel

A company reimburses its employees for weekly mileage driven in their personal cars on company business at the following rate:

$.15 per mile for the first 50 miles
$.12 per mile for the next 50 miles
$.06 per mile for the remainder

The function *MILEAGE* determines the mileage allowance due an employee for a given week if he drove M miles:

```
    ∇ AMT←MILEAGE M
[1]    AMT←.15 .12 .06×(0⌈50⌊M-0 50),0⌈M-100
[2]    AMT←AMT[1]+AMT[2]+AMT[3]
    ∇
```

For example,

```
    MILEAGE  100
13.5
```

Illustration 4.20 Monthly Retirement Income

A company has the following retirement plan. The monthly retirement income at age 65 is the greater of the amounts determined by the following computations:

1. $6.50 times the number of years of service N and
2. one-twelfth of .75% of each year's compensation YS paid up to and including $4800, plus one-twelfth of 1.5% of such compensation over $4800.

Assume that the yearly compensation YS is a previously computed average. The function $RETIRE$ computes the monthly retirement income:

```
     ∇ Z← N RETIRE YS
[1]    Z←(6.5×N)⌈((.015÷12)×0⌈YS-4800)+(.0075÷12)×YS⌊4800
     ∇
```

For example,

```
     15 RETIRE 12560'
97.5
```

Section 4.3.5 Monadic Plus

The monadic scalar function monadic plus $+$ always results in A. Its general form is

$$+A$$

where A is any array. For example,

```
     + ¯35
¯35
```
```
     +16.3
16.3
```

If necessary, monadic plus can be used as a means of specifying a numeric value to a variable and displaying that value on one line. For example,

```
     +COST←2.67  3.14  8.95
2.67 3.14 8.95
```
```
     COST
2.67 3.14 8.95
```

PROBLEMS

1. Evaluate expressions (a)–(v):

(a) 2⋆3 ¯5 4	(b) 2 4 6⋆3 2 1	(c) ¯3⋆2
(d) 2⋆¯2	(e) ¯2⋆1 0 ¯1	(f) 36⋆0.5
(g) 4 25 81⋆÷2	(h) 27⋆÷3	(i) 3⋆2⋆2
(j) 2⋆2⋆3	(k) 10⊛100	(l) 10⋆10⊛100
(m) (⋆4)÷⋆3	(n) (10⊛1000)÷10⊛100	(o) (10⊛1E6)×10⊛1E¯4
(p) 3 6 2⌈5 ¯3 2	(q) 3 6 2⌊5 ¯3 2	(r) 3 6 2⌊5
(s) 3 6 2⌈5	(t) 3 6 2⌈5 4	(u) ¯3⌊3
(v) ¯4⌊3		

2. Evaluate expressions (a)–(u):

   (a) ¯3⌈¯4

   (b) ¯3⌊¯5

   (c) (3*2)⌈2*3

   (d) 2*⌈¯3.2 4 3.2

   (e) 2 3 4|23

   (f) 2 3 4|4 5 7

   (g) 4|11 ¯11

   (h) ¯4|11 ¯11

   (i) 0|3

   (j) 1|2.25 5

   (k) 1.5|20

   (l) 3 3 ¯3 ¯3|5 ¯5 5 ¯5

   (m) !4

   (n) !3 4

   (o) !1 2 3 4

   (p) 2!4

   (q) 4!2

   (r) 0 1 2!4

   (s) 0 1 2 3 4!4

   (t) 0 1 2!3 4 5

   (u) 0 1 2!3 4

3. Write an expression to replace each component of a vector V which is an integer evenly divisible by 3 with 0. Leave the other components unchanged.

   (a) An even integer.

   (b) An odd integer.

   (c) An integer evenly divisible by 3.

4. Write an expression to replace each component of a vector V which is evenly divisible by 3 with 0. Leave the other components unchanged.

5. V is a vector of numbers. Write an expression to extract

   (a) The units digit from each component.

   (b) The tens digit from each component.

   (c) The tenths digit from each component.

   Test:

   V←10.25 56 123 578 56.7 12.4 56.9 ¯45.6 ¯68 ¯65 3.456 ¯7.897

6. Write an expression to determine the different six-position license plates that a state can create given a set of N characters to choose from for each position.

7. Suppose that a state is creating six-position license plates where the first three positions each contain any alphabetic character and the last three digits each contain any decimal digit. Write an expression to determine how many different plates the state could create.

8. A manager has seven single offices available. Write an expression to determine in how many ways he can assign them to seven different staff members.

9. Write an expression to determine how many different pairwise combinations of 15 basketball teams there can be.

10. A company has the following military benefit for its married employees: A married employee with 1 or more years of company service prior to induction receives for each month of military service up to a maximum of 24 months the greater of

    A monthly benefit of $85 or
    The difference between 75% of his former monthly company salary and the lesser monthly military pay up to a maximum of one-half of his former salary.

Assume the information variable V where

    $V[1]$ is the company service in months
    $V[2]$ is the former company monthly salary
    $V[3]$ is the military monthly salary
    $V[4]$ is the military service in months

Define a function *BENEFIT* to compute the monthly benefit that a company's married employee would receive if inducted.

    Test:

       V←27   785   120   18

       . . . .

  392.5

11. The FICA (social security) tax is levied at a rate of $R\%$ for the first I dollars of annual income. Assume an employee's to-date income is in *YTD* and that his current pay is in *PAY*. Define a function *FICA* to determine the employee's FICA tax for the current pay period and also the accumulated FICA tax paid through this current pay period. Show the result as a two-component vector whose first component is the accumulated FICA tax and the second component is the current pay period's FICA tax.

      Test:

        R←5.62
        I←10300
        YTD←9600
        PAY←345
        . . . .
  558.909 19.38919
        YTD←10000
        . . . . . .
  578.86   16.86

12. The accumulated value S on an amount of principal on which interest is compounded periodically is given by the equation

$$S = P(1 + R)^n$$

where P is the principal
      R is the rate of interest per period stated decimally
      n is the number of periods

Define a function *ACCV* to calculate the accumulated value S given P, R, and n.

    Test

    Calculate the current accumulated value of the \$24 principal paid to the Indians for Manhattan Island, assuming that it was compounded annually at 4% since 1627.

13. In installment buying the cost of the article is ordinarily paid in monthly installments. Each installment consists of the interest on the remaining unpaid balance plus an amount reducing the balance. Two equations expressing the relationships between payments P, the sum to be paid S, the number of payments n, and the interest rate per month r (at 6% per year, r is .005) are

$$P = rS \left(1 + \frac{1}{(1+r)^n - 1}\right)$$

$$n = \frac{\log\left(\frac{P}{P - rS}\right)}{\log(1 + r)}$$

(a) Define a function *PAYM* to determine the payment per month for a loan of D at PC per year for Y years.

    Test:

          $D \leftarrow 1000$
          $PC \leftarrow 10$
          $Y \leftarrow 3$
          . . . .
       32.27

(b) Define a function *PER* to determine how many months it will take to pay back K dollars at $R\%$ per year if M dollars are repaid each month. Show the answer in whole months.

    Test:

          $M \leftarrow 30$
          $K \leftarrow 1000$
          $R \leftarrow 10$
          . . . .
       39.2

(c) Define a function *REPAY* to determine the total amount repaid as a result of borrowing D dollars per year at $I\%$ per year for Y years.

(d) A loan of S dollars with simple interest I is repaid at the end of the loan period. For a year's loan the borrower pays back $S \times 1 + I$. What is the difference between borrowing $1000 on a time-credit loan at 5.5% per year for a year with payments per month and on simple interest.

14. The nominal rate of interest is the quoted rate. The effective rate depends on the frequency at which interest is compounded. The formula for effective rate (ER) is

$$\mathrm{ER} = 100 \times \left(1 + \frac{\mathrm{NR}}{n}\right)^{n} - 1$$

where

NR is the nominal rate times .01

n is the number of compounding periods

(a) What is the effective rate of interest if 6% is compounded yearly, semi-yearly, quarterly, weekly, daily?

(b) The limit of the effective rate formula is $e^{\mathrm{NR}} - 1$. Write an expression to determine how close compounding daily is to the limit for 6% nominal interest.

15. Define a function *SIGN* that tells the caller his zodiac sign lf his birth month and day are entered as a two-component vector. (The zodiac signs and dates can be found in the horoscope of your daily newspaper.)

    Test:

        SIGN 5 17
   TAURUS

16. State the following in words:

$$((A*2)-B*2) = (A+B)\times A-B$$

17. Construct an expression that states that the absolute difference between the squares of two adjacent integers is the sum of the integers.

Section 4.4 SPECIAL INTEREST FUNCTIONS

APL also provides functions which parallel the basic trigonometric operations. They are discussed in the following sections.

Section 4.4.1 Pi

The constant π is immensely important in many mathematical calculations. π is available in APL as ○1. ○1 is a special case of the scalar monadic function named *PI-Times* ○ . Its general form is

    ○B

where B is any array. The result of ○B is the value of $\pi \times B$, and so

    ○1
3.1416
    ○2
6.2832
    ○.5
1.5708

The circumference of a circle is $2\pi r$. Thus, the evaluation of the expression 2.75×○2 produces the circumference of a circle 17.279 whose radius is 2.75.

Illustration 4.21 Degrees to Radians

In higher mathematics and in the physical sciences a circular system of measurement is often used. The unit for circular measurement is the *radian*. Often, however, the size of an angle is reported in degrees instead of radians and conversion is necessary. Converting degrees D to radians can be done with this expression:

    D×○÷180

For example,

    45   90   120×○÷180
0.7854 1.5708 2.0944

And if necessary, converting radians R to degrees can be done with this expression:

    R×180÷○1

For example,

      .7854 1.5708 2.0944×180÷○1
    45 90 120

The APL trigonometric functions—sine, cosine, and tangent (a subset of the APL circular functions)—require that the argument be in radians. The inverse functions—arc sine, arc cosine, and arc tangent—return a result expressed in radians.

Section 4.4.2 Circular Functions

One function symbol ○ represents all the APL circular functions. The general form of the circular functions is

    A○B

where the left argument A denotes the function type for the right argument B. These functions are as follows:

A	Result	Domain Restriction
1	Sine	
2	Cosine	
3	Tangent	
4	(1+B*2)*.5	
5	Hyperbolic sine	
6	Hyperbolic cosine	
7	Hyperbolic tangent	
0	(1-B*2)*.5	$(\lvert B)\le 1$
¯1	Arc sine	$1\ge/B$
¯2	Arc cosine	$1\ge\lvert B$
¯3	Arc tangent	
¯4	(¯1+B*2)*.5	$1\le\lvert B$
¯5	Inverse hyperbolic sine	
¯6	Inverse hyperbolic cosine	$B\ge 1$
¯7	Inverse hyperbolic tangent	$1>\lvert B$

The functions represented by $A\in 1\ 2\ 3\ \bar{\ }1\ \bar{\ }2\ \bar{\ }3$ are, of course, the most common functions, representing as they do the sine, cosine, tangent, arc sine, arc cosine, and arc tangent.

Illustration 4.22   A Trigonometric Problem

A 13-foot pole is leaning against a vertical wall. Its foot is 4 feet from the wall. If the angle that pole makes with the wall is increased by 2.4 degrees, how far from the wall will the foot of the pole be?

The APL coding of the solution (recall that 2.4 must be converted to radians) is

        13×1○((○2.4)÷180)+¯1○4÷13
4.51446

PROBLEMS

1. State in words the meaning of expressions (a)–(j):
   (a) ○2   (b) 1○.75   (c) ¯2○.5
   (d) ¯3○.5   (e) ¯4○4   (f) ○÷3
   (g) 2○○÷4   (h) ¯3○○÷4   (i) ○○.5
   (j) 5○2

2. Evaluate expressions (a)–(f):
   (a) ○1   (b) 2○○1   (c) ¯1○1○○1
   (d) 1○○÷6   (e) 3○○÷4   (f) ÷1○○÷6

3. Write an expression for (a)–(l):
   (a) The sine of 30 degrees.
   (b) The cosine of 50 degrees.
   (c) The tangent of 30, 60, and 135 degrees.
   (d) The cotangent of 45, 70, and 105 degrees.
   (e) The number of degrees in 1 radian.
   (f) The number of radians in 1 degree.
   (g) The radian equivalent of 30 degrees.
   (h) The degree equivalent of .78539 radians.
   (i) The angle whose tangent is 1.
   (j) The angle whose cosine is one-half the square root of 3.
   (k) The secant of an angle of 2 radians.
   (l) The cotangent of a 60-degree angle.

4. For the triangle

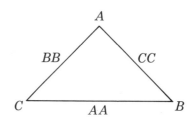

the law of cosines states that $\overline{AA}^2 = \overline{BB}^2 + \overline{CC}^2 - 2 \times BB \times CC \times \cos A$. Write in APL notation the value of AA, given the angle A in radians and the sides BB and CC.

5. The area of a triangle is equal to one-half the product of any two sides and the sine of the included angle. Define a function $AREAT$ to compute the triangular area given two sides and BB and the included angle C in degrees.

   Test:

   ```
   AA←6
   BB←10
   C←10 20 30 60 70 140
   ·······
   ```
5.2094	10.261	15	25.981	28.191	19.284

6. A 10-foot ladder leans against a wall, meeting it 3 feet from the ground. Write an expression which states the angle that the ladder makes with the wall.

7. Suppose that X and Y are the corresponding coordinates of points with respect to the usual *x-y* system. If both the *x* and *y* axis are rotated A degrees about the origin, the relationship between the old and new coordinates is defined as

$$X = \underline{X} \cos A + \underline{Y} \sin A$$
$$Y = \underline{X} \cos A - \underline{Y} \sin A$$

Define a function $OLDCO$ to compute the old coordinates X and Y given the angle of rotation A in degrees and the new coordinates $\underline{X}$ and $\underline{Y}$.

8. If $Z = X + iY$, then $\sinh Z = \sinh X \cos Y + i \cosh X \sin Y$.

   Write expressions for the real and imaginary parts of $\sinh Z$. Specify $RSINHZ$ to be the real part and $ISINHZ$ to be the imaginary part.

9. The linear velocity of a point on a circular object is equal to the product of the object's radius times the angular velocity of the point. Write an expression to determine the linear velocity (speed) of a wheel making M revolutions per minute. The diameter of the wheel is Y inches.

Section 4.5 SUMMARY

Thirteen primitive scalar monadic functions, 17 primitive scalar dyadic functions, and 1 primitive mixed dyadic function were introduced in this chapter.

Domains and Ranges

The *domain* of a function is the set of possible values of its argument(s). For example, the domain of factorial ! is all numbers but negative integers; the domain of the logic functions is 1 and 0; and the domain of membership is all numbers and all characters.

The *range* of a function is the set of the possible values of the result. For example, the range of floor is the set of integers and the range of the relational functions is 0 and 1.

Functions

The primitive functions introduced in this chapter are collected together with their related information in the following tables:

Primitive Monadic Functions Introduced in Chapter 4

Name and Syntax	Definition	Domain Restricted to	Range Restricted to	Type/Conformability
Absolute value $\lvert R$	Magnitude —no sign	Numbers	Positive numbers and zero only	Scalar
Negation $-R$	Change of sign	Numbers	Numbers	Scalar
Reciprocal $\div R$	$1 \div R$	Numbers, but not zero	Numbers	Scalar
Floor $\lfloor R$	Truncate down integer	Numbers	Integers	Scalar
Ceiling $\lceil R$	Truncate up to integer	Numbers	Integers	Scalar
Factorial $!R$	Gamma function (factorial for integer R)	No negative integers	Numbers	Scalar
Signum $\times R$	1: positive R 0: zero R $^{-}1$: negative R	Numbers	$^{-}1, 0, 1$	Scalar
π times $\bigcirc R$	$\pi \times R$	Numbers	Numbers	Scalar
Exponential $\circledast R$	e^R	Numbers	Positive	Scalar
Natural logarithm $\circledast R$	$\ln R$	$R > 0$	Numbers	Scalar
Not $\sim R$	Change value: 0 to 1; 1 to 0	$0,1$ only	$0,1$ only	Scalar (binary)
Monadic plus $+R$	No change to R	Numbers	Numbers	Scalar

Primitive Dyadic Functions Introduced in Chapter 4

Name and Syntax	Definition	Domain Restricted to	Range Restricted to	Type/Conformability
Minimum $A \lfloor B$	The lesser of A and B	Numbers	Numbers	Scalar
Maximum $A \lceil B$	The greater of A and B	Numbers	Numbers	Scalar
Residue $A \mid B$	$B-Q \times A$ for some integer Q		A to 0, inclusive (0 but not A)	Scalar
Exponentiation $A \star B$	$(A)^B$	If A is 0, B must be nonnegative; if A is negative, B must be an integer or $N \div D$, where D is an odd integer	Numbers	Scalar
Logarithm $A \circledast B$	$\text{Log}_A B$	$A>0$ only $B>0$ only if $A=1$, $B=1$	Numbers	Scalar
Combinations B things . . .	Beta function (for positive integers A and B, $-B$ things taken A at a time)		Numbers	Scalar
Less than $A<B$	1 if true; 0 if false	Numbers	0,1 only	Scalar
Less than or equal $A \leq B$	1 if true; 0 if false	Numbers	0,1 only	Scalar
Equal $A=B$	1 if true; 0 if false	None—characters permitted	0,1 only	Scalar
Greater than $A>B$	1 if true; 0 if false	Numbers	0,1 only	Scalar

Primitive Dyadic Functions Introduced in Chapter 4 (Cont'd.)

Name and Syntax	Definition	Domain Restricted to	Range Restricted to	Type/Conformability
Greater than or equal $A \geq B$	1 if true; 0 if false	Numbers	0,1 only	Scalar
Not equal $A \neq B$	1 if true; 0 if false	None— characters permitted	0,1 only	Scalar
Membership $A \in B$	1 if A is present in B; 0 otherwise	None— characters permitted	0,1 only	Mixed
And $A \wedge B$	$\begin{array}{c c\|c c} & & \multicolumn{2}{c}{B} \\ \wedge & & 0 & 1 \\ \hline & 0 & 0 & 0 \\ A & 1 & 0 & 1 \end{array}$	0,1 only	0,1 only	Scalar (binary)
Or $A \vee B$	$\begin{array}{c c\|c c} & & \multicolumn{2}{c}{B} \\ \vee & & 0 & 1 \\ \hline & 0 & 0 & 1 \\ A & 1 & 1 & 1 \end{array}$	0,1 only	0,1 only	Scalar (binary)
Nand $A \barwedge B$	$\begin{array}{c c\|c c} & & \multicolumn{2}{c}{B} \\ \barwedge & & 0 & 1 \\ \hline & 0 & 1 & 1 \\ A & 1 & 1 & 0 \end{array}$	0,1 only	0,1 only	Scalar (binary)
Nor $A \barvee B$	$\begin{array}{c c\|c c} & & \multicolumn{2}{c}{B} \\ \barvee & & 0 & 1 \\ \hline & 0 & 1 & 0 \\ A & 1 & 0 & 0 \end{array}$	0,1 only	0,1 only	Scalar (binary)
Circular $A \circ B$	Depends on value of A			Scalar
$1 \circ B$	Sine	Numbers	$(\mid 1 \circ B) \leq 1$	
$2 \circ B$	Cosine	Numbers	$(\mid 2 \circ B) \leq 1$	
$3 \circ B$	Tangent	Numbers	Numbers	
$4 \circ B$	$\sqrt{1 + B^2}$	Numbers	$(4 \circ B) \geq 1$	
$5 \circ B$	Hyperbolic sine	Numbers	Numbers	
$6 \circ B$	Hyperbolic cosine	Numbers	$(6 \circ B) \geq 1$	
$7 \circ B$	Hyperbolic tangent	Numbers	$(\mid 7 \circ B) < 1$	
$0 \circ B$	$\sqrt{1 - B^2}$	$1 \geq \mid B$	$(0 \circ B) \geq 0$	

Primitive Dyadic Functions Introduced in Chapter 4 (Cont'd.)

Name and Syntax	Definition	Domain Restricted to	Range Restricted to	Type/Conformability
^-1OB	Arc sine	$1 \geq \lvert B$	Numbers	
^-2OB	Arc cosine	$1 \geq \lvert B$	Numbers	
^-3OB	Arc tangent	Numbers	Numbers	
^-4OB	$\sqrt{B^2 - 1}$	$1 \leq \lvert B$	$(^-4OB) \geq 0$	
^-5OB	Inverse hyperbolic sine	Numbers	Numbers	
^-6OB	Inverse hyperbolic cosine	$B \geq 1$	Numbers	
^-7OB	Inverse hyperbolic tangent	$1 > \lvert B$	Numbers	

EXTENSIONS OF THE SCALAR DYADIC FUNCTIONS TO ARRAYS AND OTHER ARRAY HANDLING CAPABILITIES

CHAPTER 5

All the scalar dyadic functions have been introduced in Chapters 1 and 4. Scalar functions operate on arrays of all ranks in a component-by-component manner; that is, the scalar functions operate on components in like positions of the array arguments. Besides their use in component-by-component operations on arrays, the scalar dyadic functions are employed as the argument(s) of four operators. An operator has functions as its argument(s), whereas a function has data as its argument(s). These operators extend the user's array-handling capabilities significantly.

Section 5.1 REDUCTION

One arithmetic function often performed is that of adding a set of numbers. Consider, for example, the vector *ENROLL* whose components represent the number of students in each of four classes of a college:

$ENRÓLL$←250   207   189   170

To determine the total enrollment, the four components of *ENROLL* can be added together:

250+207+189+170

816

or

$ENROLL[1]+ENROLL[2]+ENROLL[3]+ENROLL[4]$

816

Finding the sum in these ways is possible only if the values of the components or the number of components in the vector are known in advance. Often, however, the values of the components or the number of components in the vector are not preset. For instance, a function that finds an average should work with any number of elements, rather than requiring some preset number. A function for achieving the sum without relying on the number of components of their values is the *sum-reduction* function $+/A$. In a sum-reduction, the symbols $+/$ indicate that the addition function should be inserted between the data components of the argument. Hence $+/ENROLL$ is equivalent to inserting the $+$ symbol between the components of *ENROLL*.

> $+/ENROLL$

816

Sum-reduction is equivalent to mathematical summation. $+/ENROLL$ can be represented in mathematical notation as $\Sigma_{i=1}^{4}$ *ENROLL*$_i$. As another example, the value of $\Sigma_{n=1}^{10}$ $1/n$ is $+/\div\iota 10$ or 2.929.

While the *sum* of a set of numbers is frequently required, similar types of functions, such as the *product of* a set of numbers, the *largest of* a set of numbers, or the *smallest of* a set of numbers, are also useful. The operator reduction represents a generalization of this type of function. It takes the form

> fn$/A$

where the function fn to the left of the slash (the operator symbol) may be chosen from any of the primitive dyadic scalar functions and the argument A can be a scalar or an array of any shape. The scalar dyadic function symbol and the slash (the operator symbol) make up the symbol for the reduction function. The name of the reduction comes from the name of the scalar function, such as sum-reduction, minus-reduction, maximum-reduction, and so forth. In effect, the function symbol fn in reduction is inserted between adjacent components of data; that is, the expression fn$/A,B,C,D$ is equivalent to A fn B fn C fn D.

Illustration 5.1   Range and Average

Suppose that *SAL* is a vector of salaries in a selected sample of the city's wage earners. Then $\lceil/SAL$ is the largest salary; $\lfloor/SAL$ is the smallest salary; $(\lceil/SAL)-\lfloor/SAL$ is the salary range; and $(+/SAL)\div\rho SAL$ is the average salary.

Illustration 5.2   π Represented as Alternating Sums

De Morgan in *Assorted Paradoxes* in the section on "The Curiosities of Pi" shows these alternating series:

$$\frac{\pi}{4} = 1 - \frac{1}{3} + \frac{1}{5} - \frac{1}{7} + \frac{1}{9} - \frac{1}{11} + \cdots$$

$$\frac{\pi-3}{4} = \frac{1}{2\cdot 3\cdot 4} - \frac{1}{4\cdot 5\cdot 6} + \frac{1}{6\cdot 7\cdot 8} - \cdots$$

$$\frac{\pi}{6} = \sqrt{\left(\frac{1}{3}\right)}\cdot\left(1 - \frac{1}{3\cdot 3} + \frac{1}{3^2\cdot 5} - \frac{1}{3^3\cdot 7} + \frac{1}{3^4\cdot 9} - \cdots\right)$$

Minus-reduction $-/A$ produces an alternating sum.* Then, based on the series shown above, the value of π can be determined for N terms in the series by the following expressions:

$$4\times-/\div{}^-1+2\times\iota N$$

$$3+4\times-/\div(2\times\iota N)\times(1+2\times\iota N)\times2+2\times\iota N$$

$$6\times(\div3*.5)\times-/\div(3*{}^-1+\iota N)\times{}^-1+2\times\iota N$$

Other noncommutative scalar functions when used with reduction produce some interesting and useful functions. For instance, divide-reduction produces an alternating product. Thus

$$\div/A,B,C,D$$

is equivalent to

$$\frac{A \times C}{B \times D}$$

Illustration 5.3   Determining Whether a Logic Vector Consists Entirely of 1s

That a binary vector R is made up entirely of 1s can be ascertained by and-reduction $\wedge/R$, and that R has at least one 1 by or-reduction $\vee/R$. For example,

     $B\leftarrow9\ 7\ 3\ \ 2\ 5$

     $\wedge/B>0$

1   (every component of B is positive)

     $\wedge/0=2|B$

0   (not every component of B is odd)

     $\vee/0=2|B$

1   (at least one component of B is even)

     $\vee/B<0$

0   (no component of B is negative)

Illustration 5.4   Checking Placement of Values

1. An expression for determining whether a given value N lies within a given range of values A and B is $>/N>A,B$. The result is 1 only if N lies in the range $(A,B]$; that is, N is a value greater than A and less than or equal to B. For example,

---

*To verify this recall that $-/A,B,C,D,E$ is equivalent to the APL expression $A-B-C-D-E$, which when evaluated is equivalent to the algebraic expression $A-B+C-D+E$.

```
      >/6>3 12
1
      >/¯6>3 12
0
```

2. The expression `+/×(A,B,C)-X` produces an encoding from ¯3 to 3 of the position of X relative to the values A, B, and C as follows:

Result	Meaning
¯3	Larger than the largest number
¯2	The largest number
¯1	Between the middle and largest numbers
0	The middle number
1	Between the smallest and middle numbers
2	The smallest number
3	Smaller than the smallest number

For example,

```
      +/×10 20 30-15
1
      +/×10 20 30-45
¯3
```

Illustration 5.5 Determining the Number of Dominating Components

If A and B are conformable vectors, the expression `+/A≥B` yields the number of components of A which dominate (that is, are greater than or equal to) the corresponding components of B. For example,

```
      +/6 ¯9 8 ¯3≥12 3 ¯6 ¯4
2
```

Illustration 5.6 Buffon Needle Problem

The problem known as the Buffon needle problem was proposed by Georges Louis Leclerc-Buffon (1707–1788). Buffon dropped a rod to a planked floor. The rod was shorter than the distance between the seams on the floor. Buffon discovered and later proved that, although the dropping of the rod was a random event, the ratio of seam crossings to the number of trials was twice the length of the rod to the circumference of the circle whose diameter is the width of the plank. If the rod is half the width of the plank, this ratio reduces to one over π.

The dropping of a rod can be simulated by the function *BUFFON* , which randomly selects the distance *MA* from the midpoint of a 2-inch needle to the nearer line and randomly selects the angle A in degrees that the needle makes with the line *MA*. If the cosine of that angle is greater than *MA*, the needle crosses the line. Sum-reduction is used to tally the number of crossings:

```
      ∇ RTH←BUFFON TOSSES;MA;A
[1]    MA←0.001×¯1+?TOSSESρ2001
[2]    M←¯1+?TOSSESρ91
[3]    CROSSES←+/MA<2○(○M)÷180
[4]    RTH←TOSSES÷CROSSES
      ∇
```

For example,

```
      (BUFFON 1000),(BUFFON 1000),BUFFON 1000
3.1447 3.1257  3.0041
```

Illustrations 5.1 through 5.6 have shown reduction being applied to a vector argument. However, the argument of reduction may be any array. As an example, consider the matrix *VOTES* which is the body of the election results matrix of parties versus precincts shown below:

			Precincts		
Parties	1	2	3	4	5
A	143	98	175	167	133
B	76	125	201	48	137
C	211	137	91	101	63

The number of votes each party received can be determined by summing the elements of votes by rows. Similarly, the number of votes that were cast in each precinct can be determined by summing the elements of votes by columns. Both these sums can be obtained by using reduction. The way to indicate the dimension of the array right argument along which reduction should be performed (called the *coordinate axis*) is by stating the coordinate in brackets immediately to the right of the / symbol, fn /[*I*]. The integer within brackets is an axis-specifier on the function and can be thought of as an index on the function. The expression for determining the total number of votes each party received, then, is

```
      +/[2]VOTES
716 587 603
```

The value of +/[2]*VOTES* is a three-component vector; the first component is the total vote for party A, the second for party B, and the third for party C. (The [2] indicates that the sum-reduction occurs along the second coordinate.)

The expression for determining how many people voted in each precinct is

```
      +/[1]VOTES
430 360 467  316  333
```

The value of $+/[1]VOTES$ is a five-component vector with a component for each precinct. (The $[1]$ indicates that the sum-reduction occurs along the first coordinate.)

The axis-specifier of a function is the means of specifying the coordinate axis of the argument along which the function is to be performed. There are seven APL functions that may have an axis-specifier naming the coordinate axis along which the function is to be performed. Besides reduction, they are compression, expansion, rotation, reversal, catenation, and scan. All but scan are discussed in Chapter 7; scan is discussed in Sec. 5.2. Because of its importance, two additional ways of interpreting the axis-specifier are given in the following paragraphs.

The axis-specifier may be viewed as an indicator describing which index in the set of indices associated with each element is to vary most rapidly in applying the function. To illustrate this, consider the matrix M:

```
      M
  9    8    7
 10   15   20
```

With the indices of each element stated explicitly, M is

$$9_{1\,1} \qquad 8_{1\,2} \qquad 7_{1\,3}$$

$$10_{2\,1} \qquad 15_{2\,2} \qquad 20_{2\,3}$$

The function symbol in a reduction can be placed in the matrix by rows or by columns. The first case is indicated by fn $/[2]M$, which means that the function symbol is placed between the elements of M such that the function is executed with the *second* index changing most rapidly. Those elements with the same first index are added together:

```
M[1;1] fn M[1;2] fn M[1;3]

M[2;1] fn M[2;2] fn M[2;3]
```

The effect of letting the second index vary most rapidly is an execution of the function by rows. For example,

```
    +/[2]M
24  45
```

Similarly, fn $/[1]M$ indicates that the function symbol is placed between the elements of M such that the first index changes most rapidly. Those elements with the same second index are operated on together:

```
M[1;1] M[1;2] M[1;3]

  fn      fn      fn

M[2;1] M[2;2] M[2;3]
```

The effect is an execution of the function by columns. For example,

```
    +/[1]M
19 23 27
```

A third way of interpreting the axis-specifier is to consider it an indicator of the dimension-subscript which is affected by the function. For example, the affected subscript is shown slashed in the diagram of the matrix M below:

$$\text{fn}/[1]M$$

$$9_{\not1 1} \qquad 8_{\not1 2} \qquad 7_{\not1 3}$$

$$10_{\not1 1} \qquad 15_{\not1 2} \qquad 20_{\not1 3}$$

or

$$\text{fn}/[2]M$$

$$9_{1\not1} \qquad 8_{1\not2} \qquad 7_{1\not3}$$

$$10_{2\not1} \qquad 15_{2\not2} \qquad 20_{2\not3}$$

The function is performed between all the elements with the same subscripts. For example,

```
    ×/[1]M
90   120  140
    ×/[2]M
504   3000
```

It is not always necessary to specify the direction of the reduction explicitly by using an axis-specifier. If the axis-specifier is omitted, the reduction is carried out along the *last* or rightmost index. That is, $+/M$ is equivalent to $+/[\rho\rho M]M$. The omission of the axis-specifier always produces a row reduction. For the matrix *VOTES*, shown earlier in this section, $+/VOTES$ is equivalent to $+/[2]VOTES$.

Similarly, if the operator symbol $\not{/}$ (slash, backspace, minus) is used, the reduction is carried out along the *first* dimension and no axis-specifier is needed. Thus $+\not{/}VOTES$ is equivalent to $+/[1]VOTES$. The operator symbol $\not{/}$ indicates that the function is performed along the first coordinate. For example, in a matrix this is a column reduction; in a rank-3 array, it is a plane reduction.

Reduction is often used sequentially in an expression. For instance, $\lceil/+/VOTES$ tells the largest number of votes (716) cast for one party in any precinct; $+/+/VOTES$ tells the total votes (1906) cast in the election; and $\lfloor/+/[1]VOTES$ or $\lfloor/+\not{/}VOTES$ tells the least number of votes cast (316) in a precinct.

As an example of reduction with a rank-3 array, consider *TALLY*, a 4 by 3 by 5 array representing the party vote by precinct for the last four elections. Graphically *TALLY* can be viewed as

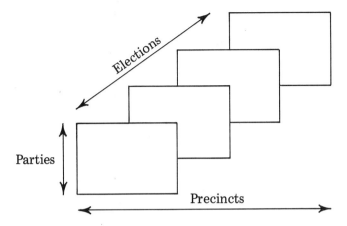

The following is some of the information available by using reduction:

Information	Expression
1. Total party vote for each party in each election	$R1\leftarrow+/[3]TALLY$ or $R1\leftarrow+/TALLY$
2. Largest vote cast for each party within each precinct over the last four elections	$R2\leftarrow\lceil/[1]TALLY$ or $R2\leftarrow\lceil\neq TALLY$
3. Total precinct vote for each election	$R3\leftarrow+/[2]TALLY$

Note that elision of the axis-specifier is possible only for the first or last coordinate. In the third example, the [2] must be shown explicitly in order to obtain the sum along the second coordinate.

An array can be reduced along any of its dimensions. The rank of the result of reduction is one less than the rank of the right argument. The dimension which is removed is the dimension along which the reduction occurs. In the example above $\rho TALLY$ is 4 3 5. The last dimension is eliminated in $R1$, leaving $\rho R1$ as 4 3; the second dimension is eliminated in $R3$, leaving $\rho R3$ as 4 5; and the first dimension is eliminated in $R2$, leaving $\rho R2$ as 3 5. Thus, if a rank-3 array is reduced, the result is a matrix. If a matrix is reduced, the result is a vector, and if a vector is reduced, the result is a scalar.

Reduction, then, can be used to make a one-component vector into a scalar. Thus

     $T\leftarrow 1\rho 5$

     ρT

1

     $R\leftarrow+/T$

     ρR

Note that this is the opposite of ravel, which makes a scalar into a vector. If a scalar is reduced, the result is that scalar.

If a null array is reduced, the result is the identity element of the function fn, if one exists, for example,

×/ι0	v/ι0	=/ι0	⊛/ι0
1	0	1	*DOMAIN ERROR*
			⊛/ι0
			∧

The identity elements for floor and ceiling are the maximum and minimum machine-representable numbers. (In APL.SV these are ‾7.237005577E75 and 7.237005577E75.) The expressions ⌈/ι0 and ⌊/ι0 can be used to describe negative and positive infinity when that concept is needed.

PROBLEMS

1. Use the following variables for evaluating expressions (a) — (z):

```
        AA
  1    2
  3    4
  5    6

  7    8
  9   10
 11   12

        U
  0  1  2
  1  2  0
  2  0  1
        V
  0  ‾1  ‾2
  1   0  ‾1
  2   1   0
        P
  7    3   2  11
  9    5   4  12
  1   12  17   8
        Q
  6  2  1
  5  4  3
  2  5  7
        W
  ‾0.5  0.5  ‾1.5  1.5
```

(a) ×/AA   (b) +/W   (c) -/W
(d) ÷/W   (e) +/[1]P   (f) ×/[2]AA
(g) ⌈/W   (h) ⌊/W   (i) +/P
(j) +≠P   (k) +/[2]P   (l) +/V
(m) +/P[1 3;3 4]   (n) -/P[1 3;3 4]   (o) +/[1]V
(p) ×/U   (q) +/[1]×/U   (r) ⌈/W,⌊/W
(s) (⌈/W),⌊/W   (t) +/ρP   (u) ×/ρP
(v) ⌈/,AA   (w) ⌈/AA   (x) ⌈/[1]AA
(y) ⌈/⌈/AA   (z) ⌈/⌈/⌈/AA

2. For

```
L1←1   1   0   1   1   0
L2←1   1   1   1   1   1
L3←0   0   0   0   0   0
```

In (a)-(c) substitute for α the functions ∧ ∨ ⍱ ⍲ = ≠.
(a) α/L1
(b) α/L2
(c) α/L3

3. Using the variables P and Q from problem 1, determine whether the expressions in each of
    the sets of expressions (a)-(h) are equivalent:
    (a) +/+/[1]P   (b) ⌈/⌊/P   (c) ⌈/⌊/[1]P
         +/+/P   ⌊/⌈/P   ⌈/⌊/P
    (d) +/×/Q   (e) +/-/Q   (f) +/-/[1]Q
         +/×/[1]Q   -/+/Q   +/-/Q
    (g) +/-/[1]Q   (h) ×/÷/Q
         -/+/Q   ÷/×/[1]Q

4. A scalar can be converted to a one-component vector by using the ravel function ,S or by
    using restructure 1ρS. Show three ways of converting a one-component vector or array T
    into a scalar.

5. On each day of the eight days of Hanukkah, the Jewish feast of lights, candles are lit. On
    the first day two candles are lit. Each day one more is lit until on the eighth day nine
    candles are lit. (New candles are lit each day.) Write an expression to determine the number
    of candles in a box of Hanukkah candles.

6. A rhyming riddle goes

    As I was going to St. Ives
    I met a man with seven wives
    Each wife had seven sacks
    Each sack had seven cats
    Each cat had seven kittens
    Kittens, cats, sacks, wives
    How many were going to St. Ives?

    The answer to the riddle is, of course, 1. Construct an expression to determine how many
    the poem's narrator met.

7. If a binary number is represented as a vector N of 0s and 1s (i.e., as a set of bits), an even parity bit P can be determined by performing an exclusive-or operation on the set of bits comprising the number. P is to be a 1 if N contains an odd number of 1-bits, while P is to be a 0 if N contains an even number of 1-bits.) Write an expression for generating P.

   Test:

   $$N \leftarrow 1 \ 0 \ 1 \ 1 \ 0 \quad \text{(i.e., } 10110_2)$$

   $$\cdots\cdots\cdots$$

   $$P$$

   $$1$$

8. State in words what the following expressions convey:

   (a) $+/WORD \in 'AEIOU'$

   (b) $(+/X*2) \neq (+/X)*2$

9. Normalization is the adjusting of data through the use of constants in order to compare the data on some common basis. For example, a set of numbers N can be normalized to unity by dividing each number in the set by the sum of the numbers. Write an expression to normalize the data N to unity. Use the test data

   $$N \leftarrow 421 \ 4.6 \ 34.5 \ 89 \ 14 \ 61.8 \ 49$$

10. A measure of forecast error is the mean absolute deviation (MAD):

    $$\text{MAD} = \frac{\text{sum of the absolute values of the deviations of each measure from the mean}}{\text{number of measures}}$$

    Write an expression to determine the MAD of data D.

11. M is a matrix representing the body of the average monthly temperature table shown below. $CITY$ is a matrix list of the city names.

Month

City	Jan.	Feb.	Mar.	Apr.	May	June	July	Aug.	Sept.	Oct.	Nov.	Dec.
Albany	22.7	23.7	33.0	46.2	57.9	67.3	72.1	70.0	61.6	50.8	39.1	26.5
Bismarck	9.9	13.5	26.2	43.5	55.9	64.5	71.7	69.3	58.7	46.7	28.9	17.8
Chicago	26.0	27.7	31.3	49.0	60.0	70.5	75.6	74.2	66.1	55.1	39.9	29.1
Denver	28.5	33.5	36.4	46.4	56.2	66.5	72.9	71.5	63.0	51.4	37.7	31.6
Houston	53.6	55.8	61.3	68.5	76.0	81.6	83.0	83.2	79.2	71.4	60.8	55.7
Minneapolis	12.4	15.7	27.4	44.3	57.3	66.8	72.3	70.0	60.4	48.9	31.2	18.1
San Francisco	50.7	53.0	54.7	55.7	57.4	59.1	58.8	59.4	62.0	61.4	57.4	52.5
Wichita	32.0	36.3	44.5	56.7	66.0	76.5	80.9	80.8	71.3	59.9	44.4	35.8

Write expressions to determine information (a)–(h):

(a) The mean for each month.

(b) The mean for each city.

(c) The city with the highest average temperature. Assume that only one city qualifies.

(d) The city with the lowest average temperature. Assume that only one city qualifies.

(e) The city with the greatest temperature variation. What is the variation? How much greater is this than the temperature variation of the other cities? Assume that only one city qualifies.

(f) The mean average temperature variation for all cities.

(g) Assume that spring includes the months April, May, and June; summer, the months July, August, and September; fall, the months October, November, and December; and winter, the months January, February, and March. Find the mean temperature for each city for each season.

(h) Test the assertion that January is the coldest month and that July is the hottest month for all cities.

12. The array *GPA* is a 4 by 10 by 4 array. Each plane represents a grade point average from high to low by class of the students at a medium sized university such that

    GPA[1;;] represents the students with grades of greater than B—level 1.

    GPA[2;;] represents the students with grades between C (2) and B(3)—level 2.

    GPA[3;;] represents the students with grades between D (1) and C (2)—level 3.

    GPA[4;;] represents students between E (0) and D (1)—level 4.

    Each column represents a class—freshmen, sophomores, juniors, seniors. Each of the 10 rows of a plane represents a decimal in the tenths position. For example, *GPA*[3;1;] represents averages of 2.0; *GPA*[3;6;] represents averages of 1.5; and *GPA*[3;10;] represents averages of 1.1. *GPA*[1;2;3] is the number of juniors who have a 3.9 average out of a possible 4 points. Assume that no student has a straight 0 average. Test data can be generated by

    GPA←4 10 4ρ10+?160ρ40

    Write expressions for information (a)-(l):
    (a) The total enrollment at the school.
    (b) The number of students in each class.
    (c) The number of students in each class in each level.
    (d) The total number of students in level 1.
    (e) The percentage of students in level 1.
    (f) The percentage of freshmen who are in level 4.
    (g) The percentage of level-3 students who are juniors.
    (h) The name of the class with the largest number of students in level 3.
    (i) The percentage of each class that was in either level 1 or level 2.
    (j) The level with the least number of students.
    (k) If students are on academic probation with a grade point average of 2.0 or less, how many students are on academic probation?
    (l) If border line is described as an integer grade level plus or minus .1, how many students are on a border line?

13. A car rental agency purchases four Darts, six Mavericks, five Novas, eight Pintos, and seven Toyotas at costs of $2250 per Dart, $2029 per Maverick, $2315 per Nova, $2195 per Pinto, and $1875 per Toyota.
    (a) Write an expression to determine the total cost of the purchase. Let the variable CP represent the total cost of the purchase.
    (b) Write an expression to determine the cost difference between the group costing the least and the group costing the most.

(c) Generalize the capability of part (a) by defining a function TC to accept as input the number of cars X and the cost per car C. Use the test data

```
X←4 6 5 8 7
C←2250 2029 2315 2195 1875
```

14. The function $HANDSQ$ describes an algorithm for an easy way to manually square a number V, which ends in a 5. State the algorithm in words.

```
    ∇ Z←HANDSQ V
[1]    Z←25+×/V+5 ‾5
    ∇
```

15. PQ is a matrix of price quotations from several vendors for an item. The price quotation varies by lot size. In the matrix PQ the rows represent the vendors and the columns represent the price quotes by lot size. If a price is not quoted for a specific lot size, the entry is zero. Define a function LPQ to determine the lowest price quote for each lot size. If no vendor quoted a price on a specific lot size, the value returned for it should be zero. (*Note*: In general terms, this problem is that of finding the lowest nonzero element in a column of of a matrix M. If all zeros, return a zero.)

> *Test:*
> ```
> PQ←3 4ρ75 70 0 50 76 0 0 40 73 60 0 45
> • • • • • ∘
> ```
> ```
> 73   60   0   40
> ```

16. MAP is an N by 2 matrix representing the X and Y coordinates of N cities on a map. The origin is at the lower left-hand corner of the map. Each row provides the X and Y coordinates of a city. Write expressions to determine
    (a) The city farthest north.
    (b) The city farthest west.

17. The three-dimensional array $DATA$ contains a year's data by month of the costs for each of six projects. $DATA$ is a 12 by 5 by 6 structure whose first dimension represents months; whose second dimension represents costs allocated to salary, machine time, travel, overtime, and overhead; and whose third dimension represents projects. Test data can be generated by

```
DATA←12 5 6ρ100+?(12×5×6)ρ900
```

Write expressions for information (a)–(h):
(a) The annual (last 12 months) individual cost components by project.
(b) The total annual cost by project.
(c) The total annual cost for project 2.
(d) The total annual machine time for project 4.
(e) The most money spent on overtime during the third month. Which project spent it?
(f) The monthly travel and overtime costs for projects 1 and 6.
(g) The largest monthly cost for machine time. Which project had it? Which month did the project use it?
(h) The monthly projects/costs matrix for the sixth month, with the columns arranged in ascending order by overtime costs.

18. Define a function *FLIP* to flip a pair of coins *C* times and to determine
    (a) How many times the first coin was a head.

    (b) The number of times the coins matched.

    (c) The number of times a pair of heads came up.

19. Fahrenheit temperatures from freezing (32) to boiling (212) can be converted to Celsius
    temperatures by scaling the Fahrenheit temperatures so that each lies in the range 0 to 1
    and then multiplying by 100. The scaling can be done by forming the ratio of temperature
    less 32 all divided by the range (212–32). Define a function *SCALE* to scale a vector *V* so
    that each value lies between 0 and 1 and each scaled number is rounded off to *P* places
    to the right of the decimal point. Use the test data

    $V \leftarrow 9$ 16 32 45 615 143
    $P \leftarrow 2$

20. For *V*, a vector of 100 random integers from 1 through 1000, define a function *STAT* to
    determine the following information:
    (a) The maximum value.

    (b) The minimum value.

    (c) The range of values.

    (d) The sum of values.

    (e) The mean of the values.

    (f) The number of elements greater than the average value.

    (g) The variance around the mean. (Variance is defined as a quotient. The numerator is
        the sum of the squares of the differences between the elements of *V* and its average.
        The denominator is one less than the number of elements in *V*.)

    (h) The standard deviation. (Standard deviation is defined as the square root of the variance.)

    (i) The number of components which are odd numbers.

    (j) The number of times the largest number occurs.

21. Define a function *PD* to determine the percentage distribution of items *Y*. For example,
    suppose that a man spends $125 on rent, $75 on savings, $95 for food, and $12.50 for
    miscellaneous per month. What percentage of the total does he spend on each category?
    Use the test data

    $Y \leftarrow 125$ 75 95 12.50

22. Construct a vector *V* of length ρY consisting entirely of underscores except for an asterisk
    where the corresponding component of *Y* is the largest component in *Y*.
          Test:

          $Y \leftarrow 9$ 12 6 5 19 16

          . . . .

          V

    _____*_

23. Write an expression to determine each of the following numbers:
    (a) The product of the first five even positive integers.

    (b) The sum of the squares of the first *K* positive integers.

    (c) The square of the sum of the first *K* positive integers.

(d) The *geometric mean* of the first K positive integers. (The geometric mean of N positive numbers is the Nth root of the product of the N numbers.)

24. Write an expression to compute the number of different sums of money one can get with a penny, nickel, dime, quarter, half-dollar, and dollar.

25. Write an expression to determine whether a vector V is a binary vector, that is, a vector whose components are 1s and 0s.

26. The table below is a frequency distribution of the nouns in the first act of Shakespeare's *Julius Caesar.* The first column indicates the occurrence categories; the second column indicates the number of words occurring once, twice, etc.

Occurrences	Number of Words
1	272
2	63
3	18
4	5
5	4
6	7
7	2
8	2
9	1
10	3
11	1
12	1
37	1

Yule's formula (in *The Statistical Study of Literary Vocabulary*, Cambridge University Press, New York, 1944) for a characteristic to measure the repetitiveness of the vocabulary of a given literary work is 10,000 times the absolute value of (a) the sum of the products of corresponding columns *less* (b) the sum of (1) the second column *times* (2) the square of the first column. The difference (a) — (b) is divided by the square of the sum of the product of the columns. Write an expression to determine the characteristic of the above table JC.

27. Define a function $ZERO$ to determine the number of consecutive terminal 0s in $!N$. (*Hint*: Consider determining the number of pairs of the factors 5 and 2 that appear in the product $!N$.)

         Test:

            $N\leftarrow 200$

            $\cdots\cdots$

    49

Section 5.2   SCAN

Often at the end of its fiscal year a company that maintains its output on a monthly basis needs monthly year-to-date totals. That is, the totals required are those for the first month, the first 2 months, the first 3 months, and so forth. For example, if the monthly output is

```
17 21 18 19 20 18 15 14 17 18 17 15
```

the year-to-date figures would be

```
17 38 56 75 95 113 128 142 159 177 194 209
```

The function sum-scan $+\backslash$ produces the accumulated output. For this example, if the monthly output is MO, the solution is

```
      YTD←+\MO
17  38 56  75  95 113 128 142 159 177 194 209
```

Besides $+$ any scalar dyadic function can be used for a scan operation; for example, $\lceil\backslash A$, $\times\backslash A$, $\wedge\backslash A$, and so forth. The general form of scan is

> fn $\backslash[I]A$

where the function fn to the left of the operator symbol $\backslash$ may be chosen from any of the primitive dyadic scalar functions and the argument A may be a scalar or an array of any shape. The axis-specifier $[I]$ defines the dimension along which the scan is performed.

In effect the function symbol fn in scan is inserted between successively additional components of A and that result makes up each successive component of the result. For example,

> fn $\backslash A,B,C,D$

results in

$A,\ (A$ fn $B),\ (A$ fn B fn $C),\ A$ fn B fn C fn D

or in terms of the year-to-date example,

$YTD[1]$	17		$MO[1]$	
$YTD[2]$	17+21	that is,	$MO[1]+MO[2]$	or $+/MO[1\ 2]$
$YTD[3]$	17+21+18	that is,	$MO[1]+MO[2]+MO[3]$	or $+/MO[1\ 2\ 3]$
$YTD[4]$	17+21+18+19	that is,	$MO[1]+MO[2]+MO[3]+MO[4]$	or $+/MO[\iota 4]$

and so forth. Scan can be considered as repeated applications of the reduction function to successively consecutive elements of the argument A. Thus if

$$R \leftarrow \text{fn} \backslash V$$

then

$$R[I] \leftarrow \text{fn} / V[\iota I]$$

The last component of fn$\backslash V$ is always equivalent to fn$/V$.

An array can be scanned along any of its dimensions. The rank and shape of the scan result is the same as that of the argument array. Thus, if $R \leftarrow \text{fn} \backslash A$, then ρR is ρA and $\rho \rho R$ is $\rho \rho A$. For matrices and arrays of higher rank an axis-specifier is used to indicate the dimension of the array along which the scan is to be performed. For example,

```
      M
 9   8   3   6
 4   2   1   5
 3   4   2   4
       +\[1]M  or  +⍀M
 9    8   3   6
13   10   4  11
16   14   6  15
       +\[2]M  or  +\M
 9  17  20  26
 4   6   7  12
 3   7   9  13
```

It is important that the definition of scan be kept in mind when working with nonassociative functions. Within each of the components that make up the components of the scan result, the standard right-to-left evaluation rule applies. For example,

```
       -\1 2 3
1   ̄1   2            (not 1  ̄1  ̄4 )

       >\3 1 2
3   1   1            (not 3 1 0 )
```

Illustration 5.7 Applications of Scan to Binary Vectors

For $B \leftarrow 0\ 0\ 1\ 1\ 0\ 1\ 0\ 1$

1. A binary vector containing all 1s after the occurrence of the first 1 in B.

```
       ∨\B
 0  0  1  1  1  1  1  1
```

2. A binary vector containing only the first 1 from B.

```
      <\B
0 0 1 0 0 0 0 0
```

3. A binary vector containing all 1s except for a 0 matching the first occurrence of 0 in B.

```
      ≤\B
0 1 1 1 1 1 1 1
```

4. A binary vector of the running even parity on B. This is equivalent to $2|+\B$.

```
      ≠\B
0 0 1 0 0 1 1 0
```

5. One of De Morgan's laws of logic may be stated as

$\sim\vee\backslash B$ is equivalent to $\wedge\backslash\sim B$

Illustration 5.8   The Evaluation of a Mathematical Expression

The mathematical expression

$$1 + \sum_{I=1}^{4} \prod_{J=1}^{I} A_J$$

can be evaluated by the following expression:

```
A←A1, A2, A3, A4
1++/×\A
```

Illustration 5.9   Inserting Zeros in a Binary Vector

The function *INSERT* has as its right argument a vector V of nonnegative integers. *INSERT* generates a binary vector B with ρV 1s such that immediately before the Ith 1 there appears $V[I]$ 0s.

```
    ∇ B←INSERT V
[1]    I←1+V
[2]    B←(ι+/I)ϵ+\I
    ∇
```

For example,

```
      INSERT 2 0 1 3 0 2
0 0 1 1 0 1 0 0 0 1 1 0 0 1
```

Illustration 5.10   Leading Zeros

A matrix of positive digits M can be converted to a binary matrix with 0s matching the leading 0s in each row and 1s everywhere else by the expression $\lceil\backslash 0 \neq M$. For example,

```
      M
 0   1   2   3
 0   0   1   0
 0   7   0   6

      ⌈\0≠M
 0   1   1   1
 0   0   1   1
 0   1   1   1
```

Illustration 5.11   First Occurrence of an Element in a Matrix

The expression $(V=' ')\iota 1$ finds the first occurrence of a blank in the vector V. To find the column indices of the first occurrence of a blank in each row of a matrix A, the expression

```
      1++/∧\A≠' '
```

can be used. If a blank does not exist in a given row, the column index for that row is one greater than the number of columns in A. For example,

```
      A
SIGN ON
SIGN-ON
ON OFF

      1++/∧\A≠' '
5   8   3
```

PROBLEMS

1. Use the following variables to answer (a)–(c):

```
      R
 9   6   3   ⁻2   1   5   7
      T
 3   6   9   4
 1   5   8   4
 2   4   6   8
      L
 1   0   1   1   0   1   1   0   0
```

(a) For fn in the expression fn\R, substitute $+$ $\times$ $-$ $\div$ $\lceil$ $\lfloor$ and evaluate the resulting expressions.

(b) For fn in the expressions fn\$[1]T$ and fn\$T$, substitute $+$ $\times$ $-$ $\div$ $\lceil$ $\lfloor$ and evaluate the resulting expressions.

(c) For fn in the expression fn\L, substitute $\vee$ $<$ $\le$ $\ne$ $\wedge$ and evaluate the resulting expressions.

2. Evaluate expressions (a) and (b):
   (a) $\times$\5ρ3
   (b) $\wedge$\1 1 1 1 0 0 0 0 0

3. Write an expression to determine the number of leading 1s in a binary vector B.
   Test:
   $$B\leftarrow 1\ 1\ 1\ 1\ 0\ 1\ 0\ 0\ 1$$
   $$\bullet\ \bullet\ \bullet\ \bullet\ \bullet$$
   $$4$$

4. The opening discussion of Sec. 4.3.1 concerned wealthy golfers. Write an expression to determine the total amount of money that had been bet after each hole was played.

5. Write an expression to determine the row subscripts in each column of the first occurrence of the scalar C in the matrix M. If C is not found in a given column, the value returned for that column should be one greater than the number of rows in M.

6. Write an expression to generate the vector
   $$1\ ^-1\ 2\ ^-2\ 3\ ^-3\ \ldots,\ N,\ -N$$

Section 5.3   OUTER PRODUCT

The first three odd powers of 3 can be obtained with the expression

```
      3*1 3 5
3    27   243
```

Likewise the cube of the first three odd numbers can be obtained with the expression

```
      1 3 5*3
1    27   125
```

But suppose that the first three odd powers of the first three odd numbers are needed. The expression 1 3 5*1 3 5 does not produce the desired result since * is a scalar function that operates on vectors component by component, that is,

```
      1 3 5*1 3 5
1    27   3125
```

The response we are looking for can be represented as a table:

$\star$	1	3	5
1	1	1	1
3	3	27	243
5	5	125	3125

The operator for achieving such a representation is *outer product*. Its symbol is made up of the symbol $\circ$, a period, and a scalar dyadic function. The general form of outer product is

      A $\circ.\mathrm{fn}$ B

where A and B can be any arrays and fn is any primitive scalar dyadic function. The expression that produces the first three odd powers of the first three odd numbers is

```
     1 3 5∘.*1 3 5
1          1           1
3         27         243
5        125        3125
```

The result of the outer product is an array whose elements are formed by applying the scalar dyadic function fn between each element of A and each element of B. This combining is performed in an orderly fashion; that is, the first element of A is combined with every element of B, then the second element of A is combined with every element of B, and so forth until every element of A has been combined with every element of B. Hence outer product can be viewed as a table-building operator. The shape of the result of outer product is $(\rho A),\rho B$, the catenation of the shape of A with that of B. The rank of the result is $(\rho\rho A)+\rho\rho B$.

Outer product, while simple in concept, is quite powerful. For instance, it can be used to generalize an algorithm. As an example of this, consider the function CYL, which computes the volume of a cylinder given the height H and the radius of the base R:

```
     ∇ Z←H CYL R
[1]    Z←H×○R*2
     ∇
```

CYL produces the volume of a cylinder for scalars H and R. If H and R are arrays, the values of H and R are paired off and a volume exists for each H and its corresponding R. Furthermore, H and R must be conformable so that $(\rho H) = \rho R$. However, if the function CYL is defined using an outer product, it provides the volumes for each H with every R, with no conformability restrictions on the arguments:

```
     ∇ Z←H CYL R
[1]    Z←H∘.×○R*2
     ∇
```

The implications of this generalizing effect of outer product can be seen by comparing the results of the two functions:

```
      2 4 6 CYL 1 2 3          |        2 4 6 CYL 1 2 3
6.2832 50.265   169.65        |     6.2832       25.133      56.549
                               |    12.566       50.265      113.1
                               |    18.85        75.398      169.65
        4 6 CYL .5 7 9         |        4 6 CYL    .5 7 9
LENGTH ERROR                   |     3.1416       615.75      1017.9
CYL[1]  Z←H×OR*2               |     4.7124       923.63      1526.8
        ∧                      |
```

Illustration 5.12 Mathematical Tables

A three-column table such that the first column contains the integers from 1 to 9, the second column contains the square of these integers, and the third column contains the corresponding square roots is generated by the following expression:

```
        (ι9)∘.*1 2 .5
1    1   1
2    4   1.4142
3    9   1.7321
4   16   2
5   25   2.2361
6   36   2.4495
7   49   2.6458
8   64   2.8284
9   81   3
```

A table of sines, cosines, and tangents of the set of angles from 0 to $\pi/2$ in increments of 30 degrees can be generated by

```
      1 2 3∘.○○○,(ι3)÷6
0.0000E0      5.0000E⁻1  8.6603E⁻1    1.0000E0
1.0000E0      8.6603E⁻1  5.0000E⁻1    1.7439E⁻16
0.0000E0      5.7735E⁻1  1.7321E0     5.7342E15
```

Illustration 5.13 An Identity Matrix

A square N by N matrix which has 1s down the main diagonal and 0s elsewhere is generated by the expression $(\iota N)\circ.=\iota N$. For example, for a 5 by 5 identity matrix,

```
      (ι5)∘.=ι5
1 0 0 0 0
0 1 0 0 0
0 0 1 0 0
0 0 0 1 0
0 0 0 0 1
```

Illustration 5.14 Accumulating Test Values

A number of circuit chips are made on a single wafer of silicon and later separated. The chips are arranged rectangularly on the wafer in R rows and C columns. For example, if the wafer has 12 chips, they might be arranged as follows

chip	chip		
1	2	. . . .	. . . .
. . . .	. . . .	. . . .	. . . .
		chip	chip
. . . .	. . . .	11	12

Each wafer is tested chip by chip. Each chip is quality-tested in W ways, getting a value of zero to W depending on the number of tests passed. Besides each chip's actual score, one of the pieces of information desired is whether certain chips in certain positions of the wafers test consistently higher or lower than others. Thus the values given to each chip are also to be related to its position on the wafer. To achieve this the testings are accumulated in a $(W + 1)$ by R by C array CUL where the Ith plane represents I number of tests passed (from zero through W). The positions in the plane represent the chip positions on the wafer. Thus, for example, if $CUL[4;2;3]$ is 15; 15 chips in the second row, third column of the wafers passed three tests.

The function $TOTAL$ accumulates in CUL the testing on the wafer $WAFER$, an R by C matrix of the test values of the chips on the wafer:

```
      ∇ Z←CUL TOTAL WAFER
[1]     Z←CUL+(0,ιW)∘.=WAFER
      ∇
```

For example,

```
        CUL←7 3 4ρ0
        W←6
        WAFER←3 4ρ3 4 2 1 3 6 6 0 1 5 4 2
CUL←   CUL TOTAL WAFER
```

There are 1s in the following positions of CUL:

$CUL[1;2;4]$, $CUL[2;1;4]$, $CUL[2;3;1]$, $CUL[3;1;3]$, $CUL[3;3;4]$, $CUL[4;1;1]$, $CUL[4;2;1]$, $CUL[5;1;2]$, $CUL[5;3;3]$, $CUL[6;3;2]$, and $CUL[7;2;2\ 3]$

Illustration 5.15 Counting Vowels

The number of vowels in a character string can be counted with the expression $+/'AEIOU'\circ.=X$. For example,

```
        WORD←'DAFFY-DOWN-DILLY HAS COME TO TOWN'
        +/'AEIOU'∘.=WORD
2   1   1   4   0
```

Illustration 5.16   Area of a Triangle

The area of a triangle given two sides a and b and the included angle C in degrees is equal to one-half the product of the two sides and the sine of the included angle:

$$\text{Area} = \frac{ab}{2} \times \sin C$$

The set of areas for all combinations of the sides and angles can be determined by two successive applications of the outer product:

```
.5×A∘.×B∘.×1○(○C)÷180
```

The result is a rank-3 array. Each plane of the result represents all possible areas holding A constant. Each row represents all possible areas holding B constant; and each column represents all possible areas holding C constant. For example, for A and B between 1 and 5 in steps of .5 and C angles of 1 5 45 60 and 90 degrees,

```
      A←B←.5+.5×ι9
      C←1 5 45 60 90
      AREA←.5×A∘.×B∘.×1○(○C)÷180
      ρAREA
9  9  5
```

Space prohibits showing the entire result as it would appear. However, this is how the first and ninth planes look if the expression is executed on a terminal:

0.0087262	0.043578	0.35355	0.43301	0.5	⎫
0.013089	0.065367	0.53033	0.64952	0.75	⎪
0.017452	0.087156	0.70711	0.86603	1	⎪
0.021816	0.10894	0.88388	1.0825	1.25	⎪
0.026179	0.13073	1.0607	1.299	1.5	⎬ plane 1
0.030542	0.15252	1.2374	1.5155	1.75	⎪
0.034905	0.17431	1.4142	1.7321	2	⎪
0.039268	0.1961	1.591	1.9486	2.25	⎪
0.043631	0.21789	1.7678	2.1651	2.5	⎭

• • • • •

0.043631	0.21789	1.7678	2.1651	2.5	⎫
0.065447	0.32683	2.6517	3.2476	3.75	⎪
0.087262	0.43578	3.5355	4.3301	5	⎪
0.10908	0.54472	4.4194	5.4127	6.25	⎪
0.13089	0.65367	5.3033	6.4952	7.5	⎬ plane 9
0.15271	0.76261	6.1872	7.5777	8.75	⎪
0.17452	0.87156	7.0711	8.6603	10	⎪
0.19634	0.9805	7.955	9.7428	11.25	⎪
0.21816	1.0894	8.8388	10.825	12.5	⎭

Illustration 5.17 A Chessboard[*]

The following function generates a chessboard with $\frac{1}{2}$-inch squares:

```
      ∇ B←CHESSBD
[1]    B←' /'[1+(2|L(1+ι26)÷3)∘.=2|L(8+ι42)÷5]
[2]    B[1;]←B[26;]←B[;1]←B[;42]←'*'
      ∇
      CHESSBD
*******************************************
*    /////     /////     /////     /////*
*    /////     /////     /////     /////*
*    /////     /////     /////     /////*
*/////     /////     /////     /////    *
*/////     /////     /////     /////    *
*/////     /////     /////     /////    *
*    /////     /////     /////     /////*
*    /////     /////     /////     /////*
*    /////     /////     /////     /////*
*/////     /////     /////     /////    *
*/////     /////     /////     /////    *
*/////     /////     /////     /////    *
*    /////     /////     /////     /////*
*    /////     /////     /////     /////*
*    /////     /////     /////     /////*
*/////     /////     /////     /////    *
*/////     /////     /////     /////    *
*/////     /////     /////     /////    *
*    /////     /////     /////     /////*
*    /////     /////     /////     /////*
*    /////     /////     /////     /////*
*/////     /////     /////     /////    *
*/////     /////     /////     /////    *
*/////     /////     /////     /////    *
*******************************************
```

Illustration 5.18 A Histogram

A histogram graph of a numeric vector V can be generated by the function *HISTO* shown below. V is the right argument and the histogram character is the left argument.

```
      ∇ Z←SYM HISTO V
[1]    Z←(' ',SYM)[1+(⌽ιΓ/V)∘.≤V]
      ∇
```

---

[*]From SHARE*APL/360 Newsletter, No. 2, July 1969, 13.

For example,

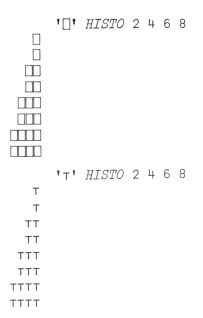

      `'□' HISTO 2 4 6 8`

      `'T' HISTO 2 4 6 8`

```
   T
   T
  TT
  TT
 TTT
 TTT
TTTT
TTTT
```

PROBLEMS

1. Use the following variables to evaluate expressions (a)–(l):

   ```
   Z←1 2 3 4 5
   Y←10 5 3 6 4
     M
   1 2 3 4
   5 6 7 8
     N
   1 2
   3 4
   5 6
   7 8
   ```

   (a) `Z∘.+M`   (b) `2 3∘.+M`   (c) `2 3∘.*¯1+Z`

   (d) `M∘.+M`   (e) `M∘.+N`   (f) `M∘.+Y`

   (g) `Z∘.>Z`   (h) `Z∘.=Z`   (i) `Z∘.≤Z`

   (j) `6|Z∘.×Z`   (k) `Y∘.⌈Z`   (l) `Z∘.⌊Z`

2. Use the following variables to evaluate expressions (a)–(m):

   ```
     A
   1 2 3
   4 5 6
     B← 1 2 3 4
     C
   1  2  3  4
   5  6  7  8
   9 10 11 12
   ```

For $R \leftarrow B \circ . + A$:

  (a) ρR

  (b) $R[1;;]$

  (c) $R[2;;]$

  (d) $R[;2;]$

  (e) $R[;;1]$

For $S \leftarrow A \circ . + B$:

  (f) ρS

  (g) $S[1;;]$

  (h) $S[2;;]$

  (i) $S[;2;]$

  (j) $S[;;1]$

For $Q \leftarrow A \circ . + C$:

  (k) ρQ

  (l) $Q[1;1;;]$

  (m) $Q[2;3;;]$

3. (a) Define a function $CREP$ to create a J by K matrix where each column is ιJ.
   Test:

$$J \leftarrow 3$$
$$K \leftarrow 4$$
$$\cdot \cdot \cdot \cdot \cdot \cdot$$

```
1 1 1 1
2 2 2 2
3 3 3 3
```

  (b) Revise $CREP$ so that each column is T.
   Test:

$$J \leftarrow 3$$
$$K \leftarrow 4$$
$$T \leftarrow 9 \quad 3 \quad 6$$
$$\cdot \cdot \cdot \cdot$$

```
9 9 9 9
3 3 3 3
6 6 6 6
```

4. Write an expression for determining which vowels V (A,E,I,O,U,Y) and how many of each appear in a given character string CS.
   Test:

$$CS \leftarrow \text{'}TWINKLE, \ TWINKLE, \ LITTLE \ STAR\text{'}$$
$$\cdot \cdot \cdot \cdot \cdot \cdot$$

```
1 3 3 0 0 0
```

5. Define a function TAB to produce a three-column table showing in the first column the integers from 1 through N; in the second column, their squares; and in the third column their square roots.

Test:

```
            N←5
            • • • • • •
    1   1   1
    2   4   1.4142
    3   9   1.7321
    4  16   2
    5  25   2.2361
```

6. Write an expression to produce a two-column kilometers-to-miles conversion table. The first column should show all kilometer values from 5 to 120 by 5s; the second column, the corresponding mile value. Round the mile values to the nearest tenth. (One mile equals 1.609 kilometers.)

7. *COST* is a vector whose components are costs per ounce of a product and *WEIGHT* is a vector of weights in ounces.
    (a) Write an expression for creating a cost-by-weight table. Such a table would provide total cost information for each size and each different price. Use the test data:

    ```
    COSTS←.015 .05 .09 .125 .23
    WEIGHTS←10 12.5 20 25.25
    ```

    (b) Write an expression for a weight-by-cost table.
    (c) Write an expression for the cost-by-weight table where weight data are given by a 2 by *N* matrix—the first row containing the amount in pounds and the second, the amount in ounces. Use the test data:

    ```
    WEIGHT←2 4ρ1 0 2 3 4 15 6 9
    ```

8. Let *N* be a matrix whose components are integers between 1 and *I*. Write an expression to determine the number of occurrences of each of these integers.

    ```
    Test:
    N←3 4ρ5 1 6 9 4 3 2 4 7 3 2 1
    I←10
    • • • • • • • • •
     2 2 2 2 1 1 1 0 1 0
    ```

9. Write an expression to determine the value of *W* for all possible combinations of given sets of values of *X*, *Y*, and *Z* in the formula

$$W = X \times Y^2 \sqrt[3]{Z}$$

Use the test data

$X \leftarrow {}^{-}2\ 2$
$Y \leftarrow 2 \times \iota 4$
$Z \leftarrow \iota 3$

10. A heat loss formula for a building is

$$\text{British thermal units per hour} = \frac{(CA + FA + WA) \times K \times TD}{I}$$

where

CA is the ceiling area in square feet
FA is the floor area in square feet
WA is the outside wall area in square feet
I is the thickness of insulation in inches
TD is the temperature difference in degrees Fahrenheit
K is the constant indicating the heat transfer of the insulation material
(for example, $K = .29$ for glass wool and $K = .22$ for styrofoam)

Define a function *HEAT* to calculate the monthly heating cost (assuming a 30-day month) for a house for all possible combinations of fuels, insulation types, insulation thicknesses, and temperature differences. (Assume that oil costs $.33 per gallon and that electricity costs $.03 per kilowatt hour; 1 gallon of oil = 100,000 British thermal units, and 1 kilowatt hour = 3414 British thermal units. Use the test data

$I \leftarrow \iota 3$
$TD \leftarrow 10 \times \iota 6$
$CA \leftarrow 1500$
$FA \leftarrow 1500$
$WA \leftarrow 3400$
$K \leftarrow .29\ .22$

11. The data rate DR of a tape drive is defined in terms of

B, the block size

G, the gap size

D, the density

S, the speed

by the formula

$$DR = \frac{S}{\dfrac{1}{D} + \dfrac{G}{B}}$$

Define a function *DR* that accepts a set of values for each of the four parameters and compute the corresponding data rates. Use the test data

```
B←1000  2500  5000
G← .3 .6
D←800 1600 2400
S←75 125 200
```

12. Most sports cars have tachometers which record the revolutions per minute of the engine.

    (a) Define a function MEQ which will, given the gear ratios in three gears, generate a table of miles-per-hour equivalents of the engine's revolutions per minute in each of the three gears. Let the revolutions-per-hour entries range from I to J in increments of X. Create the table as a revolutions-per-minute versus gears table where the miles per hour are rounded to the nearest mile. The formula to be evaluated is

    $$\text{Miles per hour} = \frac{60 \times 2\pi \times R \times \text{Revolutions per minute}}{12 \times 5280 \times GR \times AR}$$

    where R is the tire radius in inches
           AR is the axle ratio
           GR are the gear ratios

    Use the test data

    ```
    R←15
    AR←2.75
    GR←2.46 1.46 1
    I←2000
    J←6000
    X←250
    ```

    (b) Define a function REV to produce a table of miles-per-hour versus gears which yields the equivalent revolutions per minute. Let the miles per hour vary in increments of X miles per hour from I to J miles per hour. Round the resulting revolutions-per-minute values to the nearest 100. Use the test data.

    ```
    X←5
    I←5
    J←70
    ```

    (c) Modify the function REV so that it detects revolutions per minute in excess of EX and replaces them in the table by a negative 999. Use the test data

    ```
    EX←4000
    I←40
    J←120
    X←10
    ```

13. Define a function $CONV$ to convert a vector V of positive integers to a logical matrix M such that

    1. $(\rho M)=(\rho V),\lceil/V$

    2. The number of initial consecutive 1s in each row equals the corresponding component in V.

        Test:
        ```
        V←1 4 2

        . . . . . .

              M
        1 0 0 0
        1 1 1 1
        1 1 0 0
        ```

Note: This is a technique for converting decimal numbers (positive integers) to logical values and thereby saving space, since in S/360 and S/370 logical values take up 1 bit, whereas integers take 32 bits or 4 bytes. See Also Chapter 8 (Sec. 8.7.1).

14. The amount of heat H in calories conducted through a substance is defined by the equation

$$H = K \times A \times T \times DT \div L$$

   where

   K is the thermal conductivity of the substance
   A is the cross section of the substance
   L is the length of the substance
   T is the time interval of the heat flow
   DT is the temperature differential between the hot end and the cold end

The thermal conductivity coefficient K for silver is .97; copper, .92; aluminum, .50; and iron, .16. For each metal assume a uniform cross section A of 5 square centimeters and a length L of 40 centimeters.

   (a) Construct a table which states the variation in the heat flow H for the metals in the time intervals 60 to 120 seconds in steps of 10 seconds. Assume that the temperature differential is maintained at 80 degrees Celsius.

   (b) Construct a table which states the time variations for the four metals versus the temperature differences of 40 to 80 degrees Celsius in steps of 10 degrees which will produce a heat flow H of 600 calories.

15. Write an expression to produce a 1 if each component of a vector V is present in each row of a matrix M. The components of V do not have to appear in the same order in the rows of M.

   Test:

           V←2 4 1
           M←3 4ρ1 2 3 4 2 1 3 4 4 1 2 3
           ● ● ● ● ● ● ● ●
       1

16. Write an expression to determine whether all elements in a vector V are distinct. The result should be 0 if all components of V are distinct and a 1 otherwise.

   Test:

           V←9 6 3 4 5
           ● ● ● ● ● ●
       0
           V←9 6 3 4 3
           ● ● ● ● ● ●
       1

17. Write an expression to generate a square N by N matrix M such that
   (a) M has 1 down the main diagonal and 0s elsewhere.

       Test:
               N←4
               ● ● ● ● ●
       1 0 0 0
       0 1 0 0
       0 0 1 0
       0 0 0 1

(b) M is an upper triangular matrix of 0s and 1s.

    Test:

```
        N←4
        . . . . .
1 1 1 1
0 1 1 1
0 0 1 1
0 0 0 1
```

(c) M has 1s only where the sum of the indices of each component is equal to 1 plus N. This should be a matrix of 1 down the reverse diagonal and 0s elsewhere.

18. Write an expression for evaluating the following set of equations:

$$Y = \sum_{i=1}^{10} \frac{1}{i+m}$$

where $m = 1, ..., 15$.

19. Write an expression to produce an N by N lower triangular matrix, where the Ith column is defined as $((I-1)\rho 0),\iota 1+N-I$

    Test:

```
        N←4
        . . . . . .
1 0 0 0
2 1 0 0
3 2 1 0
4 3 2 1
```

20. Write an expression to produce a rank-3 N by N by N array with 1s down the main diagonal of each plane and 0s elsewhere.

21. Define a function $TABLES$ to generate the addition and multiplication tables for any given number base B less than 10. (*Hint:* Recall how to express the integral part of a number.)

    Test:

```
        B←3
        . . . . .
0    1    2
1    2   10      (addition table)
2   10   11


0    0    0
0    1    2      (multiplication table)
0    2   11
```

Section 5.4 INNER PRODUCT

    The following problem can be solved simply by reduction. A stock portfolio contains shares in three different companies. What is its total worth? If *NUM* is a vector of the number of shares in each company and *MV* is a vector of the corresponding market values of each stock, $+/MV \times NUM$ gives the total worth. For example,

```
    NUM←100    15   25
    MV←18.5  301 120.75

    +/MV×NUM
9383.75
```

But suppose, for historical reasons, that it is necessary to determine the average total worth of the stock in each of the past 4 years. Each year's average prices are collected in a 3 by 4 matrix *PRICES* where the rows represent the companies and the columns represent the years. *NUM* is a vector as previously described. While reduction can be used to solve this problem, it must be used repeatedly; that is, a reduction expression is needed for each year. For example,

```
    PRICE
  18.5     17.25    21.5     20.6
 301       285      321      331.5
 120.75   115        96       94
    +/NUM×PRICE[;1]
9383.7
    +/NUM×PRICE[;2]
8875
    +/NUM×PRICE[;3]
9365
    +/NUM×PRICE[;4]
9382.5
```

You should be familiar enough with APL by now to recognize that when a task must be performed repetitively as above, there might be a primitive function to take some of the labor out of a solution. In this case, there is—*inner product*, an operator of the form primitive scalar dyadic function, period, primitive scalar dyadic function:

$$A \ fn_2 \ \cdot \ fn_1 \ B$$

Examples of inner product with various scalar functions are

```
    +.×   ∧.∨   ⌈.×   ⌈.⌊
```

These functions are called plus-times inner product, and-or inner product, maximum-times inner product, and maximum-minimum inner product.

The solution to the average worth problem using inner product is

```
    NUM+.×PRICE
9383.7    8875    9365    9382.5
```

The execution of the inner product is basically a two-step process. First, the function fn_1 is applied to the arguments component by component. Then an fn_2 reduction is applied to the result of the first step. For matrix arguments, the left argument is operated on by rows, and the right argument, by columns. If one of the arguments is a vector and one a matrix, the vector is considered as a row or as a column depending on whether it is a left or right argument. In the example above, *NUM* is considered a row vector. Thus it combines with the columns of *PRICE*.

We have seen how the plus-times inner product can be used. As indicated earlier, any dyadic scalar functions can be used in an inner product. For example, had we wanted to know the value of the most valuable holding for each year from the example above, we could have used the expression

```
    NUM⌈.×PRICE
4515    4275    4815    4972.5
```

The illustrations at the end of this section demonstrate the use of inner product with some of the 35 × 35 (1225) combinations of functions.

The arguments of inner product may be any conformable arrays. For example, consider this problem, where the arguments are matrices:

Each of two departments within a manufacturing organization needs certain amounts of three raw materials. Their requirements are stored in a 2 by 3 matrix named *DEMAND* where the rows are departments and the columns, items. Three distributors are available from whom raw materials may be purchased. The charges that each distributor makes for each item is arranged in a 3 by 3 matrix named *SUPPLY* where the rows are items and the columns, distributors. Assuming that each department's entire requirements must be purchased from a single distributor, what are the total charges for each vendor?

A +.× inner product will solve this problem* as shown below:

	Demand		
	Item A	Item B	Item C
Dept 1	35	154	231
Dept 2	85	400	750

	Supply		
	Dist. 1	Dist. 2	Dist. 3
Item A	4.25	4	4.7
Item B	3.35	3.75	3.5
Item C	0.65	0.55	0.5

---

*+.× is the most widely used inner product. It is the same as the matrix product of matrix algebra.

```
      DEMAND+.×SUPPLY
   814.8          844.55    819
  2188.8         2252.5    2174.5
```

Notice that the 2 by 3 matrix *DEMAND* is conformable with the 3 by 3 matrix
SUPPLY. The arguments of an inner product are conformable if one of the three
following conditions is satisfied:

1. One argument is a scalar.

2. The last dimension of the left argument or the first dimension of the right
    argument is 1. Thus a 3 by 1 matrix left argument is conformable with a
    2 by 3 by 4 rank-3 array right argument. Similarly, a 2 by 3 by 4 rank-3
    array left argument is conformable with a 1 by 3 matrix right argument.

3. The last dimension of the left argument is the same as the first dimension of
    the right argument. For example, a 3 by 2 matrix left argument is conform-
    able with a 2 by 5 matrix right argument. However, a 3 by 2 matrix left
    argument is *not* conformable with a 3 by 2 matrix right argument.

A *LENGTH ERROR* results if conformability does not exist.

   The shape of the result of inner product is the catenation of all but the last dimension of the left argument with all but the first dimension of the right argument.
The rank of the result is $(\rho\rho R) = 0\lceil {}^{-}2+(\rho\rho A)+\rho\rho B$; for instance,

$\rho\rho A$	$\rho\rho B$	$\rho\rho R$
0	1	0
1	1	0
2	2	2
1	2	1
2	1	1
1	3	2
2	3	3
3	3	4

   When the ranks of the arguments are not the same, the pattern of combining is
affected by which argument has what rank. For example, a vector left argument
combines with the columns of a matrix right argument, whereas a vector right argument combines with the rows of a matrix left argument, for example, with

```
      V←3 2 1
      W←4 3 2 1
      MM←3 4ρι12
      R←V+.×MM
      R
 22    28    34    40
```

Graphically,

```
 3 2 1 +.×|1   2   3   4
 ───────→ |5   6   7   8
          |9  10  11  12
```

Each element of the result R is defined as

$$R[I] \leftarrow +/V \times M[;I]$$

On the other hand,

$$R \leftarrow MM +.\times W$$

$$R$$
20 60 100

Graphically,

```
1   2   3   4  +.× 4 3 2 1
5   6   7   8       ————————▸
9  10  11  12
   ————————▸
```

Each element of this result R is defined as

$$R[I] \leftarrow +/M[I;] \times W$$

Illustration 5.19　Locating a Word in a List

If M is a character matrix where each row contains a word, the expression $M\wedge.=W$ produces a logic vector with a 1 for each row that is identical to W. For example,

```
      M←3 4ρ'BOATCOATGOAT'
      M
BOAT
COAT
GOAT

      M∧.='COAT'
0  1  0
```

Illustration 5.20　Finding a Row of Zeros in a Matrix

Given a matrix M of data, the expression $M\vee.\neq0$ produces a binary vector where each zero indicates an all-zero row of M. For example,

```
      M
4  0  1
1  2  3
0  0  0
0  7  9

      M∨.≠0
1  1  0  1
```

The binary vectors created in Illustrations 5.19 and 5.20 can later be used either to delete such a row or to determine the row index of it.

Illustration 5.21   Resolving Illustrations 5.4(1) and 5.5

Whether you use reduction or inner product to solve problems when the arguments are vectors is a matter of personal preference. For example, illustrations 5.4(1) and 5.5 can be solved by the expressions

       $N>.>A,B$

or

       $A+.\geq B$

However, simple extensions to these illustrations make inner product the more appropriate function to use. For instance,

1. Given

        $N\leftarrow 1.75$
        R
    1 1 10 ‾4   7
  25 2 20   5 15

the expression

        $N>.>R$
  1 1 0 1 0

determines whether N lies in any of the ranges given by the columns of R.

2. Given

        B
  9 4 5 8
  1 1 5 7
      A
  2 2
  7 1
  4 6
  5 6

the expression

        $B+.\leq A$
  1 1
  2 3

determines the number of components of each column of A that dominate the corresponding components of each row of B.

Illustration 5.22   Who Knows Whom?

Consider a set of men each of whom is acquainted with some of the others. Let the logic matrix L represent who knows whom. If men I and J are acquainted, element $L[I;J]$ is 1; otherwise it is zero. Element $L[I;I]$ is necessarily 1, because we assume each man to be acquainted with himself. That a pair of men either know each other or have had an acquaintance in common can be determined by the expression

    C←LV.∧L

For example,

```
      L
  1 0 0 1 1 0 0 0
  0 1 0 0 0 1 0 1
  0 0 1 1 1 1 0 0
  1 0 1 1 1 0 1 1
  1 0 1 1 1 0 0 0
  0 1 1 0 0 1 0 0
  0 0 0 1 0 0 1 1
  0 1 0 1 0 0 1 1

     LV.∧L
  1 0 1 1 1 0 1 1
  0 1 1 1 0 1 1 1
  1 1 1 1 1 1 1 1
  1 1 1 1 1 1 1 1
  1 0 1 1 1 1 1 1
  0 1 1 1 1 1 0 1
  1 1 1 1 1 0 1 1
  1 1 1 1 1 1 1 1
```

Illustration 5.23   Meeting Demand Schedules

Departments A and B have delivery requirements on three raw components as follows:

	Demand Per Item (in Days)		
Dept A	10	6	15
Dept B	12	7	11

There are three distribution points from which delivery schedules on the three raw components can be met:

Distribution Points

	X	Y	Z
Delivery	10	8	15
schedule	5	7	6
(in days)	12	9	11

If the delivery requirements matrix is called *DEMAND* and the distribution points matrix is called *DEL*, the expression $1 \in DEMAND \wedge . \geq DEL$ determines whether any of the distribution points can meet any of the demand schedules for all the components. A 1 indicates that at least one schedule can be met and a 0 indicates that none can. The expression $DEMAND \wedge . \geq DEL$ determines a binary matrix which indicates those distribution points that can meet the various demand schedules. For example, with the matrices *DEL* and *DEMAND* defined by the tables above,

```
    1∈DEMAND∧.≥DEL
1

    DEMAND∧.≥DEL
 1  0  0
 0  1  0
```

PROBLEMS

1. Use the following variables to evaluate expressions (a)–(n):

```
    T←1 0 2
    U
0 1 2
1 2 0
2 0 1
    V
0 ‾1 ‾1
1  0 ‾1
2  1  0
    P
 7  3  2 11
 9  5  4 12
 1 12 17  8
    N
1 2
3 4
5 6
7 8
    M
1 2 3 4
5 6 7 8
```

(a) $T+.\times T$ (b) $T\wedge.=V$ (c) $V\wedge.\times V$

(d) $M+.\,|N$ (e) $(\rho T)=T+.=T$ (f) $U+.\times T$

(g) $V+.\times U$ (h) $T\wedge.>V$ (i) $T+.\times U$

(j) $U+.\times V$ (k) $N+.\times M$ (l) $V\wedge.>T$

(m) $V\vee.=U$ (n) $N+.\times P$

2. A cup of milk has 165 calories and 235 grams of calcium, and a tablespoon of cream has 50 calories and 12 grams of calcium. The ratio of milk to cream in milk is 1:0; in half-and-half, 1:1; in light cream, 1:2; and in heavy cream, 0:1. Write an expression to determine how many calories and how much calcium there is in a cup of milk, half-and-half, light cream, and heavy cream. (16 tablespoons = 1 cup)

3. Write an expression to produce a 1 if there are no duplicates in a vector V and a 0 otherwise. (This is the same as problem 17 of Sec. 5.3. This time use inner product to solve the problem.)

4. Write an expression to produce a 1 if the elements of a vector V are in ascending order, and a 0 otherwise.

     Test:

```
        V←13 16 18 35
        . . . . . . .
1
        V←13 16 11 12 18
        . . . . . . . .
0
```

5. (a) Write an expression to determine the row index of the first all-zero row in a matrix M. If the matrix has no all zero row, the expression should return the value of 1 greater than the number of rows in M.

     Test:

```
        M←3 4ρ0 1 0 5 4 3 0 2 0 0 0 0
        . . . . . . . . .
3
        N←3 4ρι12
        . . . . . . . .
4
```

(b) Write an expression to produce a binary vector where each zero indicates an all-zero column in a matrix M.

     Test:

```
        M←3 5ρ0 4 0 1 0 1 6 0 2 0 0 3 0 1 0
        . . . . . . . .
  1 1 0 1 0
```

(c) Determine the column index of the first all-zero column. If the matrix has no all-zero column, the expression should return the value of 1 greater than the number of columns in M.

     Test:

```
        With M from test (a)
        . . . . . . . .
3
        With N from test (a)
        . . . . . . .
5
```

6. PT is a two-component vector which represents the X and Y coordinates of a point on a plane. PTS is a matrix of points stated in cartesian form; each column represents a point with the first row containing the X values and the second row containing the Y values. Write an expression to determine whether PT is a member of the set of points PTS.

7. (a) A directed graph may be represented as a binary matrix. For example, the directed graph

   is equivalent to

From \ To	A	B	C	D
A	1	1	0	0
B	0	0	1	0
C	1	0	0	1
D	1	0	1	0

   Thus the matrix has a 1 wherever a path exists between the lettered nodes. Define a function $NODE$ which, when given a binary graph matrix BGM, produces another binary matrix T. The result matrix should define the nodes that may be reached from any given node by traveling along any two legs of the graph. For example, the result matrix for the above graph matrix is

```
 1 1 1 0
 1 0 0 1
 1 1 1 0
 1 1 0 1
```

7. (b) Define a function $LEGS$ which, given a binary graph matrix BGM, produces the binary matrix T defining the nodes that may be reached from any given node by traveling along any three legs of the graph. For the graph of part a, the resulting matrix is

```
 1 1 1 1
 1 1 1 0
 1 1 1 1
 1 1 1 0
```

8. The approximation of an area under a curve $f(x)$ over the interval a to b can be approximated by Simpson's rule provided that f is specified at an odd number of equidistant points n. The approximating formula is

$$A = \frac{h}{3}(f(a) + 4f(x_1) + 2f(x_2) + \cdots + 4f(x_{n-2}) + f(b))$$

where

$$h = \frac{b-a}{n-1}$$

   Note that the first and last coefficients for $f(a)$ and $f(b)$ are 1 and that all the others alternate between 4 and 2. Define a function SR which will use Simpson's rule to approximate the area under the curve $f(x)$ between points $x = a$ and $x = b$. Assume that SR accepts as arguments N, the number of evaluation points, and A and B, the range. Also, SR should assume the existence of another explicit function FX which calculates the values of $f(x)$. For example, for the function $f(x) = 3x^2$,

```
     ∇  Z←FX  X
[1]     Z←3×X*2
     ∇
```

Section 5.5 TWO FUNCTIONS THAT REPLACE COMMON OUTER AND INNER PRODUCT EXPRESSIONS

Section 5.5.1 Decode

The computation involved in answering each of the following questions is the same:

What is the decimal equivalent of the base-5 number 434?

Is 2.5 a zero of the polynomial function $6X^2 - 7X - 20$?

How many inches are there in 3 yards, 2 feet, and 4 inches?

Answering each involves the evaluation of a *polynomial function.*

A polynomial function is a function in one variable whose evaluation involves only multiplication, addition, and powers. Each term of a polynomial is the product of a constant, called a *coefficient*, and a power of the variable. The general algebraic form of a polynomial in X with coefficients arranged in descending powers of X is

$$C_n X^n + C_{n-1} X^{n-1} + \cdots + C_1 X^1 + C_0$$

There are several ways of evaluating a polynomial in APL. One way is shown in problem 6 of Sec. 2.3. Three additional ways are considered in the following paragraphs; each is shown for the evaluation at $X = 8$ of the polynomial

$$6X^3 + 7X^2 + 3X + 2$$

One way to evaluate the polynomial is to mimic the general form. Thus

```
     X←8
     (6×X*3)+(7×X*2)+(3×X)+2
3546
```

A second way of evaluating the polynomial is to use a plus-times inner product where the right argument is the vector of coefficients arranged in descending powers of X and the left argument is X raised to the appropriate powers, again arranged in descending order:

```
     (X*3 2 1 0)+.×6 7 3 2
3546
```

Both expressions shown above for evaluating a polynomial have a feature in common; namely, in each a set of products is created and then summed. This common feature underlies the primitive function *decode*, $A \perp B$, which represents a third and the most concise means of evaluating polynomials in APL. In the decode expression $A \perp B$, if A is a scalar and B is a vector, the result is the evaluation of a polynomial. A is the value for which the polynomial is to be evaluated, and B is the vector of polynomial coefficients in descending order. Thus for the above polynomial

```
      8⊥6 7 3 2
3546
```

Comparing the decode expression to the inner product expression for evaluating a polynomial shows the relationship between the two:

```
      8⊥6 7 3 2          |          (8*3 2 1 0)+.×6 7 3 2
```

With decode the powers of the variable value do not have to be stated explicitly as they do in the inner product expression. What happens during the execution of decode is that a weight vector to produce the appropriate multipliers is created. The components of the weight vector are the $(\rho B) - \iota \rho B$ powers of the left argument. This weight vector becomes the left argument of a plus-times inner product. In the example this is

```
      8*3 2 1 0
512   64   8   1
```

The decode function can be used to answer each of the questions stated at the beginning of this section. The scalar-vector use of decode discussed above can be used to answer the first two questions. To answer the first, it is necessary to know that the determination of the decimal value of a number to another base is equivalent to evaluating a polynomial. For the base-5 number 434, evaluating the polynomial

$$4X^2 + 3X + 4$$

for $X = 5$ produces the desired result. Placing a restraint on the right argument of decode that each component of it be a nonnegative integer less than the integer left argument causes the decode function to determine the decimal equivalent of a number stated in another number base. In other words, $A \perp B$ yields the decimal equivalent of a base-A number provided that the digits of the number are stated as the components of B. To find the base-10 equivalent of the base-5 number 434, then

```
      5⊥4 3 4
119
```

Note that the restraint imposed on the arguments of decode was done to achieve a particular result. The decode function places no such restraints on its arguments. It is only the user who does so.

To determine whether a value is a zero of a polynomial function, the function is evaluated at that value. If the result is 0, the value represents a zero of the function. Decode can be used to determine whether 2.5 is a zero of the polynomial $6X^2 - 7X - 20$ by evaluating the polynomial at 2.5:

```
    2.5⊥6 ‾7 ‾20
0
```

Since the value is `0`, `2.5` is a zero of the polynomial function.

Before answering the third question stated at the beginning of the section, it is necessary to consider the general form of decode. This is

```
    A⊥B
```

where `A` and `B` are arrays of any shape and rank. They are subject to the same conformability requirements as inner product: (1) The last dimension of the left argument must be the same as the first dimension of the right, or (2) one argument must be a scalar, or (3) the last dimension of the left argument or the first dimension of the right argument must be `1`.

Like the inner product, the shape of the result of decode is the catenation of all but the last dimension of the left argument with all but the first dimension of the right argument. The rank of the result `R` is `0⌈‾2+(ρρA)+ρρB`.

We have already seen that scalar-vector decode produces a polynomial evaluation. If the left argument is a vector whose components are all equal, the result is the same as if the left argument were a one-component vector or a scalar. That is, `8⊥6 7 3 2` produces the same result as `8 8 8 8⊥6 7 3 2`. If the components of the left argument differ in value, the result is a polynomial evaluation in a mixed base or *mixed radix* system. Converting yards, feet, and inches requires a mixed radix system since the relation between yards, feet, and inches is not uniform. There are 3 feet to 1 yard but 12 inches to 1 foot. An expression for converting 3 yards, 2 feet, and 4 inches to inches is

```
    1 3 12⊥3 2 4
136
```

The weight vector for the appropriate multipliers of a mixed radix evaluation can be created in the following way for a vector-vector decode expression:

```
    A←A,1
    W[I]←×/A[I+ι(ρA)-I]
```

for

```
    I∈ι(ρA)-1
```

That is, the last component of the weight vector is 1 and the Ith component of
the weight vector is the product of all but the first I components of the left argument. Thus

```
1 3 12⊥3 2 4
A←1 3 12 1

W[1]←×/A[1+ι4+1]  or  ×/3 12 1
W[2]←×/A[2+ι4-2]  or  ×/12 1
W[3]←×/A[3+ι4-3]  or  ×/1

     W
36 12 1
```

If you reexamine the general expression for a weight vector, you will see that the
first component of the left argument does not enter into its calculation. Thus
0 3 $12⊥3$ 2 4, 55 3 $12⊥3$ 2 4, and 6 3 $12⊥3$ 2 4 each produce the same
result as 1 3 $12⊥3$ 2 4.

We have used vectors and scalars for the arguments of decode. As stated in
the general form, either A or B may be arrays. If A is a scalar or vector and
B is an array, the decode evaluations are along the first coordinate of B. So,
for a matrix right argument, $R[I]$ equals $A⊥B[;I]$. To find the number of seconds
in 1 hour, 2 minutes, and 3 seconds; 2 hours, 15 minutes, and 5 seconds; and 4 hours,
21 minutes, and 45 seconds,

```
     24 60 60⊥3 3ρ1 2 4 2 15 21 3 5 45
3723   8105   15705
```

The first row of the right argument matrix is hours; the second, minutes; and the
third, seconds. One way of remembering how to arrange the data in the right
argument is to recall the relationship of decode to inner product. In an inner
product with a vector left argument and a matrix right argument, the vector
components of the left argument combine with the columns of the matrix right
argument. In decode, too, a row-by-column evaluation occurs.

Illustration 5.24 Price Comparison

A grocery store carries three brands of soap each in three sizes. The sizes
are given in pounds and ounces per brand. The price per ounce for each package
is necessary to do a cost comparison. The first step in determining the most economical purchase is to convert pounds and ounces to ounces for each of the nine
packages. Decode can be used to accomplish the conversion by arranging the data
in a 2 by 3 by 3 array WT with the first plane the pounds and the second, the
ounces. The rows are the brands; the columns, the sizes. Graphically,

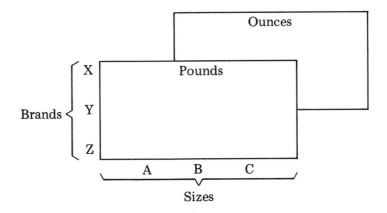

The costs are arranged in a 3 by 3 matrix COS with rows representing the brands; and columns, the sizes. The expression

$COS \div 1 \ 16 \bot WT$

produces the requested price per ounce matrix. For example, three companies market their soap in the following sizes and prices:

Brand X:

	Regular:	1 lb, 4 oz for $ .26
	Giant:	3 lb, 1 oz for $ .74
	Super King:	5 lb, 4 oz for $1.26

Brand Y:

	Regular:	13 oz for $ .35
	Giant:	2 lb, 9 oz for $ .83
	Super King:	3 lb, 6 oz for $1.35

Brand Z:

	Regular:	3 lb, 2 oz for $ .75
	Giant:	9 lb, 13 oz for $2.25
	Super King:	20 lb for $4.49

Thus:

```
    WT
 1   3   5
 0   2   3
 3   9  20

 4   1   4
13   9   6
 2  13   0
```

```
      COS
 26   74 126
 35   83 135
 75  225 449

      COS÷1 16⌊WT
1.3                1.5102        1.5
2.6923             2.0244        2.5
1.5                1.4331        1.4031
```

Illustration 5.25   Finding a Zero of a Polynomial

Suppose that we know that a zero of the polynomial

$$X^3 + 18X - 30$$

lies between 1 and 2; then decode can be used to converge on the zero. Thus

```
      (11 1ρ.9+.1×⍳11)⊥1 0 18 ‾30
‾11   ‾8.869  ‾6.672  ‾4.403  ‾2.056 0.375 2.896 5.513 8.232 11.059 14
```

By examining the result you can observe that the sign changes from negative to positive at the values corresponding to 1.4 and 1.5, thereby indicating a possible zero between those numbers. Now you can repeat the process again with a left argument of 11 1 ρ1.4:

```
      11 1ρ 1.4+0,.01+⍳10
```

for a finer resolution.

A one-column matrix was used as the left argument of decode, since it is the rows of the left argument that indicate the radices.

Illustration 5.26   Converting a Character String to a Number

A character string can be converted to a single number using decode. For example, the expression

```
      10⊥‾1+DIGITS⍳D
```

converts the character string D to a unique decimal number, where D is a character string made up of the character digits '0123456789'. For example,

```
      D←'1971'
      D
1971
      D×2
DOMAIN ERROR
      D×2
      ∧
```

```
     DIGITS←'0123456789'
     D←10⊥¯1+DIGITSιD
     D
1971
     D×2
3942
```

If the character string alphabet, the left argument of index-of, is composed of the 26 alphabetic characters, the expression

```
     26⊥¯1+ALPHABETιN
```

converts the alphabetic character string N to a decimal equivalent. For example,

```
     ALPHABET←'ABCDEFGHIJKLMNOPQRSTUVWXYZ'

     N←'CAT'
     26⊥¯1+ALPHABETιN
1371
```

Illustration 5.27   Converting a Vector Into a Single Number

Given a two-component vector V whose components are positive integers each less than $1000'$, the expression

```
     N←1000 ⊥V
```

converts V into a single number. For example,

```
     V←97 287

     1E3⊥V
97287
```

In general, for integers less than $10*N$, the expression $(10*N)⊥V$ will convert V into a single number. This can be incorporated into a function such as $CONVERT$ shown below:

```
     ∇ Z←CONVERT V
[1]    Z←(10*⌊1+10⊛⌈/V)⊥V
     ∇
```

Illustration 5.28   Replacing Scattered Elements in a Matrix

Suppose that a number of elements of a matrix need to be replaced. For example, if M is a 4 by 5 matrix, elements $M[2;3]$, $M[4;4]$, $M[3;5]$, and $M[1;3]$ may need to be replaced. The function $BUCKSHOT$ replaces elements in a matrix. The left argument is the matrix; the right argument is a matrix whose first row is the replacement elements. The second row is the row index for the replacements, and the third row is the column index for the replacements.

```
      ∇ Z←M BUCKSHOT N
[1]    Z←,M
[2]    Z[1+(ρM)⊥¯1+N[2 3 ;]]←N[1;]
[3]    Z←(ρM)ρZ
      ∇
```

In line 2, the decode function is used to convert the matrix index to the appropriate vector index. For example,

$$
\begin{array}{ccccc}
 & & M & & \\
1 & 2 & 3 & 4 & 5 \\
6 & 7 & 8 & 9 & 10 \\
11 & 12 & 13 & 14 & 15 \\
16 & 17 & 18 & 19 & 20
\end{array}
$$

$$
\begin{array}{cccc}
 & & N & \\
¯1 & ¯6 & ¯8 & ¯3 \\
2 & 4 & 3 & 1 \\
3 & 4 & 5 & 3
\end{array}
$$

$$
\begin{array}{ccccc}
 & M & BUCKSHOT & N & \\
1 & 2 & ¯3 & 4 & 5 \\
6 & 7 & ¯1 & 9 & 10 \\
11 & 12 & 13 & 14 & ¯8 \\
16 & 17 & 18 & ¯6 & 20
\end{array}
$$

*Illustration 5.29 Predicting Seats Won by a Party in the
           House of Representatives*

One of the criteria that was used in the study of the relationship between the percentage of votes gained and the number of seats won in the House of Representatives is the cube law*:

$$
Y = \frac{X^3}{3X^2 - 3X + 1}
$$

In this study, X is the percentage of the total votes that a party received and Y is the prediction of the *number of* seats won. In the 1962, 1964, and 1966 elections the Republican party had 47.5%, 42.8%, and 49.1% of the vote, respectively, and gained 177, 140, and 187 seats out of the 435 seats in the House of Representatives. The number of seats that the cube law predicts for these years is

---

*J. G. March, "Party Legislative Representative as a Function of Election Results", in *Readings in Mathematical Social Sciences*, Edited by P. F. Lozarfeld & N. W. Henry, SRA, 1966, pp. 220-241.

```
      X←.475 .428 .491
      ⌊435×(X*3)÷(((ρX),1)ρX)⊥3 ‾3 1
185   128  205
```

The floor function is used to convert the result to integer form.

Section 5.5.2 Encode

One of the uses of the decode function discussed in Sec. 5.5.1 was the determination of the decimal equivalent of a base-*N* number. At times, however, the opposite need occurs. We need to know the base-*N* representation of a decimal number. Similarly, we saw that decode could be used to convert an alphabetic character string into a unique number. At another time, however, we may need to translate a number back to a character string. The function *encode* $A \top B$ provides a means of finding the appropriate representations. Its right argument B is the value to be converted, and its left argument A is the radix.

The general form for encode is

```
      A⊤B
```

where A is an array containing the radix conversion information and B is an array containing the data to be encoded. Both A and B may be arrays of any shape and rank. The shape of the result is

```
      (ρA),ρB
```

and the rank of the result is

```
      (ρρA)+ρρB
```

For example, to find the base-5 representation of the decimal number 82,

```
      5 5 5⊤82
3  1  2
```

Or to find the character string from which the number 1371 was derived, assuming that *ALPHABET* is a character string of the alphabet,

```
R←1+26 26 26⊤1371

      R
3 1 20

      ALPHABET[R]
CAT
```

These examples illustrate the three related items of information required for converting a decimal number to its equivalent in another number base: (1) the decimal data to be encoded, (2) the base of the encoding, and (3) the number of places necessary or desired to represent the data in the new base. The last two items of information are contained in the left argument A. Consider the following sequence:

```
      5T82
2
      5 5T82
1 2
      5 5 5T82
3 1 2
      5 5 5 5T82
0 3 1 2
```

As this sequence suggests, the number of digits present for the encoding of data depends on the number of components in the left argument. While there is no conformability requirement on the arguments, an inadequate representation results if the left argument does not have a sufficient number of components, as shown in the first two examples. If the left argument contains more components than are needed for the encoding, the result is preceded by zeros, as shown in the last example. Essentially the encode function works by a repeated use of the residue function. Consider again 5 5 5T82. The computation of the solution components proceed by developing the rightmost (the least significant digit) component of the solution vector first by 5|82. The next most significant digit is computed by 5|16, where 16 is the value of ⌊82÷5, that is, the integer part of the quotient. This procedure continues until each component of the left argument has been used as a left argument of the residue function. Graphically,

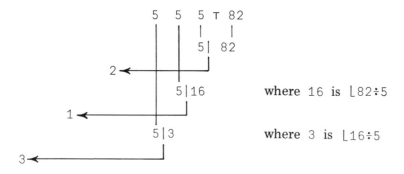

This procedure can be expressed by the outer product expression:

```
      5|⌊82∘.÷25 5 1
3 1 2
```

where 25 5 1 is a weight vector determined by

   $PLACES \leftarrow \lfloor 1 + 5 \circledast 82$

   $5 \star PLACES - \iota PLACES$
25 5 1

The expression $\lfloor 1 + R \circledast B + B = 0$ (see Illustration 4.11) is a convenient way of determining the number of components the left argument of encode must have in order
to get a complete representation of the scalar B in the base R . For example,

   $((\lfloor 1 + 5 \circledast 82) \rho 5) \top 82$
3 1 2

As with decode, the left argument of encode can indicate a mixed radix encoding. As an illustration, consider this problem:

> Mariner 4 stored picture images on magnetic tape with a storage capacity of 5
> million bits. This picture information was transmitted to the earth at the rate
> of $8\frac{1}{3}$ bits per second. How long did it take in days, hours, minutes, and
> seconds to transmit the entire tape?

This can be determined by the expression

   0 24 60 60$\top$5E6$\div$8+$\div$3
6 22 40 0

Note that the first component of the left argument in this illustration is 0 . A
zero first component has the effect of catching any overflow if the left argument
was not long enough for a complete representation. Using a zero first component is
a particularly useful device for assuring that an adequate representation will be
made with a mixed radix encoding since no simple expression exists for predeter-
mining the number of places in the result as there does for a single-base encoding.
  In the left argument 0 24 60 60 of the Mariner illustration, the rightmost
component (60) determines the number of seconds; the next rightmost (60),
the number of minutes; the next (24), the number of hours; and the 0 component (the catchall), the number of days.
  If the mariner question had been to determine the number of hours it would
take knowing that the number exceeds 24 , a zero would be used in place of 24
in the left argument; thus

   0 60 60$\top$5E6$\div$8+$\div$3
166 40 0

Had 24 been used, 144 hours would have been lost:

```
      24 60 60T5E6÷8+÷3
22 40 0
```

As we have seen, the primary form of encode is a vector left argument and a scalar right argument. However, either argument may be an array. If A is a vector and B is a vector, the result is a matrix whose Ith column is the encoding of AT$B[I]$. For example,

```
      10 10 10T124 65 83 293
   1  0  0  2
   2  6  8  9
   4  5  3  3
```

If A is a vector and B is a matrix, the first plane contains the most significant digit of the encoding of each component; the second plane, the next most significant; and so forth. Thus $R[;I;J]$ is the result of $A[I]$T$B[;J]$:

```
         N
   124      65
    82     293

      R←10 10 10TN

      ρρR
3
      ρR
3  2  2

      R
   1  0
   0  2

   2  6
   8  9

   4  5
   2  3
```

Thus
```
      R[;1;1]
1 2 4
      R[;1;2]
0 6 5
      R[;2;1]
0 8 2
      R[;2;2]
2 9 3
```

The left argument A can also be an array. It is important to note that the components for each encoding must be arranged by columns within A. The $R[;I;J]$ components are the encoded results of $A[;I]\top B[J]$, for example,

```
      M←3 2ρ8 10
      M
8   10
8   10
8   10
      R←M⊤124 65
      R
1   1
1   0

7   0
2   6

4   1
4   5
```

and

```
      R[;1;1]
1 7 4
      R[;1;2]
1 0 1
      R[;2;1]
1 2 4
      R[;2;2]
0 6 5
```

If you do not arrange the radix by columns, unanticipated results will occur. Compare the following:

```
      Q
 8    8    8
10   10   10
      Q⊤124          M⊤124
4 4 4              1 1
4 4 4              7 2
                   4 4
```

Each column of the result of $Q\top124$ is the mixed radix encoding 8 10⊤124, whereas the first column of the result of $M\top124$ is a base-8 representation of 124, and the second column is a base-10 representation of 124.

Finally, both arguments may be arrays. For example, with M and N as previously defined,

```
      R←MⳑN
      ρR
3  2  2  2
      ρρR
4

      R
  1  1
  1  4

  1  0
  0  2

  7  0
  2  4

  2  6
  8  9

  4  1
  2  5

  4  5
  2  3
```

Illustration 5.30 Breaking An Integer into a Vector of Digits

The conversion of a positive integer to a vector Z where the components represent the individual digits is accomplished by

```
Z←((1+⌊10⊛P)ρ10)ⳑP
```

If this line makes up the body of a monadic defined function with an explicit result whose header is $Z←CIV\ P$, then

```
      CIV 5678
5 6 7 8
      CIV 782
7 8 2
```

Illustration 5.31 Binary Representation

The binary scalar representation of the decimal number 13 can be obtained from the expression

```
      10⊥2 2 2 2ⳑ13
1101
```

Note that `2 2 2 2 T13` produces the binary representation `1 1 0 1` as a vector.

Illustration 5.32 Separating the Integer and Fractional Part
of a Number

A useful way of separating the integer and fractional part of a number is through the expression

        `0 1TN`

The result is a two-component vector with the first component being the integral portion of `T` and the second, the fractional. For example,

        `0  1T34.57`
`34    0.57`

        `0  1T.678`
`0     0.678`

PROBLEMS

1. Evaluate expressions (a)-(q):

   (a)   `10⌊1 9 4 6`

   (b)   `2⌊3 2 4 1`

   (c)   `1.5⌊2 7 .5`

   (d)   `3 12⌊41 11`

   (e)   `1 2 3 4⌊4 1 2 3 4`

   (f)   `6⌊2 4 5`

   (g)   `⁻3⌊1 2 0`

   (h)   `24 60 60⌊1 55 45`

   (i)   `1 ⁻2 .5⌊3 4 2`

   (j)   `3 3 3T24`

   (k)   `8 8T55`

   (l)   `3 2 4T324`

   (m)   `(4ρ3)T239`

   (n)   `(3ρ16)T1018`

   (o)   `(4ρ⁻2)T13`

   (p)   `(4ρ10)T⁻31`

   (q)   `(3ρ5)T94.5`

2. Write the expressions to evaluate polynomials (a)-(e) (written as APL expressions) for X equal to `⁻3`:

   (a)   `(5×X*3)+(⁻.2×X*2)+(17.1×X)+6`

   (b)   `(3×X*5)+(4×X*3)+13.5`

   (c)   `4+X×5+X×⁻4`

   (d)   `1+X×X×⁻2+X×X×3`

   (e)   `(3×X*⁻2)+(6×X*⁻1)+4`

3. Write the expression for converting

   (a) 14 pounds and 11 ounces to ounces.

   (b) 5 days, 12 hours, 20 minutes, and 15 seconds to seconds.

4. W is a single number representation of a two-component vector each of whose components is a positive integer less than 1000. Write an expression to convert it back to its original two-component form. (See Illustration 5.27. Note the three right most digits of W represent the second component of the two component form.)

      Test:

               $W\leftarrow356078$

               . . . . . .

      356 78

5. (a) Write an expression to separate a four-place positive integer K into a four-component vector whose components are the individual digits.

      Test:

               $K\leftarrow4312$

               . . . . . .

    4 3 1 2

   (b) Write an expression to separate the integer K into a two-component vector where the first component consists of the thousands and hundreds digits, and the second component consists of the tens and units digits.

      Test:

               $K\leftarrow2394$

               . . . .

    23 94

6. The binary vectors $L1$ and $L2$ represent binary numbers. Write an expression to form a binary vector S which is the binary sum of $L1$ and $L2$.

      Test:

            $L1\leftarrow1\ 0\ 1\ 1\ 0\ 1$
            $L2\leftarrow1\ 0\ 1\ 1$

            . . . .

            S

    0 1 1 1 0 0 0

7. (a) M is an array and $V\leftarrow,M$. For the $V[K]$ component, write an expression to find the set of indices with respect to M corresponding to the component $V[K]$.

      Test:

          $M\leftarrow2\ 2\ 2\rho2\times\iota8$
         $K\leftarrow6$

         . . . . . .

    2 1 2

   (b) IX is the set of indices of an element within an array M. Write an expression to determine the corresponding index of that element in $,M$.

      Test:

         $IX\leftarrow1\ 2\ 1$

        . . . . .

    3

8. Write an expression to convert a positive decimal integer D represented as a scalar into a binary number B represented as a scalar.

      Test:

         $D\leftarrow25$

        . . . . . .

        B

    11001

9. Write an expression to convert a character string N to a unique number. Assume $(\rho N)\leq 11$ and $\wedge/N\in\text{'}ABCDEFGHIJKLMNOPQRSTUVWXYZ\text{'}$ is a 1.

10. Define a function $NUMB$ to convert a numeric character string to its corresponding numeric value.

    Test:
    $$NCS\leftarrow\text{'}12345\text{'}$$
    $$\cdots\cdots$$
    $$12345$$

11. A Gray code binary representation of a number is a representation such that as one advances sequentially to the next number, the binary representation of it differs by only 1 bit. A commonly used Gray code is

Zero	0000
One	0001
Two	0011
Three	0010
Four	0110
Five	0111
.	.
.	.
.	.

    To encode a decimal number into Gray code, first convert it into binary. Then combine each bit of the binary code with the next highest bit such that the output is 1 only when the pair of bits are not the same. For example, for 45,

    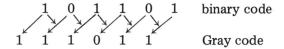

    1   0   1   1   0   1   binary code

    1   1   1   0   1   1   Gray code

    Define a function $GRAY$ which will accept a decimal integer and produce the corresponding Gray code representation. *Note:* The leftmost bit of binary code and Gray code will agree.

12. Define a function $ORDER$ to perform an upgrade-like function on the matrix M. The result should be a 2 by $\times/\rho M$ matrix whose Ith column is the row and column index of the Ith smallest component of M.

    Test:
    $$M\leftarrow2\ 3\rho 9\ 6\ 3\ 2\ 8\ 5$$
    $$\cdots\cdots$$
    $$\begin{array}{cccccc} 2 & 1 & 2 & 1 & 2 & 1 \\ 1 & 3 & 3 & 2 & 2 & 1 \end{array}$$

13. For a polynomial equation

    $$Y = A_1 x^n + A_2 x^{n-1} + A_3 x^{n-2} + \cdots + A_{n+1}$$

whose coefficients are A, define a function $YVAL$ to determine the values of Y for a given set of values X.

    Test:

    For the cubic equation $Y = 2x^3 + .5x^2 - 12$,

```
        X←ι5
        A←2 0.5 0 ¯12
        . . . . . . . . .
    ¯9.5 6 46.5 124 250.5
```

Section 5.6   TWO MATRIX FUNCTIONS

The matrix inverse and matrix divide functions discussed in this section appear in mathematically oriented applications, such as the determination of currents in an electrical network.

Section 5.6.1   Matrix Inverse

In the real number system, the reciprocal of a scalar quantity, say 5, can be found by executing the APL expression $\div 5$. The reciprocal of a given number is the number which when multiplied by that number yields 1. In algebraic terminology this number is called the *multiplicative inverse*. In linear algebra, where the basic element is not the single number but the matrix, a similar situation exists. A multiplicative inverse of a given matrix is a matrix which when multiplied* by the given matrix yields the identity matrix. An identity matrix is a matrix with 1s down the main diagonal and 0s elsewhere.

The identity matrix plays the same role in linear algebra as the number 1 does in the real number system; both are multiplicative identity elements. Unlike the real number system where every real number except zero has a multiplicative inverse, a reciprocal, not every matrix has an inverse. Matrices which do not have inverses are called *singular* matrices; matrices which have inverses are called *non-singular* matrices.

Various numeric methods have been developed for determining the inverse of a matrix, which is not so simple an arithmetic function as finding the reciprocal of a scalar. In APL finding the inverse of a matrix has been simplified by the introduction of the primitive function inverse. Its syntax is

    $\boxminus A$

where A must be of rank 2 or less ($2 \geq \rho\rho A$) and if A is a matrix, the columns of A must be linearly independent.†

------

*Recall that the multiplication of two matrices together is accomplished through a series of products and sums carried out upon the proper matrix components. In APL, this is a plus-times inner product.

†In APL/360 the requirements are that A must be a matrix ($2 = \rho\rho A$) and the columns of A must be linearly independent. If the number of columns of A exceeds the number of rows of A, which implies columnar dependency, APL/360 produces a *LENGTH ERROR* report.

If A is a nonsingular square matrix then, ⌹A is the inverse of A. For example,

```
      A
 ‾0.5   0.2  ‾1.6
 0      0.2   0.4
 0.5    0     1
```

```
       ⌹A
   2  ‾2   4
   2   3  ‾2
  ‾1   1  ‾1
```

To verify the inverse, matrix-multiply:

```
     (⌹A)+.×A
  1.0000E0      8.3267E‾17  ‾4.4409E‾16
 ‾3.3307E‾16   1.0000E0     ‾4.4409E‾16
  1.6653E‾16  ‾6.9389E‾17    1.0000E0
```

Recall that numbers with an exponent of ‾16 or smaller are rather small numbers.
In APL they should be considered as approximating zero. The display in exponential notation can be avoided by applying the floor function to the matrix product.
For example,

```
      ⌊(⌹A)+.×A
  1  0  0
  0  1  0
  0  0  1
```

The argument does not have to be a square matrix, but it must have more rows
than columns; otherwise a *DOMAIN ERROR* report is given. If A is a nonsquare
matrix such that ρA is J,K with $J>K$, the result $M←⌹A$ is a matrix which minimizes the expression

$$+/(,ID-A+.×M)*2$$

ID is the J by J identity matrix. With $(ρA)$ equal to (J,K) and $M←⌹A$,
$(ρM)$ is (K,J). The matrix M is a *left* inverse of A; that is $M+.×A$ produces
a K by K identity matrix. For example,

```
      C
 ‾0.5   0.2  ‾1.6
 0      0.2   0.4
 0.5    0     1
 1      2     1
```

```
      ⊟C
  0.6    ¯3.4     2.04    0.28
  0.05    1.05   ¯0.73   ¯0.39
 ¯0.65    1.35   ¯0.51   ¯0.07

      (⊟C)+.×C
 1.0000E0     ¯1.3878E¯16   2.2621E¯15
 1.1883E¯16    1.0000E0    ¯7.2164E¯16
 1.3878E¯16    1.3878E¯16   1.0000E0

      ⌈(⊟C)+.×C
 1  0  0
 0  1  0
 0  0  1
```

The argument A of ⊟A may also be a vector or a scalar. If A is a vector, it is treated as a one-column matrix (never as a one-row matrix, as this would violate the requirement that the columns of a matrix be independent). For example,

```
      V←⍳5

      ⊟V
0.018182  0.036364  0.054545  0.072727  0.090909
```

If A is a scalar, it is treated as a 1 by 1 matrix. For the scalar argument S, the expression ⊟S is equivalent to ÷S. For example,

```
      ⊟5
.2

      ÷5
.2
```

If A is of rank greater than 2, a *RANK ERROR* report is given.

Illustration 5.33   Inverting a Very Large Matrix

If a matrix M is too large to invert in the work space, its inverse may be achieved by subdividing or partitioning it into smaller submatrices each of which may be inverted. Let M be an R-square matrix whose inverse N is desired. Consider M and N to be partitioned into submatrices as follows:

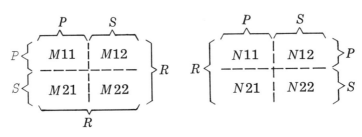

The determination of the submatrices of the inverse N is given by the equations

$$N11 = Q_1{}^{-1}$$
$$N22 = Q_2{}^{-1}$$
$$N21 = -M11^{-1} \times M21 \times Q_1{}^{-1}$$
$$N12 = M11^{-1} \times M12 \times Q_2{}^{-1}$$

where

$$Q_1 = M11 - M12 \times M22^{-1} \times M21$$

$$Q_2 = M22 - M21 \times M11^{-1} \times M12$$

The function $FN11$ computing the submatrix $N11$ is

```
     ∇ Z←FN11
[1]     Z←⌹M11-M12+.×(⌹M22)+.×M21
     ∇
```

The other submatrices can be computed similarly.
To demonstrate the function $FN11$ consider the matrix

```
      M
4   8   2   1
1   5   3   8
2   7   1   4
3   8   2   1
```

whose inverse is

```
      IM←⌹M
      IM
 1.0000E0    ¯8.1079E¯17   4.0540E¯17  ¯1.0000E0
¯3.5227E¯1   ¯7.9545E¯2    1.4773E¯1    3.9773E¯1
¯1.7045E¯1    2.8409E¯1   ¯6.7045E¯1    5.7955E¯1
 1.5090E¯1    6.8182E¯2    1.5909E¯1   ¯3.4091E¯1

      ⌊M+.×IM
1   0   0   0
0   1   0   0
0   0   1   0
0   0   0   1
```

If one partitioned M as follows,

```
      M
4   8 | 2   1
1   5 | 3   8
─────────────
2   7 | 1   4
3   8 | 2   1
```

then

```
      M11
 ι   8
 1   5

      M12
 2   1
 3   8

      M21
 2   7
 3   8

      M22
 1   4
 2   1
```

and

```
      FN11
 ‾1.0000E0      ‾5.2988E‾17
 ‾3.5227E‾1     ‾7.9545E‾2
```

Section 5.6.2 Matrix Division

Matrix division is used to solve systems of linear equations. Its general form is

$$N⊟M$$

where the left argument N may be a vector or a matrix, and the right argument M must be a matrix.

A relationship exists between the solution of the single equation $ax = b$ and the solution for the set of equations $Ax = B$. The solution of the single linear equation is $B÷A$. The solution of the set of equations is $B⊟A$. Thus consider the set of three simultaneous linear equations

$$4W + \ \ Y + 2Z = 16$$
$$W + 2Y + 5Z = 12$$
$$W + 3Y + \ \ Z = 10$$

The solution vector S for the set of equations is

$$S ← B⊟A$$

where B is the vector of *constants* and A is the matrix of coefficients of the unknowns in the three equations:

```
      B
 16   12   10
```

```
      A
4   1   2
1   2   5
1   3   1
```

Then

```
     S←B⊟A
     S
3 2 1
```

As a check $A+.×S$ should equal B :

```
     A+.×S
16 12 10
```

The expression

```
     S←B⊟A
```

is executed if

1. The first dimensions of A and B are equal.
2. The columns of A are linearly independent.

The solution vector S produced by $B⊟A$ is developed to minimize the least-squares expression $+/,(B-A+.×S)*2$.

  The left argument B may be a matrix. The shape of the result S is the same as the shape of B . For example,

```
      A
4   1   2
1   2   5
1   3   1
```

```
      B
16  1
12  2
10  3
```

```
     B⊟A
3.0000E0   4.9179E¯17
2.0000E0   1.0000E0
1.0000E0   1.2162E¯16
     ⌊B⊟A
3   0
2   1
1   0
```

Each column of the solution matrix is the solution of a set of simultaneous equations whose coefficients are given by the matrix A and constant values by the corresponding column of B. For example, $(B \boxminus A)[\;;1]$ is identical to $16\ \ 12\ \ 10 \boxminus A$.

If B is an identity matrix, the expression $B \boxminus A$ is equivalent to $\boxminus A$. When A and B are scalars, $B \boxminus A$ is equivalent to $B \div A$, except that $0 \boxminus 0$ is a *DOMAIN ERROR* not 1.

Several error situations may occur with matrix division. Both arguments must be of rank 2 or less; otherwise a *RANK ERROR* report is given. If the first dimensions of A and B are not equal, a *LENGTH ERROR* report is given; and if the columns of A are not linearly independent, a *DOMAIN ERROR* report is given.

Illustration 5.34   Determining Currents in an Electrical Network

Simultaneous linear equations arise in the determination of the currents in an electrical network. Consider the following electrical network:

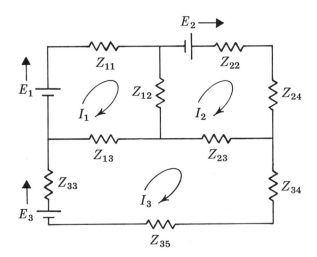

where Z_{ij} are impedances, E_i are voltage sources, and I_i are the loop currents to be determined. The determination of the I_i current values for this network results from the solution of this set of simultaneous linear equations:

$$Y_{11}I_1 + Y_{12}I_2 + Y_{13}I_3 = E_1$$
$$Y_{21}I_1 + Y_{22}I_2 + Y_{23}I_3 = E_2$$
$$Y_{31}I_1 + Y_{32}I_2 + Y_{33}I_3 = E_3$$

where

$$Y_{ii} = \sum_{j=1}^{N} Z_{ij}$$

where N is the number of impedances directly in the Ith current loop. Also notationally assume that $|Z_{ij}| = |Z_{ji}|$.

$$Y_{ij} = Z_{ij} \quad \text{or} \quad -Z_{ij}$$

where the sign is positive if both I_i and I_j flow in the same direction through Z_{ij}. Otherwise the sign is negative. Thus for the illustrated circuit:

$$Y_{11} = Z_{11} + Z_{12} + Z_{13}$$
$$Y_{22} = Z_{21} + Z_{22} + Z_{23} + Z_{24} \quad \text{(Recall } |Z_{12}| = |Z_{21}|.\text{)}$$
$$Y_{33} = Z_{31} + Z_{32} + Z_{33} + Z_{34} + Z_{35}$$
$$Y_{12} = -Z_{12}$$
$$Y_{13} = -Z_{13}$$
$$Y_{23} = -Z_{23}$$

Then with

$$Z_{11} = Z_{22} = Z_{24} = Z_{34} = 1,$$
$$Z_{13} = 0$$
$$Z_{12} = Z_{23} = 9$$
$$Z_{35} = 2$$
$$Z_{33} = 3,$$

the coefficients Y_{ij} are

```
       Y
 10   ¯9    0
 ¯9   20   ¯9
  0   ¯9   15
```

and the voltages were

```
       E
100  0  0
```

then the solution currents I are given by the expression

```
    I←E ⊟ Y
    I
22.462 13.846 8.3077
```

Illustration 5.35   Least-Squares Curve-Fitting

Least-squares curve-fitting is concerned with producing a functional representation of a set of data given as sets of points. This is done by approximating, in a

least-squares sense, the data with a curve of a known functional form. The approximations are in a least-squares sense if the sum of the squares of all the deviations is
minimum, where a deviation is the difference between a data point P and the value
P' computed from the approximating function. For example, if we choose to fit
the data by means of a quadratic equation,

$$Y = C_1 + C_2 X + C_3 X^2$$

it is necessary to determine the values of the coefficients C_1, C_2, and C_3. Suppose
that X_i, Y_i are the rectangular coordinates for the data points P_i where Y is a function of X. If the 2 by N matrix M represents the set of data points P where the
first row contains the X coordinates and the second, the Y coordinates, the following function determines the coefficients of a quadratic equation fitting the data in
a least-squares sense:

```
      ∇ Z←QUADFIT M
[1]   Z←M[2;]⊞M[1;]∘.*0 1 2
      ∇
      M
 ⁻0.9    ⁻0.5    0     1     1.5    2      3
  8.8     6.8    4.99  3.05  2.8    2.94   5.08

      QUADFIT M
5.0641 ⁻3.1164 1.0411
```

Illustration 5.36   Coefficients of the Equation of the Plane

   Three noncollinear points in 3-space determine a plane. With these three points,
the coefficients A, B, and C of the equation for the plane

$$Ax + By + Cz = 1$$

can be determined. Let PT be a 3 by 3 matrix of points where each row contains
the x, y, and z coordinates of a point. The coefficients PC of the equation for the
plane can be determined by the expression

```
      PC←1 1 1⊞PT
```

For example,

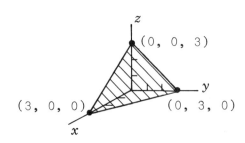

```
      PT
 3   0   0
 0   3   0
 0   0   3

      1 1 1⊞PT
0.33333 0.33333 0.33333
```

Illustration 5.37   A Forecast Equation

An approximating equation can be determined from a table of several types of inputs and their corresponding output by using matrix division. For example, consider *DATA* as the matrix in which the first three columns represent inputs *IN*1, *IN*2, and *IN*3 and the fourth column represents the observed output:

```
      DATA
 75   25   90   37
 62   24   87   28
 62   24   93   19
 58   17   88   13
 50   18   89    8
 62   20   82   15
 70   20   91   15
```

The following expression generates the coefficients of the approximating equation:

```
      COEFS←DATA[;4]⊞1,DATA[;ι3]
      COEFS
⁻16.955 0.42524 2.154 ⁻0.4061
```

Therefore the approximating equation is

$$OUTPUT = ⁻16.96 + .42IN1 + 2.15IN2 - .41IN3$$

The predicted output may be compared against the actual output as follows:

```
      PRED←(1,DATA[;ι3])+.×COEFS
      ACTUAL←DATA[;4]
      ACTUAL
37 28 19 13 8 15 15

      PRED
32.238 25.774 23.338 8.5894 6.9354 19.189 18.936
```

PROBLEMS

1. Write an expression to find the inverse of
   (a) $P\leftarrow 3\ 3\rho\ ^-1\ 4\ 5\ 0\ 2\ ^-3\ 0\ 0\ 8$
   (b) $Q\leftarrow 4\ 4\rho 4\ 8\ 2\ 1\ 1\ 5\ 3\ 8\ 2\ 7\ 1\ 4\ 3\ 8\ 2\ 1$

2. Write an expression to solve the following sets of equations:
   (a) $x + 2y + 2z = 1$ (b) $2x + z = 4$
       $2x + 2y + 3z = 3$ $x - 2y + 2z = 7$
       $x - y + 3z = 5$ $3x + 2y = 1$

3. Define a function EQ that accepts a set M of three points in 3-space and returns the coefficients of the equation of the plane, $Ax + By + Cz = 1$, determined by them.

   Test:

   $M\leftarrow 3\ 3\rho 2\ 0\ 0\ .5\ 1\ 0\ 1\ 1\ 1$ (each row of M represents a point)
   $\cdot\ \cdot\ \cdot\ \cdot\ \cdot$
   $0.5\ \ 0.75\ \ ^-0.25$

4. Given a set of values for x and the corresponding values for Y which are known to be the result of evaluating a cubic polynomial, define a function CF to determine the coefficients A, B, C, and D of the original equation

   $$Y = Ax^3 + Bx^2 + Cx + D$$

   Test:

   $X\leftarrow \iota 5$
   $Y\leftarrow\ ^-9.5\ 6\ 46.5\ 124\ 250.5$
   $\cdot\ \cdot\ \cdot\ \cdot\ \cdot\ \cdot$
   $2\ 0.5\ \ ^-1.2576E^-13\ \ \ 12$ (Here C is effectively zero so the equation
   is $2x^3 + .5x^2 - 12$)

5. The distance E from a plane $Ax + By + Cz = 1$ to a given point $P1$, (x_1, y_1, z_1), is given by the formula

   $$E = \frac{\pm Ax_1 + By_1 + Cz_1 - 1}{\sqrt{A^2 + B^2 + C^2}}$$

   where if the radical is given the sign of C, E is plus or minus according to whether $P1$ is above or below the plane. Define a function $DIST$ to provide the distance between a given point $P1$ and a plane as determined by three points M.

   Test:

   $M\leftarrow 3\ 3\rho\ 0\ 0\ .5\ 1\ 0\ 1\ 1\ 1$ (each row of M represents a point)
   $P1\leftarrow 3\ 4\ 1$
   $\cdot\ \cdot\ \cdot\ \cdot\ \cdot\ \cdot\ \cdot$
   $^-3.4744$

6. Given that the coordinate axes are rotated through an angle of α degrees, the following pair of equations relate the x and y coordinates of a point with respect to the original axes to the x' and y' coordinates with respect to the rotated axes:

   $$x = x'\cos\alpha - y'\sin\alpha$$
   $$y = x'\sin\alpha + y'\cos\alpha$$

   Define a function ROT that accepts the angle of rotation in degrees and the x and y coordinates and returns the x' and y' coordinates with respect to the rotated axes.

Section 5.7   SUMMARY

In Chapter 5 we continued the presentation of APL primitive functions, concentrating mainly on extensions to the use of the scalar dyadic functions, and introduced a new function concept—the axis-specifier.

Axis-specifier

The axis-specifier is an integer or an expression that results in an integer placed within square brackets to the immediate right of the function symbol, for example, $+/[2]A$. This integer refers to the coordinate of the array argument along which the function is to be performed. Reduction and scan, use an axis-specifier. Other functions using an axis-specifier are discussed in Chapter 7.

No axis-specifier indicates that the function operates along the last coordinate; for example, $+/A$ and $+/[\rho\rho A]A$ are equivalent expressions. An alternative means of indicating the axis-specifier if it is the first coordinate along which the function is to be performed is to overstrike the function symbol with a $-$ symbol. For example, $+\neq A$ and $+/[1]A$ are equivalent expressions.

Functions Introduced in Chapter 5

The following table summarizes the functions introduced in this chapter:

Function	Syntax	General Description	Right Argument	Left Argument	Axis-specifier	Conformability	Shape and Rank of Result
Reduction	fn /[I]A	Any scalar function can replace fn; places fn between adjacent components of Ith coordinate of argument and executes resulting expression; fn reduction of the empty vector produces the identity element of the function fn, if one exists	Data array of any shape and rank	None	Dimension along which reduction occurs		Shape: Same as ρA except that the Ith component is eliminated; Rank: $0\lceil^-1+\rho\rho A$
Scan	fn \[I]A	Any scalar function can replace fn; places fn between successively additional components of the Ith coordinate of the argument and that result makes up each successive component of the result	Data array of any shape and rank	None	Dimension along which scan occurs		Shape: ρA; Rank: ρρA
Outer product	A∘.fnB	Builds array by applying the scalar dyadic function fn between each element of A and B	Data array of any shape and rank	Data array of any shape and rank			Shape: (ρA),ρB; Rank: (ρρA)+ρρB
Inner product	Agn.fnB	Applies scalar dyadic function fn to the arguments component by component; then performs a gn reduction on that result	Data array of any shape and rank	Data array of any shape and rank		1. A or B is a scalar 2. ((ρA)[ρρA]=1 ∨(ρB)[1]=1 3. (ρA)[ρρA]= (ρB)[1]	Shape: $(\rho A)[\iota^-1+\rho\rho A]$, $(\rho B)[1+\iota\ 1+\rho\rho B]$; Rank: $0\lceil^-2+(\rho\rho A)+\rho\rho B$
Decode	A⊥B	Evaluates a polynomial function for radix A whose coefficients B are arranged in order of descending powers of the base	Data array of coefficients; may be any shape and rank	Data array of radices; may be any shape and rank		Same as inner product above	Same as inner product above
Encode	A⊤B	Finds a representation of the decimal value B in the radix system A	Data to be converted; may be any shape and rank	Radix conversion information; data array of any shape and rank; (ρA) = the number of places desired to represent the data in the new radix			Shape: (ρA),ρB; Rank: (ρρA)+ρρB
Matrix inverse	⌹A	Finds the multiplicative inverse of a nonsingular matrix	Must have rank 2 or less				Shape: Same as ρA with its components reversed. Rank: A matrix
Matrix divide	A⌹B	Solves systems of linear equations where B is a matrix of coefficients and A is a vector or matrix of constants	1. Must be of rank 2 or less. 2. (≥/ρB)=1 3. Has at least as many linearly independent rows as it has columns.	A vector or matrix		(ρA)[1]= (ρB)[1]	Shape: (ρB)[2], (ρA)[ρρA]; Rank: ρρA

CHAPTER 6

ADDITIONAL TECHNIQUES AND CAPABILITIES OF DEFINING FUNCTIONS

As we have seen, the defined function allows the user to write functions to meet his particular requirements. The range of problems solvable by defining functions can be further extended by additional defining techniques. Foremost among these are branching and output-formatting. *Branching* makes it possible to alter the sequential execution of statements so that repetitive calculations can be dealt with efficiently and so that special cases of a general solution can be handled. *Output-formatting* makes it possible to control the way data print so that reports and charts can be printed in any specified form.

Section 6.1 BRANCHING

Suppose that a survey of library usage is taken at a university and that a function is defined to summarize the results. If a summary is wanted that reflects the library usage of the students in each of the five colleges at the university, the summarizing procedure will be repeated five times, once for each college. Moreover, if the survey has some questions that are answered only by library users, the responses to these questions will have to be processed separately. The way that a defined function can handle the problems of repeating the execution of a set of statements several times or of executing one or the other of a set of statements is by using *branching* in the function definition.

Branching—as indicated by the branch statement—alters the sequential order of execution in a defined function either by directing that a line other than the next sequential one be executed or by terminating the execution before all its statements are executed. The syntax of the branch statement is

→EXPRESSION

The right-pointing arrow → is the branch symbol. It is followed by an expression whose value determines the next action taken. The relationship between the

227

allowable values of the branch expression and the action taken is shown in the table below:

Value of Expression	Action
1. A scalar positive integer I or a vector whose first component I is a positive integer	
(a) If I is less than or equal to the number of statements in the function	Statement I is the next statement to be executed in the function
(b) If I is greater than the number of statements in the function	Function execution terminates
2. A scalar zero or a vector whose first component is zero	Function execution terminates
3. An empty array	The next sequential line is executed—in other words, no branch takes place*

*In programming nomenclature, this is similar to an NOP (no operation) instruction.

To illustrate how a branch expression affects the execution of a function, suppose that a function has been defined that presents several types of problems to a student. His answer determines the kind of message he receives. After the message is given, the problem presentation continues unless the allocated time is up. The messages are collected near the end of the function. After the proper message is displayed, there is a branch back to the problem part of the function unless the message is 'TIME UP' in which case execution of the function terminates. This part of the function looks like this:

```
   .        .
   .        .
   .        .
[15]    'GOOD. NOW WE WILL TRY ANOTHER KIND OF PROBLEM'
[16]    →7
[17]    'NO. TRY THE PROBLEM ONCE MORE'
[18]    →3
[19]    'TIME UP'
[20]    →0
   .        .
   .        .
   .        .
```

Lines 16, 18, and 20 are branch statements directing the execution of the function. Line 16 says "execute line 7 next"; line 18 says "execute line 3 next"; and line 20 is a branch to a line number not in the set of line numbers of the function and so terminates execution of the function.

Whenever line 16, 18, or 20 is executed, the branch to the specific line indicated occurs unconditionally. It happens more often, however, that a branch to certain statements is needed only when a particular condition or set of conditions is met. The branch form that accomplishes this is known as a *conditional branch* statement. The condition is usually expressed by a relationship whose value is 0 if false and 1 if true.

The function *YEARS* of Illustration 4.13 for determining when two principals invested at two different rates converge is a good example since the amounts do not converge unless principal 1 is less than principal 2 *and* rate 1 is greater than rate 2. If these conditions do not hold, the function produces meaningless results. Line 1 of the function *YEARS2* shown below checks to make sure that the conditions are met before executing the function. If the conditions are not met, execution terminates. Lines 2 and 3 of *YEARS2* are the same as lines 1 and 2 of *YEARS*.

```
     ∇Z←A YEARS2 B
[1]    →2×∧/1 0=A<B
[2]    N←(⊛A÷B)[1]÷⊛((1+.01×B)÷1+.01×A)[2]
[3]    Z←N,A[1]×(1+.01×A[2])*N
     ∇
```

The vector A is a two-component vector made up of the first principal and the first rate; the vector B is a two component vector made up of the second principal and the second rate.

One of two paths is followed depending on the value of the expression in line 1.

	Result	
	Path 1	Path 2
Relationship: ∧/1 0=A<B	1 (both conditions for convergence hold)	0 (one or both conditions for convergence do not hold)
Branch value: 2×∧/1 0=A<B	2	0
Next line executed	2	Execution terminates

If principal 1 ($A[1]$) is less than principal 2 ($B[1]$) *and* rate 1 ($A[2]$) is greater than rate 2 ($B[2]$), line 2 is executed because line 1 is →2; the amounts will converge. If one or the other condition is not met, execution terminates because line 1 is →0. The form of branch statement used in *YEARS2* for executing a line or terminating function execution is

→line number × relationship

This form of branch is often used if a meaningful execution of a function depends on certain conditions existing.

Sometimes different lines within the function are to be executed based on some relationship. For example, the function *FCN1* cubes its argument if it is negative and doubles it if it is nonnegative:

```
    ∇ Z←FCN1 N
[1]    →(0>N)ρ4
[2]    Z←N×2
[3]    →0
[4]    Z←N*3
    ∇
```

For example,

```
    FCN1 ‾5
‾125
    FCN1 10
20
```

Line 1 is the branch statement that does this. Again, one of two paths is followed depending on the value of the branch expression:

	Result	
	Path 1	Path 2
Relationship: (0>N)	0 (N is nonnegative)	1 (N is negative)
Branch expression: (0>N)ρ4	empty	4
Next line executed:	2	4

The consequences of line 1 are either that lines 2 and 3 are executed if *N* is nonnegative, or line 4 is executed if *N* is negative. Note the unconditional branch to 0 at line 3. This prevents line 4 from being executed if *N* is nonnegative.

The form of branch statement used in *FCN1* for executing alternative lines within a function is

→ (relationship) ρ line number

This form of branch is quite common. Some users like to define an *IF* function based on it to use for branching when the relationship has a scalar result:

```
      ∇ Z←A IF B
[1]     Z←BρA
      ∇
```

Then the branch statement on line 1 of $FCN1$ would be

```
[1]    →4 IF 0>N
```

There are many other ways of creating a branch expression for executing alternative lines in a function. For instance, multiplication and monadic iota can be used. Line 1 of $FCN1$ using $\times\iota$ would be

```
[1]    →4×ι0>N
```

The general form of this branch statement is

    → line number $\times\iota$ relationship

$\times\iota$ can be read IF.

Or a branch statement can be written using indexing. In this case line 1 of $FNC1$ would look like

```
    [1] →2 4[1+0>N]
```

Then if N is negative, the index value is 2 and the next line executed is 4. If N is nonnegative, the index value is 1 and the line 2 is the next line executed. This form is particularly good if neither of the lines to be executed is the one following the branch statement. This could occur in a case like the problem example discussed earlier where messages were collected near the end of the function. Indexing can also be used to cause branching to more than two different lines. For example, C might be a counter that is incremented during the execution of the function. Then, a branch statement using C could be

```
    C←C+1
    →3 6 9 13 0[(ι4)ιC]
```

When C exceeds 4, function execution terminates.

The dyadic function $APRIN$ shown below computes accrued principal for the first year to the last based on the formula

$$\text{new principal} = \text{principal} + \text{principal} \times \text{rate}$$

The argument X is the vector (principal, rate); the argument Y is the vector (starting year, final year):

```
      ∇ Z←X APRIN Y;I
[1]    Z←X[1]
[2]    I←1
[3]    Z←Z×1+X[2]×.01
[4]    →3×(|-/Y)≥I←I+1
      ∇
```

For example,

```
      100 5 APRIN 1968 1971
115.76
```

Line 3 of *APRIN* is repeated again and again until the *counter* (variable *I*) is greater than the difference between the starting year and ending year.

The use of conditional branching in *APRIN* differs from that of previous examples. In those examples, the conditional branch produced a one-time branch where the branch was based on choosing which execution path to follow. This type of branch is sometimes called a *decision branch*. In *APRIN* the branch statement produces a many-time branching (as long as $1≤|-/Y$). This type of branch is called an *iterative* branch or *loop*. With looping, one of the execution paths turns back to the execution of former statements, thus causing repeated executions of a set of statements. Decision branching and looping can be illustrated graphically as follows:

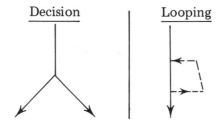

Decision branching is represented by a fork in the road; looping is represented as a turning in on itself.

Iterative branching is most often accomplished by incrementing or decreasing a counter until a desired limit is reached. The counter is usually a local variable since it serves a purpose only within the defining function. The counter has to be initialized to some value, usually 0 or 1 if it is being incremented and a maximum if it is being decreased. Often the counter can be incremented (or decreased) on the branch line as illustrated by the following three examples:

```
      →5×10≥I←I+1
      →5×0≤I←I-1
      →3 6 9 13 [C←C+1]
```

There is one danger associated with a function that has branching, especially looping, and that is the danger of an *endless loop*. As an example of an endless loop, consider the function *TRIAL*:

```
       ∇ Z←TRIAL X
[1]    Z←⍳0
[2]    I←1
[3]    Z←Z,X÷I
[4]    →(10≥I←I+1)⍴2
       ∇
```

The branch statement at line 4 directs the execution to line 2 instead of line 3. As a result *I* is always respecified to 1, and the loop exit condition in the branch is never met. *TRIAL*, then, has an endless loop.

    TRIAL is a particularly insidious function with an endless loop since there is no output within the function to suggest that there is an endless loop. The only way to detect this endless loop is to get tired of sitting in front of a locked terminal and to hit ATTN to interrupt execution. The use of ATTN always interrupts the execution of an APL expression regardless of whether it has just been entered or is a part of a defined function being executed. The function name and the number of the line that was being executed when ATTN was struck are printed. After the keyboard is released, an endless loop condition can usually be found, but it requires some effort and thought on the part of the user. One thing that can be done after hitting ATTN is to inspect the value of the test condition and the expected result. For example,

```
          ATTN struck     (this report indicates where the function was halted)
TRIAL[4]
       I
1
       ⍴Z
45
```

The length of *Z* is greater than 10, and the counter is still 1. This is a good indication that there is an endless loop in the function.

    A common cause of an endless loop is function editing. *TRIAL*, for example: may have been entered originally like this:

```
       ∇ Z←TRIAL X
[1]    I←1
[2]    Z←Z,X÷I
[3]    →(10≥I←I+1)⍴2
       ∇
```

Execution would have been interrupted by a *VALUE ERROR* report at line 2 because *Z* was not initialized; thus

```
      TRIAL 3
VALUE ERROR
TRIAL[2]    Z←Z,X÷I
               ∧
```

The function might then have been edited:

```
      ∇TRIAL[.1]Z←ι0∇
      ∇TRIAL[□]∇
    ∇ Z←TRIAL X
[1]     Z←ι0
[2]     I←1
[3]     Z←Z,X÷I
[4]     →(10≥I←I+1)ρ2
    ∇
```

After function editing, the lines are renumbered. Inserting a statement affected the line numbers for branching (thereby causing the endless loop condition). The branch at line 4 should now be to line 3 if I is less than or equal to 10, not to line 2. Line 4 should be edited to change the 2 to a 3.

Labels are a means of preserving the established branching. A *label* is a name established to identify a line in a function for branching purposes. It precedes the line and is separated from it by a colon. The format of a line with a label is

Label: Expression

With labeled branch-to lines, the branch expression is usually a branch to the label name rather than to a line number. As a consequence of labeling and branching to labels, it is possible to preserve established branch-to points regardless of changes made to the function. For example, in the edited form of *TRIAL*, line 3, the branched-to line, could be labeled

```
[3]   T1: Z←Z,X÷I
```

and the branch line would be

```
[4]     →(10≥I←I+1)ρT1
```

Then regardless of editing and line number changes, the expression branched to is that labeled $T1$.

Labels are local to the defining function. Values can not be assigned to labels by using specification within the function. A *SYNTAX ERROR* report is given if this is done. Values are assigned to labels at execution time and correspond to the line numbers of the lines containing the labels. For example,

```
      ∇  FNA
[1]     L←20
[2]     J←FNB 2+L
[3]     L
      ∇

      ∇  B←FNB N
[1]     A←3
[2]     L:B←N+A
[3]     B
[4]     L×B
      ∇

        FNA
25
50
20
```

Recall from Chapter 2 that local variable names declared by a function *FN1* are accessible in any functions that are called by *FN1* unless these functions declare these names local. This is true for labels also. For example,

```
      ∇  FN1
[1]   A: X←2
[2]     FN2
[3]     'OKAY'
      ∇
      ∇  FN2
[1]     A←ι4
      ∇
        FN1
SYNTAX ERROR
  FN2[1]    A←ι4
           ∧
```

But if *FN2* is defined with *A* as a local variable,

```
      ∇  FN2;A
[1]     A←ι4
      ∇
```

execution of *FN1* proceeds without problems:

```
FN1
OKAY
```

A final form of branch is the niladic branch →, a branch arrow not followed by an expression. The niladic branch causes a termination of not only the function currently being executed but also all functions which have called it. For example, if function *ONE* called function *TWO* which calls *THREE*, a niladic branch in *THREE* terminates execution of *THREE*, *TWO*, and *ONE*. A niladic branch is often used if a particular kind of data in one function would invalidate the data in the sequence of nested functions. For example, consider the following pair of functions:

```
      ∇ Z←X F1 Y
[1]     NUM←Y+X
[2]     DEM←X F2 Y
[3]     Z←NUM÷DEM
      ∇

      ∇ Z←X F2 Y
[1]     Z←X-Y*.5
[2]     (Z≠0)ρ0
[3]     'ERROR 1'
[4]     →
      ∇
```

Executing 2 *F1* 4 results in the *ERROR* 1 message from line 3 of *F2*; however, no bad data are passed to *F1* because line 4 of *F2* is →. Had *F2* not had a niladic branch, a *DOMAIN ERROR* report would have been given because of a division by zero at line 3 of *F1*.

Many applications require branching. A drill program in which a student is presented a number of problems to work is one example. A numerical approximation such as a Newton-Raphson approximation of square root which iteratively approaches the solution value is another. Often, however, a function that is defined using iterative branching can be redefined without branching by using the full powers of APL. For instance, Illustration 4.7 shows a situation where alternative values are needed depending on some condition. It is sometimes possible to make use of the condition as an identity element as in Illustration 4.7 or as part of an index expression as in Illustration 4.18. However, just as the decision of whether to write a one-liner should be based on the clarity of the resulting expression, so should the decision of whether to use branching. The functions of Illustrations 4.7 and 4.18 do not need branching for clarity; the function *STAR* which replaces the first occurrence of the letter *X* in the word *W* with an * would benefit from it.

Without branching:

```
      ∇ Z←X STAR W
[1]     Z←W
[2]     Z[(WιX)×ιX∈W]←'*'
      ∇
```

With branching:

```
     ∇ Z←X STAR W
[1]     Z←W
[2]     →3×XϵW
[3]     Z[WιX]←'*'
     ∇
```

As another example, consider the function $COUNT$, which counts the number of each vowel in the character string CS and prints a five-component vector Z where

$Z[1]$ is the number of As.

$Z[2]$ is the number of Es.

$Z[3]$ is the number of Is.

$Z[4]$ is the number of Os.

$Z[5]$ is the number of Us.

```
     ∇ Z←COUNT CS;I
[1]     Z←ι0
[2]     I←1
[3]     V←'AEIOU'
[4]     Z←Z,+/CS=V[I]
[5]     →4×5≥I←I+1
     ∇
```

The expression $+/'AEIOU'\circ.=CS$ accomplishes the same purpose directly and without branching. Note that use of a function like outer product might fill up a workspace if its arguments are too large, causing a $WS\ FULL$ error report. In such a case, branching, might have to be used to conserve space in the workspace.

Illustration 6.1   A Sampling of Branch Expressions

1. The expression

$$→(A,B,C)[2+×R]$$

results in a branch to the line labeled

A if expression R is negative.

B if expression R is zero.

C if expression R is positive.

Note that this is equivalent to the FORTRAN statement

IF (R) A,B,C

2. If the testing condition C is never negative, the expression

   $\rightarrow A \times \times C$

   can be used to branch to line A until $C=0$. This branch expression is useful when a counter is decreased. For example,

   $\rightarrow A \times \times CT \leftarrow CT-1$

3. The expression

   $\rightarrow (A,B,ERR)[(R,S) \iota F]$

   Branches to A if the value of F is R, to B if the value of F is S, and to ERR for all other values of F.

Illustration 6.2 I Repeats of the Ith Integer

The function $STUTTER$, when given a positive integer N less than 10, generates an N-component vector whose Ith component is a digit derived by I repeats of the Ith integer:

```
      ∇ Z←STUTTER N;V;I
[1]     V←ιN
[2]     Z←ιI←0
[3]   A:Z←Z,10⊥V[I]
        ρV[I←I+1]
[4]   →(N>I)ρA
```

For example,

```
      STUTTER 6
1 22 333 4444 55555 666666
```

Line 3 of $STUTTER$ illustrates that the branch expression may be a vector. Recall that the branch is always taken to the statement whose number matches the first component of the vector argument. In $STUTTER$, and in many other cases, this permits a one-line loop.

PROBLEMS

1. State in words the meaning of the following expressions:
   (a) $\rightarrow (N=\lfloor N)\rho INT$
   (b) $\rightarrow 0 \times \iota 'STOP' \wedge . = 4\rho ANS$
   (c) $\rightarrow 4 \ 8 \ 12[2+\times PRO]$
   (d) $\rightarrow 8 \times (C \geq 0) \wedge 0 = 2 | C$
   (e) $\rightarrow ('A' \in WORD)\rho VOW$

2. Write expressions for the following:
   (a) If the value of K is positive, go to statement 4; otherwise continue.
   (b) If the value of K is positive and less than 100, continue; otherwise stop execution.
   (c) If the value of M is negative go to statement 3; if zero, to statement 6; and if positive, to statement 9.

(d) Stop execution if T is an array greater than a matrix or if T is not a square matrix; otherwise go to statement 7.

(e) Go to the statement labeled ODD if an integer R is odd; otherwise stop execution.

3. What happens next in each of the statements shown in (a)-(d)?

    (a) Assume that $I \leftarrow \iota 4$:

      1) [3] $\rightarrow 8 \times I < 15$

      2) [3] $\rightarrow (I=0) \rho REPORT$

    (b) Assume that $J \leftarrow 23$:

      1) [2] $\rightarrow 5 \times \iota 2 | J$

      2) [2] $\rightarrow 3 \ 5 \ 9[2+\times J]$

    (c) Assume that $R \leftarrow 2 \ 3 \rho 1 \ 0$:

      1) [2] $\rightarrow OK \times 2 = \rho \rho R$

      2) [5] $\rightarrow (0 > -/\rho R) \rho ROW1$

    (d) 1) [3] $\rightarrow 13$

      2) [3] $\rightarrow 0$

      3) [3] $\rightarrow 4 \ 6 \ 8$

4. Which branch statements of the set (a)-(d) produce the same results?

    (a) [7] $\rightarrow 8 \times I \leq 10$

    (b) [7] $\rightarrow (I \leq 10) \rho 0$

    (c) [7] $\rightarrow 0 \times \iota I \leq 10$

    (d) [7] $\rightarrow 0 \times \iota I > 10$

5. (a) Define an IF function which when used within another function as $\rightarrow B \ IF \ C$ produces a branch to a given line B if condition C is true and an exit from the function if condition C is false.

      Test:

```
         C←¯3
6        6 IF C≤0
         6 IF C>0
0
```

    (b) Define a $QUIT$ function which when used within another function produces a conditional exit from the function or otherwise continues in sequence.

      Test:

```
         QUIT C=⌊C
0
         QUIT C>0
ƀ
```

    (c) Define an IF function to branch if the relationship is satisfied for each value of an array C.

      Test:

```
         C←¯3 ¯8 ¯6
         6 IF C≤0
6
         6 IF C>0
ƀ
```

6. Define a matrix product function $MPRO$ to make sure that the two numeric matrices M and N conform before $+.\times$ is applied. If they do not conform, the function should print out an appropriate message.

    Test:

```
         M←2 3ρ⍳6
         N←2 3ρ8 2 7 1 5 3
         . . . . . . .
MATRICES DO NOT CONFORM
         N←3 2 ρ N
         . . . . . .
37 13
97 31
```

7. Define a function EQU to determine whether two arrays A and B are identical.
   Test:

   $$A \leftarrow 2 \; 4 \rho \iota 8$$
   $$B \leftarrow 2 \; 2 \; 2 \rho \iota 8$$
   . . . .
   0
   $$A \leftarrow 2 \; 2 \; 2 \rho \iota 8$$
   . . . . . .
   1

8. Define a dyadic function $CONVERT$ which will accept a numeral in one base B (up to base 16) and convert it to the equivalent numeral in another base A (up to base 16). Design into the function two tests: one to indicate whether the numeral is correctly stated and one to indicate whether a base exceeds 16.
   Test:

Number	Old Base	New Base	Result
520	8	2	101010000
1501	6	4	12031
2047	8	16	427
1A2	12	16	10A
274	5	6	*IMPROPERLY REPRESENTED NUMBER*
973	10	20	*BASE TOO LARGE*

9. Define a function $LIMIT$ to determine the value L to which the expression $(1+X) \star \div X$ approaches as a value X becomes smaller or larger by a factor F. In the design of the function include controls which (1) prevent looping more than 100 times and (2) cause an exit if the difference between two successive calculations is less than $1E^- 6$. In the result, show L, X, and F.
   Test:

   $$F \leftarrow .1$$
   $$X \leftarrow .1$$
   . . . .
   2.718281798   .1   .1
   $$F \leftarrow 10$$
   $$X \leftarrow 1$$
   . . . .
   1.000000021   10   1

10. The October 1967 issue of the *American Mathematical Monthly*, Vol. 74, No. 8, contains problem E2024. It is concerned with finding the last three digits of the number $1+2 \star 2 \star 73$. Obviously it is unreasonable to compute this entire number either by hand or with a computer. However, repeatedly multiplying and truncating the result to the last three places can be carried out with ease. Define a function LFD to find the last *four* digits of the number $2 \star 2 \star N$.
    Test:

    $$N \leftarrow 73$$
    . . . .
    4896

11. Consider a picture-taking satellite in a circular orbit around the earth.

    (a) Define a function $SURFACE$, which, when given the height AF of the satellite above the earth, calculates both the actual area of the earth's surface seen and the percentage to the nearest .1% of the total earth's surface pictured in one picture. As output of the function, show the height, the area of the surface seen, and the percentage of earth seen in one picture. Assume that (1) the earth is a sphere with a radius DC of 4000 miles and (2) the height of the satellite AF is in miles. *Note:* The surface of a sphere is $4\pi DC^2$.

    In terms of the figure below, the surface area of a spherical segment is $2\pi DC^2(1 - \dfrac{DC}{AC})$:

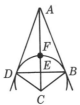

    Test:

            $AF\leftarrow100$

            $\cdot \cdot \cdot \cdot \cdot \cdot$
        100   2451974.754   1.2

    (b) Define a function $HIGH$ to determine how high the satellite must be to get at least $P\%$ of the earth's surface in one picture. Use 50-mile increments and begin searching at a height of AF miles.

        Test:

                $AF\leftarrow100$
                $P\leftarrow5$

                $\cdot \cdot \cdot \cdot \cdot \cdot \cdot$
            450   10166052.63   5

    (c) Define a function $PICT$ to generate a table containing

        1. The height of the satellite above the earth.

        2. The actual surface area enclosed in one picture.

        3. The percentage of the earth's surface so pictured.

        Begin at a height of H miles. Increase the height by 50-mile increments until a height of 500 miles has been reached. Then increase the heights by 500-mile increments until at least $P\%$ of the earth can be viewed in one picture.

12. The function $CHANGE$ shown below uses outer product successively at line 5 to determine in how many ways an amount of money AMT can be made using combinations of half-dollars, quarters, dimes, and nickels. Lines 1 – 4 of the function sets limits on the maximum value for any coin, and line 5 determines which combinations of the coins equal the amount and counts them.

```
     ∇ Z← CHANGE AMT;H;Q;D;N
[1]    H←0,.5×ι⌊AMT÷.5
[2]    Q←0,.25×ι⌊AMT÷.25
[3]    D←0,.1×ι⌊AMT÷.1
[4]    N←0,.05×ι⌊AMT÷.05
[5]    Z←+/,AMT=N∘.+D∘.+Q∘.+H
     ∇
```

CHANGE creates a rank-4 array whose size becomes quite large. For example, if the amount is $1, the array created is a 21 by 11 by 5 by 3 array. If the amount is $5, the array is an 101 by 51 by 21 by 11 array. Thus the workspace becomes full. Redefine *CHANGE* so that the workspace will not fill up.

Section 6.2 COMMENTS

As functions become more complicated and longer, it is often desirable to keep a commentary on the function along with its definition. This can be accomplished by use of the symbol (∩ overstrike ○), sometimes called the *lamp* or *comment* symbol. The symbol ⍝ must be the first symbol on the line. Everything following it is considered a comment and is not executed. For example,

⍝ *A. PREIS   STATISTICS* 101

If a comment is used within a function, it has a line number, but the line is not executed during the execution of the function. For example,

[4] ⍝ *FINDING THE MEAN AND STANDARD DEVIATION*

Because everything following the comment symbol is considered a comment, a function definition cannot be ended by placing a del at the end of a comment line. Furthermore, since the comment symbol ⍝ must be the first symbol on the line, comment lines cannot be labeled.

Illustration 6.3 Comments in a Function

A comment about the arguments of the defined function *APRIN* (of Sec. 6.1) can be placed in the definition as follows:

```
     ∇ Z←Y APRIN Y;I
[1]    ⍝X IS PRINCIPAL, RATE AS A PERCENT.
[2]    ⍝Y IS STARTING YEAR, ENDING YEAR
[3]    Z←X[1]
[4]    I←1
[5]    A1:Z←Z×1+X[2]×.01
[6]    →A1×(|-/Y)≥I←I+1
     ∇
```

Section 6.3 CONVERSATIONAL INPUT/OUTPUT

Section 6.3.1 Output from Within a Function

One means of displaying the value of an expression on a line during the execution of a function is simply to show the expression without any specification. For example,

.
.
.

```
[4]    R←+/SCORES
[5]    'THE TOTAL IS'
[6]    R
```

.
.
.

Line 5 is a display of the character vector *THE TOTAL IS*. Line 6 is a display of the value of the variable R which has been computed at line 4. During the execution of the function, the following prints out:

THE TOTAL IS
. . . .   (the value of the expression)

The monadic plus function discussed in Sec. 4.3.5 could be used to compute and display R on the same line:

.
.
.

```
[4]    'THE TOTAL IS'
[5]    +R←+/SCORES
```

.
.
.

The output is the same as that above.

Using monadic plus makes it possible to compute and assign a numeric value to a variable and to display that value on the same line. However, monadic plus cannot be used with character output; that is, an expression such as $+T←$'THE TOTAL IS' is not possible.

A more general and more recommended means for explicit display of an expression is the quad $\square$ used to the immediate left of a specification arrow. For example,

```
      □←'THE TOTAL IS'
THE TOTAL IS
      □←R
. . . . . . . .     (the value of R)
      R
. . . . . . . .     (the value of R)
```

In fact, all statements (such as R and *'THE TOTAL IS'*) are abbreviations or shorthand for complete statements (such as $\square←R$ and $\square←$'THE TOTAL IS').

Using the quad and multiple specification makes it possible to display a value and assign it to a variable on the same line. For example,

```
      □←T←'THE TOTAL IS'
THE TOTAL IS
      T
THE TOTAL IS
      □←R←+/SCORES
.......    (the value of R )
      R
.......    (the value of R )
```

The display quad can be used advantageously in multiple specification; otherwise it is typically elided. That is, we are more likely to type $9 \times 6 \div 1.75$ instead of $□← 9 \times 6 \div 1.75$ or `'HOT ISN''T IT'` instead of $□← 'HOT ISN''T IT'$.

Illustration 6.4   Tracing the Evaluation of an Expression

The quad is also a useful means of breaking a long complicated expression into smaller units so that the way the expression is evaluated can be seen. For example, the expression

```
      Z←Z,10⊥ V[I]ρV[I←I+1]
```

from line 3 of the function *STUTTER* of Illustration 6.2 creates the *STUTTER* of the *I* th integer. To see how the evaluation of this expression proceeds quads can be used to display intermediate results:

```
      □←Z←Z,□←10⊥□←V[I]ρV[□←I←I+1]
```

If *N* were 6 and the third iteration had just been completed, the output of the line shown above with quads would look like this:

```
4                     ( value of I←I+1)
4 4 4 4               ( value of V[I]ρV[I←I+1])
4444                  ( value of 10⊥V[I]ρV[I←I+1])
1   22   333   4444   ( value of Z←Z,10⊥V[I]ρV[I←I+1])
```

*Section 6.3.2   Formatting Output**

Dyadic Format

Use of the quad explicitly declares that the value of the associated expression should be displayed, but it does not control the appearance of the output. The

---

*APL.SV only. The formatting functions are not primitives in APL/360.

system's default display criteria determine the appearance of the output. For example, vectors and character matrices always begin at the left margin. Components of vectors are separated by one space. Numeric matrices are indented two spaces, and the spacing between columns depends on whether they are binary, fixed, or floating point numbers. The function *dyadic format* ⍕ (formed by ⊤ overstruck with ∘) is used to control the appearance of output. Dyadic format accomplishes this by converting the numeric array data into a corresponding character array in the prescribed format. The general form of dyadic format is

A ⍕ B

where B is the array data to be formatted and A is a control scalar or vector describing the format of the result. The result is a character array.

The format of the result is controlled in two ways: by specifying the width of the number field of each column of the array (or component in a vector) and by specifying the precision and form (either decimal or exponential) of the numbers in each column in the result. It is possible to control the appearance either of each column individually or to treat all the columns the same. All columns of the right argument are treated the same if the left argument is one control pair or a scalar. Each column of the right argument is treated individually if the left argument contains a control pair for each column in the right argument. All pairs are formed the same way. The first value of the control pair declares the width of the number field. This value should be large enough to accommodate the number in the column that requires the most space to represent. This includes besides the digits of the number, the decimal point, the negative sign, the exponential symbol, the exponent digits (with a minimum of two), and exponent sign, if any of these is present. Otherwise a *DOMAIN ERROR* report is given. For example, suppose that a column of the right argument is

```
 ‾31.8629
 934.8
   6.217
‾345
```

and that three places to the right of the decimal point are required. Then to format this column completely the value of the width control should be at least 8. Spaces between columns are indicated by increasing the width control beyond the minimum needed; for example, a width control of 12 for the above example will insert at least four spaces between adjacent columns. The spaces precede the columns, so the first column will be indented from the left margin. However, no spaces are provided before the first component of a vector. If the width control value is zero, at least one space will be inserted between adjacent columns.

The second value of the control pair declares the precision and the form of the numbers in the column. Positive numbers indicate decimal form, and negative numbers indicate exponential form. The values indicate the number of digits to the right of the decimal point for the decimal form and the number of digits in the multiplier in the exponential form. Numbers are rounded or padded with zeros to fit the specified form. In the example above where three digits to the right of the decimal point are desired, the result appears as follows:

```
 ̄31.863
934.800
   6.217
 ̄345.000
```

A single control pair or scalar specifies the format for the entire array, so that the appearance of each column is the same. For example,

```
      M
 ̄31.8629          ̄39
934.8              0
   6.217        ̄467.8191
 ̄345            0.621

      10 2⍕M
 ̄31.86        ̄39.00
934.80          .00
   6.22      ̄467.82
 ̄345.00         .62

      10  ̄2⍕M
 ̄3.2E01     ̄3.9E01
9.3E02      0.0E ̄01
6.2E00      ̄4.7E02
 ̄3.5E02     6.2E ̄01

      7 2⍕M
 ̄31.86  ̄39.00
934.80     .00
   6.22 ̄467.82
 ̄345.00    .62

      6 2⍕M
DOMAIN ERROR
      6 2⍕M
       ∧
```

A scalar left argument indicates the precision for a width of zero. If the width component of a control pair is zero, then the data right argument is formatted so that at least one space appears between adjacent numbers. The single control pair with a zero width component is equivalent to a single scalar left argument. For example,

```
      2⍕M                      0 2⍕M
 ¯31.86   ¯39.00          ¯31.86   ¯39.00
 934.80     .00           934.80     .00
   6.22 ¯467.82             6.22 ¯467.82
¯345.00     .62          ¯345.00     .62
```

The algebraic value of all numbers are used in the rounding process. Numbers are rounded to the nearest value of the specified precision.

```
        K
¯5.5 ¯4.5 ¯3.51 ¯2.54 ¯6.56 5.5 4.5 3.51 2.5 6.56
        0⍕K
¯6 ¯5 ¯4 ¯3 ¯7 6 5 4 3 7
        1⍕K
¯5.5 ¯4.5 ¯3.5 ¯2.5 ¯6.6 5.5 4.5 3.5 2.5 6.6
```

Arrays of rank 3 and higher are formatted by planes. For example,

```
       AR
 ¯31.8629                ¯39
 934.8                     0
   6.217                ¯467.8191
¯345                       0.621


 ¯63.7258                ¯78
1869.6                     0
  12.434                 135.6382
¯690                       1.242

        2⍕AR
  ¯31.86    ¯39.00
  934.80      .00
    6.22  ¯467.82
 ¯345.00      .62


  ¯63.73   ¯78.00
 1869.60      .00
   12.43   135.64
 ¯690.00     1.24
```

If each column is to be formatted separately, the left argument must have $2×(\rho B)[\rho\rho B]$ components, that is, a pair for each column of the right argument. Each pair controls a column of the result. For example,

```
        7 2 12 2⍕M
⁻31.86          ⁻39.00
 934.80            .00
    6.22       ⁻467.82
⁻345.00            .62

        7 2 10 ⁻2⍕M
⁻31.86       ⁻3.9E01
 934.80       0.0E⁻01
    6.22      ⁻4.7E02
⁻345.00       6.2E⁻01
```

The first pair controls the first column; the second pair, the second column; and so forth. If the left argument does not have a single pair, a scalar, or a pair of components for each column in the right argument, a *LENGTH ERROR* report is given.

Monadic Format

Besides wanting to control the appearance of the result as is possible with dyadic format, it is also often desirable to have numeric and character data intermixed on the same line, for example, printing

THE AVERAGE IS 6

where 6 is a calculated result. This can be achieved with the monadic format function and catenation. *Monadic format* produces a character array identical to the printing normally associated with its numeric argument. A character argument is left unchanged. The form for monadic format is

    ⍕*B*

where *B* is an array. For example,

```
      T
9 8 3 4
      ρT
4

      TF←⍕T
      ρTF
7

      TF
9 8 3 4

      TF×2
DOMAIN ERROR
      TF×2
      ∧
```

Monadic format creates a character result, and so arithmetic operations cannot be performed with it. However, the result of monadic format can be catenated with a character array to produce an intermixing of character and numeric information.* For example,

```
      'THE AVERAGE IS ',⍕(+/9 8 3 4)÷4
THE AVERAGE IS 6

      R←'THE ANSWER IS ', ⍕T×2
      R
THE ANSWER IS 18 16 6 8
```

The result of monadic format depends on the normal printing of the array argument. For different types of matrices this varies, as the following examples show:

```
        N
     2            ¯2.5
    ¯0.15          0.37
   ¯37.4          12.9
        ρN
3   2

        Q←⍕N
        ρQ
3  34

        Q
     2            ¯2.5
    ¯0.15          0.37
   ¯37.4          12.9

        W
   2   4
   6  12
   8  64
        ρW
3  2
```

---

*The mixture of numeric and character output on a line in APL/360 is accomplished by using a semicolon to separate or delimit the character and numeric parts of the expression. For example,

```
      'THE AVERAGE IS '; (+/9 8 3 4)÷4
THE AVERAGE IS 6
```

Data can be intermixed using the semicolon for display purposes only. Each value separated by semicolons is displayed. It is not possible to assign a name to a mixture of numeric and character data through the use of the semicolon. If a space appears in the quoted expression, it will be displayed. The numeric and character data may be repeatedly intermixed on a line as long as they are separated by semicolons. Use of the semicolon for intermixed data is also possible in

$E \leftarrow \Phi W$

ρE

3 6

E

2 4

6 12

8 64

T

0 1

0 1

0 0

ρT

3 2

$Y \leftarrow \Phi T$

ρY

3 4

Y

0 1

0 1

0 0

Section 6.3.3 Input During Function Execution

The functions that were defined in previous chapters required that all data to be used by the defined function during its execution had to be provided prior to or at the time of the function call. And unless there was an error or an ATTN hit, execution of the function did not stop until it was completed. Many applications, in order to be most effective, require that data be entered during the execution of the function, for instance, a CAI (computer-assisted instruction) function that asks a question to which it expects an answer or a monthly billing function that takes a line of data for each customer. Providing for values to be input during the execution of a function is accomplished by using the quad □ as part of an expression anywhere but to the immediate left of a specification arrow, such as

$$ANS \leftarrow \square \qquad ST \leftarrow (2 \times \square) \div 3 \qquad \rightarrow 0 \times \iota 12 \geq \square$$

When a quad to the right of a specification is encountered during the execution of an expression, execution halts, the symbols □: are printed, there is a line feed, the carrier indents, and the keyboard unlocks. Execution of the expression does not continue unless some expression is entered from the keyboard. (A RETURN alone causes □: to reappear.) The expression entered replaces the quad, and the entire expression is evaluated. For example,

---

APL.SV, but users of APL.SV should find monadic format and catenation a more desirable means of intermixing data.

```
     ANS←□            ST←(2×□)÷3              R←□
□:                □:                      □:
     3172                8  6  5              2×7×8
     ANS                 ST                   R
3172              5.3333   4   3.3333    112
```

□ is generally used for numeric input. Character input may also be entered in response to □:, but it must be enclosed in quotes. The system commands)*ERASE*,)*VARS*, and)*FNS* may be executed during □:. After the command has been executed, the symbols □: reappear; for example,

```
     X←□
□:
     )FNS
COST
□:
     )VARS
A     B     C      SCORE
□:
     )ERASE A
□:
     )VARS
B     C     SCORE
□:
     4
     X
4
```

If)*LOAD* is executed during □:, the □: does not reappear because the active workspace has been replaced. If)*SAVE* is executed, the execution of the expression containing the quad is halted, the report *INTERRUPT* is given, the expression containing the quad is printed with a caret pointing to the quad, and then the workspace is saved and the appropriate saved message given. For example,

```
     9+□
□:
     )SAVE
INTERRUPT
     9+□
       ∧
12.01.23  11/03/76 WSI
```

If the expression containing the quad is part of a function, execution of the function is suspended at the line containing the quad.* Execution can be resumed by branching to that or any other line of the function. Sec. 6.5 we shall discuss means of resuming execution of a function after it has been suspended.

---

*APL.SV only. In APL/360 the expressions containing the quad or the function are not interrupted following a)*SAVE* command.

Care should be exercised when the input quad is used within a function to assure that only the data that are valid for the function are entered. For example, if the function expects that a vector is entered, the structure of the data should be tested before they are used in further evaluation. Or if the data need only be put into vector form, the ravel function can be used to assure vector data; for example,

$$T \leftarrow (\iota\rho X) \leq X \leftarrow, \square$$

*Illustration 6.5 Entering an Array When the Data Exceed
       the Paper Width*

The quad catenated to the end of a vector can be used as a means of entering an array when the data exceed the paper width. For example,

```
     R←6 8ρ9 8 3 4 5 7 8 9 5 2 1 0 4 4 5 6 7 8 ,□
□:   9 7 6 1 2 3 5 7 2 0 1 3 1 3 4 5 7 9 7 6 3 4 ,□
□:   9 3 4 4 5 7 7 8

     R
 9 8 3 4 5 7 8 9
 5 2 1 0 4 4 5 6
 7 8 9 7 6 1 2 3
 5 7 2 0 1 3 1 3
 4 5 7 9 7 6 3 4
 9 3 4 4 5 7 7 8
```

Related to the input quad is the *quote-quad* ▯ (□ backspace ') placed anywhere in an expression except to the left of a specification arrow. The quote-quad indicates that the input to replace the quote-quad is character input. When a quote-quad is encountered during the execution of an expression, execution halts; there is a line feed; the carrier remains at the left margin; and the keyboard is released. Whatever is entered from the keyboard is taken as character data. For example,

```
        CHAR←▯         |        WD←'IN',▯         |          M←▯
HELLO                  |     SPECTOR              |    2×7×8
        CHAR           |        WD                |          M
HELLO                  |     INSPECTOR            |    2×7×8
                       |                          |          ρM
                       |                          |    5
```

Quotes are not necessary to indicate that the input is character data, and if a quote or a quote-quad is part of the input, it is a character. A RETURN alone results in an empty vector.

Using an input quad or quote-quad in a function can create a problem dramatically illustrated by the two endless loop functions shown on the next page:

```
        ▽ QUAD              ▽ QUOTEQUAD
[1]     X←▯          [1]     X←▯
[2]     →1           [2]     →1
        ▽                   ▽
```

Executing *QUAD* produces

```
        QUAD
▯:

        6
▯:

        7×8
▯:

        etc.
```

Executing quote-quad produces

```
(keyboard release)    FALSTAFF
(keyboard release)    STOP
(keyboard release)    I QUIT
(keyboard release)    9×7
(keyboard release)    )OFF
(keyboard release)
etc.
```

The problem is that there are no provisions within either function for stopping function execution. Compounding the problem is that it is impossible to hit ATTN fast enough to stop execution at line 2. While you are unlikely to write a function that purposely ties up the workspace as *QUAD* and *QUOTEQUAD* do, it is possible for you to create the same effect inadvertently. The best way to terminate a quad input situation is to enter a niladic branch →. The niladic branch terminates the execution of the function.

The only way to terminate the quote-quad input situation during a function execution is to enter *Ⱶ* (*O* backspace *U* backspace *T* in that order only). This interrupts the function. The report *INTERRUPT* is given, followed by the function name and line number and the expression containing the quote-quad with a caret pointing to the quote-quad.* For example,

↑ carrier waits here for keyboard entry in response to ▯

```
Ⱶ
INTERRUPT
FN[3]    X←▯
              ∧
```

---

*APL.SV only. In APL/360 *Ⱶ* immediately terminates the execution of the function.

After the function has been interrupted, the niladic branch can be used as with ☐:.

> →

The niladic branch terminates the execution of the function.

Normally quote-quad is used when character input is expected, perhaps for a list of names. Quote-quad would also be used if character data and numeric data are expected or if a specific numeric format is required. As an example of the latter, the developer of an arithmetic drill program might want to check whether the result is properly placed, such as

```
  39          39
 +62   not   +62
 101           101
```

For an arithmetic drill, using character input could also prevent an enterprising student from having a session like this:

```
    39
    62
☐:
    39+62
RIGHT
```

In the presentation of arithmetic problems and in other kinds of response situations, it is often desirable to have the input appear at some place on the line other than starting at the leftmost position. The usual output resulting from the evaluation of an expression or a ☐← includes a concluding carrier return, so that the entry that follows will be in the standard position on the following line. This carrier return can be suppressed by the use of *bare output*. Bare output, indicated by ⍞←, does not include the customary concluding carrier return if it is followed by another ⍞← or by character input, X←⍞. The carrier does not return, and input is treated as if the user had spaced over to the position occupied at the conclusion of the bare output. For example,

```
      ∇ FN
[1]    ⍞←'THE CAPITAL OF SOUTH DAKOTA IS '
[2]    ANS←⍞
      ∇

      FN
THE CAPITAL OF SOUTH DAKOTA IS PIERRE
                              ↑ user started entering data here

      ρANS
37

      ANS

                      PIERRE
```

If, however, either an unspecified expression or an expression which contains ⎕←
appears between the lines using ⍞, a carrier return will occur after the execution
of these expressions. For example,

```
      ∇ FN1
[1]    ⍞←?10
[2]    ' PLUS '  or [2] ⎕←' PLUS '
[3]    ⍞←?10
[4]    ⍞←' IS '
[5]    A←⍞
      ∇
```

```
        FN1
2 PLUS
8 IS 10
        ↑  user entry
```

But if line 2 is

```
[2]    ⍞←' PLUS '
```

execution of the function appears as follows:

```
        FN1
10 PLUS 5 IS 15
                ↑  user entry
```

The bare output or character input request may appear within an expression
without affecting its behavior; that is, it does not have to be the leftmost symbol
on the line. For example,

```
      ∇ FN4
[1]    Q←⍞←'HI.'
[2]    W←⍞←' HOW ARE YOU?'
      ∇
```

```
        FN4
HI. HOW ARE YOU?
```

```
        ρQ
3
```

```
        ρW
13
      ∇ FN5
[1]    Q←⍞←'HI. '
[2]    W←⍞←' HOW ARE YOU? '
[3]    ANS←⍞
      ∇
```

```
        FN5
HI.   HOW ARE YOU? FINE!
                        ↑ user entry

        Q
HI.

        ρQ
4

        W
HOW ARE YOU?

        ρW
14

        ρANS
23
        ANS
                    FINE!
```

Bare output can be used instead of monadic format to intermix numeric and character data on a line for display purposes, provided that the lines generating this output are separate. If they are not, monadic format must be used. For example,

```
        ∇ FN7
[1]    ⎕←2
[2]    ⎕← ' IS THE ANS'
    ∇

        FN7
2 IS THE ANS


        ∇ FN8
[1]    (⎕←2), ' IS THE ANS.'
    ∇

        FN8
2
DOMAIN ERROR
FN8[1] (⎕←2),' IS THE ANS.'
        ∧

        ∇ FN9
[1]    (⍕2), ' IS THE ANS.'
    ∇

        FN9
2 IS THE ANS.
```

The usefulness of bare output applies solely to its use within a defined function. When entered directly from the keyboard, ⎕← behaves indistinquishably from ⎕← or an unspecified expression. Each line entered from the keyboard is automatically concluded by a carrier return.

PROBLEMS

1. (a) Define a function *PARROT* to accept any single input and print it back exactly as it was input.

     Test:

     • • • • • •

     TEST
     TEST ← computer response

   (b) Modify the function *PARROT* so that it accepts repeated inputs but terminates without parroting if the four characters *STOP* are typed.

     Test:

     • • • • • • • •

     TEST
     TEST ← computer response
     AGAIN
     AGAIN ← computer response
     STOP

   (c) Modify the function *PARROT* so that it accepts repeated inputs but terminates without parroting if only a carrier return is typed.

     Test:

     Same as part (b) until last line; then carrier return only.

2. (a) Define a function *ENTER* that continues to require the entry of numeric data. Each entry should be appended to the vector *DATA* of previous entries. The function should continue to accept entries until the user types *STOP*. Assume that *DATA* is specified initially outside of the function.

     Test:
     DATA←ι3

     • • • • • • • • •

     At ⎕:,

Enter	Response
5	⎕:
8	⎕:

     STOP
     DATA
     1 2 3 5 8

   (b) Modify *ENTER* so that each entry is appended only if the entry is a positive integer less than 1000. If not, print an appropriate error message and recycle.

Test:

   $DATA \leftarrow \iota 3$

  · · · · · · · · · ·

At □:

Enter	Response
5	□:
¯9	*ENTRY MUST BE A POSITIVE INTEGER*
985	□:
1934	*ENTRY MUST BE LESS THAN* 1000
5.6	*ENTRY MUST BE AN INTEGER*

STOP

   DATA

 1 2 3 5 985

(c) Modify *ENTER* so that (1) it prompts for a four-component numeric vector and (2) it produces an error message if four components are not entered (that is, either if too few or too many components are entered) and returns to request data again.

  Test:

    $DATA \leftarrow \iota 4$

    · · · ·

  At □:

Enter	Response
9 3 4 7	□:
¯3 ¯9	*TOO FEW COMPONENTS, TRY AGAIN.*
−ι5	*TOO MANY COMPONENTS, TRY AGAIN.*
STOP	

   DATA

 1 2 3 4 9 3 4 7

3. Write an expression to compute the Nth root of X and display the output *THE NTH ROOT OF X IS* ...

  Test:

    $X \leftarrow 32$

    $N \leftarrow 5$

   · · · · · ·

  THE 5TH ROOT OF 32 IS 2

4. Define a function *GUESS* to select an integer from 1 to 10 and then prompt the user to match it. If the guess is too high or low, an appropriate message such as *TOO HIGH* or *TOO LOW* should be given before prompting again. When the guess matches, the function should display an acknowledgement such as *CORRECT!* and exit.

5. Define a conversational function *WORDS* to prompt for a word as a literal string, convert it to its unique numeric representation, and catenate that value to the previously converted words. Termination of the input is signaled by a carrier return only. All words

should be 11 characters or less and contain only alphabetics. Test each input string to determine that these conditions are satisfied. If they are not, indicate that and return for a new input. The output of this function should be explicit so that it may be used in other expressions.

Test:
· · · · · · · · ·

At keyboard release,

Enter	Response
ERNIE	Keyboard release
BIG BIRD	*ONLY ALPHABETICS. TRY AGAIN*
SNUFFLEUPAGUS	*WORD TOO LONG. TRY AGAIN.*
Carrier return	Function ends.

6. (a) Suppose that you have a student who is just learning addition. Write a drill function *ADD* on which he may practice. The drill should present only two numbers to be added. Let an input parameter of the function indicate the largest number to be added. (Notice that this will allow you to control the complexity of the addition.) For example, if the parameter is 8, the numbers appearing in the problem will be always less than or equal to 8. Design the function so that

1. The sum appears vertically, with the proper sign and underscore. For example,

$$453$$
$$+\ \ 27$$

2. It waits for the student to enter the sum from the keyboard. If the answer is correct, it presents him with a new problem. If the answer is incorrect, it returns a message to try again. An improperly aligned answer should be considered incorrect and should give a special message.

3. The student types *END* in reply to a request for a sum in order to exit from the drill program.

(b) Modify *ADD* so that if the student types *HELP*, the function responds with the correct answer before presenting a new problem. Add an accounting section as a matrix whose purpose is to keep track of the number of tries for each problem. Let the first row of it contain the problem number, and the second, the number of attempts. When the student types *END*, the function responds with this compiled count matrix.

7. State in words the appearance of the result of expressions (a)–(d) as defined by the left argument R for $R \leftarrow 2\ 3\rho 27\ 152\ 92\ 107\ 44\ 10$
    (a) $\bar{}3\overline{\overline{\nabla}}R$ (b) $8\ 2\ 0\ 0\ 7\ 4\overline{\overline{\nabla}}R$
    (c) $7\ \bar{}2\ 6\ 2\ 8\ \bar{}2\overline{\overline{\nabla}}R$ (d) $0\ 0\overline{\overline{\nabla}}R$

8. Define the left argument M of $M\overline{\overline{\nabla}}N$ for results (a)–(c).
    (a) Two places to the right of the decimal point. At least one space between columns.
    (b) Assume that every component of N is a positive integer and that $\lceil/[1]N$ is 83 3176 533 10. At least four spaces between columns. No places to the right of the decimal point.

(c) Assume that some components of N lie between $^-1$ and 1. Exponential notation with four places to the right of the decimal point in the multiplier and at least two spaces placed between each column.

9. Define a function $FORM$ which will accept a matrix M and format it so that there will be P places to the right of the decimal point and at least N places between each column of M.

Section 6.4 TRACING

For most of us, getting access to a computer and being able to use it as long as we wish is merely a dream. Since computer access is usually limited and computer time expensive, it behooves a user to be as well prepared for terminal activity as possible. Being prepared means having some activity plan laid out—knowing expressions or functions we want to enter and having test data prepared to test the functions. Some checking of expressions and functions can be done by hand to better the odds that what is entered works. For example, suppose that we want to hand-check the function $APRIN$ from Sec. 6.1 with X being 100 5 and Y being 1968 1971:

```
      ∇ Z←X APRIN Y;I
[1]     Z←X[1]
[2]     I←1
[3]     Z←Z×1+X[2]×.01
[4]     →3×(|-/Y)≥I←I+1
      ∇
```

A sample of hand checking is as follows:

Line Number	Variable or Expression	Values
	X	100 5
	Y	1968 1971
1	Z	100
2	I	1
3	Z	105 (that is, 100×1+5×.01)
4	$\|-/Y$	3
	I	2
	→	3
3	Z	110.25 (that is, 105×1+5×.01)
4	I	3
	→	3
3	Z	115.76 (that is, 110.25×1+5×.01)
4	I	4
	→	0

Thus the final result is 115.76.

Such hand calculations are effective for preliminary checking of a defined function. If the expressions in the function are long and complicated, and if there is a lot of branching in the function, it is difficult and time-consuming to hand-check extensively. We are then more apt to enter the function as it is to see if it works. Usually it does not, and the hard task of debugging begins. One feature of APL that aids in debugging is function tracing. *Tracing* provides that the value of specified lines be printed as the function executes these specified lines. The syntax of a trace statement is

$T \Delta FN \leftarrow$ line numbers (or an expression whose value is line numbers)

$T \Delta$ followed by the function name sets a trace on the line numbers indicated for that function. Every time the function is executed, the function name, line number, and value of each line indicated is printed. For example, tracing lines 3 and 4 of *APRIN* is done as follows:

```
      TΔAPRIN←3 4
      100 5 APRIN 1968 1971
APRIN[3]    105
APRIN[4]    →3
APRIN[3]    110.25
APRIN[4]    →3
APRIN[3]    115.76
APRIN[4]    →0
115.76
```

If the line being traced is a branch, the branch arrow precedes the value of the branch expression.* The trace of a function is eliminated by

```
      TΔFN←ι0
```

Continuing the *APRIN* example,

```
      TΔAPRIN←ι0
      100   5 APRIN 1968 1971
115.76
```

The trace vector is not a variable and does not appear in the variable list. Its value cannot be examined. Erasing a function also erases the trace vector for that function.

While the tracing capability is most often used for checking the execution of a function when it does not work properly, it can be used for other reasons. For instance, a trace can be set on a line of an iterative function, the function written without conditional branching and its accompanying checks and counters, and ATTN used to stop the execution of the function when enough values have been printed. The trace control is most often set before execution of a function begins.

---

*APL.SV only. In APL/360 the branch arrow is not shown.

It can, however, be set during the execution of the function. For example, it might be turned on only for certain values of a counter, perhaps by a statement like this:

```
[7]    TΔFN←4 8 12×0=5|I
```

Generally, the function lines to be traced must be stated as absolute line numbers. However, it is possible to use label names in the trace control vector if it is set during the execution of the function. For example,

```
      ∇ FN N
[1]    TΔFN←A
[2]    X←0
[3]  A :X←X+1
[4]    →A×N>X
      ∇

      FN 2
FN[3]    1
FN[3]    2
```

Section 6.5 SUSPENDED EXECUTION OF A FUNCTION

- Each of the following circumstances interrupts the execution of a function:

- One function calls another during its execution.

- An input quad or quote-quad occurs in the function.

- An error is encountered during the execution of the function or the ATTN key is struck.

In the first instance, the calling function is in a *pendent state*; it is waiting until the execution of the called function is completed. When the called function's execution is completed, the execution of the calling function resumes. In the second instance, the function is in an input or *quad state* until something is entered from the keyboard, after which execution of the function resumes. In the third instance, the function is in a *suspended state*. Execution of the function does not resume automatically as it does in the first two instances, where called functions or input quads were the cause of the interruption.

Suspended functions have a different character from functions in a pendent or input quad state. Since there are many reasons for function suspension—for example, an error requiring corrective action—the user must explicitly direct the resumption of execution of the function. Suppose that during the execution of a function an error occurs,

```
SYNTAX ERROR
FN[3]    RM←A⁻3
         ∧
```

or that an *INTERRUPT* report is given as a result of *◊* being given in response to an input quote-quad or of *)SAVE* being given in response to an input quad,*

```
INTERRUPT
TN[4]    X←⍞
              ∧
```

or

```
⎕:
    )SAVE WS
INTERRUPT
12.01.23  11/11/76
SN[6]    R←⎕
              ∧
```

In each case, execution of the function is suspended. The function name and line number constitute the suspension report. What the user does now depends on the reason for the suspension. With a function error, the safest action to take is to use a niladic branch → to wipe out function execution at the point of suspension and the execution of any pendent functions in the calling sequence, to correct the erroneous line by appropriate function editing, and to recall the function. While this method can always be used when a function is suspended, it may not be the most appropriate. For example, the function execution may almost be completed and recalling it would be time-consuming and serve no purpose. In this case, or after executing a save command in a quad state, we are likely to want to resume execution at the place it was halted. This can be achieved by an unconditional branch to the line number shown in the suspension report. The sequence of activity after the suspension of *FN* above might be

```
        ∇FN[3] RN←A-3∇
        →3
```

The error was corrected while the function was suspended, and then execution was directed to continue at statement 3. Or for function *SN* above that was suspended by an *INTERRUPT*, use

```
        →6
```

There is no error to correct, and so execution is simply directed to continue at statement 6.

In general, during suspension a branch to any line number directs execution to continue at that line. If a line number outside of the set of line numbers for the function is used, such as →0, execution of the last suspended function terminates, and if the function is called by another function, execution of the pendent function resumes. If the pendent function relies on data from the suspended function and

---

*APL.SV only. In APL/360 neither of these situations occurs.

that function was terminated prematurely, the result from the calling function may not be accurate. The niladic branch, on the other hand, causes an exit not only from the suspended function but also from the pendent function in the calling sequence. The *calling sequence* is simply the chain of nested functions leading to the suspended function. For example, function *ONE* calls function *TWO*, function *TWO* in turn calls function *THREE*, which becomes suspended. → terminates execution of *THREE*, *TWO*, and *ONE*, whereas →0 terminates execution of *THREE* only. Then execution of *TWO* resumes.

Prior to resuming execution of the suspended function by an unconditional branch or terminating execution by the niladic branch, most work that could be performed in calculation mode can be performed, such as evaluating expressions, calling functions, and editing functions with the exception that pendent functions cannot be edited. An attempt to do so results in a *DEFN ERROR* report. Thus suppose that for the nested sequence of functions *ONE*, *TWO*, and *THREE* the response had been

```
      ONE
      SYNTAX ERROR
      THREE[2] Y←X⁻3
                ∧
```

Function *ONE* is pendent and cannot be displayed or edited,

```
      ∇ONE[□]∇
DEFN ERROR
```

but function *THREE*, which is suspended, can be displayed or edited,

```
      ∇THREE [2□]
[2]      Y←X⁻3
[2]
```

Workspaces that have suspended and pendent functions can be saved.

Functions that exist in a pendent or suspended state can be executed. This creates a condition in the workspace where the function exists in two active versions, one interrupted and one executing. Usually this does not affect the performance in the active workspace, although it can limit function editing, or if the suspended function has local variables of large dimensions, the workspace may become prematurely full. The system command *)SI* presents a history called the *state indicator* of the pendent, suspended, and input-quad states of functions in the workspace. *)SI* is quite useful in keeping track of the state of interruptions of function execution in a workspace. For example, after the error report for function *FN* above,

```
      )SI
FN[3]    *
```

The asterisk indicates that the function is suspended. If *FN* had been called by *QS* at line 7, the state indicator would be

```
     )SI
FN[3]    *
QS[7]
```

QS is a pendent function. No asterisk is shown with pendent functions. The most recent interruption is always at the top of the list. If)SI is entered during □:, a □ appears at the top of the state indicator list.

There is an error report associated with the state indicator. It is *SI DAMAGE*. *SI DAMAGE* can occur in two main ways. First, an *SI DAMAGE* report is given if a function on the *SI* list, but not at the top, is edited. For example, if the state indicator in a workspace is as follows,

```
A[6]    *
B[3]
C[4]    *
D[1]
```

editing function *A* does not cause an *SI DAMAGE* report, but editing function *C* does. (An attempt to edit function *B* or *D* produces a *DEFN ERROR* report.)

Second, an *SI DAMAGE* report is given if a function on the *SI* list is erased or its header is changed or the labels of the function are affected—if labels are added or deleted or if the order of the existing labels is changed. The effect of an *SI DAMAGE* report on the state indicator is always the same. All occurrences of the function name and line number are removed, leaving only unidentified asterisks.

Clearing the state indicator means terminating all suspended functions on the list. This is most effectively done by entering one niladic branch for each ⋆ on the *SI* list. For the example above two niladic branches are needed:

```
     →
     →
```

This action clears the state indicator of functions *A*, *B*, *C*, and *D*.

Consider the following sequence of events:

```
     ∇F1[□]∇ '
   ∇ F1
[1]    A←4
[2].   B←A ¯3
   ∇
     F1
SYNTAX ERROR
F1[2] B←A ¯3
     ∧
```

```
        )SI
F1[2]  *
        ∇F1[0□9]
[0]    F1
        /1
[0]    FN1
SI DAMAGE
[1]    ∇
        )SI
        *
        FN1
SYNTAX ERROR
FN1[2] B←A ¯3
          ∧
        )SI
FN1[2] *
         *
        ∇FN1[1□6]
[1]    A←4
        2
[1]    Q:A←4
[2]    ∇
SI DAMAGE
        )SI
        *
        *
        ∇FN1[□]∇
    ∇ FN1
[1]    Q:A←4
[2]    B←A ¯3
    ∇
        FN1
SYNTAX ERROR
FN1[2] B←A ¯3
          ∧
        )SI
FN1[2] *
         *
         *
        )ERASE FN1
SI DAMAGE
        )SI
        *
        *
        *
```

The asterisks can be cleared from the state indicator with niladic branches:

```
      →
      →
      →
      )SI
```

As an illustration of how function editing and control are affected by suspended and pendent functions, consider the following events associated with the two function skeletons shown below:

```
      ∇ CALL
[1]    an expression
[2]    TEST
[3]    an expression with a SYNTAX error
      ∇

      ∇ TEST
[1]    an expression with a VALUE error
[2]    an expression with a SYNTAX error
[3]    an expression
      ∇
      CALL
VALUE ERROR
TEST[1]     .....Q.....
                 ∧

      Q←.....    giving Q a value, thereby correcting error
      )SI
TEST[1]    *
CALL[2]

      CALL    reexecuting CALL causes two versions of CALL to exist in the
              workspace
SYNTAX ERROR
TEST[2] .............
        ∧

      )SI
TEST[2]    *
CALL[2]
TEST[1]    *
CALL[2]

      ∇TEST[2] ............ ∇    error correction
SI DAMAGE
      )SI
      *
CALL[2]
```

```
        *
  CALL[2]

     CALL        reexecuting call causes three versions to exist
  SYNTAX ERROR
  CALL[3] ...........
              ∧

        ∇CALL[3] ............ ∇
  DEFN ERROR
        )SI
  CALL[3]    *

  CALL[2]    *

  CALL[2]    *
```

Since *CALL* exists in both pendent and suspended states, it cannot be edited. At this point it would be wise to clear the state indicator and start again:

```
     →
     →
     →
     )SI
```

Here is an approach to executing *CALL* that does not leave any pendent or suspended functions in the workspace:

```
     CALL
  VALUE ERROR
  TEST[1]    .....Q.....
                 ∧

     Q←.....
        )SI
  TEST[1]    *
  CALL[2]

        →1
  SYNTAX ERROR
  TEST[2] ...........
                 ∧

        )SI
  TEST[2]    *
  CALL[2]
```

```
       ∇TEST[2] ...... ∇
       →2
SYNTAX ERROR
CALL[3] ........
           ∧

       )SI
CALL[3]  *
       ∇CALL[3] ........ ∇
       →3
```

Execution resumes and is completed.

Associated with the)*SI* command is the command)*SIV*.)*SIV* lists the state indicator and beside each suspended function lists the variables local to it. Consider the following sequence:

```
     ∇ F1;A;B
[1]    A←4
[2]    B←A ⁻3
[3]    C←B 1
     ∇

A←B←C←5

     F1
SYNTAX ERROR
F1[2] B←A ⁻3
         ∧
     )SIV
F1[2] * A    B
     )VARS
     A
4
     B
VALUE ERROR
     B
     ∧
     C
5
```

Observe that the)*SIV* lists all the local variables in effect. They may not have been defined yet, for example, variable *B* in the above sequence. In a suspended state the values of the local variables take precedence over any global values of those variable names. The listing of the local variable names that is presented to a *SIV* is not necessarily alphabetic. The names are presented as they are stated in the header. These are then followed by the list of labels, again in the order used. For example,

```
      ∇ F;Q;A
[1]   R:A←5
[2]   B:Q←⁻A 1
      ∇

      F
SYNTAX ERROR
F[2] B:Q←⁻A 1
            ∧

      )SIV
F[2]   *    Q    A    R    B
```

Functions can be suspended in six common ways:

- An error is encountered during execution.

- ATTN is struck during execution.

- A *PA!:* message comes from the operator.

- The terminal is bounced, that is, is cut off by the operator or system.

- The *INTERRUPT* report is given in response to *⎕* or to *)SAVE* in the quad state.

- A *stop control* has been set for the function.

A *stop control* is a planned suspension of function execution. It is achieved with a statement similar to the trace control:

      S∆FN ← line numbers

This sets suspensions to occur just before the statements at the specified line numbers are executed. Removing the stop control is done with *S∆FN←0* or *S∆FN←⍳0.* A user might set a stop control to help him in debugging a function. The function execution can be stopped at critical points so that the value of variables can be checked and then execution resumed.

Like the trace control, the stop control is not a variable and does not appear in the variables list. Its values cannot be examined. Erasing a function also erases the stop vector for that function. The stop control is most often set before execution of a function begins. It can, however, be set during the execution of the function. For example, it might be turned on only for certain values of a counter, perhaps by a statement like this:

```
[7]   S∆FN←4 8 12×0=5|I
```

If the stop control was set during the execution of a function, labels in that function as well as absolute line numbers may be used in the stop control vector. For example,

```
      ∇ FN N
[1]    S∆FN←2,A
[2]    X←0
[3]    A:X←X+1
[4]    →A×N>X
      ∇

      FN 2
FN[2]
      →2
FN[3]
      →3
FN[3]
```

PROBLEMS

1. Consider the function $F1$ which generates a set of X binomial coefficients:

```
      ∇ Z←F1 X
[1]    Z←1
[2]    L1:Z←(0,Z)+Z,0
[3]    →L1×ιX≥ρZ
      ∇
```

   (a) What is the trace control expression for following the generation of the binomial coefficients?

   (b) If $T∆F1←3$, what possible values could appear after $F1[3]$ in the trace flow?

2. For the function PL shown below,

```
      ∇ PL X;I
[1]    I←⌈/X
[2]    ' □'[1+X≥I]
[3]    I←I-1
[4]    →2×ιI>0
      ∇
```

   with

```
      T∆PL←1 3 4
      PL 3 1 2
```

   what does the trace flow printout look like?

3. Insert a new line in the function $LOOP$ shown below which will cause line 2 to be traced every third time beginning with the first:

```
      ∇ Z←LOOP N;I
[1]    I←0
[2]    Z←2*I
[3]    →2×N>I←I+1
      ∇
```

4. The function $F1$ iterates toward a solution. As a precaution you decide to cause a suspension at a location within the main loop if the number of times through the loop exceeds N. Complete line 3 in the function $F1$ shown below so that a suspension occurs when the loop is traversed for the Nth time:

```
      ∇ F1;X
[1]     X←0
[2]     X←X+1
[3]     _ _ _ _ _ _ _
[4]     →2
      ∇
```

5. Consider the following functions and the given sequence of events:

```
      ∇ F1
[1]     2+2
[2]     F2
[3]     F3
      ∇

      ∇ F2
[1]     'ANS'
      ∇

      ∇ F3
[1]     'END'
      ∇

      SΔF1←2
      SΔF2←1
      F1
4
F1[2]
      →2
F2[1]
```

At this point in the sequence, determine the next event to follow if

    (a)   →1   **(b)**   →0   **(c)**   )SI

    (d)   →   **(e)**   ∇F1[☐]∇

6. Fill in the blanks:

```
      FS
SYNTAX ERROR
FS[3]   Z←A B
          ∧
      )SI
```

    (a) _____

```
      )ERASE FS
      )SI DAMAGE
      )SI
```

    (b) _____

Section 6.6 LOCKED FUNCTIONS

There are times when it is desirable that the users of a function not be permitted to examine the definition of a function; for example, a program simulating a lab experiment intended for students to discover a property of chemistry, such as the relationship between volume and pressure of a gas, may have the answer embedded in the function or a function that the writer intends to sell might contain some difficult and ingenious programming techniques that he does not wish to become generally available. Whatever the reason, the means of *locking* a function is to open or close function definition with a $\nabla\!\!\!\sim$ (∇ backspace $\sim$) instead of a ∇. A locked function can only be executed or erased. It cannot be edited. The trace control and stop control for a locked function are nullified.* Once locked, a function may never be unlocked. Functions should not be locked capriciously. Also, before locking a function, it is wise to obtain a display of it for your records.

If an error occurs during the execution of a locked function *FN*, a *DOMAIN ERROR* report† is given and execution of the function terminates. If *FN* was called by a locked function, execution of that function terminates also. In a calling sequence the execution of all locked functions terminate. If a function in a calling sequence is not locked, its execution is suspended.

Illustration 6.6 Locking Variables

Variables cannot be locked. However, an explicit niladic function can be created to prevent a name from having its value changed by respecification. For example,

```
    ∇Z←SERIES
[1]    Z←1 1 2 3 5 8 13 21
    ∇
```

SERIES is a constant and behaves like a variable except that it cannot be respecified.

Section 6.7 RECURSIVE FUNCTIONS

In Sec. 2.3 we gave an example of how one function could call others: the function *ATR* called the function *PI* in its defining body. Besides a function calling another function, it is possible to have a function call itself. Such a function is called a *recursive* function. A recursive function is a function that is defined in terms of itself. For example, the Fibonacci sequence 1 1 2 3 5 8 13 ... can be defined recursively. For this sequence the next term is derived by summing the previous two terms. A recursive function for the first *N* terms of the Fibonacci sequence is

---

*APL.SV only. In APL/360, the trace control and stop control can be set before the function is locked. Once the function is locked, the trace and stop controls cannot be changed.

†APL.SV only. In APL/360, the report *FN ERROR* is given.

```
      ∇ R←FIB N
[1]    R←1 1
[2]    →3×N≠2
[3]    R←FIB N-1
[4]    R←R,+/R[0 ‾1+ρR]
      ∇
```

Line 1 of *FIB* establishes the first two terms of the sequence — 1 1. Line 2 halts the execution of the function if only the first two terms of the sequence are required. Line 3 establishes the recursion. Here the function calls itself. Until $N=2$ (when execution stops) each encounter of line 3 causes another call of the function; thus, various copies or levels of the function are active, though pendent, in the workspace. After the last level of the function is executed (when $N=2$), the execution of the next higher level is completed, and so forth until all levels of the functions are executed completely. It is not until the execution of the called functions begins moving up the call levels that line 4 is executed. At line 4 the sum of the last two terms of R is catenated to R.

While the definition of a recursive function is typically short and easily stated, the concept of the execution is often difficult to comprehend. The detailed commentary below for *FIB* 6 is given to help you overcome any difficulties in understanding how a recursive function is executed.

Line Executed	Result	Comment
	FIB 6	Level 0—initial call of function
1	R←1 1	
2	→3	
3	R←*FIB* 5	Function level 0 is pendent until *FIB* 5 is evaluated
	FIB 5	Level 1—begin execution of *FIB* 5
1	R←1 1	
2	→3	
3	R←*FIB* 4	Function level 1 is pendent until *FIB* 4 is evaluated
	FIB 4	Level 2—begin execution of *FIB* 4
1	R←1 1	
2	→3	
3	R←*FIB* 3	Function level 2 is pendent until *FIB* 3 is evaluated.
	FIB 3	Level 3—begin execution of *FIB* 3
1	R←1 1	
2	→3	
3	R←*FIB* 2	Function level 3 is pendent until *FIB* 2 is evaluated

Line Executed	Result	Comment
	FIB 2	Level 4—begin execution of *FIB* 2
1	*R*←1 1	
2	→0	Recall that a branch to 0 terminates function execution and returns execution to the calling function
		The result of *FIB* 2 is 1 1; thus line 3 of level 3 can now be completed
		Return to level 3—continuing with line 3
3	*R*←1 1	
4	*R*←1 1 2	The result of *FIB* 3 is 1 1 2; thus line 3 of level 2 can now be completed
		Return to level 2—continuing with line 3
3	*R*←1 1 2	
4	*R*←1 1 2 3	The result of *FIB* 4 is 1 1 2 3; thus line 3 of level 1 can now be completed
		Return to level 1—continuing with line 3
3	*R*←1 1 2 3 5	The result of *FIB* 5 is 1 1 2 3 5; thus line 3 of level 0 can now be completed
		Return to level 0—continuing with line 3
4	*R*←1 1 2 3 5 8	Execution of all levels has been completed Result of 1 1 2 3 5 8 is printed

There are two attributes that a recursive definition must have. First, the definition must be explicit for some value of the function. In the definition of the Fibonacci sequence, the explicit value 1 1 is given for *N*=2. If an explicit value did not exist, the definition would be *circular*. This circularity arises from the second attribute of a recursive definition, namely, that the definition, except for the value which produces the explicit result, is defined in terms of itself. Thus for the Fibonacci sequence, *FIB N* is defined in terms of *FIB N*-1. If either of these attributes is ignored in a recursive definition, it will not terminate. Such a recursive definition is said to be *regressive*.*

The Fibonacci series function can be written in a nonrecursive form using looping. For example,

```
     ∇ R←FIBL N
[1]    R←1 1
[2]    N←N-1
[3]    →4×N≥2
[4]    R←R,+/R[0 ‾1+ρR]
[5]    →2
     ∇
```

---

*An excellent treatment of recursion can be found in D. W. Barron, *Recursive Techniques in Programming*, American Elsevier, New York, 1968.

The difference between *FIB* and *FIBL* is that the counting for the number of times the loop should be executed is explicitly stated in *FIBL*. In the recursive definition, it is controlled implicitly by the number of times the function gets called.

Recursive functions are not generally used because they use more workspace than a nonrecursive definition and typically take longer to execute. For a recursive function to execute properly, it must preserve its current environment for each call. And then upon completion of the innermost call, it must be able to restore a previous environment. Also, errors in recursive functions may be difficult to detect, particularly if several levels of recursion are involved.

A word of caution: An improper definition of a recursive function can cause much difficulty and confusion. For instance, suppose that the recursive function depends on a specific value for a variable. If this variable is initialized within the function, the function becomes regressive. For example,

```
      ∇ Z←RF1 Y
[1]      I←4
[2]      Z←1
[3]      →0×ι0=I←I-1
[4]      Z←Z+RF1 Y
      ∇

      RF1 3
WS FULL
RF1[4]   Z←Z+RF1 Y
                  ∧
```

Notice that line 1 initializes *I* to 4 so that for each function call *I* becomes 4. The function termination condition at line 3 for *I*=0 is never met. The *WS FULL* * report during the execution of the function means that more function calls were made than could be accommodated by the system. The function can be corrected, as follows, and reexecuted. Notice that the initial value of *I* is established outside of the definition.

```
      ∇ Z←RF1 Y
[1]      Z←1
[2]      →0×ι0=I←I-1
[3]      Z←Z+RF1 Y
      ∇

      I←4
      RF1 3
      4
```

Another source of error occurs in the definition of functions. If you forget to close the definition of a function before you call for its execution, you may

---

*APL.SV only. In APL/360, a *DEPTH ERROR* report is given.

inadvertently define a regressive recursive function. Consider the following sequence:

```
      ∇  Z←RF2 X
[1]    Z←X 2
      ∇

      RF2 4
SYNTAX ERROR
RF2[1] Z←X 2
       ∧
      ∇RF2[1□9]
[1]    Z←X 2
        1
[1]    Z←X*2
[2]    RF2 4
[3]    ∇

      RF2 4
WS FULL
RF2[2]  RF2 4
       ∧
```

Illustration 6.7 Factorial—Defined Recursively

A recursive definition for finding the factorial of N is

$$1 \text{ if } N = 0 \quad \text{or} \quad N \times \text{factorial } (N-1)$$

FACT is a function for this recursive definition:

```
      ∇  Z←FACT N
[1]    Z←1
[2]    →3×N≠0
[3]    Z←N×FACT N-1
      ∇
```

Illustration 6.8 Permutations—Defined Recursively

A recursive definition for computing the number of permutations of N things taken K at a time, $P(N, K)$, is (where $P(N, K) = 0$ for $K > N$)

$$P(N, 0) = 1$$
$$P(N, K) = (N + 1 - K) \times P(N, K - 1)$$

PERM is a function for this recursive definition:

```
      ∇  Z←N PERM K
[1]    →0×1Z←K=0
[2]    Z←(N+1-K)×N PERM K-1
      ∇
```

Illustration 6.9 Binary Addition—Defined Recursively

The actual adding of binary numbers A and B within a computer system can be defined and executed in terms of *exclusive-or* and *and* and a left shift. The algorithm consists of "exclusive-or-ing" the binary numbers A and B to get a partial sum, $Z1$. Next the carries $C1$ are determined by "and-ing" A and B together. Then the partial sum $Z1$ is "exclusive-or-ed" with the carry vector $C1$ left-shifted by 1 to get a new partial sum $Z2$. A new carry vector is created by again "and-ing" the partial sum $Z1$ with the left-shifted carry vector $C1$ to get a new vector, $C2$. This process continues until the carry vector is all zeros. The recursive function *ADDER*, shown below, defines this algorithm:

```
     ∇ Z←A ADDER B
[1]    Z←A≠B
[2]    →3×1∊C←A∧B
[3]    Z←Z ADDER (C,0)[1+ιρC]
     ∇
```

For example,

```
     ADDEND← 0 0 1 1
     AUGEND← 0 1 1 1
     AUGEND ADDER ADDEND
1 0 1 0
```

Illustration 6.10 Tower of Hanoi Puzzle

In *The World of Mathematics*,* J. R. Newman discusses the Tower of Hanoi puzzle. He repeats the following little story from W. W. R. Ball.† "In the great temple at Benares beneath the dome which marks the center of the world, rests a brass plate in which are fixed three diamond needles, each a cubit high and as thick as the body of a bee. On one of these needles, at the creation, Brahma placed 64 disks of pure gold, the largest disk resting on the brass plate and the others getting smaller and smaller up to the top one. This is the tower of Brahma. Day and night unceasingly, the priests transfer the disks from one diamond needle to another, according to the fixed and immutable law of Brahma, which requires that the priest on duty must not move more than one disk at a time and that he must place this disk on a needle so that there is no smaller disk below it. When the 64 disks shall have been thus transferred from the needle on which, at the creation, Brahma placed them, to one of the other needles, tower, temple, and Brahmas alike will crumble into dust, and with a thunderclap, the world will vanish."

The recursive function, *BRAHMA*, prints out the steps that the priests should follow in moving the disks. The function has as its left argument N the number of

---

World of Mathematics, J. R. Newman, (New York: Simon and Schuster, 1956), Vol. 4, p. 2425.

† W. W. R. Ball, *Mathematical Recreations and Essays*, 11th ed. (New York: Macmillan, 1939).

disks on the first needle and as its right argument *NEEDLES* a three-component vector giving the numbers of the first, auxiliary, and receiving needles, respectively:

```
    ∇ N BRAHMA NEEDLES
[1]    →0×ιN=0
[2]    (N-1)BRAHMA NEEDLES[1 3 2]
[3]    'MOVE DISK ';N;' FROM NEEDLE ';NEEDLES[1];' TO ';NEEDLES[3]
[4]    (N-1)BRAHMA NEEDLES[2 1 3]
    ∇
```

Since, for *N*=64, as specified by the story, there are ‾1+2*64 moves required, we show a test of the function on a smaller *N*:

```
    4 BRAHMA 1 2 3
MOVE DISK 1 FROM NEEDLE 1 TO 2
MOVE DISK 2 FROM NEEDLE 1 TO 3
MOVE DISK 1 FROM NEEDLE 2 TO 3
MOVE DISK 3 FROM NEEDLE 1 TO 2
MOVE DISK 1 FROM NEEDLE 3 TO 1
MOVE DISK 2 FROM NEEDLE 3 TO 2
MOVE DISK 1 FROM NEEDLE 1 TO 2
MOVE DISK 4 FROM NEEDLE 1 TO 3
MOVE DISK 1 FROM NEEDLE 2 TO 3
MOVE DISK 2 FROM NEEDLE 2 TO 1
MOVE DISK 1 FROM NEEDLE 3 TO 1
MOVE DISK 3 FROM NEEDLE 2 TO 3
MOVE DISK 1 FROM NEEDLE 1 TO 2
MOVE DISK 2 FROM NEEDLE 1 TO 3
MOVE DISK 1 FROM NEEDLE 2 TO 3
```

PROBLEMS

1. The number of combinations of *N* things taken *K* at a time can be defined recursively as follows:

$$C(N, 0) = 1$$
$$C(N, N) = 1$$
$$C(N, K) = 0 \text{ for } K > N$$
$$C(N, K) = C(N-1, K) + C(N-1, K-1)$$

Define a recursive function *COMB* to compute the number of combinations of *N* things taken *K* at a time.

2. Bessel functions $J(N, X)$ of the same argument and different orders can be defined recursively as follows:

$$J(N, X) = \left(\frac{2(N-1)J(N-1, X)}{X}\right) - J(N-2, X)$$

For $X = 6$, $J(0, 6)$ is 0.1506452572 and $J(1, 6)$ is -0.2766838581. Define a recursive function $BESSEL$ to compute the Nth order Bessel function for $X \leftarrow 6$.

       Test:

             $N \leftarrow 5$

             $X \leftarrow 6$

           $\cdots \cdots$

       0.36209

Section 6.8   SUMMARY

The defined function capabilities discussed in Chapter 6 expand the variety and complexity of function definition available to the user and provide additional techniques for function debugging. Additionally, in Chapter 6 we have presented two primitive functions for formatting output.

Branching

Branching alters the sequential order of execution of a function. The syntax of a branch statement is

     $\rightarrow$ expression

The value of the expression following the branch arrow determines the next line to be executed is as follows:

Value	Next Action
Positive integer N or vector whose first component is N	Line N is executed (if N is in the set of line numbers of the function)
0 or Q, where Q is a number outside the set of line numbers of the function	Execution terminates
Empty array	Next sequential line is executed

There are three types of branches—unconditional, conditional, and niladic. An unconditional branch is a branch which always results in the same line being executed next; that is, the value of the branch expression is a constant. A conditional branch is a branch where the next line to be executed is dependent on the value of a relationship. There are several forms of conditional branches. Some of these are illustrated below. The vertical lines indicate the sequential execution. $\rightarrow$ indicates a branch point. R stands for a relationship whose value is 0 or 1.

1. "Fork-in-the road," where at some point in the execution of the function, one of two paths is followed:

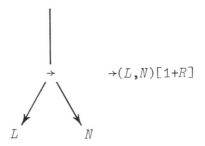

$$\rightarrow(L,N)[1+R]$$

2. "Go on or quit," where at some point either execution continues at some line L or execution terminates;

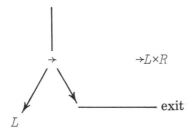

$$\rightarrow L \times R$$

— exit

3. "Jump or continue," where at some point either execution skips forward or backward or the next sequential line is executed:

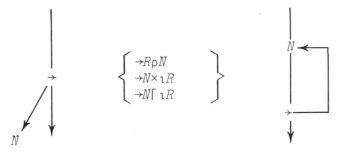

$$\left\{ \begin{array}{l} \rightarrow R \rho N \\ \rightarrow N \times \iota R \\ \rightarrow N \lceil \iota R \end{array} \right\}$$

The niladic branch, a branch arrow without a succeeding value or expression, terminates execution of all nested functions in the calling sequence.

One danger associated with branching is an *endless loop*. This occurs if, because of the programming, the exit condition for terminating function execution is never met. Once an endless loop is suspected, hitting ATTN interrupts execution of the function, and corrective action can be taken.

Labels

A label is a name preceding an expression and separated from it by a colon. A label is a constant whose value is the line number on which it appears. Editing which affects the line numbers of a function causes the value of the label to be changed. Labels are local to the function containing them. Labels are usually used at branch-to points in a function so that the branch statement shows a branch to a label instead of to a number.

Comments

The symbol ⍝ preceding a line indicates that the line is a comment and is not to be executed. A comment in a function has a line number.

Output

⎕←E is an explicit command to display the value of E, the expression to the right of the specification arrow. It is generally elided except in cases of multiple specification or mixed branching and specification.

In the execution of a function the output of an expression to the right of the specification arrow in ⎕←T does not include the customary concluding carrier return if the next expression executed is ⎕← or VAR←⍞. Thus the next output or keyboard entry continues on the same line as that generated by ⎕←T. This is called *bare output*.

Input

The quad ⎕ for numeric input and the quote-quad ⍞ for character input anywhere but to the immediate left of a specification arrow interrupts execution of the expression containing them until something to replace them is entered from the keyboard. If ⎕ is used, ⎕: is typed as a signal that input is required. If ⍞ is used, the keyboard releases and the carrier remains at the left margin. All data entered to replace quote-quad are taken as character data. Besides numeric data to replace the quad, character data can be used if they are enclosed in quotes. System commands can also be executed. To stop an input quad, use a niladic branch →. To stop an input quote-quad, use ⍚ (O backspace U backspace T in that order only) to interrupt the evaluation of the expression; then use a niladic branch →.

Tracing

A trace on a line in a function causes the value of the line to be printed each time it is executed. T∆ followed by the function name is the trace control vector.

T∆FN← line numbers

sets the trace control for the lines indicated.

T∆FN←⍳0

turns off the trace.

Suspension

The six common causes of suspended execution of a function are

- An error.

- A $PA!$: message from the operator.

- ATTN is struck.

- The terminal is bounced, disconnected by the operator.

- $\square$ in response to an input quote-quad or $)SAVE$ in response to an input quad.

- A stop control vector is set.

The stop control vector is set by $S\Delta FN\leftarrow$ line numbers. It is removed by $S\Delta FN\leftarrow\iota 0$. Function execution is suspended at each line represented in the stop control vector. Execution of a suspended function can be terminated by using a niladic branch → or a branch to a line number not in the set of line numbers of the function. Or execution can be resumed by a branch to a line number in the set of line numbers of the function, usually to the line number indicated in the suspension report.

The state indicator is a list of the functions currently suspended or pendent. A function is pendent if its execution is interrupted so that a function that is called can be executed. The system command $)SI$ lists the state indicator with the most recently interrupted function first. The system command $)SIV$ lists the state indicator giving the suspended and pendent function together with the variables local to it. The most recently interrupted function appears first. If the function is a suspended function, an asterisk follows its name and line number. Only suspended functions on the list, functions with an asterisk, can be edited. Pendent functions cannot be edited. The report $SI\ DAMAGE$ is given if function editing or $)ERASE$ disrupts the state indicator.

Locked Functions

Opening or closing a function definition with ∇ locks a function; that is, it prohibits the function from being edited or displayed. Once locked, a function cannot be unlocked. It can only be erased. If an error occurs in a locked function FN, the report $FN\ ERROR$ is given and execution of the function and all locked functions in the calling sequence terminates. If a function in the calling sequence is not locked, function execution is suspended at that function.

Recursive Functions

A function which calls itself is called a recursive function. Any APL defined function may be recursive. Such a defined function is characterized by containing in the body of the function a call to itself and an explicit result for some given value of the function.

An inadvertent source of error arises when the user calls a function which he may have just edited before he closes the definition. When he does close the definition, he has created an accidental recursive function. When called, it will continue to execute until the workspace is full.

New Primitive Functions

The two primitive functions, monadic and dyadic ⍌, introduced in Chapter 6 are summarized in the table on the next page.

Function	Syntax	General Description	Right Argument	Left Argument	Conformability
Dyadic format	$A\,\mathbf{\bar{\phi}}\,B$	Formats a numeric array into a character array of same rank; puts spaces between the columns of B and controls precision and form of values in each column of B	Numeric array of any shape and rank	Scalar or vector defining format of result; each pair of components of A specifies the controls for the corresponding column of B; first value of pair declares width of number field; second value of pair declares precision and form of numbers in column; positive numbers indicate decimal form—value indicates number of digits to right of decimal point; negative numbers indicate exponential form—value indicates number of digits in the multiplier If first value of a pair is zero, one space is automatically provided between columns If the left argument is a scalar, width of zero is assumed for all columns, and value controls precision and form; if only one pair, it applies to all columns.	A is a scalar or two-component vector or $(\rho A) = 2\times(\rho B)[\rho\rho B]$
Monadic format	$\mathbf{\bar{\phi}}\,B$	Produces a character array identical to printing normally associated with its numeric argument; leaves character argument unchanged	Data array of any shape and rank		

DATA SELECTION
AND REARRANGEMENT

Indexing, introduced in Chapter 3, is a powerful multipurpose function. It can be used for selecting certain data from an array as well as for changing the relationship among the components of an array. For instance, the index expression can be established so that only the components satisfying certain conditions are selected from the indexed array as when even-numbered components are selected from a vector V by the expression $V[2\times\iota\lfloor.5\times\rho V]$. Or the components of an array can be rearranged by an appropriate index expression as when a vector V is sorted in ascending order by the expression $V[\underline{\textstyle{\Delta}}V]$. Indexing, however, is a rather cumbersome means of selecting certain data from an array or for making certain rearrangements of the data. The functions in this chapter represent other means of selecting specific data from arrays and other means of changing the relationship among the components of an array.

Section 7.1 DATA SELECTION

Section 7.1.1 Compression

The function *compression* L/A is used to eliminate components from an array that do not satisfy the stated conditions, leaving only those that do. The right argument A defines the original data, and the left argument L is a logical vector defining the rule of the compression. The elements of A are matched with the corresponding components of L. Where the component of L is a 1 that corresponding element of A is retained; where the component of L is 0, the corresponding element of A is discarded or compressed out. In a sense, L is an overlay or a mask placed upon the right argument data. For example,

```
      0 1 0 1 0 1 0 1/6 2 ‾3 ‾4 1 5 ‾2 9
2 ‾4 5 9
```

```
      1 1 0 1 0 0 1/'CULTURE'
CUTE
```

Generally, the left argument is created through an expression. For instance, if V is a vector, the expression $(V \geq 0)/V$ removes the negative components of V. For example,

```
      V←9 ¯8 3.2 ¯4.1 ¯7
      (V≥0)/V
9 3.2
```

The expression $((\rho V)\rho 0\ 1)/V$ eliminates the odd-indexed components of V:

```
      ((ρV)ρ0 1)/V
¯8 ¯4.1
```

The right argument may be any array, and the compression may be performed along any of its dimensions by using an axis-specifier. The axis-specifier defines the dimension along which the compression is to be carried out. The general form of compression is

```
      L/[I]A
```

where

A is the data to be compressed. It may have any rank and shape.

I indicates the dimension along which compression is to occur.

L is the binary scalar or vector defining the rule of the compression.

The arguments are conformable if $(\rho L) = (\rho A)[I]$. That is, L must state what is to be done with each element in the dimension along which compression is to occur. For example,

```
      MAT
ABCD
EFGH
IJKL

      0 1 0/[1]MAT
EFGH
```

MAT has three rows. To compress along rows requires a three-component left argument.

```
      0 1 1 0/[2]MAT
BC
FG
JK
```

MAT has four columns. To compress along columns requires a four-component left argument.

Note: If no explicit axis-specifier is stated, the compression is along the last index, the column index. Thus the expression `0 1 1 0/MAT` is identical to the expression `0 1 1 0/[2]MAT`. Also, the symbol $\neq$ indicates that compression is along the first dimension. Thus the expression `0 1 0≠MAT` is identical to the expression `0 1 0/[1]MAT`.

The shape of the result of compression is the same as the shape of the right argument except for the dimension in which compression occurs. In this dimension, the degree of freedom is $+/L$. The rank of the result is the same as the rank of the right argument.

If the left argument is a binary scalar, the right argument is totally accepted or totally compressed. For example,

```
      1/'ALL'
ALL
      0/'ALL'
ƀ
```

*Illustration 7.1   Selecting Even-Subscripted Components
              of a Vector*

In the beginning of this chapter the even-subscripted components of a vector V were selected by indexing. The expression $(\sim2|\iota\rho V)/V$ accomplishes the same thing by compressing out the odd-subscripted components of V. For example,

```
      V←6 2 ¯3 ¯4 1 5 ¯2
      (~2|ιρV)/V
2 ¯4 5
```

Illustration 7.2   Conserving Space by Compressing Out Blanks

Often blanks or other characters are compressed out of a character string to preserve storage space. For example, the labeled S/360 instruction $RET\ LR\ 4,3$ can have its blanks compressed out:

```
      M←'RET LR 4,3'
      C←(L←' '≠M)/M
      C
RETLR4,3
```

$$L$$
1 1 1 0 1 1 0 1 1 1

Illustration 7.3 A Multiple-Way Branch

The compression function can be used as part of a branching statement. For example, the expression $\rightarrow(I>0)/17$ results in a branch to line 17 if $I>0$. Otherwise the next sequential line of the function is executed. A four-way branch depending on whether a variable is 1000, positive, negative, or 0 can be accomplished with a statement like this:

$$[12] \quad \rightarrow((R=1000),(R>0) \;\; R<0)/0 \;\; 31 \;\; 22$$

If R is 1000, function execution terminates; if it is positive and not equal to 1,000, a branch to line 31 occurs; if negative, a branch to line 22 occurs; and if 0, the next sequential line, line 13, is executed.

Illustration 7.4 A Selective Output Message

The compression function can be used in constructing a character string for printout. For example, in a prompting environment, assuming the response and solution are scalars, the expression

$$(SOLUTION{\neq}ANSWER)/\text{'}INCORRECT \;\; ANSWER\text{'}$$

produces the message $INCORRECT \;\; ANSWER$ if the user's solution does not match the answer. A more elaborate expression

$$((SOLUTION{\neq}ANSWER)/\text{'}IN\text{'}),\text{'}CORRECT \;\; ANSWER\text{'}$$

produces either the message $CORRECT \;\; ANSWER$ or the message $INCORRECT$ $ANSWER$ depending on whether the solution agrees or disagrees with the answer.

Illustration 7.5 Finding the Indices of Duplicate Components
in a Vector

Given a vector V with duplicate components, the expression $(S{=}V)/\iota\rho V$ produces the indices of all occurrences of the scalar S in V. For example,

$$V \leftarrow 4 \;\; 7 \;\; 8 \;\; 4 \;\; 6 \;\; 4 \;\; 2 \;\; 1 \;\; 4$$
$$(4{=}V)/\iota\rho V$$
1 4 6 9

Note: This can be considered as an extension to the index-of function since it provides the indices of all occurrences of a scalar instead of only the index of the first occurrence. For example,

$$V\iota 4$$
1

PROBLEMS

1. Use the following variables to evaluate expressions (a)–(r):

```
Z←1 2 3 4 5
Y←10 5 3 6 4
        AA
    1   2
    3   4
    5   6

    7   8
    9  10
   11  12
        AL
ADG
BEH
CFI
A←0 0 0 0 1 1 1 1
B←0 0 1 1 0 0 1 1
C←0 1 0 1 0 1 0 1
```

(a)	$A/\iota 8$	(b)	$B/\iota 8$
(c)	$(3>\iota 8)/\iota 8$	(d)	$1\ 0\ 1/AL$
(e)	$0\ 1\ 0/[2]AA$	(f)	$0\ 1/AA$
(g)	$(A\vee C)/B\vee C$	(h)	$(Z\in Y)/Y$
(i)	$(Y\in Z)/Z$	(j)	$(\sim A)/\iota 8$
(k)	A/B	(l)	$(3<\iota 8)/\iota 8$
(m)	$1\ 0\ 1/[1]AL$	(n)	$\rho 0\ 1\ 0/[2]AA$
(o)	$\rho 0\ 1/AA$	(p)	$A\vee C/B\vee C$
(q)	$1\ 0\ 0\ 0\ 1\ 0\ 1\ 0\ 0/\text{'}CONTAINER\text{'}$	(r)	$1\ 0\ 1\ 0\ 1\ 1\ 0\ 0\ /\text{'}INDOLENT\text{'}$

2. Write an expression to select from V the components with the following properties (if you wish, use test data $V←\bar{}2.5\ 3\ \bar{}0.5\ 2\ 1\ \bar{}2$):

   (a) Not equal to 3.   (b) Not less than negative .6.

   (c) Less than 2.   (d) Positive.

   (e) Positive or less than negative .6.   (f) Equal to 3.

   (g) Less than 2 and not less than negative .6. (h) Positive and not equal to 3.

3. Write the expressions to delete from a vector V of integers the following (if you wish, use test data $V←5\ 6\ 2\ \bar{}4\ 8\ \bar{}3\ 2\ 4\ \bar{}8$):

   (a) All negative components.

   (b) All even components.

   (c) All odd components.

   (d) All components divisible by 3.

   (e) All components between negative 5 and 5.

4. (a) Define a function DEL to delete from a binary matrix M all leading and trailing rows and columns of zeros.

Test:

```
         M
 0  0  0  0
 0  0  0  0
 0  1  1  0
 0  1  0  0
 0  0  0  0
     . . . . . . . . .
 1  1
 1  0
```

(b) Modify DEL to handle all numeric matrices.

Test:

```
          M
 0  0  0  0  0
 1  1  2  0  0
 8  5  3  0  0
 3  2  6  0  0
 0  0  0  0  0
      . . . . . . . . .
 1  1  2
 8  5  3
 3  2  6
```

5. (a) Define a function PD to determine all the positive divisors of a given positive integer N.

   Test:
   ```
              N←24
           . . . . . . .
    1  2  3  4  6  8  12  24
   ```

   (b) Define a function PV to return a 1 if the given positive integer N is a *prime number* (a number divisible only by 1 and itself) and a 0 if it is not a prime number. Use function PD.

   Test:
   ```
              N←53
           . . . . . .
    1
              N←33
           . . . . . .
    0
   ```

   (c) Define a function LM to list the prime numbers that lie between the integers R and S, inclusive. Use function PV.

6. Define a function RD to remove all duplicate elements from a vector V.

   Test:
   ```
         V←1  2  3  4  1  3  4  1  2  6  1
          . . . . . . .
    1  2  3  4  6
   ```

7. Assume that vectors $S1$ and $S2$ are two sets (that is, vectors that have no duplicate elements). Write the expression for each of the following:
   (a) The intersection of $S1$ and $S2$.

Test:

$$S1 \leftarrow 9 \ 6 \ 2 \ 8 \ 3$$
$$S2 \leftarrow 1 \ 3 \ 8 \ 5 \ 6$$

. . . . . .

3   8   6

(b) The union of $S1$ and $S2$.
    Test:

. . . .

1   2   3   5   6   8   9

(c) The symmetric difference of $S1$ and $S2$.
    Test:

. . . .

9   2   1   5

(d) That $S1$ and $S2$ are identical. Set the result equal to 1 if they are, and to 0 otherwise.
    Test:

. . . .

0

8. (a) Define a function $FIND$ for finding the longest word in a character string CS. In other words, find the longest string of consecutive nonblank characters. Display this string. If there is a tie, display the leftmost string.
    Test:

$$CS \leftarrow \text{'}TRIAL \ AND \ ERROR\text{'}$$

. . . .

5
TRIAL

(b) Modify the function $FIND$ so that each longest word is displayed.
    Test:

. . . .

5
TRIAL
ERROR

9. Define a function OUT to delete a given name N from a matrix NMS.
    Test:

            NMS

JOAN
PETER
CARL
SCOTT
ADAM

          $N \leftarrow \text{'}JOAN\text{'}$

. . . .

PETER
CARL
SCOTT
ADAM

10. Define a function $LOCATE$ to determine the number and locations of the vowels $A\ E\ I\ O\ U$ in a character vector CV.

> *Test:*
> $$CV \leftarrow 'HOW\ NOW\ BROWN\ COW'$$
> $\cdots\cdots$
> ```
> A  0
> E  0
> I  0
> O  4  2  6  11  16
> U  0
> ```

11. Write an expression to delete the rows of a matrix M whose first component is a duplicate of a first component of some previous row of M.

> *Test:*
> ```
>        M
>     1  2  2
>     0  0  0
>     2  2  1
>     0  0  0
>     0  1  2
> ```
> $\cdots\cdots$
> ```
>     1  2  2
>     0  0  0
>     2  2  1
> ```

12. Define a function $SIMUL$ to replace the commas in a character vector V containing variable-length items each separated by a comma (or other suitable separator) by a carrier return character so that on display it appears as if it were a matrix.

> *Test:*
> $$V \leftarrow 'TOM,\ DICK,\ HARRY'$$
> $\cdots\cdots$
> ```
> TOM
> DICK
> HARRY
> ```

13. When instructions are given within a function it is often useful to have two forms of the instructions—a long form with much detail and a short form. Define a function EXP to select the long form $LONG$ or the short form $SHORT$ depending on the setting of a previously specified global binary variable SW.

14. Write an expression to compress out all the blanks from a character string S.

Test:

$$S \leftarrow 'S \; Q \; U \; E \; E \; Z \; E'$$

. . . .

SQUEEZE

15. Illustration 5.23 illustrated a means of determining whether any of the distribution points can meet any of the demand schedules for all requirements of a department. Define a function *MATCH* to determine which distribution points can satisfy the delivery requirements of each department.

Test:

$$DEMAND \leftarrow 2 \; 3\rho10 \; 6 \; 15 \; 12 \; 7 \; 11$$
$$DEL \leftarrow 3 \; 3\rho10 \; 8 \; 15 \; 5 \; 7 \; 6 \; 12 \; 9 \; 11$$

. . . . . .

FOR DEPT. A DIST PT. X
FOR DEPT. B DIST PT. Y

Section 7.1.2 Expansion

Compression, as we saw in the preceding section, is a function that eliminates or compresses elements out of an array. At times, an opposite need arises: An expansion of the array data is required. For instance, Illustration 7.2 removed all the blanks for the character vector M, leaving $RETLR4,3$. For a printout, however, the blanks should be restored. The function expansion $L\backslash A$ will do this. For example,

```
      1 1 1 0 0 0 1 1 0 0 1 1 1\'RETLR4,3'
RET   LR  4,3
```

The right argument of expansion is the data whose shape is to be expanded. The left argument is a binary vector or scalar which defines the rule of the expansion. The location of zeros within this left argument indicates the places where zero or blank components are to be inserted. Zeros are inserted if the right argument is numeric. Blanks are inserted if the right argument is character.

The left argument of expansion is essentially an overlay or a mask defining the structure of the result relative to the original structure. For example,

```
      V←213  75  ¯89
      1 0 1 0 0 1\V
213 0 75 0 0 ¯89
      (9ρ1 0 0)\V
213 0 0 75 0 0 ¯89 0 0
      H←'HIHOHO'
      1 1 0 1 1 0 1 1\H
HI HO HO
```

The general **form** for the expansion function is

$$L\backslash[I]A$$

where:

A is the data over which expansion is to occur. The rank and shape of A are arbitrary.

I is the dimension along which expansion is to occur.

L is the binary vector defining the rule of the expansion.

The arguments are conformable if $(+/L) = (\rho A)[I]$, that is, the number of binary 1s in L must match the dimension along which the expansion is to occur. Otherwise there is a *LENGTH ERROR* report. How the axis-specifier works is shown with the following examples:

```
        MAT
ABCD
EFGH
IJKL
        1 0 1 0 1\[1]MAT
ABCD

EFGH

IJKL
```

There are three rows in *MAT*, and so to expand rows requires that the left argument contain three 1s. The expression 1 0 1 0 1↑*MAT* produces the same result. The symbol ↑ indicates that the expansion occurs along the first dimension:

```
        1 1 0 1 0 0 1\MAT    (or 1 1 0 1 0 0 1\[2]MAT)
AB C  D
EF G  H
IJ K  L
```

There are four columns in *MAT*, and so to expand columns requires four 1s in the left argument. The omission of the axis-specifier indicates that the expansion occurs along the last or column dimension.

Illustration 7.6 Inserting Data into an Array

Expansion, combined with indexing, makes it possible to insert data into an array. Consider the following examples:

```
        I←ι5
J←(10ρ1 0)\I
```

```
      J
1 0 2 0 3 0 4 0 5 0
      J[2×ι5]←.5+ι5
      J
1 1.5 2 2.5 3 3.5 4 4.5 5 5.5
      H←'SMILE'
      M←(9ρ1 0)\H
      M
S M I L E
      M[2×ι4]←'*'
      M
S*M*I*L*E
      R←2 3ρι6
      S←1 0 1 0 1\R
      S
  1 0 2 0 3
  4 0 5 0 6
      S[;2 4]←2 2ρ-8 7 6 5
      S
  1 ‾8 2 ‾7 3
  4 ‾6 5 ‾5 6
```

Illustration 7.7 Distinguishing Between a Character and a
Numeric Null Vector

While there is no visible distinction between a numeric null vector and a character null vector, an internal distinction is made. The expansion function allows us to determine which it is:

```
      0\''
ϸ
      0\ι0
0
```

The expression $0=0\backslash0\rho V$ produces a 0 if V is a character vector and a 1 if V is a numeric vector. The function *DIAGNOSE* shown below incorporates this information to print the determination of whether its argument is a character or numeric vector:

```
    ∇ DIAGNOSE V;MSG
[1]   MSG← 2 9 ρ'CHARACTER NUMERIC '
[2]   'THE VECTOR IS A ',(, MSG[1+0=0\0ρV;]),' VECTOR.'
    ∇
```

For example:

```
      R←6 8 12 15
      T←'FULL STEAM AHEAD'
      DIAGNOSE R
THE VECTOR IS A NUMERIC VECTOR.
      DIAGNOSE T
THE VECTOR IS A CHARACTER VECTOR.
```

Illustration 7.8 Producing More Readable Printout

The function *HISTO* shown in Illustration 5.18 produces a bar graph representation of the integer argument. For example,

```
      'T' HISTO 3 2 4 1 2
   T
 T T
 TTT T
 TTTTT
```

The graph is displayed with the columns adjacent to each other. A visually better picture can be achieved if each column of the graph is separated by two spaces. This can be achieved using the expand function and adding another line to the function as follows:

```
[2]    Z←((3×(ρZ)[2])ρ1 0 0)\Z
```

Then

```
      'T' HISTO 3 2 4 1 2
      T
 T    T
 T  T  T     T
 T  T  T  T  T
```

Illustration 7.9 Underscoring a Character String

The function *US* illustrates a technique for underscoring character data without backspacing:

```
    ∇ Z←US W
[1]    CR←' (A CARRIER RETURN IS ENTERED HERE)
'
[2]    Z←W,CR,(' '≠W)\(W+.≠' ')ρ'‾'
    ∇
      US 'AN UNDERSCORE FUNCTION'
AN UNDERSCORE FUNCTION
```

PROBLEMS

1. Use the following variables for evaluating expressions (a)–(g):

```
CC←'THE YEAR 1776'
     AA
 1  2
 3  4
 5  6

 7  8
 9 10
11 12

      AL
ADG
BEH
CFI
```

   (a) 1 0 1 0 1\3ρCC   (b) 1 0 1 0 1\AL

   (c) 1 0 0 1 1\[1]AL   (d) 1 0 1\AA

   (e) ρ1 1 0 1\AL   (f) 1 0 1\[1]AA

   (g) 1 1 0 1 0 1 1 1 1\'AMIABLE'

2. Define a function *INTO* to insert an arbitrary character N between each character in a vector V.

       Test:

```
           V←'LOOK HERE'
           N←'!'

           . . . . . . .
       L!O!O!K! !H!E!R!E!
```

3. For a numeric matrix M,

   (a) Write an expression to insert a zero column after every given column.

   (b) Write an expression to insert a zero row after every given row.

   (c) Write an expression to insert a zero row and column after every given row and column.

       Test:

```
             M
       1  2  3
       4  5  6

       . . . . . . .
       1 0 2 0 3 0
       0 0 0 0 0 0
       4 0 5 0 6 0
       0 0 0 0 0 0
```

4. Define a function *MESH* to mesh together two numeric vectors V and W as prescribed by a binary mesh vector K. A value of 1 for a component of K implies the placement of a component of V and a 0 component of K implies a placement of a component of W.

   Test:

   $$V \leftarrow 1 \ 3 \ 5 \ 7$$
   $$W \leftarrow {}^-2 \ {}^-4 \ {}^-6$$
   $$K \leftarrow 1 \ 1 \ 0 \ 0 \ 1 \ 0 \ 1$$
   $$\cdots\cdots$$
   $$1 \ 3 \ {}^-2 \ {}^-4 \ 5 \ {}^-6 \ 7$$

5. Define a function *REPLACE* to replace in a given character string S all the occurrences of any of the characters of a string C by blanks.

   Test:

   $$S \leftarrow {}'SMITH,J.P.$$
   $$C \leftarrow {}',.'$$
   $$\cdots\cdots$$
   $$SMITH \ J \ P$$

Section 7.1.3 Take

Compression, as we have seen in Sec. 7.1.1, permits the selection of elements from anywhere in an array. Often, however, simply the first or last of so many elements is needed from an array. This more restrictive selection process is obtained more directly using the mixed dyadic function *take—* $A \uparrow B$. For vector right arguments, take selects the *first* or *last* /A sequential components from B. For example,

```
      Q←'MARSHALL'
      5↑Q
MARSH
      ‾5↑Q
SHALL
```

The right argument of take may be any array. The general form of the function is

$$A \uparrow B$$

where

B is the array data from which selection occurs.

A is a scalar or a vector whose components describe the rule of the selection in each dimension of B.

The arguments are conformable if the number of components in A is equal to the rank of B, that is, $(\rho,A) = \rho\rho B$, or if B is a scalar. The shape of the result is the absolute value of the left argument, and the rank of the result is ρ,A.

The left argument must be integral. (A nonintegral value of the left argument A results in a *DOMAIN ERROR* report.) If $A[I]$ is a positive integer, the *first* $A[I]$ components are selected from the Ith dimension of B. For example,

```
        M
NOWHERE
BEDEVIL
INKNEED
BARKING

        ρM
4  7

        2 3↑M
NOW
BED
```

In this example, the first two rows and the first three columns of M are selected.

If $A[I]$ is a negative integer, the *last* $|A[I]|$ components are selected from the Ith dimension of B. For example, with M as specified above,

```
        ¯3 ¯4↑M
EVIL
NEED
KING
```

The last three rows and the last four columns of M are selected. The components of A may be positive and negative. For example,

```
        2 ¯4↑M
HERE
EVIL

        ¯2 3↑M
INK
BAR
```

A may have any integral value—even greater than the number of components of B, that is, $(|A)>\rho B$, for example, $5↑\iota 3$. When this occurs, the take function pads out the resulting array. When the data right argument is numeric, the padding elements are zeros; when the data right argument is character, the padding elements are blanks. When the left argument A is a positive integer, the padding elements appear to the right of the original elements of B; when the left argument A is a negative integer, the padding elements appear to the left of the original components of B. For example,

	5↑ι3							‾5↑ι3			
1	2	3	0	0		0	0	1	2	3	

5↑'*HI*'	‾5↑'*HI*'
HI	*HI*

If a component of the left argument is greater in absolute value than the corresponding dimension of the array B, padding occurs in that dimension of B. This padding occurs if $(|A[I])>(\rho B)[I]$. Thus

```
        N
 1   2   3   4
 5   6   7   8
 9  10  11  12
```

	4 2↑*N*			‾4 2↑*N*
1	2		0	0
5	6		1	2
9	10		5	6
0	0		9	10

		2 5↑*N*					2 ‾5↑*N*				
1	2	3	4	0		0	1	2	3	4	
5	6	7	8	0		0	5	6	7	8	

As the examples illustrate, the padding appears after the selected elements if $A[I]$ is positive, and before if $A[I]$ is negative. If B is character data, the padding characters are blanks. For example,

```
        W
HI
HO
        ρW
 2   2
```

□←*R*←3 2↑*W*	□←*S*←1 ‾4↑*W*
HI	*HI*
HO	
ρ*R*	ρ*S*
3 2	1 4

The elements in the last row of R are spaces. The first two elements of S are spaces.

The take function does not change the rank of the result from that of the original data array. For example, with the result S shown above,

$$\rho\rho S$$
2

If A is zero, no elements are taken from B. The result is a null array. Thus $0\uparrow B$ is another way of creating an empty vector.

Illustration 7.10 A Function for Entering Data

An R by C matrix of names of variable lengths (no greater than C) can be created using the function $MAKE$ shown below:

```
    ∇ M←R MAKE C;I
[1]    M←(R,C)ρ' '
[2]    I←1
[3]    M[I;]←C↑⎕
[4]    →(R≥I←I+1)ρ3
    ∇
```

The take function in line 3 pads out short names or truncates long ones.

Illustration 7.11 Extracting the First and Last Dimensions
from a Shape Vector

The expressions

$$1\uparrow\rho M \quad \text{and} \quad {}^{-}1\uparrow\rho M$$

extract the first and last dimensions of an array M. The main conformability of inner product, for example, can be expressed as $({}^{-}1\uparrow\rho A) = 1\uparrow\rho B$ (see Sec. 5.4).

Illustration 7.12 Converting Names to Unique Numbers

At times it is desirable to convert names into unique numbers, perhaps to sort them or to save internal space. If the names are made up from the alphabet and the blank, each name must be less than 11 characters in length in order to convert it to a unique number representable in System/370 [that is, $((27\star11)<2\star56)$ but $(2\star56)\geq27\star12$]. The conversion can be accomplished in this way:

```
    ALF←' ABCDEFGHIJKLMNOPQRSTUVWXYZ'
    27⊥⁻1+ALFι11↑NAME
```

The first 11 components of the character vector $NAME$ are converted to a unique numeric equivalent.

Illustration 7.13 A Binary Matrix With 1*s in the
Upper Left Quadrant*

An N by N matrix with 1s in the upper left quadrant [that is, the first $(\lfloor N \div 2)$ rows and columns] and 0s elsewhere can be generated by the function $QUAD$:

```
    ∇ Z←QUAD N;I
[1]    I←⌊.5×N
[2]    Z←(N,N)↑(I,I)ρ1
    ∇
```

For example,

```
    QUAD 4
 1 1 0 0
 1 1 0 0
 0 0 0 0
 0 0 0 0
```

PROBLEMS

1. State in words the results of the following expressions:

   (a) 0↑V

   (b) 1 0↑M   for M a matrix

   (c) 1↑0ρV   for V a character vector

   (d) 1↑0ρV   for V a numeric vector

2. Use the following variables to evaluate expressions (a)–(i):

   ```
          V←'ABCDE'
          M
   ABCDE
   FGHIJ
   KLMNO
   ```

   (a) 2↑V   (b) ‾2↑V   (c) 7↑V

   (d) ‾7↑V   (e) 1 2↑M   (f) ‾2 2↑M

   (g) 2 ‾2↑M   (h) 2 ‾1↑M   (i) ‾1 ‾1↑M

3. Define a function RES that reshapes an array Q into a matrix M. If Q is a scalar, the shape of the resulting matrix is 1 1. If Q is a vector, the shape of the result is 1,ρQ. If Q is an array of rank 3 or greater, accept the first plane of Q. Thus whatever the previous rank of Q had been, it becomes rank 2.

4. Redefine the function $PAGE$ of problem 12(b) of Secs. 3.2–3.4 so that a heading $HEAD$ prints on the right side of odd pages followed by the page number PN and on the left side of even-numbered pages preceded by the page number. Leave three spaces between the heading and the page number. The page number should always be flush with the margin.

Test:

```
HEAD←'OUR BOOK'
PN←15
. . . . . . . .
                      OUR BOOK    15  (assuming a page width of 32)
PN←16
. . . . . . .
16    OUR BOOK
```

5. (a) Define a function $CENTER$ to center a page number X on a page of width W.

   (b) Modify $CENTER$ so that a decoration such as – surrounds the page number.

6. The technique for determining the indices of all occurrences of a scalar S in the vector V shown in Illustration 7.5 is

   $(V=S)/\iota\rho V$

   However, if S is not present in the above expression, the result is the null vector. Modify the expression so that it will return a zero if S is not present in V.

   Test:

```
S←5
V←1 2 4 7 9 1 4 7
. . . . . . .
0
```

7. (a) Write an expression to border a numeric matrix M with zeros on all four sides.

   Test:

```
M←2 3ρ\iota6
. . . .
0 0 0 0 0
0 1 2 3 0
0 4 5 6 0
0 0 0 0 0
```

   (b) Write an expression to border a rank-3 numeric array A with zeros on all six sides.

   Test:

```
A←2 2 2ρ\iota8
. . . . . . .
0 0 0 0
0 1 2 0
0 3 4 0
0 0 0 0

0 0 0 0
0 5 6 0
0 7 8 0
0 0 0 0
```

   (c) Write an expression to create a new array T by appending an all-zero first plane and an additional all-zero row in each plane.

Test:
```
        T←2 2 3ρ⍳12
        · · · · · · · ·
    0   0   0
    0   0   0
    0   0   0

    1   2   3
    4   5   6
    0   0   0

    7   8   9
   10  11  12
    0   0   0
```

Section 7.1.4 Drop

Just as the take function represents a specialized selection of the first or last so many components from a vector, a specialized selection can be obtained by deleting or dropping *all but* the last or first of so many components. The function *drop* $X↓Y$ accomplishes this. Consider again:

```
        Q
MARSHALL
        3↓Q
SHALL
        ⁻3↓Q
MARSH
```

The right argument of drop may be any array. The general form of the function is
```
        X↓Y
```

where

    Y is the array data to be operated on.
    X indicates the number of successive elements to drop.

The following expressions summarize the relationship between the variables for the result R:

$$(\rho R) \; = \; 0\lceil(\rho Y)-|X$$
$$(\rho X) \; = \; \rho\rho Y$$
$$(\rho\rho R) \; = \; \rho X$$

The left argument X must be integral. (A nonintegral value for X results in a *DOMAIN ERROR* report.) If $X[I]$ is a positive integer, the first $X[I]$ components of the Ith dimension of Y are dropped. For example,

```
        N
BOWLEGGED
BOATHOUSE
BLUEBERRY

        ρN
3 9

       1 4↓N
HOUSE
BERRY
```

This is, of course, the same thing as

$$^-2 \ ^-5\uparrow N$$

There are occasions, however, when using take results in a more concise expression than using drop and vice versa. For example, to take all but the first component of a vector V could be expressed as $(-^-1+\rho V)\uparrow V$. Obviously, the expression $1\downarrow V$ is more concise.

If $X[I]$ is a negative integer, the last $|X[I]$ components of the I th dimension of Y are deleted. For example,

$$^-1 \ ^-5\downarrow N$$

```
BOWL
BOAT
```

If $X[I]$ is zero, no dropping occurs in the I th dimension of Y. If Y is a matrix, this means that selection is in only one dimension. This property makes for some rather concise selections. For example to select all but the first two rows of a matrix M,

```
         M
   1    2    3    4
   5    6    7    8
   9   10   11   12
  13   14   15   16
       M[2+ι^-2+1↑ρM;]
   9   10   11   12
  13   14   15   16
       2 0↓M
   9   10   11   12
  13   14   15   16
```

If $X[I]$ is an integral value not less than the number of elements of Y (that is, $(|X)\geq\rho Y)$, all the elements in the I th dimension of Y are dropped. The result is an empty array.

Illustration 7.14   Finding the Original of a Sum-Scanned Vector

Let V be a vector whose components represent the sum scan of the vector W. Thus if V is 1 3 6 10 15, W was originally 1 2 3 4 5. The expression

$$W \leftarrow V - 0, \bar{} 1 \downarrow V$$

produces the original vector W, given V.

Illustration 7.15   Suppressing Leading Zeros

Given a numeric character string Z, the expression

$$NZ \leftarrow (\bar{} 1 + (Z = {}' 0 {}') \iota 0) \downarrow Z$$

suppresses leading zeros. For example,

```
        Z←'00175'
        NZ
175
        Z←'04076'
        NZ
4076
```

PROBLEMS

1. Use the following variables to evaluate expressions (a)–(j):

```
           V←'DATE'
           N
   TEA
   ATE
   TEE
   EAT
```

    (a) $1 \downarrow V$ (b) $\bar{} 2 \downarrow V$ (c) $2 \downarrow V$

    (d) $5 \downarrow V$ (e) $0 \downarrow V$ (f) $1 \ 2 \downarrow N$

    (g) $\bar{} 3 \ 1 \downarrow N$ (h) $3 \ 0 \downarrow N$ (i) $1 \ \bar{} 2 \downarrow N$

    (j) $1 \ 0 \downarrow \bar{} 2 \ \bar{} 1 \downarrow N$

2. Define a function $VTOM$ which deletes the item-delimiter character C in a character vector V and then converts V into a matrix where each item appears as a separate line. (*Note:* Such a vector could arise by defining it as the input from an IBM magnetic card selectric typewriter (MCST) card where the carrier returns are variably spaced on each line.)

Test:

$$V \leftarrow 'ONE, TWO, THREE, FOUR'$$
$$C \leftarrow ','$$

. . . . . .

ONE
TWO
THREE
FOUR

3. (a) Define a function IN to determine whether a character string CS is in the character string R. Design the function so that it returns the message CS NOT $FOUND$ if CS is not in R and the message CS $FOUND$ if CS is present in R.

Test:

$$CS \leftarrow 'RANGE'$$
$$R \leftarrow 'STRANGER'$$

. . . .

RANGE   FOUND
$$CS \leftarrow 'RUNG'$$

. . . .

RUNG   NOT   FOUND

   (b) Rewrite IN so that the result is the index value of where CS begins in R. If CS is not found, return a zero.

Test:

$$CS \leftarrow 'RANGE'$$

. . . . . .

3

$$CS \leftarrow 'RUNG'$$

. . . . . .

0

4. Define a function REP to replicate numbers in a vector such that only the numbers and an indication of the number of times they are to be replicated need to be entered.

Test:

          100 3 *REP* 90 80 2 *REP* 60 2 *REP* 50 70
    100 90 90 90 80 60 60 50 50 70

5. Define a function SEL to select from an arbitrary array A an element whose indices are indicated by V. Assume that $(\rho V) = \rho \rho A$.

Test:

$$A \leftarrow 2\ 3\ 4 \rho \iota 24$$
$$V \leftarrow 2\ 2\ 3$$

. . . . . .

    19

6. (a) Write an expression for shifting a vector V, I places to the left and inserting into the vacated components an arbitrary scalar quantity X.

Test:

$$V \leftarrow 9\ 8\ 7\ 6\ 3\ 2$$
$$I \leftarrow 2$$
$$X \leftarrow {}^-3$$

. . . . . .

    7 6 3 2 ‾3 ‾3

(b) Define a function *SHIFT* that shifts a given vector V left or right N places filling in the vacated places with an arbitrary character or number X. Define a positive N to mean a left shift and a negative N to mean a right shift.

Test:

```
        V←'SPOKE'
        N←2
        X←'*'
        . . . . . .
OKE**
            N←¯2
        . . . . . .
**SPO
```

7. Without using indexing, write two different expressions to extract the first two rows of a matrix M.

Test:

```
        M←5 3ρι15
        . . . . .
    1 2 3
    4 5 6
```

8. Write an expression to remove the border of zeros from a matrix M bordered on all four sides by zeros.

Test:

```
            M
    0 0 0 0
    0 4 5 0
    0 3 2 0
    0 0 0 0
        . . . . . .
    4 5
    3 2
```

9. Modify the function *WORDS* of problem 5 of Sec. 6.3 so that each word entered may be up to 22 characters in length and as a result each word is converted into a pair of numbers. The first number represents the first 11 characters of the word; the second, the last 11 characters. If any word is shorter than 22 characters, pad it with blanks on the right.

10. Define a function *PLURAL* to form the plural of a singular common noun. Consult a dictionary or English handbook for plural-forming rules. *Hint:* You may wish to treat some words by listing their plurals or by having a set of words that produces a "consult your dictionary" message.

Test:

Word	Plural
CHILD	*CHILDREN*
SISTER-IN-LAW	*SISTERS-IN-LAW*
MATCH	*MATCHES*
SKY	*SKIES*
ALTO	*ALTOS*
KNIFE	*KNIVES*
LEAF	*LEAVES*
MOOSE	*MOOSE*
BY-PRODUCT	*BY-PRODUCTS*

11. A perfect number is a number whose factors excluding itself add up to the number. Write an expression to verify that 28 is a perfect number.

12. Modify the expression given in Illustration 7.15 so that leading zeros are still suppressed from numeric character strings N but that in the case of all-zero characters, a single zero character results.

    Test:

$$N \leftarrow \text{'0000'}$$

    . . . . . .

   0

13. In Sec. 7.1.1 the shape of the result of a compression

$$R \leftarrow L/[I]A$$

was defined to be the same as the shape of the right argument A except for the I th dimension in which compression is to occur. In this dimension, the degree of freedom is $+/L$. Write an expression which is equivalent to ρR.

14. (a) Define a function CNT to determine how many times each word appears in a matrix of words $WORDS$.

    Test:

          $WORDS$

    $GLAD$
    $HAPPY$
    $JOYFUL$
    $GLAD$
    $HAPPY$
    $GLAD$

          . . . .

    $GLAD$ 3
    $HAPPY$ 2
    $JOYFUL$ 1

  (b) Modify CNT to count the occurrences in a list of words, considering that a list of suffixes SUF do not count as separate words—so that, for example, walk, walking, walked, and walks would be counted under the word walk if SUF contained –s, –ing, –ed.

15. Define a function SUB to select the element from a matrix M whose row and column indices are given by a two-component vector V.

    Test:

$$M \leftarrow 4 \ 5\rho\iota 20$$
$$V \leftarrow 3 \ 4$$

   14

Section 7.1.5   Catenation and Lamination

In Chapter 1 catenation was introduced as a means of appending a scalar or vector expression to another scalar or vector expression. In this section, we shall discuss how catenation is used to catenate all arrays. For our discussion, consider the matrix $STOCKS$, which contains information about four stock holdings:

```
      STOCKS
 31.625    27.72    14.25    301.5
  2         0.2      0.17    11.08
```

The first row of *STOCKS* contains the current price per share for each stock. The second row contains the corresponding latest 12 months' earnings. When new stock is purchased, the data on this new stock should be added to the *STOCKS* matrix as new columns. This can be done by using an axis-specifier of [2] for the catenation function to indicate appendage along the second or column coordinate:

```
      NEWSTOCK
116.375 6.31
      STOCKS←STOCKS,[2]NEWSTOCK

      STOCKS
 31.625    27.75   14.25    301.5    116.375
  2         0.2     0.17    11.08      6.31
```

If the information on each stock in *STOCKS* were to be increased to include its current dividend, a third row would be needed. Additional rows can be added by using an axis-specifier of [1] for the catenation function to indicate appendage along the first or row coordinate:

```
      DIVIDEND
1.11    0.6    0    5.2    0.8
      STOCKS←STOCKS,[1]DIVIDEND

      STOCKS
 31.625    27.75   14.25    301.5    116.375
  2         0.2     0.17    11.08      6.31
  1.11      0.6     0        5.2       0.8
```

As the above example illustrates, catenation is possible along any dimension of an array. The general form for the catenation function is

```
      A,[I]B
```

where

   A is the data to which catenation is to occur. *A* may be an array of any rank and shape.

   B is the data being catenated to *A*. *B* may assume any rank or shape provided it conforms with *A*.

   I indicates the dimension along which catenation is to occur.

The arguments are conformable under any of the following conditions:

1. A or B is a scalar, $\vee/0=(\rho\rho A),\rho\rho B$ yields a 1.

2. If A and B have the same rank, $(\rho\rho A) = \rho\rho B$,

    a. I must be a positive integer less than or equal to the rank of $A - I\in\iota\rho\rho A$ holds true

    b. All the dimensions of A and B except the Ith must agree— $\wedge/(I\neq\iota\rho\rho A)/(\rho A)=\rho B$ yields a 1.

    c. A or B is a one-component array.

3. If A and B do not have the same rank, $(\rho\rho A)\neq\rho\rho B$. If neither A nor B is a scalar, their ranks may differ only by 1: $1=|(\rho\rho A)-\rho\rho B$. Furthermore, each dimension of the smaller array, say B, must be equal to the corresponding dimension of the other array A excluding the dimension along which catenation is to occur— $\wedge/(\rho B)=(I\neq\iota\rho\rho A)/\rho A$ yields a 1.

The shape and rank of cantenation $R\leftarrow A,[I]B$ follows. If A and B are scalars, ρR is the shape of the array with the greater rank except that $(\rho R)[I]$ is equal to $(\rho,A)[I]+(\rho,B)[I]$. And $(\rho\rho R)$ = $/\lceil(\rho\rho A)\lceil\rho\rho B$

As an example of conformability of arguments under catenation, suppose that three stocks were purchased whose data needed to be appended to the matrix *STOCKS* discussed earlier:

```
      NEWSTOCKS
 33        24.75    19.5
  1.26      .81      1.31
  0.52     0.45     0.85
```

NEWSTOCKS can be catenated to the columns of *STOCKS*, since the two matrices have the same number of rows:

```
      STOCKS,[2]NEWSTOCKS
 31.625   27.75   14.25   301.5   116.375   33     24.75   19.5
  2        0.2     0.17    11.08    6.31     1.26   0.81    1.31
  1.11     0.6     0         5.2    0.8      0.52   0.45    0.85
```

NEWSTOCKS cannot be catenated to the rows of *STOCKS*, since the two matrices do not have the same number of columns.

As another example, consider the array *ENROL* as the yearly enrollments array of the years 1970, 1969, and 1968 for the four classes of a college on a semester basis. Thus $\rho ENROL$ is 3 4 2. Suppose that *ENROL71* is the enrollment data for 1971. $\rho ENROL71$ is 4 2. To update the *ENROL* array, *ENROL71* should be catenated as the first plane of *ENROL*. The expression

    ENROL71,[1]ENROL

accomplishes this. The arrays are conformable for catenation along planes since

$$|(\rho\rho ENROL) - \rho\rho ENROL71 \text{ is } 1$$

and

$$\wedge/(\rho ENROL71)=(1\neq\iota\rho\rho ENROL)/\rho ENROL \text{ is } 1$$

As with other functions which have axis-specifiers, the explicit statement of the axis-specifier may be omitted. In this case, the function of catenation is defined to occur along the last or rightmost dimension. Therefore A,B is equivalent to $A,[\rho\rho A]B$ where $(\rho\rho A)= \rho\rho B$. For example, if $\rho\rho A$ and $\rho\rho B$ are 3, A,B is identical to $A,[3]B$.

Illustration 7.16   Creating a Variable-Length List of Names

The function *MAKE* for creating a matrix of names described in Illustration 7.10 required the number of names to be known in advance. The function *MAKE2* shown below bypasses this requirement by using catenation. An asterisk typed in instead of a name terminates the function.

```
     ∇ Z←MAKE2 C
[1]    Z←(1,C)ρC↑⎕
[2]    Z←Z,[1]C↑⎕
[3]    →('*'≠,¯1 1↑Z)ρ2
[4]    Z←¯1 0↓Z
     ∇
```

Lamination

The axis-specifier of catenation was discussed as being a positive integer. An extension to catenation—called *lamination*—occurs if the axis-specifier is not an integer. Lamination joins the arguments A and B together by creating a new dimension whose value is 2. The placement of the new dimension depends on the value of I, the axis-specifier. It is placed before the $\lceil I$th coordinate, if there is one. Otherwise the new dimension becomes the $\lceil I$th one. The first index of the new dimension is filled by A; the second index by B. For example, using lamination two vectors of equal length can be combined directly to form a matrix. Thus

```
       V
ABC

       W
XYZ

       R←V,[.1]W

       ρR
   2 3
```

The new dimension is placed before the $\lceil.1$ or first dimension:

```
        R
ABC
XYZ
```

V fills $R[1;]$ and W fills $R[2;]$.

```
     S←V,[1.1]W

     ρS
3 2

     S
AX
BY
CZ
```

V fills $S[;1]$ and W fills $S[;2]$.

The conformability conditions for lamination with a syntax of

$$A,[I]B$$

where

I is a positive number

are

Case 1: Both arguments have the same rank—$(\rho\rho A)= \rho\rho B$:
1. All the dimensions of A and B must agree—$(\rho A)\wedge.=\rho B$ yields a 1.
2. I is not an integer—$I\neq\lfloor I$ yields a 1.
3. I must lie between zero and one plus the rank of the arguments—$(I>0)\wedge(\lfloor I)<1+\rho\rho A$ yield a 1.

Case 2: The arguments are not of the same rank—$(\rho\rho A)\neq \rho\rho B$:
1. Either A or B must be a scalar—$0\vee.=(\rho\rho A),\rho\rho B$ yields a 1.
2. I is not an integer—$I\neq\lfloor I$ yields a 1.
3. I must lie between zero and the rank of the nonscalar argument—plus one $(I>0)\wedge(\lfloor I)<\lceil/(\rho\rho A),\rho\rho B$ yields a 1.

The shape and rank of lamination $R←A,[I]B$ follows. For (ρR) a new dimension of 2 is placed before the $\lceil I$th and the rest of the dimensions are the same.

$$(\rho\rho R)=1+1\lceil(\rho\rho A)\lceil\rho\rho B$$

As an example of conformability under lamination, consider the matrices $M1$ and $M2$:

```
        M1
ABC
DEF
GHI

        M2
JKL
MNO
PQR
```

Here $(\rho\rho M1) = \rho\rho M2$, $(\rho M1) = 3\ 3$, and $(\rho M2) = 3\ 3$. Therefore

```
        M1,[.3]M2
ABC
DEF
GHI

JKL
MNO
PQR
```

The two matrices $M1$ and $M2$ are laminated together to form a rank-3 array where the new dimension is the first. The value of the axis-specifier associated with the function may be any decimal value less than 1 in order to make the new dimension the first. Similarly,

```
        M1,[1.82]M2
ABC
JKL

DEF
MNO

GHI
PQR
```

Here the new dimension is the second. Again the decimal portion of the axis-specifier may be any decimal.

Illustration 7.17 Interleaving Two Vectors

Two vectors can be interleaved by using lamination with an axis-specifier of 1.1 and the ravel function. For example,

```
        F←'BOXED IN'

        G←8ρ'□'

        ,F,[1.1]G
B□O□X□E□D□ □I□N□
```

Illustration 7.18 Heading Reports

The matrix *DATA* is a 4 by 3 matrix of four weekly summaries of a library's lending record. Before the report is printed, title information is appended to the data so that the report appears as

<u>*LIBRARY STATISTICS*</u>

<u>*BORROWERS BOOKS-LENT FINES*</u>

WEEK 1	218	356	9.76
WEEK 2	383	563	10.92
WEEK 3	239	323	6.06
WEEK 4	119	363	12.45

The function *REPORT* produces such a tabular output:

```
      ∇  Z←REPORT X;R1;R2;C1;C2;X1
[1]    R1←'      LIBRARY STATISTICS   ]'
[2]    R2←'BORROWERS BOOKS-LENT FINES'
[3]    C1←4 7ρ'WEEK 1 WEEK 2 WEEK 3 WEEK 4 '
[4]    C2←4 7ρ' '
[5]    ⍝ASSUMING BORROWERS<500, BOOKS LENT<1000 AND FINES <100
[6]    X1←6 0 10 0 10 2⍕X
[7]    Z←(C2,[1] C1),((R1,[0.1] ' '),[1] R2,[0.1]' '),[1] X1
      ∇
```

PROBLEMS

1. Use the variable *M* to evaluate expressions (a)-(e):

```
       M
   2   4   6   8
  10  12  14  16
   1   3   5   7
```

(a) *M*,⍳3   (b) (⍳3),*M*   (c) (⍳3),*M*,⍳3

(d) (⍳4),*M*   (e) (⍳4),[1]*M*

2. Define a function *INS* to insert a vector *R* into a matrix *M* after the *I*th row.

Test:

```
        R← ¯9 ¯6 ¯3
        M←3 3ρ⍳9
        I←1

       . . . . . . . .
    1   2   3
   ¯9  ¯6  ¯3
    4   5   6
    7   8   9
```

3. Define a function *EVAL* to evaluate a polynomial whose coefficients in descending powers of the variable are P for a set of points S. The result should be a two-column matrix whose first column is the set of evaluation points and the second column is the value of the polynomial at the corresponding points.

    Test:

```
       P←6 3 2 ‾2
       S←ι4
       . . . . . . .
   1   9
   2   62
   3   175
   4   458
```

4. Define a function *BORDER* to border a matrix M on all sides with the character or number Y (depending on whether M is character or numeric). Use catenate.

    Test:

```
       M←3 3ρ'TEAEATATE'
       Y←'o'
       . . . . . . . .
 OOOOO
 oTEAo
 oEATo
 oATEo
 OOOOO
```

5. Write an expression to create a rank-3 array from the matrices N, E, S, and W, each of the same shape, such that the four planes are the N, E, S, and W planes, respectively.

6. Using the matrices *ENGINE*, *FREIGHT*, and *TANK*, construct a seven-car train, made up of an engine and some combination of freight and tank cars.

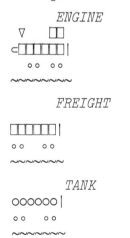

Section 7.2 REARRANGEMENT OF DATA

Section 7.2.1 Reversal

We have already reversed the components of a vector in Chapter 2 using downgrade and indexing. For example,

$V \leftarrow 'KNITS'$

$V[\Psi \imath \rho V]$

$STINK$

The function of reversing the order of data can be accomplished more directly using the monadic mixed function *reversal* ϕB. Then

ϕV

$STINK$

The general format for the reversal function is

$\phi[I]A$

where

A is the array data to be reversed.

I indicates the dimension along which the reversal is to occur.

If the axis-specifier is omitted, the reversal occurs along the last dimension. The symbol $\ominus$ can be used to specify reversal along the first dimension.

Consider the matrix $ENROL$ which contains the body of the table of the enrollment of each class in a college for the 6 years 1966–1971:

		Class		
Year	Fr.	So.	Jr.	Sr.
1966	167	162	161	152
1967	170	165	164	153
1968	190	166	159	156
1969	201	195	160	154
1970	269	206	198	162
1971	289	258	199	189

The expression $\phi[2]ENROL$ or $\phi ENROL$ rearranges the data so that the senior class enrollment appears in the first column; the junior class, in the second; the sophomore class, in the third; and the freshman class in the fourth column; that is,

$\phi[2]ENROL$ (or $\phi ENROL$)

152	161	162	167
153	164	165	170
156	159	166	190
154	160	195	201
162	198	206	269
189	199	258	289

The expression $\phi[1]ENROL$ or $\ominus ENROL$ reverses the data so that the most recent year appears in the first row, that is,

$\phi[1]ENROL$ (or $\ominus ENROL$)

289	258	199	189
269	206	198	162
201	195	160	154
190	166	159	156
170	165	164	153
167	162	161	152

Reversal rearranges the data but does not change the data values. This rearrangement is accomplished by performing a permutation on the indices associated with the data. As an example, consider the matrix CH:

CH

ABC
DEF
GHI

ρCH

3 3

If CH is written with the subscripts stated explicitly beneath the elements, it appears as

A_{11} B_{12} C_{13}

D_{21} E_{22} F_{23}

G_{31} H_{32} I_{33}

$\phi[1]CH$ results in a rearrangement of CH produced by doing a reversal along the first of each of the subscript pairs. After the reversal, the subscripts on the data are

A_{31} B_{32} C_{33}

D_{21} E_{22} F_{23}

G_{11} H_{12} I_{13}

Then the data are placed in their row-major order. This results in the reversal of the data along the rows or the first dimension:

$$
\begin{array}{lll}
G_{11} & H_{12} & I_{13} \\
D_{21} & E_{22} & F_{23} \\
A_{31} & B_{32} & C_{33}
\end{array}
\quad ; \text{that is,}
\quad
\begin{array}{l}
GHI \\
DEF \\
ABC
\end{array}
$$

Similarly, $\phi[2]CH$ results in a reversal on the second of the subscript pair.

$$
\begin{array}{lll}
A_{13} & B_{12} & C_{11} \\
D_{23} & E_{22} & F_{21} \\
G_{33} & H_{32} & I_{31}
\end{array}
$$

Placing the data in row-major order results in the reversal of the data along the second dimension:

$$
\begin{array}{lll}
C_{11} & B_{12} & A_{13} \\
F_{21} & E_{22} & D_{23} \\
I_{31} & H_{32} & G_{33}
\end{array}
\quad ; \text{that is,}
\quad
\begin{array}{l}
CBA \\
FED \\
IHG
\end{array}
$$

Illustration 7.19   Applying Reversal Successively

Reversal can be applied successively to a matrix either as $\ominus\phi M$ or $\phi\ominus M$. Both produce the same result. The effect is a flipping of the matrix vertically and horizontally around the center of the matrix. For example, recall that the matrix *ENROL* represented a table of enrollments at a college from the first year (1966) to the last year (1971) and from freshmen to seniors. The expression $\phi\ominus ENROL$ rearranges the data of *ENROL* from last year (1971) to first year (1966) and from senior to freshmen:

```
     φ⊖ENROL
189    199    258    289
162    198    206    269
154    160    195    201
156    159    166    190
153    164    165    170
152    161    162    167
```

Illustration 7.20   Calculating Depreciation by Sum-of-the-Years

One of the methods of calculating depreciation is the sum-of-the-years method. With this method, if an investment P is depreciated over N periods, the first period's depreciation is

$$P\times N\div+/\iota N$$

The second period's depreciation is

$P \times (N-1) \div +/\iota N$

And so forth, until the last period, where the depreciation is

$P \times 1 \div +/\iota N$

The function *SUMOFYRS* computes an N-component vector which is the sum-of-the-years depreciation of the value P:

```
    ∇ Z←N SUMOFYRS P
[1]   Z←P×(ϕιN)÷+/ιN
    ∇
```

For example,

```
    5 SUMOFYRS 5000
1666.7 1333.3 1000 666.67 333.3
```

Illustration 7.21   The Evaluation of a Mathematical Expression Again

Illustration 5.8 presented an APL expression equivalent to the mathematical expression

$$1 + \sum_{I=1}^{4} \prod_{J=1}^{I} A_J$$

Another APL expression equivalent to this mathematical expression is

$(0,\phi A)\bot 1$

PROBLEMS

1. Use the following variables to evaluate expressions (a)–(l):

```
     P
 1   5   9  13  17
 2   6  10  14  18
 3   7  11  15  19
 4   8  12  16  20
     M
 1   2   3   4
 5   6   7   8
```

```
        AA
    1    2
    3    4
    5    6

    7    8
    9   10
   11   12
        AL
ADG
BEH
CFI
```

(a) $\phi 0, \iota 5$	(b) $\phi(0, \iota 5) + \iota 6$	(c) $\phi\phi\iota 6$
(d) $\phi[1]M$	(e) ϕP	(f) ϕAL
(g) ϕAA	(h) $\phi[2]AA$	(i) $(\phi 0, \iota 5) + \iota 6$
(j) ϕM	(k) $\phi[1]AL$	(l) $\phi[1] \ AA$

2. The matrix M consisting of only 1s and 0s is an event/time matrix. Each row represents a different event, and each column represents a specific time. Within the matrix each row has a 1 in the column that corresponds to the times that the event occurred. Zeros appear elsewhere in each row. For example,

	$T(1)$	$T(2)$	$T(3)$
$E(1)$	0	1	0
$E(2)$	1	0	1

Event $E(1)$ occurred at time $T(2)$, and event $E(2)$ occurred at times $T(1)$ and $T(3)$.

(a) Given the matrix M, define a function $WHEN$ to determine the first occurrence of each event. As output, print a logical matrix with only the first occurrence in each row.
Test:

```
          M
    1  0  1  0
    1  1  0  0
    0  1  0  0
    0  0  1  1
       . . . . . . . . .
    1  0  0  0
    1  0  0  0
    0  1  0  0
    0  0  1  0
```

(b) Assume that there exists a time vector T which matches the number of columns in M. Define a function $OCCUR$ which when given M and an event number E outputs the message

$$EVENT \ NUMBER \ \_\_FIRST \ OCCURRED \ AT \ TIME \ \_\_$$

If the event did not occur, set the time to zero in the output message.

Test: M as defined in part (a)

```
T←5 10 15 20
E←2
```

```
. . . . . . .
```

EVENT NUMBER 2 FIRST OCCURRED AT TIME 5

3. The function $RANK$ when presented a set of scores yields a ranking of them. Its definition is shown below:

```
    ∇ Z←RANK X
[1]   Z←⌊.5×(⍋⍋X)+⌽⍋⍋⌽X
    ∇
```

What does the function ϕ do in $RANK$? (See illustration 3.12 for meaning of ⍋⍋.)

4. If CC is a binary vector, write an expression to determine the last occurrence of 1 in CC.

Test:

```
CC←1 0 1 1 0 0 1 1 0 1 0 0 0
. . . . . .
```

```
10
```

5. Define a function PA to produce a 1 if a character string S is a perfect palindrome, that is, reads the same forward and backward, spaces and punctuation included; a $^-1$ if a character string S is an imperfect palindrome, that is, reads the same disregarding spaces and punctuation; and a 0 if S is not a palindrome at all.

Test:

For	Result
LEWD DID I· LIVE – EVIL I DID DWEL	1
HE LIVED AS A DEVIL, EH?	$^-1$
CARBON PAPER	0

6. Write an expression to produce a rank-3 N by N by N array with a 1 down the main diagonal and 0s elsewhere. (The main diagonal of an array is defined as all elements whose subscripts are the same.)

Test:

```
        N←2
      . . . . . .
  1 0
  0 0

  0 0
  0 1
```

Section 7.2.2 Rotation

While completely reversing the order of the elements of an array is useful, a more common rearrangement is that of rotating the order of the elements. The function *rotation*, $A\phi B$, where A is the amount of the rotation on the array B, provides this facility. For example, consider the vector W:

        $W \leftarrow 'CAT\ DOG\ MAN\ '$

        ρW
12

        $4 \phi W$
$DOG\ MAN\ CAT$

The rotation on W is four positions, cyclically to the left. And

        $^{-}4 \phi W$
$MAN\ CAT\ DOG$

The rotation on W is four positions, cyclically to the right. The sign of the left argument determines the direction of the rotation.

The above examples show rotation on a vector right argument. However, there are no restrictions on the shape that the right argument of rotation may assume. The general form of rotation is

        $A \phi [I] B$

where

B is the array data being rotated.

I is the axis-specifier, indicating the dimension along which the rotation occurs.

A is a scalar or an array whose rank is 1 less than the rank of B and whose shape is that of B with the Ith component eliminated.

The components of the left argument must be integers. These components describe displacements and their directions. The amount of rotation to be performed (the displacement) is specified by the magnitude of the left argument. For example,

        $1 \phi 'SMILE'$
$MILES$

        $^{-}1 \phi 'TRAPS'$
$STRAP$

The direction of the rotation is specified by the sign on the value of the left argument. For example, if the right argument is a vector, a positive left argument indicates a cyclic rotation of the components, moving them leftward. A negative left argument indicates a cyclic rotation of the components, moving them rightward. If the left argument is zero, no rotation occurs.

If the right argument is a matrix, rotation can occur in either one of the dimensions. The rotation function symbol $\phi[1]$ or $\ominus$ produces a rotation upon the first or row dimension. A positive left argument indicates a cyclic rotation, moving them upward; a negative left argument indicates a cyclic rotation, moving them downward. For example,

```
       CHR
ABCD
EFGH
IJKL

       1ϕ[1]CHR  or  1⊖CHR
EFGH
IJKL
ABCD

       ‾1ϕ[1]CHR
IJKL
ABCD
EFGH
```

The rotation function symbol $\phi[2]$ or ϕ produces a rotation on the second or column dimension. A positive left argument indicates a cyclic rotation leftward; a negative left argument indicates a cyclic rotation rightward. For example,

```
       1ϕCHR  or  1ϕ[2]CHR
BCDA
FGHE
JKLI

       ‾1ϕCHR
DABC
HEFG
LIJK
```

The amount of rotation for each item in the dimension along which rotation occurs can be specified. For example,

```
       1 2 1ϕCHR
BCDA
GHEF
JKLI

       1 2 1 2ϕ[1]CHR
EJGL
IBKD
AFCH

       ‾1 ‾2 1ϕCHR
DABC
GHEF
JKLI

       ‾1 2 ‾1 ‾2ϕ[1]CHR
IJKH
ABCL
EFGH
```

Another way of determining the direction of the rotation is to consider how the left argument affects the subscripts of the data in the dimension along which the rotation occurs. The left argument of the rotation function can be thought of as a value which is subtracted from each of the subscripts of the data. To illustrate this, consider the vector W again with its subscripts stated explicitly:

$$C_1 A_2 T_3 \; {}_4 D_5 O_6 G_7 \; {}_8 M_9 A_{10} N_{11} \; {}_{12}$$

To obtain $4\phi W$, subtract 4 from each subscript. The subscripts then are

$$\bar{3} \; \bar{2} \; \bar{1} \; 0 \; 1 \; 2 \; 3 \; 4 \; 5 \; 6 \; 7 \; 8$$

Next take the subscripts modulo (residue function) the length of the vector, which is the degree of freedom on the subscripts. For W, ρW is 12; therefore

$$12 | \; \bar{3} \; \bar{2} \; \bar{1} \; 0 \; 1 \; 2 \; 3 \; 4 \; 5 \; 6 \; 7 \; 8$$
$$9 \; 10 \; 11 \; 0 \; 1 \; 2 \; 3 \; 4 \; 5 \; 6 \; 7 \; 8$$

Thus the subscripts on W for $4\phi W$ are

$$C_9 A_{10} T_{11} \; D_0 \, O_1 \, G_2 \; {}_3 M_4 A_5 N_6 \; {}_7 \; {}_8$$

The result of rotation is stated by arranging the components sequentially with respect to their new subscripts. Zero is considered as the last or rightmost component.* Thus for $4\phi W$,

$$D_1 O_2 G_3 \; {}_4 M_5 A_6 N_7 \; {}_8 C_9 A_{10} T_{11} \; {}_0$$

The result of rotation by manipulating the subscripts for $A\phi B$ can be described by this APL expression:

$$(A\phi B)=B[1+(\rho B)|\bar{1}+A+\iota\rho B]$$

For matrices and arrays of higher ranks, the axis-specifier is an indicator of the dimension affected by rotation. Considering just the affected subscripts, a positive left argument indicates a cyclic rotation of the subscripts from right to left; a negative left argument indicates a cyclic rotation of the subscripts from left to right. For example, rotating the 3 by 2 by 4 array T by $\bar{1}\phi[1]T$,

---

*In modulo work, one usually considers the modulo vaues as running from 0 to $N-1$ in modulo N. However, one could also consider the values as running from 1 to N in modulo N. Zero is equivalent to N modulo N.

$$T$$
ABCD
EFGH

IJKL
MNOP

QRST
UVWX

Consider the plane (dimension 1) subscripts:

        1   2   3

Under the rule of the rotation $^-1$, the subscripts of the rotated planes are

        3   1   2

Thus

        $^-1\phi[1]T$
QRST
UVWX

ABCD
EFGH

IJKL
MNOP

The axis-specifier can be elided in two cases. For rotation along the last coordinate, the symbol ϕ is sufficient. For rotation along the first subscript, the function symbol $\phi[1]$ may be replaced by $\ominus$.

The amount of rotation can be specified for each item in the affected dimension. The argument A must be a scalar or an array whose rank is 1 less than that of B. The shape of A is the same as the shape of B except that the element corresponding to the value of the axis-specifier is not present. For example, if B is a 2 by 3 by 4 array being rotated along the second dimension, A must be a scalar or a 2 by 4 array: where the first row defines the column rotations on the first plane and the second row defines the column rotations on the second plane:

        $\square \leftarrow B \leftarrow 2$ 3 $4\rho \iota 24$
    1   2   3   4
    5   6   7   8
    9 10 11 12

   13 14 15 16
   17 18 19 20
   21 22 23 24

```
      □←A←2 4ρι3
 1 2 3 1
 2 3 1 2

      AΦ[2]B
 5 10  3  8
 9  2  7 12
 1  6 11  4

21 14 19 24
13 18 23 16
17 22 15 20
```

Illustration 7.22 Rotation in a Branch Expression

Rotation can be used in a branch expression for branching to multiple locations. For instance, let B be a vector of possible branch locations. If I is an integer value, then the expression

```
    →IΦB
```

branches to one of the components of B. The actual component taken as a branch will be the one whose subscript is $1+(\rho B)|I$. For example,

```
    B←10  7  4  12
    →2ΦB
```

The branch is to line 4 of the function.

Illustration 7.23 Symmetrical Rearrangement of Elements
                                  Along the Main Diagonal

The expression $N←1Φ[1]1ΦM$ produces a symmetrical rearrangement of the elements of M about the main diagonal. For example, if $M←4$ $4ρι16$, N is

```
   6   7   8   5
  10  11  12   9
  14  15  16  13
   2   3   4   1
```

N is derived from $M←4$ $4ρι16$ by rotating all its elements one place upward parallel to the main diagonal. Each of the diagonals is considered to have the same number of elements but distributed about the main diagonal. The movement created by 1⌽[1]1⌽*M* on *M* is displayed graphically below:

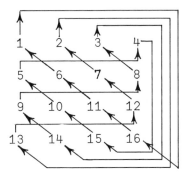

Illustration 7.24   Best Grades First

The function *TOP* shown below rearranges its argument so that the largest number in each column appears in the first row:

```
      ∇ Z←TOP X;I;K
[1]    I←ρX
[2]    K←(ι1↑I)⌈.×X=Iρ⌈⌿X
[3]    Z←(¯1+K)⌽[1]X
      ∇
```

For example, the matrix *GRADES* contains the grades of four students in three exams. *TOP* can be used to rearrange *GRADES* so that the best grade that each student received appears in the first row:

```
      GRADES
 75   88   65   93
 85   88   80   89
 78   80   85   98

      GRADES←TOP GRADES
      GRADES
 85   88   85   98
 78   80   65   93
 75   88   80   89
```

Repeated calls of this function to successively fewer rows of a given matrix results in each column being rearranged independently in descending order. For example,

```
      GRADES[2 3;]←TOP GRADES[2 3;]
      GRADES
 85   88   85   98
 78   88   80   93
 75   80   65   89
```

PROBLEMS

1. Use the following variables to evaluate expressions (a)–(t):

```
Y←10   5   3   6   4
         P
 1    5    9   13   17
 2    6   10   14   18
 3    7   11   15   19
 4    8   12   16   20
         M
 1   2   3   4
 5   6   7   8
         AA
  1    2
  3    4
  5    6

  7    8
  9   10
 11   12
        AL
ADG
BEH
CFI
```

(a) ‾4⌽ι6   (b) ⌽‾3⌽ι6

(c) (3⌽ Y)[ι3]   (d) 0 1 2⌽[1]AL

(e) 1⌽[2]AA   (f) (3 2ρ1)⌽[1]AA

(g) ‾1⌽P   (h) 0 1 2⌽[1]0 1 2⌽AL

(i) 2⌽(‾2+ι3),3ρ0   (j) 2⌽ι6

(k) 1⌽⌽ι6   (l) 3⌽Y[ι3]

(m) 0 2⌽M   (n) 0 1 2 ‾1⌽P

(o) 0 1 2⌽AL   (p) 1⌽AA

(q) (2 3ρ1)⌽AA   (r) (2 2ρ1)⌽[2]AA

(s) ‾2⌽[1]P   (t) 0 1 2⌽0 1 2⌽[1]AL

2. Write an expression to rotate the rows of only the first plane of AR one place to the left. Assume that AR is a rank-3 array and that ρAR is 3 4 5.

3. Define a function DLT to delete the Ith row from a matrix M.

Test:

```
M←4 3ρι12
I←2
```

. . . .

```
 1    2    3
 7    8    9
10   11   12
```

4. Given a rank-3 array $AR3$ such that ρ$AR3$ is 7 5 6, build a matrix M such that ρM is 5 6, where each element of M is chosen from one of the possible seven choices of those

corresponding row and column elements of $AR3$. The selection is defined by a selection matrix A (where ρA is 5 6). Its elements define from which plane an element is to be selected for the corresponding row and column of M.

5. (a) Write an expression to remove surplus blanks within a character string S.

Test:

$$S\leftarrow'TOO \quad MANY \quad SPACES \quad BETWEEN \quad\quad WORDS'$$

....

TOO MANY SPACES BETWEEN WORDS

(b) Define a function REM to remove leading, trailing, and surplus blanks from a character string S.

Test:

$$S\leftarrow' \quad CLOSE \quad UP \quad\quad THESE \quad\quad SPACES \quad\quad '$$

....

CLOSE UP THESE SPACES

6. Define a function $UNDUP$ to remove duplicates from a vector R.

Test:

$$R\leftarrow6 \ 7 \ 9 \ 8 \ 6 \ 5 \ 6 \ 7 \ 5 \ 6 \ 8 \ 6 \ 5 \ 5 \ 7 \ 6$$

....

6 7 9 8 5

7. (a) Define a function $ENCODE$ to encode a message M by shifting the alphabet I places.

(b) Define a function $DECODE$ to decode a message M written by the encoding procedure of part (a).

8. Define a function $MULT$ to multiply two polynomials together. Assume as input the co-efficients $C1$ and $C2$ arranged in descending order of powers of the variable of each polynomial. Let the output be the vector of coefficients of the resulting product polynomial.

Test:

$$C1\leftarrow4 \ 5$$
$$C2\leftarrow3 \ 2 \ 1$$

....

12   23   14   5

9. M is a matrix of values representing a temperature grid. For example M might be

```
25   30   41   29
23   40   42   30
24   42   44   29
22   21   23   25
```

New values on the temperature grid are to be computed by averaging the four perpendicular points directly surrounding each grid point. For the matrix above, the point whose current value is 40 would be replaced by $(+/30 \ 42 \ 42 \ 23)\div4$.

Define a function $NEWGRID$ to replace each current grid value by its newly computed grid value. Try to write the function without branching.

Hint: Respecify the matrix to have a border of zeros for the calculations. However, the function should return only the grid values without any border.

Section 7.2.3 Transposition

Reversal and rotation change the relation among the elements of an array by permuting the subscripts or indices within one dimension. The data in matrices and higher rank arrays can be rearranged in yet another way—by permuting the dimensions of the array. This is done with the monadic or dyadic transpose functions. There are three transposition conditions possible: (1) where the order of all the dimensions is reversed, (2) where any dimensions are interchanged with any other dimensions, and (3) where certain subsets of components are interchanged. These three conditions are discussed in the following section under the headings monadic transpose, general dyadic transpose, and specialized dyadic transpose.

Monadic Transpose

The monadic transpose function reverses the order of all the dimensions in an array. Its syntax is

> ⍉Q

where Q is the array data to be transposed. For example,

```
        M
    1   2   3   4
    5   6   7   8
    9  10  11  12

        ρM
3 4

        N←⍉M
        ρN
4 3

        N
    1   5    9
    2   6   10
    3   7   11
    4   8   12
```

What monadic transpose does is to interchange the row and column indices for each element of a matrix. For instance, consider the matrix W:

```
        W
ABCD
EFGH
IJKL
```

With the subscripts on the elements indicated explicitly W is

$$
\begin{array}{cccc}
A_{11} & B_{12} & C_{13} & D_{14} \\
E_{21} & F_{22} & G_{23} & H_{24} \\
I_{31} & J_{32} & K_{33} & L_{34}
\end{array}
$$

The result of $\lozenge W$ is created by interchanging the subscripts:

$$
\begin{array}{cccc}
A_{11} & B_{21} & C_{31} & D_{41} \\
E_{12} & F_{22} & G_{32} & H_{42} \\
I_{13} & J_{23} & K_{33} & L_{43}
\end{array}
$$

and then reordering the data with the subscripts in row-major order:

```
AEI
BFJ
CGK
DHL
```

The monadic transpose function completely reverses the dimensions of the argument. An example of this transpose on a rank-3 array AR is shown below:

```
        AR                              T
ABCD                            AM
EFGH                            EQ
IJKL                            IU

MNOP                            BN
QRST                            FR
UVWX                            JV

        ρAR
2 3 4                           CO
                                GS
        T←ΦAR                    KW

        ρT
4 3 2                           DP
                                HT
                                LY
```

Illustration 7.25   Testing for a Symmetric Matrix

A square matrix M is defined to be symmetric if all the elements are such that

$$M[I;J] = M[J;I]$$

The expression

$$\sim 0 \in M = \lozenge M$$

returns a 1 if the matrix M is symmetric and a 0 otherwise. For example,

```
        M
OH
HO

        ~0∈M=⍉M
1

        N
HI
HO

        ~0∈N=⍉N
0
```

Monadic transpose is often used with the function decode and encode to create more readable results, as shown in Illustrations 7.26–7.29.

Illustration 7.26   Alphabetizing a List of Names

N is a matrix of names where each row represents a single name. Assume that short names are padded out with blanks. The function *SORT* shown below arranges the names in alphabetic order:

```
     ∇ Z←SORT N;R;TN
[1]    R←' ABCDEFGHIJKLMNOPQRSTUVWXYZ'
[2]    TN←⍉N
[3]    NI←R⍳TN
[4]    Z←⍉TN[;⍋(1+⌈/[1]NI)⊥NI]
     ∇
```

For example,

```
        NAMES
JONES
SMITH
JOHNSON
WILLIAMS

        SORT NAMES
JOHNSON
JONES
SMITH
WILLIAMS
```

Illustration 7.27 N-Place Binary Numbers

All N-place binary numbers are produced with the following expression:

$$\lozenge(N\rho2)\top^{-}1+\iota2*N$$

For example, for four-place binary numbers,

```
        ⍉(4⍴2)⊤¯1+⍳16
 0 0 0 0
 0 0 0 1
 0 0 1 0
 0 0 1 1
 0 1 0 0
 0 1 0 1
 0 1 1 0
 0 1 1 1
 1 0 0 0
 1 0 0 1
 1 0 1 0
 1 0 1 1
 1 1 0 0
 1 1 0 1
 1 1 1 0
 1 1 1 1
```

Illustration 7.28 Addition of Two Binary Numbers

The function *ADDB* adds two binary numbers represented in a two-row binary matrix:

```
     ∇ Z←ADDB M;Q
[1]    Z←((⌊1+2⍟Q)⍴2)⊤Q←+/2⊥⍉M
     ∇
```

```
      M
  1   0   1   0   1
  1   0   1   1   0
      ADDB M
  1 0 1 0 1 1
```

Illustration 7.29 Hexadecimal Addition

The function *HEXSUM* performs hexadecimal addition of any character matrix argument whose rows represent valid hexadecimal numbers:

```
      ∇ Z←HEXSUM M
[1]   HEX←'0123456789ABCDEF'
[2]   DEC←+/16⊥¯1+HEXιⱯM
[3]   Z←HEX[1+((⌊1+16⊛DEC)ρ16)⊤DEC]
      ∇

      M
1F2
20A
713

      HEXSUM M
B0F
```

Had transpose not been used with each of the Illustrations 7.26–7.29 the input and output would have been by columns instead of by rows.

General Dyadic Transpose

With arrays of rank 3 and higher, the transpose need not be restricted to reversing the dimensions of the array. All or any of the dimensions and their corresponding degrees of freedom can be interchanged by using the dyadic transpose function. The syntax of the dyadic transpose function is

$$V \mathbb{Q} B$$

where

B is the data array to be transposed.

V is a vector whose components define the rule of the transformation; that is, it describes how the dimensions of B are to be permuted.

Thus the general dyadic transpose function reorders the dimensions of the right argument as indicated by the left argument.

The domain of definition of the components of V is the set of positive integers less than or equal to the rank of B. Any other components result in a *DOMAIN ERROR* report. The vector left argument V contains information relating the original dimension to the new dimension after the transpose. Our discussion of dyadic transpose uses the rank-3 array AR for illustration:

```
      AR
  1    2    3    4
  5    6    7    8
  9   10   11   12

 13   14   15   16
 17   18   19   20
 21   22   23   24

      ρAR
2 3 4
```

A mechanical way of determining the shape of R for $R \leftarrow 3\ 1\ 2 \lozenge AR$ in relation to the shape of AR is as follows:

Write down the values of ρAR, and under each, the corresponding components of V.

Then move the values of ρAR to the position indicated by the matching value of V.

The resulting reordering is ρR. Thus

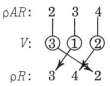

```
ρAR:   2   3   4
 V:    ③   ①   ②
ρR:    3   4   2
```

In determining the shape of R, the transposed array, the *index* of each component of V is equated to the original dimensions of AR and the *value* of each component of V is equated to the dimensions of R into which AR was transformed. Again for $R \leftarrow 3\ 1\ 2 \lozenge AR$:

The first dimension of AR (index 1 of V) is transformed into the third dimension of the result R ($V[1]$ is 3).

The second dimension of AR (index 2 of V) is transformed into the first dimension of the result R ($V[2]$ is 1).

The third dimension of AR (index 3 of V) is transformed into the second dimension of the result R ($V[3]$ is 2).

Thus

```
     ρR
3 4 2
```

This means that   for $R\leftarrow 3$ 1 2 ⍉ AR

- The first dimension of AR
  becomes the third of the result.———

- The second dimension of AR
  becomes the first of R. ———

- The third dimension of AR
  becomes the second of R.———

$$
\begin{array}{rr}
 & R \\
1 & 13 \\
2 & 14 \\
3 & 15 \\
4 & 16 \\
\\
5 & 17 \\
6 & 18 \\
7 & 19 \\
8 & 20 \\
\\
9 & 21 \\
10 & 22 \\
11 & 23 \\
12 & 24 \\
\end{array}
$$

The equivalence $(\rho R)[V] = \rho B$ between the variables of $R\leftarrow V\text{⍉}B$ is the formal statement of the discussion above. Thus $(\rho R)[3\ 1\ 2]$ is the shape of AR:

$$3\ 4\ 2[3\ 1\ 2] = 2\ 3\ 4$$

We have been considering the shape of the transformed data and how to determine what the transpose should be to order the elements into a specific relation. It is also important to be able to determine the new position of each element in a transposed array. This can be done by looking at the transposition as an exchange of indices. The basic relation $(\rho R)[V] = \rho B$ can be restated as

(new indices) [left argument] = old indices

This relation can be applied to the indices of each element. For example, the element of AR whose subscripts are 1 2 4 has the new indices 2 4 1 under the transposition 3 1 2⍉AR. Graphically,

a set of indices of an element in AR

the transformation vector 3 1 2

the set of indices for the corresponding elements of the result of the transposition

The position of each element of an array after its transposition can be determined by applying this technique to each component. Let us look at the rank-3 array $R3$ as an example:

```
        R3
DOG
MAN

PAL
JOE
```

Or graphically,

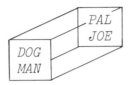

To determine the position of each component of $R3$ under the transposition

$$NR \leftarrow 1 \ 3 \ 2 \lozenge R3$$

first list each component of $R3$ in row-major order with its indices explicitly stated:

$$D_{111} \ O_{112} \ G_{113} \ M_{121} \ A_{122} \ N_{123} \ P_{211} \ A_{212} \ L_{213} \ J_{221} \ O_{222} \ E_{223}$$

Then apply the transposition as defined by the left argument, here $1 \ 3 \ 2$, to each set of indices. The $1 \ 3 \ 2$ transposition can be illustrated graphically as

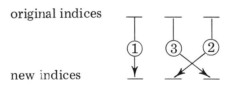

The transposed indices are

$$D_{111} \ O_{121} \ G_{131} \ M_{211} \ A_{212} \ N_{213} \ P_{211} \ A_{221} \ L_{231} \ J_{212} \ O_{222} \ E_{232}$$

Thus

```
        NR
DM
OA
GN

PJ
AO
LE
```

Or graphically,

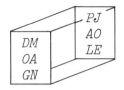

The 2 1 3 transpose of a rank-3 array then interchanges rows and columns in each plane.

Illustration 7.30 Subdividing Each Row of Data in a Matrix

The function $FLIP$ changes a matrix X whose elements are positive integers less than 9999 into a rank-3 array Z whose shape is $(1 \uparrow \rho X), 2, 1 \downarrow \rho X$. The Ith plane of the result array corresponds to the Ith row of X. $Z[I;1;]$ contains the leftmost two digits of each component of $X[I;]$; $Z[I;2;]$ contains the rightmost two digits of each component of $X[I;]$:

```
    ∇ Z← FLIP X
[1]   Z←2 1 3⍴100 100⊤X
    ∇
```

For example,

```
        M
 1492    2003    345
  156    7896     34

        FLIP M
 14   20    3
 92    3   45

  1   78    0
 56   96   34
```

Illustration 7.31 Determining Whether a Set of Coordinates
Is an End Point of a Line in a Plane

$LINES$ is a 2 by 2 by N array containing the beginning and end points of line segments in a plane. $LINES[1;;]$ contains the initial points and $LINES[2;;]$ contains the terminal points. That PT is an end point can be determined by the following expression:

```
    1∊PT∧.=2 1 3⍴LINES
```

Illustration 7.32   Rearranging a Table for Varying
                     Management Purposes

The rank-3 array *EXPENSES* represents the monthly costs over the last 6 months in the four categories labor, services, overhead, and miscellaneous for the three departments purchasing, personnel, and computer center. *EXPENSES* is a 6 by 4 by 3 array where each plane is a month, rows are costs and columns are departments. That is, *EXPENSES* is a costs versus departments on a monthly basis array. The expression

    ⍉*EXPENSES*

rearranges *EXPENSES* as a costs versus months by department array. And the expression

    2 3 1⍉*EXPENSES*

rearranges *EXPENSES* as a months versus costs by department array.

Specialized Dyadic Transpose

In addition to transforming an array by permuting each element's indices, the dyadic transpose can also be used first to select and then to transpose certain subsets of elements from the array. This is accomplished by making one or more of the integers in the vector left argument the same. For example,

          M
PAT
RAY
SAM

          ⍴*M*
3 3

          1 1⍉*M*
PAM

In the case of a matrix right argument as above, a pair of 1s for the left argument yields the elements on the main diagonal of the matrix. In effect the left argument of 1 1 can be interpreted as a selection of those elements of *M* whose first and second indices have the same value. For *M* this is

    P_{11} A_{22} M_{33}

For matrix right arguments, there are three permissible left argument forms:

    1 2⍉*M*   Equivalent to *M*.
    2 1⍉*M*   Equivalent to ⍉*M*.
    1 1⍉*M*   The main diagonal of *M*.

The full nature of the specialized dyadic transpose is not seen until arrays of rank 3 or greater are considered. To illustrate, let us use the 2 by 3 by 4 rank-3 array *AR* again:

```
      AR
    1    2    3    4
    5    6    7    8
    9   10   11   12

   13   14   15   16
   17   18   19   20
   21   22   23   24
```

The vector left argument V of a transposition on *AR* must have three components. For the specialized dyadic transpose two or more of the components are identical. The values which the three-component vector left argument may assume are governed by the following two conditions:

1. $V\epsilon\iota\rho\rho B$: Each component of the left argument V must be a positive integer less than or equal to the rank of the array right argument B.

2. $(\iota\lceil/V)\epsilon V$: All the positive integers up to the largest in V must appear in V. Thus 3 1 2 and 2 1 2 are valid left arguments, but 3 1 1 and 2 2 2 are not. Any invalid combination produces a *DOMAIN ERROR* report. Valid left arguments for the specialized dyadic transpose $V\lozenge AR$ are 1 1 1, 1 1 2, 2 2 1, 2 1 1, 1 2 2, 1 2 1, and 2 1 2.

The result of a specialized general transpose is formed in two steps: selection and transposition. First the indices are coalesced in the dimensions indicated by the position of identical components of V. Thus for a rank-3 array,

1 1 1 indicates selection of all elements whose first, second, and third indices are the same.

1 1 2 and 2 2 1 indicate selection of all elements whose first and second indices are the same.

2 1 1 and 1 2 2 indicate selection of all elements whose second and third indices are the same.

1 2 1 and 2 1 2 indicate selection of all elements whose first and third indices are the same.

Similarly, the left argument is reduced by coalescing like elements:

Original	Coalesced
1 1 1	1
1 1 2	1 2
2 2 1	2 1
2 1 1	2 1
1 2 2	1 2
1 2 1	1 2*
2 1 2	2 1*

Next the selected array from the first step is transposed according to the coalesced V. For example, the transpositions 1 1 2$\lozenge AR$ and 2 2 1$\lozenge AR$ both select the matrix in the first step of obtaining a specialized general transpose:

$$\begin{array}{cccc} 1 & 2 & 3 & 4 \\ 17 & 18 & 19 & 20 \end{array}$$

Finally this matrix is transposed by 1 2 for 1 1 2$\lozenge AR$ and by 2 1 for 2 2 1$\lozenge AR$. Recall that a 1 2 transpose of B is the same as B. Thus

1 1 2$\lozenge AR$
$$\begin{array}{cccc} 1 & 2 & 3 & 4 \\ 17 & 18 & 19 & 20 \end{array}$$

But 2 1$\lozenge B$ interchanges columns and rows. Thus

2 2 1$\lozenge AR$
$$\begin{array}{cc} 1 & 17 \\ 2 & 18 \\ 3 & 19 \\ 4 & 20 \end{array}$$

The possible transpositions of a rank-3 array are illustrated in the table below. The elements indicated by ⋆ are not selected.

Transpose	Result	A Graphic Representation of the Selection
AR	1 2 3 4 5 6 7 8 9 10 11 12 13 14 15 16 17 18 19 20 21 22 23 24	

*The right term coalesces into the left term.

Transpose	Result	A Graphic Representation of the Selection

1 1 1◊*AR*   1   18

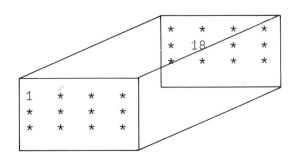

1 1 2◊*AR*   1   2   3   4
              17   18   19   20

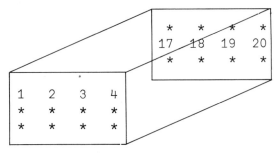

2 2 1◊*AR*   1   17
                2   18
                3   19
                4   20

Transpose	Result	A Graphic Representation of the Selection

2 1 1◊*AR*

```
 1   13
 6   18
11   23
```

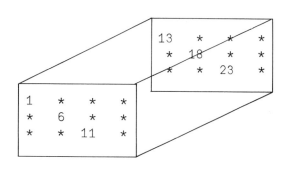

1 2 2◊*AR*

```
 1    6   11
13   18   23
```

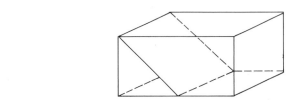

1 2 1◊*AR*

```
 1    5    9
14   18   22
```

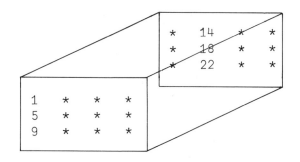

2 1 2◊*AR*

```
1   14
5   18
9   22
```

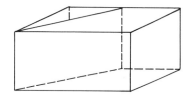

Illustration 7.33   Adding a Vector to a Matrix

Let M and V be a numeric matrix and vector respectively, where

$$(\rho V) = 1\uparrow\rho M$$

The expression

        1 1 2⍉V∘.+M

adds the Ith component of V to each of the components in the Ith row of M.
For example,

        V←⍳4

        M←4 3ρ⍳12

        1 1 2⍉V∘.+M
     2   3   4
     6   7   8
    10   11   12
    14   15   16

Substituting any scalar function for + in the outer product will cause that function
to be performed between V and M.

PROBLEMS

1. Use the following variables to evaluate expressions (a)–(z):

        Z←1 2 3 4 5
              P
     1   5   9   13   17
     2   6   10   14   18
     3   7   11   15   19
     4   8   12   16   20
              M
     1   2   3   4
     5   6   7   8
             AA
     1   2
     3   4
     5   6

     7   8
     9   10
    11   12
             AL
    ADG
    BEH
    CFI

(a) ⍴P   (b) ⍴AA   (c) ⍫⍴P

(d) 1 1⍴AA   (e) 1 1⍴P   (f) 1 1⍫1⍫AL

(g) ⍴[1]AA   (h) ⍴M   (i) 1 2 3⍴AA

(j) ρ2 1 3⍴AA   (k) ρ1 3 2⍴AA   (l) ρ2 3 1⍴AA

(m) 1 1 2⍴AA   (n) 2 1 1⍴AA   (o) 1 2 1⍴AA

(p) 1 3 1⍴AA   (q) ⍴Z   (r) ⍴⍫AL

(s) ⍴⍫[1]AL   (t) 1 1⍴AL   (u) 1 1⍴⍫AL

(v) 1 1 1⍴AA   (w) 2 1⍴M   (x) 2 1 3⍴AA

(y) 1 3 2⍴AA   (z) 2 3 1⍴AA

2. Let M be an N by 2 matrix representing the X and Y rectangular coordinates of cities on a map. Each row provides the X and Y coordinates of a city. Assume that the origin is at the lower left-hand corner of the map.

(a) Determine the matrix D of straight-line distances between any two cities. Round to the nearest mile.

(b) Assuming the distance matrix D from part (a), determine the maximum and minimum distances between the cities.

3. (a) Define a function *POS* to produce a list of the successive three position base-N integers from 0 0 0 to $(N{-}1)$, $(N{-}1)$, $(N{-}1)$.

Test:

    $N \leftarrow 3$

    . . . .

    0 0 0
    0 0 1
    0 0 2
    0 1 0
    0 1 1
    0 1 2
    0 2 0
        .
        .
        .
    2 2 2

(b) Modify *POS* so that it produces a list of C-position base-N integers.

Test:

    $N \leftarrow 2$
    $C \leftarrow 4$

    . . . .

    0 0 0 0
    0 0 0 1
    0 0 1 0
    0 0 1 1
        .
        .
        .
    1 1 1 1

4. Define a function BIG which, when given a character vector V, will print out horizontally each of the input characters as a 5 by 7 grid character. Use the character G as the grid element.

> *Test:*
>
> $$V \leftarrow 'APL'$$
> $$G \leftarrow '\Box'$$
>
> . . . .

5. Define a function $COMP$ which, when given a vector V and a matrix M, will compare the Nth element of V with each element of the Nth row of M. The result should be a binary matrix which records in the Nth row which elements of the Nth row of M match the Nth element of V.

> *Test:*
>
> $$V \leftarrow 4 \quad 5 \quad 6 \quad 7$$
> $$M$$
>
> | | | | |
> |---|---|---|---|
> | 4 | 7 | 8 | 3 |
> | 6 | 5 | 2 | 5 |
> | 3 | 0 | 4 | 7 |
> | 6 | 5 | 4 | 7 |
>
> . . . .
>
> | | | | |
> |---|---|---|---|
> | 1 | 0 | 0 | 0 |
> | 0 | 1 | 0 | 1 |
> | 0 | 0 | 0 | 0 |
> | 0 | 0 | 0 | 1 |

6. Define a function TD to generate a rank-3 array A where $(1 \uparrow \rho A) = \rho V$ and $(1 \downarrow \rho A) = X$ such that the first plane consists entirely of the component $V[1]$, the second plane consists entirely of $V[2]$, and so forth. In general, the Ith plane consists entirely of $V[I]$, where $I \in \iota \rho V$.

> *Test:*
>
> $$V \leftarrow 1 \quad 2 \quad 3$$
> $$X \leftarrow 2 \quad 4$$
>
> . . . .
>
> | | | | |
> |---|---|---|---|
> | 1 | 1 | 1 | 1 |
> | 1 | 1 | 1 | 1 |
>
> | | | | |
> |---|---|---|---|
> | 2 | 2 | 2 | 2 |
> | 2 | 2 | 2 | 2 |
>
> | | | | |
> |---|---|---|---|
> | 3 | 3 | 3 | 3 |
> | 3 | 3 | 3 | 3 |

7. Define a function *ISIN* that returns a 1 if a name vector *N* is in the name array *AR*.

> *Test:*
>
> > *N←'SCOTT'*
> > *AR*
>
> *JOHN*
> *TERRY*
> *SCOTT*
> *SHAW*   . . . . . .
>
> 1

8. Define a function *COM* which produces a binary matrix *B* of the same shape as a given matrix *M*. The ones in *B* reflect where within each column the element equates to a corresponding element of a given vector *V*.

> *Test:*
>
> > *V←1 2 3 4*
> > *M*
>
> 2 4 1 5
> 6 7 2 4
> 3 9 3 1
> 1 2 4 4
>   . . . .
> 0 0 1 0
> 0 0 1 0
> 1 0 1 0
> 0 0 1 1

9. Write expressions for the following expressions using the square matrix *M*:

> > *M*
>
> *ABCD*
> *EFGH*
> *IJKL*
> *MNOP*

(a) Transpose it about the major (main) diagonal.

(b) Transpose it about the vertical center axis, that is,

> *DCBA*
> *HGFE*
> *LKJI*
> *PONM*

(c) Transpose it about the horizontal center axis, that is,

> *MNOP*
> *IJKL*
> *EFGH*
> *ABCD*

(d) Transpose it symmetrically about the center point. In other words, produce a 180-degree rotation about the center point, that is,

PONM
LKJI
HGFE
DCBA

(e) Transpose it about the reverse diagonal, that is,

PLHD
OKGC
NJFB
MIEA

10. Let M be the matrix

EAN
TAO
CAR

Write expressions to extract

(a) The main diagonal.

(b) The first column.

(c) The last column.

(d) The last row.

(e) The reverse main diagonal (that is, from lower-left to upper-right).

11. Write the expressions which will create a vector V from a matrix M by

(a) Raveling M by rows.

(b) Raveling M by columns.

(c) Raveling M in a direction parallel to the main diagonal.

Begin with the elements on the main diagonal.

Test:

        M←3 3ρι9

        . . . .
    1 5 9 2 6 7 3 4 8

12. For the array AA defined as $AA←3\ 3\ 3ρ'ABC...Z□'$,

(a) Find the main diagonal.

(b) Find the major plane, that is, all the elements where row and column indices are the same.

(c) Transpose the array so that the planes and rows are interchanged.

(d) Transpose the array so that the rows become columns, the columns become planes, and the planes become rows.

(e) Transpose the array so that the rows and columns are interchanged.

13. Let M be a character matrix where each of the N rows represents an N-place decimal number between 0 and 1.

    (a) Define a function NEW to form as a character vector a new N-place decimal numeral Z. This numeral Z is to be constructed from the set of N-place decimal numerals in M by selecting as the Ith digit of Z the Ith digit of the Ith numeral of the matrix M. Arrange the display of the result so that a decimal point appears in the leftmost position.

    Test:

    ```
            M
    1435
    9278
    0836
    6104
          ......
    .1234
    ```

    (b) Define another function DEC to form as a character vector a new N-place decimal numeral Z. This time the numeral Z is to be constructed from the given set of N place decimal numerals such that its Ith digit differs from the Ith digit of the Ith decimal numeral by 1. (*Note*: The construction of such a number forms the basis of the proof that the real numbers are not countable.)

    Test:

    ```
           M
    035
    791
    624
          ......
    .105
    ```

14. Modify the function $EXPOSE$ of problem 14 of Sec. 4.2 so that given the camera f-stops $FSTOP$ the output will show the nearest f-stop available on the camera.

    Test:

    ```
        FSTOP←22 16  11 8 5.6 4 2.8 1.4
          .......
    22  16  11  11  11  11
    ```

Section 7.2.4 Execute

At times it is desirable to convert a vector of characters representing numbers to numbers or to examine input from the keyboard during function execution prior to attempted execution or to use the name of an APL object, rather than its value, as an argument of a defined function. Each of these situations can be handled by using the monadic function *execute* $\pm$ ($\circ$ overstruck $\bot$).

The function execute evaluates or executes the APL statement represented by its character argument. The general form of execute is

$$\pm B$$

where B is a character scalar or character vector. For example,

```
      ⍎'6 3+2 1'
8 4
      '6 3+2 1'
6 3+2 1
```

For execute to complete successfully B must represent a well-formed APL expression. In addition to incomplete expressions such as $3+$, system commands and the opening of a function definition within the quotes are not considered well-formed expressions.

Error reports may occur indirectly through the execute function because of an error in the expression represented by its argument. In such cases, the actual error type is preceded by the symbol ⍎. For example,

```
      ⍎'3+'
⍎ SYNTAX ERROR
      3+
       ∧

      ⍎'4÷0'
⍎ DOMAIN ERROR
      4÷0
        ∧

      ⍎'⍳3.8'
⍎ DOMAIN ERROR
      ⍳3.8
       ∧

      ⍎')SAVE'
⍎ VALUE ERROR
      ) SAVE
         ∧
```

The argument must be character; otherwise a DOMAIN ERROR results:

```
      ⍎2+4
DOMAIN ERROR
      ⍎2+4
       ∧
```

The execute function may appear anywhere within an expression, but the expression represented by the character vector argument must by syntactically correct in its context for execute to complete successfully. Thus, execute produces an explicit result except when

- The argument is the empty vector, or
- The argument is composed solely of blanks, or
- The argument contains either the branch character → or the comment character ⍝

With such arguments, the execute function can appear only at the extreme left of an expression. If it does not, an error report is given. For example.

```
        Q←⍎' '
VALUE ERROR
        Q←⍎' '
        ∧

        Q←⍎2 3ρ'56'
DOMAIN ERROR
        Q←⍎2 3 ρ'56'
          ∧

        T←⍎'→6'
VALUE ERROR
        T←⍎'→6'
        ∧

        ⍎'∇FN'
DOMAIN ERROR
        ⍎'∇FN'
        ∧
```

Some of the versatility of execute can be seen in the following illustrations.

Illustration 7.34   Name Generation

In the course of computation a name or a set of names may be required. Perhaps such names are to be established based on some computed value, batch number, or date. The function *NEWNAME* forms the kernel of such name generation:

```
      ∇ NEWNAME X
[1]     ⍎X,'←⍳10'
      ∇
```

For example:

```
      )VARS
A   H

      NEWNAME 'ZEBRA'

      )VARS
A   H   ZEBRA
```

Illustration 7.35   Selective Specification

Without the execute function, a conditional setting of a variable X requires that the variable be previously specified. For example,

$$X \leftarrow (X,A)[1+C=0]$$

Here $X \leftarrow A$ if $C=0$ and $X \leftarrow X$ if $C \neq 0$ with X previously defined. By using execute, X no longer needs to be previously defined. The expression

$$\pm(C=0)/'X \leftarrow A'$$

specifies X if $C=0$; otherwise no X is created.

Illustration 7.36　Character-to-Numeric Conversion

In data manipulation, one could carry the data in character form and return it to numeric form later. For example,

```
DATA←?10ρ999
CDAT←⍕DATA
DATA←⍎CDAT
```

In S/370, $DATA$ requires 40 bytes whereas $CDAT$ requires at most 33 bytes.

Illustration 7.37　Graphing

The function $GRAPH$ prompts for both an algebraic expression in one unknown X and a set of values for the unknown X. Given such information, it produces a plot of Y as a function of X : Y must have integral values.

```
    ∇ GRAPH;X;Y;R
[1]     'SUPPLY EXPRESSION WITH ''X'' AS INDEPENDENT VARIABLE'
[2]     Y←⍞
[3]     'SUPPLY VALUES OF ''X'' TO BE GRAPHED'
[4]     X←⎕
[5]     R←⌽(¯1+⌊/Y)+ι1+(⌈/Y)-⌊/Y←⍎Y
[6]     ' *'[1+R∘.=Y]
    ∇
```

For example,

```
    GRAPH
SUPPLY EQUATION WITH 'X' AS INDEPENDENT VARIABLE
(X-3)×(X-5)
SUPPLY VALUES OF 'X' TO BE GRAPHED
⎕:
    1+ι5
*    *


  *  *
   *
```

Illustration 7.38   Conditional IF *Function*

With the execute function an expression or function may be conditionally executed. The function IF is typical of what may be done:

```
    ∇ Z←ΔE IF ΔC
[1]    →0⌊⍳0=ρZ←⍳ΔC
[2]    ⍎'Z←',ΔE
    ∇
```

For example:

```
    X←3
    Y←3

    'X+Y' IF X=Y
6
```

Such a function can be used to define recursive functions. For example, the factorial function can be written as follows using IF:

```
    ∇ Z←FAC N
[1]    Z←('1' IF N=0),'N× FAC N-1' IF N>0
    ∇
```

For example:

```
    FAC 4
24
```

PROBLEMS

1. Evaluate expressions (a)–(k):

   (a) $⍎'3←4'$ (b) $⍎'''3+4'''$ (c) $⍎⍎'''3+4'''$

   (d) $⍎X←'4+5'$ (e) $⍎X,X←'3+4'$ (f) $⍎X,X←' 3+4'$

   (g) $⍎'X←','3+4'$ (h) $X←⍎'3+4'$ (i) $Y←⍎X←⍎'''3+4'''$

   (j) $⍎''3+4''$ (k) $⍎'→7'$

2. Define a function $SWAP$ which, when presented two arbitrarily named variables X and Y, interchanges their associated values.

3. Define a function $ASSIGN$ which generates a specified named variable X and assigns to this newly created variable a specified arbitrary value Y.

4. In another programming language such statements as IF...THEN...ELSE...can be used. Define three functions IF, $THEN$, and $ELSE$ so that one may write, for example,

   ```
   IF (C=0) THEN 'R←12' ELSE 'R←23'
   IF (C≠0) THEN 'R←12' ELSE 'R←23'
   ```

5. In FORTRAN the equal symbol = is used for the APL specification symbol and .EQ. is used for logical equality. Define a function *FORTRAN* which will accept such FORTRAN statements, convert them to the corresponding APL equivalent, and execute them. Design the function so it will continue to accept and execute such statements until *END* is typed.

    Test:

           $R=3$
           $P=4$
           $Q=R.EQ.P$
           Q
    0
           $W=4$
           $W.EQ.P$
    1
           END

Section 7.3 SUMMARY

In Chapter 7 we have completed the discussion of APL primitive functions with a presentation of additional mixed functions for data manipulation. These are summarized in the following table:

Function	Syntax	General Description	Right Argument	Left Argument	Axis-specifier	Conformability	Shape and Rank of Result
Compression	$L/[I]A$	Compresses out elements from an array by removing certain elements as prescribed by a binary mask	Data array to be compressed; may be any shape and rank	Binary vector or scalar defining nature of compression; an element of A whose corresponding element of L is a 1 is kept, while an element of A whose corresponding element of L is a 0 is discarded; a scalar 1 takes all of A, and a scalar 0 discards all of A	Dimension along which compression occurs	$(\rho L)=(\rho A)[I]$	Shape: Same as ρA except that $(\rho A)[I]$ is $+/L$ Rank: $\rho\rho A$
Expansion	$L\backslash[I]A$	Enlarges one of the dimensions of an array by inserting into it zeros for numeric data and blanks for character data; the position of the insertion items is prescribed by a binary mask	Data array to be expanded; may be any shape and rank	Binary vector defining nature of expansion; zeros or blanks are inserted among the elements of A to match the occurrence of zeros in L	Dimension along which expansion occurs	$(+/L)=(\rho A)[I]$	Shape: Same as ρA except that $(\rho A)[I]$ is ρL Rank: $\rho\rho A$
Take	$V\uparrow A$	Selects the first or last $|V[I]|$ components from the I th dimension of the array argument	Data array from which selection occurs; may be any shape and rank	A vector of integers whose I th element describes the selection in the I th dimension of A; if $V[I]$ is positive, the first $V[I]$ elements are selected, and if $V[I]$ is negative, the last $|V[I]|$ elements are selected; if $V[I]>(\rho A)[I]$, zeros for numeric arrays and blanks for character arrays are used for padding out		$(\rho,V)=\rho\rho A$ or A is a scalar	Shape: $|V$ Rank: ρ,V
Drop	$V\downarrow A$	Deletes or drops all but the first or last $|V[I]|$ components from the I th dimension of the array argument	Data array from which selection occurs; may be any shape and rank	A vector of integers whose I th element describes the selection in the I th dimension of A; if $V[I]$ is positive, all but the first $V[I]$ elements are selected, and if $|V[I]|$ is negative, all but the last $V[I]$ elements are selected		$(\rho V)=\rho\rho A$	Shape: $(\rho A)-|V$ Rank: ρV

Function	Syntax	General Description	Right Argument	Left Argument	Axis-specifier	Conformability	Shape and Rank of Result
Catenation	$A,[I]B$	Appends the right argument to the left	Data array of any shape and rank	Data array of any shape and rank	Must be an integer; if $(\rho\rho A)=(\rho\rho B)$, $I\in\iota\rho\rho B$; if $(\rho\rho A)\neq\rho\rho B$, $I\in\iota(\rho\rho A)\lceil \rho\rho B$	1. A or B is a scalar 2. If $(\rho\rho A)=\rho\rho B$; $\wedge/(I\neq\iota\rho\rho A)/(\rho A)=\rho B$; 3. If $(\rho\rho A)\neq\rho\rho B$, $1=\mid(\rho\rho A)-\rho\rho B$ **and** $\wedge/(\rho B)=(I\neq\iota\rho\rho A)/\rho A$ **or** A or B is one-component array	If A and B are scalar, the shape is 2 and rank is 1. Otherwise, the same as the shape of the array of the greater rank except that $(\rho R)[I]=(\rho A)[I]+(\rho B)[I]$
Lamination	$A,[I]B$	Joins the arguments by creating a new dimension with value 2; A fills first index of new dimension; B fills second index of new dimension	Data array of any shape and rank	Data array of any shape and rank	Must not be an integer; $(I>0)\wedge I<1+(\rho\rho A)\lceil \rho\rho B$	1. $(\rho A)\wedge.=\rho B$ 2. A or B is a scalar	Shape: Same as the arguments except a new dimension of 2 is added before the $\lceil I$ th component. Rank: $1+(\rho\rho A)\lceil \rho\rho B$
Reversal	$\phi[I]A$	Reverses the order of the components in the I th dimension of an array	Data array of any shape and rank	None	Dimension along which reversal occurs		Shape: ρA Rank: $\rho\rho A$
Rotation	$A\phi[I]B$	Cyclic rotation of components in the I th dimension of an array	Data array of any shape and rank	Must be integral; describes the displacement and direction of rotation; positive element indicates cyclic movement of affected subscripts from left to right; negative element indicates cyclic movement of affected subscripts from right to left	Dimension along which rotation occurs	1. A is a scalar 2. $(\rho A)=1+\rho\rho B$ $(\rho A)=\rho B$ with the I th element eliminated	Shape: ρB Rank: $\rho\rho B$

Function	Syntax	General Description	Right Argument	Left Argument	Axis-specifier	Conformability	Shape and Rank of Result
Monadic transpose	$\mathbb{\oslash}B$	Reverse the coordinates of the argument	Data array of any shape and rank	None			Shape: The same as ρB except that the elements are reversed Rank: $\rho\rho B$
General dyadic transpose	$R \leftarrow V\mathbb{\oslash}B$	Interchanges coordinates of B as defined by V	Data array of any shape and rank	Defines how dimensions of B are to be permuted; $V\in\iota\rho\rho B$; the $V[I]$th coordinate of the result is the I th coordinate of B		$(\rho V)=\rho\rho B$	Shape: $(\rho R)[V]=\rho B$ Rank: $\rho\rho B$
Specialized dyadic transpose	$V\mathbb{\oslash}B$	First selects, then transposes subsets of components from B	Data array of any shape and rank	One or more elements are the same; the elements are selected in the dimensions indicated by where identical components of V are. $(\iota\lceil/V)\in V$ must hold true; identical elements of V are coalesced, producing the transposition for the selected elements		$(\rho V)=\rho\rho B$	Rank: $\lceil/V$
Execute	$\underline{\epsilon}B$	Evaluates the APL statement represented by B.	Character scalar or vector	None			Depends on APL statement represented by B

CHAPTER

8

COMMUNICATIONS WITH THE
APL SUPPORTING SYSTEM

The language definition of APL is considered separate from the APL supporting system—the host computer. The functions and data structures of APL as facilities of the language have been discussed at length in Chapters 1–7, but only in Chapter 1, in the brief section on system commands, did we deal with communication with the supporting system.

There are two ways of communicating with the supporting system: through system commands which are outside the language definition and must be issued manually from the terminal at the time they are needed and through system variables and system functions which provide the means to utilize the facilities of the language for the management of portions of the supporting system. That is, certain elements of the interfaces between the language and the supporting system are identified and defined as system variables or as system functions.

Communications with the APL supporting system via system commands for such things as saving and loading workspaces are identified by a leading right parenthesis. System commands are present in APL systems for direct communication with the supporting system. They cannot be a part of a defined function.

Communications with the APL supporting system via system variables and system functions for such things as varying the characteristics of a workspace possess distinguished names which are identified by a leading □. Distinguished names are reserved for system communications and have specific system-related meanings. Like other variables and functions in the language, system variables and functions can be used in APL expressions and defined functions.

In this chapter we shall discuss communications with the system that supports APL.SV: all the system commands and the system variables and system functions available to users of APL.SV.

Section 8.1 WORKSPACE CONTENTS

The APL-user sits at a terminal—usually one far removed from the computer system—to do his work. His work is transmitted to a work area created for him in the computer system known as the *active workspace*. It is through the active workspace that the user makes known to the APL system what he wants done.

The contents of a workspace are variables and defined functions. The contents of a workspace can be modified by

1. Specifying variables

2. Defining functions

3. Copying in variables and functions from another workspace

4. Erasing variables or functions

5. Grouping variables and functions into useful units

Section 8.1.1 Copying

The preceding chapters have demonstrated the more common way of getting variables and functions into a workspace—by specifying them and defining them. Another way of bringing variables and functions into a workspace is by using the system commands)*COPY* or)*PCOPY*.

The)*COPY* command is used to bring into the active workspace either the contents of another workspace—)*COPY NAME*—or a set of objects from another workspace—)*COPY NAME OBJ*1 *OBJ*2...*OBJ*n.* After the copy takes place a saved message is given indicating the time and date that the workspace being copied from was last saved. Requested objects which were not found are so listed after the saved message as *NOT FOUND*:, for example,

```
      )VARS
V1   V2   V3
      )FNS
F1    F2

      )COPY THIS NEWF
SAVED 11.33.04 11/29/99
      )VARS
V1   V2   V3
      )FNS
F1    F2    NEWF


      )COPY CONTINUE W Z
SAVED 11.33.09 11/29/99
NOT FOUND: Z

      )VARS
V1   V2   V3   W
```

---

*In APL/360 only a single object may be copied with each copy command.

The function *NEWF* from the workspace *THIS* has been copied into the active workspace, as was the variable *W* from the workspace *CONTINUE*, but *Z* was not found in *CONTINUE*.

```
      )COPY THIS
SAVED 12.12.12  08/10/99

      )VARS
V1 V2 V3 V4 V5 V6 V7
      )FNS
F1 F2 F3 NEWF
```

All the variables and functions from the workspace *THIS* have been copied into the active workspace.

Generally, copying does not interfere with the contents of the active workspace. Copying does interfere with the contents of the active workspace, however, if a name being copied in is the same as a name already in the workspace. In this case the name takes its meaning from the copied name, and the meaning it had previously in the active workspace is obliterated, for example,

```
      A←'TEST'
      )COPY THIS A
SAVED 8.11.10 12/20/99
      A
763
```

The use of the protect-copy command)*PCOPY* avoids this interference. Only those names which do not conflict with names already in the workspace are copied. Those names that do conflict are not copied and are so listed after the *SAVED* report as *NOT COPIED:*.

```
      A←'TEST'
      )PCOPY THIS A
SAVED 8.11.10 12/20/99
NOT COPIED:A
      A
TEST
```

Section 8.1.2 Grouping

Grouping is the bringing together of a set or group of variables and/or functions under a single name. The primary purpose of grouping is to facilitate copying a set of variables and functions into another workspace. For example, a workspace *LESSONS* may contain three sets of functions and variables. During any one class session only one set is needed. If *LESSON1* is a group of functions and variables needed for using Lesson 1, the command

```
      )COPY LESSONS LESSON1
```

brings into the workspace those functions and variables that had been grouped under the name *LESSON*1.

A group is defined by the *)GROUP NAME LIST* command, where *NAME* is the name of the group and *LIST* is a list of names which may be names of variables, names of functions, names of groups, or names unassociated with an object, for example,

> *)GROUP LESSON1 DRILL PRAC TEST STAT A̲ B̲ ANS COMPAR*

The term *object* is used to mean a variable, a function, or a group. It is possible to put a name unassociated with an object into a group. Such a need may arise when the use of a defined function creates data that will have to be copied out of the workspace. For example, *LESSON*1 may have in it functions that create several variables that contain statistics on a student's performance as he works through the functions in *LESSON*1. *LESSON*1 might contain the group name *STAT* which is a group of the names *SCORES* and *TIMING*. After the student has completed lesson 1 and saved his workspace, the teacher or proctor can copy the group *STAT*, which now contains variables *SCORES* and *TIMING*, into his statistics-gathering workspace.

The name of a group must be unique to the workspace. The message *NOT GROUPED*, *NAME IN USE* is given if a function or variable in the workspace already has the name, for example,

```
      )FNS
F1   F2   F3
      )GROUP F1 A B
NOT GROUPED, NAME IN USE
```

The group definition can be eliminated or dispersed by *)GROUP NAME* , which means that the objects in *NAME* no longer form a group. The *)GROUP NAME* command does not affect the value or definition of any objects in the group being dispersed. Using the *)ERASE* command on a group deletes the group identification as well as the names of the objects in a group and their meanings. (The discussion of the erase command is found in Sec. 8.1.4.)

The command *)GRP NAME* lists the names in the group *NAME*, for example,

```
      )GRP LESSON1
DRILL PRAC TEST STAT A̲ B̲ ANS COMPAR
```

Names can be added to a group by repeating the group name as the first name in the list of the *)GROUP NAME LIST* command, for example,

```
      )GROUP LESSON1 LESSON1 TRIES

      )GRP LESSON1
DRILL PRAC TEST STAT A̲ B̲ ANS COMPAR TRIES
```

If a group *NAME* is copied into a workspace that already has an object *NAME*, the group referents are copied, but the group definition is not. The message

NOT GROUPED, NAME IN USE is given.

```
      )LOAD WS1
SAVED 12.12.12 08/10/99
      )GRPS
SET
      )GRP SET
X  Y  Z
      )LOAD WS2
SAVED 11.11.11 08/10/99
      )VARS
      SET

      )COPY WS1 SET

NOT GROUPED, NAME IN USE

      )VARS
SET X  Y  Z
```

If a group is protect-copied, only the nonconflicting referents are copied.

Section 8.1.3 Inquiring About the Objects in a Workspace

Three inquiry commands available for identifying the types of objects in a workspace are)*VARS* for a variables listing,)*FNS* for a defined function listing, and)*GRPS* for a group listing. The)*VARS* command lists only global variables. Each of these commands lists the names of the objects in alphabetical order A to Z and $\underline{A}$ to $\underline{Z}$, for example,

```
      )VARS
AL AME GRY MLT RESET SET TEST TRIAL
      )FNS
GULLY STY UNCL VALUE ZILCH
      )GRPS
METHOD STYLE
```

Optionally each of these commands can be followed by a letter, in which case only names from that letter on are listed, for example,

```
      )VARS R
RESET SET TEST TRIAL
      )FNS U
UNCL VALUE ZILCH
      )GRPS S
STYLE
```

There are no system commands available that tell whether a variable is numeric or character, or what its size and shape is, or which of the six types of defined function a particular function is. Use of ρ tells the shape of a variable; then indexing can be used to examine one component to determine whether it is numeric or character. The function header can be displayed by ∇*FN*[0□]∇ to determine what the function type is.

Finally the inquiry command)*SI* or)*SIV* lists the condition of the state indicator. (This is discussed in detail in Sec. 6.5.)

Section 8.1.4 Erasing Objects

We have already used the)*ERASE* command to erase variables and functions from a workspace. This is done by listing all the names to be erased, for example,

)*ERASE FN*1 *VAR*1 *FN*2 *VAR*2 *VAR*3

The erasing of a group erases the group definition and the referents of the group. If a group is a member of a group being erased, its definition is eliminated but its referents are not, for example,

```
        )GROUP ADJ ART IVE ING AL
        )GROUP ART AN THE
        )GRPS
ADJ ART
        )VARS
AL AN ING IVE THE
        )ERASE ADJ
        )GRPS
        )VARS
AN THE
```

Since the erase command acts upon any global object, pendent functions may also be erased. In such a case, an *SI DAMAGE* report is given.

Section 8.2 THE LIBRARY

In the preceding section we discussed the contents of a single workspace. The structure for collecting and keeping workspaces is known as the *library*. There are two types of libraries in APL: public libraries and private libraries. Each public library contains workspaces available to all users. Each private library is accessible only to the holders of the library's number. Libraries are referred to by number rather than by name, as individual workspaces are.

Each user has a private library in which to store his workspaces. The identification of this library is the user's sign-on number. (Although the user's sign-on usually consists of two parts—the unique sign-on number and a key—only the number becomes the library number and identifies the user's library.) Anyone who knows this library number can access the workspaces in that user's library, except for workspaces that are protected with a password. (Passwords are discussed in Sec. 8.2.2.) However, no one but the user himself may store into his private library.

The *workspace quota* is the number of workspaces a user can store in his library. This is an amount set by the installation; it can usually be increased by a request to the administrator of APL. In addition to the workspace quota, each library has room for a workspace named *CONTINUE* built into its quota. *CONTINUE* is automatically established if the user's line is disconnected, or it can be established explicitly with a *)SAVE CONTINUE* or *)CONTINUE* command (see Sec. 8.4). If the user's line is disconnected, the work in the active workspace is automatically placed into the workspace *CONTINUE*. Thereafter the user's library has a workspace named *CONTINUE*. When the user signs on again after a prior line drop, he gets a saved message indicating that the *CONTINUE* workspace was automatically reactivated.

If the work from the previous active workspace is not needed, the command *)CLEAR* can be executed to make the active workspace a clean, unused workspace.

The command *)SAVE CONTINUE* is executed even though the name of the active workspace is not *CONTINUE*. Compare

)SAVE LESSONS	*)SAVE CONTINUE*
NOT SAVED, THIS WS IS CLEAR WS	*SAVED* 12:12:12 08/10/99

CONTINUE can be used like any other workspace in the user's library—loaded, copied from, and so forth, except that *CONTINUE* may not be activated or copied by anyone not signed on with the library number.* Since any line drop automatically loads the current active workspace into *CONTINUE*, wiping out whatever was there, it is advisable to use *CONTINUE* only for temporary storage.

Public libraries are not associated with user sign-on numbers. They are numbered from 1 to 999, although not all of them may have workspace quotas. Anyone can use the public libraries; however, restrictions on their use may be established by the installation. For example, library 360 may be reserved for workspaces that contain functions concerned with various aspects of the system 360, such as timing and throughput. Workspaces are usually put into public libraries because their contents are for general use. For example, *LESSONS*, discussed earlier, would probably be placed in a public library so that the teacher's sign-on number would not have to be given to the students.

Section 8.2.1 Library List

The command *)LIB* lists the names of the named workspaces in the user's library. The command *)LIB* **number** lists the names of the named workspaces in the public library whose number is provided. There is no indication in the library list of any vacancies in the user's library, that is, workspaces alloted but not used. Any workspaces that the user has created for any public libraries are not listed, even though creating a public workspace uses up a workspace in the user's workspace quota. Passwords to locked workspaces are never listed in the *)LIB* list. (See Sec. 8.2.2.) It is not possible for a user to list the contents of another user's private library.

---

*In APL/360 access to the *CONTINUE* workspace in another library is possible.

sign-on
.

.

.

　　　)*LIB*
WSI
CONTINUE
LESSON 2

　　　)*LIB* 10
PLOTFORMAT
.

.

.

　　　)*LIB* 246810
IMPROPER LIBRARY REFERENCE

Section 8.2.2 Workspace Saving

Workspace saving is the only way to get a workspace into a library except for the workspace *CONTINUE*. The primary save command)*SAVE NAME* assigns *NAME* to the active workspace and stores a copy of the active workspace in the library under the name *NAME*. Once *NAME* is an established workspace in the library, a)*SAVE NAME* command is executed only if the workspace name is *NAME*. Since this is the case, the abbreviated)*SAVE* command can be used. The effect of)*SAVE* is the same as)*SAVE NAME*.

The first 11 characters of a workspace name are significant. More characters can be used as desired. However, names not differing until the twelfth character or beyond are not regarded as unique. For example, *PROBS△TO△CH1* and *PROBS△TO△CH2* are not unique workspace names, since they do not differ until the twelfth character.

A workspace is saved in a public library by the command

　　　)*SAVE* number *NAME*

where the number is less than 1000. If the name of the active workspace is *CONTINUE*, it cannot be placed into a public library.* Only the creator of the public workspace can save into it. The name does not appear in the private library)*LIB* list but does appear in the public library)*LIB* number list.

It is not possible to save a workspace in another user's private library. One may save only into one's own library or into a public library. Whether a new workspace is saved in a public library or in the user's private library, it is reckoned against the total number of workspaces allocated to the user's account number.

A workspace can be protected from unauthorized use by attaching a password to the name. The password name must consist of eight or less letters. It is separated from the name of the workspace by a colon, for example,

----

*In APL/360 a *CONTINUE* workspace can be stored in a public library.

```
      )SAVE PORTFOLIO:MINE
SAVED 12.12.12  08/0/99
```

Thereafter, an attempt to load *PORTFOLIO* without the password results in the message *WS LOCKED*. *)SAVE NAME* without the lock discontinues the protection. *)SAVE* retains the lock. To change a lock, simply resave the workspace again with a new password, for example,

```
)SAVE PORTFOLIO:FAMILY
```

Workspace protection is common when several people share a user number or when the workspace contains some form of confidential information. A locked workspace can be saved in a public library.

     Within a defined function, the expression $X \leftarrow \square$ results in a prompting request to the user. Should he issue a *)SAVE* in response to such a prompt, the function containing the prompt is interrupted and then the *SAVE* command is executed. If this occurs, the report *INTERRUPT* is issued,[*] for example,

```
      FL
□:
      )SAVE
INTERRUPT
FL[2] Y←□
         ∧
   34.55.26 12/15/74 PORTFOLIO
```

     To resume the execution of the interrupted function, a branch to the line containing the prompt is necessary. Also when the saved workspace is next loaded, function execution does not automatically resume.

Section 8.2.3   Loading Workspaces

     The command *)LOAD NAME* brings into the active workspace a copy of the library workspace *NAME*. Loading obliterates whatever was in the active workspace in contrast to copying, which augments the contents of the workspace.

     If the workspace *NAME* had been saved with a password, that password is needed with an *)LOAD NAME* command as a key, for example,

```
      )LOAD PORTFOLIO:FAMILY
SAVED 12.15.12  08/10/99
```

Failure to provide the key results in the message *WS LOCKED*.

     If the name, library number, and key of a workspace are known, that workspace can be loaded, for example,

---

[*]In APL/360 the function is not interrupted before the *)SAVE* is executed.

```
    )LOAD 345678 HIS:WORK
SAVED 12.12.12  08/10/99
```

If *CONTINUE* received a locked workspace as a result of a disconnect, it is not automatically loaded but must be loaded with the key.

Section 8.2.4   *Dropping Workspaces*

The command)*DROP NAME* drops the workspace *NAME* from the library. Any workspace in the user's library can be dropped at any time, even if it is password-protected. Knowledge of the password is not necessary to drop the workspace. The drop command is also used to drop a public workspace that the user created. It cannot be used to drop a workspace from a private library that is not the user's own, nor can it be used to drop a public library workspace that the user did not create.

Section 8.2.5   *Copying from Other Libraries*

The copy commands and protect-copy commands are discussed in Sec. 8.1.1 for copying from the unlocked workspaces in the user's own library. Preceding the workspace name with the library number makes it possible to copy from other libraries. Following the workspace name with :*PASSWORD* makes it possible to copy from a locked workspace.

Section 8.3   THE WORKSPACE, THE WORK UNIT OF APL

A newly assigned workspace has these attributes:

1. The name *CLEAR WS*

2. A storage space (assigned by the operator at the system location) for functions, variables, calculations, and so forth

3. A symbol table allowing 256 names to be used in the workspace

4. Displays of 10 significant digits, if necessary

5. A maximum of 120 characters of output per line

6. Indexing in origin 1 (which means that the index of the first component of a vector is 1)

7. Fuzz of $1E^{-}13$ after which apparent equality exists

8. A random seed of $7*5$

Either system variables or system commands are available to the user to modify all the attributes of the workspace (except storage space, which can be modified only by the system operator and applies generally to all users). However, while both system variables and system commands can be issued manually (that is, in execution mode) from the terminal, only system variables can be specified within defined functions. System commands cannot be part of a function definition.

System variables are assigned values by using the specification arrow in the same way as values are assigned to all other variables in APL. For example, $\Box PW \leftarrow 100$ sets the page width to 100 characters. Moreover, as with any variable, the value of a system variable can be ascertained by typing its name, for example,

$\quad\Box PW$
100

System variables always have a value. If an explicit specification has not been made, the value of the system variable is its default value, for example,

$\quad\Box PP$
10

The printing precision in the workspace of the example is the default value of 10 significant digits.

Within defined functions, the system variables may be declared local. If a system variable is local, any use of it before a prior specification results in an *IMPLICIT* error report. This report also occurs if the system variable is specified ignoring the system's set restrictions.

The system commands and system variables for modifying a workspace are shown in the table below. The details of their usage follows the table.

| Attribute | Modifiable by | | Restrictions |
	System Variable	System Command	
NAME		)WSID NAME)SAVE NAME)LOAD NAME)CLEAR	Eleven characters to NAME
STORAGE Storage space			Only by system operator Cannot be done on individual basis
Symbol table (default 256)		)SYMBOLS N	$26 \leq N \leq 4241$ — must be executed before any names are used in the workspace

DISPLAY
  Significant digits
  (default 10)
	$\Box PP$
	Print precision
		)DIGITS N	$1 \leq N \leq 16$

Width of output line (default 120)	$\Box PW$ Page width	)WIDTH N	$30 \leq N \leq 390$

CALCULATION
  Index origin
  (default 1)
	$\Box IO$
	Index origin
		)ORIGIN N	$N \in 0\ 1$

Fuzz (default $1E^{-}13$)	$\Box CT$ Comparison tolerance		$0 \leq N < 1$
Random seed (default $7 \star 5$)	$\Box RL$ Random link		$N \in \iota^{-}1 + 2 \star 31$

Section 8.3.1 Name

Workspace Identification

The name of a workspace can be determined by the system command *)WSID*.
)WSID is an inquiry command. It provides information about the workspace, but it
does not modify the name attribute of the workspace. The system response to *)WSID*
is the name currently associated with the active workspace, for example,

```
      )WSID
TOSSES
      )WSID
10 PLOTFORMAT
```

The abbreviation *WSID* stands for workspace identification. It is used to indicate
the name and library number currently associated with the active workspace. If the
library number is the same as the account number, it is omitted.

A fresh workspace always has the name *CLEAR WS* associated with it. The name
CONTINUE is associated with a workspace when the previous work session was terminated prematurely by a line disconnect or when the command *)CONTINUE* was used
to sign off.

To change the name associated with the active workspace, the system command

```
      )WSID NAME
```

is used, where *NAME* is the name to be assigned to the workspace, for example,

```
      )WSID TRIAL
WAS TOSSES
```

Changing the name is often done if the workspace *CONTINUE* is automatically loaded
at sign-on time.

The system command *)WSID* can also be used to protect a workspace by permitting the attachment of a password to its name.[*] This is accomplished in the same
way as adding a password with the *)SAVE* command. For example,

```
      )WSID TRIAL:LK
```

protects the workspace *TRIAL* with the password *LK*. Any inquiry via *)WSID* only
returns the name of the workspace, never its password.

Saving

A *)SAVE NAME* command changes the name of the active workspace to match
that of the workspace saved, for example,

---

[*]This is not possible in APL/360.

```
    )WSID
CLEAR WS
    )SAVE NEW
 12.12.12  05/10/99
    )WSID
NEW
```

Note: A *)SAVE NAME* command can be used to save either a workspace under a new name or to save in a workspace that has the same name as the active workspace. (For the complete discussion of the save command, see Sec. 8.2.2.) A sequence of commands illustrating this is

```
    )WSID
CLEAR WS
    )SAVE OLD
NOT SAVED, THIS WS IS CLEAR WS
    )WSID OLD
WAS CLEAR WS
    )SAVE
 12.12.12  05/10/99 OLD
```

Loading

The command *)LOAD NAME* replaces the contents of the active workspace with the contents of the workspace name and assigns to the active workspace the name *NAME*. (For the complete discussion of the load command, see Sec. 8.2.3.)

Clearing

The command *)CLEAR* clears out the contents of the active workspace and creates a fresh workspace with the attributes listed in Sec. 8.1. After *)CLEAR*, the name of the active workspace is *CLEAR WS*.

Section 8.3.2 Storage

The symbol table is the storage location of the names used in the workspace. The smaller the size of the symbol table, the fewer the names that can be used in the workspace. A small-sized symbol table, however, provides additional room in the workspace for storing variables and functions and for doing calculations.

The symbol table contains all the names—both local and global—that were created in the workspace from the time it was first used. With the first specification of a name, an entry in the symbol table occurs for it. Erasing the name does not remove it from the symbol table.

The symbol table size can be changed by the command

>)*SYMBOLS N*

where N lies between 26 and 4241. This command can be executed in a workspace only before any names are used, that is, in a *CLEAR* workspace.

If it becomes necessary to change the size of the symbol table or to remove names no longer specified from the symbol table, the following procedure should be followed:

>)*SAVE WS*1
>
>)*CLEAR*
>
>)*SYMBOLS N*   (Only if size of the symbol table should be changed.)
>
>)*COPY WS*1

All names appearing in the symbol table of *WS*1 but which are no longer specified are effectively removed from the symbol table as a result of)*COPY*. Then

>)*WS*1*D WS*1
>)*SAVE WS*1

The size of the symbol table can be determined by using the command)*SYMBOLS* without a number. The response is the number of names that currently can be accommodated.* Thus

>)*SYMBOLS*
IS 256

Section 8.3.3   Display

Significant Digits

Calculations for APL on IBM Systems 360 and 370 are carried out to approximately 17 digits. The number of significant digits that can be displayed ranges from 1 to 16, with a 10 significant digit display as the default condition. The system variable $\Box PP$, print precision, in an expression $\Box PP \leftarrow N$ for N between 1 and 16 changes the number of significant digits displayed. For example, to check the examples in this book, we typed

> $\Box PP \leftarrow 5$

before executing any problems.

The value of $\Box PP$ affects the result of monadic format $\bar{\Phi}$ and the nature of numeric output. Any number that is equal to or greater than $10 \star \Box PP$ is displayed in exponential format, regardless of how it was entered:

----

*This is not permitted in APL/360.

```
        □PP←10

        2÷3
0.6666666667

        V←7 1E6
        V
7 1000000
```

With $\square PP$ it is possible to change the digit setting dynamically within a function, for example,

```
     ∇ F1;□PP
            ·
            ·
            ·
[4]     □PP←5
            ·
            ·
            ·
[7]     □PP←12
            ·
            ·
            ·
     ∇
```

In this example, all numeric output is displayed to 5 significant digits after line 4 is executed. After line 7 is executed, 12 digits are displayed. When the function is successfully completed, the global setting for print precision is reestablished because $\square PP$ was declared local to the function in the header. If no setting had been made explicitly, the default value would have been 10.

The system command $)DIGITS$ N performs the same function as $\square PP$. The response to the $)DIGITS$ command is the previous digits setting, for example,

```
        )DIGITS 5
WAS 10
        2÷3
0.66667
        V
7 1E6

        □PP←5
        2÷3
0.66667
        V
7   1E6
```

Output Line

The width of the output line can be varied between 30 characters per line and 390 characters per line by using the system variable $\Box PW$, page width, in an expression $\Box PW \leftarrow N$, for example,

$\quad \Box PW \leftarrow 30$

Output that exceeds the line width setting is continued indented 12 spaces on successive lines. Input is not affected by the width setting.

The system command $)WIDTH\ N$ can also be used to set the width of the output line. If the width is not set explicitly by either $)WIDTH$ or $\Box PW$, the default setting is 120. Some common width settings are

- 75: This ensures that the length of a line with 1/2-inch margins does not exceed the width of standard size paper ($8\frac{1}{2} \times 11$) since most terminals give 10 characters to the inch.

- 30 to 50: This low width setting is used if output from a terminal is being televised to ensure that everything will be on the screen.

- 130: This is the maximum width setting for an IBM 2741 terminal and is often used when lines of a function are quite long, since only single lines can be line-edited, or when large matrices are to be printed, since a matrix whose rows exceed the line width is difficult to read.

Section 8.3.4   Calculation

Index Origin

The index origin is the number assigned to the first position in each coordinate of an array. This may be either 0 or 1. The default condition in APL is origin 1. This means that, for example, in the vector V

$\quad V$
$1.9\ 6\ 3\ 5\ 4$

the index of 1.9 is $V[1]$. The last component of V is $V[\rho V]$. And in the matrix M

$\quad\quad M$
$\quad 8\quad 3\quad 2$
$\quad 1\quad 7\quad 4$

the indices of 8 are $M[1;1]$.

The system variable $\Box IO$ changes the index origin, for example,

$\quad \Box IO \leftarrow 0$

In origin 0, the index of `1.9` in the vector V is `V[0]`. The last component of V is `V[¯1+ρV]`. The index of `8` in the matrix M is `M[0;0]`.

The `)ORIGIN N` system command can also be used to change the index origin. The response is the previous index setting, for example,

```
    )ORIGIN 0
WAS 1
```

Besides indexing, all primitive functions that are concerned with indices are affected by the change in origin. These functions and an example in each origin are listed in the table below:

Function	Result in Origin 0	Result in Origin 1
Index generator `ι7`	`0 1 2 3 4 5 6`	`1 2 3 4 5 6 7`
Index-of, `'ABC' ι 'CAT'`	`2 0 3`	`3 1 4`
Grade up, `⍋9 6 3 8 4`	`2 4 1 3 0`	`3 5 2 4 1`
Grade down, `⍒9 6 3 8 4`	`0 3 1 4 2`	`1 4 2 5 3`
Roll, `?10 10 10 10`	`0 4 9 0`	`10 1 1 5`
Deal, `5?5`	`3 1 0 2 4`	`3 5 1 4 2`

Dyadic transpose,
`1 2 0⍉2 2 2ρι8`
	`0 2`
	`4 6`
	
	`1 3`
	`5 7`
		DOMAIN ERROR

`2 3 1⍉2 2 2ρι8`	*DOMAIN ERROR*	`1 3`
		`5 7`
		
		`2 4`
		`6 8`

The axis-specifier, which may appear in reduction, scan, catenation, lamination, rotation, reversal, compression, and expansion, is also affected by a change in origin. As an example of how the axis-specifier is affected by the change in origin, consider plus – reduction of the matrix M:

Origin 0	Origin 1
$+/[1]M$	$+/[1]M$
13 12	9 10 6

In origin 0 the first coordinate is the zero coordinate.

Defined functions that are written for one origin often do not work in the other. It is possible, however, to write functions that can work in either origin. These may require more coding. For example, selecting the last component of a vector via indexing with either origin cannot be done simply by $V[\rho V]$ or $V[^-1+\rho V]$. Rather an expression like the following must be used:

$$V[\lceil/\iota\rho V] \quad \text{or} \quad V[\square IO+^-1+\rho V]$$

However, the use of an origin-independent function may also serve the purpose. The function, take, for example, is origin-independent. The expression

$$^-1\uparrow V$$

selects the last element from a vector V regardless of origin. To avoid extra coding the primitive functions were defined in this text for origin 1 and may not be quite the same for origin 0. For example, the conformability on the axis-specifier of lamination is given as $(I>0)\wedge I<1+\rho\rho A$. To make the expression independent of origin requires $(I>^-1+\iota 1)\wedge I<1+\lceil/\iota\rho\rho A$.

An alternative to making a function origin–independent is to specifically set the origin for the function. This can be done during function definition by making the first line of the function $\square IO\leftarrow 0$ or $\square IO\leftarrow 1$, as needed. If $\square IO$ is made local to the function, the origin returns to what it was previously after execution of the function is completed.

Many people feel more comfortable using origin 1. However, some defined functions are written more simply for origin 0, for example, functions that simulate computers or functions that do a lot of converting from numeric to character and vice versa. As an example of the latter, consider the following. In origin 0, this expression converts the character vector '365' to the number 365:

```
      10⊥'0123456789'ι'365'
365
```

whereas in origin 1, the same result requires an additional function:

```
      10⊥^-1+'0123456789'ι'365'
365
```

Fuzz

Within a computer the difference between the ideal and the actual is often encountered. One such difference lies in the representation of numbers within a computer. Errors creep in because of the finite precision and inexact representation imposed upon numbers by the computer. For instance, finite decimal values may not always be representable finitely in a binary. The decimal number .1, for example, can be represented only by a nonterminating binary string of digits.

```
.000110001100011...
```

Because of this, anomalies such as .5 ≠1÷2 could occur in calculations on a computer. APL.SV avoids such anomalies through the use of *fuzz* whereby a set of binary values is made to represent a given decimal value.

Within a binary machine, in determining all but the last N binary digits are used whether a string of binary digits represents a decimal number. These last N bits are referred to as *fuzz*. Any binary string which differs only by fuzz, that is, in the last N bits, represents the same number. This concept of fuzziness establishes a tolerance which permits a relative comparison between numbers. If two numbers are within this tolerance or fuzz of each other, the relationship between them is considered to be true.

Fuzz is used with the relational functions in the comparison of numbers and in the determination of the floor and ceiling of numbers. In APL.SV, the fuzz provided automatically for each workspace is $1E^-13$.

For situations in which the system measure of fuzziness is not desirable, for instance, numerical error analysis, the system variable $\Box CT$, comparison tolerance, is available to alter it. The values which may be assigned to $\Box CT$ are values between 0 and 1, inclusive of 0 but exclusive of 1. The value assigned to $\Box CT$ is used in computing the relative fuzz between two numbers. The measure of relative fuzz involves the magnitude of the numbers taking part in the comparison. The following function is a formal definition of relative fuzz as it is used in APL.SV:

```
    ∇ Z←A RFUZZ B
[1]    Z←□CT×NB*⌈NB⊛(|A)⌈|B
    ∇
```

NB is the base used by the computer system to represent the internal floating point fraction. In System/370, NB is 16.

Relative fuzz is used in determining the proper response to the relational functions and the floor and ceiling functions. For example, the formal definition of equality can be stated as the function FEQ:

```
    ∇ Z←A FEQ B
[1]    Z←(A RFUZZ B)≥|A-B
    ∇
```

The symbol ≥ is assumed to represent the exact mathematical function of greater than or equal to. Thus for $\Box CT←1E^-5$ and $NB←10$, that is, for a decimal machine implementation, with $A←1000$ and $B←999.9999$, A $RFUZZ$ B results in $1E^-2$, whereas $|A-B$ results in $1E^{-}4$. Hence A FEQ B produces 1. But with $A \leftarrow 1$ and $B \leftarrow .9999$, A $RFUZZ$ B results in $1E^{-}5$, which is not greater than $1E^{-}4$. Hence A FEQ B produces 0. *

The following tables illustrate some of the effects of different settings for $\Box CT$ on different sized numbers within System/370 ($NB \leftarrow 16$):

Comparison

Setting of $\Box CT$ \ $2=$	2.1	2.01	2.001	2.0001
$1E^{-}5$	0	0	0	1
$1E^{-}6$	0	0	0	0

Comparison

Setting of $\Box CT$ \ $20=$	20.1	20.01	20.001	20.0001
$1E^{-}5$	0	0	1	1
$1E^{-}6$	0	0	0	1
$1E^{-}7$	0	0	0	0

Comparison

Setting of $\Box CT$ \ $2000=$	2000.1	2000.01	2000.001	2000.0001
$1E^{-}5$	0	1	1	1
$1E^{-}6$	0	0	1	1
$1E^{-}7$	0	0	0	1

For example, with $\Box CT \leftarrow 1E^{-}6$ and $NB=16$ the tables state that

        20=20.001
0

but that

        2000=2000.0001
1

---

*For further detail, see R. H. Lathwell and J. E. Mezei, "A Formal Description of APL," *IBM Philadelphia Scientific Center Report 320–3008*, Nov. 1971.

The difference between a number and its actual internal representation can occasionally cause some mysteries. For example, both the residue and encode functions seem to produce occasional inaccuracies. For the residue function recall that for

$$R \leftarrow A \mid B$$

the solution is either the smallest nonnegative or the largest nonpositive value R such that the equation

$$B = R + A \times Q$$

is satisfied where Q takes on integer values. If B is a decimal number such that its internal floating point representation cannot be exactly represented within the confines of the computer, the residue function may not seem to produce the correct value, for example,

```
      60|1000×3÷25
60
```

where one should have expected a zero. This peculiarity arises in the display of the data. The exact result cannot be represented internally as a finite binary floating point number, and here this internal representation is slightly less than 60. Thus when the data are displayed under the influence of the $\square PP$ or $)DIGITS$ setting, the result is rounded to that number of significant digits. Thus

```
      □PP←16
      60 | 1000 × 3 ÷ 25
59.99999999999999
      □PP←10
      60 | 1000 × 3 ÷ 25
60
```

The underlying difficulty is that the value of $1000 \times 3 \div 25$ is represented as a floating point number which is not exact. In the case where the right argument was to have been an integral value, this difficulty can be overcome through the use of the ceiling or floor function. These functions convert the inexact internal floating point representation into an internal integer representation. This integer representation is exact because fuzz is applied in the conversion. Thus

```
      □PP←10
      60 | ⌈1000 × 3 ÷ 25
0
```

If this difficulty arises where the arguments are not integral, then besides using the ceiling function some scaling may be necessary to make the data integral. Thus

```
      □PP←10
      .1 | 1.2
0.1
```

It should have appeared as 0:

```
      .1 × 1 | ⌈ 10 × 1.2
0
```

This same sort of situation also occurs with the encode function and the corresponding corrective measures should be taken to ensure a proper display. Note that

```
      □PP←10
      0 1 ⊤ 34.9999999997
34 0.9999999997
```

but that

```
      ⌈0 1 ⊤ 34.9999999997
34 1
```

Random Seed

The random seed is discussed at length in Sec. 2.9.3. The algorithm used in APL.SV* to generate a random number Z from the set ιB is

$$B←(\bar{\ }1+2\ast31)|\underline{B}×7\ast5$$
$$Z←□IO + \lfloor B×\underline{B}÷\bar{\ }1 + 2\ast31$$

where $\underline{B}$ is the last pseudo-random value generated.

The system variable $□RL$, random link, can be used to change the value of the random seed. It accepts as a value any integer between 1 and $\bar{\ }1+2\ast31$.

PROBLEMS

1. Fill in the blanks describing the system response in the following sequence:

```
            )CLEAR
      CLEAR WS
            )LIB
      WS0

       •
       •
       •
            )SAVE
```

---

*From R. H. Lathwell and J. E. Mezei, "A Formal Description of APL," *IBM Philadelphia Scientific Center Report 320–3008*, Nov. 1971.

(a) _____

```
      )SAVE CONTINUE
```

(b) _____

```
      )SAVE WS1
```

(c) _____

```
      )CLEAR
CLEAR WS
      )LIB
WS0
WS1

         .
         .
         .

      )SAVE WS1
```

(d) _____

```
      )WSID WS1
WAS CLEAR
      )SAVE
```

(e) _____

2. Consider the following sequence. Fill in the blanks and answer the questions.

```
      )CLEAR
CLEAR WS
      Q←ι3
      )SAVE CONTINUE
SAVED .....

    ∇ F;Q;□IO
[1]   □IO←0
[2]   Q←'OWE'
[3]   'DONE'
    ∇
      Q←12
      SΔF←3
      F
F[3]
      Q
```

(a) _____

(b) Why?

```
      )PCOPY CONTINUE Q W
SAVED .....
```

(c) *NOT FOUND*: _____

(d) Why?

(e) *NOT COPIED*: _____

(f) Why?
```
      )COPY CONTINUE Q
SAVED .....
      Q
```

(g) _____

(h) Why?
```
      )SIV
```

(i) _____
```
      Q
```

(j) _____

(k) Why?
```
      F
F[3]
      Q←12
      )COPY CONTINUE Q
SAVED .....
      Q
```

(l) _____
```
      )ERASE Q
      Q
```

(m) _____

(n) Why?
```
      →
      Q
```

(o) _____

(p) Why?
```
      ∇F[1]
[1]
      ∇ (that is, ATTN/RETURN)
[2] ∇
      ∇F[□]∇
      ∇ F;Q;□IO
[1]   Q←'OWE'
[2]   'DONE'
      ∇
      F
```

(q) $F[\_\_\_\_\_]$

(r) Why?

(s) $\Box IO$

(t) Why?

(u) $\iota 3$

(v) Why?

3. On S/360 the following sequence occurred:

```
      U←10⊛100
      U
2
      2|U
2
      2|2
0
```

(a) What caused this difference?

(b) If a terminal is available, perform the following sequence filling in the blanks:

```
      )DIGITS 16
WAS 10
      U←10⊛100
      2|U
2
_____
      U|2
_____
      U÷2
_____
      U÷2
_____
      U-2
_____
      2-U
_____
```

4. Given that the data and shape associated with the name *ONE* has remain unchanged. What occurred within the workspace at point (a) in the following sequence to account for the behavior in the rest of the sequence?

```
      ρONE
3 4
      ×/[1]ONE
1 1 1 1
      .
      .
      .
```

(a)

       •
       •
       •

     $\times/[1]ONE$

$1\ 1\ 1$

5. When will $\times/M$ and $\times/[1]M$ not produce the same result?

6. Indexing is normally an origin dependent function. Modify the expression $V[I]$ to make it origin independent.

7. The axis-specifier is origin dependent. Modify the expression $+/[I]AR$ to make it origin independent.

8. Determine the effective branch value in the expression

     $[14]\ \to 3\times \iota C=0$

under the stated conditions:

(a) 1–origin and $C\neq 0$

(b) 1–origin and $C=0$

(c) 0–origin and $C\neq 0$

(d) 0–origin and $C=0$

9. Replace the $\times$ symbol in the branch expression

     $[15]\ \to A\times \iota C=0$

to make it origin independent. Assume that $A > 0$.

10. What is the sequence of system commands to change the size of the symbol table to accommodate 512 names for workspace $WS1$?

11. After the following sequence

         $)LOAD\ WS1:LK$

 • • • • • • • • • •

         $)WSID\ WS1$

 • • • • • • • • • •

         $)SAVE$

What must be typed in to reload $WS1$?

Section 8.4   ON AND OFF

Presumably the reader already knows how to sign on with a *) number* command and how to sign off with a *)OFF* command. This section considers signing on with a password and other means of signing off.

Section 8.4.1 Signing On

The main portion of the sign-on command is the user-account number. *)number* signs the terminal on the APL system if the number is a recognized account number and if the sign-on number is not protected by a password. *)number* *:PASSWORD* signs the terminal on if the number is a protected one, for example,

```
     )999999:NIKAP
018)    12.12.12.  10/10/99    RJONES
        APLSV    ...
```

The computer response to a valid sign-on command is an information line containing (1) the access port number, which is used in other communications; (2) the time on a 24-hour clock in hours, minutes, and seconds; (3) the date; and (4) the user's name as it appears for accounting purposes—usually one or two initials (no periods or spaces) and a last name. The active workspace at sign-on is either *CLEAR WS* or *CONTINUE*. If it is *CONTINUE*, an additional saved message is given in the acknowledgement to the sign-on. (See also Sec. 8.2.)

Section 8.4.2 Signing Off

There are four signing off commands. An ending report is received as a final communication from the system for each, for example,

```
     018     15.15.15  10/10/99    RJK
CONNECTED    2.21.45   TO DATE  15.12.15
CPU TIME     0.10.10   TO DATE   1.13.07
```

The first line of the sign-off report includes the port number, sign-off time and date, and the user code, which is the first three letters of his sign-on name. The second and third lines are statistics for connect time, the actual time that the terminal was signed on, and CPU time, the time that the central processing unit was engaged for this user.

For each line, a pair of values is given. The first states the time used during the current terminal session. The other figure is a cumulative value. Each value is in hours, minutes, and seconds.

The four signing off commands are

1. a. *)OFF* This command simply signs the terminal off and disconnects the line. The contents of the active workspace are lost.

    b. *)OFF:LOCK* This command is the same as *)OFF* except that *LOCK* is a password that must be used with the sign-on number in order to get back on the system. The password can be up to eight letters in length. *)OFF:* eliminates the password; *)OFF:NEWLOCK* changes it.

2. a. *)OFF HOLD* This command is the same as *)OFF* except that the line is held for a minute so that another user can sign on without redialing.

b.)*OFF HOLD:LOCK* This command is the same as)*OFF HOLD* except that it establishes a password. Again)*OFF HOLD:* eliminates the password;)*OFF HOLD:NEWLOCK* changes it.

3. a.)*CONTINUE* This command saves the active workspace in *CONTINUE*, gives a saved report, and then signs the terminal off.

b.)*CONTINUE:LOCK* This command is the same as)*CONTINUE* except that it establishes a password.)*CONTINUE:* eliminates the password.

4. a.)*CONTINUE HOLD* This command is the same as)*CONTINUE* except that the line is held for a minute so that another user can sign on without re-dialing.

b.)*CONTINUE HOLD:NEWLOCK* This command is the same as)*CONTINUE HOLD* except that it establishes a new password.

If either of the commands)*CONTINUE* or)*CONTINUE HOLD* is used, a subsequent sign-on results in an automatic activating of the continue workspace, for example,

```
      )FNS
F1    F2  F3
      )VARS
A  B    C
      )CONTINUE
      .
      .
      .
      )123456:LK1
015)   17.54.30  10/22/99   STUDENT
      APLSV
SAVED  15.21.47  10/21/99
      )FNS
F1    F2   F3
      )VARS
A    B   C
```

However, if a password is associated with the *CONTINUE* workspace, *CONTINUE* is not automatically activated at a subsequent sign-on.

A sign-off command involving *HOLD* is usually used when someone is waiting to get on the system. If this is the case, a good practice to follow is to have the current user type)*OFF HOLD* without depressing the RETURN key until the new user sits down ready to sign on. In this way the new user can get established at the terminal without using up the minute available to him.

Section 8.5 MESSAGES

Messages can be sent to other terminals using system commands. There are two types of messages: *)OPR* and *)OPRN* for sending messages to the operator and *)MSG* and *)MSGN* for sending messages to other users' terminals. Messages can be received only when the keyboard of the recipient is locked. The sending terminal's keyboard remains locked until the message is received. When it is, the report *SENT* is printed and the sender's keyboard unlocks. If attention is struck before the message is received, the report *MESSAGE LOST* is given and the sender's keyboard unlocks.

An ordinary message received from the operator is prefaced by *OPR:*. A public address message is sent by the operator to all terminals and is prefaced by *PA..* A *PA.* message interrupts execution of a function; other messages do not. A message sent from a user's terminal is prefaced by his port number, such as 31. What ports are signed on the system and the user code associated with the port can be determined by the command *)PORTS*, for example,

```
        )PORTS
18      RJO
21      SPA
25      RJB
31      STP
42      RJO
51      RPO
```

The command *)PORTS user code* lists all the port numbers associated with the code, for example,

```
        )PORTS   RJO
18      RJO
42      RJO
```

Section 8.5.1 Message to the Operator

The command *)OPRN* followed by some text sends a message to the operator's terminal. The sender's keyboard unlocks after the message is sent.

The command *)OPR* followed by some text sends a message to the operator's terminal. The user's keyboard remains locked until either a message is sent or ATTN is hit.

Section 8.5.2 Message to Another Terminal

The command *)MSGN number* followed by some text sends a message to the terminal whose port number is given. The sender's keyboard unlocks after the message is sent. If the message is sent to a port that is signed off, the sender's port number and the message are printed.

The command)*MSG number* followed by some text sends a message to port *number*. The sender's keyboard remains locked until either a message is returned or ATTN is hit.

At the receiver's terminal the incoming message is prefaced by either the port number of the sending terminal followed by the letter R, for instance $021:R$, or just the port number, $021:$. The letter R appears to indicate that the sender's keyboard is locked awaiting a reply; that is, the sender had issued a)*MSG* command. If he had used a)*MSGN* command, the R would not have appeared.

Consider the following sequence as an illustration of the uses of the message system commands:

```
       )OPR FORGOT LOCK ON MY WORKSPACE. HELP
OPR: SORRY I CAN'T HELP YOU

       )OPRN THANKS

       )PORTS
18     RJO
21     SPA
33     RPP
         .
         .
         .
       )MSG 21 SANDY, IS THAT YOU?  RAY
021:R   YES, WHAT'S UP?
       )MSG 21 WHAT IS THE LOCK ON WS-PROBLEMS?
021:    ANS
       )MSGN 21  OF COURSE, THANKS
```

Illustration 8.1   Keyboard Locking

Only when a keyboard is locked can messages be received on it. Normally the user's keyboard is in an unlocked state. Occasionally a user may be waiting for an incoming message. Instead of periodically depressing the RETURN key to see if the message has arrived, the user can send a message to himself to lock his keyboard. In doing so, either his port number or port 0 suffices, for example,

```
       )MSG 0 HI
085:RHI
SENT
```

or

```
       )MSG 85 HIYA
085:RHIYA
SENT
```

The keyboard remains locked until a message comes in or until the user strikes the ATTN key to unlock the keyboard.

*Section 8.5.3 Message Control**

With the commands *)MSG* and *)MSGN* any user can send a message to another user. However, it can be very inopportune for a message to appear between lines of a final output. In such cases, and others, a user may wish to block off incoming messages. The command *)MSG OFF* blocks off all incoming messages, although a message may arrive before the keyboard unlocks after *)MSG OFF* is entered.

A user attempting to send a message to a keyboard which has had its incoming messages inhibited will not be able to get the message through. The terminal to which he is sending appears always to be unlocked, and so his keyboard remains locked waiting for delivery of the message. (ATTN unlocks his keyboard and causes the message to be lost.)

The command *)MSG ON* enables the user to again accept messages. After *)MSG ON*, the last *PA:* (public address message) issued during the *MSG OFF* interval is printed.

The inhibition of incoming messages established by the *)MSG OFF* command is not saved when the workspace is saved. Thus any workspace when loaded always accepts incoming messages. An explicit request via *)MSG OFF* is always required to inhibit incoming messages.

Section 8.5.4 Messages Associated with Workspaces†

As workspaces are developed for different applications, they are accessed by many people other than their creator. Often information about a workspace, such as operational details, needs to be supplied to the person who loads it. The system variable *□LX*, *latent expression*, enables such information to be automatically presented when the workspace is activated. After *□LX* has been assigned meaningful information, the workspace is saved. Thereafter, when a workspace is activated, the expression previously assigned to *□LX* is executed, for example,

```
)LOAD WS1
         .
         .
         .
□LX←'''CONTENTS CHANGED ON 6/30/99'''
         .
         .
         .
)SAVE
         .
         .
         .
)LOAD WS1
         .
         .
CONTENTS CHANGED ON 6/30/99
```

---

*This section is not applicable to APL/360.

†This section is not applicable to APL/360.

Or if the following defined function D existed in the workspace $WS1$,

```
      ∇D
[1]   'FOR FURTHER INFORMATION'
[2]   'TYPE   DESCRIBE'
      ∇
```

then

```
      )LOAD WS1
         •
         •
         •
      □LX←'D'
      )SAVE WS1
         •
         •
         •
      )LOAD WS1
         •
         •
         •
FOR FURTHER INFORMATION
TYPE   DESCRIBE
```

Note in the first example that the expression began and ended with three quotes. This was necessary since the expression specified to $□LX$ was to appear as a character string after execution. Also recall that a quote in a character string must be stated as a pair of quotes.

$□LX$ acts as if it were the right argument of an execute function; that is, its behavior can be compared to $⍎□LX$. Thus any expression assigned to $□LX$ must be a character string. The only restrictions placed upon it are those of the execute function. Namely, the character string assigned to $□LX$ may be the character representation of an executable expression, the name of a function, or a character string comment.

PROBLEMS

1.   Fill in the missing expression at point (a).

```
      ∇INFO
[1]   'TYPE ''DESCRIBE'''
      ∇
```

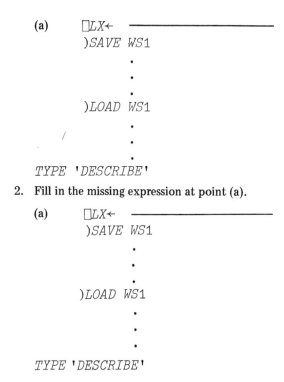

(a)   □*LX*← ─────────────────
)*SAVE WS1*

                    .
                    .
                    .
)*LOAD WS1*
                    .
    /   .
                    .
TYPE 'DESCRIBE'

2. Fill in the missing expression at point (a).

(a)   □*LX*← ─────────────────
)*SAVE WS1*

                    .
                    .
                    .
)*LOAD WS1*
                    .
                    .
                    .
TYPE 'DESCRIBE'

Section 8.6 TROUBLE REPORTS

The table below lists the trouble reports associated with system commands.
The problem that caused the report is usually evident from the report. Suggestions
for correcting the problem are given.

Report	To Correct the Problem Try
ALREADY SIGNED ON	$1\uparrow$□*AI* (see Sec. 8.7.1) or ɪ29 (see Sec. 8.7.2) to determine the sign-on number. Find the owner of that number or)*CONTINUE HOLD.*
IMPROPER LIBRARY REFERENCE	Avoiding)*SAVE*,)*DROP*, and)*LIB number* for a private library other than the one signed on.
INCORRECT SIGN ON	Entering a right parenthesis) followed by the account number and password, if any.
MESSAGE LOST	Reentering the message. Do not signal ATTN until the SENT report appears.

Report	To Correct the Problem Try
NOT GROUPED, NAME IN USE	Changing the name of the group or erasing or changing the name of the conflicting object.
NOT SAVED, THIS WS IS WSID	Changing the name of the active workspace using *)WSID* command.
NOT SAVED, WS QUOTA USED UP	Asking to have workspace allotment increased, using the workspace *CONTINUE*, or dropping an unused workspace from your library.
NOT WITH OPEN DEFINITION	Closing the definition.
NUMBER IN USE	Checking the number to be sure it is the one you meant to enter, reentering the number, or notifying the APL operator.
NUMBER LOCKED OUT	Contacting the person who gives authorization.
NUMBER NOT IN SYSTEM	Entering the number with the proper password or contacting the APL operator.
OBJECT NOT FOUND	Checking variables, functions, and groups lists in the workspace you are copying out of.
WS LOCKED	Loading or copying with the proper password.
WS NOT FOUND	Checking the *NAME* entered as part of the load or copy command.
SYMBOL TABLE FULL	Enlarging the symbol table via the *)SYMBOLS* or clearing the symbol table of unspecified names via *)CLEAR* and *)COPY*

Section 8.7   SYSTEM INFORMATION

Section 8.7.1 is devoted to the material which is applicable only to APL.SV. Section 8.7.2 contains material applicable to APL/360. Many of the illustrations appearing in Sec. 8.7.1 are duplicated in Sec. 8.7.2 in terms of what is available in APL/360. The reader need not read both sections.

Section 8.7.1 System-Dependent System Variables

A set of system variables are available to provide information related to the host processor supporting the language. Each variable has a distinguished name. While each name may be localized and set by a user, such action is immaterial since the host processor always resets it before the user can use it again. The table below states each system variable and the information it provides. Following the table are illustrations using each.

Distinguished Name	Meaning	Value
□WA	Work area	The number of bytes unused in the active workspace
□UL	User load	The number of users currently signed on the system
□TS	Time stamp	A seven-component vector containing year, month, day, hour, minute, second, and millisecond
□AI	Account information	A four-component vector containing 1. User sign-on number 2. Computer time 3. Connect time 4. Keying time All times are in milliseconds and are cummulative.
□TT	Terminal type	3 for 1050, 1 for Selectric, and 2 for PTTC/BCD
□LC	Line counter	A vector of line numbers, of functions in execution, suspended functions, or pendent functions.
□AV	Atomic vector	A 256-component vector containing all the possible characters representable on System/370.

System Variables for Timing and Accounting

The system variable □AI, *account information*, contains useful accounting information consisting of

1. The account number of the user

2. The amount of computer system time used since the user signed on

3. Connect time, the amount of time that the terminal has been signed on

4. The keying time, the accumulated time that the keyboard was released for entering data

All times, in milliseconds, are cummulative from sign-on.

The system variable $\square TS$, *time stamp*, makes available a time clock setting. This time information is a seven-component vector with the year first and the millisecond last. Thus the components of $\square TS$ are year, month, day, hour, minute, second, and millisecond.

Illustration 8.2   Timing Typing Speed

$TYPE$ is a function that times a person's typing speed. The portion which is directly related to the timing is

```
        ∇TYPE
[1]     KT←¯1↑□AI
[2]     'TYPE THIS EXPRESSION'
                   •
                   •
                   •
[.]     R←□
[.]     SPEED←(¯1↑□AI)-KT
                   •
                   •
                   •
        ∇
```

Illustration 8.3   Restricting a Function's Use

If a function's use is restricted to only certain users, the expression

$$\rightarrow CONT \times \square AI[1] \in NUMBERS$$

will continue with the function execution only if the sign-on number is contained in the vector $NUMBERS$.

Illustration 8.4   Adding Security to a Limited Use Function

The function $F1$ executes only if a required password is given. To add more security to that provided by the password only a limited amount of keying time is allowed. This helps prevent guessing and experimentation to find the password.

```
        ∇F1
[1]     TPWD
[2]     'ENTERED CORRECTLY IN TIME'
        ∇
        ∇TPWD;KT
[1]     'ENTER WORD -YOU HAVE 1 MINUTE'
[2]     KT←¯1↑⎕AI
[3]     Z←⍞
[4]     →TOOLATE×ι60000<(¯1↑⎕AI)-KT
[5]     →0×ι'GO'∧.=2↑Z
[6]     'WRONG PASSWORD'
[7]     →
[8]     TOOLATE:'YOU TOOK TOO LONG'
[9]     →
        ∇
        F1
ENTER WORD -YOU HAVE 1 MINUTE
GO
ENTERED CORRECTLY IN TIME
        F1
ENTER WORD -YOU HAVE 1 MINUTE
HI
WRONG PASSWORD
        F1
ENTER WORD -YOU HAVE 1 MINUTE
GO
YOU TOOK TOO LONG
```

Illustration 8.5   Limiting Time Spent in Using a Function

Suppose that the typing drill of Illustration 8.2 has the constraint that the person should not work more than 15 minutes. The following expressions would be added to the function to accomplish this:

```
        ∇TYPE
          .
          .
          .

[7]     ET←900000+⎕AI[3]    (NOTE:    900,000 is the number of milliseconds
          .                           in 15 minutes.)
          .
          .
[9]     →(ET<⎕AI[3])ρEND
          .
          .
          .
        ∇
```

Illustration 8.6   Curtailing CPU Time Used in a Function

Since CPU time is usually an extra charge, stopping a function's execution after the CPU time reaches an established limit is often desirable. For example,

> →(6*E*4<□*AI*[2])ρ*QUIT*

branches to *QUIT* when CPU time exceeds 1 minute.

Illustration 8.7   Testing to Determine the Solution Taking the
Least CPU Time

Often the solution to a problem can be solved in several alternative ways. □*AI* can be used to determine which alternative uses the least CPU time during execution. The following example illustrates the timing of two ways of reversing the order of an iota vector:

```
      ∇ N TEST M;I;J;T;Q
[1]      'NO. OF EXECUTIONS: ',⍕N
[2]      J←1
[3]    A:I←1
[4]      T←□AI[2]
[5]    B:Q←⍝M[J;]
[6]      →B×ιN>I←I+1
[7]      T←□AI[2]-T
[8]      M[J;],' ',(⍕T),' MILLISEC.'
[9]      →A×ι(1↑ρM)≥J←J+1
[10]     □UL, □TS
      ∇
```

```
      ∇ Z←F1                  ∇ Z←F2
[1]      Z←⌽ι500     [1]       Z←⍉ι500
      ∇                       ∇
```

```
      10 TEST 2 2ρ'F1F2'
NO. OF EXECUTIONS: 10
F1 184 MILLISEC.
F2 667 MILLISEC.
32 1974 1 14 9 50 57 100
```

Illustration 8.8   Length of Time a Terminal User
Has Been Signed On

The expression below determines how long a terminal user has been signed on in hours, minutes, seconds, and milliseconds:

```
      0 60 60 1000⊤□AI[3]
0 1 0 567
```

The expression

```
      ⌽0 60 60 1000⊤ ⎕AI[3 2]
0   8   37   933
0   0    9   583
```

produces the hour, minute, second, and millisecond matrix where the first row states how long a user has been signed on and the second row how much CPU time has been consumed.

Illustration 8.9 Printing the Date

A function that produces a report can have the date printed in any of the following ways:

1.   `⎕TS[2 3 1]`
   1 15 1974   numeric

2.   `⍕⎕TS[2 3 1]`
   1 15 1974   character

3.   `(' '≠T)/T←,(0,1↓⍕3 1⍴⎕TS[2 3 1]),'// '`
   1/15/1974

4.   `MONTH[⎕TS[2];],(⍕⎕TS[3]),',',⍕1↑⎕TS`
   JANUARY 15, 1974

In 4, *MONTH* is assumed to be a matrix whose rows are the names of the months and whose last column is blank.

The Workspace Information System Variable

`⎕WA`, *working area*, determines the number of bytes yet available in the user's active workspace. The amount of space occupied by the various data types depends on the internal representations assigned to each data type. This is very system-dependent. For APL on System/370 the assignments are as follows:

Each character occupies 1 byte.

Each integer in magnitude less than or equal to `2*31` occupies 4 bytes.

Each decimal number or integer in magnitude greater than `2*31` occupies 8 bytes.

Each binary digit occupies one-eighth of a byte.

Illustration 8.10 Space Determination

`⎕WA` enables one to determine the amount of space occupied by different representations of the same data. Consider the following sequence:

```
      )CLEAR                      )CLEAR
CLEAR WS               CLEAR WS
      □WA                         SP←□WA
60300                             SP
      SP←□WA              60300
      SP                          M←⍳0
60300                             SP←□WA
      M←⍳0                        M←1=5⍴1.0
      SP-□WA                      SP-□WA
32                         4
      SP←□WA                      )CLEAR
      M←5⍴1.0            CLEAR WS
      SP-□WA                      SP←□WA
40                                SP
      )CLEAR              60300
CLEAR WS                          M←⍳0
      SP←□WA                      SP←□WA
      M←⍳0                        M←⌊5⍴1.0
      SP-□WA                      SP-□WA
32                        20
      M←1=5⍴1.0
      SP-□WA
36
```

Illustration 8.11 Pretesting for a Workspace Full Situation

Consider a function in which data are entered and catenated to an existing matrix, M. A *WS FULL* report could occur during the execution of this function. The following sequence within a function could detect such a potential danger in advance and issue a warning.

```
             •
             •
             •
[5]   M←M,[1]V
             •
             •
             •
[9]   T←M
[10]  →12×⍳(16××/⍴M)>□WA
[11]  →CONT,T←⍳0
[12]  'DO NOT ENTER ANY MORE DATA'
[13]  'THE WORKSPACE WILL NOT CONTAIN IT'
             •
             •
             •
[16]  →OUT
[17]  CONT: ......    (Here normal execution resumes.)
```

Note: The 16 used in line 10 is a worst case situation assuming that the internal representation of the data is floating point.

System Variables Related to Terminal Usage

$\Box UL$, *user load*, defines the number of users currently signed on.

Illustration 8.12   Anticipating the Number of Names in the PORTS List

Executing $\Box UL$ before $)PORTS$ tells how many names to expect in the *PORTS* list.

$\Box TT$, *terminal type*, defines the nature of the terminal in use as follows: 3 for 1050, 1 for Selectric, and 2 for PTTC/BCD.

Illustration 8.13   Giving Instructions Based on Terminal Type

In a program designed to teach how a terminal is used, $\Box TT$ can be used to branch to the proper set of instructions.

Line Sequencing System Variable

$\Box LC$, *line counter*, produces a vector of line numbers of the functions in execution, suspended, and pendent. $\Box LC$ yields a snapshot of the function line numbers with the most recently executed function line number first. Consider the following set of functions:

```
        ∇ F1                    ∇ F2                    ∇ F3
[1]       □LC           [1]       □LC           [1]       □LC
[2]       F2            [2]       □LC           [2]       □LC
[3]       □LC           [3]       F3                    ∇
        ∇               [4]       □LC
                                ∇
        F1
1
1 2
2 2
1 3 2
2 3 2
4 2
3
```

Illustration 8.14   Relative Branching

1. Relative branching can be achieved with the expression

$$\rightarrow N+1\uparrow \Box LC$$

where N, a positive or negative integer, is the distance beyond or before the current line number to which branching is to occur. This expression is an unconditional branch.

2. The expression

$$\rightarrow(2+1\uparrow\square LC)\times\iota X=0$$

illustrates one form of conditional relative branching.

3. An alternative way of accomplishing this is through the following function:

```
      ∇Z←RL RBR C
[1]   Z←RL+C/1↑1↓□LC
      ∇
```

With this function the preceding branch statement becomes

```
   →2 RBR X=0
```

4. The following expression produces a four-way branch in that if $A=B$, a branch to three statements ahead occurs; if $A=C$, a branch to two statements back occurs; if $A=D$, a branch to four statements ahead occurs; and finally if A does not equal any of these, no branching occurs and the next statement in the sequence is executed.

$$\rightarrow(A=B,C,D)/3 \; {}^{-}2 \; 4+1\uparrow\square LC$$

Note: It is very important to use the expression $1\uparrow\square LC$ since $\square LC$ is generally a vector, and otherwise a *LENGTH ERROR* might occur or, far worse, an incorrect and undetected branch location might be computed.

5. If a function calls another function, $\square LC[1]$ is the line currently being executed in the called function; $\square LC[2]$ is the line number of the pendent function. If a function is written with a lot of relative branching, the function *HERE* can take the place of $\square LC[2]$:

```
      ∇Z←HERE
[1]   Z←□LC[2]
      ∇
```

Then $\rightarrow HERE+N$ results in a branch N statements before or beyond the current statement.

Illustration 8.15   Function Resumption

There are times in a prompting function when one would like to halt the function and resume later at the point of the prompt. The following set of functions and variables permits this if *STOP* is typed in response to a prompting request:

```
        ∇MAINFCN;STOP
[1]     STOP←⁻.29845
              •

              •

              •
[4]     'ENTER DATA'
[5]     →(S̲×ιSTOP=1↑X←⎕),1+L̲←1↑⎕LC
              •

              •

              •
[8]     'ENTER NAME'
[9]     →(S̲×ι'STOP'∧.=4↑Y←⍞),1+L̲←1↑⎕LC
              •

              •

              •
[21]    S̲:STOPM;RESTART
[22]     →L̲-1
              •

              •

              •
        ∇

        ∇STOPM
[1]     'THE FUNCTION HAS BEEN HALTED'
[2]     'IF YOU WISH TO RESUME LATER'
[3]     '  )SAVE    NOW'
[4]     'WHEN YOU RELOAD,   TYPE'
[5]     '→RESTART'
[6]     RESTART←8
[7]     S̲∆STOPM←8
[8]     'NOW TO CONTINUE'
        ∇
```

Illustration 8.16 Automatic Function Resumption

$\quad\quad$ $\square LC$ in conjunction with $\square LX$ can be used to produce an automatic resumption of a function at the point of suspension:

```
        ∇MAINFCN;⎕LX
[1]     ⎕LX←'→⎕LC'
[2]     'IF YOU WISH TO SUSPEND THIS FUNCTION AND RESUME IT AT'
[3]     'A LATER POINT IN TIME, THEN INTERRUPT IT VIA THE'
[4]     ' ATTN KEY  AND THEN'
[5]     '   )SAVE      '
[6]     'UPON RELOADING THIS SAVED WORKSPACE RESUMPTION'
[7]     ' OF EXECUTION WILL OCCUR AUTOMATICALLY AT THE '
[8]     'POINT OF SUSPENSION.'
              •

              •

              •
        ∇
```

$\quad\quad\quad\quad\quad\quad\quad\quad\quad\quad\quad\quad$ *Note:* With $\square LX$ local, the meaning assigned to a global $\square LX$ is unaffected.

System Variable for Internal Representation

The *atomic vector*, $\Box AV$, is a 256-component vector containing all the possible characters represented in System/370. Each character is represented in System/370 as a byte, 8 binary digits. Each of the representable characters is assigned a unique set of 8 binary digits. Currently not all the possible 256 combinations have been assigned a character representation. The assignment in System/370 is called Z code. $\Box AV$ allows the user access to any of the defined characters and its Z-code representation. This permits access to the terminal control codes such as carrier return, backspace, linefeed, tabulate, and idle. The following table shows the Z-code representation of the defined characters.

Z-code	APL character	Meaning*
0		Idle
1		End of statement character†
2		End of statement containing a label†
3		Left arrow in definition header when no result—dummy character†
4		Buffer end character
5		Unused—idle
6		Unused—idle
7	:	Fake colon in internal representation†
8	.	Fake period in internal representation†
9		Floating point constant (E-format)†
10		Logical constant†
11		Integer constant†
12		Floating constant†
13		Character constant†
14	[	Left bracket
15	]	Right bracket
16	(	Left parenthesis
17	)	Right parenthesis
18	;	Semicolon
19	/	Slash: compression; reduction
20	\	Reverse slash: expansion; scan
21	←	Left arrow: specification
22	→	Right arrow: branch
23	E	Fake 'E' for E-format numbers†
24	‾	Fake overbar (negative sign or high minus)†
25	··	Dieresis
26	+	Plus sign: addition

---

*The reader is advised that this definition is implementation-dependent. The one stated here is that used by APL.SV at the time of publication.

†This has meaning only to the APL interpreter. It is included here merely for completeness.

Z-code	APL Character	Meaning
27	−	Minus sign: subtraction; negation
28	×	Times sign: multiplication; signum
29	÷	Divide sign: reciprocal; division
30	*	Star: power; exponential
31	⌈	Ceiling; maximum
32	⌊	Floor; minimum
33	|	Residue; modulus
34	∧	And
35	∨	Or
36	<	Less than
37	≤	Less than or equal
38	=	Equal
39	≥	Greater than or equal
40	>	Greater than
41	≠	Not equal
42	α	Alpha
43	∈	Epsilon: membership
44	ι	Iota: index-of; index generator
45	ρ	Rho: restructure; shape
46	ω	Omega
47	,	Comma
48	!	Exclamation point: combinations; factorial
49	ϕ	Rotation; reversal
50	⊥	Decode
51	⊤	Encode
52	○	Large circle: circular; Pi-times
53	?	Question mark: deal; roll
54	~	Not
55	↑	Up arrow: take
56	↓	Down arrow: drop
57	⊂	Subordination
58	⊃	Implication
59	∩	Cap

Z-code	APL Character	Meaning
60	∪	Cup
61	_	Underscore
62	⍉	Transpose
63	⌶	I-beam
64	∘	Little circle—null
65	⎕	Quad
66	⍞	Quote-quad
67	⍟	Logarithm
68	⍲	Nand
69	⍱	Nor
70	⍝	Lamp: comment
71	⍋	Upgrade
72	⍒	Downgrade
73	⊖	First dimension rotation; reversal
74	⌿	First dimension compression; reduction
75	⍀	First dimension expansion; scan
76	⌹	Matrix multiply; matrix inverse
77	⍕	Format
78	⍎	Execute
79		Unused
80		Unused
81		Unused
82		Unused
83		Unused
84	*T*Δ	Trace (T Delta)
85	*S*Δ	Programmed Stop (S Delta)
86	*A*	A
87	*B*	B
88	*C*	C
89	*D*	D
90	*E*	E
91	*F*	F
92	*G*	G

Z-code	APL Character	Meaning
93	H	H
94	I	I
95	J	J
96	K	K
97	L	L
98	M	M
99	N	N
100	O	O
101	P	P
102	Q	Q
103	R	R
104	S	S
105	T	T
106	U	U
107	V	V
108	W	W
109	X	X
110	Y	Y
111	Z	Z
112	Δ	Delta
113	$\underline{A}$	A underscore
114	$\underline{B}$	B underscore
115	$\underline{C}$	C underscore
116	$\underline{D}$	D underscore
117	$\underline{E}$	E underscore
118	$\underline{F}$	F underscore
119	$\underline{G}$	G underscore
120	$\underline{H}$	H underscore
121	$\underline{I}$	I underscore
122	$\underline{J}$	J underscore
123	$\underline{K}$	K underscore
124	$\underline{L}$	L underscore
125	$\underline{M}$	M underscore

Z-code	APL Character	Meaning
126	$\underline{N}$	N underscore
127	$\underline{O}$	O underscore
128	$\underline{P}$	P underscore
129	$\underline{Q}$	Q underscore
130	$\underline{R}$	R underscore
131	$\underline{S}$	S underscore
132	$\underline{T}$	T underscore
133	$\underline{U}$	U underscore
134	$\underline{V}$	V underscore
135	$\underline{W}$	W underscore
136	$\underline{X}$	X underscore
137	$\underline{Y}$	Y underscore
138	$\underline{Z}$	Z underscore
139	$\underline{\Delta}$	Δ underscore
140	0	0
141	1	1
142	2	2
143	3	3
144	4	4
145	5	5
146	6	6
147	7	7
148	8	8
149	9	9
150	.	Period
151	‾	Overbar
152		Space
153	'	Quote mark
154	:	Colon
155	∇	Del
156		Carrier return
157		End of block
158		Backspace

Z-code	APL Character	Meaning
159		Linefeed
160	⍫	Protected del
161		Prefix (circle D for 1050)
162		Tab
163		Uppercase idle
164		Lowercase backspace
165		Reverse half linefeed (for MCST)
166		Track link (for MCST)
167		Card eject (for MCST)
168		Length of Z-symbol table

Thus, for the binary number 10101 represented as a binary vector V, $V \leftarrow 0\ 0\ 0\ 1\ 0\ 1\ 0\ 1$, the expression $\Box AV[2\bot V]$ or $\Box AV[21]$ in origin 0 yields the character $\leftarrow$. In general $\Box AV[2\bot V]$ yields the character represented by the 8-component binary vector V. Conversely, $\Box AV\iota'Q'$ yields the zero origin index of the character Q, and $(8\rho 2)\top\Box AV\iota'Q'$ produces the 8-element binary encoding of the character Q.

Illustration 8.17   Terminal Control Characters

In zero origin,

```
⎕AV[156 158 159 0 162]
```

are carrier return, backspace, linefeed, idle, and tab.

Illustration 8.18   The Dollar Sign

One cannot directly create illegal overstrikes as part of a character vector. But with $\Box AV[158+\Box IO]$ any overstruck graphic may be built. Thus the character vector

```
'S',⎕AV[158+⎕IO],'|'
```

produces $ a reasonable approximation for the dollar sign, for example,

```
    COST←432.57
    'S',⎕AV[158+⎕IO],'|',0 2⍕ COST
$432.57
```

PROBLEMS

1. Assume that before each specification a $)CLEAR$ was executed. Fill in the blanks.

$A \leftarrow 1$
$\square WA$

(a) _____

$A \leftarrow 1 \ 1$
$\square WA$

(b) _____

$A \leftarrow ,1$
$\square WA$

(c) _____

$A \leftarrow 8 \rho 1$
$\square WA$

(d) _____

$A \leftarrow 32 \rho 1$
$\square WA$

(e) _____

$A \leftarrow 33 \rho 1$
$\square WA$

(f) _____

$A \leftarrow 1 \ 1 \rho 1$
$\square WA$

(g) _____

$A \leftarrow 1 \ 1 \ 1 \rho 1$
$\square WA$

(h) _____

$A \leftarrow 1 = 1$
$\square WA$

(i) _____

$A \leftarrow 1 = 1 \ 1$
$\square WA$

(j) _____

$A \leftarrow 1 = 32 \rho 1$
$\square WA$

(k) _____

$A \leftarrow 1 = 33 \rho 1$
$\square WA$

(l) _____

$A \leftarrow 1.0$
$\square WA$

(m) _____

$A \leftarrow 32 \rho 1.0$
$\square WA$

(n) _____

$A \leftarrow 33 \rho 1.0$
$\square WA$

(o) _____

$A \leftarrow 2 - 1$
$\square WA$

(p) _____

$A \leftarrow 2 - 2 \rho 1$
$\square WA$

(q) _____

$A \leftarrow 2 - 32 \rho 1$
$\square WA$

(r) _____

$A \leftarrow 2 - 33 \rho 1$
$\square WA$

(s) _____

$A \leftarrow \iota 0$
$\square WA$

(t) _____

$A \leftarrow 1 \ 0 \ \rho 1$
$\square WA$

(u) _____

$A \leftarrow 0 \ 0 \rho 1$
$\square WA$

(v) _____

$AA \leftarrow ,1$
$\square WA$

(w) _____

$AAA \leftarrow ,1 \lrcorner$
$\square WA$

(x) _____

2. Fill in the blanks.

$)CLEAR$
    $\square WA$

(a) _____

$X \leftarrow 1$
$\square WA$

(b) _____

$)CLEAR$
$X \leftarrow 100 \rho 1$
$\square WA$

(c) _____

$)CLEAR$
$X \leftarrow 100 \rho 1.$
$\square WA$

(d) _____

$)CLEAR$
$X \leftarrow 'A'$
$\square WA$

(e) _____

$)CLEAR$
$X \leftarrow 100 \rho 1$
$\square WA$

(f) _____

$X \leftarrow X+1$ $X \leftarrow X=2$ $X \leftarrow X+1.$
$\square WA$ $\square WA$ $\square WA$

(g) _____   (h) _____   (i) _____

$X \leftarrow \lfloor X$
$\square WA$

(j) _____

3. On your system via a terminal
   (a) Half the current size of the symbol table and determine the additional workspace gained

   (b) Make the symbol table as small as possible, then determine the additional workspace gained

   (c) Make the symbol table as large as possible, then determine the amount of workspace available.

4. Consider the following sequences:

```
      )CLEAR
CLEAR WS
      SP←□WA
      M←1=5ρ1
      SP-□WA
36
      )CLEAR
CLEAR WS
      M←ι0
      SP←□WA
      M←1=5ρ1
      SP-□WA
20
      )CLEAR
CLEAR WS
      SP←□WA
      M←ι0
      SP←□WA
      M←1=5ρ1
      SP-□WA
4
```

Why do the number of bytes shown at the end of each sequence differ?

5. Define a function $SPACE$ to determine the minimum number of bytes required to store the result of an expression.

```
      Test
      X←ι6
      . . . . .
40
```

Section 8.7.2 System-Dependent Functions

System-dependent functions provide various information about the system. The general format of system-dependent functions is

$$I N$$

where, I, called *I-beam*, is the symbol formed by $\bot$ overstruck $\top$ and N is a number between 19 and 29. The value of N determines the type of information given. The table below states the type of information given for each N. Following the table are illustrations using each.

$I19$	Keying time	The accumulated time in 60ths of a second since sign-on that the keyboard was released so that data could be entered
$I20$	Time of day	The time of day in 60ths of a second
$I21$	CPU time	Central processing unit time in 60ths of a second since sign-on
$I22$	Bytes unused	The number of bytes unused in the workspace
$I23$	Number of users	The number of users currently signed on the system
$I24$	Sign-on time	Sign-on time in 60ths of a second
$I25$	Date	Today's date as an integer MMDDYY
$I26$	Line counter	Current line being executed in a defined function
$I27$	State indicator	Vector of line numbers of pendent and suspended functions
$I28$	Terminal device	1—2741 correspondence; 2—2741 BCD; 3—1050; 4—console typewriter
$I29$	User sign-on number	User sign-on number expressed as an integer

System-Dependent Functions for Time and Date

    $I19$, Keying Time

Illustration 8.19 Timing Typing Speed

    TYPE is a function that times a person's typing speed. Then

```
      ∇TYPE
  •
  •
  •
[ ]   KT←⍳19
[ ]   'TYPE THIS EXPRESSION'
[ ]   ..........
[ ]   R←⎕
[ ]   SPEED←(⍳19)-KT
  •
  •
  •
      ∇
```

Illustration 8.20 Adding Security to a Limited Use Function

The function $F1$ executes only if a required password is given. To add more security to that provided by the password only a limited amount of keying time is allowed. This helps prevent guessing and experimentation to find the password.

```
      ∇F1
[1]   TPWD
[2]    'ENTERED CORRECTLY IN TIME'
      ∇
      ∇TPWD;R;KT
[1]   'ENTER PASSWORD-YOU HAVE 1 MINUTE'
[2]   KT←⍳19
[3]   Z←⎕
[4]   →TOOLATE×⍳3600<(⍳19)-KT
[5]   →0×⍳'GO'∧.=2↑Z
[6]   'WRONG PASSWORD'
[7]   →
[8]   TOOLATE:'YOU TOOK TOO LONG'
[9]   →
      ∇
      F1
ENTER PASSWORD-YOU HAVE 1 MINUTE
GO
ENTERED CORRECTLY IN TIME
      F1
ENTER PASSWORD-YOU HAVE 1 MINUTE
HI
WRONG PASSWORD
      F1
ENTER PASSWORD-YOU HAVE 1 MINUTE
GO
YOU TOOK TOO LONG
```

ɪ20, Time of Day

Illustration 8.21   Limiting Time Spent in Using a Function

Suppose that the typing drill of Illustration 8.19 has the constraint that the person should not work for more than 15 minutes. Then

```
      ∇TYPE
[1]   ET←54000+ɪ20
  ·
  ·
  ·
[N]   →(ET<ɪ20)ρEND
  ·
  ·
  ·

      ∇
```

ɪ21, CPU time

Illustration 8.22   Curtailing CPU Time Used in a Function

Since CPU time is usually an extra charge, it is often useful to stop a function's execution after the CPU time reaches an established limit. For example,

→(3600<ɪ21)ρQUIT

branches to *QUIT* when CPU time exceeds 1 minute.

Illustration 8.23   Testing to Determine the Solution Taking the Least CPU Time

Often the solution to a problem can be solved in several alternative ways. ɪ21 can be used to determine which uses the least CPU time during execution, e.g.,

```
      ∇  TEST N;K;Q;T;I;T1;T2
[1]      ⍝N IS THE NUMBER OF TIMES EACH
[2]      ⍝FUNCTION IS TO BE EXECUTED.
[3]      I←0
[4]      T←ɪ21
[5]   A:Q←F1
[6]      →A×ιN>I←I+1
[7]      T1←(ɪ21)-T
[8]      I←0
[9]      T←ɪ21
[10]  B:Q←F2
[11]     →B×ιN>I←I+1
[12]     T2←(ɪ21)-T
[13]     'F1 FCN: ';T1
[14]     'F2 FCN: ';T2
      ∇
```

```
        ∇ Z←F1                    ∇ Z←F2
[1]       Z←⌽ι500        [1]       Z←⍒ι500
        ∇                         ∇
```

```
     TEST 10
F1 FCN:  88
F2 FCN:  323
```

ιΙ24, Sign-on Time

Illustration 8.24 Length of Time the Terminal Has Been Signed on

The expression below determines how long a terminal has been signed on in hours, minutes, seconds, and sixtieths of a second:

```
     24 60 60 60⊤(Ι20)-Ι24
```

Ι25, Today's Date

Illustration 8.25 Printing the Date

A function that produces a report can have the date printed in any of the following ways:

1. `,(3 2ρ'0123456789'[1+(6ρ10)⊤Ι25]),'// '`

2. `'/0123456789'[1+1 1 0 1 1 0 1 1 \1+(6ρ10)⊤Ι25]`

3. `A←10⊥⌽3 2ρ(6ρ10)⊤Ι25`
   `MONTH[1↑A;];A[2];', ';19;‾1↑A`

The result of the first two expressions if today's date is January 3, 1972 is

```
01/03/72
```

The result of the last expression, assuming that *MONTH* is a matrix whose rows are the names of the months and whose last column is a blank, is

```
JANUARY 3, 1972
```

System-Dependent Functions for Workspace Information

Ι22, Number of Unused Bytes

The amount of space occupied by the various data types depends on the internal representations assigned to each data type. This is quite system-dependent. For APL/360, these assignments are as follows:

Each character occupies 1 byte, but space is allocated in multiples of 4 bytes.
Each integer in magnitude less than or equal to $2*31$ occupies 4 bytes.
Each decimal number or integer greater than $2*31$ occupies 8 bytes.
Each binary digit occupies one-eighth of a byte, but space is allocated in multiples of 4 bytes.

Illustration 8.26   Space Determination

I22 enables one to determine the amount of space occupied by different representations of the same data. Consider the following sequence:

```
      )CLEAR
CLEAR WS
      I22
32308
      SP←I22
      SP
32304
      M←ι0
      SP-I22
32
      SP←I22
      M←5ρ1.0
      SP-I22
40
      )CLEAR
CLEAR WS
      SP←I22
      M←ι0
      SP-I22
32
      M←1=5ρ1.0
      SP-I22
36
      )CLEAR
CLEAR WS
      SP←I22
      SP
32304
      M←ι0            (Establish name M .)
      SP←I22
      M←1=5ρ1.0
      SP-I22          (Space required to store value of 1=5ρ1.0)
4
      )CLEAR
CLEAR WS
      SP←I22
      SP
32304
      M←ι0
      SP←I22
      M←⌊5ρ1.0
      SP-I22
20
```

Illustration 8.27   Pretesting for a Workspace Full Situation

Consider a function in which data are entered and catenated to an existing matrix M. An exposure exists in that a *WS FULL* report could occur. The following sequence within the function could detect such a potential danger in advance and issue a warning:

```
        •
        •
        •
[5]     M←M,[1]V
        •
        •
        •

[9]     T←M
[10]    →(12)×ι(16××/ρM)>ι22
[11]    →CONT,T←ι0
[12]    'DO NOT ENTER ANY MORE DATA'
[13]    'THE WORKSPACE WILL NOT CONTAIN IT'
        •
        •
        •
[16]    →OUT
[17]    CONT: ⍝NORMAL EXECUTION RESUMES
```

Note: 16 used in line 10 is a worst case situation, assuming that the internal representation of the data is floating point.

ι26, Current Value of Line Counter, and ι27, State Indicator

Illustration 8.28   Relative Branching

1. Relative branching can be achieved by the expression

   $$→N+ι26$$

   where N is the distance beyond or before the current statement that a branch to point is located.

2. The expression

   $$→(2+ι26)×ιX=0$$

   illustrates one form of conditional relative branching.

3. An alternative way of accomplishing this is through the following function, which uses ι27:

```
        ∇Z←RL RBR C
[1]     Z← RL+C/1↓ι27
        ∇
```

   With this function the preceding branch statement becomes

   $$→2 RBR X=0$$

4. If a function calls another function, (ι27)[1] is the line currently being executed in the called function; (ι27)[2] is the line number of the pendent function. If a function is written with a lot of relative branching the function *HERE* can take the place of ι26, for example,

```
      ∇Z←HERE
[1]    Z←(I27)[2]
      ∇
```

Then →*HERE*+*N* creates a branch *N* statement before or beyond the current statement.

Illustration 8.29 Function Resumption

There are times when in a prompting function one would like to halt the function and resume later at the point of the prompt. The following set of functions and variables permits this if *STOP* is typed in response to a prompt request:

```
      ∇MAINFCN;STOP
[1]    STOP←-0.25
        .
        .
        .
[12]   'ENTER DATA'
[13]   →(S×ιSTOP=1↑X←□),1+L←I26
        .
        .
        .
[21]   'ENTER NAME'
[22]   →(S×ι'STOP'∧.=4ρN←□),1+L←I26
        .
        .
        .
[31]   S:STOPM
[32]   →L-1
        .
        .
        .
      ∇
      ∇STOPM
[1]    'THE FUNCTION HAS BEEN HALTED'
[2]    'IF YOU WISH TO RESUME LATER'
[3]    '   )SAVE    NOW'
[4]    'WHEN YOU RELOAD, TYPE'
[5]    '      →RESTART'
[6]    RESTART←8
[7]    S∆STOPM←8
[8]    'NOW TO CONTINUE'
      ∇
```

System-Dependent Functions for Terminal Usage

I23, Number of Users

Illustration 8.30 Anticipating the Number of Names in PORTS *list*

Executing I23 before)*PORTS* will tell how many names to expect in the *PORTS* list.

⍳28, Terminal device

Illustration 8.31   Giving Instructions Based on Terminal Type

In a program designed to teach how a terminal is used, ⍳28 can be used to branch to the proper set of instructions.

⍳29, User Sign-on Number

Illustration 8.32   Restricting a Function's Use

If a function's use is restricted to only certain users, the expression

→CONT×⍳29∊NUMBERS

will continue with the function execution only if the sign-on number is contained in the list NUMBERS.

PROBLEMS

1. Assume that before each specification a)CLEAR was executed. Fill in the blanks.

A←1	A←1 1	A←,1
⍳22	⍳22	⍳22
(a) _____	(b) _____	(c) _____

A←8⍴1	A←32⍴1	A←33⍴1
⍳22	⍳22	⍳22
(d) _____	(e) _____	(f) _____

A←1 1⍴1	A←1 1 1⍴1	A←1=1
⍳22	⍳22	⍳22
(g) _____	(h) _____	(i) _____

A←1=1 1	A←1=32⍴1	A←1=33⍴1
⍳22	⍳22	⍳22
(j) _____	(k) _____	(l) _____

A←1.0	A←32⍴1.0	A←33⍴1.0
⍳22	⍳22	⍳22
(m) _____	(n) _____	(o) _____

```
    A←2-1                    A←2-2ρ1                   A←2-32ρ1
    I22                      I22                       I22
```

(p) _____   (q) _____   (r) _____

```
    A←ι0                     AA←,1                     AAA←,1
    I22                      I22                       I22
```

(s) _____   (t) _____   (u) _____

```
    AAAA←,1
    I22
```

(v) _____

2. Fill in the blanks.

```
    )CLEAR                   X←1                       )CLEAR
    I22                      I22                       X←100ρ1
                                                       I22
```

(a) _____   (b) _____   (c) _____

```
    )CLEAR                   )CLEAR                    )CLEAR
    X←100ρ1.                 X←'A'                     X←100ρ1
    I22                      I22                       I22
```

(d) _____   (e) _____   (f) _____

```
    X←X+1                    X←X=2                     X←X+1.
    I22                      I22                       I22
```

(g) _____   (h) _____   (i) _____

```
    X←⌊X
    I22
```

(j) _____

3. On your system via a terminal
   (a) Half the current size of the symbol table and determine the additional workspace gained.
   (b) Make the symbol table as small as possible, then determine the additional workspace gained.
   (c) Make the symbol table as large as possible, then determine the amount of workspace available.

4. Consider the following sequences:

```
        )CLEAR
CLEAR WS
        SP←I22
        M←1=5ρ1.
        SP-I22
```
36

```
      )CLEAR
CLEAR WS
      M←⍳0
      SP←⎕22
      M←1=5⍴1.
      SP-⎕22
20
      )CLEAR
CLEAR WS
      SP←⎕22
      M←⍳0
      SP←⎕22
      M←1=5⍴1.
      SP-⎕22
4
```

Why do the number of bytes shown at the end of each sequence differ?

5. Define a function of $SPACE$ to determine the minimum number of bytes required to store the result of an expression.

   Test

```
      X←⍳6
      • • • • •
40
```

Section 8.8 THE SYSTEM FUNCTION

In addition to the set of system variables APL.SV provides a set of system functions for manipulating defined functions, for providing information about the names in a workspace, and for affecting the execution of a function. Like the system variables, each system function has a distinguished name beginning with ⎕. System functions are like ordinary locked user-defined functions: their definitions cannot be edited. Syntactically, each system function is either monadic or dyadic with a space separating the function name from its argument(s) for the function call. Each has an explicit result, and some system functions have an additional implicit result; that is, an action occurs during the function execution that is not apparent from looking at the explicit result.

Section 8.8.1   Function-Manipulating System Functions

Canonical Representation and Function Establishment

In Chapter 6, we introduced the format functions, monadic and dyadic ⍕ for converting output to character form. At times, it would also be advantageous to convert a function definition to character form. For example, when using data sets for auxiliary data storage, such as those discussed in Chapter 9, function definitions can be first converted to character forms and then stored as data. The system function *canonical representation* $\Box CR$ provides for converting function definitions to character form. Canonical representation is a monadic system function of the form

      $R \leftarrow \Box CR \ V$

where the right argument V must be a character scalar or a character vector representing the name of the function. For example, if the workspace contains a function named $EQUAL$, V would be represented as $'EQUAL'$. The explicit result of the function is a character matrix representation of the function named in the argument. Neither the ∇ symbol nor the bracketed line numbers appear in the result. For example, the function $EQUAL$ determines whether any two arbitrary variables are equal in rank, shape, and element-by-element:

```
      ∇ Z←A EQUAL B;I;J
[1]    Z←(ρJ←ρA)=ρI←ρB
[2]    →0×ι~Z
[3]    →0×ι~Z←JΛ.=I
[4]    Z←~0∈A=B
    ∇

      V←ι8
      A←8 1ρι8
      A EQUAL V
0

      Q←□CR 'EQUAL'
      Q
Z←A EQUAL B;I;J
Z←(ρJ←ρA)=ρI←ρB
→0×ι~Z
→0×ι~Z←JΛ.=I
Z←~0∈A=B

      ρQ
5 15
```

The result Q is a 5-by-15-character matrix. The first line represents the function header. Each line is made as long as the longest line by padding shorter lines with blanks on the right. Once a defined function has been converted into a character matrix, it may be manipulated in any of the ways available to manipulate character data.

   $\Box CR$ does not erase the function it has converted to character form.

```
      )FNS
EQUAL
      )VARS
Q
```

If the function is no longer required in the workspace, it should be erased.

```
)ERASE EQUAL
)FNS
)VARS
```
Q

If the argument does not represent the name of an unlocked defined function, $\square CR$ returns as an explicit result a null matrix whose shape is `0 0`. If the right argument is not a character matrix, a *DOMAIN ERROR* results. And if the argument is neither a scalar nor a vector, a *RANK ERROR* results.

The system function *function establishment* $\square FX$ attempts to fix or transform a character matrix into an executable function, and as such can be considered the converse of $\square CR$. The format of function establishment is

```
R←□FX X
```

where the right argument X is a character matrix which is to be converted into an executable function. The system function $\square FX$ produces an explicit result and an implicit result. The explicit result is a character vector representing the name of the newly fixed function. Simultaneously and implicitly it establishes the named function as an executable function. After the function is established by $\square FX$, it may be called in the normal fashion. For example, suppose

```
          R
Z←TEST A
Z←(A>100)∧A<1000

          ρR
2 16
          )VARS
R
          )FNS
```

Then to fix the matrix R as a function

```
          □FX R
TEST
          TEST
SYNTAX ERROR
          TEST
          ∧
          )VARS
R
          )FNS
TEST
          ∇TEST[□]∇
      ∇ Z←TEST A
[1]       Z←(A>100)∧A<1000
      ∇
          TEST 75
```
0

The argument to $\Box FX$ must be a character matrix. If the argument is not character, a *DOMAIN ERROR* occurs. If the argument is not a matrix, a *RANK ERROR* occurs. Moreover, the matrix argument must be a valid representation of a function. If it is not, $\Box FX$ returns the row number in the matrix where the fault occurs. For example, suppose

```
      M
Z←FLIN V
Z←1+(ρV)-(⌽V≠0)ι1V
```

Then,

```
      □FX M
2
```

If there is a function in the workspace with the same name as that produced by $\Box FX$, its definition is replaced by the newly established one. For example, suppose that the matrix Q is that which was created earlier in this section by $Q←\Box CR$ '*EQUAL*' and that the workspace now contains the following definition of *EQUAL*,

```
      ∇ Z←A EQUAL B
[1]     Z←A=B
      ∇
```

Then,

```
      □FX Q
EQUAL
```

and

```
      ∇EQUAL[□]∇
      ∇ Z←A EQUAL B;I;J
[1]     Z←(ρJ←ρA)=ρI←ρB
[2]     →0×ι~Z
[3]     →0×ι~Z←J∧.=I
[4]     Z←~0∈A=B
      ∇
```

$\Box FX$ cannot establish an executable function in the workspace if the name which would be its result represents the name of

1. a function currently suspended or pendant

2. a label

3. a group name

4. a variable name

In these cases □*FX* returns as an explicit result a scalar number representing the row of the matrix argument in which the conflict appeared. Thus, had the workspace contained

```
      EQUAL←5
      □FX Q
1
```

The one indicates that the first line of the matrix contains the conflict; in this example, the function name is the same as that of a variable in the workspace.

□*FX* does not erase the variable it has converted to character form. If the variable is no longer required in the workspace, it should be erased.

□*FX* allows for the local establishment of functions in this way. If the name to be established by □*FX* has been declared local to the function in which □*FX* occurs, the named established function exists only within the function. When that function successfully terminates, this established function disappears. For example:

```
      )CLEAR
CLEAR WS
      ∇ Z←A EQ B
[1]   Z←A=B
      ∇

      M←□CR 'EQ'
      )ERASE EQ
      )FNS
      )VARS
M
      ∇ NONS;EQ
[1]   N←□FX M
[2]   C←3
[3]   D←4
[4]   ⍎'D    ',N,' C'
      ∇

      S∆NONS←2
      NONS
NONS[2]
      )FNS
NONS
      3 EQ 4
0
      →2
0
      )FNS
NONS
      3 EQ 4
SYNTAX ERROR
      3 EQ 4
      ∧
```

Illustration 8.33   Selective Line Erasure Within a Defined Function

The function *LINEERASE* deletes from a named function a set of lines as prompted.

```
      ∇ LINEERASE FN;M;□IO
[1]    □IO←0
[2]    □←'WHICH LINES TO BE REMOVED?  '
[3]    N←□CR FN
[4]    M←(1↑ρN)ρ1
[5]    M[⍕□]←0
[6]    N←M≠N
[7]    M←□FX N
      ∇
```

```
      ∇ TEST
[1]    'LINE 1'
[2]    'LINE 2'
[3]    'LINE 3'
[4]    'LINE 4'
      ∇
```

```
      LINEERASE 'TEST'
WHICH LINES TO BE REMOVED?  1 3
      TEST
LINE 2
LINE 4
```

Illustration 8.34   Editing Comments Out of a Function

As functions are defined, comments are often interspersed to explain the actions of some of the lines. For example

```
      ∇ Z←SILLY T;ONESAT
[1]    Z←T
[2]   ⍝DO NOTHING IF THERE ARE NO ONES
[3]    →ON×∨/1=Z
[4]   ⍝FIND THE ONES
[5]    ON:ONESAT←(1=Z)/⍳ρZ
[6]   ⍝REPLACE THE ONES WITH SUCCESSIVE INTEGERS
[7]    Z[ONESAT]←⍳ρONESAT
      ∇
      SILLY 9 1 6 1 3 5 1 2 3 1
9 1 6 2 3 5 3 2 3 4
```

Later, if desired, the comments can be edited out of the function by using □*CR* and □*FX* .

```
      ∇ Z←EDIT IT;M
[1]     M←□CR IT
[2]     COMMENTS←(M[;1]='ค')/[1]M
[3]     Z←□FX (M[;1]≠'ค')/[1]M
      ∇
```

```
      EDIT 'SILLY'
SILLY
      ∇SILLY[□]∇
      ∇ Z←SILLY T;ONESAT
[1]     Z←T
[2]     →ON×∨/1=Z
[3]   ON:ONESAT←(1=Z)/ιρZ
[4]     Z[ONESAT]←ιρONESAT
      ∇
```

```
      COMMENTS
ค DO NOTHING IF THERE ARE NO ONES
ค FIND THE ONES
ค REPLACE THE ONES WITH SUCCESSIVE INTEGERS
```

Dynamic Erasure □EX

In the preceding discussion of □*CR* and □*FX*, we noted that neither system function erases the object it has converted to another form. Erasing the unneeded object must be explicit. The system command)*ERASE* can be used for removing objects from a workspace. However it has the drawback that, like all system commands, it requires user intervention; that is, it is not dynamic. A dynamic erasure capability is the ability to remove objects from within an executing function. It is provided by the system function *expunge* □*EX*. Expunge is a monadic function of the form

```
      R←□EX M
```

where *M* is a character scalar, vector, or matrix. If the argument is a scalar or vector, it represents the name of an object to be erased. If the argument is a matrix, each row represents the name of an object to be erased. □*EX* returns as an explicit result a 0 or 1 to indicate whether the named objects were actually erased. A result of 1 indicates that the object was erased, while a result of 0 indicates that it was not. For matrix arguments, □*EX* returns a logic vector whose *I*th element is 1 or 0 depending on whether the name represented by the *I*th row of *M* has been erased or not. For example,

```
      )FNS
FN1    FN2    FN3
      )VARS
A      B      C      M
```

```
        M
A
FN2
FN3
C
        ⎕EX M
1  1  1  1
        )FNS
FN1
        )VARS
B       M
```

An object is not erased (1) if it names a label, a group, a pendent or suspended
function, or system variables or system functions or (2) if the name is not well
formed according to the established naming conventions. If the argument of ⎕EX
is not a character array, a *DOMAIN ERROR* results. If the rank of the argument is
greater than 2, a *RANK ERROR* occurs.

⎕EX differs from the system command)ERASE in one way. Since ⎕EX may
be used within a defined function, it may erase either local or global objects;)ERASE
erases only global objects. For example consider the following sequence which com-
pares)ERASE to ⎕EX:

```
        ∇ F1;A;B;I
[1]     A←10
[2]     B←50
[3]     I←⎕EX 'A'
[4]     B
        ∇

        A←B←2
        S∆F1←3  4
        F1
F1[3]
        )VARS
A       B
        A
10
        B
50
        )ERASE B
        )VARS
A
        B
50
        →3
F1[4]
        )VARS
A
```

```
        A
VALUE ERROR
        A
        ∧
        B
50
        →4
50
        )VARS
A
        A
2
        B
VALUE ERROR
        B
        ∧
```

Illustration 8.35   Conversion of Named Function to a Named Variable

The function *FNTOVR* converts the named function *F* into a named variable *N*. If the conversion is successful, the function is erased. If the conversion cannot be accomplished, a 'no conversion' message is given.

```
      ∇ N FNTOVR F;X;□IO
[1]     □IO←1
[2]     X←□CR F
[3]     →ER×ι0∧.=ρX
[4]     ⍕N,'←X'
[5]     X←□EX F
[6]     →0
[7]   ER:'NO CONVERSION'
      ∇
      ∇ FN;Q
[1]     Q←1
[2]     'DONE'
      ∇
        )VARS
        )FNS
FN        FNTOVR F1
        'DF' FNTOVR 'FN'
        )VARS
DF
        )FNS
FNTOVR  F1
        DF
FN;Q
Q←1
'DONE'
```

Section 8.8.2 Information-Yielding System Functions

Name List □*NL*

    The dynamic display of variables and functions within a workspace is provided by the system function *Name List* □*NL* which produces a character matrix of names of the objects in the workspace. The format of name list is

       R←□*NL X*

Where the argument *X* indicates the objects which may be requested as follows:

    1 indicates a request for labels

    2 indicates a request for variables

    3 indicates a request for functions

X may be either a scalar or vector whose values must be either 1, 2 or 3. The result is a matrix of names listed in accidental order; that is, they are not alphabetized. For example:

```
      )VARS
A AT BET STOP   VIE   WAIT   ZERO
      □NL 2
STOP
VIE
A
AT
BET
ZERO
WAIT
```

    If the workspace does not contain any object of the specified type, □*NL* returns a null matrix of dimension 0 0.

    Name list may also be a dyadic function which permits some selection from the list indicated by the left argument. Its format is

       R←C □*NL X*

Where the argument *X* is the same as the argument of the monadic name list and the argument *C* is used to limit the listed names of objects to only those beginning with one of the letters in *C*. For example:

```
      'ASZ' □NL 2
ZERO
AT
STOP
A
```

Illustration 8.36 Automatic Function Display

The function *DISPLAYF* displays all the functions in the current environment.
In the display the functions are separated by a row of blanks and ∗∗∗∗∗∗.

```
      )FNS
DISPLAYF FNTOVR F1
    ∇ DISPLAYF;□IO;L;K;I
[1]    □IO←1
[2]    L←□NL 3
[3]    →0×ι0∧.=ρL
[4]    □←K← 2 6 ρ'        ∗∗∗∗∗∗'
[5]    I←1↑ρL
[6]  A:□CR,L[I;]
[7]    K
[8]    →A×ι0≠I←I-1
    ∇
      DISPLAYF
∗∗∗∗∗∗
F1;A;B;I
A←10
B←50
I←□EX 'A'
B

∗∗∗∗∗∗
DISPLAYF;□IO;L;K;I
□IO←1
L←□NL 3
→0×ι0∧.=ρL
□←K← 2 6 ρ'        ∗∗∗∗∗∗'
I←1↑ρL
A:□CR,L[I;]
K
→A×ι0≠I←I-1

∗∗∗∗∗∗
N FNTOVR F;X;□IO
□IO←1
X←□CR F
→ER×ι0∧.=ρX
⍎N,'←X'
X←□EX F
→0
ER:'NO CONVERSION'
∗∗∗∗∗∗
```

Name Classification □NC

The system function □NL presents a list of names of a specified type. Now, let us consider the converse: given a name, what is its classification?

The system function *name classification* □NC supplies the facility for determining how a name is being used. Name classification is a monadic function of the form

    R←□NC A

where A is a character array of rank 2 or less. The argument contains row by row the names whose classification is sought. For each name, □NC returns a classification number, ranging from 0 to 4. Thus R[I] corresponds to the I th row of A. The meaning of these values is as follows:

   0 indicates that the name is not associated with any object in the workspace

   1 indicates that the name is associated with a label

   2 indicates that the name is associated with a variable

   3 indicates that the name is associated with a function

   4 indicates that the name is not available because it is a group name, a system variable name, or an invalidly constructed name

For example,

```
        )FNS
EQUAL    TAX     WA
        )VARS
A    AM    RATE    TRY
        )GRPS
PACK
        A
TAX
PACK
RATE
DO-IT
NEW
        □NC A
3  4  2  4  0
```

Illustration 8.37 Dynamic Generation of a New Name

The need to know how a name is being used becomes important in defined functions which use the execute function ±. In such functions, new names can be defined dynamically, but should not be if the new name conflicts with a name that already exists in the workspace.

The function *CRTNAME* establishes the name X (presented to it as a character argument) provided that the name is available. If the name is not available, the message *NA* (for not available) followed by the current classification of the name is returned.

```
      ∇  Z←CRTNAME X;M;J;□IO
[1]      □IO←0
[2]      M← 5 8 ρ'NAME OK NA-LABELNA-VAR NA-FCN NA          '
[3]      →A+ιJ←□NC X
[4]      ⍕X,'←ι0'
[5]   A:Z←M[J;]
      ∇
      )VARS
AS        Q
      )FNS
CRTNAME NN
      CRTNAME 'DATA'
NAME OK
      )VARS
AS        DATA      Q
      CRTNAME 'DATA'
NA-VAR
```

Section 8.8.3 Execution-Affecting System Function

Delay □*DL*

In a situation where two functions in separate active workspaces can interact with each other, one function may have to wait for the other or in a computer-assisted-instruction function, a pause may be needed to give the student an opportunity to consider his answer before he is presented with a new problem. The monadic system function *delay* □*DL* produces a pause in the execution of the statement in which it occurs. The format of delay is

```
      R←□DL S
```

The amount of the pause given in seconds is specified by the right argument S. Since system contention and other system overhead is not directly controllable by the user, the actual wait will only approximate S. The explicit result returned from □*DL* is the scalar value which represents the actual time delay in seconds. The delay function □*DL* uses only a negligible amount of computer time regardless of the value of S.

If a delay is initiated and has not completed, the user at the terminal may terminate it through the use of the attention signal. As always, use of ATTN results in a suspended function. If the argument S is not a scalar or a one-component vector, a *RANK ERROR* results. If the argument is not numeric, a *DOMAIN ERROR* results.

Illustration 8.38   A Continuous Display

Occasionally for an open house for example, an unattended continuously running display on the terminal would be useful. The function *SHOW* produces a set of appropriate prose on the terminal every N seconds. At approximately $N \div 2$ seconds, the typing element spaces twice followed by two backspaces to give some assurance of activity.

```
       ∇ SHOW N;□IO;TOD;J
[1]    □IO←0
[2]    TOD← 3 9 ρ'MORNING  AFTERNOONEVENING  '
[3]    R:'GOOD ',TOD[+/□TS[3]> 12 18 ;]
[4]    PROSE N
[5]    J←□DL N÷2
[6]    □AV[152 158 152 158]
[7]    J←□DL N÷2
[8]    →R
       ∇
```

```
       ∇ PROSE N
[1]    'THIS IS A DEMONSTRATION'
[2]    'IT WILL BE REPEATED EVERY ',(⍕N),' SECONDS'
       ∇
```

```
       SHOW 12
GOOD AFTERNOON
THIS IS A DEMONSTRATION
IT WILL BE REPEATED EVERY 12 SECONDS

GOOD AFTERNOON
THIS IS A DEMONSTRATION
IT WILL BE REPEATED EVERY 12 SECONDS

GOOD AFTERNOON
THIS IS A DEMONSTRATION
IT WILL BE REPEATED EVERY 12 SECONDS
```
                                        (*ATTN* used here)
```
SHOW[8]
     →
```

PROBLEMS

1. Define a function *SPLIT* to subdivide a function into two individually named functions.

2. What would happen in Illustration 8.33 if a user responds with a request to remove lines 0 and 3?

3. Modify the function *LINEERASE* of Illustration 8.33 to shelter the user from accidentally putting a line removal request for line 0 or a line beyond the length of the function. For either case, issue a warning message.

4. Define a function *LOCKEDFCN* to list all the locked functions in the active workspace.

5. Define a function *COMMENTS* to accept a defined function name and produce only the header of the function and the comment lines. The function should associate the line numbers in which the comment occurred in the given function.

6. Define a function name *WHAT* which takes a name and tells whether it is a variable or a function. If it is a variable, give its shape and rank. If it is a function, show its header.

Section 8.9   SUMMARY

System Commands

Contents of a Workspace

Command	Purpose
)*COPY NAME*	Copies the contents of the workspace *NAME* into the active workspace
)*PCOPY NAME*	Like)*COPY*, except it is protective
)*COPY NAME* 1...*OBJ*∩	Copies list of objects from the workspace *NAME* into the active workspace
)*PCOPY NAME OBJ*1...*OBJ*∩	Like)*COPY NAME OBJECT*, except it is protective
)*GROUP NAME FI DAT*	Groups under *NAME* the names *FI* and *DAT*
)*GROUP NAME*	Breaks up the *GROUP* called *NAME*
)*VARS*	Lists variables in the workspace
)*FNS*	Lists functions in the workspace
)*GRPS*	Lists groups in the workspace
)*GRP NAME*	Lists the members of the group called *NAME*
)*ERASE OBJ*1...*OBJ*∩	Deletes *OBJ*1...*OBJ*∩ and associated information from the workspace

Libraries

Command	Purpose
)*LIB*	Lists the names of the workspace in the user's library
)*LIB N*	Lists the names of the workspaces in the public library whose identification number is *N*

Libraries (Cont'd.)

Command	Purpose
)*SAVE NAME*	Establishes the name of the active workspace and saves a copy in the user's library
)*SAVE NAME:LOCK*	Same as above, but *LOCK* is a password that protects workspace usage by unauthorized people
)*SAVE N NAME*	Saves the active workspace in the library *N* as *NAME*
)*LOAD NAME*	Brings a copy of the library workspace *NAME* into the active workspace
)*LOAD NAME:KEY*	Same as above, but *KEY* is the password with which that workspace has been saved
)*LOAD N NAME*	Brings a copy of the workspace *NAME* from library *N* into the active workspace
)*DROP NAME*	Drops the workspace *NAME* from the library
)*DROP N NAME*	Drops the workspace *NAME* that the user had created for the public library *N*

Workspace Attributes

Command	Purpose
)*WSID NAME*	Changes the name of the active workspace to *NAME*
)*WSID*	Gives name of the active workspace
)*CLEAR*	Makes the active workspace a clear unused workspace named *CLEAR WS*
)*SYMBOLS N*	Changes the size of the symbol table to *N* for $26 \leq N \leq 4241$
)*DIGITS N*	Changes the number of significant digits displayed to *N* for $1 \leq N \leq 16$
)*WIDTH N*	Changes the width of an output line to *N* for $30 \leq N \leq 390$
)*ORIGIN N*	Changes the origin of indexing and related functions to *N* for $N \in 0 \ 1$
)*MSG ON*	Permits any transmitted messages to be received
)*MSG OFF*	Inhibits the transmission of any incoming messages

System Variables

System Variables for Workspace Attributes

Distinguished Name	Meaning	Purpose
□*PP*	Printing precision	To specify the number of significant digits displayed (for $1 \leq N \leq 16$)
□*PW*	Page width	To specify page width (for $30 \leq N \leq 390$)
□*IO*	Index origin	To specify the index origin (for $N \in 0 \ \ 1$)
□*CT*	Comparison tolerance	To specify fuzz for comparisons (for $0 \leq N < 1$)
□*RL*	Random link	To specify a random seed (for $N \in \iota^{-}1 + 2 \star 31$)

System Variables Providing Information about the System

Distinguished Name	Meaning	Value
□*WA*	Work area	The number of bytes used in the active workspace
□*UL*	User load	The number of users currently signed on the system
□*TS*	Time stamp	A seven-component vector containing year, month, day, hour, minute, second, and millisecond
□*AI*	Account information	A four-component vector containing 1. User sign-on number 2. Computer time 3. Connect time 4. Keying time All times are in milliseconds and are cumulative
□*TT*	Terminal type	3 for 1050; 1 for Selective; and 2 for PTTC/BCD
□*LC*	Line counter	A vector of line numbers of suspended functions, pendent functions, or functions in execution
□*AV*	Atomic vector	A 256-component vector containing all the possible characters representable on System/370

System Functions

Function	Syntax	General Description	Right Argument	Left Argument
Canonical representation	⎕CR B	Converts a defined function into a character matrix representation of the function definition with blanks padding short lines. Line numbers and ∇s are not included.	Character scalar or vector representing the name of a function.	
Function establishment	⎕FX B	Attempts to fix the matrix B as a defined function. Returns the name of the function as an explicit result. The implicit result is to create an executable function from the matrix.	Character matrix representing a function definition.	
Expunge	⎕EX B	Erases the objects named in the argument. Returns a 1 for each object erased and a 0 otherwise.	Character scalar, vector, or matrix representing the name(s) of objects in the workspace. Each row of a matrix corresponds to a name.	
Name list	⎕NL B	Lists the objects in a workspace.	Scalar or vector such that $B \in \iota 3$, with the following meanings: 1 –labels; 2 –variables; 3 –functions.	
Name list	A ⎕NL B	Lists the objects in a workspace beginning with the characters in A.	Same as for ⎕NL B	Character scalar or vector indicating beginning letter(s) of objects to be listed.
Name classification	⎕NC B	Gives the type of object associated with the name(s) provided in B as follows: 0 –name not in use; 1 –label; 2 –variable; 3 –function; 4 –name not available.	A character scalar, vector, or matrix representing names. Each row of a matrix corresponds to a name.	
Delay	⎕DL B	Pauses for B seconds. Returns the actual amount of delay taken.	Scalar or one-component vector.	

CHAPTER 9

DATA COMMUNICATION—
THE SHARED VARIABLE FACILITY

As the APL-user moves from developmental work with its emphasis on algorithms and processes to production work with its emphasis on data and resource management, he requires additional services from the APL system, such as

- The ability to transmit to and receive data from another APL user.

- The ability to use the data management facilities of the host operating system (the non-APL system, such as OS/VS, within which APL.SV operates).

- The ability to manipulate a collection of data which is larger than can be accommodated in the workspace.

- The ability to use input and output equipment other than the APL terminal.

Each of these needs involves transmitting and receiving information, that is, data communications. The APL shared variable facility (APL.SV) is a means by which data communications like those listed above are realized. In this chapter we shall discuss the system functions that implement the shared variable facility and its application to data communications.

Section 9.1 PROCESSORS AND THE NATURE OF THE
SHARED VARIABLE

A processor is anyone or anything that uses data: A processor accepts data input and produces data output. Under this definition a processor is an APL user, a non-APL system, such as OS/VS, or a piece of equipment such as a disk drive or printer. Communication between processors involves the transmission of data between them over an established interface.

In APL.SV the interface for communication between processors is the shared variable. Communication between two processors is established when each processor, agreeing to share, uses the system function $\square SVO$, naming the same variable as that which it wishes to share. This variable becomes the *shared variable*—shared because when sharing is established, it appears simultaneously in both processors. The shared variable is the communication link between the processors.

Syntactically, the shared variable is no different from any other variable in the user's workspace: it may be local or global, and it may appear to either side of the specification arrow. But the value of the variable is that which is assigned last by either owner. For example, consider the following sequence with the variable *SHARE* as the communication interface for *USERA* and *USERB* , each operating out of his own workspace:

USERA:		*SHARE*←12	(shared variable *set*)
USERB:		*SHARE*	(shared variable *used*)
	12		
		T←*SHARE*	(used)
		T	
	12		
USERA:		*SHARE*÷3	(used)
	4		
		SHARE←7	(set)
USERB:		*T*=*SHARE*	(used)
	0		
		SHARE←*T*	(set)
USERA:		*SHARE*	(used)
	12		

Each processor may independently assign values to the variable. When the shared variable appears to the left of the specification arrow, its value is being *set*. When it appears to the right of the specification arrow, its value is being *used*. Either a set or a use of a shared variable is called an *access*. A variable is defined to be a shared variable if it can be accessed by two concurrent processors.

Any processor may share several variables simultaneously. This sharing may be with the same processor or several different processors. But any one shared variable may have only two owners. That is, all sharing is *bilateral*.

As an example of a communication system using shared variables, consider a reservation system in which students may sign up for exclusive use of one or more devices or rooms, such as a graphics terminal, audio visual equipment, or a rehearsal room. The reservation scheduler is one processor. It resides in an active APL workspace. Each registering student (himself a processor) makes his request to the scheduler at his APL terminal through a defined function that uses the shared variable communication link. The request may be an inquiry about the state of the schedule, a reservation for a particular time slot, or a change or deletion of a former entry made by this student. The scheduler acts on the request and returns a reply, again through the shared variable communication link. The relationship between the scheduler-processor and the student-processor is illustrated by the accompanying diagram.

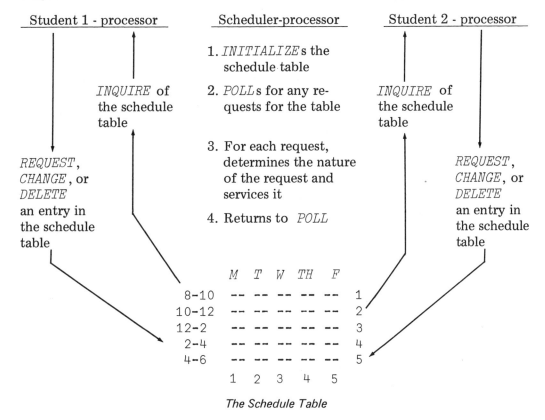

The Schedule Table

Each of the names in APL type font represents a function which contains system functions for manipulating shared variables to affect a satisfactory communication between the processors described for the reservation system.

The system functions for shared variables are

□*SVO*, to establish sharing between processors.

□*SVQ*, to inquire about any sharing requests.

□*SVC*, to control sharing between processors.

□*SVR*, to terminate sharing between processors.

In the next four sections we shall discuss each of these system functions for shared variables. The section following this discussion illustrates the reservation system outlined above.

9.1.1 Establishment of Sharing

To establish sharing between two processors, each of the processors must make a matching offer which includes the name of the variable to be shared and the identity of the processor with which it wishes to share. Offers to share are made through the dyadic system function S hared V ariable O ffer, $\Box SVO$. The format of this system function is

$$I \ \Box SVO \ C$$

The left argument I is a scalar number or a vector of numbers representing the identification of the processor(s) to which offers (or an offer) are being made. If I is a nonzero scalar, an offer is being made to one processor. If I is a vector, an offer is being made to each processor represented as a component of the vector. If I is zero, a general offer is being made, which may be accepted by any processor.

The processor identification for APL users is usually the unique user account number. For example, the user whose sign-on number is 932145 has 932145 as his processor identification. The identification numbers between 1 and 1000 are reserved for auxiliary processors such as non-APL host systems, printers, OS data sets, and disk drives. The matching of auxiliary processors with identification numbers is usually made at the installation. For example, 370 might be the identification number of OS/370.

If I is a scalar or one-component vector, the right argument C is a character scalar or vector representing the name of the variable to be shared. For example,

932145 $\Box SVO$ 'TALK'

offers to share the variable $TALK$ with the processor whose identification is 932145. If I is a vector, C must be a character matrix. Each row of C corresponds to a component of I and names the variable to be shared with that processor. For example,

1234 6789 $\Box SVO$ 2 4ρ'SV5 SV10'

offers to share the variable $SV5$ with processor 1234 and the variable $SV10$ with processor 6789. Leading or trailing blanks in the right argument names are ignored. For example, 'A1 ', ' A1', and 'A1' each represent the same variable name.

$\Box SVO$ returns an explicit result of 0, 1, or 2 to indicate the state of the offer. The integer result is called the *degree of coupling* and the meaning of its value is as follows:

Degree of Coupling	Meaning
0	No offer was made because the name used for the shared variable exists as the name of a label, function group, or a variable shared with another processor.
1	The offer is *pending* because the processor to which the offer has been made has not reciprocated with a matching offer.
2	Sharing has been established because both processors have issued acceptable matched offers to share.

Note 1:   The processor which initiates the offer to share receives a response of
0 or 1 when he executes $\square SVO$. The second processor can get any of
the responses when he makes his reciprocating offer.

Note 2:   An offer is always made to a processor whether or not the processor is
available. For example, it is not necessary for your sharing partner to
be signed on before you make an offer to share with him.

Examples of offers to share follow.

```
      932145 []SVO 'TALK'
1
```

The offer is pending until processor 932145 reciprocates the offer with

```
      546723 []SVO 'TALK'
2
```

Sharing has been established.

```
      1234 6789 []SVO 2 4ρ'SV5 SV10'
1 0
```

The result is a two-component vector giving the degree of coupling for each of the
components of the left argument. The offer is pending for processor 1234; no offer
has been made to processor 6789.

The result R of $\square SVO$ is a scalar or a vector with as many components as there are
names or name pairs being offered, that is,

$$(\rho R) \text{ is } \times/^{-}1\downarrow\rho C.$$

The processor to whom an offer is being made is not automatically informed of
the offer. If offers are anticipated, he can use the system function $\square SVQ$ to determine which processors have offered what variables for sharing. $\square SVQ$ is discussed in
Sec. 9.1.2. This section assumes that each processor involved in sharing knows that
an offer has been made and what the shared variable name is.

In the example above where *TALK* has been established as the shared variable,
neither processor 932145 or processor 546123 has assigned a value to it. If either
processor tries to use the variable, he gets a *VALUE ERROR*. For example,*

Processor 932145	Processor 546723
TALK	*TALK*
VALUE ERROR	*VALUE ERROR*
TALK	*TALK*
∧	∧

But if one of the processors assigns a value to *TALK*, that value appears in both
workspaces.

```
      TALK←'HI'
                                    TALK

                              HI
```

---

*The timed sequence of events which occur for each user is indicated in separate columns.
In this and the following illustrations the earlier events appear on lines before the later events.

If, prior to sharing, one user had assigned a value to the variable, it becomes the value of the shared variable. For example,

USERJ (*USERK*←932145)	*USERK* (*USERJ*←546723)

```
            C1                              C1←67
   VALUE  ERROR
            C1
            ∧
            USERK ⎕SVO 'C1'
    1

                                            USERJ ⎕SVO 'C1'
                                        2
            C1                              C1
    67                                  67
```

If, prior to sharing, both users have assigned values to the variable, the value associated with the variable is that which is associated with the user who first offered to share. For example,

USERJ	*USERK*

```
        A1←34                           A1←'AB'
        B1←56                           B1←'CD'
        USERK ⎕SVO 'A1'
    1

                                        USERJ ⎕SVO 'B1'
                                    1
        USERK ⎕SVO 'B1'                 USERJ ⎕SVO 'A1'
    2                               2
        A1                              A1
    34                              34
        B1                              B1
    CD                              CD
```

The vector right argument or each row of the matrix right argument can contain a second name which is used as an alias or stand-in name. This second name is called the *surrogate name*. For example,

    'MINE YOURS'

YOURS is the surrogate name of *MINE*. The processor to which the offer is being made knows the shared variable only by the surrogate name. Thus the surrogate name permits sharing between two processors even though one processor does not have direct knowledge of the variable name the other processor is using. For example, suppose that processor 1234 wishes to share a variable named *RECORD* with processor 5678. If processor 5678 was designed to operate with a shared variable named *BLOCK*, 1234 must establish *BLOCK* as the surrogate name for *RECORD*. The sharing offer that 1234 issues is

```
      5678 □SVO 'RECORD BLOCK'
1
```

5678's reciprocating offer is

```
      1234 □SVO 'BLOCK'
2
```

Sharing is established. Processor 1234 knows the shared variable as *RECORD*, and processor 5678 knows the same variable as *BLOCK* and does not know that 1234 knows it as *RECORD*.

Each processor can use the surrogate name. For example, *BLOCK* could be a surrogate name for both processors:

```
          USERJ                                      USERK


      RECORD←12
      USERK □SVO 'RECORD BLOCK'
1
                                         USERJ □SVO 'DATA BLOCK'
                                    2
      )VARS
RECORD                                       )VARS
      RECORD                    DATA
12                                    DATA
                                    12
                                         DATA←1 2 3
      RECORD
1 2 3
```

The same surrogate name may be used to establish sharing of different variables with the same user. In this case offers are matched in sequence with the reciprocating offers of the other user, each using the surrogate name. For example,

```
          USERJ                                      USERK

      A←17                              M←'AB'
      B←79                              N←'CD'
      USERK □SVO 'A S'
    1
      USERK □SVO 'B S'
    1
                                         USERJ □SVO 'M S'
                                    2
                                         USERJ □SVO 'N S'
                                    2
                                         M
                                    17
                                         N
                                    79
```

The same surrogate name may be used to share different variables with different processors, but the surrogate name must be associated with different variable names if it is to be associated with different processors. For example,

USERJ	*USERK*	*USERM*

```
     USERK □SVO 'A S'
1
     A←'HI'                 USERJ □SVO 'D S'
                    2
                        D
                    HI
     USERM □SVO 'B S'
1
     B←'BYE'                                   USERJ □SVO 'E S'
                                           2
                                               E
                                          'BYE'

     USERK □SVO 'B S'
0
```

The following table illustrates different ways to use the right argument to establish the name of the shared variable for two processors.

Right Argument for Sharing Between

USERJ	*USERK*	Result
'*A*'	'*A*'	The shared variable is known by the name *A* to both users.
'*A B*'	'*B*'	The shared variable is known to *USERJ* as *A* and to *USERK* as *B*. *USERK* does not know *USERJ*'s name for the shared variable.
'*A*'	'*B A*'	This is the same situation as above, only here *USERJ* does not know *USERK*'s name.
'*A X*'	'*B X*'	A variable is shared. It is known to *USERJ* as *A* and to *USERK* as *B*. But neither knows the other's name for the shared variable.
'*A*'	'*B*'	Two offers to share are outstanding, one by each user.
'*A*'	'*B X*'	This is the same as the previous case.
'*A X*'	'*X A*'	Two offers to share are outstanding, one by each user. (The surrogate name is always the second of a pair of names.)

The left argument of $\square SVO$ may also be zero. A zero argument indicates a general offer to share with any processor which accepts it by making a reciprocating offer. When a general offer is responded to, a reciprocating offer must be made to the processor which issued the general offer. For example,

USERJ	USERK
$0\ \square SVO\ 'Z1'$	
1	
	$USERJ\ \square SVO\ 'Z1'$
	2

If two processors offer a general share of the same variable, neither can be the accepting processor for the variable. Only a third processor can accept the offer, and then because sharing is bilateral with only one of the offerers. For example,

USERJ	USERK	USERM
$0\ \square SVO\ 'ZW'$		
1	$0\ \square SVO\ 'ZW'$	
	1	
$USERK\ \square SVO\ 'ZW'$		
0	$USERJ\ \square SVO\ 'ZW'$	
	0	$USERJ\ \square SVO\ 'ZW'$
		2

No user can share an unlimited number of variables. The number that can be shared is a parameter set by the installation. If a user attempts to share more variables than his quota, he receives the error report *INTERFACE QUOTA EXHAUSTED*. The error report *NO SHARES* appears if the shared variable facility of the APL system is not available.

Illustration 9.1   A Skeleton of a Share-Offering Function

The function named *OFFER* builds a shared variable name from the characters SV catenated with the user's account number, assigns data to it, and offers to share it. The explicit result is 0, 1, or 2 depending on the response to the share offer.

```
    ∇ Z←X OFFER Y;□IO;T;SVN
[1]   ∧ Y IS THE OFFEREE
[2]   ∧ X IS DATA
[3]   □IO←0
[4]   SVN←'SV',⍕1↑□AI
[5]   ⍎SVN,'←X'
[6]   Z←Y □SVO SVN
    ∇
```

$\square SVO$ may also be used as a monadic function. Monadic $\square SVO$ serves as a means of determining what the current degree of coupling is on the specified name, name pair, or matrix of name pairs. For example,

```
M←3 2ρ'A1A2A3'
□SVO M
2 0 1
```

The result indicates that the variable $A1$ is shared, that $A2$ is a nonshared variable, and that $A3$ has an offer to share associated with it.

> *Note*: Either the monadic or dyadic form of $\square SVO$ may be used to inquire into the degree of coupling of the variable. If the explicit result to a dyadic $\square SVO$ is 1 or 2, no further implicit actions are taken. Any further use of the dyadic $\square SVO$ returns only the current degree of coupling.

Illustration 9.2   Compilation of a List of Shared Variables

The function $SVOFFERED$ produces a list of the names of the shared variables which have been offered from this workspace:

```
      ∇Z←SVOFFERED
[1]   Z←□NL 2
[2]   Z←(× □SVO Z)≠Z
      ∇
```

Illustration 9.3   Determining and Classifying Offered and
Accepted Shared Variables

The following function produces a character matrix listing of the names of all the shared variables in the active workspace. All those variables for which an outstanding offer existed are prefaced by a 1, while those for which sharing had been established are prefaced by a 2.

```
      ∇ Z←SEARCH;M
[1]   M←□NL 2
[2]   Z←((1=□SVO M)≠'1',M),[1](2=□SVO M)≠'2',M
      ∇

      SEARCH
1S
1A1
2SHVAR
```

9.1.2   Sharing Inquiries

Since sharing can be offered, established, and retracted at any time, a user needs to know the status of the shared variables in his workspace, whether any offers to share have been made to him, and what the names of the variables being offered are.

We have already seen that the degree of coupling for any variable can be determined by using the monadic system function $\Box SVO$. Information about offers and variable names is acquired through the use of the monadic system function S hared V ariable Q uery, $\Box SVQ$. The format of $\Box SVQ$ is

> $R \leftarrow \Box SVQ \;\; V$

The argument may be an empty vector, a scalar, or a one-component vector.

    If V is an empty vector, $\Box SVQ$ returns a vector of processor numbers of those processors with outstanding offers to the processor issuing the inquiry. For example,

> $\Box SVQ \;\; \iota 0$
>
> 1009 1003

Processors 1009 and 1003 have made offers to share to this processor. If no offers are outstanding, $\Box SVQ$ returns an empty vector.

    If V is a scalar or one-component vector representing a processor identification, $\Box SVQ$ returns as a character vector or matrix the variable name(s) being offered by that processor. If a processor has not made any offers to the processor issuing the inquiry, $\Box SVQ$ returns an empty vector. For example,

> $\Box SVQ \;\; 1003$
>
> *DATA*
>
> *A1*

The variables *DATA* and *A1* have been offered by processor 1003 to this processor.

> $\Box SVQ \;\; 1004$
>
> ɫ

No variables have been offered by processor 1004 to this processor.

    $\Box SVQ$ returns only the names of variables for which an outstanding offer exists to the issuer of the inquiry. If the issuer of the inquiry subsequently accepts the offer of a variable, any later use of $\Box SVQ$ to that processor does not produce that variable name. Furthermore, if the issuer of the inquiry has an outstanding offer to the other processor, $\Box SVQ$ does not indicate it. For example,

> $\Box SVQ \;\; 1003$
>
> *DATA*
>
> *A1*
>
>
>
> 1003 $\Box SVO \;\; 'A1'$
>
> 2
>
>
>
> 1003 $\Box SVO \;\; 'B1'$
>
> 1
>
>
>
> $\Box SVQ \;\; 1003$
>
> *DATA*

A1 is not included in the result of the second $\Box SVQ$ expression, because it is an established shared variable. *B1* is not included in the result of the second inquiry expression because it is a variable being offered by the issuer of the inquiry.

Illustration 9.4 Associating Processors with Shared Variables

After sharing of a variable has been established, it is impossible to determine with which processor each variable is shared. At the time the offer is made, this information is available and should be recorded. The function *GENACC* is an illustration of a general acceptance function. This function queries to determine whether there is an offer to share, accepts the variables being offered, and builds a character matrix for each processor. The matrix contains as its first row the processor number, and each succeeding row contains the name of the variable it offered to share. The name created for each such matrix is *P* followed by the processor number.

```
     ∇ GENACC;I;J;R;P;Q;S
[1]    I←ρR←,□SVQ⍳0
[2]    →(0=ρR)/0
[3]  A:J←R[I] □SVO Q←□SVQ R[I]
[4]    P←⍕R[I]
[5]    S←(ρP)⌈¯1↑ρQ
[6]    ⍕'P',P,'←(S↑P),[1]((1↑ρQ),S)↑Q'
[7]    →A×⍳0≠I←I-1
     ∇
```

9.1.3 Access Control for Sharing

It is quite important in sequencing communication events to have the access of a shared variable controlled, that is, to control the set or use of the shared variable by the sharing partners. For example, perhaps the communication requires that each processor be allowed to use a shared variable only once between successive sets by its sharing partner. The dyadic system function *S* hared *V* ariable *C* ontrol, *□SVC* , is used to define an access control for a shared variable. The controls possible are controls imposed on successive sets or successive uses by either processor and can be represented by the following table, where processor *ME* is this processor and processor *YU* is the sharing partner:

	Processor	
	ME	*YU*
	Requires an intervening	
Successive sets by	access by *YU*	access by *ME*
Successive uses by	set by *YU*	set by *ME*

For example, one of the ways that the table can be read is that successive sets by processor *ME* require an intervening access (either a set or use) by processor *YU*.

Thus, with this form of control, the following sequence for the shared variable *SHARE* would hold:

	Processor *ME*	Processor *YU*
	SHARE←35	
	SHARE×2	
70		
	SHARE← ¯15	
	Keyboard locks until an access	*SHARE*
	by *YU*	35
	SHARE	
¯15		

Either or both sharing partners may participate in establishing control over the shared variable. The control that governs the shared variable is a summary of the controls desired by both processors.

The form of □*SVC* is

$R←B$ □*SVC* C

where C is a character vector representing the shared variable whose access is to be controlled. The form of the control desired by the issuing processor is defined by the *rules vector* B, a four-component Boolean vector, where a 1 indicates that the control represented by that component should exist. The first two components of B define the set rules for the two processors, and the last two components define the use rules. The meaning of each of the components is as follows:

Component of B	Meaning
$B[1]$	Another set by this processor is not permitted until the sharing partner accesses the variable C.
$B[2]$	Another set by the sharing partner is not permitted until this processor accesses the variable C.
$B[3]$	Another use by this processor is not permitted until the sharing partner sets the variable C.
$B[4]$	Another use by the sharing partner is not permitted until this processor sets the variable C.

If the access rules vector is restructured as a matrix, the meaning of each of the elements corresponds to the control table shown above, where processor *ME* is the issuing processor and processor *YU* is the sharing partner.

	Processor	
	ME	*YU*
	Requires an intervening	
Successive sets by	*B[1]* access by *YU*	*B[2]* access by *ME*
Successive uses by	*B[3]* set by *YU*	*B[4]* set by *ME*

The result of □*SVC* is the access control vector of the shared variable as viewed by the issuing processor. The meaning of each of the components in the access control vector is the same as that for the access rules vector. For example,

Processor *ME*	Processor *YU*
1 0 0 0 □*SVC* *'SHARE'*	1 0 0 0 □*SVC* *'SHARE'*
1 0 0 0	1 1 0 0

The rules defined by *ME* are the same as the control on the variable, namely, that a second set by processor *ME* is not permitted until an access by processor *YU* has occurred. The rules defined by processor *YU* are that a second set by processor *YU* is not permitted until an access by processor *ME* has occurred. The result, the control on the shared variable, is that successive sets by either sharing partner are controlled and cannot occur without an intervening access by the other partner.

Each processor will see the access control vector from its point of view. Thus the access control vector may not appear to have the same value for each processor. For example, if the access control is such that successive sets by processor *ME* require an intervening access by processor *YU* and successive uses by processor *ME* require an intervening set by processor *YU*, the access control vector appears as 1 0 1 0 to processor *ME* and as 0 1 0 1 to processor *YU*. The meaning of the access control vector to both processors, however, is the same. Graphically this might be visualized as

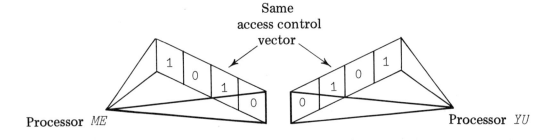

The monadic use of $\Box SVC$ is an inquiry about the current access control on the shared variable. The form of monadic $\Box SVC$ is

$R \leftarrow \Box SVC \ C$

The result is the access control vector for the shared variable C. It is a summary of the controls defined by both processors as viewed by the issuing processor. Formally, if BME is the four-component access rules vector used by processor ME in defining control and BYU is the four-component access rules vector used by processor YU in defining control, the access control vector for the shared variable, as viewed by ME, is defined as

$BME \lor BYU[2 \ 1 \ 4 \ 3]$

The following sequence of events shows the monadic and dyadic use of $\Box SVC$ for shared variable $A1$:

Processor ME		Processor YU
$YU \leftarrow 2222$		$ME \leftarrow 1111$
$YU \ \Box SVO \ 'A1'$		
1		
		$ME \ \Box SVO \ 'A1'$
	2	
		$\Box SVC \ 'A1'$
	0 0 0 0	No control exists when a shared variable is established.
1 0 0 0 $\Box SVC \ 'A1'$		
1 0 0 0 Control established on successive sets by ME.		
$A1 \leftarrow 12$		
$A1 \leftarrow 34$		
This statement is not completed; the keyboard remains locked.		$A1$
	12	At this point the statement $A1 \leftarrow 34$ issued by processor ME will be accepted.
		$A1$
	34	
$\Box SVC \ 'A1'$		$\Box SVC \ 'A1'$
1 0 0 0	0 1 0 0	

Note that the access control vector for each processor states that processor ME cannot make two successive sets without an intervening access by YU.

        1 0 0 0 $\Box SVC \ 'A1'$ Control defined on successive sets by YU.

   1 1 0 0 Control on successive sets by both ME and YU exists.

<u>Processor *ME*</u>   <u>Processor *YU*</u>

```
                                        A1←33
                                        A1←44
                              The keyboard remains locked until an
                                 access by ME.
      A1
33    Now YU's keyboard unlocks.
      A1
44                                                        A1
                                                   44
      ☐SVC 'A1'
1  1  0  0
```

A sharer can reset only those components of the access control vector which he first set. For example, if *ME* does the following,

```
      0  0  0  0  ☐SVC 'A1'
0  1  0  0
```

he removes only the control on successive sets by *ME* which he had originally defined. The control defined by *YU* still exists. Either sharer can only increase the degree of control on the shared variable or reset that portion which he set.

Consider now several possible access control vector settings and their meanings. Let *ACVME* be the access control vector as seen by user *ME* and *ACVYU* be the corresponding access control vector as seen by the sharing user *YU*:

Setting	Meaning
ACVME= 0 0 0 0 (*ACVYU*= 0 0 0 0)	There exists no constraints upon the shared variable.
ACVME= 1 1 1 1 (*ACVYU*= 1 1 1 1)	The shared variable is completely constrained. This is called a *full interlock*. Neither sharer can make a second set or use until his partner intervenes with an access or set.
ACVME= 1 0 1 0 (*ACVYU*= 0 1 0 1)	User *ME* can neither set nor use the variable a second time without an intervening access or set by user *YU*. User *YU* has no restrictions upon his use of the variable.
ACVME= 0 1 0 1 (*ACVYU*= 1 0 1 0)	User *YU* can neither set nor use the shared variable a second time without an intervening access by user *ME*.

Setting	Meaning
ACVME= 1 1 0 0 (*ACVYU=* 1 1 0 0)	Neither *ME* nor *YU* can set a second time without an intervening access by the other partner.
ADVME= 0 1 1 0 (*ACVYU=* 1 0 0 1)	User *YU* cannot set a second time without an intervening access by user *ME*. Also, user *ME* cannot access a second time without an intervening set by user *YU*.

In our discussion of □*SVC*, a single control vector was applied to a single shared variable via a single □*SVC* to simplify the explanation of the control process. However, a single □*SVC* can set several control vectors for several shared variables. The control vectors must appear as rows of a binary four-column matrix. This matrix is the left argument of □*SVC*. The right argument is a character matrix where each row is the corresponding shared variable name to which the control vector is associated. For example, with

```
      ACV
  1 1 1 1
  1 1 0 0
      SVNAMES
A1
B12
      ACV □SVC SVNAMES
```

imposes a maximum constraint on shared variable *A1*. The shared variable *B12* has placed upon it the constraint of 1 1 0 0, permitting successive sets by either partner only if the other has an intervening access.

Also, as a matter of convenience, the left argument of □*SVC* may be either the scalar 0 or 1, which is extended to represent 0 0 0 0 and 1 1 1 1, respectively.

9.1.4 Retraction of Sharing

A user who has offered to share a variable with another needs to be able to retract such an offer. The termination of sharing can occur explicitly through the issuance of the system function *S*hared *V*ariable *R*etraction, □*SVR*, or implicitly through other acts of either user, such as signing off or loading a new workspace.

The form of □*SVR* is

```
      R←□SVR C
```

The result is the retraction of sharing of the variables named in the character array *C*. Each variable name must appear as a separate row of the array *C*. If the shared variable for which retraction is desired has a surrogate, both the name and its surrogate must be provided. □*SVR* returns as an explicit result the degree of coupling which existed on the variable before retraction occurred. The implicit result is to reduce the degree of coupling on the variable to zero. For example,

USERA	*USERB*
`B ⎕SVO 'A1'`	
`1`	
	`A ⎕SVO 'A1'`
	`2`
	`⎕SVO 'B1 S'`
	`2`
`⎕SVR 'A1'`	
`2`	
	`⎕SVR 'A1'`
	`1`
`M←3 2 ρ'A1A2A3'`	
	`⎕SVR 'B1 S'`
	`2`
`⎕SVO M`	
`0 2 1`	
`⎕SVR M`	
`0 2 1`	
`⎕SVR M`	
`0 0 0`	

`⎕SVR` reduces the degree of coupling to zero.

The retraction of sharing also occurs automatically in the following circumstances:

1. One of the sharing user's connection with the computer was terminated. (Such actions as signing off or powering the terminal off terminates the connection.)

2. One of the sharers loaded a new workspace.

3. One of the sharers erased the shared variable.

4. One of the sharers has defined the variable being shared as a local variable within his function. When this function successfully completes, sharing is retracted.

The user who did not produce any of these conditions will get a response of `1` as the degree of coupling of the previously shared variable when he executes `⎕SVR`.

9.1.5 Some Functions for a Reservation System

Section 9.1 describes a reservation system that uses shared variables to provide on-line communications between active APL workspaces. The functions *INITIALIZE*, *POLL*, *INQUIRE*, and *REQUEST*, shown in the diagram in Sec. 9.1, have been defined and are shown later in this section. The functions *CHANGE* and *DELETE* have not been implemented in this illustration. Each student-processor needs only the functions *INQUIRE* and *REQUEST* and the supporting functions *IF* and *OFFER* (not shown on the diagram). The scheduler-processor uses the function *INITIALIZE* to establish a new named schedule table. The main function for the scheduler-processor is the *SCHEDULER* function. It uses the supporting functions *POLL*, *BLANKSUPRS*, *IF*, *INQ*, and *RES*. A sequence of events using these functions is shown below:

Student 1-Processor   **Scheduler-Processor**

```
                                      SCHED1←INITIALIZE
                                      SCHED1

                                           M   T   W  TH  F
                                    8-10  --  --  --  --  --   1
                                   10-12  --  --  --  --  --   2
                                   12-2   --  --  --  --  --   3
                                    2-4   --  --  --  --  --   4
                                    4-6   --  --  --  --  --   5
                                           1   2   3   4   5

                                      SCHEDULER
```

```
        )VARS
OWNER      SH
        SH
SCHED1
```

OWNER is the scheduler-processor
  identification number

```
      SH INQUIRE OWNER

        M   T  'W  TH  F
 8-10  --  --  --  --  --   1
10-12  --  --  --  --  --   2
12-2   --  --  --  --  --   3
 2-4   --  --  --  --  --   4
 4-6   --  --  --  --  --   5
        1   2   3   4   5
```

```
      SH REQUEST OWNER
WHAT TIME SLOT? (ENTER ROW NUMBER)
2
WHAT DAY? (ENTER COLN NUMBER)
4
STUDENT NO. (2 DIGITS)
42
        M   T   W  TH   F
 8-10  --  --  --  --  --   1
10-12  --  --  --  42  --   2
12-2   --  --  --  --  --   3
 2-4   --  --  --  --  --   4
 4-6   --  --  --  --  --   5
        1   2   3   4   5
```

The functions which permit this sequence of events are shown at the end of the section. The line numbers given in the following discussion refer to these functions.

The main function for the scheduler-processor is *SCHEDULER*. It calls *POLL*, which goes into a nonending loop, seeking any offers to share with the scheduler processor. There is a built-in .5-second delay in the polling loop. When a request does arrive from a student-processor, *SCHEDULER* determines the name of the variable to be shared (line [7]). It puts a control upon it to prevent *STUDENT* from reading it until *SCHEDULER* has served it (line [11]). In doing this, *SCHEDULER* immediately sets the shared variable to the null vector. Then *SCHEDULER* analyzes the message passed to it via the shared variable from *STUDENT*. The format of the message is that of a character vector with at least two fields. The first field is the digit 1 to 4 defining the nature of the request. A 1 indicates an *INQUIRY* request; 2, a *RESERVE* request; 3, a *CHANGE* request; and 4, a *DELETE* request.

The second field is the name of the schedule table. In this illustration the variable *LIST* is a matrix of eligible table names. For the *REQUEST*, *CHANGE*, and *DELETE* requests there are three other fields, the row and column numbers of the entry and a two-digit student number to be placed in the designated entry. The digit of the first field results in the call of the corresponding functions *INQ*, *RES*, *CHG*, or *DEL* (line [18]). These functions, of which only *INQ* and *RES* are illustrated here, perform the necessary request from the student-processor. They return the proper information or an error message via the shared variable to the student-processor.

Having accomplished this, *SCHEDULER* interlocks until the student-processor retracts sharing (line [21]). Then *SCHEDULER* retracts sharing, erases the shared variable, and returns to *POLL*. The interlock is important—otherwise a race condition could occur in that *SCHEDULER* could get back to *POLL* before the student-processor can retract sharing.

The student-processor has as its primary functions *INQUIRE* and *REQUEST*. They build the necessary message to be passed to *SCHEDULER*. Then, via the supporting function *OFFER*, the shared variable is built. This shared variable name is built by prefacing the characters *SV* to the user's account number. Following that, sharing is offered. Then, since *SCHEDULER* first returns an ιO, *OFFER* attempts to read the shared variable twice. The second read will not be successful until there was an intervening set by *SCHEDULER*. The second read of the shared variable contains the requested information from the scheduler-processor. Thereafter, the student-processor retracts sharing and erases the variable.

```
      ∇ Z←INITIALIZE;HR;DAY;FC;BR;ENT;B
[1]     B←6ρ' '
[2]     HR← 7 6 ρB,' 8-10 10-12 12-2   2-4   4-6   ',B
[3]     ENT← 5 15 ρ'__'
[4]     DAY←' M   T   W   TH  F '
[5]     FC←' 12345 '
[6]     BR←' 1   2   3   4   5 '
[7]     Z←DAY,[1] ENT,[1] BR
[8]     Z←HR,Z,FC
      ∇
```

```
     ∇ SCHEDULER;T;I;J;WHO;WHAT;RSP;CT;TYPE;□IO;TW
[1]    TYPE← 6 3 ρ'INQRESCHGDELERR'
[2]    □IO←1
[3]   ⍝ POLL
[4]  PL:WHO←POLL 0.5
[5]    CT←ρWHO
[6]    I←1
[7]  OTHER:WHAT←□SVQ WHO[I]
[8]  ⍝ASSUMING ONLY 1 VARIABLE TO SHARE PER STUDENT
[9]  CHK:RSP←WHO[I] □SVO WHAT
[10]   →CHK IF 2≠RSP
[11]   RSP← 0 0 0 1 □SVC WHAT
[12] ⍝TO PREVENT STUDENT FROM READING W/O A SET BY SCHEDULER
[13]   TW←⍎WHAT[1;]
[14]   ⍎WHAT[1;],'←⍳0'
[15] ⍝ANALYZE THE MESSAGE
[16]   TW←BLANKSUPS TW
[17]   J←⍎(TW⍳' ')↑TW
[18]   ⍎TYPE[(⍳4)⍳J;]
[19]   RSP← 0 0 0 0 □SVC WHAT
[20] ⍝ A HOLD UNTIL STUDENT RETRACTS SHARING
[21] HD:→HD IF 2=□SVO WHAT[1;]
[22]   RSP←□SVR WHAT
[23]   RSP←□EX WHAT
[24]   →OTHER IF CT≥I←I+1
[25]   →PL
     ∇

     ∇ WHO←POLL X;T
[1]   ⍝X IS A DELAY IN THE POLL LOOP
[2]  PL:WHO←□SVQ⍳0
[3]    →0 IF 0≠ρ,WHO
[4]    T←□DL X
[5]    →PL
     ∇

     ∇ Z←BLANKSUPS S
[1]    Z←S≠' '
[2]    Z←(Z∨(1↓Z),0)/S
[3]    Z←(' '=1↑Z)↓Z
     ∇

     ∇ INQ;J;RSP
[1]    J←(TW⍳' ')↓TW
[2]    →OK IF 1∈LIST∧.=6↑J
[3]    ⍎WHAT[1;],'←''NAME NOT IN LIST'''
[4]    →0
[5]  OK:⍎WHAT[1;],'←',J
     ∇
```

```
      ∇ Z←SCHED INQUIRE OWNER;□IO;T
[1]     □IO←0
[2]     T←'1 ',SCHED
[3]     Z←SCHED OFFER OWNER
      ∇


      ∇ RES;I;J;K;T
[1]   ⍝TW SUPPLIED BY SCHEDULER FCN
[2]   ⍝TW IS THE MESSAGE PASSED BY STUDENT
[3]   ⍝ WHAT[1;] IS NAME OF SHARED VARIABLE
[4]     J←(TWι' ')↓TW
[5]     T←(¯1+Jι' ')↑J
[6]     →OK1 IF 1∈LIST∧.=6↑T
[7]     ⍕WHAT[1;],'←''NAME NOT IN LIST'''
[8]     →0
[9]   OK1:I←⍕(Jι' ')↓J
[10]    →OK2 IF 3=ρI
[11]    ⍕WHAT[1;],'←''INCOMPLETE REQUEST INFORMATION'''
[12]    →0
[13]  OK2:K←⍕T
[14]    K[1+I[1]; 7 8 +3×¯1+I[2]]←⍕I[3]
[15]    ⍕T,'←K'
[16]  ⍝RETURN UPDATED SCHEDULE TO STUDENT
[17]    ⍕WHAT[1;],'←K'
      ∇


      ∇ Z←SCHED REQUEST OWNER;T;□IO
[1]     □IO←0
[2]   ⍝ PROMPT FOR TIME AND DAY SLOT
[3]     'WHAT TIME SLOT? (ENTER ROW NUMBER)'
[4]     →ER IF 5<⍕RN←⎕
[5]     'WHAT DAY? (ENTER COLN NUMBER)'
[6]     →ER IF 5<⍕CN←⎕
[7]     'STUDENT NO. (2 DIGITS)'
[8]     SN←BLANKSUPS ¯2↑⎕
[9]   ⍝BUILD A MSG TO SCHEDULER
[10]    T←'2 ',SCHED,' ',RN,' ',CN,' ',SN
[11]  ⍝OFFER RETURNS UPDATED SCHEDULE TO THE REQUESTOR
[12]    Z←SCHED OFFER OWNER
[13]    →0
[14]  ER:'INCORRECT ENTRY'
      ∇
```

```
      ∇ Z←SHED OFFER OWNER;DEL;SVNAME
[1]   ⍝BUILD SV NAME
[2]    SVNAME←'SV',⍕1↑⎕AI
[3]   ⍝ASSIGN SV NAME THE MESSAGE
[4]    ⍎SVNAME,'←T'
[5]   ⍝OFFER TO SHARE
[6]    T←OWNER ⎕SVO SVNAME
[7]   ⍝CHECK RESPONSE
[8]    →(R0,R1,R2)[T]
[9]   ⍝SHARING ESTABLISHED
[10]  ⍝  A WAIT FOR SCHEDULE OWNER TO RETURN THE
[11]  ⍝  REQUESTED SCHEDULE IS BUILT IN.
[12]  ⍝  N.B. OWNER 1ST RETURNS ⍳0
[13]  R2:T←⍎SVNAME
[14]   →R2 IF 0=⍴,T
[15]   Z←T
[16]   T←⎕SVR SVNAME
[17]   T←⎕EX SVNAME
[18]   →0
[19]  ⍝OFFER OUTSTANDING  WAIT FOR 1 MINUTE BEFORE EXITING
[20]  R1:T←⎕TS[4]
[21]  R11:→R2 IF 2=⎕SVO SVNAME
[22]   →R0 IF ⎕TS[4]≥T+1
[23]   DEL←⎕DL 0.1
[24]   →R11
[25]  ⍝ OFFER NOT ACCEPTED
[26]  R0:'ACCESS TO SCHEDULE NOT GRANTED'
[27]   '  TRY AGAIN - LATER'
[28]   DEL←⎕SVR SVNAME
      ∇


      ∇ Z←A IF B
[1]    Z←B⍴A
      ∇
```

PROBLEMS

1. What will the possible degree of coupling values be in each of the following situations:

   (a) 1234 ⎕SVO 'ABC'   (initial offer)   (d)   1234 ⎕SVO 'A1'

   (b) 2468 ⎕SVO 'ABC'   (accept offer)   1

   (c) 1234 ⎕SVO 'A.C'   3456 ⎕SVO 'A1'

2. In the sequence, fill in the blanks

User *J*	User *K*

```
                   A1←10
                   A2←20                        A2←'XY'
                   A3←30                        A3←'WZ'
                   USERK □SVO 2 2ρ'A1A2'
(a) _____
                                                USERJ □SVO 2 2ρ'A2A3'
                                         (b) _____

                   USERK □SVO 2 2ρ'A3B1'
(c) _____
                                                USERJ □SVO 2 2ρ 'A1B1'
                                         (d) _____

                      A1                            A1
(e) _____                                   (f) _____
                      A2                            A2
(g) _____                                   (h) _____
                      A3                            A3
(i) _____                                   (j) _____
                      B1                            B1
(k) _____                                   (l) _____
```

3. Fill in the blanks. Assume that time increases as one steps down the page.

Processor 1001	Processor 1002

```
             MV←2 5ρ'BL R1BL R2'
             1002 1003 □SVO MV
(a) _____
             BL←123                           □SVQ ι0
             R1                        (b) _____
                                               □SVQ □SVQ ι0
(c) _____
                                        (d) _____
                                               1001 □SVO 'CL R1'
                                        (e) _____
                                               BL
                                        (f) _____
                                               CL
                                        (g) _____
                                               R1
                                        (h) _____
```

4. (b)

Processor 1001	Processor 1003
	$NV \leftarrow 2\ 2\rho\,'R3R4'$
	$1001\ \Box SVO\ NV$
	(a) - - - - -
$SV \leftarrow 2\ 2\rho\,'R3R4'$	
$1003\ \Box SVO\ SV$	$R3 \leftarrow 456$
	$R4 \leftarrow 789$
(b) - - - - -	
$R3$	
(c) - - - - -	
	$\Box EX\ 'R3'$
	(d) - - - - -
	$\Box EX\ 'R4'$
$R4$	(e) - - - - -
(f) - - - - -	
$\Box SVO\ SV$	$\Box SVO\ NV$
(g) - - - - -	(h) - - - - -

5. Suppose user ME wishes to pass/share the function $FN1$ with user YU. Write a set of expressions to permit this.

6. Suppose that user ME is sharing variable SV with user $YU1$. Then user ME via $\Box SVQ$ determines that user $YU2$ also wishes to share a variable SV with user ME.

   (a) If user ME issues

   $YU2\ \Box SVO\ 'SV'$

   what is the response?

   (b) Why?

   (c) What must user ME do to accept user $YU2$'s sharing offer of variable SV? (write the $\Box SVO$ expression)

7. Suppose that user ME and user YU are sharing the variable SV with no control setting. Now ME wishes to enter a function FCN, and while he is within that function he wishes to control YU's access to SV.

   (a) What control can ME set on SV to prevent YU from setting SV more than once?

   (b) What control can ME set on SV to prevent YU from accessing SV more than once?

   (c) Suppose that ME wishes to use SV repeatedly within the function FCN and yet he wishes to prevent any setting of SV by YU while he is within FCN. What can ME do?

8. Modify the function of Illustration 9.1 so that if the response to $\Box SVO$ is 0, the function will exit with the message $NOT\ OFFERED$, and if the response to $\Box SVO$ is 1, the function will delay 10 seconds and then test for acceptance again. This time if the response is not 2, it will exit, retracting the offer and issuing the message $OFFER\ WITHDRAWN$.

9. In the shared variable comprehensive illustration in Sec. 9.1.5 the RES function inserts a student number into the proper entry in the schedule table (line $[14]$). However, it does not examine the entry to see if it is occupied by another student number. It simply overwrites it. Modify the RES function so that it does not overwrite a previous student entry.

10. Implement the *CHANGE* and *DELETE* functions for the reservation scheduling illustration. The *CHANGE* function permits a given reservation to be replaced, while the *DELETE* function removes a previous reservation. Also, the corresponding functions *CHG* and *DEL* for use by the *SCHEDULER* function need to be implemented.

Section 9.2   TSIO—AN APL.SV PROCESSOR FOR DATA SET MANIPULATION

TSIO—time sharing input/output—is an auxiliary processor making available to the APL.SV user many of the data management facilities of OS/VS, its host operating system. The first feature of the TSIO processor discussed in this section is that which allows the user to overcome the workspace size limitation of APL by permitting him to use remote files or *data sets* for auxiliary storage of functions and variables not currently needed in his workspace and to return these functions and variables to the active workspace when needed; that is, TSIO is considered as an APL file system.*

Other features of TSIO such as the allocation of data sets in the host system, the transfer of data to it, the printing on a printer, and the automatic translation of data encoding between APL and other common encoding representations are built on the base of the storage facilities but require a knowledge of OS/VS for their full use.† These features are summarized in Sec. 9.2.5.

9.2.1   *Terminology and Procedural Overview*

Data Sets

A *data set* is a named collection of data items. The creation of a data set occurs with the assignment of a name to this entire set of data items. Thereafter, the data

---

*A file system manages data sets (files). It represents another means of organizing, controlling and sharing access to data. Several APL file systems exist. They may be divided roughly into two categories. Both extend APL service facilities by overcoming workspace imposed restrictions. The first category of file system achieves this while keeping the user entirely within the APL environment. In such a file system the user addresses his file through a simple set of instructions. The APL*PLUS file subsystem and the Burroughs APL/700 system are examples of such a system. In both of these systems the user creates his file and reads and writes to it without needing to know where the file is or how it is stored and manipulated. Appendices E and F summarize the APL*PLUS and Burroughs APL/700 file systems. The second category of file system, as exemplified by TSIO, extends the service facilities further. It also permits the APL user to move back and forth between the APL workspace and the operating system. In TSIO the file mechanism is designed to accommodate both file activity and communication with the operating system through OS data sets or physical end-use devices, such as a printer.

†Full details concerning OS/VS facilities pertinent to TSIO can be found in *OS/VS Data Management Services Guide*, IBM publication GC26–3783, and *APL Shared Variables Users Guide* IBM publication SH20–1460.

set is referred to by name, the assigned *data set name*. A data set is composed of *records*. Each record is that collection of data which the creator or writer of the data set wishes to consider as a single entity. The records of a data set may be heterogeneous: the rank, shape, and data type of each item are independent of each other. For example, one record in a data set may be a numeric vector, and another, a character matrix. Within the host system records are transferred to and from auxiliary physical storage devices in larger groupings called *blocks*. A data set containing only blocks, each having one record, is called an *unblocked data set*.

Writing to a data set means putting records on it. *Reading* from a data set means taking records from it. Before a data set can be written to or read from, it has to be *opened*. Opening a data set supplies the supporting system with enough information so that proper supporting programs and physical devices may be allocated to it. When use of a data set is completed, it is *closed*. Closing a data set enables the supporting system to free resources for other uses. Closing a data set does not destroy it.

The organization of data sets is considered *sequential* when the records can be accessed only in the sequence of their physical relationship. The organization of data sets is considered *direct* or *indexed* when the records can be accessed by naming their position in the data set. Data sets for direct access are created and records appended to them sequentially. The direct access applies only to reading and re-writing records.

The data set differs from a workspace in several important aspects:

1. The data set, once created, continues to exist after the creator signs off.

2. The data set's existence is unaffected by the)*SAVE* and)*LOAD* commands.

3. Several data sets may be open at the same time.

4. The data set may be used simultaneously by several users.

It is these characteristics which make a file system a desirable accompaniment to the workspace.

Communications with TSIO

Basically, all communication with the TSIO processor is through a shared variable called the *control variable*. The user sends the control information necessary to open a data set for reading or writing records or for renaming or deleting a data set to TSIO through this control variable. The TSIO processor assumes the role of translating the control variable into a form understandable to OS/VS. After the data set has been opened, the same control variable can be specified with data to write a record sequentially on a data set or to indicate the index of a record on an indexed data set. The following sequence of events occurs when writing records sequentially on a data set:

- A data set is named and opened using the control variable.

- The data for a record are assigned to the control variable; that is, a record is written to the data set. (This step is repeated for each record being written.)

- The data set is closed.

A use of the control variable reads a record sequentially from a data set. The following sequence of events occurs when reading records sequentially from a data set:

- The data set is opened using the control variable.

- The control variable is used; that is, a record from the data set is read into the workspace. (This step is repeated for each record being read.)

- The data set is closed.

A second shared variable called a *data variable* can be specified with data to rewrite a record to an indexed data set and used to read a record from an indexed data set. The following sequence of events occurs when rewriting a record to an indexed data set:

- The data set is opened using the control variable.

- The control variable is specified with the position of the record in the data set.

- The data variable is specified with data.

- The data set is closed.

The following sequence of events occurs when reading a record from an indexed data set:

- The data set is opened using the control variable.

- The control variable is specified with the position of the record in the data set.

- The data variable is used.

- The data set is closed.

The details of how these events for sequential and indexed data sets are realized are presented in Sec. 9.2.2 and 9.2.3. Section 9.2.6 provides an extended illustration of data set maintenance.

9.2.2   The Control Variable and Sequentially Accessed Data Sets

The control variable is the shared variable which serves as the communication interface with the TSIO processor. The name of the control variable must begin with the characters *CTL* and then may be followed by any alphameric characters, for example, *CTL1* or *CTLMINE*. A full interlock (an access control vector of 1 1 1 1) must be associated with the control vector so that successive sets by either processor must have an intervening access by the other processor and successive uses by either processor must have an intervening set by the other processor. The TSIO processor issues a full interlock control vector after it accepts sharing.

The APL user-processor specifies the control variable with

1. Control information in the form of a character vector to open a data set,

2. Data to write to an opened data set, or

3. The empty vector to close a data set.

The TSIO processor assigns to the control variable

1. A response code indicating the success or failure of the command or data transfer request or

2. Data from an opened data set.

The control variable exists in two modes: *command mode* and *data transfer mode*. In command mode, the value of the control variable is interpreted as a command with the control information necessary to carry out the command. In data transfer mode, the value of the control variable is interpreted as data to be transmitted or received. The control variable shifts to data mode after the issuance of a successful read or write command in command mode.

When the control variable is in command mode, the character vector assigned to it is interpreted as information necessary to initiate a data management operation. The character vector must be in a prescribed form. The structure of the control variable for sequential reading and writing of unblocked data sets is shown below:

$$' \left\{ \begin{array}{l} SW \\ SR \\ RENAME \\ DELETE \end{array} \right\} DSNAME = \text{xxxxxxxx} \, [\, , NEWNAME = \text{xxxxxxxx} \,] \, [\, , DISP = \left\{ \begin{array}{l} NEW \\ OLD \\ MOD \\ SHR \end{array} \right\} \,] \, [\, , BLKSIZE = \text{n} \,] \, '$$

Within the command structure of the control variable exists a *main action command* identifying the data management operation and one or more phrases identifying the data set attributes and usage. Each phrase consists of a *key word* identifying a particular attribute or usage, the equal sign, and the desired value for that attribute. In the structure shown above, brackets indicate optional phrases—phrases which may not be necessary for every operation. All phrases but *DSNAME=* are optional. Braces indicate parameter values; that is, when only a few values are possible, they are listed as alternatives. X indicates alphameric values, and n, numeric values.

In specifying a control variable in command mode, only those phrases necessary are included in the specification. The brackets and braces must not be included. The main action command must be first; the order of the phrases is immaterial. A space separates the main action command from the phrases. Each phrase must be separated from the others by a comma. For example, the character vector,

   ' SW DSNAME=SET,DISP=NEW,BLKSIZE=550 '

creates (*DISP=NEW*), a sequential (*SW*) data set named *SET* (*DSNAME=SET*) whose blocks are to contain no more than 550 bytes (*BLKSIZE=550*). The next action expected is a specification of the control variable with data (because the main action command is a write command).

The main action command and the key words are discussed separately in the following paragraphs. Illustration 9.5 following this discussion contains samples of control variables for various operations.

Main Action Commands

The character vector required in command mode must begin with a mnemonic defining a data management operation to be performed. For sequential data sets these are

Mnemonic	Meaning	Purpose
SW	Sequential write	Commands the creation of a new data set or the sequential writing to an already existing one
SR	Sequential read	Commands sequential reading from an existing data set
RENAME	Rename data set	Commands that the name of the data set be changed
DELETE	Delete data set	Commands the deletion of an existing data set

DSN or DSNAME

The data set name phrase *DSN*=xxxxxxxx or *DSNAME*=xxxxxxxx defines the name of the data set involved in the command. It must be present with each main action command. When used with *SW* (sequential write) it may be establishing the name of a new data set. When used with the other commands, it is reopening an existing data set. The naming conventions for the data set are those of the host system. Each name must be eight characters or less in length; the first character must be alphabetic, and the remaining characters, alphameric. If the user is accessing another user's data set, that user's account number must precede the rest of the data set name, separated from it by a space. For example,

DSN=54321 *DATA*

NEWNAME

The data set identification phrase *NEWNAME*=xxxxxxxx is used only with the *RENAME* command. The phrase defines the new name to be given to the data set named in the data set phrase.

DISP

The disposition phrase *DISP*= determines the positioning of the data set and whether it may be accessed by other users besides its creator. The parameters assignable to *DISP* are

Value	Meaning
NEW	A data set is to be created for exclusive use.
OLD	Access to a previously created data set, when opened, will start at the beginning of the data set.
MOD	Access to a previously created data set, when opened, will start at the end of the data set.
SHR	The data set is permitted shared access; when opened, access starts at the beginning of the data set.

BLKSIZE

The block size parameter *BLKSIZE*= n defines the largest size block to be used in the data set, that is, the maximum number of bytes in a block. This parameter must be stated explicitly in the control variable when creating a new data set and is generally not included when the data set is subsequently opened.

Illustration 9.5   Sample Control Vectors

1. Create a new data set:

    CTL1←'SW DSN=SET,DISP=NEW,BLKSIZE=550'

    The *BLKSIZE* value selected for the example has been selected arbitrarily.

2. Read sequentially from the beginning of the data set:

    CTL1←'SR DSN=SET'

3. Append further records onto a data set:

    CTL1←'SW DSN=SET,DISP=MOD'

4. Rewrite over a data set:

    CTL1←'SW DSN=SET'

    Note with care the difference between the control vectors of items 3 and 4. If *DISP=MOD* is not present, the previously named data set *DSN=SET* is overwritten.

5. Rename a data set:

    CTL1←'RENAME DSN=SET,NEWNAME=NEWSET'

6. Delete a data set:

    CTL1←'DELETE DSN=NEWSET'

With the four key words described thus far, writing and reading of unblocked sequential data sets is possible. For example, the write sequence of events described in Sec. 9.2.1 might appear as follows:

TSIO □*SVO* '*CTL1*' 1	Sharing of *CTL1* is offered to the TSIO processor (whose processor number is represented by *TSIO*).
1 1 1 1 □*SVC* '*CTL1*' 1 1 1 1	A full interlock is associated with *CTL1*.

The above two expressions represent the establishment of sharing and do not have to be included each time a data set is opened.

CTL1←'*SW DSNAME=FCNS,DISP=NEW,BLKSIZE=550*'	A data set named *FCNS* is created and opened.
CTL1 0	Response code indicates success of command.
CTL1←*RESULTS*	The data specified to *CTL1* is a record written on the data set *FCNS*.
CTL1 0	Response code indicates success of the write.
CTL1←''	The data set is closed.

The response code represents TSIO's set after each access by the user-processor (to fulfill the full interlock requirements). Table 5 in Section 9.2.5 contains the non-zero response code returnable to a command mode control variable. Table 6 in Section 9.2.5 contains the nonzero response codes returnable to a data transfer mode control variable. In either mode, a response code of 0 indicates normal completion.

The control variable is in command mode under three circumstances:

1. It is initially in command mode immediately following the acceptance by TSIO of the offer to share. For example,

    > *TSIO* □*SVO* '*CTL1*'
    > .
    > .
    > .
    > □*SVO* '*CTL1*'
    > 2

At this point *CTL1* is in command mode.

2. The control variable remains in command mode after the execution of a command mode control variable which requested a simple single command such as renaming or deleting a data set.

3. The control variable reverts to command mode when data access has been terminated. For example,

```
CTL1←RESULTS
CTL1←⍳0
CTL1
```
```
0
```

At this point *CTL1* reverts to command mode from data transfer mode.

Normally the user terminates data reading or writing by assigning the empty vector to the control variable. TSIO can also terminate data reading. If a data set is being read sequentially, TSIO terminates the reading after the last record on the data set is read. A subsequent use of the control variable produces an empty vector. A further *use* of the control variable, after TSIO sets it to the empty vector, results in a numeric response code. A response code of 0 indicates a normal termination. A nonzero response code indicates an abnormal termination. For example,

```
⎕IO←1
A: ...
⍝ MORE RECORDS TO BE READ

   .

   .

   .

RESULT←CTL1
→(0≠ρ,RESULT)/A
⍝ READING TERMINATED
RESPONSE←CTL1
→(0=RESPONSE)/0
⍝ ABNORMAL READ TERMINATION

   .

   .

   .

ER∆MSG∆MATRIX[20|RESPONSE;]

   .

   .

   .
```

If a data set is written sequentially and an error occurs, TSIO terminates data transfer immediately and responds with a nonzero response code to the next use of the control variable. For example,

```
⎕IO←1

A:  .

    .

    .

  CTL1←RESULT
  RESPONSE←CTL1
  →A×ι0=RESPONSE
ᴀ ABNORMAL WRITE TERMINATION
  ERRMSGMATRIX[ 20|RESPONSE;]
    .

    .

    .
```

In this example a check on the response code is made after each record is written. This is not mandatory but ensures that the record was actually written. In both of the previous examples, the names *ERΔMSGΔMATRIX* and *ERRMSGMATRIX* represent character matrices whose rows are phrases matched against the numeric response codes. The numeric response codes and their meanings are described in Tables 5 and 6 in Sec. 9.2.5.

If the control variable involves a data transfer, its successful acceptance shifts the control variable to data transfer mode. On occasion, within a function due to an error the control variable may remain in the data transfer mode rather than changing into command mode. If that is the case, presenting the control variable a command character vector is interpreted as data rather than as a command. One way to ensure that this does not happen is to preface the sequence by *CTL1←' '*, which always returns *CTL1* to command mode.

9.2.3 The Data Variable and Direct-Accessed Data Sets

Occasions frequently arise in which accessing a data set in a sequential manner is highly inefficient. For example, suppose that only the next to last record of a data set is desired. Quite a few records would have to be read sequentially and discarded before the next to last was obtained. A better technique for such an occasion is one which allows direct access to the desired record. Direct access is possible via indexed reading and writing. With indexed reading and writing, the records of a data set are assumed to be numbered or indexed just as components of a vector are indexed in origin 0. Then reference is made to records by index numbers. Direct access permits nonsequential reading and writing of records.

Any data set, whether it is to be read sequentially or directly, must be created or extended in a sequential manner using the *SW* command. An additional requirement for data sets that will be accessed directly is that the records be unblocked and of a uniform length. Thus when the data set is created an additional attribute phrase is needed. This is *RECFM=F*.

The phrase *RECFM=x* defines the format of the data set. The use of this phrase permits records to be formatted as blocked or unblocked records, of fixed or variable length, and with or without appended length information. The format possibilities for the format phrase are

Value	Meaning
U	Undefined length, unblocked records
F	Fixed-length records with one per block
FB	Fixed-length blocked records
V	Variable-length unblocked records
VB	Variable-length blocked records

RECFM=U is the default provided by TSIO; thus it was not necessary to include this parameter in our discussion of sequentially accessed, unblocked, variable-length data sets in Sec. 9.2.2.

Creating a data set for direct access would require, then, a control variable of the form

'*SW DSN*= xxxxxxxx ,*DISP=NEW*,*RECFM=F*,*BLKSIZE*= n '

The length of each record would be that of the block size.

The main action commands *IR* and *IRW* are defined for use in the command mode portion of the control variable for established data sets.

Mnemonic	Meaning	Purpose
IRW	Indexed read or write	Commands reading or writing of records from an existing data set in an arbitrary indexed manner
IR	Indexed read	Commands only reading records from an existing data set in an arbitrary indexed manner

After the data set has been opened for indexed reading and/or writing (by using main action command *IR* or *IRW*), an additional item of information is needed, namely, what record is involved. This information is assigned to the control variable in data transfer mode after an indexing main action command. It is a two-component numeric vector: The first component defines whether the indexed operation is to be a read, 0, or a write, 1. The second component is the index number of the desired record. The records within a data set are numbered from 0.

Since the use of the control variable is prescribed in both command and data transfer modes for indexed data sets, a second shared variable is necessary for transmitting the data involved. This variable is called the *data variable*. Its name must begin with the characters *DAT*, and its suffix must match the suffix of its corresponding *CTL* control variable. For example, if *CTLXY* is the control variable name, the data variable must be named $DATXY$. For example, the sequence to read the fourth record of the data set called FCN is

```
CTL1←'IR DSN=FCNS'
     .
     .
     .
CTL1←0 3
     .
     .
     .
TEMP←DAT1
```

The following sequence of statements first opens a named data set, writes into it, and then reads back record number 2:

```
CTL1←''
CTL1←'SW DSN=INDSET,DISP=NEW,RECFM=F,BLKSIZE=550'
→(0≠CTL1)/ERR
CTL1←'FIRST RECORD'
CTL1←'SECOND RECORD'
CTL1←'THIRD RECORD'
CTL1←''
TSIO □SVO 'DAT1'
```
1
```
CTL1←'IR DSN=INDSET'
CTL1←0 2
DAT1
```
THIRD RECORD

Note that this sequence began with $CTL1←''$. A useful technique to assure that the control variable $CTL1$ is in command mode is to issue $CTL1←''$ immediately before specifying $CTL1$ with a command mode character vector. Also within the sequence note that the response to $TSIO \ □SVO \ 'DAT1'$ is 1. Any further querying of $DAT1$ would continue to return a 1. TSIO does not accept the sharing offer for $DAT1$ until it is needed.

Continuing the above sequence, suppose that the second record, which is the character vector $SECOND \ RECORD$, is to be rewritten as $RECORD \ TWO$. The sequence would continue

```
     .
     .
     .
CTL1←''
CTL1←'IRW DSN=INDSET'
CTL1
```
0
```
DAT1←'RECORD TWO'
CTL1←1 1
```

The first statement, *CTL1←' '* , is necessary in order to close the data set *INDSET* . It is not possible to have a data set open to several data movement commands simultaneously. Also in doing an indexed write, the data should be specified to *DAT1* before the write request is issued via *CTL1* . It is not necessary to place any control upon the shared variable *DAT1* since TSIO uses it in conjunction with *CTL1* , which has a complete interlock.

An indexed write enables one only to rewrite existing records. It cannot be used to append new records onto the data set. If such an attempt is made, error code 24, *FILE INDEX ERROR* , is given. For example, continuing the previous illustration,

```
     DAT1←'FOURTH'
     CTL1←1 4
     CTL1
24
```

9.2.4 *User Levels*

Any user on an APL.SV system does not have automatic access to TSIO. First, the user must be assigned a nonzero quota of shared variables. Second, he must be authorized to use TSIO. This assignment of a shared variable quota and authorization to access TSIO is installation-managed. When the installation authorizes a user to access TSIO, he is given a *user level*. The user level discriminates as to what the TSIO user may or may not do. The following table defines the major discriminant levels:

Discriminant	Code	Meaning
SPACE	8	Permits a user to create new direct access data sets
DEVICE	4	Permits allocation of specific physical devices via *UNIT* and *VOLUME*
ACCESS	2	Permits indexed or sequential reading of other TSIO user's data sets
SYSTEM	1	Permits use of four additional main action commands and access to any data set

Associated with each discriminant level is a code number. Each user's discriminant level is specified by a numeric value. Each user's access is further qualified by combining these four code numbers. Thus the user level is given as an integer between 0 and 15, which is constructed by summing the corresponding code numbers of the desired discriminants. For example, a common user level is 10. This means that the user has been assigned the *SPACE* and *ACCESS* discriminants. A level 10 user can both create new data sets on the storage device assigned to hold TSIO data sets and read or write other TSIO users' data sets, given proper knowledge of them. He can use all six of the main action commands described in the previous section.

If the user's discriminant level includes *SYSTEM*, that is, code 1, he has the use of four additional main action commands, *CATALOG*, *UNCATALOG*, *READVTOC*, and *MSG*.

The *CATALOG* main action command allows the issuer to relate a data set name with a direct access volume. This association established by the *CATALOG* command is placed into the system catalog. Thereafter any further references to that data set can be by data set name only. For example, the data set *MYDATA* can be associated with the direct access volume named *ABC*555 on the 3330 as follows:

    CTL1←'*CATALOG DSN=MYDATA*,*VOL=ABC*555,*UNIT*=3330'

The *UNCATALOG* main action command removes the name, volume, and unit correspondence from the system catalog. For example, the opposite of the above control variable is

    CTL1←'*UNCATALOG DSN=MYDATA*'

The *READVTOC* main action command enables its user to get a listing of the data set names on a particular direct access volume. Thus

    CTL1←'*READVTOC VOL=ABC*555,*CODE=C*'

Finally, the *MSG* main action command enables its user to send a message to the OS/VS operator's console. For example,

    CTL1←'*MSG PLEASE MOUNT TAPE LABELED APL*; *ACKNOWLEDGE*'

The next reference to *CTL1* contains the operator's reply. Note that the variable *CTL1* remains unusable until the operator replies.

Further details as to the meanings of the user levels is found in the APL.SV TSIO reference manual.

9.2.5 Other Features of the TSIO Processor and Summary Tables

The TSIO processor can be used for other activities such as reading or writing on a magnetic tape or printing on a high-speed printer. These activities require use of some additional knowledge of and communication with the host operating system. Such activities should also involve the system operator since direct control of an output device like the printer or tape drive may not be desirable without the installation's knowledge. In any case, the effective use of TSIO for such activities requires that the user be familiar with the terminology and conventions of the host system.

Other parameters are introduced in TSIO in order to achieve this communication with the underlying host system. These are described below.

CODE defines the nature of the transformation that the data representation must undergo in moving between an APL workspace and the operating system environment.

LRECL defines the record size for fixed-length records or the maximum size for variable-length records.

SPACE defines the amount of physical storage space reserved for a data set.

VOLUME defines the name of the associated direct access device.

UNIT defines the specific device unit address or device type. Also there are the more specialized parameters *EXPDT*, *KEYLEN*, *DEN*, *LABEL*, and *TRTCH*.

EXPDT defines expiration data before which an associated data set cannot be deleted or overwritten without operator intervention.

KEYLEN defines the length in bytes of keys used in a data set with keyed records.

DEN defines the track width and recording density of tape.

LABEL defines the nature of the tape label.

TRTCH defines the nature of parity checking and data conversion.

These last three parameters apply specifically to magnetic tape. For example, a control variable to read from a magnetic tape with a standard label might be

```
CTLTAPE←'SR DSN=TAPEDATA,CODE=C,UNIT=2400,VOLUME=XYZ123''
```

Illustration 9.6   *Reading Records from a Tape*

The function *READ△TAPE* is a prompting function which will read a designated data set from a previously written magnetic tape.

```
     ∇ READ△TAPE;D;L;U;V;C;T;S;MSG;CTL
[1]    ⎕←'DATASETNAME='
[2]    D←12↓⎕
[3]    ⎕←'UNIT='
[4]    U←5↓⎕
[5]    ⎕←'VOLUME='
[6]    V←7↓⎕
[7]    ⎕←'SEQUENCE NUMBER='
[8]    L←16↓⎕
[9]    ⎕←'CODE='
[10]   C←5↓⎕
[11]   T←370 ⎕SVO 'CTL'
[12]   T← 1 1 1 1 ⎕SVC 'CTL'
[13]   T←⎕DL 4
[14]   (S←2≠⎕SVO 'CTL')/'TSIO NOT READY'
[15]   →S/0
[16]   T←'SR DSN=',D,',UNIT=',U,',VOL=',V
[17]   CTL←T,',LABEL=(',L,',SL),CODE=',C
[18]   →(0≠MSG←CTL)/ERROR
[19]   →(0=ρ⎕←CTL)/DONE
[20]   →‾1+⎕LC
[21] ERROR:'***ERROR CODE ',(⍕MSG),'***'
[22] DONE:T←⎕SVR 'CTL'
     ∇
```

The function prompts for *DSN*, *UNIT*, *CODE*, and finally the data set sequence number used in the *LABEL* parameter. From this information the control character vector in line 17 is built. The *UNIT* parameter defines the device type, for example, 2400. The *VOLUME* parameter defines the name assigned to the storage device. The

LABEL parameter defines the sequence number of the desired data set on the tape and also the nature of labels on the tape. The execution of line 17 results in a message being sent to the computer system's operator terminal. The message requests that the operator mount the proper tape on the appropriate tape drive. After that has been accomplished, the appropriate data set is read. Line 19 results in its display. A sample execution could look like this:

```
     READΔTAPE
DATASETNAME=DSN2
UNIT=2400
VOLUME=APLTAP
SEQUENCE NUMBER=2
CODE=E
THIS IS DATA SET 2 FROM THE TAPE. THIS DATA SET IS CHARACTER DATA.
```

Illustration 9.7   Removal of Undesired Data Sets

Often in developmental work, data sets become established on a file. These data sets continue to exist on a physical storage device once written there until their creator explicitly deletes them. The following function performs such an explicit deletion:

```
     ∇ DELETE Y;T
[1]    TSIO □SVO 'CTLDS'
[2]    CTLDS← 'DELETE DSN=',Y
[3]    'DATA SET ',Y,((CTLDS≠0)/' NOT'),' DELETED'
[4]    T←□SVR 'CTLDS'
     ∇
```

Tables 1–4 summarize the TSIO main action commands and the parameters. They are included here as an overview of the controls available to users of the TSIO processor. Tables 5 and 6 define the possible error responses.

Table 1 TSIO Command Forms

Parameter Usage	Meaning	Comments
[$BLKSIZE$=block size]	Number of bytes in the block	Required with $DISP=NEW$ or $LABEL=NL$ or BLP
[$CODE=$ $\begin{Bmatrix} A \\ B \\ C \\ E \\ F \\ I \end{Bmatrix}$] APL – APL (default) APL – Boolean APL – Character APL – EBCDIC APL – Floating Point APL – Integer	Data transformation	Required when reading non-APL data sets
[$DEN=$ $\begin{Bmatrix} 0 \\ 1 \\ 2 \\ 3 \end{Bmatrix}$] 7 track, 200 bpi 7 track, 556 bpi 7 or 9 track, 800 bpi 9 track, 1600 bpi	Recording density	Used only with $UNIT=$ tape and $DISP=NEW$
[$DISP=($ $\begin{Bmatrix} NEW \\ OLD \\ MOD \\ SHR \end{Bmatrix}$ [, $\begin{Bmatrix} LEAVE \\ REREAD \end{Bmatrix}$])]	Positions device with respect to data set and defines nature of data set	See Table 2 for defaults
$\begin{Bmatrix} DSN \\ DSNAME \end{Bmatrix}$ = [user no.] $\begin{Bmatrix} dsname \\ dsname\ (member) \end{Bmatrix}$	Data set name	Required except for $READVTOC$
[$EXPDT$=yyddd]	Expiration date	Only with $SW\ DISP=NEW$
[$KEYLEN$=keylength]	Access key	Only with $DISP=OLD$ or SHR and $UNIT=$ direct access
[$LABEL=($ data set seq no.[, $\begin{Bmatrix} BLP \\ NL \\ SL \end{Bmatrix}$])]	Label on tape	Only with $UNIT=$ tape
[$LRECL$=record size]	Number of bytes on each record	With $RECFM=FB$ and $DISP=NEW$ or $LABEL=BLP$ or NL
[$NEWNAME$=[user no.] $\begin{Bmatrix} dsname \\ dsname\ (member) \end{Bmatrix}$]	New data set name	With $RENAME$ command
[$RECFM=$ $\begin{Bmatrix} U \\ \begin{Bmatrix} F \\ V \end{Bmatrix}[B] \begin{bmatrix} A \\ M \end{bmatrix} \end{Bmatrix}$]	Record format	Only with $DISP=NEW$ or $LABEL=BLP$ or NL
[$SPACE$=(blocklength, (primary[,secondary[,directory]]))]	Amount of space allocated for data set	Default (1061,(120,11))
[$TRTCH=$ $\begin{Bmatrix} C \\ E \\ T \\ ET \end{Bmatrix}$]	Parity check, data conversion feature, and EBCDIC-BCD translation for tape	Seven-track tape only, normally not required
[$UNIT=$ $\begin{Bmatrix} device\ type \\ group\ name \\ unit\ address \end{Bmatrix}$]	Type of storage device	
[$\begin{Bmatrix} VOL \\ VOLUME \end{Bmatrix}$ = [$SER=$]volume serial]	Identification of disk pack or tape	Use prevents cataloging a non-TSIO data set

Legend: NL: No Label; SL: Standard Label; BLP: Bypass Label Processing

     [ ]   indicates an optional phrase

     { }   indicate alternative values

Table 2
Data Set Operations, Parameter Usage, and Default Values

	BLKSIZE (1),	CODE	DISP (2),	DSN	LRECL (1),	NEWNAME	RECFM (1),	SPACE (2)
Range of Values	≤Unit Size (3)	A B C E F I	NEW OLD MOD SHR		≤Unit Size (3)		F FB U V VB (4)	
DELETE	O		C T OLD	R		.	O	
IR	C	O T A	O T SHR	R	C		C	
IRW	C	O T A	O T OLD	R	C		C	
RENAME			C T OLD	R		R		
SR	O L (5)	O T A	O T SHR	R	O L		O L	
SW New	R	O T A	R	R	R for blocked data		O T U	O T (6)
Not new	C L	O T A	O T OLD	R	C L		C L	

Legend

Use

C   With caution
E   Error
O   Optional
R   Required
Blank   Ignored

Default

T   From TSIO (parameter values shown in APL font)
L   From label

Operations

DELETE   Expunge the data set
IR   Read with index
IRW   Read and write with index
RENAME   Change the data set name
SR   Read sequentially
SW   Write sequentially

Notes

1. See Table 3.
2. Parameter value may be compound.
3. Upper limit is 32760.
4. *A* or *M* appended to any *RECFM* value treats the first character of a record as a control character.
5. *BLKSIZE* is required for data sets that do not have standard labels.
6. (1061,(120,11,15)) default.

Table 3 Parameters Related to Format

RECFM	Meaning and Usage	LRECL	BLKSIZE
F	Fixed-length records, one per block. Structural data carried in label. Best format for creating indexed data sets. For any *CODE* other than *A*, the data must exactly fit the record length.	Not required	Unit size
FB	As for *F* except that records are blocked. Not suitable for indexing since blocks may be incomplete.	Required ≤*BLKSIZE*	≤ Unit size Multiple of *LRECL*
V	Variable-length unblocked records. First 4 bytes carry block length and next 4 carry record length.	Not required	Sets upper limit; must be ≤Unit size
VB	As for *V* except records are blocked and each record is prefaced by 4-byte length information.	Required Estimated average size	Sets upper limit; must be ≤Unit size
U	Undefined length, unblocked records. Can be used to read data with any format.	Not required	Sets upper limit; must be ≤Unit size

Table 4 Main Action Commands

Main Action Command	Meaning
DELETE	Expunge the data set
IR	Read with index
IRW	Read and write with index
RENAME	Change the data set name
SR	Read sequentially
SW	Write sequentially
CATALOG	Places a data set name and its location onto the system catalog
UNCATALOG	Removes a data set name from the system catalog
READVTOC	Read the table of contents of a specific direct access volume
MSG	Send message to the OS/VS console

Table 5
Command Mode Error Responses

Response Code	Meaning
0	Successful completion.
1,N	Parse of the command failed. The second element, N, numbers the point of failure in the command.
2,N	Command requires a different user authorization. N numbers the point of difficulty.
3	*DSN* parameter is missing.
4	*BLKSIZE* parameter is missing or too large.
5	*LRECL* error.
6	*DISP* error.
7	*RECFM*≠*F* where it was required to be *F*.
8	*UNIT* error.
9	*VOLUME* parameter needed.
10	*NEWNAME* missing where required.
11	Duplicate data set name (i.e., *DISP=NEW* and the name was previously used).
12	Data set name not found for *DISP≠NEW*.
13	Member of a partitioned data set, PDS,* not found.
14	System's I/O buffers full; try later.
15	Data set in use with *DISP≠SHR*.
16	Volume full.
17	PDS* directory is full.
18	Volume not available (not allocated or mounted).
19	Name already cataloged (for *DISP=NEW*) or a name conflict exists.
20	Control variable is in use

*See *APL Shared Variables Users Guide.*

Table 6
Data Transfer Mode Error Responses

Response Code	Meaning
0	Successful transmission
21	Data type not appropriate to *CODE* value
22	Data length error
23	Data rank error (*CODE*≠*A* and data not a vector)
24	File index error
25	*CTL* domain error because (ρCTL)≠2 or the first component was not 0 or 1
26	*DAT* variable required
27	Variable too large for the system's shared variable storage
28	Physical I/O error occurred in data transfer
29	Data set full
30,N	System error, $N\in\iota 8$; N numbers the type of system failure

9.2.6 A Comprehensive Illustration

The set of functions described in this section form the basis for the writing and reading of functions from a data set onto an auxiliary storage device. Users of these functions merely issue the following statements

```
CREATE 'FNSFILE'
PUT 'FN1 FN3 FN4' ON 'FNSFILE'
GET ' FN3 FN1' FROM 'FNSFILE'
```

in order to move functions to or from a data set.

The *CREATE* function is issued once to establish a new data set with the name *FNSFILE*. Thereafter the statement *PUT 'FN1 FN3 FN4' ON 'FNSFILE'* results in the placement of the named functions *FN1 FN3 FN4* onto the data set *FNSFILE*. The *PUT* function responds with an acknowledgment of the successful or unsuccessful placement. After they are placed there, they are erased from the workspace. The actual work is done by the *ON* function. The *ON* function also builds a catalog of the functions placed on the data set. The name of the catalog is the name of the data set with *CAT* suffixed to it. In this catalog the names of the functions are kept as base-37 numbers. As it is now constructed, only function names made from the plain alphabetics and integers are converted properly. Also no test was included to handle names of greater than 10 characters. Each catalog entry consists of the number representation of the name and a chain value. Since the block size is fixed at 900, some functions when converted to their character form may not fit. In such a case the chain entry is nonzero and indicates which additional record must be fetched from the data set to get the rest of the function. This portion has not been implemented in the *ON* function. The *ON* function calls upon several auxiliary functions: *OFFER*, *COMPRESS*, *CONVERT*, and *RETRACT*. The *OFFER* function establishes a shared variable with TSIO. The *COMPRESS* function takes the left argument and removes superfluous blanks within the character string of function names. The *CONVERT* function establishes the canonical representation of a function. *RETRACT* breaks sharing with TSIO.

The *GET* and *FROM* functions are the opposites of the *PUT* and *ON* functions. The *GET* function acknowledges the successful or unsuccessful fetching of a set of functions from an auxiliary storage device. The actual work of fetching the set of functions is done by the *FROM* function. It searches the function catalog for the requested names, does an indexed read of the requested data set, and finally establishes the records read as true functions.

The *DELETE* function is a simple form of the function of Illustration 9.7. It is present to remind the user of the potential for pollution of the storage device by unwanted data sets. These data sets will remain until their creator deletes them.

Finally, two global variables are created, *ERRFLAG* and *RECNO*. *ERRFLAG* has a binary value indicating success or failure of the *ON* or *FROM* functions. It is used by the *PUT* and *GET* functions, respectively. *RECNO* is the running count of the number of records on the data set.

What follows is a sample terminal session followed by the set of defined functions.

```
    )FNS
COMPRESS CONVERT CREATE DELETE FROM FTOC GET NONCE OFFER
ON PUT RETRACT TEST1 TEST2

    ∇ Z←FTOC X
[1]    Z←(X-32)×5÷9
    ∇

    ∇ TEST1
[1]   ⍝ THIS IS A NEW FNS
[2]   ⍝ A TEST CASE
    ∇

    ∇ TEST2
[1]    QQ←90
[2]   ⍝ ABSOLUTE NONSENSE
    ∇

    CREATE 'FNSFILE'

    PUT 'FTOC' ON 'FNSFILE'
RECORDS WRITTEN ON FNSFILE

    )FNS
COMPRESS CONVERT CREATE DELETE FROM GET NONCE OFFER ON
PUT RETRACT TEST1 TEST2

    PUT 'TEST1 TEST2' ON 'FNSFILE'
RECORDS WRITTEN ON FNSFILE
```

```
      )FNS
COMPRESS CONVERT CREATE DELETE FROM GET NONCE OFFER ON
PUT PUTF RETRACT
      )VARS
CHAIN   CT    CTLFNS    DATFNS    ERRFLAG FNSFILECAT    NAMETABLE
RECNO   TSIO   Z
      FNSFILECAT
  331856    0
37763264    0
37763265    0

      )FNS T

      GET 'TEST1' FROM 'FNSFILE'
A RECORD READ FROM FNSFILE
      )FNS T
TEST1
      GET 'TEST3' FROM 'FNSFILE'
FCN TEST3 NOT FOUND ON FNSFILE
A RECORD NOT READ FROM FNSFILE

      PUT 'TEST1' ON 'FNSFILE'
RECORDS WRITTEN ON FNSFILE
      )FNS T

      GET 'TEST1 TEST2' FROM 'FNSFILE'
A RECORD READ FROM FNSFILE
      )FNS T
TEST1    TEST2


     ∇ Z←FNS ON DATASET;SIZE;⎕IO;T;J;N;D;S;ALF;CT;CHAIN
[1]    Z←DATASET
[2]    ALF←'ABCDEFGHIJKLMNOPQRSTUVWXYZ0123456789'
[3]    ⎕IO←1
[4]    ERRFLAG←0
[5]    OFFER 'CTLFNS'
[6]    CTLFNS←''
[7]    CTLFNS←'SW DSN=',DATASET,',DISP=MOD'
[8]    →OK1×⍳0∧.=J←CTLFNS
[9]    'CMD MODE ERR ',⍕J
[10]   →OUT
[11] OK1:S←FNS
[12]   S←COMPRESS S
[13]   CT←RECNO++/' '=S←S,' '
[14] A:N←(¯1+J←S⍳' ')↑S
[15]   S←J↓S
```

```
[16]    T←CONVERT N
[17]    SIZE←×/ρT
[18]    →BYPASS×ιSIZE≤1000
[19]    NONCE
[20]    →□LC+2
[21] BYPASS:CHAIN←0
[22]    CTLFNS←T
[23]    →OK2×ι0∧.=J←CTLFNS
[24]    'DATA TRANSFER ERR ',⍕J
[25]    →OUT
[26] OK2:D←37⊥ALFιN
[27]    ⍎DATASET,'CAT←',DATASET,'CAT,[1]D,CHAIN'
[28]    T←□EX N
[29]    →A×ιCT>RECNO←RECNO+1
[30]    CTLFNS←''
[31]    →OK3×ι0∧.=T←CTLFNS
[32]    'CLOSING ERR ',⍕T
[33] OUT:ERRFLAG←1
[34] OK3:RETRACT 'CTLFNS'
      ∇


     ∇ PUT X
[1]    (ERRFLAG/'NO '),'RECORDS WRITTEN ON ',X
     ∇


     ∇ Z←FCNS FROM DATASET;□IO;T;S;ALF;N;CT;CATN;CV;K
[1]    Z←DATASET
[2]    □IO←1
[3]    ALF←'ABCDEFGHIJKLMNOPQRSTUVWXYZ0123456789'
[4]    ERRFLAG←0
[5]    OFFER 'CTLFNS'
[6]    T←TSIO □SVO 'DATFNS'
[7]    CATN←DATASET,'CAT'
[8]    CTLFNS←''
[9]    CTLFNS←'IR DSN=',Z
[10]   →OK1×ι0∧.=T←CTLFNS
[11]   'CMD MODE ERR ',⍕T
[12]   →OUT
[13] OK1:S←FCNS
[14]   S←COMPRESS S
[15]   CT←+/' '=S←S,' '
[16] A:N←(¯1+J←Sι' ')↑S
[17]   S←J↓S
[18]   CV←⍎CATN,'[;1]'
[19]   K←CVι37⊥ALFιN
[20]   →(K≠1+ρCV)/OK2
```

```
[21]    'FCN ',N,' NOT FOUND ON ',Z
[22]    →OUT
[23] OK2:CTLFNS←0,K-1
[24]    →(0∧.=J←CTLFNS)ρOK3
[25]    'DATA TRANSFER ERR ',⍕J
[26]    →OUT
[27] OK3:T←DATFNS
[28]    →(0=≢CATN,'[K;2]')ρOK4
[29] ⍝FETCH AND CATENATE NEXT PART OF FCN
[30]    NONCE
[31]    →OUT
[32] OK4:J←⎕FX T
[33]    →OK5×⍳0≠0\0/J
[34] `'FCN: ',N,' NOTFIXED'
[35]    '   ERR IN ROW ',⍕J
[36]    →OUT
[37] OK5:→A×⍳0≠CT←CT-1
[38]    CTLFNS←''
[39]    →OK6×⍳0∧.=T←CTLFNS
[40]    'CLOSING ERR ',⍕T
[41] OUT:ERRFLAG←1
[42] OK6:RETRACT 'CTLFNS'
[43]    RETRACT 'DATFNS'
     ∇


     ∇ GET DATASET
[1]    'A RECORD ',((1=ERRFLAG)/'NOT '),'READ FROM ',DATASET
     ∇


     ∇ Z←COMPRESS S;A;B
[1]    A←S≠' '
[2]    B←(A∨(1↓A),0)/S
[3]    Z←(' '=1↑B)↓B
     ∇


     ∇ OFFER N;I;J
[1]    I←1
[2]  A:→A0×⍳2=370 ⎕SVO N
[3]    J←⎕DL 1
[4]    →A×⍳60>I←I+1
[5]    N,' OFFER NOT ACCEPTED'
[6]    RETRACT N
[7]    →
[8] A0:J← 1 1 1 1 ⎕SVC N
     ∇
```

```
      ∇   CREATE DATASET;□IO;T
[1]    □IO←1
[2]    OFFER 'CTLFNS'
[3]    ⍙DATASET,'CAT←0 2ρ1'
[4]    RECNO←0
[5]    T←TSIO □SVO 'DATFNS'
[6]    CTLFNS←'SW DSN=',DATASET,',BLKSIZE=900,RECFM=F,DISP=NEW'
[7]    →OK×ι0∧.=Z←CTLFNS
[8]    DATASET,' NOT OPENED ',⍕Z
[9]    →
[10] OK:CTLFNS←''
[11]   →0×ι0∧.=CTLFNS
[12]   DATASET,'NOT CLOSED ',⍕Z
[13]   RETRACT 'CTLFNS'
[14]   RETRACT 'DATFNS'
[15]   →
      ∇


      ∇ Z←CONVERT X;T
[1]    Z←□CR X
[2]    →ER×ι0∧.=ρZ
[3]    →0
[4]  ER:'FCN. ',X,' NOT CONVERTED'
[5]    RETRACT 'CTLFNS'
[6]    →
      ∇


      ∇ RETRACT N;J
[1]    J←□SVR N
      ∇


      ∇   DELETE DATASET;J
[1]    TSIO □SVO 'CTLFNS'
[2]    CTLFNS←'DELETE DSN=DATASET'
[3]    CTLFNS
[4]    □SVR 'CTLFNS'
      ∇
```

PROBLEMS

1. Consider the following sequences for users 1002 and 1003.
   (a) Fill in the blanks with the proper information in order that user 1003 might read from user 1002's data set *CRC*.

   USER 1002

   .

   .

   .

   CTL2←'SW DSN=CRC,DISP=NEW,BLKSIZE=600,VOLUME=555555'
   CTL2

   0

   CTL2← ...
   CTL2← ...

   .
   .   *USER* 1003
   .

   CTL2←''

                       CTL3←'SR DSN=_____,DISP=_____'

   (b) What user level must user 1002 be?

2. In the discussion on $\square EX$, it was observed that while $\square CR$ converted a defined function into a character matrix form in order to place it out on a data set, both its character matrix form and its executable form continue to exist in the workspace. The $\square EX$ was necessary to expunge both from the workspace. In the illustration of Sec. 9.2.6 the canonical representation of the function was not explicitly expunged. Why?

3. In the illustration of Sec. 9.2.6 there exists a defect in the *ON* function. Every time it is used it places the function out on the named data set. It does this regardless of the fact that the function may already reside on the data set. Modify the *ON* function to prevent writing duplicate functions on the data set.

4. In Problem 3, the modification of *ON* was stated, such that if a function to be placed on the file already existed, it would not be written on the file a second time. This is not satisfactory if the function on the file were to be modified and then returned to the file. Modify the *ON* function such that if a function in the argument of *ON* were already on the file, this file version would be replaced by the current workspace version.

5. To supplement the illustration of Sec. 9.2.6, write the functions to delete a named function from the data set. Design them so that to delete the function *FN3* from the data set *FNSFILE* the user would enter

   DELETE 'FN3' IN 'FNSFILE'

6. (a) In Illustration 9.6, what must the user level be for the issuer of the function in order for the function to be successively executed?
   (b) What must the minimum user level be for a user to use the functions of the illustration of Sec. 9.2.6?

7. Modify the function of Illustration 9.7 so that it can accept and delete a given set of data sets.

Section 9.3   SUMMARY

In Chapter 9 we have discussed the shared variable facility and the TSIO application built upon it. The shared variable system functions and TSIO facilities are summarized in the following tables.

SHARED VARIABLE SYSTEM FUNCTIONS

Function	Syntax	General Description	Left Argument	Right Argument	Response
Share Offer	I $\Box SVO$ C	**Offers to share or accepts a previous offer to share**	Numeric scalar or vector identifying the processors with whom sharing is being established. Zero means a general offer. Rank: $1 \geq \rho\rho I$ Domain: $I \in {}^{-}1 + \iota 2\star 31$ Length: $(\times/\rho I) \in 1, {}^{-}1 \downarrow \rho C$	Character scalar, vector or matrix containing the names (and surrogates) of the shared variables. Each row of a matrix must represent a name or pair of names. Rank: $2 \geq \rho\rho C$	The degree of coupling for each variable. 0 –no offer made 1 –offer made 2 –offer accepted Shape of result: $\times/ {}^{-}1 \downarrow \rho C$
Share Couple Query	$\Box SVO$ C	**Reports on the current degree of coupling on the shared variables**	–	Character scalar, vector or matrix containing the names (and surrogates) of the shared variables. Rank: $2 \geq \rho\rho C$	The degree of coupling for each variable. 0 –no offer made 1 –offer made 2 –offer accepted Shape of result: $\times/ {}^{-}1 \uparrow \rho C$
Share Query	$\Box SVQ$ V	**Reports the processor numbers with outstanding offers to the inquirer, or reports the variable names which a specific processor is offering to the inquirer.**	–	An empty vector or numeric scalar or one component vector. Rank: $1 \geq \rho\rho V$ Domain: $V \in {}^{-}1 + \iota 2\star 31$, Length: $1 \geq \rho, V$	For $0 = \rho V$: A vector of processors with outstanding offers to the issuer. For $1 = \times/\rho V$: A character matrix of names offered by processor V, but not yet accepted.
Share Retract	$\Box SVR$ C	**Retracts sharing of the named variables**	–	Character scalar, vector or matrix containing the names (and surrogates) of the shared variables. Rank: $2 \geq \rho\rho C$	The degree of coupling of each variable as it existed before retraction. Shape of result: $\times/ {}^{-}1 \downarrow \rho C$

SHARED VARIABLE SYSTEM FUNCTIONS (Cont'd.)

Function	Syntax	General Description	Left Argument	Right Argument	Response
Share Control	$B \ \square SVC \ C$	Establishes a set and/or use control on the named shared variables	A Boolean scalar, 4 component vector, or 4 column matrix. It contains the access control. 0: no control 1: control First two elements relate to sets by the partners. Last two elements relate to use by the partners Rank: $2 \geq \rho \rho B$ Domain: $\wedge / B \in 0 \ 1$. Length: either $(1 \geq \rho \rho B) \wedge 1 = \times / \rho B$ or $(\rho B) = (^{-}1 \downarrow \rho C), 4$	Character scalar, vector or matrix containing the names (and surrogates) of the shared variables. Rank: $2 \geq \rho \rho C$	The access control vector as seen by the issuing processor for each shared variable. Shape of result: $(^{-}1 \downarrow \rho C), 4$
Share Control Query	$\square SVC \ C$	Reports the current access control vector for the shared variables.		Character scalar, vector or matrix containing the names (and surrogates) of the shared variables. Rank: $2 \geq \rho \rho C$	The access control vector as seen by the issuing processor for each shared variable. Shape of result: $(^{-}1 \downarrow \rho C), 4$

TSIO

Sequentially Accessed Data Sets

One shared variable called a control variable is required. It must begin with the characters CTL. This control variable defines the nature of the request and serves as the means for data transfer.

Control Variable in Command Mode

$CTL\leftarrow$ 'main action command $DSN=\cdots$,keyword parameters'

> •Main Action Commands
>
> | | | |
> |---|---|---|
> | SW | : | Sequential Write |
> | SR | : | Sequential Read |
> | $DELETE$ | : | Delete the Data Set |
> | $RENAME$ | : | Rename the Data Set |
>
> •$DSN=\cdots$: the data set name
>
> •Keyword Parameters
>
> | | | | | |
> |---|---|---|---|---|
> | $BLKSIZE=$ | block size | | $NEWNAME=$ | new name of data set |
> | $LRECL=$ | logical record | | $SPACE=$ | physical space |
> | $DISP=$ | disposition | | $EXPDT=$ | expiration date |
> | $CODE=$ | code translation | | $KEYLEN=$ | key length |
> | $RECFM=$ | record format | | $LABEL=$ | tape label type |
> | $UNIT=$ | physical unit | | $DEN=$ | tape density |
> | $VOLUME=$ | volume of storage | | $TRTCH=$ | parity check type |

Control Variable in Data Transfer Mode

$CTL\leftarrow$ data: a record transferred to a data set

$R\leftarrow CTL$: a record transferred from a data set:

Directly Accessed Data Sets

Two shared variables are required to access records in an indexed fashion from a data set. The first, the control variable, must begin with the characters CTL. The second, the data variable, must begin with DAT. Each pair must have the same suffix.

Control Variable in Command Mode

$CTL\leftarrow$ 'main action command $DSN=\cdots$,keyword parameters'

> •Main Action Commands
>
> | | | |
> |---|---|---|
> | IR | : | Indexed Read |
> | IRW | : | Indexed Read or Rewrite |
>
> •$DSN=\cdots$: the data set name

• Keyword Parameters

    Same as those for sequentially accessed data sets

Control Variable in Data Transfer Mode

$CTL \leftarrow V$ where

$$V[1] \quad \text{is} \quad \left\{ \begin{array}{l} 0 - \text{indexed read} \\ 1 - \text{indexed rewrite} \end{array} \right\}$$

$V[2]$ is I, the Ith record to be manipulated (in zero origin)

The Data Variable

$DAT \leftarrow$ data: the record to be rewritten directly into the data set.

$R \leftarrow DAT$: the record read directly from a data set.

APPENDICES

The first four appendices form a reference section describing briefly the APL symbol set, the error reports, and accessing an APL system. The appendices sketch rather than summarize APL functions and concepts. Full summaries of APL functions and concepts are given at the ends of the chapters in which they were introduced.

The last two appendices summarize two file system approaches which differ from that of the APL.SV TSIO processor (described in Section 9.2). Appendix E summarizes the Scientific Time Sharing Corporation APL*PLUS file subsystem. Appendix F summarizes the Burroughs Corporation APL/700 file system.

APPENDIX

A

THE APL SYMBOL SET

The digits are used to make numbers. The letters unless otherwise indicated are used to make names. All other symbols are named and briefly described in the order in which they appear on the keyboard. If a symbol represents both monadic and dyadic functions, the monadic name is listed first. References indicate text discussion and chapter summary of the function or symbol. The chapter summary page number is followed by *. Composite symbols and multiple symbols are explained separately. Every character on the keyboard whether defined or not can be used as character data. Additionally, the composite characters (formed by typing one character over another), the space, and the return can be used as character data. A few symbols are used only to form composite or multiple symbols; these are listed as being undefined symbols in the keyboard section and are described under "composite" or "multiple" symbols.

The keyboard is divided as follows:

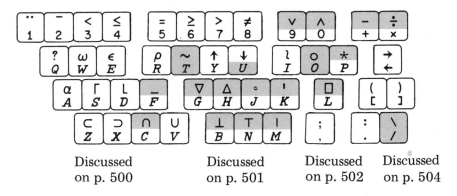

Discussed on p. 500   Discussed on p. 501   Discussed on p. 502   Discussed on p. 504

The shaded characters are used in the formation of composite symbols.

Keyboard Symbols

The part of the keyboard described on this page is

¨ 1	Undefined	‾ 2	Negative sign	< 3	—Less than	≤ 4	—Less than or equal
? Q	Roll—deal	ω W	Undefined	∈ E	—Membership, Exponential notation		
' α A	Undefined	⌈ S	Ceiling—maximum	⌊ D	Floor—minimum	_ F	Underscore
⊂ Z	Undefined	⊃ X	Undefined	∩ C	Undefined	∪ V	Undefined

Name	Syntax or Example	Meaning	See Pages
Negative sign	‾3	Sign for numbers less than zero	9
Less than	A<B	Relationship: 1 if true, 0 if false	125, 153*
Less than or equal	A≤B	Relationship: 1 if true, 0 if false	125, 153*
Roll	?B	Integer selected randomly from set 1 through B	114, 120*
Deal	A?B	A distinct integers selected randomly from set 1 through B	114, 120*
Membership	A∈B	1 if A is present in B, 0 if not	127, 154*
Exponential notation	3.4E8	"times 10 to the"	8
Ceiling	⌈B	The least integer greater than or equal to B.	124, 152*
Maximum	A⌈B	The greater value of A and B	143, 153*
Floor	⌊B	The greatest integer less than or equal to B.	124, 152*
Minimum	A⌊B	The lesser value of A and B	142, 153*
Underscore	_APL_	Creates alternate alphabet set	36

The part of the keyboard described on this page is

`=` `5` —Equal	`≥` `6` —Greater than or equal	`>` `7` —Greater than	`≠` `8` —Not equal
`ρ` `R` Shape—reshape	`~` `T` Not—	`↑` `Y` —Take	`↓` `U` —Drop
`∇` `G` Del	`∆` `H` Delta	`∘` `J` Undefined	`'` `K` Quote
`⊥` `B` —Decode	`⊤` `N` —Encode	`|` `M` Absolute value—residue	

Name	Syntax or Example	Meaning	See Pages
Equal	$A=B$	Relationship: 1 if true, 0 if false	125, 153*
Greater than or equal	$A \geq B$	Relationship: 1 if true, 0 if false	125, 154*
Greater than	$A > B$	Relationship: 1 if true, 0 if false	125, 153*
Not equal	$A \neq B$	Relationship: 1 if true, 0 if false	125, 154*
Shape	ρB	Number of components in each dimension of B	73, 120*
Reshape	$A \rho B$	Array of shape A with data B	74, 120*
Not	$\sim B$	Logical: (~ 0) is 1; (~ 1) is 0	128, 152*
Take	$A \uparrow B$	The first or last $|A$ components of B are selected	299, 357*
Drop	$A \downarrow B$	B with the first or last $|A$ components removed	305, 357*
Del	∇FN	Enter and end function definition mode	38, 64*
Delta	$\Delta F \leftarrow 78$	Additional naming symbol	36
Quote	$'HI'$	Used to form character input	9, 13
Decode	$A \perp B$	Value of a polynomial whose coefficients are B at A	198, 226*
Encode	$A \top B$	Base-A representation of the value B	205, 226*
Absolute value	$|B$	The magnitude of B	121, 152*
Residue	$A|B$	The A modulo value of B lying between A and 0	140, 153*

The part of the keyboard described on this page is

| ∨ 9 | —Or | ∧ 0 | —and |

| ι I | Index generator—index-of | | ○ O | π times—circular | | ⋆ P | Exponential—exponentiation |

| ▯ L | Quad |

| ; , | Delimiter Ravel—catenation |

Name	Syntax or Example	Meaning	See Pages
Or	$A \vee B$	Logic: 0 if A and B are 0; 1 otherwise	128, 154*
And	$A \wedge B$	Logic: 1 only if A and B are 1; 0 otherwise	128, 154*
Index generator	ιB	The integers from 1 through B	14, 35*
Index-of	$A \iota B$	The index in A of the first occurrence of component B. $1 + \rho A$ if B is not in A	101, 120*
π times	$\circ B$	$B \times \pi$	148, 152*
Circular	$A \circ B$	One of 15 functions —square roots, trigonometric, and hyperbolic; angles for the trigonometric functions in radians; A declares the function; B, the argument	149, 154*
Exponential	$\star B$	$e \star B$	138, 152*
Exponentiation	$A \star B$	A raised to the B power	136, 153*
Quad	$\square \leftarrow A$	Display A	243, 282*
	$A \leftarrow \square$	$\square$: is printed; keyboard unlocks for data input	250, 282*
		In editing: $[\square]$ —function display; $[N\square]$ —line display; $[\square N]$ —function display from specified line to the end of the function; $[N\square K]$ —line editing	41, 65*
	$\square CR$	Begins name of system variable or system function	360

Table (Cont'd.)

Name	Syntax or Example	Meaning	See Pages
Delimiter	*FN*;*I*;*J*	Separates local variables from syntax in function header	54, 65*
	A[*T*;*S*;*R*]	Separates indices for each dimension in an array	70, 90
	2;' *AND* ';3	Separates numeric and character data on a line for output	249
Ravel	,*B*	Structures *B* as a vector	105, 120*
Catenation	*A*,*B*.	The elements of *B* appended to *A*	27, 35*, 311, 358*

The part of the keyboard described on this page is

–	Negation—minus		÷	Reciprocal—divide
+	Monadic plus—plus		×	Signum—multiply

→	Branch
←	Specification

(	Left parenthesis		)	Right parenthesis
[	Left bracket		]	Right bracket

:	Label indicator		\	—Expansion
.	Decimal		/	—Compression

Name	Syntax or Example	Meaning	See Pages
Negation	$-B$	Changes sign of B	122, 152*
Minus (Subtract)	$A-B$	The difference of A and B	2, 35*
Monadic plus	$+B$	B without change	144, 152*
Plus (Add)	$A+B$	The sum of A and B	2, 35*
Reciprocal	$\div B$	1 divided by B	123, 152*
Divide	$A \div B$	The quotient of A divided by B	2, 35*
Signum	$\times B$	¯1, 0, 1 for B negative, zero, positive, respectively	129,152*
Multiply	$A \times B$	The product of A and B	2,35*
Branch	$\rightarrow B$	Branch to statement whose number is the value of B	227, 280*
Specification	$A \leftarrow B$	Assign value B to variable A	17
Left parenthesis	$(3+4) \div .3$	Enclose expression when necessary with matching right parenthesis	4
Right parenthesis	)$SAVE$	Begins system command	21, 361
Left bracket Right bracket	$A[B]$	Indexing; the components of A in positions B	70, 87, 120*
	fn $[I]$	Axis-specifier; following functions \ / , φ; I indicates the dimension of the array along which function is performed	161
	$[3 \square 9]$	Function editing; instructions for editing in brackets	41, 66*

Table (Cont'd.)

Name	Syntax or Example	Meaning	See Pages
Label indicator	ST:	The line label precedes the colon	234, 281*
Decimal	3.456	For expressing mixed decimal	10
Expansion	$A\backslash B$	Inserts zeros (or blanks) in B corresponding to zeros in A	294, 357*
Compression	A/B	Selects elements of B corresponding to ones in A	286, 357*

Composite Symbols

Composite symbols are formed by typing one symbol, backspacing, and typing another symbol over the first. The order of typing is immaterial.

Composite Symbol	Formed by	Name	Syntax or Example	Meaning	See Pages
⍱	∨ ~	Nor	$A⍱B$	Logic: 1 if both A and B are zero; otherwise 0	128, 154*
⍲	∧ ~	Nand	$A⍲B$	Logic: 0 if both A and B are 1; otherwise 1	128, 154*
⌹	⎕ ÷	Matrix inverse	⌹B	The inverse of B	214, 226*
⌹	⎕ ÷	Matrix divide	A⌹B	Solution to system of linear equations $Ax = B$, where B is array of coefficients and A is array of components	218, 226*
⍟	○ *	Logarithm	⍟B	Natural logarithm, base e of B, $\log_e B$	138, 152*
			A⍟B	Logarithm of B to base A	137, 153*
⌽	○ |	Reversal	⌽B	The elements of B in reverse order	318, 358*
⌽	○ |	Rotation	A⌽B	The elements of B rotated A positions in some direction	323, 358*
⊖	○ −	Reversal	⊖B	Reversal along first coordinate	318
⊖	○ −	Rotation	A⊖B	Rotation along first coordinate	324
⍋	∆ |	Grade up	⍋B	The indices of B which will arrange B in ascending order	109, 120*
⍒	∇ |	Grade down	⍒B	The indices of B which will arrange B in descending order	109, 120*
⍞	⎕ '	Quote-quad	$A←$⍞	Keyboard releases for character input	252, 282*

Table (Cont'd.)

Composite Symbol	Formed by	Name	Syntax or Example	Meaning	See Pages
⍞	⎕ '	Quote-quad	⍞←A	Bare output; return suppressed if followed by input quote-quad or another ⍞←A	254, 282*
⍎	⊥ ∘	Execute	⍎B	Removes quotes from character string B and attempts to execute resulting expression	351, 359*
⍕	⊤ ∘	Monadic format	⍕B	A character matrix representation of the output form of B	248, 285*
⍕	⊤ ∘	Dyadic format	A⍕B	B formatted to precision and field size specified by A	245, 285*
⍉	∘ \	Monadic transpose	⍉B	The dimensions of B in reverse order	332, 359*
⍉	∘ \	General transpose	A⍉B	The dimensions of B ordered by A	336, 359*
!	' .	Factorial	!B	The product of integers 1 through B	139, 152*
!	' .	Combinations	A!B	The number of combinations of B things taken A at a time	140, 153*
⍝	∩ ∘	Comment	⍝PAGE 3	Characters following symbol are not evaluated	242, 282*
⍢	∇ ~	Function protect	⍢FN	Function editing not permitted	273, 283*
I	⊥ ⊤	I-beam	I23	System dependent functions in APL/360; see System Variables (p. 451) for APL.SV system dependent functions	412

Table (Cont'd.)

Composite Symbol	Formed by	Name	Syntax or Example	Meaning	See Pages
$\underline{A}$	A _	Alternate alphabet	$\underline{FG}$←6	An alternate alphabet is formed by underscoring any alphabetic letter or $\triangle$	36
⌿	/ -	Reduction	+⌿B	Reduction along the first coordinate	162
⌿	/ -	Compression	A⌿B	Compression along the first coordinate	288
⍀	\ -	Scan	+⍀B	Scan along the first coordinate	172
⍀	\ -	Expansion	A⍀B	Expansion along the first coordinate	295
⍞	O U T	Quote-quad interrupt		Interrupts an input quote-quad; cannot be used as character data	253, 282*

Multiple Symbols

Multiple symbols are used for operators, control vectors, and distinguished names for system variables and system functions.

Multiple Symbol	Name	Meaning	See Pages
Operators			
fn $/B$	Reduction	Places scalar dyadic function fn between components of B and evaluates the resulting expression	157, 226*
fn $\backslash B$	Scan	Places scalar dyadic function fn between successively more consecutive components of B and evaluates resulting expression	170, 226*
$A \circ .$fn B	Outer product	Each element of A combined by scalar dyadic function fn with each element of B	176, 226*
A fn$_1 \cdot$ fn$_2 B$	Inner product	Element-by-element application of scalar dyadic function fn$_2$ to A and B, then scalar dyadic function fn$_1$ reduction is applied	188, 226*
Control Vectors			
$S\triangle FN$	Stop control	Sets stop control for defined function FN; function is suspended at lines indicated	270, 283*
$T\triangle FN$	Trace control	Sets trace control for defined function FN; value of lines indicated are printed as the function executes	261, 282*
System Variables			
$\Box CT$	Comparison tolerance	Sets relative comparison for $\lfloor \ \lceil \ < \ \le \ = \ \ge \ > \ \ne$	378, 437*
$\Box IO$	Index origin	Sets index origin for indexing; affects functions $? \ \iota \ \Psi \ \underline{\Delta} \ \Diamond$	375, 437*
$\Box LX$	Latent expression	Executes an expression when workspace is activated	390
$\Box PP$	Printing precision	Sets printing precision of numbers	373, 437*
$\Box PW$	Printing width	Sets width of printed line	375, 437*

Table (Cont'd.)

Multiple Symbol	Name	Meaning	See Pages
$\Box AV$	Atomic vector	All possible characters represented in System/370	403
$\Box RL$	Random link	Sets random seed for roll and deal	381, 437*
$\Box AI$ ɪ29 21 24 19	Account information	Gives account information: identification and computer time, connect time, and keying time accumulated during the session in milliseconds	394, 437*
$\Box LC$ ɪ27 26	Line counter	Gives line numbers of functions in execution, innermost first	400, 437*
$\Box TS$ ɪ25 20	Time stamp	Gives year, month, day, hour minute, second, millisecond	395, 437*
$\Box TT$ ɪ28	Terminal type	Gives terminal type: 0 = 1050; 1 = Selectric; 2 = PTTC/BCD	400, 437*
$\Box UL$ ɪ23	User load	Gives number of users on system	400, 437*
$\Box WA$ ɪ22	Working area	Gives number of bytes remaining in active workspace	398, 437*

General System Functions

$\Box CR$ B	Canonical Representation	Gives canonical representation of object B	422, 438*
$\Box FX$ B	Function Establishment	Establishes definition of function represented by B	423, 438*
$\Box EX$ B	Expunge	Erases objects named by rows of B	427, 438*
$\Box NL$ B	Name list	Identifies names representing (1) labels, (2) variables, and/or (3) functions, according to the value of B—1, 2, or 3	430, 438*
A $\Box NL$ B	Name list	As monadic $\Box NL$ but identifies only names beginning with the letters in A	430, 438*
$\Box NC$ B	Name classification	Gives usage 0, 1, 2, 3, 4 (none, label, variable, function, other) of name in each row of B	432, 438*
$\Box DL$ B	Delay	Requires B seconds to complete —a delay	433, 438*

Table (Cont'd.)

Multiple Symbol	Name	Meaning	See Pages
System Functions for Management of Sharing			
$A\ \square SVO\ B$	Share offer	Makes offer to processor A if name(s) B has not been previously offered	442, 492*
$\square SVO\ B$	Share couple query	Gives degree of coupling now in effect for name pair B	448, 492*
$A\ \square SVC\ B$	Share control	Sets access control	450, 493*
$\square SVC\ B$	Share control query	Gives existing access control	453, 493*
$\square SVR\ B$	Share retract	Ends sharing	455, 492*
$\square SVQ\ B$	Share query	Produces a matrix of names offered by the processor or the processor number with an offer outstanding to the issuer of $\square SVQ$	449, 492*

APPENDIX

B

ERROR REPORTS

These are the error reports that are given for APL expressions:

Name	Meaning
CHARACTER	Undefined overstrike character
DEFN	Improper attempt at function definition or editing
DOMAIN	Argument not in domain of function
IMPLICIT	Inappropriate value or no value to system variable
INDEX	Invalid index expression
INTERFACE QUOTA EXHAUSTED	Attempt to share more variables than the quota allotted
INTERRUPT	Function execution interrupted as result of *O* in response to input quote-quad or)*SAVE* in response to input quad
LENGTH	Arguments not conformable
NO SHARES	Shared variable facility is not available
RANK	Function not defined for arguments of this rank

Table (Cont'd.)

Name	Meaning
SI DAMAGE	Label lines of a suspended function are edited or function not at the top of *SI* list is edited, erased, or copied, or a function on *SI* list has its header edited
SYMBOL TABLE FULL	Too many names in use for the current symbol table capacity
SYNTAX	Improperly constructed expression
SYSTEM	Indeterminate problem internal to the supporting system
VALUE	Value not assigned to object
WS FULL	Workspace overloaded

Note: An error which occurs during the attempted execution of an expression (using the execute function ⍎) results in a report prefaced by the symbol ⍎.

APPENDIX

C ERROR REPORTS GIVEN
WITH SYSTEM COMMANDS

Report	Meaning	See Pages
For)*SAVE*:		
NOT SAVED, THIS WS IS wsid	The active workspace must have the same name as that of the library workspace; use)*WSID* to change the name of the active workspace	21, 367, 393
NOT SAVED, WS QUOTA USED UP	All workspaces assigned to this library have been named; drop unused workspaces or request more workspaces	21, 367, 393
NOT WITH OPEN DEFINITION	A workspace cannot be saved during function definition; close definition with ∇, and then save	21, 367, 393
IMPROPER LIBRARY REFERENCE	Workspaces in other users' private libraries cannot be saved	21, 367, 392
For Sign On:		
NUMBER IN USE	A terminal is already signed on with this number; check to make sure you entered your own number; contact operator for help; add password to your number to assure privacy	386, 393
NUMBER NOT IN SYSTEM	Number is not recognized; possibly because it has a password attached	386, 393
ALREADY SIGNED ON	The terminal is already signed on; sign off	386, 392
INCORRECT SIGN ON	Procedure followed is not correct; make sure a right parenthesis precedes sign-on number	386, 392

Table (Cont'd.)

Report	Meaning	See Pages
For)*ERASE*		
NOT ERASED: names	A function is pendent or function definition is open; clear state indicator or close function definition	365
For)*GROUP*:		
NOT GROUPED, NAME IN USE	The name selected for the group is already being used; change the name	363, 393
For)*COPY*,)*PCOPY*:		
NOT FOUND: names	The variables, functions, or groups named are not in the workspace. Check workspace contents or spelling	361
NOT COPIED: names	The response to)*PCOPY* when named items already appear in the workspace	361
WS FULL	There is not enough room in the active workspace for the objects requested; erase unneeded variables and functions and clear state indicator	361
For)*LOAD*:		
WS LOCKED	The workspace was saved with a password; use the password with the load command	368, 393
WS NOT FOUND	There is no workspace by this name in the library; check library contents; check spelling	368, 393
For)*OPR*,)*MSG*:		
MESSAGE LOST	Attention was signaled before message was sent; try again	388, 392
For)*DROP*:		
IMPROPER LIBRARY REFERENCE	Workspace in other users' private libraries cannot be dropped	369

APPENDIX

D

SIGNING ON AN IBM 2741 COMMUNICATIONS TERMINAL EQUIPPED WITH A DATA · PHONE ACOUSTIC COUPLER

The terminal needs continuous form paper, a ribbon, and an IBM #1167-987 or #1167-988* Selectric typeball.

1. *Set Switches on Terminal:*
   a. LCL/COM to COM
   b. ON/OFF to ON

2. *Call Up:*
   a. Take Data·Phone receiver off the cradle
   b. Press talk button
   c. Dial number provided
   d. At high-pitched steady tone, press the data button (if line is busy or there is no response, hang up and try again or try another number)
   e. Place receiver back on the cradle

3. *Sign-On:*

   When keyboard unlocks, type your sign-on number. It is) followed by some digits and password, if any

4. *APL Activities Can Begin*

5. *Sign-Off:*
   a. Type)*OFF* or other appropriate command (see Sec. 8.4)
   b. Turn terminal ON/OFF switch to OFF
   c. Press the talk button on the Data·Phone

---

*The last three digits are imprinted on the typing element.

APL * PLUS FILE SUBSYSTEM

An alternative to the TSIO file system described in Chapter 9 is that offered by Scientific Time Sharing Corporation as part of its APL*PLUS service.* The material which follows is a concise summary. It is based on the *APL*PLUS File Subsystem Instruction Manual*, copyright 1971 by the Scientific Time Sharing Corporation.†

The APL*PLUS system has in workspace 1 *FILES* a set of defined functions with mnemonic names to perform the necessary file manipulation functions. Underlying each such defined function is a primitive file function named $F\underline{F}$. The first component of its right argument indicates the file function. $F\underline{F}$ can be used in place of the more mnemonic defined file function, resulting in some saving of workspace storage and execution efficiency. However, use of $F\underline{F}$ does produce a definite loss in readability. In the following presentation only the mnemonic names are used. The concluding tabular summary matches the mnemonic name with its corresponding primitive file function $F\underline{F}$.

Introduction

A *file* is a named collection of data items. These data items are APL arrays. Each such item is independent of any other in content, form, shape, and rank. A file as an entity is completely separate from a workspace. Once created, a file continues to exist after its creator has signed off. It is independent of any *)LOAD* or *)SAVE* system commands. Furthermore, several files may be active at one time, and any individual file may be in simultaneous use by several users. Each data item, an APL array, in a file is referred to as a *file component*, and each component has a

---

unique *file component number*. All references to the file components are by
number. The file name along with the library number of the creator or common
library number go to make up the *file-id*. Before the files can be used a one-to-one
correspondence must be established between the file-id and a unique positive
integer. This integer is referred to as the *file number*. Once this correspondence
has been established, all further references to the file are by the unique file number.
A file which has such a file number associated with it is said to be *tied*. Up to 10
files may be tied at the same time. Furthermore, to protect a user from going into
a file creation loop, the system places upon any account number a total file space
limit, normally about 500 Kb.* Also, for user protection each established file has
a file size limitation of approximately 50,000 bytes assigned to it. In either case, no
physical storage is actually set aside.

File Manipulation

Before any activity can occur the file has to be created. The creation of a file
involves naming it and tying it to a unique file number. The defined function

'file-id [reservation]' *FCREATE* file-number

results in the creation of a file. The character string left argument contains the name
of the new file, and optionally the number of bytes of file storage to be reserved.
If no value is stated, the system assumes the default option and establishes a file size
limit of 50,000 bytes. The file-id may consist of just a name. In this case, the named
file is associated with the user's private library. However, the named file may also be
associated with a public library. Here, then, the file-id character string consists of the
public library number preceding the file-name. For example,

'46 *LESSON*1'

would place the file named *LESSON*1 in the public library 46 . The name given the
file should differ from any other name in that library.

The right argument is a positive integer not currently in use as a file number.
Thus,

'*DATA*1' *FCREATE* 4

creates a new file named *DATA*1 and exclusively ties it to the file number 4 . Hereafter any further reference to this file is via the file number 4 . Similarly,

'*DATA*2 20000' *FCREATE* 22

creates a new file named *DATA*2, ties it to the file number 22 , and establishes a file
size limit of 20,000 bytes for it.

A newly created file does not contain any components. Any file continues to
exist even though the creator signs off. To delete a file an explicit action is required.
Thus the function

'file-id' *FERASE* file-number

*1 Kb = 1024 bytes.

destroys all file components, unties the file number from the file name, deletes the file name, and frees up the space occupied by it. Before a file can be erased it must be tied exclusively. To erase the file, both the file-id and its tied file number must be given. Of course, each must represent the same file. Thus

> *'DATA2' FERASE* 22

erases the file *DATA2*.

Also if access to this file by the user account has a passnumber associated with it, this passnumber must be present. A more detailed discussion of the passnumber will come in the summary on file control. For most applications the use of a pass-number is not necessary. An important use of the passnumber is to give access to a file only to certain locked functions provided by the file designer. Hereafter mention of this optional field is omitted. The reader should consult the tabular summary to determine which file functions may use a passnumber.

After creation a file may be disassociated or *untied* from its file number without erasing it. Essentially this disassociation is equivalent to the closing of the file. An untied file cannot be accessed. The function which unties a file from its file number is

> *FUNTIE* file-numbers

The right argument may be a vector of file numbers. These file numbers should be distinct and represent tied functions. Thus

> *FUNTIE* 4

unties the file *DATA1* from the file number 4. Also, any sign-off, voluntary or otherwise, implicitly unties any file tied by that account number. Other system commands such as)*LOAD* do not affect the tie status.

Since a file may be untied arbitrarily after creation, one must be able to retie it again. The function

> 'file-id' *FTIE* file-number

ties the previously created file to a new file number. This new file number need not be the same one that had previously been associated with the file. In the following sequence, a file *DAT3* is created, untied, and retied to a new file number:

> *'DAT3' FCREATE* 33
> *FUNTIE* 33
> *'DAT3' FTIE* 66

The establishment of a file tie with *FTIE* produces an exclusive tie. Thus only the issuer can use that file. There also exists a file tie function which permits shared usage of the file:

> 'file-id' *FSTIE* file-number

The arguments are defined as they are for *FTIE*. The role that a shared file tie plays is covered in the section on file control.

Not only may a new file number be associated with a given file but so may a new name. The file rename function is

'file-id [reservation]' *FRENAME* file-number

Such renaming capability performs four useful functions. It can

1. Change the file-id associated with a file in the user's library.

2. Place the file into a public library.

3. Change the owner of a file by moving the file-id from another's library to the issuer's library.

4. Change the file size limit for a file.

In any case, the renaming of a file must occur when the file is exclusively tied. The renaming process does not create a copy of the file. It renames the existing file, which means that the former name disappears. Consider the following illustrations:

```
'DATA1' FTIE 10
'OLDDATA' FRENAME 10
FUNTIE 10
```

Here the file *DATA1* has been renamed *OLDDATA* in the user's library. The explicit use of *FTIE* and *FUNTIE* is to emphasize that renaming can be accomplished only while the file is exclusively tied. Now

```
'DATA2' FTIE 20
'30 DATA2' FRENAME 20
FUNTIE 20
```

This time the file *DATA2* is removed from the user's library and placed into public library 30. Finally,

```
'1009 DATA3' FTIE 30
'DATA3 30000' FRENAME 30
FUNTIE 30
```

Here the file *DATA3* is moved from library 1009 to the issuer's library. In the process the file size limit was set at 30,000 bytes.

Component Manipulation

The purpose of the creation and tying of a file is to establish an object in which the system can hold data. A file that has been created and tied does not contain any data in the form of file components. In general, then, functions which permit the creation, retrieval, replacement, and removal of file components are necessary.

New file components can be added to a file via the file function

data *FAPPEND* file-number

As a result of such a function the value of the left argument is appended to the end of the file whose file number is stated in the right argument.   The newly appended component is given the file component number one greater than the largest previous file component number. For example,

```
'DATA2' FTIE 5
(R←FCN) FAPPEND 5
```

results in the addition of the output of function *FCN* as the newest file component of the *DATA2* file. Thus the file-append function permits its users to enter sequentially into a file a set of file components. While the writing of file components is essentially a serial process, reading back existing file components may be in any order. The file function which permits this is

> *R←FREAD* file-number, component-number

The file-read function requires both the file number of the file and the specific file component number to be read. Only one file component may be read with each issuance of the file-read function. Since this function produces an explicit result, the data in that file component, it may be used within larger expressions. The sequence

```
'DATA1' FTIE 66
VR←,FREAD 66 2
```

results in the assignment of the name *VR* to the ravel of the second file component read from file *DATA1*. Reading a component merely brings a copy into the workspace; it does not destroy it in the file.

The replacement of an existing file component can be accomplished via

> data *FREPLACE* file-number,component-number

This function replaces the numbered file component of the numbered file by the value specified by the left argument. Only one component at a time can be replaced by the function. Continuing the previous illustration,

```
'DATA1' FTIE 66
VR←, FREAD 66 2
VR FREPLACE 66 2
FUNTIE 66
```

The ravel of the second file component is put back as the second file component.

Finally, the problem of removal of file components from a file must be considered. Should one wish to remove a specific component from within the file, a replacement by ⍳0 would by the most straightforward way. Thus

```
'DATA1' FTIE 66
(⍳0) FREPLACE 66 2
FUNTIE 66
```

In addition to this technique, the file function

> *FDROP* file-number,integer

permits the dropping of consecutive components from either the beginning or the end of a file. The integer which is the second element of the vector right argument may be positive, negative, or zero. It defines the number of consecutive components to be dropped from the file. If the integer is positive, the components are dropped from the beginning (the low-numbered components) of the file. If the integer is negative, the components are dropped from the end (high-numbered components) of the file. If the integer is zero, no components will be dropped. The integer must be less than or equal to the total number of components in the file. Dropping components from the file does not cause a renumbering of the remaining file components.

Suppose that file *DATA1* has 12 file components. Then

> *'DATA1' FTIE 77*
> *DROP 77 5*

results in the dropping of the first 5 file components from file *DATA1*. The remaining 7 file components are numbered 6, 7, 8, 9, 10, 11, and 12. On the other hand,

> *FDROP 77 ⁻5*

would have dropped the last five file components, leaving the numbered file components 1, 2, 3, 4, 5, 6, and 7. Finally,

> *'DATA1' FTIE 88*
> *FDROP 88 5*
> *FDROP 88 ⁻5*

produces a file *DATA1* with only two file components, numbered 6 and 7.

File Query

The procedures related to the establishment of a file and the manipulation of data within it have been presented. However, in order to use the file more conveniently certain types of inquiries are necessary. For example, answers to such questions as

What files are accessible to this account?

What files are tied?

What is the tie number?

What component numbers exist in the file?

What file size limit has been established for the file?

How much physical space does the file actually occupy?

are all at some point very desirable or necessary. There exists a set of file functions which addresses such questions as these. Paramount, of course, is determining whether the file system is up and available. The file function

> *R← FAVAIL*

returns a 1 if the file system is available and a 0 if it is not. Use of this function within an application package can avoid error messages when the file system is not yet up.

The file function

> *R←FLIB* library-number

returns the file names in the specified library to which the issuer of the functions has authorized access. The result is a character matrix where each row is essentially a file-id. The character matrix has 22 columns of which the first 10 columns contain, right-justified, the library number; column 11 is always blank; and the remaining columns, 12–22, contain the left-adjusted file name. Shorter library numbers and file names are filled out with leading and trailing blanks, respectively. For example, for user 1004

> *FLIB* 1004

could return the character matrix

> 1004 *DATA1*
> 1004 *DATA2*

If the current user issues a library request to a library in which he has no authorized files, a null matrix is returned, for example,

> *Q←FLIB* '77458'
> ⍴*Q*
0 22

Working with a file requires that it be tied. If one were to attempt to tie a file that was already tied, a *FILE TIED* error message would be given. To avoid that error message one can use the file function

> *R←FNAMES*

This function returns a character matrix where each row contains the file-id of the files which are currently tied. The row entries are in the order in which they were tied. Like the result returned for *FLIB*, the character matrix has 22 columns. The first 10 columns contain the right-justified library number, and the last 11 columns contain the left-justified file name. If no files are currently tied, then the result is an empty matrix, for example,

```
        Q←FNAMES
        ρQ
3 22
        Q
1004 DATA2
1004 DATA1
1009 SET9
```

Here the issuer of *FNAMES* has 3 tied files *DATA2*, *DATA1*, and *SET9* which were tied in that order. The first two are in user 1004's library, while the last is in user 1009's library.

Recall that tying a file requires the use of a unique number. If a tie were attempted with a number already in use as a file number, a *FILE TIE ERROR* message would occur. To avoid that message one can use the file function

```
        R←FNUMS
```

This function produces a numeric vector of file numbers used in tying files. The file numbers appear in the vector in the order in which they were used. Therefore they match the corresponding rows of the file-ids produced by *FNAMES*. Thus if

```
        'SET2' FCREATE 81
        'SET1' FCREATE 164
        '46 LESSON3' FCREATE 35
```

then

```
        FNUMS
81 164 35
```

and

```
        FNAMES
1002 SET2
1002 SET1
  46 LESSON3
```

where the account number of the issuer of the *FCREATE* is 1002. Observe that

```
        FUNTIE FNUMS
```

unties all three files *SET2*, *SET1*, and *LESSON3*. When a file was created, the creator was free to establish a file size limit. As components are appended and/or dropped, the actual amount of physical storage occupied fluctuates. Also, when file components are dropped from a file, the file components are not renumbered. Thus one must keep track of these changes, or one can resort to the file instructions

```
        R←FSIZE  file-number
        F←FLIM   file-number
```

FSIZE returns a four-component numeric vector. The first element is the file component number of the first component. The second element is an integer one greater than the last file component. The third element states the number of bytes of physical storage actually occupied. Finally, the fourth element is the maximum size established for the file. The function *FLIM* returns the first two elements returned by *FSIZE*.

After a creation these first values are 1 1. Then as components are appended to the file the second value increases. Until a drop function is used, the first component is 1. Consider the following sequence:

```
      'DATA1' FTIE 88
      FSIZE 88
1 11 5027 30000
      FLIM
1 11
      FDROP 88 4
      FLIM 88
5 11
      FDROP 88 ‾3
      FLIM 88
5 8
```

Should the file size limit previously established for the file at creation time be inadequate, the file function

> reservation *FRESIZE* file-number

can be used to change it. Continuing the previous sequence,

```
      FSIZE 88
5 8 3852 30000
      10000 FRESIZE 88
      FSIZE 88
5 8 3852 10000
```

Inquiries to this file had been with respect to the whole file. Information concerning the individual file components would be valuable also. The file function

> R←*FRDCI* file-number, component-number

could be useful. The result from this function is a three-component vector. The first element states the amount of physical space in bytes required by that file component. The second element is the account number of the last user who issued a *FAPPEND* or *FREPLACE* for a numbered component. The third element is the time in sixtieths of a second of the most recent *FAPPEND* or *FREPLACE*. The time is measured from the initial point of midnight 1 March 1960.

File Control

As long as a file is created and used solely by one account, the foregoing material is sufficient. Often, however, a file is established to be shared among several users. The sharing could be either serial or parallel in nature. With serial sharing, several users have access to a file—but only one at a time. With parallel sharing, several users have concurrent access to the same file. With either form of sharing further restrictions may be placed upon the individual users to permit them to use only a subset of the totality of file functions.

The determinations of whether a given user may access a given file and, if so, which functions he may use on the file are both kept within a table called an *access matrix*. An access matrix is associated with every file. At create time, the created file has associated with it an access matrix with a shape of 0 3.

The access matrix is numeric and contains three columns. The first column contains the account numbers which have been authorized to access the file. The second column contains an encoded number representing the nature of the access for the account number listed in that row. The third column contains the passnumber which that account must use with the various file functions.

The creator and owner of a file need never appear in the access matrix. He thereby has complete and unlimited access to the file. Conversely, no other user has any access because his account number does not appear in the access matrix. Thus at creation time only the creator has access to the file.

If several users are authorized access via the access matrix to the same file, serial access to the file is achieved via the *FTIE* function. This function ties the issuer exclusively to the file. Any attempt by another account to tie the same file results in a *FILE TIED* message.

Earlier, in the introduction of *FRENAME* an example was given using *FRENAME* to move a file from one library to another. To do this the original owner of the file had to agree to such renaming. In the example cited, the user renaming the file issued a *FTIE* function. This allowed him exclusive control over that file and thus the ability to rename it. Suppose that the original owner wishes to prevent such a transfer from occurring. He can forbid this as long as he stays tied exclusively to the file via a *FTIE*.

However, an owner of the file may still wish to share the file with others. To achieve concurrent sharing, the file must be tied to several users simultaneously. The file function

    'file-id' *FSTIE* file-number

accomplishes this. It establishes a file tie permitting shared use. The file may be share-tied only if it is not currently exclusive-tied by any user. If this is the case, a *FILE TIED* message occurs.

Each user who wishes to share the file must have issued an *FSTIE* function. Even if a file exists in a shared mode, there are times when a user wishes exclusive access to the file. Suppose that one user *MFG* wishes to change the sixth cost per unit component in his *PRICELIST* file. When he does this, he does not want another user to use the *PRICELIST* file. In this case the file function

    FHOLD file-numbers

can be used. This function places an interlock on each file mentioned by file number in the vector argument. This file-hold function does not allow any other sharing user to issue a hold to get exclusivity. Thus sharing users can establish exclusive locking situations among themselves by the proper use of *FHOLD* . The hold is honored only if the file or files are not currently held by any other user. The second issuer of *FHOLD* is *delayed* in execution until the first user has released his hold. Thus for

	User *MFG*		User *DISTRIB*
	.		.
	.		.
	.		.
[*N*]	*FHOLD* 95		.
	(proceed)	[*M*]	*FHOLD* 95
	.		.
	.		(this user is delayed)
	.		.
[*P*]	*FHOLD* ⍳0		.
	.		.
	.		.
	.		

user *DISTRIB*'s function becomes pendent at line [*M*] since user *MFG* issued a prior *FHOLD*. To release a hold on a file, the argument of *FHOLD* should be null, ⍳0. This occurred at line [*P*] above in user *MFG*'s function. At this point in time, user *DISTRIB*'s function resumes executing at line [*M*]. Thus, for example, the user *DISTRIB* to assure exclusive use of the file *PRICELIST* while he replaces the 6th component could use the following sequence:

```
User DISTRIB
'PRICELIST' FSTIE 123
        .
        .
        .
FHOLD 123
NEWCOST FREPLACE 123 6
FHOLD ⍳0
        .
        .
        .
```

When *FHOLD* is issued by, say, user *A* , any previous *FHOLD* issued by user *A* is nullified. Then user *A* is placed on a FIFO queue behind other users who are holding or waiting to hold one or more of the requested files. User *A*'s program is delayed until there is no hold on *any* of the files requested. When that is the case the interlocks requested by user *A* are set on the desired files and user *A*'s program resumes. Consider the following illustration:

User A	User B	User C
`'DATA1' FSTIE 45`	`'DATA1' FSTIE 45`	`'DATA1' FSTIE 45`
`'DATA2' FSTIE 67`	`'DATA2' FSTIE 67`	`'DATA2' FSTIE 67`
	.	.
`FHOLD 45`	.	.
.	.	.
.	`FHOLD 67`	.
.	.	.
	.	`FHOLD 67 45`
(function continues)	.	
.		(function delayed)
.	(function continues)	
.	.	.
.	.	.
`FHOLD ι0`	.	.
	`FHOLD ι0`	(function can now
		continue)

The release of a hold on a file is done explicitly by the `FHOLD ι0` function but also implicitly when the user signs off voluntarily or involuntarily. The release is also implicit when the user's function

1. Issues another `FHOLD`,

2. Becomes suspended, or

3. Successfully completes its execution.

One final note: `FHOLD` provides an interlocking mechanism on a file whose use is established by user conventions. This function does not prevent an `FREAD`, `FAPPEND`, or `FREPLACE` from occurring. If another user sharing a file should choose not to use the `FHOLD` function, he could proceed reading and writing indiscriminately.

Earlier the access matrix was introduced. Several details have yet to be examined. The access matrix for a given file is set by the left argument in the file function

data `FSTAC` file-number

This function makes a total replacement of the access matrix. The left argument must be a three-column integer matrix, where the first column contains the account number of the authorized users of this file, the second column contains an encoded number defining which of the file functions a user may use on the file, and the third column contains a passnumber which the user must use as part of the right argument for most of the file functions. This passnumber is usually zero, which means that no passnumber need be used in any of the file functions. Omitting the passnumber in the functions is equivalent to providing a passnumber of zero.

Suppose that user `1004` were an entry in the access matrix for the file *DATA* which has a file number `55`. The entry might be

> `1004 3 1492`

Then, to read file component `12` user `1004` issues

> `'DATA' FTIE 55 1492`
> `RESULT← FREAD 55 12 1492`

Here `1492` is the passnumber that user `1004` must use with most of the file functions. In fact, all file functions except

> *FHOLD*
> *FLIB*
> *FNAMES*
> *FNUMS*
> *FUNTIE*

must be used with a passnumber if a nonzero one appears in the third column of the user's entry row of the access matrix.

The second column of the access matrix permits a finer degree of restriction on a given file. While several users may have access to a file, they may not have access to all the file functions. The second column contains an integer which defines which file functions are permitted. The following table defines the correspondence between integers and the permitted file functions:

Integer Value	Permitted File Function
1	*FREAD,FLIM, FSIZE*
2	*FTIE*
4	*FERASE*
8	*FAPPEND*
16	*FREPLACE*
32	*FDROP*
64	*FHOLD*
128	*FRENAME*
256	*FRDAC, FSTAC*
512	*FRDCI*
1024	*FRESIZE*

The integer values are all powers of 2. Therefore the number which represents the authorization of a subset of the file functions is derived by summing the corresponding subset of integer values. For example, in the previous illustration the second column value of 3 (1 + 2) authorized user `1004` to use file functions *FREAD*, *FLIM*, *FSIZE*, and *FTIE*. For a file user to be able to *FTIE*, *FREAD*, *FAPPEND*, and *FREPLACE*, the encoded integer would be 27 (1 + 2 + 8 + 16). An encoded integer of 2047 permits all file functions to be applied to the file. While the *FSTIE* function does not appear in the table, its use does require a nonzero entry in column 2 of the access matrix. Also, *FCREATE* is not present since one cannot use the *FCREATE* function on a file that already exists.

The individual row entries cannot be replaced or inserted. The file function *FSTAC* replaces the whole matrix. Since each file has an access matrix, reading of the related access matrix would be very desirable. The file function

$F{\leftarrow}FRDAC$ file-number

returns the access matrix associated with the file number.

Summary

The 21 defined file functions just presented along with the access matrix comprise the APL*PLUS file subsystem. This set of defined file functions is found in the APL* PLUS library 1 under the name *FILES*. Each file function has a matching primitive file function whose mnemonic begins with *FF*. However, it is not necessary to *)COPY 1 FILES* to use the primitive file functions. While they have less mnemonic meaning, their use requires less storage and they perform more efficiently.

The APL*PLUS file subsystem provides another means of organizing, sharing, and controlling access to data. In so doing, this system provides a convenient way of overcoming workspace limitations. This is accomplished while keeping the user within an APL environment. APL*PLUS service does provide additional facilities for conversion between APL and non-APL files, but it requires the cooperation of the computer operations staff; it is not part of the APL*PLUS file subsystem. For example, APL*PLUS service provides a file-printing facility in *1 FILEPRINT*. This workspace contains APL functions for controlling page formats and for requesting printouts. For details on these facilities and others, consult the Scientific Time Sharing Corporation.

APL*PLUS File Subsystem Instruction Summary

Syntax	Meaning	Access Code Number
File manipulation		
'f-id [lim]' $\left\{ \begin{array}{l} FCREATE \\ F\underline{E}\ 1, \end{array} \right\}$ f-n	Create and tie a new file	—
'f-id' $\left\{ \begin{array}{l} FERASE \\ F\underline{E}\ 5, \end{array} \right\}$ f-n [,pn]	Erase a file	4
$\left\{ \begin{array}{l} FUNTIE \\ F\underline{E}\ 3, \end{array} \right\}$ f-n	Break the file tie association	—
'f-id' $\left\{ \begin{array}{l} FTIE \\ F\underline{E}\ 2, \end{array} \right\}$ f-n [,pn]	Tie a file to a file number for exclusive use	2
'f-id' $\left\{ \begin{array}{l} FSTIE \\ F\underline{E}\ 4, \end{array} \right\}$ f-n [,pn]	Tie a file to a file number for shared use	—
'f-id [lim]' $\left\{ \begin{array}{l} FRENAME \\ F\underline{E}\ 15, \end{array} \right\}$ f-n [,pn]	Change the file-id or file size limit on a file	128
Component manipulation		
data $\left\{ \begin{array}{l} FAPPEND \\ F\underline{E}\ 7, \end{array} \right\}$ f-n [,pn]	Add a new component to the end of a file	8
result ← $\left\{ \begin{array}{l} FREAD \\ F\underline{E}\ 6, \end{array} \right\}$ f-n, c-n [,pn]	Read a file component value	1
data $\left\{ \begin{array}{l} FREPLACE \\ F\underline{E}\ 8, \end{array} \right\}$ f-n, c-n [,pn]	Replace a numbered file component	16
$\left\{ \begin{array}{l} FDROP \\ F\underline{E}\ 13, \end{array} \right\}$ f-n, n [,pn]	Drop n consecutive file components from the beginning or end of a file	32
File query		
result ← $\left\{ \begin{array}{l} FAVAIL \\ F\underline{E}\ 25 \end{array} \right\}$	Determine if the file system is available	
result ← $\left\{ \begin{array}{l} FLIB \\ F\underline{E}\ 9 \end{array} \right\}$	State file names to which issuer has access in the specified library	—
result ← $\left\{ \begin{array}{l} FNAMES \\ F\underline{E}\ 19 \end{array} \right\}$	State the names of the currently tied files	—
result ← $\left\{ \begin{array}{l} FNUMS \\ F\underline{E}\ 18 \end{array} \right\}$	State the numbers of the currently tied files	—
result ← $\left\{ \begin{array}{l} FSIZE \\ 4 \uparrow F\underline{E}\ 10, \end{array} \right\}$ f-n [,pn]	Return first and last + 1 file component number, the space used, and the space reserved	1

APL*PLUS File Subsystem Instruction Summary   (Cont'd.)

Syntax	Meaning	Access Code Number
result ← $\left\{\begin{array}{l} FLIM \\ 2\uparrow F\underline{E}\ 10, \end{array}\right\}$ f-n [,pn]	Return first and last + 1 file component number	1
result ← $\left\{\begin{array}{l} FRDCI \\ 3\uparrow F\underline{E}\ 11, \end{array}\right\}$ f-n, c-n [,pn]	Provide the amount of space occupied, who filled it, and when	512
lim $\left\{\begin{array}{l} FRESIZE \\ F\underline{E}\ 24, \end{array}\right\}$ f-n	Change the file size limit established for the file	

File control

Syntax	Meaning	Access Code Number
$\left\{\begin{array}{l} FHOLD \\ F\underline{E}\ 14, \end{array}\right\}$ f-n	Release and set sharing interlock	64
data $\left\{\begin{array}{l} FSTAC \\ F\underline{E}\ 17, \end{array}\right\}$ f-n	Set the access matrix	256
result ← $\left\{\begin{array}{l} FRDAC \\ F\underline{E}\ 16, \end{array}\right\}$ f-n	Read the access matrix	256

f-id: [library number] file name   data: numeric data
lim: file space limit   n: integer value
f-n: file number   c-n: component number
pn: passnumber   [ ]: optional item

APPENDIX

F

APL/700 FILE SYSTEM

The APL/700 system is an APL system that the Burroughs Corporation developed for use on the B6700 and B7700 computers. Incorporated within it is a file system different from those described in Chapter 9 and Appendix E which enables the user to retain and access APL-created items outside the workspace.

The material which follows is a concise summary. It is based on the Burroughs Corporation's *APL/700 Users Reference Manual*, Document No. 5000813. Further details and information should be obtained from the Burroughs Corporation.*

Introduction

Each user account is assigned a quota of *files*. A file consists of a name and a set of numbered components. At any point in time each component is either null or contains an APL data item. These APL data items do not have to be related. Any given file may be simultaneously open to several users. A file becomes opened for an account when the first file primitive other than File Create, Rename, Destroy, or File Existence Test is issued to it. The file remains open until it is explicitly released or until the user signs off.

File Characteristics

The file name is the name by which all users of the file refer to the data in that file. In general a file name consists of

(account name) file name [password]

where both the proper name of the file and the optional password may consist of 1 to 12 alphameric characters with the first being an alphabetic. The account

---

*Burroughs Corporation, Computer Systems Group, Tredyffrin Plant, P. O. Box 203, Paoli, Pa. 19301.

name is a 1 to 6 alphameric name defining the owner of the file. Every file has one owner. Any other user of that file must include the owner's account name.

Any file is restricted to having a maximum of 1000 components. Furthermore, the system installation defines the maximum number of files any account may be allocated. It also sets the maximum number of bytes per file for that account. Then, too, the system installation also defines a maximum number of files that may be concurrently opened by any one user.

The actual members of a file are referred to as the *file components*. These file components are sequentially numbered. This numbering is origin-dependent. Each file component may contain any APL data item. What one component contains is independent in content, type, shape, and rank from what any other contains. In fact the existence of a file component does not imply that it contains anything. A file component may be *null*. Note that this is different from stating that a file component contains an empty vector. Any request for a null file component results in a *FILE VALUE ERROR* message.

The File System Primitives

The APL/700 system supplies a set of primitive file operators for file management. The symbol used for each primitive consists of the quad symbol, □, overstruck with another primitive function symbol. With one exception, System Query, the right argument to the primitive file operators is the file name. Some of the file operators return the file name if it is required. Such a requirement exists when the file operator is part of a simple compound expression. For example, this permits a sequence of file operations to be performed on the same line of a defined function. If the file name is not required, then the file primitive operator does not return it.

File Manipulation

The first act must be the creation of a file. The file primitive *Create File*

   ⍈ *F*

creates a file. *F* is the name assigned to the file. This name, of course, must not already exist. ⍈ *F* merely establishes the file name; it neither opens a file nor establishes any components for it. Thus

   ⍈ *'FILE1'*

establishes the file name, *FILE1*, whereas

   ⍈ *'FILE2[KY1]'*

establishes the file *FILE2* with the password *KY1*. To change the password on a file requires a new create stating both the old and new passwords. Thus

   ⍈*'FILENAME[OLDPASSWD/NEWPASSWD]'*

Therefore

   ⍈*'FILE2[KY1/KY2]'*

changes the password on *FILE2* from *KY1* to *KY2*. Also

    ⍈ *'FILE1 [/PW1]'*

assigns a password of *PW1* to a previously unlocked file. Finally,

    ⍈ *'FILE2 [KY2/]'*

deletes the password.

    Only the creator-owner of the file can change the password but only if the file is not held by another account. Besides changing the password on a file, renaming the file is useful.

    'NEWNAME' ⍈ *'OLDNAME'*

results in the file previously named *OLDNAME* being renamed *NEWNAME*. However, renaming the file can occur only if the file is inactive, that is, not open to any account. Renaming a file does not open it.

    The opposite of creation is destruction. The file primitive *Destroy File*

    ⍒ *F*

results in the destruction of the file named *F* provided it exists and is not held by any other user. It returns an explicit result of 1 if successful and 0 if not. One must use the password when calling for destruction. Thus

    ⍒ *'FILE1[PW1]'*

destroys the file named *FILE1* whose password was *PW1*. Only the creator and owner of a file may destroy it. That is, a file owned by one account cannot be destroyed by another.

    In addition to the implicit opening and closing of a file, the primitives *Open File* and *Close File*

    ⍐ *F* and ⍗ *F*

explicitly open and close the file *F*.

File Component Manipulation

File Component Write, Read, and Nullify

    Recall that file creation neither establishes any file components nor fills them with values. To do this, the three primitives File Write, File Read, and File Nullify are provided. The structure of the *File Component Write* is

    A ⊞*[K] F*

where *A* is the APL data item, *K* is the file component number, and *F* is the file name. *K* must either be an existing file component number or one greater than the largest previously written file component. When used monadically,

⊟[*K*] *F*

nullifies the *K*th component of file *F*. Here *K* must again be an existing file component number.

The structure of the file primitive *File Component Read* is

⊞[*K*] *F*

Here *K* must be an existing file component number. Also the component to be read must be nonnull; otherwise a *FILE VALUE ERROR* message occurs. In the following sequence three file components are established; the third one is read back, and the second one is nullified:

```
     ⬛ 'FILE1'
     (2 3⍴⍳6) ⊟[1] 'FILE1'
     (FN ←⎕CR'FCN') ⊟[2] 'FILE1'
     'THIRD RECORD' ⊟[3] 'FILE1'
     R←⊞[3] 'FILE1'
     R
THIRD RECORD
     ⊟[2] 'FILE1'
```

File Component Take and Drop

Instead of building up a set of file components sequentially, one could build up a set of null file components. This can be accomplished through the *File Component Take* function. The format for this function is

I ⬛ *F*

where *F* is the file name and *I* is an integer of magnitude ≤1000. The result of a File Component Take is a file *F* with *I* components. The File Component Take behaves like the Take function, ↑, in that if the magnitude of *I* exceeds the number of file components already on the file, a sufficient number of null components are appended to the file. The null components are appended before or after depending whether *I*<0 or *I*>0.

With *I*>0, File Component Take takes the first *I* components from the start of the file. With *I*<0, the *I* components come from the end of the file. However, those components *not* taken are destroyed. Thus

5 ⬛ 'FILE1'

results in a five-component file.

```
     ⬛ 'FILE3'
     6 ⬛ 'FILE3'
```

Here *FILE*3 consists of six null file components. Then

```
'FIRST'  ⊟[1] 'FILE3'
'2ND'    ⊟[2] 'FILE3'
'5 TH'   ⊟[5] 'FILE3'
'6TH '   ⊟[6] 'FILE3'
```

results in the file *FILE*3 having two null components and four nonnull components, but if

```
¯2⊟ 'FILE3'
```

then *FILE*3 now has only two file components.

```
        ⊟[1] 'FILE3'
5 TH
        ⊟[2] 'FILE3'
6TH
```

Finally, continuing the sequence,

```
¯6⊟ 'FILE3'
```

results in a six-component file where the first four components are null.

Complementary to the File Component Take is the *File Component Drop* primitive. Its format is

```
I ⊽ F
```

where *I* and *F* have the same meaning as in ⊟. The result of this function is that *I* file components are dropped from file *F*. The components dropped are destroyed. Should

```
6 ⊽ 'FILE3'
```

then

```
¯2⊽ 'FILE3'
```

produces a four-component file named *FILE*3. Finally, for both File Component Take and File Component Drop, the file name is returned when required.

File Component Compress and Expand

The *File Component Compress* and *Expand* primitives behave in an analogous fashion with the primitive functions of compression and expansion. The general format of these primitives is

```
B ⌿ F
B ⍀ F
```

where *F* is the file name and *B* is a Boolean vector. With File Component Compress the length of *B* must match the number of components of *F*. With File Component

Expand the number of 1s in B must match the number of file components in F. Wherever a 0 appears in B for expansion a null component is inserted into the file F. If *FILE4* had 4 nonzero file components, then

       1 0 1 0 ⍀ *'FILE4'*

compresses *FILE4* to a two-component file, the second and fourth file components being compressed out. Then

       1 0 1 0 ⍀ *'FILE4'*

expands *FILE4* into a four-component file where the second and fourth components are null components. For both File Component Compress and File Component Expand, the file name is returned when it is required.

File Component Reverse and Rotate

     Conceptually it is possible to consider a file as a vector of heterogeneous elements. In that sense it becomes possible to consider reversing or rotating the order of the file components in a given file, just as one can do with a vector within a workspace. The *File Component Reverse*,

       ⊖ F

and the *File Component Rotate*,

       I ⊖ F

permit this to be done on files. The File Component Reverse does a complete reversal of the file component order in a file. The File Component Rotate does a circular rotation among the file components of the file. The left argument, I, is an integer. A positive integer is essentially a left circular rotation. A negative integer is a right circular rotation. Thus let

        ⊟[1] *'FILE4'*
FIRST RECORD
        ⊟[2] *'FILE4'*
SECOND RECORD
        ⊟[3] *'FILE4'*
THIRD RECORD
        ⊟[4] *'FILE4'*
*** *FILE VALUE ERROR* ***

Then

        ⊖ *'FILE4'*
        ⊟[1] *'FILE4'*
THIRD RECORD
        ⊖ *'FILE4'*
        ⊟[1] *'FILE4'*
FIRST RECORD
      1 ⊖ *'FILE4'*
        ⊟[1] *'FILE4'*
SECOND RECORD'

Again for either function, the file name is returned when it is required.

File Component Pop and Append

Not only may the file be considered as a vector, it may be thought of as having stack-like or queue-like characteristics. A queue can be viewed as a vector of items with a retrieval discipline associated with it. Two common retrieval disciplines are LIFO (last in, first out) and FIFO (first in, first out). A stack is a queue with a LIFO retrieval discipline.

The File Component Pop and the File Component Append primitives treat the file as if it were a queue. There are two file component primitives. The *File Component Append Before* primitive

        A ◁ *F*

appends the data item *A* before all components of the file *F*. The *File Component Append After* primitive

        A ▷ *F*

appends the data item *A* after all components of the file *F*. In either case the number of components of the file is increased by 1. Furthermore, if the file component is appended before the rest of the file components of the file, the file component number associated with each is increased by 1. Thus

```
      ⊟[1] 'FILE4'
FIRST RECORD
      (⍳3) ◁ 'FILE4'
      ⊟[1] 'FILE4'
1 2 3
```

The File Component Append primitive returns the file name if required.

The File Component Read and Pop primitives permit the reading of either the first or last component of the file. Thus the *File Component Read and Pop First* primitive

        ◁ *F*

reads the first component of the file and removes (pops) it from the file. The *File Component Read and Pop Last* primitive

        ▷ *F*

reads the last component of the file and removes (pops) it from the file. In either case the component must be nonnull. If the Read and Pop First primitive removed the first component of the file, then the file component number associated with each of the remaining file components is decreased by 1. For example,

```
      (ı4) ◁ 'FILE4'
      'XYZ' ◁ 'FILE4'
      ◁[1] 'FILE4'
XYZ

      ◁ 'FILE4'
XYZ

      ◁[1] 'FILE4'
1 2 3 4
      ◁ 'FILE4'
1 2 3 4
```

Hence to treat the file as a stack of entries the File Component Append primitives and the File Component Read and Pop primitives should be applied to the same end of the file: This produces a LIFO discipline. The application of the File Component Append primitives and the File Component Read and Pop primitives to opposite ends of the file establishes a queue with a FIFO retrieval discipline.

File Query and Control

In addition to being able to create a file and manipulate the file components, the file system needs to be controlled and capable of being queried.

Any application placed upon a computer system has system-imposed restrictions. With this file system there exist installation-imposed restrictions on the maximum number of accounts permitted to use files and the maximum number of files that may be active at a given time. Since that is the case, the *File System Interrogate* primitive

```
      ⌻ I
```

exists to furnish such information about the file system. I must be an integer which currently may be either 1 or 2. For $I=1$, ⌻ I returns the current number of accounts using files. For $I=2$, ⌻ I returns the total number of currently active files. Such primitives would be quite useful in monitoring the usage of the system.

To use the file system, a file has to be created. This is done via the File Create primitive Ⓝ F, where F is the file name for the file being created. To do this properly, one should determine that the name F does not currently exist as a file name. The *File Existence* primitive

```
      ⌻ F
```

where F is the file name, provides this information. The response from ⌻ F is binary. It returns a 0 if the file name F does not exist and a 1 if the file name F does exist. Thus

```
      ⌻ 'FILE4'
1
      ⌻ 'FILE8'
0
```

After it has been determined that the file name F exists, determining some of the file characteristics is desirable. This is accomplished through the dyadic primitive *Query File Attribute*,

$I \ \boxdot \ F$

F is an integer defined over the set of integers 1 through 7. The significance of the query is determined by the value of I. Thus

I	The result is —
1	— the current size of the file in bytes
2	— the maximum file size in bytes (an installation set option)
3	— the current number of file components (including null components)
4	— a 1 if any file modification occurred after the file had been reorganized; a 0 otherwise
5	— the cycle number of the last reorganization
6	— the number of accounts for which the file is open
7	— the time stamp, $\Box TS$, of the most recent file modification.

Recall that $3 \ \boxdot \ F$ can never return a value greater than 1000.

File modification results from all the file component primitives except File Component Read. In handling such modifications an update file is maintained as a separate entity from the main file. File reorganization results in the merging of the update file with the main file, producing a compact indexed sequential new file. Reorganization occurs when the file becomes inactive or the file ceases to be open to any account.

The use of such query primitives can detect potential problems early. For example, the two expressions can detect a nearly full file situation.

$\rightarrow OK \times \iota (2 \boxdot \ 'FILE1') > 100 + 1 \ \boxdot \ 'FILE1'$
$'FILE \ IS \ WITHIN \ 100 \ BYTES \ OF \ FULL'$

Now recall that a file may contain both null and nonnull file components. Thus it is necessary to determine which components are null and which are not. The primitive *Value Component Map*

$\boxminus \ F$

results in a binary map vector with a 1 where the corresponding file component is nonnull. If a file component is null, the corresponding component of $\boxminus \ F$ is 0. The primitive *Empty Component Map*

$\boxtimes \ F$

provides a binary vector where a 1 corresponds to a null file component and a 0 corresponds to a nonnull file component. Consider the sequence

```
      ⍲ 'FILE5'
      'FIRST' ⍅ 'FILE5'
      '2ND' ⍅ 'FILE5'
      (⍳3) ⍅ 'FILE5'
      ⊟ 'FILE5'
1 1 1
      4 ⍔ 'FILE5'
      ⊟ 'FILE5'
1 1 1 0
      ⍒[2] 'FILE5'
      ⊟ 'FILE5'
1 0 1 0
      ⍂ 'FILE5'
0 1 0 1
```

File Control

Since a file may be shared by several users, file control is necessary to assure exclusive use by one user in order, perhaps, to update that file. The monadic primitive *Hold File*

```
      ⍲ F
```

establishes a hold on the file permitting exclusive use by the issuer. Such an exclusive-use hold can only be placed on the file if it is not currently being held. If a hold is issued on a file currently held by some other account, the present hold causes a wait until the file is freed. A hold exists only while execution continues in a defined function. A return to desk calculator mode breaks the hold.

A held file is freed implicitly when a return to calculator mode occurs or when the file is destroyed. It may be explicitly freed by the primitive *Free File*

```
      ⍱ F
```

This primitive must be issued by the issuer of the Hold File. However, the owner of the file is more privileged than other users of the file. The owner of the file can preempt his file through the use of the primitive *Preempt Hold*

```
      ⍞ F
```

When issued, Preempt Hold breaks any existing hold on the file by another account and place its own hold on the file. This should be issued with discretion since any file update in progress by another user is discarded.

Again for all three primitives, Hold File, Free File, and Preempt Hold, the file name is returned if it is required.

The following sequence determines whether the file *FILE*1 is currently being shared, issues a Hold File, checks to see if the new component *DATA* will fit into the file without exceeding the maximum file size, puts the *DATA* item at the end of the file, and finally frees the file:

.
.
.

```
[8]   →OK1 ×ι 0=5 ⊡ 'FILE1'
[9]   ⍝ 'FILE1'
[10]  →OK1 ×ι(2 ⊡ 'FILE1')≥ DATA+1 ⊡ 'FILE1'
[11]  'NEW ENTRY TOO LARGE FOR FILE'
[12]  →END
[13]  OK1: DATA ⊠ 'FILE1'
[14]  END: ⍝ 'FILE1'
```

.
.
.

Illustration F.1   A Skeleton Function for Putting Workspace
Functions on a File

Chapter 9 contained a detailed set of functions for moving APL functions between a data set (file) and a workspace in APL.SV. The following function forms the skeleton for writing an APL function on a file in APL/700:

```
      ∇ DUMP FILE;INDEX;FNS;T
[1]   INDEX←0
[2]   FNS←⎕NL 3
[3]   LOOP:→((1↑ρFNS)<INDEX+←1¹·)/0
[4]   (⎕VR ²· FNS[INDEX;]) ⊠ FILE
[5]   T←⎕EX FNS[INDEX;]
[6]   →LOOP
      ∇
```

1. This is equivalent to $INDEX←INDEX+1$ in APL.SV.

2. This is equivalent to ,$⎕CR$ in APL.SV.

Illustration F.2   A Skeleton Function for Getting a Workspace
from a File

This function forms the basic skeletal function for getting an APL function from a file:

```
      ∇ RESTORE FILE
[1]   LOOP:→(0=ρ⊟ FILE)/0
[2]   ⎕FX ◁ FILE
[3]   →LOOP
      ∇
```

Summary of APL/700 File Primitives

Name	Symbol	Comment*	Role
Create File	⎕ F	A, B	Creates a file with the name F
Change Password	⎕ [O/N] F	A, B	Changes password O to N on existing file F
Destroy File	⎕ F	B	Destroys unheld existing file; returns a 1 if successful, and a 0 otherwise
Rename File	NF ⎕ OF	B	Renames inactive file OF to NF
Open File	⎕ F	A	Opens a file
Close File	⎕ F	A, B	Closes an inactive file
File Component Write	D ⎕ [K] F	A	Writes datum D as Kth component of file F
File Component Nullify	⎕ [K] F	A	Sets the Kth component of file F to null
File Component Read	⎕ [K] F	A	Reads the Kth component from file F
File Component Take	I ⎕ F	A	Takes I consecutive components from either end of the file F
File Component Drop	I ⎕ F	A	Drops I consecutive components from either end of file F
File Component Compress	B ⎕ F	A	Compresses out components of F corresponding to 0 in B
File Component Expand	B ⎕ F	A	Expands in an order-preserving manner file F, inserting null components wherever a 0 exists in B
File Component Reverse	⎕ F	A	Reverses the component order of the file F
File Component Rotate	I ⎕ F	A	Rotates circularly the components of file F
File Component Read and Pop First	⎕ F		Reads and removes the first component of file F
File Component Read and Pop Last	⎕ F		Reads and removes the last component of file F
File Component Append Before	D ⎕ F	A	Appends datum D before component of file F
File Component Append After	D ⎕ F	A	Appends datum D after components of file F
File System Interrogate	⎕ I	B	I=1: current number of file users; I=2: current number of active files
Value Component Map	⎕ F		Provides a binary map indicating nonnull components; 1 for nonnull, 0 for null
Empty Component Map	⎕ F		Provides a binary map indicating the null components; 1 for null, 0 for nonnull
File Existence	⎕ F	B	Returns a 1 if file name F exists, and a 0 otherwise
Query File Attribute	I ⎕ F	B	Returns one of seven-defined attributes depending on I being 1 through 7
Hold File	⎕ F	A	Holds file F for exclusive use
Free File	⎕ F	A	Frees hold on file F
Preempt Hold	⎕ F	A	Owner preemptively holds file F

*A: File names as explicit result when required.
B: Does not open file.

BIBLIOGRAPHY

This APL Bibliography is organized in sections as follows:

General: Articles that tell about APL or that describe it generally.

Texts: Books for learning APL.

Applications: Books and articles discussing uses of APL and applications in education, business, engineering and science, computers and computing, mathematics and statistics, and miscellaneous.

APL developments: Articles discussing extensions to APL and/or the APL terminal system.

Miscellaneous: Articles of interest to the APL programmer.

Collections: APL journals and conference proceedings.

The bibliography is rich in source materials with the following exceptions. No books or articles written prior to 1968 are included. 1968 was chosen as a cutoff date because APL/360 was not made publicly available by IBM until then. Earlier references tend to use Iverson notation (as formulated in *A Programming Language*, Wiley, New York, 1962) rather than APL. Neither articles nor manuals discussing specific implementations of APL on various machines or by various companies or universities nor how APL is used at various installations are included since such information tends to be transient. No foreign language articles are included. Finally no articles whose distribution is restricted are included.

General: Articles that Tell About APL—Describe or Discuss It Generally

"APL: The Controversial, Powerful Interactive Language," *Computing Newsletter, IV*, No. 7, 1971, 1-2.

"APL—The Language of the 4th Generation?," *Computing Newsletter*, March 1972, 1-2.

Bairstow, J. N., "Mr. Iverson's Language and How it Grew," *Computing Decisions*, Sept. 1969, 42-45.

Couger, J. D., "Schools, Colleges Attest to APL Growth," *Computer World*, March 29, 1972, 16.

"Creating Plain Talk for Computers," *IBM Magazine*, Feb. 16, 1970.

DeVries, W., "Watch Your (Computer) Language," *The Actuary*, March 1971.

Falkoff, A., "APL/360 History," in *APL Users Conference at S.U.N.Y. Binghampton*, Binghampton, N. Y., July 1969, 8-15.

Falkoff, A. D., and K. E. Iverson, "The Design of APL," *IBM Journal of Research and Development, 17*, No. 4, July 1973, 324-334.

Foster, G. H., "APL—A Perspicuous Language," *Computers and Automation*, Nov. 1969, 24-29.

Griffith, E. V., "APL—A Programming Language," *Chemical Engineering*, March 6, 1972, 99-104.

Iverson, K. E., "The Story of APL," *Computing Report, 6*, No. 3, 1970, 14-18.

McCracken, D. D., "Whither APL?," *Datamation*, Sept. 15, 1970, 53-57.

McMurchie, T. D., "Applause for APL," *Computers and Automation*, March 1970, 4.

Reeves, R. J. D., "APL, A Potential Liability," *Datamation*, Sept. 15, 1971, 71-72.

Robertson, R. E., "A Programming Language Just for Everybody," *College Management*, April 1971, 32-34, 38.

Rueter, D., "Array for APL," *Datamation*, Nov. 15, 1971, 17.

Sammet, J., "APL/360 and PAT," in *Programming Languages, History and Fundamentals*, Prentice-Hall, Englewood Cliffs, N. J., 1969, pp. 247-253.

Standish, T. A., *An Essay on APL*, Dept. of Computer Science, Carnegie-Mellon University, Pittsburgh, March 1969.

Stickler, G. P., "Real-World APL," *Datamation*, Dec. 1, 1971, 19.

Taylor, A., "APL, A Complex or Simple Language," *Computerworld*, April 1, 1970, 11.

Texts: Teaching APL

Anger, A., *The APL Language*, Wiley, New York, 1971.

APL Audio Education Package, Form No. SR20-9382, SR20-9383, SR20-9384, IBM Corp., 1971.

Berry, P. C., *APL/1130 Primer*, Form No. GC-20-1967, IBM Corp., 1968.

Berry, P. C., *APL/360 Primer*, 2nd ed., Form No. GH-20-0689-1, IBM Corp., Jan. 1970.

Buckley, J. W., D. L. Sharp, M. R. Nagaraj, and J. Schenck, *Management Problem Solving with APL*, Wiley/Becker and Hayes, New York, 1974.

Falkoff, A. D., and K. E. Iverson, *APL/360 User's Manual*, Form No. GH-20-0683, IBM Corp.

Gilman, L., and A. J. Rose, *APL—An Interactive Approach*, 2nd ed., Wiley, New York, 1974.

Gray, L. D., *A Course in APL/360 with Applications*, Addison-Wesley, Reading, Mass., 1973.

Henson, J. C., and W. F. Manny, *APL—An Introduction*, 2nd ed., Altanta Public Schools, Atlanta, April 1971.

Katzan, H., *APL Programming and Computer Techniques*, Van Nostrand Reinhold, New York, 1970.

, *APL User's Guide*, Van Nostrand Reinhold, New York, 1971.

Pakin, S., *APL/360 Reference Manual*, 2nd ed., Science Research Associates, Chicago, 1971.

Pakin, S., and Staff of Computer Innovations, *APL: A Short Course*, Prentice-Hall, Englewood Cliffs, N.J., 1973.

Prager, W., *An Introduction to APL*, Allyn and Bacon, Boston, 1970.

Rose, A. J., *APL for Users of Basic*, Scientific Timesharing Corp., Washington, D.C., 1969.

Smillie, K. W., *An Introduction to APL/360 with Some Statistical Applications*, Publ. No. 19, Dept. of Computing Science, University of Alberta, Edmonton, Alberta, Canada, Jan. 1970.

Education: Uses of APL and Applications in

Adams, W. S., "The Use of APL in Teaching Programming," *Programming Teaching Techniques*, W. M. Turski, ed., American Elsevier Publishing Co., New York, 1973, 1–13.

Bartoli, G., L. Bartolo, and V. Spadavecchia,"Design of a Simulator for Open Use of an APL Computer in Science Teaching," in *Proceedings of the Fifth International APL Users' Conference*, Toronto, Canada, APL Technical Committee, May 1973, pp. 8.1–8.9.

Bartoli, G., L. Bartolo, P. Berry, and V. Spadavecchia, "APL Functions in Teaching Science: Tools of Analysis and Simulation," in *APL Congress 73*, P. Gjerlov, H. J. Helms, and J. Nielsen, eds., American Elsevier Publishing Co., New York, 1973, pp. 41–48.

Berry, P. C., A. D. Falkoff, and K. E. Iverson, "Using the Computer to Compute, a Direct but Neglected Approach to Teaching Mathematics," *Report No. 320-2988*, IBM Scientific Center, New York, May 1970.

Berry, P. C., G. Bartoli, C. Dell'aquila, and V. N. Spadavecchia, "APL and Insight, a Strategy for Teaching," *Colloque APL*, Institut de Recherche d'Informatique et Automatique, Rocquencourt, France, Sept. 1971, 251–272.

Berry, P. C., G. Bartoli, C. Dell'aquila, and V. Spadavecchia, "APL and Insight: The Use of Programs To Represent Concepts in Teaching," *Report No. 320-3020*, IBM Philadelphia Scientific Center, Philadelphia, March 1973.

Carolan, K. P., "Teaching APL," in *Proceedings of the Fifth International APL Users' Conference*, Toronto, Canada, May 1973, pp. 1.1-1.5.

Charmonman, S. and D. K. Reed, "A Table-Driven Program to Play a Game of Logical Deduction," in *Proceedings of the Fifth International APL Users' Conference*, Toronto, Canada, May 1973, pp. 6.1-6.18.

Clark, J., and R. Mercer, "Computers in Instruction at the Coast Community Colleges," in *Proceedings of the Fifth International APL Users' Conference*, Toronto, Canada, May 1973, pp. 5.1-5.18.

Conklin, R. F., "Instant CAI," in *Proceedings of the Sixth International APL Users' Conference*, Anaheim, Coast Community College District, May 1974, pp. 100-105.

Davis, L. N., J. Eskinazi, and D. J. Macero, "APL as a Teaching Tool: Two Versatile Tutorial Approaches," in *Proceedings of the Fourth International APL Users' Conference*, Atlanta, Board of Education of the City of Atlanta, June 1972, pp. 59-66.

, "Communication, Computers, and the Classroom," in *Proceedings of the Fifth International APL Users' Conference*, Toronto, Canada, May 1973, pp. 7.1-7.11.

Davis, L., and D. Macero, "Techniques for Computer Administered Examinations of Restricted or Confidential Material," in *Proceedings of the Sixth International APL Users' Conference*, Anaheim, May 1974, pp. 124-132.

DeBarthe, D., "Application of APL/360 in Junior High School," in *Proceedings of the Sixth International APL Users' Conference*, Anaheim, May 1974, pp. 133-138.

DeVahl Davis, G., and W. N. Holmes, "The Use of APL in Engineering Education," *Colloque APL*, Publication IRIA, Sept. 1971, 179-307.

Dehner, T. R., and B. E. Norcross, "The Evolution of an Interactive Chemistry Laboratory Program," in *Proceedings of the Fourth International APL Users' Conference*, Atlanta, June 1972, pp. 67-72.

Edwards, E. M., "APL, A Natural Language for Engineering Education, Part II," *IEEE Transactions on Education*, Nov. 1971, 179-180.

Falkoff, A. D., and K. E. Iverson, "The Use of Computers in Teaching Mathematics," *Report No. 320-2986*, IBM Philadelphia Scientific Center, Philadelphia, April 1970.

Foster, G. H., "APL, A Natural Language for Engineering Education, Part I," *IEEE Transactions on Education*, Nov. 1971, 174-185.

, "Motivating Arrays in Teaching APL," in *Proceedings of the Fifth International APL Users' Conference*, Toronto, Canada, May 1973, pp. 3.1-3.8.

Iverson, K. E., "The Role of the Computer in Teaching," *Queen's Papers on Pure and Applied Mathematics*, No. 13, Kingston, Ontario, Canada, 1968.

, "Introducing APL to Teachers," *Report No. 320-3014*, IBM Philadelphia Scientific Center, Philadelphia, July 1972.

, "An Introduction to APL for Scientists and Engineers," *Report No. 320-3019*, IBM Philadelphia Scientific Center, Philadelphia, March 1973.

———, "The Use of APL in Teaching," *Report No. 320-0996-0*, IBM Corp., 1969.

Kellerman, Anne, and Jeanine Meyer, "Teaching Beyond Elementary APL to Applications Users," in *Proceedings of the Sixth International APL Users' Conference*, Anaheim, May 1974, pp. 266–279.

Konstam, A. H., and J. E. Howland, "APL as a LINGUA FRANCA in the Computer Science Curriculum," *SIGCSE Bulletin*, 6, No. 1, Feb. 1974, pp. 21–27.

LePage, W. R., "APL, A Natural Language for Engineering Education, Part III," *IEEE Transactions on Education*, Nov. 1971, 180–183.

Levine, R., "APL Instruction for the Class of History 330," in *Proceedings of the Sixth International APL Users' Conference*, Anaheim, May 1974, pp. 292–300.

Liknaitzky, R., "APL Functions for Use in Junior High School Mathematics," *Report CAI 3-69*, Division of Education Research, Faculty of Education, University of Alberta, Edmonton, Alberta, Canada, Nov. 1969.

Lippert, H. T., and E. V. Harris, "APL: An Alternative to the Multi-Language Environment for Education," *CAI-Systems Memo-4*, Florida State University, Tallahassee, Aug. 1970.

Orgass, R. J., "APL in the Teaching of Computational Complexity," in *APL Congress 73*, P. Gjerlov, H. J. Helms, and J. Nielsen, eds., American Elsevier Publishing Co., New York, 1973, pp. 339–346.

Peelle, H. A., "Teaching Children Thinking via APL," in *Proceedings of the Fifth International APL Users' Conference*, Toronto, Canada, May 1973, pp. 0.1–0.2.

———, "A Generalized Learning Game," in *Proceedings of the Sixth International APL Users' Conference*, Anaheim, May 1974, pp. 424–428.

Penfield, P., "Use of APL in Teaching Electrical Network Theory," in *Proceedings of the Fourth International APL Users' Conference*, Atlanta, June 1972, p. 191.

Peterson, S. R., "A CAI System Based on Modifications to York/APL," in *Proceedings of the Sixth International APL Users' Conference*, Anaheim, May 1974, pp. 429–437.

Plum, T. W. S., and G. M. Weinberg, "Teaching Structured Programming Attitudes, Even in APL, By Example," *SIGCSE Bulletin*, 6, No. 1, Feb. 1974, pp. 133–143.

Raucher, S. M., "APL and Its Use in the Classroom," *AEDS Journal*, Dec. 1968, 3–11.

Rudberg, D., "APL, A Natural Language of Engineering Education, Part IV," *IEEE Transactions on Education*, Nov. 1971, 183–185.

Savary, J. R., "APL as an Aid to the Teaching of Undergraduate Economics," in *Proceedings of the Fifth International APL Users' Conference*, Toronto, Canada, May 1973, pp. 9.1–9.9.

———, "APL, A Natural Language of Engineering Education, Part V," *IEEE Transactions on Education*, Nov. 1971, 185.

Schmidt, K., and M. M. Vijay, "Development of Some New Functions in APL for Computer-Aided Individualized Instruction," *SIGCUE Bulletin*, 8, No. 1, ACM, Jan. 1974, pp. 23–26.

Searle, C. L., "Teaching of Transistor Circuit Design Using a Digital Computer," *IEEE Transactions on Education*, Sept. 1969, 216–219.

Smillie, K. W., "The Use of APL in the Teaching of Probability," in *Proceedings of the Sixth International APL Users' Conference*, Anaheim, May 1974, pp. 475–483.

Spadavecchia, V. N., P. C. Berry, and G. Bartoli, "An Abstract Machine for the Introduction to Computer Science," *Colloque APL*, Institut de Recherche d'Informatique et D'Automatique, Rocquencourt, France, Sept. 1971, 273–278.

Sprowis, R. C., "APL in Management Education," *APL Congress 73*, P. Gjerlov, H. J. Helms, and J. Nielsen, eds., American Elsevier Publishing Co., New York, 1973, pp. 431–438.

Taylor, R. W. W., "APL as a Coursewriting Language," *APL Quote-Quad*, June 1972, 3–12.

Vaskevitch, D., "APL/CAT: APL for Computer Assisted Teaching," *Proceedings of the Sixth International APL Users' Conference*, Anaheim, May 1974, pp. 544–557.

Business: Uses of APL and Applications in

Andersen, H., 0. Bjarkild, and E. Holsøe, "CBC Plan, an APL Application," *APL Congress 73*, P. Gjerlov, H. J. Helms, and J. Nielsen, eds., American Elsevier Publishing Co., New York, 1973, pp. 25–32.

Barasz, J-P., and F. Lapadu-Hargues, "A Multi-Network Pert Program," *APL Congress 73*, P. Gjerlov, H. J. Helms, and J. Nielsen, eds., American Elsevier Publishing Co., New York, 1973, 275–278.

Carlson, J. G. H., and R. Gilman, "Management Information/Decision Systems Using APL," in *Proceedings of the Sixth International APL Users' Conference*, Anaheim, May 1974, pp. 65–78.

Courtney, H., "A Generalized Multi-Stage Cost Minimization Model in APL," in *Proceedings of the Sixth International APL Users' Conference*, Anaheim, May 1974, pp. 106–111.

Courtney, H. M., and C. M. Cheney, "An Application of the Binomial Distribution to Labs Planning," in *Proceedings of the Fifth International APL Users' Conference*, Toronto, Canada, May 1973, pp. 16.1–16.17.

Dyer, D. "The Use of APL in the Management of a Time Sharing Company," in *Proceedings of the Sixth International APL Users' Conference*, Anaheim, May 1974, pp. 148–150.

Flower, D., "The Brown Box Data Management System," in *Proceedings of the Fifth International APL Users' Conference*, Toronto, Canada, May 1973, pp. 15.1–15.17.

Grazis, D. C., "A Computer Model for the Financial Analysis of Urban Projects," *Report No. RC-2850*, IBM Research Center, Yorktown Heights, N.Y.

Hahn, S. G., "Minipert," *Proceedings of Share XXXVII, 1*, Aug. 1971, 371–379.

Halmstad, D. G., "APL/Solid. A Life Insurance Management Game," *APL Congress 73*, P. Gjerlov, H. J. Helms, and J. Nielsen, eds., American Elsevier Publishing Co., New York, 1973.

Henselyn, R. G., "Pert Project Scheduling in APL*PLUS," *APL Congress 73*, P. Gjerlov, H. J. Helms, and J. Nielsen, eds., American Elsevier Publishing Co., New York, 1973, pp. 211–214.

Hirschberg, D., "A Conversational APL Program for Decision Analysis," *APL Congress 73*, P. Gjerlov, H. J. Helms, and J. Nielsen, eds., American Elsevier Publishing Co., New York, 1973, pp. 215–222.

Hurtabise, R. A., and Y. Poulin, "APL and MIS: Two Compatible Concepts," in *Proceedings of The Sixth International APL Users' Conference*, Anaheim, May 1974, pp. 201-213.

Jarvis, W., and H. Wobbe, "APL as a Foundation for a Marketing Planning and Analysis System," in *Proceedings of the Sixth International APL Users' Conference*, Anaheim, May 1974. pp. 214-217.

Lee, J. H., "Advanced Decision-making for Private Real Estate Construction Management—An APL Program," in *Proceedings of the Southwestern IEEE Conference*, April 1970, pp. 272-276.

Løken, S. A., "An Interactive Long Range Planning Model Written in APL," *APL Congress 73*, P. Gjerlov, H. J. Helms, and J. Nielsen, eds., American Elsevier Publishing Co., New York, 1973, pp. 289-292.

McAllister, C., "APL Based On-Line Manpower and Budget Planning," *APL Congress 73*, P. Gjerlov, H. J. Helms, and J. Nielsen, eds., American Elsevier Publishing Co., New York, 1973, pp. 293-298.

McLean, E. R., "The Use of APL in Management Education," in *Proceedings of the Sixth International APL Users' Conference*, Anaheim, May 1974, pp. 324-333.

Mezei, J. E., "Structure in the Traveling Salesman's Problem—The Shklar Algorithm," *Report No. 320-3003*, IBM Philadelphia Scientific Center, Philadelphia, Sept. 1971.

Mock, J. T., and M. A. Vasarhelyi, *APL for Management*, Melville Publishing Co., Los Angeles, 1972.

Montalbano, M. S., "Conversational Linear Programming—A User's Manual for LP-APL, Computers in Management Education, Report No. 1," *Report No. G320-3272*, IBM Palo Alto Scientific Center, Palo Alto, Calif., March 1970.

Ohayon, S. and P. A. LaVallee, "APL Data Management Systems (APLDMS)," in *Proceedings of the Sixth International APL Users' Conference*, Anaheim, May 1974, pp. 393-404.

Redwood, P. H. S., "APL for Business Applications," *Datamation*, May 1972, 82-84.

Richter, J. A., "APL for Synthesis in Corporate Dynamics," *APL Congress 73*, P. Gjerlov, H. J. Helms, and J. Nielsen, eds., American Elsevier Publishing Co., New York, 1973, pp. 369-376.

Riedy, J. E., "Dynamic Job Tracking Using APL," *APL Congress*, P. Gjerlov, H. J. Helms, and J. Nielsen, eds., American Elsevier Publishing Co., New York, 1973, pp. 385-394.

Rough, J. W., "Xerox Financial Planning and Control System in APL," in *Proceedings of the Fifth International APL Users' Conference*, Toronto, Canada, May 1973, pp. 14.1-14.11.

Seaberg, R. A., "Computer Assisted Forecasting—How Business Is Using APL," *Canadian Data Systems*, Jan. 1971, 30-31.

——, "APL in Financial Forecasting Is Base for Eventual MIS," *Canadian Data Systems*, Feb. 1971, 50-53.

——, "Computer Assisted Forecasting (CAF) at Xerox," *Proceedings of Share XXXVII, 2*, Aug. 1971, 756-761.

Sharon, E., and M. S. Montalbano, "The Formal Description of Data Processing Procedures: An APL/360 Income Tax Program," *Report No. 320-3242*, IBM Scientific Center, Palo Alto, Calif., May 1968.

Tava, P. A., "The Financial Planning System—The Application of APL to Financial Modeling," in *Proceedings of the Sixth International APL Users' Conference*, Anaheim, May 1974, pp. 487–498.

Taylor, R., "Budget Planning and Costing in Xerox APL," in *Proceedings of the Sixth International APL Users' Conference*, Anaheim, May 1974, pp. 499–528.

Vaskocvitch, D., "APL for CAL and Information Management," in *Proceedings of the Fifth International APL Users' Conference*, Toronto, Canada, May 1973, pp. 18.1–18.12.

Wahi, P. N., "AIMS—Applied Information and Management Simulation, A General Business Simulation in APL," *Report No. G320-2066*, IBM Cambridge Scientific Center, Cambridge, Mass., April 1971.

———, "A General Management Business Simulation in APL," *IBM Systems Journal, 1*, No. 2, 1972, 169–180.

Weaver, K. R., "Shared Information Management System," in *Proceedings of the Sixth International APL Users' Conference*, Anaheim, May 1974, pp. 558–561.

Engineering and Science: Applications and Uses of APL in

Beam, W. R., "An APL Implementation of Microwave Circuit Analysis," *IEEE NEREM Record*, 1970, 99–105.

Bork, A. M., "Physics Computer Development Project," *Technical Summary Report*, University of California, Irvine, June 1972.

Buchheit, E. A., and R. B. Roden, "APL Routines for Evaluating Functions in Mathematical Physics," *Research Report CSRR 2029*, Dept. of Applied Analysis and Computer Science, University of Waterloo, Ontario, Nov. 1970.

Desblache, A. and V. Riso, "Simulation of Automatic Equalizers to be Used in Data Transmission Systems," *APL Congress 73*, P. Gjerlov, H. J. Helms, and J. Nielsen, eds., American Elsevier Publishing Co., New York, 1973, pp. 91–98.

Fancher, E. J., "Controlling Numerically Controlled Machines Using APL," in *Proceedings of the Sixth International APL Users' Conference*, Anaheim, May 1974, pp. 151–160.

Foster, G. H., "APL as a Descriptive Language for Associative Processing and Systems Design," *APL Congress 73*, P. Gjerlov, H. J. Helms, and J. Nielsen, eds., American Elsevier Publishing Co., New York, 1973, pp. 133–140.

Ghez, R., "Data Fitting Thin Film Oxidation and Tarnishing Reactions with APL," *Report No. RC-3817*, IBM Research Center, Yorktown Heights, N.Y., April 1972.

Hansler, E., "Using APL for Network Reliability Calculations," *APL Congress 73*, P. Gjerlov, H. J' Helms, and J. Nielsen, eds., American Elsevier Publishing Co., New York, 1973, pp. 223–230.

Jensen, R. W., T. A. Higbee, and P. M. Hansen, "ECAPL: An APL Electronic Circuit Analysis Program," in *Proceedings of the Fourth International APL Users' Conference*, Atlanta, June 1972, pp. 161–190.

Jones, A. L., "The Use of APL/360 in Mechanical Analysis," in *Proceedings of 1970 IEEE International Computer Group Conference*, June 1970, pp. 195–204.

Jones, A. L., and A. J. Lavin, "Effect of Hammer Length and Nonlinear Paper-Ribbon Characteristics on Impact Printing," *IBM Journal of Research and Development*, March 1971, 108-115.

LePage, W. R., and L. E. Linge, "Power System Load Flow in APL," in *Proceedings of the Sixth International APL Users' Conference*, Anaheim, May 1974, pp. 287-291.

Meldal, K. G., "APL/360 Used for Sewer Design in Danish Cities," *APL Congress 73*, P. Gjerlov, H. J. Helms, and J. Nielsen, eds., American Elsevier Publishing Co., New York, 1973, pp. 319-324.

Penfield, P., "A Set of APL Programs for Use in Network Theory," *APL Quote-Quad*, June 1971, 4.

Posdamer, J. L., and R. Riesenfeld, "The Application of APL in Graphics Computation," *APL Congress 73*, P. Gjerlov, H. J. Helms, and J. Nielsen, eds., American Elsevier Publishing Co., New York, 1973, pp. 353-360.

Spence, R., "Patterns in the Development of Insight: An Experimental Text on Electrical Circuit Theory," *APL Congress 73*, P. Gjerlov, H. J. Helms, and J. Nielsen, eds., American Elsevier Publishing Co., New York, 1973, pp. 421-430.

Thornton, R. D., "Computer Flavored Circuit Theory," *IEEE Transactions on Education*, Sept. 1969, 219-222.

Wende, C. D., "Modeling a Satellite Experiment in APL," in *Proceedings of the Fourth International APL Users' Conference*, Atlanta, June 1972, pp. 45-57.

Computers and Computing: Uses and Applications of APL in

"Aaims' Utilizes Power of APL, Provides Flexible MIS Facility," *Computerworld*, Oct. 4, 1972, 11.

Abrams, P. S., "Program Writing, Rewriting, and Style," *APL Congress 73*, P. Gjerlov, H. J. Helms, and J. Nielsen, eds., American Elsevier Publishing Co., New York, 1973, pp. 1-8.

Aguzzi, G., F. Cesarini, R. Pinzani, G. Soda, and R. Sprugnoli, "An APL Implementation of an Interpreter Writing System," *APL Congress 73*, P. Gjerlov, H. J. Helms, and J. Nielsen, eds., American Elsevier Publishing Co., New York, 1973, pp. 9-16.

Bartel, D., H. W. Homrighausen, and L. Richter, "Simulation of a Class of Computers and Their Assembly Languages," *APL Congress 73*, P. Gjerlov, H. J. Helms, and J. Nielsen, eds., American Elsevier Publishing Co., New York, 1973, pp. 376-384.

Bingham, H. W., "Use of APL in Microprogrammable Machine Modeling," *ACM Sig Plan Notices*, Oct. 1971.

Blaauw, G. A., "The Use of APL in Computer Design," in *MC-25 Information Symposium*, Mathematical Center, Amsterdam, 1971, 2.1-2.36.

Bouricius, W. G., W. C. Carter, K. A. Duke, J. P. Roth, and P. R. Schneider, "Interactive Design of Self-Testing Circuitry," in *Proceedings of the Purdue Symposium on Information Processing*, April 1969, pp. 73-80.

Brame, J. L., and C. V. Ramamoorthy, "An Interactive Simulator Generating System for Small Computers," *SJCC*, 1971, 425-449.

Brown, J. A., "Using the Ackerman Function to Rate Programming Languages," *APL Quote-Quad*, April 1970, 4-5.

Burkley, R. M., "Implementation of a Numerical Control Application Language (APT) by Direct Use of APL," *Report No. G320-2652*, IBM Corp., Los Angeles, Calif., Aug. 1971.

Compton, M. Y., "APL in PL/1," *Report No. RC4481*, IBM T. J. Watson Research Center, Yorktown Heights, N.Y., Aug. 1973.

Correia, M., D. Cossman, F. Putzolu, and T. S. Nethen, "Minimizing the Problem of Logic Testing by the Interaction of a Design Group with User Oriented Facilities," in *Seventh Design Automation Workshop*, June 1970, pp. 100-107.

Day, W. H. E., "Compiler Assignment of Data Items to Registers," *IBM Systems Journal, 9,* No. 4, 1970, 281-317.

Demars, G., E. Girard, and J. C. Rault, "APL in a Two-Step Programming Technique for Developing Complex Programs," *APL Congress 73*, P. Gjerlov, H. J. Helms and J. Nielsen, eds., American Elsevier Publishing Co., New York, 1973, pp. 83-90.

Dhatt, G., and L. Robichaud, "Finite Elements, Flow-Graphs and APL," *Colloque APL*, IRIA, Recquencourt, France, Sept. 1971, 37-69.

Duke, K. A., H. D. Schnurmann, and T. I. Wilson, "System Validation by Three-Level Modeling Synthesis," *IBM Journal of Research and Development*, March 1971, 166-174.

Falkoff, A. D., "Criteria for a System Design Language," *Software Engineering Techniques*, ed. J. N. Buxton and B. Randell, Pub. NATO Science Committee, Brussels, Belgium, 1970. pp. 88-92.

Falster, P., "A New Approach in System Design by Utilizing APL," *APL Congress 73*, P. Gjerlov, H. J. Helms and J. Nielsen, eds., American Elsevier Publishing Co., New York, 1973, pp. 109-118.

Fisher, R. A., "Automated Testing of Software Systems," in *Proceedings of the Third Hawaii International Conference on System Science*, Jan. 1970, part 2, 886-889.

Foster, G. H. and W. J. Jones, "On the Efficiency of Language Processors," in *Large Scale Information Processing System*, Vol. II (*Systems: Theory, Advanced Concepts and Designs*), Rome Air Development Center, Griffiss Air Force Base, N.Y., Report RADC-TR-68-401, April 1969, pp. 1-24.

Foster, G. H., "Using APL to Investigate Sequential Machines," IEEE *NEREM Record*, 1970, 121-127.

Foster, G. H., A. E. Spaanenburg, and W. E. Stumpf, *Computer Enhancement Through Interpretive Techniques* (NASA Grant NGR 33-022-125), Dept. of Electrical and Computer Engineering, Syracuse University, N.Y., Jan. 1972.

Friedman, T.D., "A System of APL Functions to Study Computer Networks," *AFIPS Conference Proceedings, 42*, 1973, pp. 141-148.

Friedman, T. D., and S. C. Yang, "Methods Used in an Automatic Logic Design Generator—(Alert)," *IEEE Transactions on Computers*, July 1969, 593-614.

Gerhart, S., "Verification of APL Programs," *APL Congress 73*, P. Gjerlov, H. J. Helms and J. Nielsen, eds., American Elsevier Publishing Co., New York, 1973, pp. 141-149.

Ghandour, Z. J., "Formal Systems and Analysis," *Report No. 320-3002*, IBM Philadelphia Scientific Center, Philadelphia, June 1971.

Goncharsky, R. S., A. Rauch, and W. W. White, "Large Scale Mathematical Programming in an APL Environment," in *Proceedings of the Sixth International APL Users' Conference*, Anaheim, May 1974, pp. 161–172.

Grant, C. A., M. L. Greenbert, and D. E. Redell, "A Computer System Providing Microcoded APL," in *Proceedings of the Sixth International APL Users' Conference*, Anaheim, May 1974, pp. 173–179.

Grebert, A., F. Gerbstadt, and P. Colen, "Space Programming Language Machine Architecture Study," CIRAD Report No. WS-10 300-2, Vol. 1, Claremont, Calif., April 1972.

Haegi, H. R., "Euler Files—Simulation of a File System with APL," *APL Congress 73*, P. Gjerlov, H. J. Helms and J. Nielsen, eds., American Elsevier Publishing Co., New York, 1973.

Hake, R. B., and D. R. Page, "Tasking in APL," *Report Tr-12.102*, IBM World Trade Corp., Hursley, England, May 1972.

Hall, F. J., and G. R. Peterson, *Digital Systems: Hardware Organization and Design*, Wiley, New York, 1973.

Hassitt, A., "Microprogramming and High Level Languages," *International IEEE Computer Conference*, Sept. 1971, 91–92.

Hasterlik, R. L., "Algorithm Evaluation: A Practical Use for APL/360," *Report No. Tr-01.1182*, IBM Systems Development Division, Endicott Laboratory, Endicott, N.Y., Oct. 1969.

Hellerman, H., "Some Principles of Time Sharing Scheduler Strategies," *IBM Systems Journal, 8*, No. 2, 1969, 94–117.

Hellerman, H., and Y. Ron, "A Time-sharing System Simulation and Its Validation," *Report No. 320-2984*, IBM Philadelphia Scientific Center, Philadelphia, April 1970.

Juran, W., and C. Moore, "An APL Program for Remote Job Entry," in *Proceedings of the Sixth International APL Users' Conference*, Anaheim, May 1974, pp. 233–238.

Kelly, R. A., and J. R. Walters, "APLGOL-2 A Structured Programming System for APL," *Report No. 320-3318*, IBM Scientific Center, Palo Alto, Aug. 1973.

———, "A Structured Programming Language System for APL," in *Proceedings of the Sixth International APL Users' Conference*, Anaheim, May 1974, pp. 275–280.

Konnerth, K. L., "Use of a Terminal System for Data Acquisition," *IBM Journal of Research and Development*, Jan. 1969, 132–138.

Laws, B. H., "A Parallel BCH Decoder," *Report No. ERL-603-T2-0670*, Montana State University, Bozeman Electronics Research Lab, June 1970.

Lehman, M. M., "Syscom, An APL Program for System Evaluation," *Report No. RC-3375*, IBM Research Center, Yorktown Heights, N.Y., May 1971.

Leiner, A. L., "Supermod—An Analytic Tool for Modeling the Performance of Large Scale Systems," *Report No. RC-2796*, IBM Research Center, Yorktown Heights, N.Y., Feb. 1970.

Levy, S., R. H. Doyle, and R. M. Heller, "APL as a Development Tool for Special Purpose Processors," in *Proceedings of the National Computer Conference*, May 1974, pp. 279–284.

Lewis, P. A. W., and P. C. Yue, "Statistical Analysis of Series Events in Computer Systems," *Report No. RC-3606*, IBM Research Center, Yorktown Heights, N.Y., Nov. 1971.

Lorie, R. A., "APL as a Language for Handling a Relational Data-Base," *Report No. G320-2067*, IBM Cambridge Scientific Center, Cambridge, Mass., March 1971.

Lorie, R. A., and A. J. Symonds, "Use of a Relational Access Method Under APL," *Report No. G320-2071*, IBM Cambridge Scientific Center, Cambridge, Mass., May 1971.

MacDonald, Geraldine, "Evaluating the Equality or Inequality of Symbol Strings in APL," in *Proceedings of the Sixth International APL Users' Conference*, Anaheim, May 1974, pp. 301–306.

Marchal, A., "Data Structure Techniques in an Implementation of APL," Unpublished Ph.D. Thesis, Dept. of Electronical Engineering, Division of Computer Science, University of Utah, Provo, June 1973.

Maybury, W. J., "Programming Aids in Xerox APL," in *Proceedings of the Sixth International APL Users' Conference*, Anaheim, May 1974, pp. 307–315.

McFarland, C., "A Language-Oriented Computer Design," *AFIPS Conference Proceedings*, 37, 1970, 629–640.

Milville-DeChene, A., and L. P. A. Robichaud, "Subtasking in APL," in *Proceedings of the Fourth International APL Users' Conference*, Atlanta, June 1972, pp. 135–141.

Moore, C. R., "Character String Manipulation in APL," in *Proceedings of the Sixth International APL Users' Conference*, Anaheim, May 1974, pp. 349–353.

Nielsen, C. P., T. H. Burnett, and W. Vernon, "APL and Fortran: A Symbiotic Mix for a Small Machine," in *Proceedings of the Sixth International APL Users' Conference*, Anaheim, May 1974, pp. 387–392.

Nissen S. M., and S. J. Wallach, "The ALL Applications Digital Computer," *Proceedings of a Symposium on HIgh-Level-Language Computer Architecture, SIGPLAN Notices*, 8, No. 11, Nov. 1973, pp. 43–51.

Owens, J. L., "Bulk I/O and Communications with Livermore Time Sharing System," *APL Quote-Quad*, June 1971, 7–8.

Peccoud, D. M., and G. L. Noguez, "An Array Processor Design for APL-like Data Structure," *Information Processing 71*, ed. C. V. Freiman, North-Holland, Amsterdam, 1972, pp. 717–720.

Penfield, P., "General Purpose Electric Circuit Analyzer Imbedded in APL," *Electrodynamics Memo No. 15*, Research Lab of Electronics, M.I.T., Cambridge, Mass., Feb. 1971.

Polivka, R., and K. Haralson, "Microprogramming Training—An APL Application," in *Proceedings of the Fourth International APL Users' Conference*, Atlanta, 1972, pp. 154–160.

Puckett, T. H., "Improved Security in APL Applications Package," in *Proceedings of the Sixth International APL Users' Conference*, Anaheim, May 1974, pp. 438–441.

Raynaud, J., L. P. A. Robichaud, and G. Simian, "APL in the Description and Simulation of Computer Systems," *SIGMICRO Newsletter*, 3, No. 4, Jan. 1973, 5–24.

Robichaud, L.P.A., "Lexical and Syntactic Analysis of APL, Generation of a Prefix Polish String," in *Proceedings of the Sixth International APL Users' Conference*, Anaheim, May 1974, pp. 447–451.

Roth, J. P., W. G. Bouricius, W. C. Carter, and P. R. Schneider, *Phase II of an Architectural Study for a Self Repairing Computer*, SAMSO-Tr-67-106, Air Force Systems Command, Los Angeles, Calif., Nov. 1967.

Saal, H. J., "Simulating Computers in Symbolic Assembler Notation," in *Proceedings of the Fifth International APL Users' Conference*, Toronto, Canada, May 1973, pp. 20.1-20.6.

Schaefer, M., *A Mathematical Theory of Global Program Organization*, Prentice-Hall, 1973.

Schmidt, R. O., "Collection of Walsh Analysis Programs Information Theory," *IEEE Transactions in Electromagnetic Compatibility*, Aug. 1971, 88-94.

Schroeder, S. C., and L. E. Vaughn, "A High Order Language Optimal Execution Processor," *Proceedings of a Symposium on High-Level-Language Computer Architecture, SIGPLAN Notices*, 8, No. 11, Nov. 1973, pp. 109-116.

Smillie, K. W., "APLISP: A Simple List Processor in APL," *APL Quote-Quad*, Feb. 1972, 16-20.

Surkan, A. J., "A Virtual-Variable Name-Specification Operator for High Level Languages," in *Proceedings of the Sixth International APL Users' Conference*, Anaheim, May 1974, pp. 484-486.

Thistle, W. G., and D. S. Galbraith, "APL Flowcharting Functions," *Report No. DREV M-2191/72*, Defense Research Establishment Valcartier, Valcartier, Quebec, Canada, 1972.

Tuckerman, B., "A Study of the Vigenere-Vernam Single and Multiple Loop Enciphering Systems," *Report No. RC-2879*, IBM Research Center, Yorktown Heights, N.Y., May 1970.

Wadia, N. C., "Theory of Improvement in System Reliability," *Report No. TR-27.089*, IBM Corp., Kingston, N.Y., Feb. 1972.

Waldbaum, G., "Evaluating Computing System Changes by Means of Regression Models," *Report No. RC-4060*, IBM Research Center, Yorktown Heights, N.Y., Sept. 1972.

Woodrum, L. J., "Internal Sorting with Minimal Comparing," *IBM Systems Journal*, 8, No. 3, 1969, 189-203.

, "A Model of Floating Buffering," *IBM Systems Journal*, 9, No. 2, 1970, 118-144.

, "Representing Negative Integers in Bit Vectors—A Short Note," in *Proceedings of the Fourth International APL Users' Conference*, Atlanta, June 1972, p. 58.

Zaks, R., and D. Steingart, "A Language Machine," *APL Quote-Quad*, Oct. 1971, 34-39.

Mathematics and Statistics: Applications and Uses of APL in

Alleman, G. B., and J. Richardson, "A Time Study in Numerical Methods Programming," in *Proceedings of the Sixth International APL Users' Conference*, Anaheim, May 1974, pp. 6-27.

Anscombe, F. J., "Use of Iverson's Language APL for Statistical Computing," *Technical Report No. 4*, Dept. of Statistics, Yale University, New Haven, Conn., July 1968.

Bergquist, J. W., "Algebraic Manipulation," in *Proceedings of the Sixth International APL Users' Conference*, Anaheim, May 1974, pp. 45-49.

Bickert, T. A., "Function to Accelerate and/or Induce Sequence Convergence," *APL Quote-Quad*, April 1970, 8-9.

Casarosa, V., and S. Trumpy, "Interactive Interpolation and Display of Surfaces," *APL Congress 73*, P. Gjerlov, H. J. Helms, and J. Nielsen, eds., American Elsevier Publishing Co., New York, 1973, pp. 59–66.

Chen, T. C., "The Automatic Computation of Exponentials, Logarithms, Ratios, and Square Roots," *Report No. RJ-970*, IBM Research Center, San Jose, Calif., Feb. 1972. Also *IBM Journal of Research and Development,* July 1972, 380–388.

Cousineau, F. G., J. F. Perrot, and J. M. Rifflet," APL Programs for Direct Computation of a Finite Semigroup," *APL Congress 73*, P. Gjerlov, H. J. Helms, and J. Nielsen, eds., American Elsevier Publishing Co., New York, 1973, pp. 67–74.

Dell'Orco, P., "A Syntatic Approach to Automatic Theorem Proving," *APL Congress 73*, P. Gjerlov, H. J. Helms, and J. Nielsen, eds., American Elsevier Publishing Co., New York, 1973, pp. 75–82.

Edwards, E. M., and W. R. Tinga, "An APL Complex Arithmetic Package," IEEE *NEREM Record*, 1970, 106–112.

Feldbrugge, F. H. J., "An Interactive APL System (ISVAP) for the Verification of APL Programs Using Floyd's Method," *APL Congress 73*, P. Gjerlov, H. J. Helms, and J. Nielsen, eds., American Elsevier Publishing Co., New York, 1973, pp. 119–126.

Fontanella, F., "An APL Polyalgorithm for Function Approximation by Some Interpolating Functions," *APL Congress 73*, P. Gjerlov, H. J. Helms, and J. Nielsen, eds., American Elsevier Publishing Co., New York, 1973, pp. 127–132.

Girard, E., D. Bastin, and J. C. Rault, "A Collection of Graph Analysis APL Functions," in *Proceedings of the Fourth International APL Users' Conference*, Atlanta, June, 1972, pp. 73–102.

Halpern, M. M., "Permutations," in *Proceedings of the Fifth International APL Users' Conference*, Toronto, Canada, May 1973, pp. 13.1–13.15.

———, "Algebra and the Properties of Scans," *APL Congress 73*, P. Gjerlov, H. J. Helms, and J. Nielsen, eds., American Elsevier Publishing Co., New York, 1973.

Hassitt, A., and L. E. Lyon, "Efficient Evaluation of Array Subscripts of Arrays," *IBM Journal of Research and Development*, Jan. 1972, 45–57.

Heath, J. S., "Planayse—An APL Program for the Analysis of Planar Structures," *Report No. TR-12,103*, IBM World Trade Corp., Hursley, England, June 1972.

Heilberger, R. M., "APL Functions for Data Analysis and Statistics," *Research Report CP-5*, Dept. of Statistics, Harvard University, March, 1971.

Horvath, A., "A Conversational Regression Analysis Program in APL," *Report No. TR-22.1400*, IBM Corp., East Fishkill, N.Y., Dec. 1971.

Iverson, K. E., "Use of APL in Statistics," in *Statistical Computations*, R. C. Milton and J. A. Nelder, eds., Academic Press, New York, 1969, pp. 285–299.

———, "Elementary Algebra," *Report No. 320-3001*, IBM Philadelphia Scientific Center, Philadelphia, June 1971.

———, "Algebra as a Language," *Collogque APL*, IRIA, Rocquencourt, France, Sept. 1971, 5–16.

Jenkins, M. A., "The Solution of Linear Systems of Equations and Linear Least Squares Problems in APL," *Report No. 320-2989*, IBM New York Scientific Center, New York, June 1970.

Jones, A. L., "The Fast Fourier Transform Algorithm—Applications and an APL Implementation," IBM Systems Development Divisions, Endicott, N.Y., Report No. TR-01.1560, March 1972.

Kellerman, Anne, "An Investigation of Curve Fitting Methods Using an APL Graphics Terminal," in *Proceedings of the Sixth International APL Users' Conference*, Anaheim, May 1974, pp. 249-265.

Kellerman, E., and W. C. Rodgers, "APL Tools for Combinatorics," in *Proceedings of the Sixth International APL Users' Conference*, Anaheim, May 1974, pp. 239-248.

Korsan, R. J., "On the Design of a Function to Solve Large Linear Systems of Equations Using the APL*PLUS File Subsystem," *APL Congress 73*, P. Gjerlov, H. J. Helms, and J. Nielsen, eds., American Elsevier Publishing Co., New York, 1973, pp. 251-258.

Korsan, R. T., "A Spline Package in APL," in *Proceedings of the Sixth International APL Users' Conference*, Anaheim, May 1974, pp. 281-286.

Laflamme, A. K., *Symbolic Differentiation with APL*, DREV, Quebec, Canada, 1971.

Levy, L. S., "An APL Program for the Multiple Output Two Level Minimization Problem," *Report No. RC-2323*, IBM Research Center, Yorktown Heights, N.Y., Dec. 1968.

Linden, T. A., "The Ackerman Function in APL," *APL Quote-Quad*, Jan. 1971, 10-11.

McAuliffe, G. K., "APL Fast Fourier Program," *Report No. RC-2832*, IBM Research Center, Yorktown Heights, N.Y., March 1970.

McDonnell, E. E., "Complex Floor," *APL Congress 73*, P. Gjerlov, H. J. Helms, and J. Nielsen, eds., American Elsevier Publishing Co., New York, 1973, pp. 299-306.

McIntyre, D. B., "Introduction to the Study of Data Matrices," *An Introduction to Mathematical Geology*, AGI Short Course Lecture Notes, American Geological Institute, Nov. 1969.

Michel, J. Y., "APLAMBDA: A Lambda-Calculus Machine for APL-Operators," *APL Congress 73*, P. Gjerlov, H. J. Helms, and J. Nielsen, eds., American Elsevier Publishing Co., New York, 1973, pp. 325-332.

More, T., "An Interactive Method for Algebraic Proofs," *Report No. 320-3005*, IBM Philadelphia Scientific Center, Philadelphia, Sept. 1971.

———, "Axioms and Theorems for a Theory of Arrays," *IBM Journal of Research and Development*, *17*, No. 2, March 1973, 135-175.

———, "Notes on the Development of a Theory of Arrays," *Report No. 320-3016*, IBM Philadelphia Scientific Center, Philadelphia, May 1973.

———, "Notes on the Axioms for a Theory of Arrays," *Report No. 320-3017*, IBM Philadelphia Scientific Center, Philadelphia, May 1973.

Murray, M. D., "ISP/1: A Conversational Statistical Package," in *Proceedings of the Sixth International APL Users' Conference*, Anaheim, May 1974, pp. 364-372.

Myers, H. J., and M. Y. Hsiao, "APL Algorithm for Calculating Boolean Difference," in *Proceedings of 1968 Automatic Support Symposium for Advanced Maintainability*, paper 5D, IEEE, Nov. 1968.

Page, P.D., "An On-line Proof Checker Operating Under APL/360, with Educational Applications in Logic, Mathematics, and Computer Science," *APL Quote-Quad*, Oct. 1971, 30–34.

Prins, J., "General K Factor Analysis of Variance Program Package for APL Users," Computer Center, State University of New York at New Paltz, Dec. 1972.

Richardson, J. L., "The Newton Coefficients in APL," in *Proceedings of the Sixth International APL Users' Conference*, Anaheim, May 1974, pp. 443–446.

Schatzoff, M., "Interactive Statistical Data Analysis-APL Style," *Report No. G320-2079*, IBM Cambridge Scientific Center, Cambridge, Mass., April 1972.

Schatzoff, M., P. Bryant, and A. P. Dempster, "Interactive Statistical Computation with Large Data Structures," *Report No. 320-2085*, IBM Cambridge Scientific Center, Cambridge, Mass., March 1973.

Smillie, K. W., "An APL Algorithm for the Critical Path," *Quarterly Bulletin of the Computer Society of Canada*, 8, No. 2, 1968, 6–13.

———, "Statpack 1, An APL Statistical Package," Dept. of Computing Science, Alberta University, Edmonton, Alberta, Canada, Jan. 1968.

———, "The APL Language and Statistical Computations," *Computer Bulletin*, 13, No. 8, 1969, 896–897.

———, "Statpack 2, An APL Statistical Package, *Publication No. 17*, Dept. of Computing Science, University of Alberta, Edmonton, Alberta, Canada, Feb. 1969.

———, "Some APL Algorithms for Orthogonal Factorial Experiments," *Publication No. 18*, Dept. of Computing Science, University of Alberta, Edmonton, Alberta, Canada, June 1969.

———, "Statistical Programs in APL/360," *Computer Bulletin*, 14, No. 5, 1970, 151–152.

———, "APL and Statistics, Programs or Insight," *Colloque APL*, IRIA, Rocquencourt, France, Sept. 1971, 17–35.

———, "Lines Through a Cube and Tic-Tac-Toe," *APL Quote-Quad*, Sept. 1972, 18–28.

———, "APL as a Notation for Statistical Analysis," in *Proceedings of the Fourth International APL Users' Conference*, Atlanta, June 1972, pp. 146–149.

Smith, R., "Interpretations of All Possible Reductions of a Boolean Vector Where the Result is 0 or 1" and "Similarities Between Reduction and Scan of Boolean Vectors," *APL Quote-Quad*, Jan. 1973, 34–35.

Snyder, M., "Interactive Data Analysis and Non-Parametric Statistics," *APL Congress 73*, P. Gjerlov, H. J. Helms, and J. Nielsen, eds., American Elsevier Publishing Co., New York, 1973, pp. 483–488.

Stockwell, R. K., and K. E. Vanbee, "Use of APL to Implement Algorithms for Sparse Linear Systems," IEEE *NEREM Record*, 1970, 113–119.

Surkan, A. J., "On Line APL Realization of Nonnumeric Algebraic Operations for Recursively Deriving Polynomial Coefficient Series of Orbital Motion," *Report No. RC-2048*, IBM Research Center, Yorktown Heights, N.Y., April 1968.

———, "Symbolic Polynomial Operations with APL," *IBM Journal of Research and Development*, March 1969, 209–211.

, "Discrete Fast Fourier Transformation Made Simple by a Single Reliable APL Function," *Report No. RC-2591*, IBM Research Center, Yorktown Heights, N.Y., Aug. 1969.

Tang, D. T., and C. N. Liu, "Distance Two Cyclic Chaining of Constant Weight Codes," *Report No. RC-3448*, IBM Research Center, Yorktown Heights, N.Y., July 1971.

Vervoort, W., "Correctness Proofs of APL Programs Using the Assertion Method of Floyd," *APL Congress 73*, P. Gjerlov, H. J. Helms, and J. Nielsen, eds., American Elsevier Publishing Co., New York, 1973, pp. 465–472.

Von Maydell, U. M., "An Introduction to Probability and Statistics Using APL," *Publication No. 21*, Dept. of Computing Science, University of Alberta, Edmonton, Alberta, Canada, June 1970.

Wilhelmi, G., "Formal Differentiation Using APL," in *Proceedings of the Fifth International APL Users' Conference*, Toronto, Canada, May 1973, pp. 11.1–11.9.

Other Applications and Uses of APL

Brown, J. A., and B. Warner, "An Application of a Specialized Data Bank for Information Retrieval," in *Proceedings of the Sixth International APL Users' Conference*, Anaheim, May 1974, pp. 58–64.

Coffey, C. E., J. Eskinazi, F. H. Fraser, and D. J. Macero, "A Program for Filing and Searching Literature References," *APL Quote-Quad*, Jan 1973, 28–32.

Dell'Orco, P., and L. Bartolo, "APL/Info: A System for Automatic Documentation," in *Proceedings of the Sixth International APL Users' Conference*, Anaheim, May 1974, pp. 139–147.

Gray, B. C., "A Military Enlisted Manpower Projection and Simulation Model," *APL Congress 73*, P. Gjerlov, H. J. Helms, and J. Nielsen, eds., American Elsevier Publishing Co., New York, 1973.

Gregersen, O. V., "Temperature-Level in Airconditioned Room," *APL Congress 73*, P. Gjerlov, H. J. Helms, and J. Nielsen, eds., American Elsevier Publishing Co., New York, 1973.

Gull, W. E., "The Solution of Rational Equations Using Text Processing," *APL Congress 73*, P. Gjerlov, H. J. Helms, and J. Nielsen, eds., American Elsevier Publishing Co., New York, 1973.

Hagamen, W. D., and D. J. Linden, "Encoding Verbal Information as Unique Numbers," *IBM Systems Journal*, *11*, No. 4, 1972, 278–315.

Hopkins, M. J. D., H. G. Moria, and T. V. Narayana, "A First APL Tournament Package," in *Proceedings of the Sixth International APL Users' Conference*, Anaheim, May 1974, pp. 185–200.

Jones, A. L., "Cross-Country Scoring and Timing Using APL," in *Proceedings of the Sixth International APL Users' Conference*, Anaheim, May 1974, pp. 218–220.

Kellerman, E., "An Adaptive Query System," in *Proceedings of the Fourth International APL Users' Conference*, Atlanta, June 1972, pp. 150–153.

Kolsky, H. G., "Problem Formulation Using APL," *IBM Systems Journal*, *8*, No. 3, 1969, 204–219.

Kvaternik, R., "An APL Terminal Approach to Computer Mapping," *Technical Report CSRG-21*, Toronto University, Canada, Dec. 1972.

LePage, W. R., "APL Simulation of Musical Staff Notation," *APL Congress 73*, P. Gjerlov, H. J. Heims, and J. Nielsen, eds., American Elsevier Publishing Co., New York, 1973, pp. 281-288.

Lorie, R. A., and A. J. Symonds, "Interactive Problem Solving Using a Relational Data-Base in APL," in *Conference Digest of International IEEE Computer Conference*, IEEE, Boston, Sept. 1971, pp. 191-92.

Niehoff, W. H., "Contour Plotting in Rectangular Domains," in *Proceedings of the Sixth International APL Users' Conference*, Anaheim, May 1974, pp. 373-386.

Pages, J-C., "Individualized Documentation Application," *APL Congress 73*, P. Gjerlov, H. J. Helms, and J. Nielsen, eds., American Elsevier Publishing Co., New York, 1973, pp. 347-352.

Pages, J-C., and A. Mauboassin, "Flexible Building of Specialized Retrieval Systems," in *Proceedings of the Sixth International APL Users' Conference*, Anaheim, May 1974, pp. 414-423.

Petersen, T. I., "The Ecology Decision Game Introduction," *Report No. G320-2073*, IBM Cambridge Scientific Center, Cambridge, Mass., Sept. 1971.

Price, R., "APL Processing of Traffic Data Within a PBX (IBM 3750 System)," *APL Congress 73*, P. Gjerlov, H. J. Helms, and J. Nielsen, eds., American Elsevier Publishing Co., New York, 1973, pp. 361-368.

Raynaud, Y. G., and L. P. A. Robichaud, "Scalar Segment Processor," in *Proceedings of the Sixth International APL Users' Conference*, Anaheim, May 1974, p. 442.

Rogers, G., "Adaptive Data-Classifying Systems," *APL Congress 73*, P. Gjerlov, H. J. Helms, and J. Nielsen, eds., American Elsevier Publishing Co., New York, 1973, pp. 395-400.

Rosenkrands, B., "Graphics by APL," *Colloque APL*, IRIA, Rocquencourt, France, Sept. 1971, 91-113.

Rueter, D. B., "Speech Synthesis Under APL," in *Proceedings of the Sixth International APL Users' Conference*, Anaheim, May 1974, pp. 585 ff.

Rux, W. A., and E. Baelen, "Casper," in *Proceedings of the Sixth International APL Users' Conference*, Anaheim, May 1974, pp. 452-470.

Sandi, C., "From the Free Optimum to the True Optimum: A Direct Search Method for the Transportation Problem," *APL Congress 73*, P. Gjerlov, H. J. Helms, and J. Nielsen, eds., American Elsevier Publishing Co., New York, 1973, pp. 415-420.

Schench, J., J. Peetz, and C. Caluson, "APL Catalog System," in *Proceedings of the Sixth International APL Users' Conference*, Anaheim, May 1974, pp. 471-474.

Smart, J. S., "An APL Version of JABOWA, the Northeastern Forest Growth Simulation," *Report No. RC-3985*, IBM Research Center, Yorktown Heights, N.Y., Aug. 1972.

Thomson, N. D., "The Use of APL in Constructing School Time-Tables," *APL Congress 73*, P. Gjerlov, H. J. Helms, and J. Nielsen, eds., American Elsevier Publishing Co., New York, 1973, pp. 439-446.

Thygesen, S., and N. C. Mortensen, "APL in Local Government Economical and Physical Planning," *APL Congress 73*, P. Gjerlov, H. J. Helms, and J. Nielsen, eds., American Elsevier Publishing Co., New York, 1973, pp. 447-456.

Wahi, P. N., and T. I. Petersen, "The Ecology Decision Game Management Science and Gaming," *Report No. G320-2076*, IBM Cambridge Scientific Center, Cambridge, Mass., Oct. 1971.

Weaver, K. R., "An Information Retrieval System Using One File," *APL Congress 73*, P. Gjerlov, H. J. Helms, and J. Nielsen, eds., American Elsevier Publishing Co., New York, 1973, pp. 465-472.

Wende, C. D., "A Modest Information System Implemented on APL," in *Proceedings of the Sixth International APL Users' Conference*, Anaheim, May 1974, pp. 568-580.

APL Developments

Abrams, P. S., "An APL Machine," Ph.d. dissertation, *SLAC Report No. 114*, Stanford University, Stanford, Calif., Feb. 1970.

Adams, M. F., "The Extended File System at GSFC," in *Proceedings of the Sixth International APL Users' Conference*, Anaheim, May 1974, pp. 1-5.

Alfonseca, M., "An APL-Written APL-Subset to System/7-MSP Translator," *APL Congress 73*, P. Gjerlov, H. J. Helms, and J. Nielsen, eds., American Elsevier Publishing Co., New York, 1973, pp. 17-24.

Amram, Y., B. deCosnac, J. L. Granger, and A. Smoucovit, "An APL Interpreter for Mini-Computers. A Microprogrammed APL Machine," *APL Congress 73*, P. Gjerlov, H. J. Helms, and J. Nielsen, eds., American Elsevier Publishing Co., New York, 1973, pp. 33-40.

Ashcroft, E. A., "Towards an APL Compiler," in *Proceedings of the Sixth International APL Users' Conference*, Anaheim, May 1974, pp. 28-38.

Battarel, G., and D. Tusera, "APL Optimization: A Unified Approach," in *Proceedings of the Sixth International APL Users' Conference*, Anaheim, May 1974, pp. 39-44.

Battarel, G., M. Delbreil, and D. Tusera, "Optimized Interpretation of APL Statements," *APL Congress 73*, P. Gjerlov, H. J. Helms, and J. Nielsen, eds., American Elsevier Publishing Co., New York, 1973, pp. 49-58.

Bauer, A. M., and H. J. Saal, "Does APL Really Need Run-Time Checking?," *Dept. Memo 59-73*, Dept. of Computer Science, State University of New York at Buffalo, April 1972.

Bernecky, B., "Speeding Up Dyadic IOTA and Dyadic EPSILON," *APL Congress 73*, P. Gjerlov, H. J. Helms, and J. Nielsen, eds., American Elsevier Publishing Co., New York, 1973, pp. 479-482.

Bonyum, D. A., "Mark-Sense APL," *APL Quote-Quad*, June 1971, 18-19.

Breed, L. M., "Generalizing APL Scalar Extensions," *APL Quote-Quad*, March 1971, 5-7.

———, "Design of the APL*PLUS File Subsystem," *Colloque APL*, IRIA, Rocquencourt, France, Sept. 1971.

———, "APL-ASCII: An ASCII Overlay Stanford for APL Terminals," *APL Quote-Quad*, Jan. 1973, 13-19.

Brown, J. A., *A Generalization of APL*, Ph.D. dissertation, Systems and Information Science Dept., Syracuse University, Syracuse, N.Y., 1971.

Charmonman, S., "Sixty-Character Representation of APL Symbols," *APL Quote-Quad*, July 1970, 5–10.

———, "A Generalization of APL Array-Oriented Concept," *APL Quote-Quad*, Sept. 1970, 13–17.

Clement, J. F., P. Sandery, and B. James, "Development of a Batch APL System," in *Proceedings of the Sixth International APL Users' Conference*, Anaheim, May 1974, pp. 85–99.

Clementi, J. F., and P. P. Fletcher, "Modifications to the APL/1130 System To Provide More Convenient Operating on a Fortran User's Machine," *APL Quote-Quad*, June 1971, 16–18, and Oct. 1971, 40–42.

Colle, A., "Increasing the Flexibility of HI and PA Messages," *APL Quote-Quad*, Sept. 1972, 29–34.

Crayton, J., "APL Unary Matrix Operators," in *Proceedings of the Sixth International APL Users' Conference*, Anaheim, May 1974, pp. 112–116.

Edwards, E. M., "Generalized Arrays (Lists) in APL," *APL Congress 73*, P. Gjerlov, H. J. Helms, and J. Nielsen, eds., American Elsevier Publishing Co., New York, 1973, pp. 99–106.

Falkoff, A. D., "Design of a Format Function with a Pictorial Argument," *APL Congress 73*, P. Gjerlov, H. J. Helms, and J. Nielsen, eds., American Elsevier Publishing Co., New York, 1973, pp. 107–108.

———, "A Survey of Experimental APL File and I/O Systems in IBM," *Colloque APL*, IRIA, Roequencourt, France, Sept. 1971, 365–374.

Falkoff, A. D., and K. E. Iverson, "Communication in APL Systems," *Report No. 320-3022*, IBM Philadelphia Scientific Center, Philadelphia, May 1973.

Fletcher, J., "An 8-Bit ASCII Code," *APL Quote-Quad*, June 1971, 13.

Foster, G. "File Action in APL," *Sigplan Notices*, 8, No. 4, April 1973, pp. 6–15.

Gerhart, S. L., *Verification of APL Programs*, Ph.D. dissertation. Dept. of Computer Science, Carnegie-Mellon University, Pittsburgh, Nov. 1972.

Ghandour, Z., and J. Mezei, "General Arrays, Operators, and Functions," *IBM Journal of Research and Development*, July 1973, 335–352.

Hail, J. D., and J. D. Kirscher, "A Batch Processing Version of APL/1130 for Student Use," in *Proceedings of the Sxith International APL Users' Conference*, Anaheim, May 1974, pp. 180–184.

Harbinson, M. D., "A Magnetic Tape Format for Communication of APL Functions," *APL Congress 73*, P. Gjerlov, H. J. Helms, and J. Nielsen, eds., American Elsevier Publishing Co., New York, 1973, pp. 195–202.

Harris, L. R., "A Logical Control Structure for APL," *APL Congress 73*, P. Gjerlov, H. J. Helms, and J. Nielsen, eds., American Elsevier Publishing Co., New York, 1973, pp. 203–210.

Hassitt, A., J. W. Lageshulte, and L. E. Lyon, "A Microprogrammed Implementation of an APL Machine," *APL Quote-Quad*, June 1970, 11–12.

Hassitt, A., J. W. Lageshulte, and L. E. Lyon, "Implementation of a High Level Language Machine," *CACM*, *16*, No. 4, April 1973, 199–212.

Iverson, E. B., "APL/4004 Implementation," *APL Congress 73*, P. Gjerlov, H. J. Helms, and J. Nielsen, eds., American Elsevier Publishing Co., New York, 1973, pp. 231–236.

Jenkins, M. A., "Domino—An APL Primitive Function for Matrix Inversion—Its Implementation and Applications," *Proceedings of Share XXXVII*, *1*, Aug. 1971, 379–388, and *APL Quote-Quad*, Feb. 1972, 4–15.

———, "Numerical Analysis and APL, Can They Coexist?," *APL Congress 73*, P. Gjerlov, H. J. Helms, and J. Nielsen, eds., American Elsevier Publishing Co., New York, 1973, pp. 237–244.

Juran, W., "A Fast Formatter for APL," in *Proceedings of the Sixth International APL Users' Conference*, Anaheim, May 1974, pp. 228–232.

Kalfon, P., "On a Bottom-Up Method for Evaluation of APL Expressions," *APL Congress 73*, P. Gjerlov, H. J. Helms, and J. Nielsen, eds., American Elsevier Publishing Co., New York, 1973, pp. 245–250.

Korsan, R. J., "A Proposed APL Extension," *APL Quote-Quad*, Oct. 1971, 21–23.

———, "APL, the FFT and Ordinary Differential Equations (Odes)," *APL Congress 73*, P. Gjerlov, H. J. Helms, and J. Nielsen, eds., American Elsevier Publishing Co., New York, 1973, pp. 259–268.

Lathwell, R. H., "System Formulation and APL Shared Variables," *IBM Journal of Research and Development*, *17*, No. 4, July 1973, pp. 353–359.

———, "File Processing in Terms of Concurrent Processors with Shared Variable Interfaces," *APL Congress 73*, P. Gjerlov, H. J. Helms, and J. Nielsen, eds., American Elsevier Publishing Co., New York, 1973, pp. 279–280.

Leibovitz, C., "Suggestions for a 'Mapped' Extension of APL," in *Proceedings of the Fourth International APL User's Conference*, Atlanta, June 1972, pp. 142–145.

Liu, Y., "Reverse Operator in APL," *Computing Center News* (Syracuse University, Syracuse, N.Y.), March 1, 1971, 9–10.

Marchal, A., and R. A. Keir, "The Design of a Structured APL Interpreter," *APL Congress 73*, P. Gjerlov, H. J. Helms, and J. Nielsen, eds., American Elsevier Publishing Co., New York, 1973, pp. 313–318.

McDonnell, E. E., "The Caret Functions," in *Proceedings of the Sixth International APL Users' Conference*, Anaheim, May 1974, pp. 316–323.

McEwan, A., and D. Watson, "APL/360 Recurse, Part I," *APL Quote-Quad*, July 1970, 11–16.

McMurchie, T. D., "A Limited Character APL Symbolism," *APL Quote-Quad*, Nov. 1970, 3–4.

Mezei, J., "General Arrays Operators and Functions," in *Proceedings of the Sixth International APL Users' Conference*, Anaheim, May 1974, pp. 334–348.

Moore, C., W. Juran, C. Orndorff, and L. Rice, "The PCS APL Shared File System," in *Proceedings of the Sixth International APL Users' Conference*, Anaheim, May 1974, pp. 354–363.

Murray, R. C., "On Tree Structure Extensions to the APL Language," *APL Congress 73*, P. Gjerlov, H. J. Helms, and J. Nielsen, eds., American Elsevier Publishing Co., New York, 1973, pp. 333–339.

O'Dell, M. D., "APL/XAD: An Extension of APL for Abstract Data Manipulation," in *Proceedings of the Sixth International APL Users' Conference*, Anaheim, May 1974, pp. 405–413.

Penfield, P., "Proposed Notation and Implementation for Derivatives in APL," in *Proceedings of the Fifth International APL Users' Conference*, Toronto, Canada, May 1973, pp. 12.1–12.5.

Perlis, A., "APL as a Conventional Language—What is Missing?," *APL Quote-Quad*, June 1971, 3–4.

Pettus, C., "Indeterminate (0÷0) Check in APL," *APL Quote-Quad*, Feb. 1972, 15–16.

Ruggiu, G., and P. Aigrain, "Description of APL Operators," *APL Congress 73*, P. Gjerlov, H. J. Helms, and J. Nielsen, eds., American Elsevier Publishing Co., New York, 1973, pp. 401–406.

Ryan, J., "Generalized Lists and Other Extensions," *APL Quote-Quad*, June 1971, 8–10.

——, "Secure Applications Within an APL Environment," *APL Congress 73*, P. Gjerlov, H. J. Helms, and J. Nielsen, eds., American Elsevier Publishing Co., New York, 1973, pp. 407–414.

Stohr, E. A., "Simulation of Some APL Operators," *Report LR-16*, Center for Research in Management Science, University of California, Berkeley, Calif., Feb. 1971.

Thurber, K. J., and J. W. Myrna, "System Design of a Cellular APL Computer," *IEEE Transactions on Computers*, April 1970, 291–303.

Van Hedel, H., "An APL Batch Processor," *Colloque APL*, IRIA, Rocquencourt, France, Sept. 1971, 339–364.

Vasseur, J. P., "Extension of APL Operators to Tree-Like Data Structures," *APL Congress 73*, P. Gjerlov, H. J. Helms, and J. Nielsen, eds., American Elsevier Publishing Co., New York, 1973, pp. 457–464.

Wiedman, C., "The Case for APL Standards," in *Proceedings of the Sixth International APL Users' Conference*, Anaheim, May 1974, pp. 581–584.

Williams, J., "Conditional Branch APL Compiler," *APL Quote-Quad*, June 1971, 5–6.

Zaks, R., D. Steingart, and J. Moore, "Firmware APL Timesharing System," *SJCC*, 1971, 179–190.

Zaks, R., "Microprogrammed APL," *Conference Digest of International IEEE Computer Conference*, Boston, Sept. 1971, IEEE, pp. 192–194.

*Miscellaneous: Of Interest to the APL-Programmer or
APL-Related Information*

Alercia, R., R. Swiatek, and G. M. Weinberg, "Every Little Bit Hurts: Saving Money by Saving Space in APL," in *Proceedings of the Fourth International APL Users' Conference*, Atlanta, June 1972, pp. 118–119.

Bork, A. M., "Graphics in APL," in *Proceedings of the Fourth International Users' Conference*, Atlanta, June 1972, pp. 33–36.

——, "APL as a Language for Interactive Computer Graphics," in *Proceedings of the Sixth International APL Users' Conference*, Anaheim, May 1974, pp. 50–57.

Casarosa, V., and S. Trumpy, "Conversational Building and Display of Solid Objects," in *Proceedings of the Sixth International APL Users' Conference*, Anaheim, May 1974, pp. 79-84.

Charmonman, S., "A Comparison of the Structures of APL, Fortran, Algol, and PL/I," *APL Quote-Quad*, Jan. 1970, 2-4.

Charmonman, S., and S. E. Bell, "A PL/I Batch Processor for APL," in *Proceedings of the Fourth International APL Users' Conference*, Atlanta, June 1972, pp. 123-134.

Creveling, C. J., "APL and Its Entry Into the World," in *Proceedings of the Sixth International APL Users' Conference*, Anaheim, May 1974, pp. 117-123.

Dayton, M., "A Plotter of APL," *APL Quote-Quad*, June 1971, 13.

Embley, D. W., "APL Graphics," unpublished M.S. thesis, Dept. of Computer Science, University of Utah, Provo, 1971.

Gerhart, S. L., "Verification of APL Programs," unpublished Ph.D. Thesis, Dept. of Computer Science, Carnegie-Mellon University, Pittsburgh, University Microfilms, Ann Arbor, 1972.

Greenberg, S. G., and C. I. Johnson, "An Interactive APL Graphics System," in *Proceedings of the Fourth International APL Users' Conference*, Atlanta, June 1972, pp. 37-44.

Hagerty, P. E., "On the Portability of APL Packages," *APL Quote-Quad*, Jan. 1973, 22-27.

Haralson, K. N., "Useful APL Defined Functions," *Report No. TR-00.2409*, IBM Poughkeepsie Laboratory, Poughkeepsie, N.Y., Feb. 1973.

Higgins, J., and A. Kellerman, "Management of APL Time-sharing Activities," in *Proceedings of the Fourth International APL Users' Conference*, Atlanta, June 1972, pp. 103-114.

Hunter, G. T., "Found in an Empty APL Workspace," *APL Quote-Quad*, Jan. 1971, 5-8.

Iverson, K. E., "APL in Exposition," *Report No. 320-3010*, IBM Philadelphia Scientific Center, Philadelphia, 1971.

Jones, A. L., and R. H. Katyl, "A Graphical Input Capability for APL," in *Proceedings of the Sixth International APL Users' Conference*, Anaheim, May 1974, pp. 221-227.

Jones, A. L., and W. H. Niehoff, "APL/360 Graphpak-Interactive Graphics in the Terminal Environment," *Report No. TR-01.1502*, IBM Systems Development Division, Endicott, N.Y., Aug. 1971.

Katzan, H., "A Prose Glossary of APL," *Computers and Automation*, Aug. 1970, 39-42.

———, "Representation and Manipulation of Data Structures in APL," in *Proceedings of a Symposium on Data Structures in Programming Languages*, ACM, Feb. 1971, pp. 366-397.

Kupka, I., and N. Wilsing, "An APL Based Syntax Form for Dialog Languages," *APL Congress 73*, P. Gjerlov, H. J. Helms, and J. Nielsen, eds., American Elsevier Publishing Co., New York, 1973, pp. 269-274.

Lathwell, R. H., and J. E. Mezei, "A Formal Description of APL," *Colloque APL*, IRIA Rocquencourt, France, Sept. 1971, 181-215.

Macon, H. P., "A Survey of APL Compatible Terminals," *APL Quote-Quad*, Oct. 1971, 12-20.

Mahanti, B. K., and M. E. Sandfelder, "Interactive Data Processing Application Implementation Using APL," *APL Congress 73*, P. Gjerlov, H. J. Helms, and J. Nielsen, eds., American Elsevier Publishing Co., New York, 1973, pp. 307–312.

McDonnell, E. E., "The Variety of Alternative Definitions of a Single Function," in *Proceedings of the Fifth International APL Users' Conference*, Toronto, Canada, May 1973, pp. 4.1–4.23.

Moruzzi, V. L., "APL/Fortran Translations," *Report No. RC-3644*, IBM Corp., Yorktown Heights, Dec. 1971.

Niehoff, W. H., and A. L. Jones, "An APL Approach to Interactive Display Terminals," in *Proceedings of the Fourth International APL Users' Conference*, Atlanta, June 1972, pp. 23–32.

Penfield, P., "Security of APL Application Packages," in *Proceedings of the Fourth International APL Users' Conference*, Atlanta, June 1972, pp. 119–122.

Rault, J. C., and G. Demars, "Is APL Epidemic? or a Study of its Growth Through an Extended Bibliography," in *Proceedings of the Fourth International APL Users' Conference*, Atlanta, June 1972, pp. 1–22.

Riedy, J. E., "Some Solved Problems in Intermediate APL," *Report No. TR-01.1544*, IBM Systems Development Division, Endicott Laboratory, Endicott, N.Y., June 1972.

Rose, A. J., "Teaching the APL/360 Terminal System," *Proceedings of Share XXXII*, Part II, March 1969, 543–554.

Rowley, J. R., "An APL-ASCII Graphics Terminal," *APL Quote-Quad*, Jan. 1973, 20–21.

Ryan, J. L., "Enhanced Interaction for an APL System," in *Proceedings of the Fourth International APL Users' Conference*, Atlanta, June 1972.

Sant, D., "The MRX 1240 Communication Terminal and 1270 Transmission Control Unit," *APL Quote-Quad*, June 1971, 13.

Schreiber, G. P., and R. Polivka, "Experiences and Observations with a Self-Teaching Course in APL," *Colloque APL*, IRIA, Rocquencourt, France, Sept. 1971, 77–90.

Thanhouser, N., and L. Koeningsberg, "A Graphics System for APL Users—APL/Graph-II," in *Proceedings of the Sixth International APL Users' Conference*, Anaheim, May 1974, pp. 529–543.

Weiss, C., "Communications Between Users in a Dispersed APL Network," in *Proceedings of the Sixth International APL Users' Conference*, Anaheim, May 1974, pp. 562–567.

Collections

APL Congress 73, P. Gjerlov, H. J. Helms, and J. Nielsen, eds., American Elsevier Publishing Co., New York, 1973.

APL Quote-Quad, an informal publication for APL-users, published quarterly.

Proceedings APL Conference, York University, Downsview, Ontario, Canada, Jan. 1972.

Proceedings of the APL Users' Conference at S.U.N.Y., Binghamton, N.Y., July 1969.

Proceedings of the Fifth International APL Users' Conference, Toronto, Canada, May 1973.

Proceedings of the Fourth International APL Users' Conference, Atlanta, June 1972.

Colloque APL, IRIA (Institut de Recherche d'Informatique et d'Automatique), Rocquencourt, France, Sept. 1971.

Proceedings of the Sixth International APL Users' Conference, Anaheim, May 1974, Coast Community College District.

INDEX

DATE DUE

GAYLORD			PRINTED IN U.S.A.